Physical Activity and the Social Sciences

Edited by:
W. Neil Widmeyer
Department of Kinesiology
University of Waterloo

Mouvement Publications, Inc.
109 E. State St.
Ithaca, N.Y. 14850

Woodstock
19 Oaks Way, Gayton
Heswall, Wirral
L60 3SP England

Woorkarrim
Lot #7 Strathmore Drive
Torquay 3228
Australia

Copyright © 1983 by Mouvement Publications.
Layout by: Sandy Sharpe
Typeset by: Strehle's Computerized Typesetting, Ithaca, New York
Printed in the United States of America
by McNaughton Gunn, Ann Arbor, Michigan.

ISBN   0-932392-13-X

Dedicated to: *Carol*
                 Dave
                 Debbie
                 E. J.
                 Gunther
                 Jack
                 Jan
                 Jeff
                 Judi
                 Marilyn
                 Sandy
                 Sheila
                 Vicki

and all the other great teaching assistants who have helped me so much with this course.

Acknowledgements

This custom-book of readings has been prepared for university courses examining the relationships between the social sciences and physical activity. The first version of this text was published in 1976 by the MSS Information Corporation, 655 Madison Avenue, New York, New York 10021. Subsequent volumes were published in 1978, 1979 and 1980 by the University of Waterloo Printing Press, Waterloo, Ontario, Canada.

The editor wishes to express his appreciation to the editors of the journals and textbooks in which these articles first appeared for granting their permission to reproduce the articles for this collection. Naturally, appreciation is also extended to the authors who wrote each of the articles which appear in this volume.

A very special "thank you" is expressed to Karri Deckert for the many hours she spent in obtaining the permissions for the articles contained in this volume. Without her efforts the present version of this text would not exist.

PREFACE

WHY "PHYSICAL ACTIVITY AND THE SOCIAL SCIENCES?"

"What do you teach at the University?"
"Kinesiology"
"Kin_____what?"
"Kin-ee-see-aw-low-gee."
"What's that?"
"Kinesiology is the study of human movement and the factors which influence and which are influenced by that movement."
"Oh yeah, you study joints and muscles and fitness and that stuff.'"
"Not really. Some of our faculty members study those things, but I'm interested in the relationships between the social sciences and physical activity."
"I don't understand what you mean by that.?
"Well, I'm interested in . . . ."

I have had that conversation at least one hundred times during each of the past five years and I'm certain I'll have it another hundred times during the next five years. The comments of my conversational partners suggest that people do recognize that associations exist between biological or physical factors and physical activity. Further evidence of the wide spread recognition of these associations lies in the fact that words such as "aerobics", "isometrics" and "ergonomics" are creeping into everyday speech. The desire of the public to know how to attain and/or maintain physical well being has made it "all right" for academics to study the physiological factors which influence and which, in turn, are influenced by physical activity. But how can the social sciences be related to physical activity? Although most will agree that physical activity does not occur within a social vacuum, it has only been recently that there has been any sort of wide spread recognition given to the fact that social and psychological factors influence and are influenced by human participation in and performance of physical activities. In most cases, the study of such factors has been in connection with rather highly structured forms of physical activity such as dance and sport. In the case of sport, recognition of the pervasiveness of the activity has led to the establishment of such sub-disciplines as the history of sport, the psychology of sport, and the sociology of sport and to talk of anthropology of sport, and a geography of sport. Kinesiology 103 at the University of Waterloo is a first year course designed to introduce students to the types of questions that social scientists are, can and might be able to answer concerning physical activity.

WHY A "COLLECTION OF READINGS" FOR A COURSE DEALING WITH PHYSICAL ACTIVITY AND THE SOCIAL SCIENCES?

At present, to the best of this professor's knowledge, there is no text in existence that contains material dealing with the relationships between physical activity and each of the social sciences. To have students purchase six or more different texts, each dealing with one social science and its relationship to physical activity would be extremely costly and probably quite wasteful, as only a section of each book would be examined. The placing of readings "on reserve" in the library is an accepted practice with graduate courses or small undergraduate classes, but is totally impractical, regardless of the number of duplicates made of each article, for a class of two hundred students.

ON WHAT BASIS WERE ARTICLES SELECTED FOR THIS COLLECTION?

No one criteria was used in the selection process. Sometimes a recent review article was chosen in order to give the student an appreciation of the scope of the topic before delving into any specific study in depth. At other times, articles were selected that were very specific to a particular activity or population. The inclusion of such articles, be they recent "tangents" or "classic oldies", opens the doors to an inductive teaching approach.

It must be recognized that some articles should be included but were not, either because of their length or due to an inability to obtain copyright privileges. Therefore, students should be prepared to extend their knowledge of the social sciences and physical activity by reading beyond this particular compilation.

Table of Contents

SECTION I
FRAMES OF REFERENCE

Often writers and lecturers, in their haste to tell their audience about certain relationships that have been found to exist between certain entities, do not take the time to define these entities. For example, the statement that religious people tend to shun the theatre is very confusing until one knows what is meant by a religious person and if the theatre refers simply to a building which houses anything from a town meeting to a movie, or if it is a universal institution involving the acting of roles. If this collection of readings is going to deal with physical activity and the social sciences, one must have a clear understanding of physical activity and know what is meant by the social sciences. Consequently the first section of this course, entitled "Frames of Reference", is devoted to delineating these entities.

Before one can appreciate inter-relationships that exist between any one of the social sciences and physical activity, one must not only comprehend the social sciences as a collectivity, but also one must understand what is meant by "science". Entire textbooks and graduate courses at university are devoted to the philosophy of science, therefore, it would be folly to expect that a student could gain more than a basic appreciation of the term in one lecture supplemented by a few readings. Nevertheless, it is still hoped that the student will recognize that although science has made certain aspects of life more pleasant, the betterment of mankind is not the aim of science. Instead science seeks to describe, explain, predict and even control humans and their universe.

Physical activity means different things to different people. Biological scientists see physical activity manifested as a muscle twitch whereas to physical scientists physical activity may be a joint extension. Social scientists, on the other hand, are usually interested in grosser and more structured forms of physical activity such as play, work, sport and dance. At times, the social scientist is concerned with how participation and performance in all or any one of these forms of physical activity influence human social life, whereas at other times these scholars seek to determine how social-psychological factors influence human participation and performance in any one or all of these forms of physical activity.

Introduction: The Domain of the Social Sciences *

Science is a vast enterprise involving innumerable persons in literally every country of the world. Science advances understanding and enables people to explain their behavior and the environment in which they live. Through the application of scientific findings, people have developed an extensive number of products and procedures that extend life, improve our physical and psychological well-being and give us more control over our destinies. Unfortunately, the same approach has led to the development of lethal weapons and other destructive devises. The constructive or destructive use of science has come to depend, however, upon ethical and moral questions.

Precisely because science is so vast, no scientist or group of scientists can be technically competent in all areas. For this reason science is generally separated into three families or domains — the physical and biological sciences and the social sciences — which may or may not overlap. Within each of these three families there is further specialization.

The Social Scene provides an introduction to the social sciences which can be defined briefly as the study of the behavior of people in human society. As we shall see, the social sciences are sometimes also called the behavioral sciences. We will begin by defining more completely the term social sciences and then by considering the major disciplines — psychology, sociology, anthropology, economics, and political science — that are encompassed by this term.

WHAT ARE THE SOCIAL SCIENCES?

A recent report of a distinguished commission to the National Science Foundation offered the following definition of the social sciences.

The *social sciences* are intellectual disciplines that study man as a social being by means of the scientific method. It is their focus on man as a member of society and on the groups and societies he forms, that distinguishes the social sciences from the physical and biological sciences (National Science Foundation, 1969, p. 7).

A review of the outlook and needs of the *social sceinces* describes them as *dealing with the behavior of people, their relations with other human beings and the environment they share* (National Academy of Sciences — Social Science Research Council, 1969, p. 19).

The five *social science* generally regarded as essential social science

Browne, Freeman, Hamilton, Kogan, Kamney. Introduction: The Domain of the Social Sciences, in *The Social Scene,* Cambridge, Mass.: Winthrop Publishers, 1972, pp 1-10. Printed with permission of the editors.

2

disciplines — pyschology, sociology, anthropology, economics and political science — are in many ways difficult to define and to distinguish from one another. They share a concern with *social processes* and the products and consequences of *social relationships.* The bonds between the various diciplines are real. They provide the different perspectives necessary to obtain a rounded picture of human behavior and of human societies. An individual's actions take place within an environment and this environment is composed of people, the traditions they have inspired, and the objects they have produced.

It bears emphasis that there are large overlaps between the social science diciplines, as well as overlaps with several of the biological and physical sciences. Indeed, a number of special disciplines, areas that fall between the more traditionally established ones, have grown up and achieved an autonomy of their own. Perhaps the best-known such discipline is *social psychology,* which is concerned with the individudal in relation to his group behavior and group processes. Social psychology has dual parentage in psychology and sociology and both disciplines continue to contribute to its development (Sherif and Sherif, 1969, pp. 18-19).

We will continue to emphasize the interrealtionships between the various *social sciences;* it is necessary, however, both for analytical purposes and to achieve an effective allocation of work, to split the *social sciences* into diciplines, and to consider each one separately.

PSYCHOLOGY

Psychology can be thought of as a science of individual behavior and mental processes; it studies the individual as he acts in his natural environment or in the laboratory. It includes observable phenomena, such as gestures and speech, physiological changes like heart rate and sweating, and thought processes that must be inferred from answers to problems and dreams. Psychologists study the nature and organization of *mental processes* in people; they also determine his *motivations.* Psychologists deal with the *mental abilities and aptitudes* of individuals; their capacities for learning, thinking and emotional expression. The most common application of psychology concerns learning and education problems, problems of personnel selection in industry, and concerns of clinical assessment and care of mental illness.

Psychology is interrelated with sociology; it deals with individual behavior as it takes place in a complex social environment. The investigations of psychologists working in laboratories on experiments with birds, lower mammals and primates provide us with a knowledge of the brain and its mechanisms, the forces that motivate individuals, the problems of mental disorders and the ways that we learn. These studies can then be applied to human infants, growing children, and adults of all ages. Psychology is in part also a life science closely related to biology. The behavior of people naturally depends on neurological and physiological processes.

3

SOCIOLOGY

Sociology is the discipline that investigates the collective behavior of individuals. We have seen that psychologists study the individual in his environment. Sociologists also study the behavior and motivation of individuals as they relate to each other and undertake activities in groups and organizations. Sometimes sociology is referred to as the science of *society.* it studies the structure, functions and various features of *societies* and *communities* such as families, religious *groups,* professions, occupations, race relations, and so on. In addition, sociology is applied to a large extent to the many social problems in the *community* such as crime, violence, and poverty. In this sense sociology is interrelated with anthropology, economics and political science, because *poverty* is a cultural, political and economic as well as a sociological problem.

ANTHROPOLOGY

Anthropology sometimes is difficult to distinguish from sociology; both disciplines study the societies in which people live and the social forms and structures within which individual and group behavior takes place. Anthropology is a generic name for a number of even further specialized fields including *social anthropology, archaeology, physical anthropology and linguistics.* Traditionally, anthropologists have studied pre-literate and developing cultures. More recently anthropologists are studying *cultures* of industrialized *societies,* such as the United States. While many anthropologists continue to study pre-literate societies, Indian tribes, South Sea Islanders, and so on, more and more anthropologists are focusing their work on urban *groups* and seeking to understand *kinship* patterns, friendship relationships, the values and beliefs that characterize the contemporary urban center. Anthropologists have produced fruitful work on important contemporary problems such as *poverty,* ghetto life, minority groups and mental health.

Anthropologists who specialize in *physical anthropology* are concerned with the evolution of the human body, the antiquity of people and the development of human and social qualities. Archaeology is closely linked to physical anthropology. Archaeologists are concerned with early people and their culture. Through the physical residue of earlier times, they are putting together art objects, buildings, and burial mounds in an effort to reconstruct earlier civilization which have no recorded histories. *Social and cultural anthropology* is concerned with the organization, arrangement, beliefs and values of groups of people. In *linguistics,* anthropologists study the universals of human language and thought and their links to the behavior and social life of people.

ECONOMICS

Economics is sometimes defined as the study of the allocation of available productive resources among competing uses. The work of economists is focused on employment, *inflation and deflation,* ecomomic growth, fiscal and monetary policies, international payments, taxation, monopolies, manpower, labor markets, union movements, agricultural and industrial production and the inequities resulting from the distribution of income.

The theories and work of economists strongly influence the domestic and international policies of our government and the workings of both large and small businesses in the United States. Although many economists are engaged in generalized economic studies of a national or international scope, a number of them focus on highly specific topics, such as the problems involved in producing goods or of marketing and selling products. Economic indicators such as prices, wages and unemployment figures are well-know to us, and the public is probably more familiar with the areas of examination of economists than with any of the other social sciences. We worry constantly, for example, about inflation or recession. Economists provide indicators on these economic problems for persons and local or national governments.

POLITICAL SCIENCE

Political science investigates the ways in which people govern themselves. It is concerned with the goals of the political system, the structural relationships in that system, the patterns of *individual and group behavior* which help explain how the system functions, and the development of laws and social policies. Political scientists study a variety of phenomena involved in the process of government including political parties, interest groups, communication and public opinions, *bureaucracy,* and public administration.

In the United States, political scientists have provided us with considerable information about voting habits, such as the reasons underlying which persons vote and why they vote for certain individuals. They have also analyzed problems associated with the way local and national governments are developed and organized, as well as problems of international tensions such as those between competing ideologies. Some political scientists study the local communities in which they live; others are concerned with the development and processes of government in new nations or in remote *communities.* Some political scientists focus on broad ideological issues such as the emergent organizations of governments under *communism, socialism* and various other ideologies. Others are more microscopic in that they investigate and concern themselves with the way particular departments operate at a city or state government level. The political scientist, then, investigates political processes that set up and enforce various rules of collective behavior to realize group interests and to protect individual rights. He is concerned with patterns of interpersonal and group behavior which contribute to the ways in which various political systems function, and with the goals and structural relationships of political systems.

THE CONCEPT OF THE BEHAVIORAL SCIENCES

We have mentioned that the social sciences are sometimes described as the behavioral sciences. Many persons use the terms interchangeably. For a significant number, however, the concepts have somewhat different meanings, although the definitions of both are fuzzy. The term *behavioral sciences* was invented both to eliminate from consideration those aspects of the *social sciences* that are not directly concerned with behavior (such as *archaeology)* and to allow such fields as psychiatry and physiology to be included as *behavioral sciences.* The term is a more recent one than the *term social sciences.*

HOW SOCIAL SCIENTISTS WORK

Basically all scientists follow the same rules in their work (Freeman and Jones, 1970, pp. 3-4). They subscribe to a methodology or philosophy, if you will, which is commonly know as the scientific method.

Social scientists are trained to share a common outlook and to be aware of a wide set of techniques, although between disciplines there are differences in the emphasis given to the range of these techniques.

There are a number of rules in common, as Berelson and Steiner (1964) note. Their discussion is as brief and clear-cut as any:

The procedures are public: The results and the methods are both communicable and communicated. The scientific report contains a detailed description of just what was done and how. The description is adequate if, and only if, another competent practitioner of the science can follow each step of the investigation. In addition:

The definitions are precise: Here again, the procedure must be crystal-clear. As an example, the statement "aggressive subjects were found to have greater dependence on their fathers than non-aggressive subjects" is inadequate as a scientific report. How was aggressive defined and measured? By what test or procedures and by what specific scores? Where was the cut-off point between aggressive and non-aggressive subjects? How was dependence on the father revealed?

The data-collecting is objective: Once the investigation is underway, the investigator is bound to follow the data, whatever way they may fall—for or against his hypothesis (however cherished), and for or against his personal perferenes. Biased procedures in collecting data has no place in science, nor has biased perception of the results. As a result:

The findings are replicable: Because of the openness of the inquiry another scholar can test the findings by seeking to reproduce them. This is why "artistic sensitivity" or "clinical insight" is itself not sufficient, though it may of course suggest hypotheses. And, although all persons in the social sciences strive for replicability, the ability to repeat is more difficult in studying certain problems.

The purposes are explanation, understanding, and prediction: The scientists wants to know why and how, and to be able to prove it. if he can, then he can predict the conditions under which the specified behavior will occur. And if he can do that, then the question of control enters in as well. We have achieved a great deal of control over nature in the physical and biological sciences, and some in economic affairs; but the matter inevitably becomes more sensitive with the prospect that the behavioral science will enable us to control ourselves, or each other.

Thus, there are a variety of procedures and techniques used by social scientists. In broad terms, one can think about three different approaches which are commonly employed in the social sciences; the experiment, the survey, and the case study.

An *experiment* is any investigation that includes two elements: manipulation or control of some variable and systematic observation or measurement of the results. Experiments are common to all fields of science and those undertaken in the social sciences differ only by subject matter from ones in other fields. However, particularly in psychology, and to some extent in sociology, much of the investigation which is undertaken is by experiment. The basic design is the same. Some experiments in social sciences are carried out in laboratories; these are mainly studies undertaken with animals and are conducted under conditions that are as sterile and as well-controlled as research of a biological or physical nature. Other experiments are carried out in communities which are being investigated. Many of these experiments are complicated because of the realities of the everyday environment. One of the limitations of such experiments is the difficulty of manipulating and controlling the complex world in which we live. Another limitation is the concern for the well-being and privacy of subjects which might be otherwise affected by experiments.

The *survey,* known to many of us because of public opinion polling, is a common means of assessing political views, consumer preferences and the like. A wide variety of surveys are undertaken each year by social scientists, mainly by economists and political scientists. The surveys differ greatly in the topics considered and in their extent. (They also differ in whether they are carried out with selected subgroups from the population, or whether they are broad national studies of representative samples.) Generally, however, surveys are more concerned with factual and behavioral data rather than with delving deeply into the psychological recesses of individuals regarding their beliefs, values and motives.

Finally, there are case studies, either of single individuals or organizations, or of comparisons of several different people or groups. Much of the work of anthropologists consists of case studies. The survey measures many persons on a few characteristics, usually on one point in time. The case study typically examines quite intensively many characteristics of one or a few units, such as a community. Usually, case studies extend over relatively long periods of time. They may be of a particular person, perhaps during adolescence, or of a particular community during a period of rapid change in its ethnic or racial composition, or of a particular social class of persons in a city, or of any other special or definable group.

In addition an important source of information to social scientists is regularly collected information, public reports or other types of public records. For example, much economic analysis is based upon the information uniformly and regularly collected by federal, state and local governments. Sociologists often make use of statistics collected by police departments, the FBI and other law enforcement agencies in trying to understand deviant behavior and the crime problem. Many of these records are quite suitable for research; others are limited in accuracy and specificity.

It should be noted that there are widely divergent methods and techniques used in collecting data. *One of the dimensions running throughout the social sciences is the extent to which a particular study is quantitative — reported in numerical terms — or qualitative — reported in verbal statements.* Descriptions in terms of statistics, such as averages, and those reported in terms of "more" or "less" are equally valuable. However, the use of quantitative methods depends to a large extent on the particular field of inquiry. Likewise sometimes events, behavior or incidents are directly observed. At other times they are reported by the subjects themselves, and still at other times by individuals who are only marginally involved in some particular process or event. Some social scientists depend heavily on what is called participant observation, where the scientists literally become or have been and continue to be a part of the groups that they study. Others are much more detached and sit in their offices, directing large staffs of highly-trained interviewers who seek out appropriately designated informants. Both in terms of scope and intensity the key attribute of all scientific investigation seems to be systemization and replicability.

Any discussion of scientific method, however brief, must explicitly acknowledge the limitations that exist within all of the social sciences in conforming to generally-accepted ideas of scientific rigor. In certain of the disciplines, and when studying a number of critical research problems, opportunities for replication and precision are very limited. For example, anthropologists who use a semi-participant observation approach in studying a particular society at a particular time simply cannot repeat their investigations exactly. Limitations of time and money require that some studies be undertaken with less than perfectly developed instruments, or with measures whose reliability and validity are questionable. Nevertheless, regardless of the limitations of particular studies or work in the particular disciplines, social scientists hold in common with all scientists the attitude that it is important to strive to meet the general criteria for scientific work.

Finally, it should be pointed out that while social scientists try to operate with a set of procedures that emphasize objectivity, the choice of the problems they study and sometimes the way they go about studying these problems are related to who they are and what their *values* are. *Social science* is not "value free' in the sense of deciding what to study and when to undertake an investigation. However, scientific rigor is important in determining how one conducts a study. Indeed, there are continual accusations from both the radical right and left that the problem-selection process is dominated by persons whose *values* do not represent theirs. They feel that the "wrong" problems are often worked on and that they are being disenfranchised from using *social science* to advance their interest. Whether or not their accusations are justified is not a matter for this volume. However, perhaps the fact that these accusations exist clarifies the difference between objectivity in how *social science* operates and subjectivity in what *social science* emphasizes.

THE BASIC AND APPLIED SOCIAL SCIENCES

As is probably apparent from the discussion so far, the *social sciences,* like all science, contribute *both* to the knowledge base and to the solution and resolution of practical problems and issues. Often, a distinction is made between basic and applied science. The difference lies not so much in the actual steps or procedures that the scientists employ, but rather in the problems they select for their study and their concern for immediate practical applications. There is certainly a great difference between a social scientist who analyzes poverty in the biblical era and one who is concerned with *poverty* now. Different also are the investigator who studies public administration in the colonial period and the political scientist who studies problems of governmental adminstration in Washington today.

Recently, the *social sciences* and related disciplines have been more concerned with the immediacy of their work. There is a tendency on the part of social scientists and government, industry and community leaders to apply the knowledge, theories, techniques and procedures of the *social sciences* to the contemporary *community* and its many problems. (Freeman and Sherwood, 1970). The applied emphasis of the *social sciences* differs considerably. For instance, economics has long-term and historical links to government, industry and people of action, while sociology and anthropology have been traditionally more distant from the policy-maker and practitioner. Psychologist serve as therapists, vocational counselors and assessors of aptitudes and mental ability.

The *social sciences* like all science have a dual function. They serve to help people cope with their environment and at the same time to explore and to understand the world about them. In other words, simultaneously there is an interest in application and an interest in understanding. The balance between basic work and applied activities is often the subject of controversy among persons identified with the various social science disciplines. But while many social scientists hold that the primary goal of the *social sciences* is the discovery and verification of generalizations on social behavior, whether or not they are immediately useful in programs to improve social life and social conditions, given our troubled times, the applied perspective seems to be gaining adherents.

As we have noted, the *social sciences* were reviewed by the National Academy of Sciences and the Social Science Research Council (1969) which determined how useful they were in dealing with the many interpersonal and social problems that we face today. For the purpose of their report they chose an example from each of the social sciences to show how that particular *social science* has been useful:

Psychology—it is largely the work of psychologists that led to the development of computer instruction and reading improvement programs. This approach has raised the reading levels of hundreds of thousands of children throughout the country and revolutionized a part of our general educatonal system.

Sociology—Sociologists' studies of segregation in schools provided infor-

9

maton that led to both federal and local efforts to modify the racial composition of public schools.

Anthropology—Comparative studies of child rearing by anthropologists in which differences were found from one culture to the next have proved valuable to therapists and counselors in providing guidance to parents on the development of their children.

Economics—the development of economic indicators which provide figures at regular intervals on such matters as the cost of living, unemployment, and production of manufactured goods, are invaluable in planning the industrial and technical development of the country.

Political Science—Information and analysis by political scientists on national building and the ramification of social change in educational programs, occupational distributions and the like around the world have been used by our government, international organizations and private groups in establishing policies toward the developing nations.

The *social sciences* are far from having all the answers to the problems facing contemporary society. They are limited in method, theory and the manpower necessary to meet the many demands made upon them for new knowledge and improved application of existing knowledge. Social scientists in many ways have not been able to meet the expectations of persons in the community who are convinced that the very existence of people and progress toward better social conditions can come from the so-called "scientific method." But the potential is there and the work and accomplishments we can now see are convincing evidence of the promise of the *social sciences*.

Finally, it should be noted that there are a wide variety of practicing professionals—social workers, educators, persons in the medical specialities such as psychiatry, public health and rehabilitation, lawyers engaged in a variety of criminal and civil practices, city planners, recreation workers and the like whose knowledge base is drawn primarily from the *social sciences*. These practicing professionals and technicians, as well as, of course, responsible and intelligent laymen, gain much from an understanding of the *social sciences*. Many of their clinical and practice techniques, their procedures and perspectives are predicated on principles derived from the theories and research of the *social sciences*. In fact, in recent years, there has been a growing awareness and understanding of the *social sciences* on the part of socially concerned individuals, as well as professionals and technicians, in the fields of health, education and welfare, and medicine.

We have mentioned both the complex interrelationships between the *social sciences* and their potential contributions to problem-solving. Many of the problems that the world faces today require the combined efforts of persons in all of the social science disciplines, since these problems are beyond the interest and abilities of persons in any single discipline. Sometimes, one *social science* has more to offer than another; generally all of the *social sciences* can be brought into play in analyzing complex social problems. This is certainly true of such complex crises as international conflict in Viet Nam or the Middle East, or of our ecological environment, where noise pollution is of great concern to psychologists, air and water pollution of concern to economists and especially political scientists, who are concerned with the many political aspects of pollution. The *social sciences* cannot individually or collectivley pretend to have pat solutions to any of these very complicated issues. Rather, their contribution to any solution is to provide a detailed analysis of the problem. They can also present options which can be elected to reduce the problem, and the benefits and consequences of implementing alternate programs. For example, the social sciences have made important contributions to understanding the causes and effects of poverty.

A Conceptual Model for Characterizing Physical Activity[1] *

Gerald S. Kenyon
University of Wisconsin
Madison, Wisconsin

It is the purpose of this paper to report efforts to construct a model characterizing physical activity as a sociopsychological phenomenon. The work was based upon the assumptions that physical activity can be reduced to more specific components, i.e., a set of all physical activities can be reduced to logical subsets; and that a meaningful basis for such a procedure is the instrumental value physical activity is perceived to have for the individual. A rationale is given for each of the six dimensions of the model. In addition to construct validity, the integrity of the model was assessed by determining the degree of univocality and independence of the postulated subdomains.

The study of gross motor behavior frequently requires dealing with such concepts as *play, game, physical activity, sport,* and other similar terms. Yet the meaning of any one of these is complex; a fact that quickly becomes apparent upon even the most superficial analysis. Is adult play the same as child play, or football the same as craps? Is everything that appears on the sports page sport? Although difficulties seldom arise in their informal use, serious inquiry demands explicit definitions of all essential terms.

Review of Literature

Some writers have been satisfied with somewhat general definitions such as the meaning Huizinga (14) attaches to the concept *play*. Others have seen the utility in reducing a term to more fundamental components, such as the classifications of games by Caillois (4), Roberts and Sutton-Smith (25), and McIntosh (22).

When a conceptual domain is reduced to a logical system of subdomains the nature of the resultnig components depends upon the use to which the classification is to be put. For example, the term *physical activity,* when used in an instructional setting, such as in physical education, is often reduced to such heuristic categories as "individual and dual activities," "team games," rhythmics," "aquatics," and "dance." However, a structure based solely upon

* Kenyon, G. S. "A conceptual model for characterizing physical activity," *Research Quarterly*, 1968, *39*, 96-105. Reprinted by permission of the publisher.

pedagogical considerations may be of limited use in another context. Wrestling and tennis are "dual" activities, but beyond this fact they may have little else in common.

Purpose

It is the purpose of this paper to report efforts to construct a model characterizing physical activity as a sociopsychological phenomenon. The work was based upon the assumptions that physical activity can be reduced to more specific components; i.e., a set of all physical activities can be reduced to logical subsets, and that a meaningful basis for such a procedure is the instrumental value physical activity is perceived to have for the individual. That is, it was postulated that different classes of physical activities are perceived to provide different sources of satisfaction — a "perceived instrumentality" (28).

Definitions

For this study *physical activity* donotes organized, (structured), nonutilitarian (in an occupational or maintenance sense), gross human movement, usually manifested in active games, sports, calisthenics, and dance. Although the term *model*[2] has come to have a variety of meanings, for the work described herein, it is a system of representation for a phenomenon (in this case, physical activity) which furnishes new ways of regarding or thinking about empirical objects and events (17: 78-80).

PROCEDURE

The work reported herein was precipitated by a need for a more adequately defined "psychological object" about which one has positive or negative feelings (attitude). In developing a scale for assessing attitude toward physical activity, the question faced immediately was, "What does one mean by physical activity?" In an attempt to answer this question a combination of formal, empirical, and (admittedly) intuitive methods were employed.

RATIONALE

Since the object was to determine whether the domain *physical activity* can be reduced to several independent or quasi-independent subdomains, the first step was to formulate structural models, the components of which were to represent various hypothesized instrumental values of physical activity, manifest or latent. Such multidimensional models would be tested empirically by acquiring responses to verbal stimuli thought to represent each of the dimensions. If subdomains were independent of each other, responses should correlate within dimensions (internal consistency) but not between.

In all, three hypothetical models were postulated, the first two of which are described only briefly. The initial attempt consisted of six subdomains. These were: *physical health, mind-body dichotomy, cooperation-competition, mental health, social intercourse,* and *patriotism.* The basis for these was a combination of intuitive and traditional conceptions of the dimensions of the physical activity. Statements thought to represent each of the subdomains were incorporated in an inventory which was administered to a randomly selected sample of 756 adults[3] and to a convenient group of approximately 100 college students. Intercorrelations and factor analysis of each set of data provided little evidence of a meaningful structure. Reflection upon this failure suggested several explanations for this result, including the use of too few stimuli, the possiblity that subdomain were in themselves multidimensional, or the possibility that the deduced subdomains were not all on the same level of discourse.

Based in part upon an analysis of the results of the first attempt, and in part upon further reflection upon the instrumental value of physical activity, a second structure was formulated, also consisting of six subdomains: physical activity as a *social experience,* for *health and fitness,* as *the pursuit of vertigo,* as an *aesthetic experience,* as a *recreational experience,* and as a *competitive experience.* To test the integrity of this configuration, the universe of content was more systematically defined for each subdomain. Seventy-three Likert-type attitude statements were evaluated by judges, revised, incorporated into an inventory, and administered to 176 college men and women. A factor analysis of the item intercorrelation matrix yielded a solution that warranted the assumption of multidimensionality. For two of the subdomains — physical activity as a recreational experience and as a competitive experience — the results were still unsatisfactory, in that collecting the items thought to represent each did not account for any sizable amount of the common factor variance, again suggesting imprecision in the original definitions. The revision of the conceptual basis for these subdomains together with the apparent efficacy of the other four, was the basis of a third model (Figure 1) the nature and integrity of which will be described in some detail.

Although not all of equal logical rigor, the rationales underlying each of the six subdomains thought to represent the perceived instrumental value of physical activity were as follows:

1. *Physical activity as a social experience.* Claims that participation in physical activity can meet certain social needs of individuals have long emanated from professional sources (13, 24, 29). For this study it was postulated that lay opinion would be similar, that is, physical activity engaged in by groups of two or more is perceived by many as having some social value. To the extent that physical activity is play, Huizinga writes that such experiences provide opportunities for "sharing something important" (14:12). Thus physical activity as a social experience was characterized by those physical activities *whose primary purpose is to provide a medium for social intercourse,* i.e., *to meet new people and to perpetuate existing relationships.* Although such events as school or college dances and bowling im-

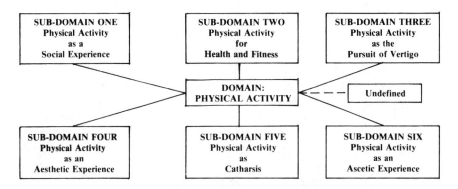

Figure 1. Structure of model for the characterization of physical activity.

14

mediately come to mind, almost any physical activity can serve such a purpose, either incidently or by design.[4]

2. *Physical activity for health and fitness.* That a sizable proportion of contemporary Western people, whether active themselves or not, believe that physical activity has the capacity to enhance personal health probably needs little documentation. The formation of the President's Council on Physical Fitness, the widely prevalent health studio, the writings of physical educators (6) and the statements of the medical profession (1), all serve to suggest that it is plausible to believe that many consider health through physical activity as both possible and desirable. Therefore, it was posited that some physical activity can be characterized primarily by its *contribution to the improvement of one's health and fitness.* Obviously, calisthenics and other conditioning exercises are for such a purpose, but conceivably, many activities could be similarly oriented.

3. *Physical activity as the pursuit of vertigo.* The suggestion that certain physical activities can provide a medium for pursuing vertigo comes from Caillois (4). Games based on the pursuit of vertigo.

. . . consist of an attempt to momentarily destroy the stability of perception and inflict a kind of voluptuous panic upon an otherwise lucid mind. In all cases, it is a question of surrendering to a kind of spasm, seizure, or shock which destroys reality with sovereign brusqueness . . .

Various physical activities . . . provoke these sensations, such as the tight rope, falling or being projected into space, rapid rotations, sliding, speeding, and acceleration of vertilinear movement separately or in combination with gyrating movement.

. . . men surrender to the intoxication of many kinds of dance, from the common but insidious giddiness of the waltz to the many mad, tremendous [sic] and convulsive movements of dances. They derive the same kind of pleasure from the intoxication stimulated by high speed on skis, motor cycles, or in driving sport cars. (4: 23-25).

McIntosh (22), has criticized Caillois' concept of games for the pursuit of vertigo pointing out that the sensation one receives on an amusement park device (classified by Caillois as vertiginous) is not the same as an activity over which the participant has some control.

Caillois' category of vertigo is thus seen not to be fundamental but to sub-divide within his classification of competition and chance depending on whether resourcefulness or resignation is the dominant factor. (22:126).

Despite such criticism, physical activity as the pursuit of vertigo has been retained as a category in the present model, since early empirical evidence showed it to have considerable promise. However, the chance element has been attenuated so that physical activity as the pursuit of vertigo is considered to be *those physical experiences providing, at some risk to the participant, an element of thrill through the medium of speed, acceleration, sudden change of direction, or exposure to dangerous situations, with the participant usually remaining in control.* In that he usually approaches vertigo without actually achieving it, the experience becomes the *pursuit* of vertigo. It is possible that the instrumental value here is latent. The participant may not recognize vertigo as the common element, but rather views sports such as skiing, diving from a high platform, heavy weather sailing, mountain climbing, sky diving, etc., as apparently unrelated.

4. *Physical activity as an aesthetic experience.* The proposition is advanced here that many people believe that at least some forms of physical activity are generally pleasing to the eye, and have a capacity for satisfying aesthetic tastes (7, 18). Although some may consider skilled movement as beautiful in a broad perspective from ballet to Olympic gymnastics, others would insist on a much narrower range of physical activites — perhaps restricted to the creative and expressive movements primarily found in the dance. The important point is that physical activity is often perceived of as having *aesthetic value for the individual — that is activities are conceived of as possessing beauty or certain artistic qualities.*

5. *Physical activity as catharsis.* Upon analysis of the results of using "recreational activities" as a category of physical activity, it became apparent that the concept was too nebulous to be useful, and that it did not sufficiently characterize the function of a certian kind of activity for the individual. It seemed that both these difficulties might be overcome by narrowing the conception to *physical activity perceived as providing a release of tension precipitated by frustration through some vicarious means.* The notion that a reduction in tension is achieved by expressing hostility and aggression, either directly, by attacking the instigator of the frustration, or more commonly, through venting one's hostilities through some equivalent form of aggressive behavior, is the "catharsis hypothesis" (3). The use of catharsis in this sense, however, departs somewhat from the meaning the term has in the context of Greek drama. Nevertheless, writers from philosphers to psychiatrists, have, for some time, been employing *catharsis* in a more general sense, often with respect to physical activity and sport. Nietzeche wrote of ". . . simple outlets for getting rid of sudden congestion by a violent muscular exertion . . ." (23:291). Menninger (10:343) claimed that " . . . competitive games provide an unusually satisfactory social outlet for the instinctive aggressive drive . . . " Wenkert (28:403) alluded to catharsis through sport spectatorship. Despite the frequently made claims for catharsis through substitute aggression, including the use of play and sport (8, 9, 15, 19), the findings of Berkowitz (3) cast doubt upon the existence of the phenomenon. Again, however, what is important is whether or not physical activity is *perceived* as having a cathartic function, that is, the belief that physical activity can provide a release from frustration and so called pent-up emotions created by pressures of modern living.

6. *Physical activity as an ascetic experience.* An attempt to conceive of certain forms of physical activity as providing a "competitive" experience did not prove successful. Either the choice of stimuli was poor, or the concept *competition* is not a unitary phenomenon. The later position is supported in part by McIntosh (22). In his analysis of Caillois' category "com-

petition," he discusses four subcategories of competitive games, all of which provide a means for expressing the "desire for superiority." It was reasoned that if sport provides a medium for the expression of superiority as McIntosh suggests, then those who aspire to high levels of achievement, regardless of the sport, recognize the need to delay gratification and to be able to endure long and strenuous periods of training.[5] The associated punishment of the body (although seldom inflicting permanent damage) is seen by some to be somewhat akin to religious ascetism (19).

. . . by detaching the senses [from objects of enjoyment] . . . and by rigorously practicing austerities [men] gain that state [even] in this [world].
—The Laws of Manu, (26:183).

It would seen that contemporary sport provides and analogy. Championship performance today requires athletes to undergo a kind of "ascetic" experience whereby physical activity for him involves long strenuous, and often painful training and stiff competition demanding a deferment of many gratifications.[6]

EVALUATING THE INTEGRITY OF THE STRUCTURE

If the conceptual structure proposed above is to have merit as a model serving to represent the sociopsychological characteristics of physical activity, two conditions need to be met: (a) each subdomain must be univocal, i.e., internally consistent, and (b) the various subdomains must be relatively independent of one another. In essence, this approach represents the testing of the model for construct validity (5). To accomplish this objective, data were acquired from college freshmen (353 men, 215 women) consisting of responses to Likert-type attitude statements thought to be representative of each of the subdomains of the hypothesized model. Many of these stimuli were revisions of statements used to test previous forms of the model. Separate inventories for men and women were used, using sex-appropriate statements where necessary. Response styles were evaluated, and item analyses performed[7] providing criteria for selecting the best statements for subsequent analyses. The degree of internal consistency of each subdomain was determined using Hoyt's analysis of variance approach. Coefficients were maximized by rescaling the priori weights of the best items using a reciprocal averages procedure (2). The structural integrity of the model was tested using an incomplete image analysis (10, 11) followed by an oblique rotation (12) of the first six factors.[8]

RESULTS

Internal Consistency

The degree of internal consistency for each of the six subdomains is given in Table 1. For each form maximized Hoyt r's were determined both for the original 84 items and for the "best items" based upon item analysis. For both men and women, r's for the "social experience" dimension were lowest, while those for "pursuit of vertigo" were highest.

Independence of Subdomains

Although item reliabilities are generally low[9] and thus precipitate a large error variance (21), an oblique rotation of the first six factors following an incomplete image analysis yielded clusters of items clearly corresponding to each of the six postulated subdomains. Table 2 presents for each factor the number of items with loadings of .30 or higher compared to the number of items predicted to represent each subdomain.[10] The greatest consistency was with the *pursuit of vertigo* scale. Although the six domains appeared to be relatively independent some of the factors were correlated, as seen in Table 3. The stronger relationship appeared to be among the *catharsis, health and fitness* and *ascetic* dimensions. However, no two factors shared more than 32 percent of the variance — usually much less. The "social" and "aesthetic" dimensions showed the greatest independence.[11]

Table 1. Hoyt Reliabilities for Each of Six Scales Based on Samples of 353 Men and 215 Women.

Scale	Original items (Form C)		Best items (Form D)	
	n_1[a]	Hoyt r	n_1	Hoyt r
1. Social experience				
Men	14	.70-72[b]	10	.70-.72
Women	14	.70-.74	8	.68-.72
2. Health and fitness				
Men	14	.74-.77	10	.79
Women	14	.79-.82	11	.83
3. Pursuit of vertigo				
Men	14	.88-.89	10	.88-.89
Women	14	.83-.84	9	.86
4. Aesthetic experience				
Men	14	.80-.82	10	.82
Women	14	.83-.85	9	.87
5. Catharsis				
Men	14	.69-.78	9	.77
Women	14	.72-.80	9	.79
6. Ascetic experience				
Men	14	.82-.82	10	.81
Women	14	.74-.79	8	.74-.78

[a]Number of items used to represent each scale.
[b]The first coefficient is based upon a priori weights, the second, based upon weights rescaled to optimize reliability. Where rescaling did not increase r, only the original coefficient is given, i.e., based upon the [a] priori weights 1 through 7.

Table 2. Number of Items Loading on Each Factor Contrasted with Number Predicted to Represent Each Subdomain (Forms CM and CW).

Subdomain	No. of items predicted	Number of items with loading of .30 or better on first six factors					
		1	2	3	4	5	6
1. Social experience							
Men	10	3	0	0	1	0	6
Women	9	3	0	0	0	0	7
2. Health and fitness							
Men	10	3	0	0	1	6	0
Women	11	3	0	1	9	0	0
3. Pursuit of vertigo							
Men	10	0	10	0	1	0	0
Women	9	1	0	0	0	0	0
4. Aesthetic experience							
Men	10	0	0	9	0	0	0
Women	9	0	9	0	0	0	0
5. Catharsis							
Men	9	9	0	0	0	0	0
Women	9	4	0	0	0	5	1
6. Ascetic experience							
Men	10	0	0	0	10	0	0
Women	8	8	0	1	0	1	0

Table 3. Factor Intercorrelations Resulting from Oblique Rotation of Six Incomplete Image Factors—Independent Cluster Solution (Forms CM and CW)

Men	1	2	3	4	5	6
1. Catharsis	1.00	.18	.14	.45	.52	.18
2. Vertigo		1.00	.07	.17	.15	.16
3. Aesthetic			1.00	.04	.22	.39
4. Ascetic				1.00	.44	.01
5. H and F					1.00	.03
6. Social						1.00

Women	1	2	3	4	5	6
1. Ascetic	1.00	.20	.45	.57	.57	.44
2. Aesthetic		1.00	.02	.11	.08	.18
3. Vertigo			1.00	.28	.29	.16
4. H and F				1.00	.38	.12
5. Catharsis					1.00	.36
6. Social						1.00

DISCUSSION

Although some success was met in developing a model for characterizing physical activity as a sociopsychological phenomenon, the work described herein represents only a crude beginning. First, no claim is made that the entire domain of physical activity has been exhausted. The model presented here may represent only a few of the actual dimensions. Second, the test of a model lies in its application. Although attitude scales have been developed based upon the characterization of physical activity as described in this paper, it is not known whether the model would have other uses, such as the classification of interests. Thus considerable caution is in order.

SUMMARY

An attempt was made to develop a multidimensional conceptual model for characterizing physical activity from the standpoint of its perceived instrumental value for individuals. The two necessary conditions for testing the worth of the hypothesized structure, namely, internal consistency and subdomain independence, were sufficiently met to warrant the conclusion that the conceptual model postulated herein has some validity. This does not imply that all the dimensions of physical activity have been accounted for, nor does it imply that this is the only approach to characterizing physical activity.

REFERENCE NOTES

1. The writer is indebted to Jacqueline Damgaard, John W. Loy, Jr., Robert Pruzek, and Albert Solomon, for their assistance with one or more phases of the research; to Professors Owen Bergsrud, State University of Wisconsin — River Falls, and Phillis Roney, State University of Wisconsin — Oshkosh, and their colleagues for providing subjects; and to Professor Frances Z. Cumbee of the University of Wisconsin, for reading the manuscript. The research upon which this paper is based has been supported by National Institute of Mental Health Grants MH 08214-01 and MH 11038-01, and University of Wisconsin Graduate School Research Committee Grant 63-851.
2. Although not without difficulties, the term *model* was felt to be more suitable than *frame of reference, analogy,* or *paradigm.* It would be greatly premature to employ the term *theory,* even in a limited sense. Although a model is often regarded as a "separate system" the structure described in this paper was formulated in conjunction with the development of scales to measure attitude toward physical activity. The latter work is described in a companion paper written by the author, "Six scales for assessing attitude toward physical activity," *Research Quarterly,* in press.
3. As part of a survey of adult opinion based upon Project 120 of Wisconsin Survey Research Center. Population: all noninstitutionalized, nonmilitary adults over the age of 21 in the state of Wisconsin.
4. See companion paper for example of verbal stimuli used to represent each subdomain.
5. Caillois himself alludes to this element of competition, but does not see the need for a separate category (4:16).
6. No claim is made that physical activity as an ascetic experience represents all elements of competition.
7. Details are given in the companion paper.
8. For exploratory purposes, a second approach was attempted. A multidimensional scaling analysis of the first four subdomains was carried out based upon dissimilarity data acquired from inventories developed especially for this purpose.

9. For this study squared multiple correlations based upon loadings for as many as twenty factors seldom exceeded 0.50 for a given item. Thus common factor variances were expectedly small — between 40 and 50 percent, depending upon the number of factors considered.

10. Pattern matrices are available upon request.

11. When the multidimensional scaling approach was used a meaningful solution was obtained, although the level of "stress" was only "fair to good."

REFERENCES

American Medical Association, Resolutions on health and fitness. Passed by house of delegates, June 1960.

Baker, F. B. Univac scientific computer program for scaling of psychological inventories by the method of reciprocal averages. *Behav. sci.* 5:268-69, 1960.

Berkowitz, L. *Aggression: a social psychological analysis.* New York: McGraw-Hill, 1962.

Caillois, R. *Man, play, and games.* New York: The Free Press of Glencoe, 1961.

Cronbach, L., and Meehl, P. E. Construct validity in psychological tests. *Psychol. bull.,* 52:281-302, 1955.

Cureton, T. K. *Physical fitness an dynamic health.* New York: Dial Press, 1961.

H'Doubler, M. *Dance, a creative art experience.* Madison: University of Wisconsin Pess, 1962.

Gardner, G. E. Recreation's part in mental health. *Recreation.* 45:446-48, 1952.

Gerstl, J. E. Leisure, taste, and occupational milieu. In E. O. Smigel (Ed.), *Work and leisure.* New Haven, Conn.: College and University Press, 1963.

Guttman, L. Image theory for the structures of quantitative variates. *Psychometrika.* 18:277-96, 1953.

Harris, C. W. Some Rao-Guttman relationships. *Psychometrika.* 27:247-63, 1962.

Harris, C. W., and Kaiser, H. F. Oblique factor analytic solutions by orthogonal transformations. *Psychometrika.* 29:347-62, 1964.

Hetherington, C. W. *School program in physical education.* Yonkers on Hudson, New York: World Book Co., 1922.

Hutzinga, J. *Homo ludens.* Boston: Beacon Press, 1950.

Husman, B. F. Aggression in boxers and wrestlers as measured by projective techniques. *Res. quart.* 26:421-25, 1955.

Kenyon, G. S. A multidimensional scaling approach to validating an a priori model for characterizing values held for physical activity. Paper presented at national convention, AAHPER, Dallas, Texas, March 20, 1965. Mimeographed.

Lachman, R. The model in theory construction. In M. H. Marx (Ed.), *Theories in contemporary psychology.* New York: Macmillan Co., 1963.

Langer, S. K. *Philosophy in a new key.* New York: Mentor, 1942.

Meheu, R. Sport and culture. *J. hlth, phys. educ., rec.* 34:30-32, Oct. 1963.

Menninger, W. C. Recreation and mental health. *Recreation.* 42:340-46, 1948.

Messick, S., and Ross, J., (eds.) *Measurement in personality and cognition.* New York: Wiley, 1962.

McIntosh, P. C., *Sport in society.* London: Watts, 1963.

Nietzsche, F. *The dawn of day* (1881). In D. Levy (Ed.), *The complete works of Friedrich Nietzsche.* Edinburgh: Foulis, 1909-1913.

Oberteuffer, D., and Ulrich, C. *Physical education.* New York: Harper and Row, 1962.

Roberts, J., and Sutton-Smith, B. Child training and game involvement. *Ethnology.* 1:166-85. 1962.

Radhakrishnan, S., and Moore, C. A. (eds.) *A source book in Indian philosophy.* Princeton: University Press, 1957.

Rosenberg, M., and others. *Attitude organization and change.* New Haven: Yale University Press, 1960.

Wenkert, S. The meaning of sports for contemporary man. *J. exist. psychiat.* 3:397-404, 1963.

Williams, J. F. *The principles of physical education.* Philadelphia: Saunders, 1964.

Play, Games, Sport, And Athletics In Perspective*

Stephen K. Figler

Since we will be using these terms throughout the text, it is important that we understand the similarities and differences among play, games, sport, and athletics. A number of writers attempt to define these terms by looking to their etymology. This is done particularly with *sport* where the Latin, Greek, or French roots are often used to clarify definition. This tactic is often more confusing than helpful because the form of words and their meaning, both denotation and connotation, change over time and geo-political context. Thus, while the French *desport* may originally have meant "to divert oneself" in the French cultural context, it does not necessarily follow that its derivative, *sport,* carries the same meaning in late 20th century America, or France for that matter. Therefore, in defining key words, we will avoid their etymology and focus instead upon present context.

Johan Huizinga in *Homo Ludens* describes the characteristics of play as follows (1955:13):

. . . a free activity standing quite consciously outside "ordinary" life as being "not serious," but at the same time absorbing the player intensely and utterly. It is an activity connected with no material interest, and no profit can be gained by it. It proceeds within its own proper boundaries of time and space according to fixed rules and in an orderly manner. It promotes the formation of social groupings which tend to surround themselves with secrecy and to stress their differences from the common world by disguise or other means.

Caillois (1961:9-10) analyzed Huizinga's conception of the characteristics of play and restated them as follows:

1. Free involvement — play is voluntary.

2. Separated from "non-play" by spatial and temporal limits (lines, ropes, walls, goals, innings, holes, maximum or minimum points).

3. Uncertainty of outcome — especially where competition is an element of the play activity, efforts are often made to insure that both or all sides begin evenly and that the process is "fair." Thus, play is not play if it is not fair play.

4. Unproductive — no material gain comes from playful activity.

*From *Sport and Play in American Life* by Stephen K. Figler. Copyright © 1981 by CBS College Publishing. Reprinted by permission of CBS College Publishing.

5. Rules govern the procedures.

6. Make-believe — play stands apart from "real life."

More recently, Garvey (1977:4-5) attributed to play these characteristics:

1. Play is pleasurable, enjoyable. Even when not actually accompanied by signs of mirth, it is still positively valued by the player.

2. Play has no extrinsic goals. Its motivations are instrinsic (sic) and serve no other objectives. In fact, it is more an enjoyment of means than an effort devoted to some particular end. In utilitarian terms, it is inherently unproductive.

3. Play is spontaneous and voluntary. It is not obligatory but is freely chosen by the player.

4. Play involves some active engagement on the part of the player.

5. Play has certain systematic relations to what is not play.

While many more scholars have attempted to analyze play[1] and its components, one characteristic seems to appear often: its separateness from "reality." Huizinga, Caillois, and Garvey all seem to agree on this thought. For example, in Garvey's last characteristic listed above, attacking behavior during play is accepted as mock attack (unreal or nonliteral) rather than as literal attack with its consequent dangers. Play ceases when the attack or the danger become real.

In contrast, theologian Michael Novak in *The Joy of Sports* (1976:40) insists that "Play is reality. Work is diversion and escape." Play, according to Novak, is real because it concerns living and life in the present tense. Work, on the other hand, is unreal because it is motivated by and directed toward something past, such as paying bills and debts, or future-oriented toward goals such as saving, security, and improvement.

Reality only exists in the present tense. We can only "be" now. Our "becoming" is oriented toward a future non-reality, something that we hope to become but are not yet. Play and sport, for Novak, are pure "nowness." All that matters is what is going on now, within the confines of the activity. Indeed, one of the difficult tasks of coaches is to keep players' minds on and in the game or match at hand. When we leave the mental state of "play," we return to activities that attempt to cover for our past debts or plan for our as-yet-unrealized future.

> The serious ones say that sports are escape. It seems far more true to the eye, the ear, the heart, and the mind that history is an escape. Work is an escape. Causes are an escape. Historical movements are an escape. All these escapes must be attempted; I take part in as many as I can. But the heart of human reality is courage, honesty, freedom, community, excellence: the heart is sports (Novak, 1976:42).

Novak's perspective is refreshing and introduces a possible resolution to Huizinga's unsatisfactory view of play as unreal. However, Novak's view is not wholly satisfactory either, since he fails to distinguish between play and sport. We can readily imagine sports in the future used as a means for improving one's life, as a tool of politics, and for other worldly purposes ulterior to play. We might suggest that sport is not a unitary concept, but rather like a chameleon, it takes on the hue of its environment. Play, on the other hand, has a hue of its own.

How do play and sport, games and athletics resemble each other? How do they differ? In common parlance these terms may be used interchangeably or in the same context. It would be naive to think that by defining them more carefully, we could change their common usage. Our purpose in defining them more closely is not to change common usage, but rather to allow the readers of this text to see the shadings of difference among these terms so that our communication may be more precise and shared.

Edwards (1973) provides a useful distinction among three key terms: play, games, and sport. I feel it is necessary to distinguish further between sport and athletics. These four categories should not be conceived as distinct, but rather as positions upon a continuum of physical activity possessing the aura, if not the reality, of leisure (see Fig. 1.1).

Edwards points out that although some aspects of these activities are different in gradation only, other categories have particular aspects that absolutely distinguish one form of activity from the others. For example, each category or position on the continuum is characterized more or less by *fun.* That is, while we may have fun in all categories, in play fun is a necessary component. It is not a necessary component for the other three categories. To explain this more fully

1. In play, fun is essential; play ceases when fun ceases (i.e., when the activity becomes drudgery or work).

2. In games, fun is usually present, although compulsion or obligation to finish the game may keep participants involved even after their pleasure ceases.

3. In sport, fun is hoped for and expected, but is not a necessary ingredient of the activity.

4. In athletics, fun is completely irrelevant and may be unlikely considering the pressures involved.

Rather than being present to a lesser or greater extent in all categories, certain characteristics exist in some categories but are totally absent in others. Competition, for example, is a necessary component of games, sport, and athletics since each points to a particular outcome or culmination of the activity. Play, on the other hand, is non-competitive in its purest state, since play has no set beginning and set ending and has only the state of enjoyment as its goal, rather than a victory of some sort.

Keeping in mind that we are conceiving the four forms of activity as areas on a continuum, rather than as mutually exclusive categories, what

Figure 1-1.   Continuum of Physical Leisure Activity.

| Play | Games | | Sport | Athletics |

are the attributes most characteristic of each area and what are the particular characteristics that distinguish given categories from the others?

PLAY

Freedom. Play tends to be free. Participants enter and exit of their own volition. To the extent that play is ordered or controlled by some external authority figure such as an elementary school teacher ("Playtime!") or one's mother ("Go out and play in the street."), the activity may be less "playful," unless the player wants to play anyway. In other words, it is difficult truly to play if you do not want to play.

Limits. Play tends not to be limited in time and space. One can, if not may, play anywhere at any time. A ballpark with foul lines designating "out of play" is unnecessary. Play occurs in a field, at home, at school, in a business office (more or less surreptitiously), and on the surface of the moon. Play may become less playful or less free when someone says, "Time to stop playing!" but we know that such edicts do not necessarily and immediately put an end to the play activity, although fear of punishment might put a severe crimp in the joyfulness of the play.

Rules and authority. In play there are few and flexible rules. Such rules as there are often change at a player's whim. So long as the new rule is agreed upon, play continues. Disagreement and conflict bring an end to the playfulness of play.

Play has no imposed authority figure. Authority resides within the players during play. A well-meaning adult who tries to interject or impose his or her own conception of "the rules" simply interferes with the play in progress.

Outcome. Play is devoid of competition since competition implies a degree of gain or loss that is difficult to pursue given the freedom of time, space, rules, entry, and exit inherent in play.

Motivation. The primary motivation of play is pleasure. If the activity is not fun, it is not play. In the absence of fun, any activity becomes work.

Investment. Finally, play is characterized by an absence of investment. True play requires no money, planning, training, or ego-investment. While play may occur in their presence, play is quite possible, if not more probable, in their absence.

GAMES

Freedom. While games tend also to be free, there is less complete freedom than in play because games usually have a specific beginning and a specific end. Therefore, when one enters a game, one is implicitly obligated as a player to participate until the end (although there is less obligation to oneself in a game such as solitaire).

Limits. Games tend to be confined within specific limits of space (i.e., boundaries) and time (either temporal limits or completion of designated activities such as capturing other players or holes or innings played).

Rules and authority. Games tend to be played by rules that may be changed on agreement. However, this is less likely to occur than in pure play because games are pointed toward a specific outcome which may be obscured or subverted by mid-game rules changes.

Outcome. When a game is begun, it is understood that there will be a winner and a loser, requiring some degree of competition to determine the winner. This is the key distinction between games and play. While in pure play there are only participants, not winners and losers, in a game all entrants begin their game with the shared assumption that each is trying to win, whether or not the game actually culminates in a definitive outcome.

Investment. Since games imply winners and losers, there may be a degree of emotion or ego-investment, although such investment tends to be light relative to the next two categories. In other words, games are primarily recreational, with relaxation, exercise, human interaction, and enjoyment providing the primary motivations.

Games, like play, need not be physical, while sport and athletics require physical exertion. For our purposes, however, we will consider primarily play and games of the physical type in order to compare them with sport and athletics.

SPORTS

The difference in character between games and sports increases dramatically over the difference between play and games (thus the greater distance between the two in Fig. 1.1), with sports tending to take on more of the character of work while relinquishing some of the appearance of play and games.[2]

Structure. Sports imply a structure of teams and of leagues. There are more restrictive controls over entry into and exit from sports participation than there are in the two prior categories.

Authority. Sports tends to have a hierarchical authority pattern within given competing groups. Coaches exist to guide and/or dictate to players. At least one level of external authority (Little League Baseball, the AAU, high school state sports associations) also exists to dictate regulations, schedules, and conduct. While rules in games may or may not be codified (i.e., written), by agreement among players in a particular game these rules may be altered or transgressed. This is not so in a sport where rules changes must be channeled through an authority that governs the sport.

Investment. Sports are significantly more competitive than games, and it follows that there is significantly more investment of time, energy, money, and ego in sports. This greater degree of investment in sports than in games, and a concern for won-lost records in addition to the outcome of the contest at hand, is a key distinguishing feature of sports, as Edwards (1973), among others, points out.

Quite often, the investment aspect of sports equals or outweighs its recreational aspect. The recreational Sunday golfer, tennis player, or runner who has significant ego-investment (and often monetary investment in equipment) may be clothing his or her "game" in the raiments of sports. On the other hand, many weekend participants legitimize their sports involvement by joining sports clubs or tournaments with achievement as their express goal. Problems can occur when some recreationally inclined players engage in contests with more ego-invested opponents, or when the motivation changes in mid-contest. What began as "just a game" sometimes becomes something more.

This scenario illustrating possible crossed lines of communication among participants might be a problem among middle class adults or possibly in intramural sports. In such situations as inner city basketball contests, the games are seldom "just games" because of the long-range goals of many of the players and often because of the scarcity of playing space and the need to work or play hard in order to keep playing.

ATHLETICS

Sports and athletics are often conceived as synonymous and tend to be used interchangeably (Edwards, 1973). A distinction, however, is not only useful but necessary in a world seemingly exploding with sportive activities of all kinds and degrees.

In simple terms, we may conceive of athletics as sports in spades. Athletics out-sports sport. If sports are highly structured, the category of athletics is virtually rigid. If sports limit access and exit, athletics is absolutely restrictive. This is particularly apparent in the rigid guidelines that allow and prevent participation in college and Olympic athletics.

Although sports have their modest forms of authority hierarchy, systems of athletics place athletes on the lowest status level of an extensive authority structure with the least voice in procedures, despite the fact that athletes are the essence of athletics. In recent years, athletes and social critics such as Hoch (1972), Scott (1971), and Edwards (1969) have publicly bemoaned the pawn-like status of players.

Regarding goals and motivations, athletics also outdistances sport. Sports require some investment, while athletics is big business. Sports are competitive, while in athletics, "Winning is the only thing." It would be nice but totally irrelevant in athletics if the athletes were having fun.

The distinction between sports and athletics, in Keating's words (1964:28), is based on a difference in "attitude, preparation, and purpose of the participants." Sports are basically pleasurable diversions characterized by moderate effort, while participation in athletics is characterized by intense dedication and sacrifice.

The term sports, as used in this text, will refer to the category of activities that is more conducive to fun than athletics and is, at least by degree, less serious and consuming than athletics. *Sport* (in the singular form) will be considered a generic term for sports, athletics, and even some competitive physical games.

REFERENCE NOTES

1. The interesting topic of *why* humans play is tangential to our present concern with how we play. Sage (1979) discusses briefly but thoroughly theories of why people play.
2. Jaeggi (1967) has found some empirical support for this contention in Europe.

Backyard Versus Little League Baseball: Some Observations on the Impoverishment of Children's Games in Contemporary America *

Edward C. Devereux

In this presentation, I plan to focus on a few more general issues. Most generally, my critique of Little League Baseball, and other such major sports programs for children, will be based not so much upon what participation in such activities does for the child-participants as upon what it does *not* do for them. I will argue that "Little Leaguism" is threatening to wipe out the spontaneous culture of free play and games among American children, and thus that it is robbing our children not just of their childish fun but also of some of their most valuable learning experiences.

On the impoverishment of children's games in America. One way to gain insight about what is happening in contemporary America is to look at ourselves in cross-cultural and historical perspective. Earlier this year, I spent two months in Japan, carrying out a survey among Japanese school children. While there, I spent as much time as I could observing children in informal play settings, such as parks, neighborhood playgrounds, school yards, apartment court yards and city streets. What struck me most forcefully was the observation that Japanese children seem to spend very little time just "hanging around"; whenever two or more children found themselves together, they seemed to move very quickly into some kind of self-organized but rule-oriented play. Though I made no formal inventory, I was impressed with the great variety and richness of the games I observed. Although the Japanese also have Little League Baseball, most of the games I observed were carried out wholly without adult instigation or supervision.

On one occasion my wife and I observed a group of some dozen kindergarten children playing ring games in a public park. I have no doubt

* Devereux, E. C. "Backyard versus Little League Baseball: Some Observations on the Impoverishment of Children's Games in Contemporary America," In D. M. Landers, *Social Problems in Athletics: Essays in the Sociology of Sport*. Urbana, Illinois: University of Illinois Press, 37-56, 1976. Reprinted by permission of the author.

28

that these children were brought to the park by some teacher or adult supervisor, and I kept waiting for some adult to appear to structure the next game for them. But during the forty-five minutes we remained in the vicinity no adult ever approached or spoke to the children. Evidently the game repertory, the motivation to play, and the ability to organize and pace their own activities were well rooted in the children's own heads.

Later in the year, I went to Israel on another research project, and again I spent as much time as I could observing the informal play activities of the Israeli children. Here also I was impressed with the enormous variety of spontaneous games and play activities I observed. On this, we also have some impressive research documentation in the work of the Israeli psychologist Rivka Eifermann (1971a). In her study, a team of some 150 observers recorded the play activities of some fourteen thousand Israeli school children, in Kibbutzim, Moshavim and cities, in school yards, playgrounds and streets, over a two year period. One result of this research was the compilation of an encyclopedia of over 2000 games the children were observed to be playing, including many bewildering variants on such well-known games as soccer, tag and hop-scotch, as well as hundreds of less well known games, also in endless variations (Eifermann, 1971b). Most of the games, moreover, were being played wholly without adult instigation or supervision.

All this challenges us to raise the question: What has happened to the culture of children's games in America? Looking back to my own childhood, some fifty years ago, I can recall literally dozens of games we played regularly and with enthusiasm — puss in the corner, red rover, capture the flag, one-o-cat, statues, stealing sticks, blind man's bluff, croquet, leap frog, duck on the rock, prisoner's base, and many, many more. No doubt some of these are still around, in vestigial form; but my impression is that I rarely see these, or other games like them, being played spontaneously by children. Those which are played seem to be adult-instigated and supervised, in schools, camps or other organized play settings, or in party settings in homes. And even here, our game culture has become sadly impoverished. Ask any group of children what they did at a birthday party and nine out of ten will say they pinned the tail on the donkey. Halloween? Bob for apples and tricks or treats! What ever happened to the tricks, incidentally? We have institutionalized and sterilized Halloween, and thereby killed most of its creativity and fun. Most generally, it appears that our game culture has become sadly impoverished from lack of use and from an excess of adult supervision and control. "Come on, children, we're all going to play a game now!" "Do we *have* to?" You can almost hear the groans.

On these trends, there is also some research evidence in a fascinating study by Sutton-Smith and Rosenberg (1971). In their monograph, these authors compare game preferences of American children as documented in four different research studies spanning a sixty-year period from the late 1890s to the late 1950s. Even though these four studies are not strictly comparable, nevertheless certain general trends are impressively clear. The great variety of once-popular indoor and backyard skill games, such as croquet and quoits, have all declined in interest, to be replaced by the ubiquitous ping-pong. Leader games, such as Simon Says, statues, and follow the leader, are now of little interest for boys. Chasing games, like tag, are now acceptable only to very little children. Central person parlor games, such as hide the thimble, forfeits and twenty questions, have mostly disappeared, as have the endless varieties of ring games, such as drop the handkerchief and London Bridge, and the team guessing and acting games, like charades. Individual games of skill — remember mumble-de-peg? — are withering away. Virtually all of the undifferentiated team games, such as hare and hound, prisoner's base, etc., have either disappeared or declined in interest, as boys have devoted more of their attention to a few major sports. And even here, the authors conclude, the range of choice has narrowed significantly:" . . . trends would indicate that boys are spending more and more time on fewer sports. Bowling, Basketball, and Football improve in rank positions, but all other sports decline. . . . This would appear to be further evidence of the increasing circumscription of the boy's play role." (p. 47)

How can we account for this apparently very real constriction in the game culture of American children? How do American children realy spend their spare time? In the presence of this audience, I am tempted to say that they are all out there on the baseball and football fields, or on the hockey rinks, participating according to season in the sports programs organized for them by schools and other adult sponsoring agencies. In fact, as we all know, several hundred thousand of them are doing just that, for example, as members of the now more than forty thousand Little League Baseball teams. For these children, there can be no doubt that such team activities capture a very large share of their time and attention. In one study reported by Skubic (1956), for example, 81 out of 96 Little League players in the Santa Maria area "reported that half to most of their leisure time during the whole year is spent on baseball." (p. 102)

But even conceding that a very large absolute number of children are now involved in such organized sports, the fact remains that the vast majority of children in the 8 to 12 age range are not. What do they do instead? A great deal of unstructured, non-rule-oriented play: bike riding, for example, still ranks very high with both boys and girls. In American homes, toys, hobby kits and various proprietary games such as Monopoly still find wide acceptance among children. Just hanging around and talking, or very informal horseplay with friends, now occupies a very large share of the typical preadolescent's time. Finally, and by far the most important, there is television watching, to which this age group now devotes some twenty hours per week.

On this, I would spectulate that the availability of a mass television audience has had a lot to do with the extraordinary ascendency of Big Leaguism in America, and perhaps indirectly, of Little Leaguism as well. By focusing the attention of millions of viewers on a handful of major sports, and on the heroic teams and individual stars within them, we have converted ourselves to a nation of spectators. For most of us, sports are

30

something to be watched, not played — or at least not by amateurs.

Personaly, I doubt that very many children in the 8-12 range are television sports addicts, though some undoubtedly are. But children surely perceive where their father's interests are focused, and by 10 or 12 are well aware of the extraordinary pay-off value of success in major sports in America. They see how the star athletes are rewarded in college and high school sports, and how pleased their fathers are at any athletic achievements of their own. I suspect that Little Leaguism for elementary school children is fostered more by the parents than by the children themselves, though for some it falls on well-cultivated ground. Here is a chance to "play" at something really important that parents and adults generally seem to take very seriously.

But even for the children who have no special interest or competence in any major sport, probably a majority of all children, or who are actually alienated by the whole sub-culture of organized, competitive sports, the model is still there and highly salient. Against the heroic, if perhaps somewhat myopic, standards of Big League or Little League sports, who would dare propose a simple game of puss in the corner, capture the flag or red rover? Kid stuff, unworthy of the time and attention of any red-blooded American boy past the age of seven or eight!

On the educational functions of play and games. Why should we care about what has been happening to the recreational and spare time activities of our children? In approaching an answer to this question, I would like to say just a bit about the functions of games and informal play activities in childhood and comment specifically about the kinds of learning which may occur in spontaneous, self-organized children's games. I will then go on to assess how organized, adult sponsored competitive sports stack up against this model.

It has long been recognized that children's games and play activities represent miniature and playful models of a wide variety of cultural and social activities and concerns. To take a familiar example, the activities of little girls revolving about dolls and playing house undoubtedly serve some function in the process of anticipatory socialization to future roles as mothers and housekeepers. Similarly, in the games of boys, such elemental social themes as leading and following, of capturing and rescuing, of attacking and defending, of concealing and searching, are endlessly recombined in games of varying complexity in what Sutton-Smith (1971) has called a syntax of play. For example, the chase and elude themes of tag are combined with the capture and rescue elements of relievo in the more complex game of prisoner's base. When the chase and elude themes of tag are combined with the attack and defend themes of dodge ball, we have the more complex game type represented in football.

As Roberts and Sutton-Smith (1962) have pointed out, games of different types represent microcosmic social structures in which various different styles of competing, and of winning or losing, are subtly encoded. Through their participation in a wide variety of *different* game types, in which the various elements of skill, chance, and strategy are variously

31

recombined in gradually increasing complexity, children find an opportunity to experiment with *different* success styles, and gain experience in a variety of cognitive and emotional processes which cannot yet be learned in full scale cultural participation.

I would stress in particular, at this point, that for game experiences to serve their socialization functions effectively, it is essential that children engage in a wide variety of different types of games, and at varying levels of complexity appropriate to their stage of development. If the American game culture is becoming overly constricted, will our coping styles and success strategies as adults also become constricted? Could it be, as journalists have speculated, that America's inability to cope with the realities of world politics stems in part from the fact that our president, a football addict, is committed to a narrow-gage game plan and success style which is grossly inadequate to deal with those of opponents who are skilled in such sophisticated games as chess and go?

There is another feature of spontaneous games which renders them especially effective in serving as "buffered learning experiences" for our children: The fact that the models they embody are miniaturized and rendered relatively safe by the "having fun" context in which they typically occur. As Lewin (1944) noted, games tend to occur on a "plane of unreality,' a fact which renders them especially well suited as contexts in which to "toy" with potentially dangerous psychological and emotional problems. Thus Phillips (1960) has observed that many children's games provide a miniature and relatively safe context in which children may gain useful experience in the mastery of anxiety. Consider in this connection the titillating joys of peek-a-boo, the universally popular game in which infants toy with the anxieties associated with mother-absence, and the happy resolution achieved in the discovery that one can bring her back by uncovering one's eyes. In playful games, older children deliberately project themselves into situations involving risk, uncertainty and insecurity, and the tensions generated by the conflicting valences of hope and fear. Particularly where some element of chance is involved, as it is in many children's games, failure is less invidious and hence more easily bearable. Similarly, in games involving mock combat, aggression may be safely expressed because, as Menninger (1942, p. 175) pointed out, "one can hurt people without really hurting them"; and of course without too much danger of being really hurt yourself.

I must stress in particular the point that children's games are effective as expressive models for gaining experience in the mastery of dangerous emotions very largely because of their miniature scale and their playful context. They are rendered safe by remaining on a plane of unreality, in which "reality consequences" do not have to be faced.

I would like to go on to argue that "child's play," far from being a frivolous waste of time as is so often pictured in our task-oriented, Puritan culture, may in fact represent an optimum setting for children's learning.

To gain some perspective on this matter, consider what psychologists are saying about the kinds of conditions in which optimum learning may occur. In designing their famous computer-typewriter-teaching-machine, or "automatic reflexive environment," O.K. Moore and A. R. Anderson (1969) were careful to take into account what they believe to be the essential features of a really good learning environment: That it should permit free and safe exploration; that it should be self-pacing; that it should be "agent-responsive"; that it should provide immediate and directly relevant feedback; that it should be "productive," that is to say, so structured that a wide variety of ramifying principles and interconnections can be learned; that it should be "autotelic" or self-rewarding, that is to say, related directly to the child's own spontaneous interests and motivations; and finally, that it should be responsive to the child's own initiatives in a way which will permit him to take a "reflexive view of himself." Otherwise put, the environment should be such that the child may alternate in the roles of "active agent" and "patient," and at times may step back and view the whole setting from the viewpoint of an "umpire."

If we take these principles seriously, as I believe we must, it is easy to see why many children do not learn very much in traditionally-structured school settings. For in such traditional schools, the pupils are "patients" and the teacher is the active agent. The "principles" to be learned are explained, perhaps even demonstrated by the teacher, rather than being discovered by the children themselves. Learning is defined as "work," with all the implications that the children, left to follow their own motivations and interests freely, would rather be doing something else. The pacing of activities is rigidly controlled by the teacher, or by the school schedules, or by the tyranny of the lesson plan. And the evaluative feedback, coming from the teacher rather than from the materials themselves, is often delayed, irrelevant and peculiarly invidious.

I will try to show you that these principles, so widely violated in the regular educational settings in which children are supposed to be learning, are all admirably incorporated in a spontaneous, self-organized and self-paced game of backyard baseball, and in many other children's games and play activities. And I will argue that Little League Baseball — and other adult-organized and supervised sports — do a pretty good job of bankrupting most of the features of this, and other, learning models.

But first I would call your attention to the observations of another eminent child psychologist about the functions of spontaneous, self-organized children's games. In this classic study of the moral development of children, Jean Piaget (1932) noted that social rules, for the young child, originally appear as part of the external situation, defined and enforced by powerful adults. At an early stage of "moral realism," the child conforms because he must, to avoid punishment and to maintain the needed goodwill of his parents. But he feels no internalized moral commitment to these rules, because he had no share in defining them, because they often seem arbitrary or unnecessary, and because they are often imposed in an arbitrary and punitive fashion. Piaget argued that the experiences children have in informal games and play activities with their own age mates play an essential role in moving them beyond this stage of moral realism. In an informal game of marbles, for example, where there is no rule book and no adult rule-imposer or enforcer, and where the children know "the rules" only vaguely or have differences of opinion about what they really are, the children must finally face up to the realization that some kinds of rules really are necessary; they must decide for themselves what kinds of rules are "fair," to keep the game going, and interesting, and fun for all; they must participate in establishing the rules and must learn how to enforce them on themselves and others. Experiences like this, Piaget theorized, play a vital role in helping the child grow to a more mature stage of moral development based on the principles of cooperation and consent.

Along somewhat similar lines, Parsons and Bales (1955) have argued that the enormous power differentials between adults and children present serious obstacles to certain kinds of essential learning. For example, adult authority usually appears to young children to be heavily ascriptive in character; authority flows from the fact that one is a parent, a teacher, a coach, or simply an "adult," possessed by awesome powers to punish or reward. But the relevance of this power is not always obvious. Within the peer group, however, where differences in power are on a much smaller scale, leadership is much more likely to be based on relevant, universalistic criteria. A child leader is accepted and followed only by the extent that he effectively expresses the children's own values and helps them to work or play together in self-satisfying ways. It is largely within the framework of informally organized peer groups, these authors reason, that the child learns to conceive of social relationships as being patterned on relevant, universalistic principles in which people must get along in common subjection to general rules.

Kohlberg (1962) has pointed to yet another feature of unstructured children's play for the processes of moral development. If the "rules" are rigidly fixed once and for all by parents, teachers, coaches, or rule books, the child may learn them and perhaps accept them. But he will not gain much experience in the development of mature moral judgment. According to Kohlberg, it is only with some real experience with dissonance, as when the rules are ambiguous or when there is some cross-pressure or opinion difference about which rules should apply, that children learn to understand how certain more general moral principles must be formulated to help them decide for themselves what they should do. Much of my own recent research has tended to support the notion that informal peer group experiences and their accompanying dissonance contribute to the development of moral autonomy in children (Devereux, 1970) and that authoritarian control by adults has precisely the opposite effect (Devereux, 1972).

Backyard versus Little League Baseball, viewed as learning settings. In the light of what has been said thus far, I would now like to comment on what I see as some crucial differences between an informal and spontaneous version of backyard baseball and the organized and adult-controlled Little League version of the same game. Let me grant at once that the latter form of the game is obviously much better equipped, better coached and probably also a good deal safer. No doubt Little League children really do get better training in the official rules and strategies of our national sport, and better experience in the complex physical skills of ball handling, fielding, and so on. If the purpose of the game is to serve as an anticipatory socialization setting for developing future high school, college and professional ball players, the Little League sport is clearly the winner.

But if we look at the matter in a more general educational perspective, it appears that those gains are not achieved without serious cost. In educational terms, the crucial question must always be not what the child is doing to the ball, but what the ball is doing to the child. My most general point must be that in Little League baseball this is often not the case. Almost inevitably, in a highly organized, competitive sport, the focus is on winning and the eye is on the ball. How often does the well-intentioned volunteer coach from the phys-ed department really think about what kind of total experience his boys are having, including those who have warmed the bench all afternoon, or who were not selected for League competition?

Of that, more shortly. But first let me describe a typical variant of backyard baseball, as played in my own neighborhood some fifty years ago. We called it One-o-Cat. There were no teams. With a minimum of five kids you could start up a game, though it was better with seven or eight; once the game got started, usually a few more kids would wander over to join in, often kids of the wrong age or sex. But no matter: It was more fun with more kids, and the child population was a bit sparce back then. One base — usually a tree, or somebody's sweater or cap. Home plate usually a flat stone. Two batters, a catcher, a pitcher, a first baseman. If other kids were available, you had some fielders, too. If someone had a catcher's mit, we'd use a hard ball; otherwise a softball, or tennis ball or anything else. If someone had a face mask, the catcher would play right behind the batter; otherwise way back. There was no umpire to call balls and strikes, so the pitcher was disciplined mostly by shouts of "put it over!" Fouls were balls that went to the right of the tree marking first base or to the left of a shrub on the other side; in other yards or fields, other foul markers would have to be agreed upon.

The "rules" of the game, as we vaguely understood or invented them, were fairly simple. Pitched balls not swung at didn't count either as balls or strikes. Three swings without a hit and you were out. In principle you could go on hitting fouls indefinitely, but after a while the other kids would complain and make you go shack a wild one. A caught fly put you out. A good hit could get you to the tree and back for a home run; a lesser hit could leave you stranded at first, to be hit in, maybe, by the other batter. Or you could be put out either at first base or at the home plate in the usual fashion. Since there were no fixed base lines, when a runner was caught between the first baseman and the catcher, a wild chase all over the yard frequently ensued. When you went out, you retired to right field and everybody moved up one notch, catcher to batter, pitcher to catcher, first baseman to pitcher, left fielder to first, etc. There were no teams and nobody really bothered to keep score, since the personnel of the game usually changed during the session anyway, as some kids had to go do their chores or as others joined in. The object seemed to be to stay at bat as long as you could; but during the afternoon every kid would have plenty of opportunities to play in every position, and no one was ever on the bench. If a few more kids showed up, the game was magically transformed to Two-o-Cat, now with three rotating batters and a second base somewhere over there where third would have been; the runners now had to make the full triangular circuit before completing their run.

Maybe we didn't learn to be expert baseball players, but we did have a lot of fun; moreover, in an indirect and incidental way, we learned a lot of other kinds of things which we probably more important for children in the eight to twelve age range to learn. Precisely because there was no official rule book and no adult or even other child designated as rule enforcer, we some how had to improvise the whole thing all by ourselves — endless hassles about whether a ball was fair or foul, whether a runner was safe or out, or more generally, simply about what was fair. On the anvil of experience we gradually learned to control our affect and to understand the invisible boundary conditions of our relationships to each other. Don't be a poor sport or the other kids won't want you to play with them. Don't push your point so hard that the kid with the only catcher's mit will quit the game. Pitch a bit more gently to the littler kids so they can have some fun too; and besides, you realize it's important to keep them in the game because numbers are important. How to get a game started and somehow keep it going, so long as the fun lasted. How to pace it. When to quit for a while to get a round of cokes or just to sit under a tree for a bit. How to recognize the subtle boundaries indicating that the game was really over — not an easy thing, since there were no innings, no winners or losers — and slide over into some other activity. "Let's play tag" — "Not it!" Perhaps after supper, a game of catch with your father, who might try to give you a few very non-professional pointers. Perhaps for a few, excited accounts to the family of your success at bat that day and momentary dreams of later glory in the big leagues. But mostly on to the endless variety of other games, pastimes and interests which could so engage a young boy on a summer afternoon or evening.

In terms of the learning models proposed by Roberts, Sutton-Smith, Moore, Paiget, Parsons, Kohlberg, and many others, it was all there. It was fun; the scale was small, and the risks were minimal; we felt free and relatively safe (at least psychologically); it was spontaneous, autotelic, and agent responsive; it was self-pacing and the feedback was continuous and relevant; and the game was so structured that it required us to use our utmost ingenuity to discover and understand the hidden rules behind the rules — the general principles which make games fair, fun and interesting, and which had to govern our complex relationships with each other; the recognition of the subtle differences in skills, including social skills, which gave added respect and informal authority to some; the ability to handle poor sports, incompetents, cry-babies, little kids, and girls, when the easy out of excluding them from the game entirely was somehow impractical. How to handle it when your own anger or frustrations welled up dangerously close to the point of tears. Most generally, although the formal structure of the game was based on a model of competition and physical skill, many of its most important lessons were in the social-emotional sector — how to keep the group sufficiently cohesive to get on with the play, and how to handle the tensions which arose within us and between us.

All those are things which were happening to the boys when left to themselves in this informal game situation. And it seems to me that they are far more important than what was happening to the ball. By now the ball is lost, anyway, somewhere in the bushes over by the left field. Perhaps some-one will find it tomorrow. And besides, its too hot for baseball now, and the kids have all gone skinny-dipping in the little pond down the road a bit.

How does Little League Baseball stack up against this model? Rather badly, in my opinion. The scale is no longer miniature and safe, what with scoreboards, coaches, umpires, parents, and a grandstand full of spectators all looking at you and evaluating your every move with a single, myopic criterion: Perform! Win! The risks of failure are large and wounding. And in the pyramidal structure of league competition only a few can be winners and everybody else must be some kind of loser.

In Little League ball, the spontaneity is largely killed by schedules, rules, and adult supervision — a fixed time and place for each game, a set number of innings, a commitment to a whole season's schedule, at the expense of all alternative activities. Self pacing? Obviously not. Fun? Yes, in a hard sort of way; but please, no fooling around or goofing off out there in-right field; keep your eyes on the ball. Instant feedback? Yes, loud and clear from all sides, if you make a mistake; but mostly from adults in terms of their criteria of proper baseball performance.

But the major problem with Little League Baseball, as I see it, is that the whole structure of the game is rigidly fixed once and for all. It's all there in the rule books and in the organization of the League and of the game itself. It is all handed to the children, ready-made, on a silver platter, together with the diamonds, the bats and the uniforms. It is all so carefully supervised by adults, who are the teachers, coaches, rule enforcers, decision makers, and principal rewarders and punishers, that there's almost nothing left for the children to do but "play" the game. Almost all of the oppor-tunities for incidental learning which occur in spontaneous self-organized and self-governed children's games have somehow been sacrificed on the altar of safety (physical only) and competence (in baseball only).

Competition and Little Leaguism in Contemporary America. No doubt there are some who will argue that ours is a tough, competitive society and that somehow, during the educational process, children must be hardened up and readied for the rigorous competition of real life they will face later on. It is certainly true that competition has indeed played a central role in American society, and for generations there were many, like Theodore Roosevelt, who thought of it as the backbone of American character and achievement. But at what cost to other values? More than thirty years ago the great psychoanalyst, Karen Horney, in her classic analysis of *The Neurotic Personality of Our Time* (1937) saw fit to devote an entire chapter to "neurotic competitiveness." But while Horney saw the problem clearly enough, most psychologists and educators of that generation did not. It is interesting to note that among the 23 experimental studies of competition reported by Murphy, Murphy and Newcomb (1937), the focus is almost invariably upon the effects of competition on the performance of some task; not a single one of these studies dealt with any measures of the effects of competition upon the subjects themselves!

But effects there undoubtedly are, among them the apparent inability of American children, reared in a competitive style, to know when *not* to compete. This point was neatly demonstrated in an experiment by Madsen and Shapira (1970) in which an apparatus was so arranged that no child could get any reward at all without cooperating with the others. Mexican children, and in another study by Shapira and Madsen (1969), Israeli Kibbutz children, were quick to fall into a cooperative plan to everybody's mutual advantage, but the American children continued to compete even after it became quite obvious that no one could "win" anything at all.

The time has surely come to reasses the heavy stress we have placed on competition in our educational system, and in our culture generally. In this connection it is interesting to note that recent movements toward educational reform call for a drastic reduction in the role of competition. More generally, the new "counter culture" flourishing on our college campuses is strongly anticompetitive in basic orientation. Somehow a whole generation of fathers, still deeply involved in major sports and other facets of the old American dream, has managed to rear a generation of sons among which a very substantial segment will have no part of it.

What can we say, more specifically, of the effects of Little League competition for children? I shall not take space here to consider such measurement physiological side-effects as the famous Little League elbow; or the evidences of measured Galvanic Skin Responses of young boys before and after competition (Skubic, 1955); or the reported losses of sleep and appetite before or following competition (Skubic, 1956). I have no reason to doubt that first rate child athletes, like the adult athletes studied by Ogilvie and Tutko (1971), are better built physically, better coordinated and have fairly well integrated, if somewhat aggressive, personalities, in comparison with less athletic peers.

But the crucial question must be whether participation in Little League sports helps make them that way, or whether the reported differences are a result of the selection processes involved. In the adult study cited above, the authors believe that most of observed differences result from the selection processes rather than from the character-molding experiences of athletic competition. Hale's (1956) finding that the Little League players who made it to the Williamsport national competition had more, darkest and curlier pubic hair than non-playing age mates almost certainly reflects a selective factor rather than a consequence of ball playing.

Similarly, in Seymour's (1956) study, it is clear that all the major reported differences between the Little Leaguers and their classmates, all documenting the "superiority" of the League players, existed *before* the season began. On all the self-rating scales used in this study, moreover, the non-participants actually *improved more* than the participants, ending ahead of the participants in their post-season self-ratings of their feelings about "me and my school" and "me and my home." In this study, the non-participants also gained somewhat more than the participants in the teacher ratings on "social consciousness," "emotional adjustment," and "responsibility." On the sociometric ratings, as expected, the boy athletes were the sociometric stars in their classrooms both before and after the season. The author does note, however, that on the post-season sociometric test, the Little League boys were somewhat *less* accepting of their peers, as measured by ratings they extended to others, than they had been before the season started. Could these results represent a gentle forecast of the Ogilvie-Tutko description of adult athletes: "Most athletes indicate low interest in receiving support and concern from others, low need to take care of others and low need for affiliation. Such a personality seems necessary to achieve victory over others." (p. 61-62.)

If some processes of selection are at work in sifting out the children who get to play in League or interscholastic competition, as they quite obviously are; and if both the adult and peer culture shower these children with special attention and kudos, as they surely do, then responsible educators must have some concern about all the other children, who are losers or non-participants in this one-dimensional competition. How sure are we that the values and character traits selected and carefully reinforced in Little League sports are really the best for wholesome child development? In a culture as fanatically dedicated to excellence in competitive sports as we have become in modern America, are we needlessly and cruelly punishing the children who are physically smaller or less mature, or less well coordinated or aggressive, who can't compete successfully and perhaps don't even want to. Many will no doubt turn into fine and productive adults, but only following a childhood in which they were never able to live up to the myopic values of the peer culture or to the expectancies of their sport-addicted fathers.

Let me not be misunderstood. I am certainly not coming out against baseball as such, though for reasons indicated, I believe the informal, backyard variants have far more learning values for children than the formally organized, adult-supervised version. My most fundamental opposition to Little League Baseball, however, is based not so much to what it does by way of either harm or good to the player, as it is upon what Little Leaguism is doing to the whole culture of childhood, to participants and non-participants alike, and to the schools, families, neighborhoods and communities where Little Leaguism has taken root.

Look first at what has happened to organized sports in high schools, and the picture is perhaps clearer. In a high school of two thousand students, only a relative handful get to participate even on the squads of any of the major sports teams. All the rest are consigned to the role of frenzied spectators at interscholastic meets, or still worse, in many sport-minded communities, to non-participant-non-spectators, perceived by adults and peers alike as odd-balls, pariahs, or queers. As Coleman (1961) showed, this group may in fact include some of the best students, but they get precious little reward for their academic efforts. And the kids who do go out in earnest for a high school sport find that, to compete at all effectively against our fanatic standards of excellence, they have to make it almost a full time job both in season and out, at the expense of virtually *all* other extra-curricular and leisure time activities. In one way, you're damned if you don't participate; in another way, you're damned if you do. . . .

In Little League and other variations of organized interscholastic sport, we now see clear indications of the invasions of this sports culture into the much more precious and vulnerable world of little children. Like the bad currency in Gresham's famous law, it is an inferior product which ends by driving out the good. Because of its peculiar fascination, more of the parents than for the children themselves, it ends by nearly monopolizing the field and driving almost to bankruptcy the natural and spontaneous culture of play and games among American children.

REFERENCE NOTE

1. Paper presented by Edward C. Devereux (Dept. of Human Development and Family Studies, Cornell University) to the *Conference on Sport and Social Deviancy,* sponsored by the State University of New York College at Brockport, December 9-11, 1971. This paper also published in Daniel Landers, ed. *Social Problems in Athletics,* University of Illinois Press, Urbana, Ill., 1976.

REFERENCES

1. Coleman, J., *The Adolescence Society,* Glencoe, Ill.: Free Press, 1961.
2. Dervereux, E. C., "Authority and moral development among American and West German children," *Journal of Comparative Family Studies,* Vol. III, Spring, 1972. In press.
3. _____, "The role of peer-group experience in moral development," in J. P. Hill, ed., *Minnesota Symposia on Child Psychology,* Minneapolis: University of Minnesota Press. 1970. Vol. IV, pp. 94-140.
4. Eifermann, Rivka R., *Determinants of children's game styles.* Jerusalem: The Israel Academy of Sciences and Humanities, 1971b. In press.
5. _____, "Social play in childhood," in R. E. Herron & Brian Sutton-Smith, eds., *Child's Play,* New York: John Wiley & Sons, 1971a, pp. 270-297.
6. Hale, C. J., "Physiological maturity of Little League baseball players," *Research Quarterly,* 1956, 27, 276-282.
7. Herron, R. E., and Sutton-Smith, B., *Child's Play,* New York: Wiley & Son, 1971.
8. Horney, Karen, *The Neurotic Personality of Our Time,* New York: W. W. Norton & Co., 1937.
9. Kohlberg, L., "Development of moral character and moral ideology," in M. L. Hoffman and L. W. Hoffman, eds., *Review of Child Development Research,* New York: Russell Sage Foundation, 1964, Vol. I, pp. 383-431.
10. Lewin, Kurt, et al., "Level of Aspiration," in J. M. Hunt, ed., *Personality and Behavior Disorders,* New York: Ronald Press, 1944.
11. Madsen, M. C., and Shapira, A., "Cooperative and competitive behavior of urban Afro-American, Anglo-American, Mexican-American and Mexican village children," *Developmental Psychology,* 1970, 3(1), 16-20.
12. Menninger, Karl, *Love Against Hate,* New York: Harcourt, 1942.

13. Moore, Omar Khayyam & Anderson, A. R., "Some principles for the design of clarifying educational environments," in D. Goslin, ed., *Handbook of Socialization Theory and Research,* New York: Rand McNally, 1969, pp. 571-613.

14. Murphy, G., Murphy, L. B. & Newcomb, T. M., *Experimental Social Psychology,* New York: Harper Bros., rev. ed., 1937.

15. Ogilvie, B. C., and Tutko, T. A., "If you want to build character, try something else," *Psychology Today,* 1971, Vol. 5, pp. 60-63.

16. Parsons, T., and Bales, R. F., *Family, Socialization and Interaction Process,* Glencoe, Ill.: Free Press, 1955.

17. Phillips, R. H., "The nature and function of children's formal games," *Psychoanalytic Quarterly,* 1960, 29, 200-207.

18. Piaget, J., *The Moral Judgment of the Child,* New York: Harcourt, 1932.

19. Roberts, J. M., & Sutton-Smith, B., "Child training and game involvement," *Ethnology,* 1962, *1,* 166-185.

20. Seymour, E. W., "Comparative study of certain behavior characteristics of participants and non-participants in Little League Baseball," *Research Quarterly,* 1956, 27, 338-346.

21. Shapira, A., and Madsen, M. C., "Cooperative and competitive behavior of Kibbutz and urban children in Israel," *Child Development,* 1969, 40, 609-617.

22. Skubic, E., "Emotional responses of boys to Little League and Middle League competitive baseball," *Research Quarterly,* 1955, 26, 342-352.

23. _____, "Studies of Little League and Middle League Baseball," *Research Quarterly,* 1956, 27, 97-110.

24. Sutton-Smith, B., "A syntax for play and games," in R. E. Herron and B. Sutton-Smith, eds., *Child's Play,* New York: John Wiley & Sons, 1971, pp. 298-307.

25. Sutton-Smith, B., and Rosenberg, R. G., "Sixty years of historical change in the game preferences of American children," in R. E. Herron and B. Sutton-Smith, eds., *Child's Play,* New York: John Wiley & Sons, 1971, pp. 18-50.

Sport In American Society: Its Pervasiveness And Its Study*

George H. Sage

THE PERVASIVENESS OF SPORT IN THE UNITED STATES

Sport is such a pervasive activity in contemporary America that to ignore it is to overlook one of the most significant aspects of this society. It is a social phenomenon which extends into education, politics, economics, art, the mass media, and even international diplomatic relations. Involvement in sport, either as a participant or in more indirect ways, is almost considered a public duty by many Americans.

A stranger to America would soon realize that sport involvement is ubiquitous in our culture. Primary involvement in sport begins for most boys while they are still in elementary school. The Little League baseball program initiates boys to the world of organized sport at seven or eight years of age, and if a boy shows a little interest and aptitude for the sport, he will likely pass through the Pony League, Babe Ruth League, and American Legion baseball programs on his way to adulthood. Pop Warner football programs capture the efforts of young boys who are inclined toward rough, contact activity. Bitty basketball, Pee Wee Hockey, age group swimming, soccer, gymnastics, track and other sports are available in most communities to youngsters who wish to participate. Within the past decade similar programs have emerged for girls, and youth sports programs for girls are growing rapidly. An estimated 20 million boys and girls participate in youth sports programs.

The programs mentioned above are sponsored by community, club, or service groups, but American schools also provide abundant opportunities for sports involvement. Most states have legislation requiring the teaching of physical education through high school, and sports activities form the basic curriculum of the physical education programs. In addition to the required physical classes, most schools throughout the country sponsor interschool athletic programs beginning in the junior high school and continuing through college. According to recent (1978) statistics compiled by the National Federation of State High School Associations, more than 6.4 million boys and girls participate on interscholastic athletic teams each year. The

*Sage, G. H. "Sport in American Society: Its Pervasiveness and Its Study," *Sport and American Society,* 3rd ed., Reading, Mass.: Addison-Wesley Publishing Company, 1980, pp. 4-15. Reprinted with permission.

significance of these programs in the life of high school students is best exemplified in Coleman's statement that a visitor to a typical American high school "might well suppose that more attention is paid to athletics by teenagers, both as athletes and as spectators, than to scholastic matters. He might even conclude . . . that the school was essentially organized around athletic contests and that scholastic matters were of lesser importance to all involved" [Coleman, 1961, p. 34]. Although his comments were made some 20 years ago, they are as appropriate today as when they were written.

Professional sports are responsible for an enormous amount of sports involvement in American society. During the past 20 years professional sports teams have multiplied at a bewildering rate, thus providing job opportunities for an increasing number of professional athletes. The growth of professional sports may be exemplified by noting that the National Hockey League began the 1960s with six teams and the 1970s with 14. Also during the 1960s professional basketball proliferated from one league to two and from 12 teams to a total of 22 teams, when the leagues merged in the mid-1970s; major league baseball broke the longstanding 16-team tradition and went to 24 teams; professional football witnessed the birth of a new league, the merger of that league with the NFL, and a new 28-team league, thus more than doubling the teams which existed in 1960. The growth of other professional sports could be described but the pattern is the same.

The major form of involvement with professional sport, however, is through watching the contests, either by actually attending the contests or by viewing them on television. Professional football attracts some 16 million spectators each year, and major league baseball 32 million, but horse racing and auto racing attract the most sports fans with some 50 million paid admissions to each sport each year. Television is probably the single way in which most adults are involved in sport, especially professional sport. Up to 25 hours of professional sports are beamed into home television sets per week and it is not unusual for six to eight hours of professional sports to be aired on a single Sunday.

The economic impact of sport in the United States is awesome; sport is big business. It is a commercial interest with a commanding position in the entertainment industry. Professional sports are one of the most successful and expanding industries in the United States. As has already been noted, in the past ten years the numbers of professional football, baseball, and hockey teams have more than doubled. Horse racing, golf, and bowling have moved into the big business arena and sundry other sports give evidence of capturing more sports dollars in the future. Professional athletes' salaries reflect the value placed on sports. A minimum salary of over $20,000 is guaranteed in several sports and annual salaries of over $100,000 are not uncommon. A few of the so-called "super stars" receive salaries in excess of $300,000. The average salary in the National Football League in 1979 was over $45,000, while professional golfers compete for over 8 million dollars in prize money each year. Professional sports franchises are worth anywhere from 5 million to 20 million dollars. But few professional sports franchises could exist without television revenue. Television contracts with professional sports is a billion dollar-a-year business. Professional sports virtually is television.

Big business is not just confined to professional sports. In the process of fostering wholesome recreation, high school and college sports have unwittingly entered the field of professional entertainment. Over 170,000 student-athletes participate in NCAA-sponsored competitions in 35 different sports each year at a dollar investment of 5 billion dollars. Sport, in the form of participant recreation, is promoted by companies for their employees to the extent that industry buys more sports goods and equipment than United States schools and colleges combined, and it schedules more entertainment than the nation's night clubs. Americans spend about 60 billion dollars on recreation annually. This money is spent primarily in the purchase of equipment, supplies, and memberships, in the payment of dues, and in other necessities of active engagement in sports. Even gambling on sports is a major economic activity; estimates of the amount of money that Americans wager on sports range from 15 billion to 50 billion dollars per year. Between 12 and 15 million Americans bet on pro-football games on any given weekend.

Sport is a prominant feature of American politics. In their own way, of course, politicians realize the pervasiveness of sport and make every effort to use it for political gain. Presidents are well aware of the political potential of big-time sports, and this is why they seldom miss an opportunity to publically associate themselves with sports. Nixon's telephone calls to the locker rooms of sports victors garnered publicity for him as well as for sport. Gerald Ford capitalized on his background as a football player at the University of Michigan. But the President is only the most visible politican to be linked with sport. Politicians from the local level to the national level capitalize as much as possible on sport for political self-promotion.

The linking of politics and sport extends beyond the local, state, and national levels and into international affairs. Today, most countries of the world use sport to some extent as an instrument of international policy. Communist countries make quite clear their motive for supporting and promoting national and international sports: sport is used as a visible example of the success of the ideological political system. As Morton (1963) says: "The Soviets have made serious business out of sport competition. . . . They have forged a direct propaganda link between sport triumphs on one hand and the viability of a social system on the other." [p. 82] Perhaps the most visible example of blatant sport diplomacy is the German Democratic Republic (Kirshenbaum, 1976; Chapman, 1978). The Communist countries are not, of course, the only countries who practice sports diplomacy. Canada has undertaken a federally financed program of support to amateur athletics designed to enhance the caliber of athletes and thus bring prestige and respect to the nation (Report of Task Force, 1969). The United States supports international level competitors and teams largely through the U.S. State Department and the military services. Although the federal government does not directly support American participation in the Olympic

Games, untold millions of dollars are spent to indirectly assist the Olympic team so that the United States may field teams to impress other nations throughout the world. The Final Report of the President's Commission on Olympic Sport issued in 1977 recommends governmental intrusion into amateur sports in America and calls for an enormous expenditure of taxpayer money to support elite athletes.

While there may seem to be little in common between sport and religion, each institution is actually making inroads into the traditional activities and prerogatives of the other. Churches have had to alter their weekend services to accommodate the growing involvement in sport. Frank Deford (1976), in a three-part series for *Sports Illustrated,* noted that "the churches have ceded Sunday to sports. . . . Sport owns Sunday now, and religion is content to lease a few minutes before the big games." Contemporary religion uses sport by sponsoring sports events under religious auspices and/or proselytizing athletes to religion and then using them as missionaries to spread the Word and recruit new members.

Sport is even making a considerable impact on the literary and art fields. Although sport has occupied a prominent place in the newspapers for the past 70 years, serious writers have tended not to use sport to any extent, although the most powerful passages in Hemingway deal with blood sports and Fitzgerald captures an atmosphere and perception of an American in Paris with the term "football weather." But sport themes were tangential to the writings of noted novelists, but with the rise of mass sport interest, there is a trend toward serious writing about sport, and in the past decade American novelists have increasingly employed sport themes in their writing (Higgs and Isaacs, 1977; Chapin, 1976); indeed, over 30 novels since 1960 have either referred to football or used it as a central theme (Burt, 1975). Perhaps the greatest impact of sport in the literary field, however, is coming from former athletes and sports journalists. Within the past decade there has been a virtual deluge of books by professional athletes (most are actually ghost written) who describe their experiences in sports. A number of former athlets have written "kiss and tell" books which have either mocked their sports experiences or have been highly critical of them. The underpaid, unheralded sport journalist has also gotten into the publishing windfall of sports books in recent years, and several have written what might be called expose or muckraking type of books.

Sport has even invaded Broadway and shows evidence of making a happy marriage with drama. Several years ago, the story of Jack Johnson, the first Black heavyweight boxing champion, came to life in the play *The Great White Hope* and became an immediate success. This was followed up with several other dramas about sport. Jason Miller's grimly funny account of a high school basketball team's 20th reunion, *The Championship Season,* was voted the best play of 1972 by the Drama Critics Circle. In 1972, *The Jockey Club Stakes,* and *The Changing Room* became two of the most popular plays in New York. Sports themes are increasingly used in motion pictures. Movies such as *Rollerball, Slap Shot, Rocky,* and *Black Sunday*

45

are only a few of the movies of the past few years that involved sports themes.

Even everyday language reflects the influence of sport. One who goes beyond normative behavior is said to be "off side" or "out-of-bounds." A person who begins an activity before the agreed-upon time is said to have "jumped the gun" or engaged in "foul play." Politicians and businessmen frequently sprinkle such euphemisms as "taking a cheap shot," "laying the ground rules," "game plan," and "fumbled the ball" into their professional conversations. The swain can gain nods of appreciation among his friends by saying he "scored" or gestures of sympathy if he admits he "struck out."

James Reston wrote in *The New York Times:*

Sport in America plays a part of our natonal life that is probably more important than even the social scientists believe. Sports are now more popular than politics in America, increasingly so since the spread of television. The great corporations are now much more interested in paying millions for sports broadcasts than they are for all political events except for the nominations and inaugurations of Presidents, because the general public is watching and listening.

He appears to be a very insightful observer of American society.

STUDY OF THE SOCIAL ASPECTS OF SPORT

Since sports involvement consumes so much of the daily activity of American people, it seems logical that it should be of major importance to our understanding of their behavior. It would seem that social scientists would probably have devoted a great deal of their scholarly energy to it. In this regard, sport sociologist, John Loy (1972), said:

One would think that the sheer magnitude of the public's commitment to sport would attract the attention of a number of social observers of human conduct. Moreover, sport seems to be an ideal proving ground for the testing of many social theories, and it also appears to offer several suitable settings for the development of formal theories of social behavior [p. 229].

Unfortunately, the serious study of sport has been virtually nonexistent in the social sciences until the past decade. Thus a body of knowledge, from a social science perspective, is in its infancy.

In surveys conducted by the American Sociological Association in 1950 and 1959 (Riley, 1969) each member of this association was asked to list three sociological fields in which he felt qualified to teach or to do research. The sociologists were asked to describe their competencies in their own terms, thus the categories which emerged were not predetermined. Sport as a topic for teaching or research did not appear in enough cases to be classified as a topic.

By 1970 the American Sociological Association classified its membership into 33 areas of competence, and area #14 was entitled "Leisure, Sports, Recreation, and the Arts" and, according to a survey of its membership (Stehr and Larson, 1972), 50 sociologists out of 8,350 who returned the questionnaires marked this area as an area of personal competence. This represents 0.7 percent of the total group and places this area as the 30th out of 33 categories, in terms of rank position. Loy (1972) reports that the actual specialization of sociologists within this "grab bag" area divides up something like this:". . . approximately one-third identify the arts as their special area of competence, another one-third leisure, while a final one-third cite sport as their specific domain of interest and expertise [p. 50]." According to Loy (1978), more recent analyses of ASA membership lists indicate that the number of sociologists with a special area of competence in sport is not increasing appreciably. He says: "In sum, at the time of this writing, only two dozen members (excluding students) of the American Sociological Association are identified with the sociology of sport and less than half of this number can be considered productive researchers (i.e., at least one paper per year)" [p. 41].

Comparable conditions exist in the other social sciences. In psychology, for example, the American Psychological Association does not have a separate section on sport psychology, although it has a multitude of sections for the various specialties within the field of psychology. Historians, anthropologists, economists, etc. have not given much recognition to sport as a special topic for study either.[1]

There are undoubtedly several reasons why the study of sport has not been in the mainstream of any of the social sciences. American philosopher, Paul Weiss (1969) and French philosopher Rene Maheu (1962) both suggest that the relative neglect of sport by scholars is largely due to the prevailing tradition in Western Civilization which views sport as a lower form of culture and not worthy of serious study. Second, even though sport may be considered a socially significant aspect of society, it is often seen as frivolous and ephemeral and thus not easily incorporated into the prevailing theoretical frameworks of the social sciences. Third, the study of sport, since it has not been in the mainstream of the social sciences, has not provided the scholar with opportunities to earn prestige with colleagues. The "proper" scholar in a given field is expected to study topics that scholars in that field are studying because it is by following this path that one gains recognition, rewards, and prestige in the field of study. Although there are certainly exceptions to this pattern in every discipline, it is easy to find a few topics that are well mined by the majority of scholars in that field. The social science scholar who chose to study sport was not only isolating himself from the "proper" topics for study in his field but he was also laying himself open to ridicule for studyinig "a frivolous children's pastime." The limitations on publishing outlets for sport research may be a fourth reason for the reluctance to study sport. Prior to 1966, there were no journals specifically concerned with sport social science. Sociologist Gregory Stone (1972) humorously described the difficulty a scholar has had in getting a piece of research on this topic published in the sociology journals. He says: "When sociologists speak of play, those ghosts who control and patrol the journals strike terror into their hearts! . . . it is very difficult to find a resting

47

place for an article on play in the graveyards staked out by major journals of sociology. Consult the gravestones — I mean, of course, the table of contents" [pp. 3-4]. A fifth reason for the unwillingness to study sport may be related to the same reluctance in studying the sociology of education which Gross (1959) identified, namely the quality of the literature is poor, consisting mainly of essays, and the scant research has little or no relevance to existing social science theory and research.

A final reason that sport has not been seriously studied until recently may be related to its recent rise to omnipresence. Until the last generation or so, sports participation was primarily a recreation of the upperclasses, when it was engaged in by adults. Long working hours, physically exhausting labor, and limited income made sports prohibitive for the working class. Except for major league baseball, professional sports were not prominent until after World War I. Even in baseball, since only 16 major league teams existed throughout the United States and transportation was rather cumbersome, very few persons actually got to see the games. It was not until the 1920s that radio began reporting live-action baseball games, and while this was an improvement over newspaper accounts of games, it could not compare with the impact that television had on the development of professional sports. College football has been popular since the late 19th century with the college students and alumni, but mainstream America was not really a part of the college scene until after World War II, and even here TV had the greatest impact on popularizing college sports. So, although sports interests certainly existed prior to television, this particular mass media has had the most dramatic effect on the sports mania of today, and television is a phenomenon of the past thirty years.

Although the study of the social aspects of sport is in its infancy, recent trends indicate that progress in developing a cogent body of knowledge is increasing at an accelerating rate. Physical education departments throughout the United States are now offering courses in sport sociology, sport history, sport psychology, and other courses with a social science perspective, and this general field has become a favorite area for specialization among graduate students in physical education. A few sociology departments now have professors within the department who are making sport their primary interest. Several sociology departments are cooperating with physical education departments by employing a sport sociologist on a dual appointment basis; that is, the faculty member is assigned to both physical education and sociology departments. Another evidence that interest in the study of sport is growing is that in their conventions national and regional professional social science associations are including sessions devoted to research papers and seminars on sport.

Development of a Sociology of Sport

Although it is always difficult, as well as risky, to identify a given incident or piece of writing as being the first of its kind, Steinitzer's book, *Sport and Kultur,* published in Germany in 1910, may be identified, as one of the pioneer works in the sociology of sport because it was concerned with the relationship of sports and culture. A better known book entitled *Soziologie des Sports* written by Risse in 1921 and published in Germany is often referred to as the first treatise on the sociology of sport. Both of these books lacked systematic and empirical research data for the ideas which were discussed. They were, Wohl (1966) says, "reflections on social phenomena and social consequences of sports, inspired by the fact that this subject was particularly thrown into relief at this time. Thus . . . we can safely consider both belonging to the type of publicistic works, based only on one's own suggestions, that are the outcome of generally accepted opinions and prejudices about sports" [p. 5]. However, Risse did discuss various social issues related to sports and recommended that these phenomena be given systematic scientific study.

These books did not stimulate any immediate substantive study of sport but they did trigger a number of publications, especially in Europe, concerned with the relationship between sport and various social issues. Although most of these publications were not empirically based, the social sources and consequences of sport were thoroughly analyzed.

Few physical educators have devoted their careers to a study of the social aspects of sport. While the early 20th century leaders of the so-called "new physical education" such as Thomas Wood, Clark Hetherington, Jesse Feiring Williams, and Rosalind Cassidy gave a privileged position to "social development," the term went largely undefined and the social outcomes of physical education and inter-school sports programs went unmeasured. These physical educators were not researchers; they did not document the claims they made with regard to the social outcomes of physical education. Actually, they were more interested in justifying programs of physical education than they were of studying the broad scope of social behavior in sport contexts, and they did not attempt to develop a basic subject matter on the social science of sport. Charles Cowell (1937, 1959), a physical educator at Purdue, published a few empirical studies between 1935 and 1960 and a book entitled *Sports in American Life* (1953) by two physical educators, Frederick Cozens and Florence Stumpf, was a pioneering effort to discuss the social role of sport in American society. However, it was not until the publication of an article entitled "Toward a Sociology of Sport" in the *Journal of Health, Physical Education, and Recreation* in 1965 by Gerald Kenyon and John W. Loy that physical educators began to seriously pursue this subject.

The first generation of American sociologists gave passing attention to sport. For example, W. I. Thomas (1901) published an article in the *American Journal of Sociology* entitled "The Gaming Instinct," and in his book, *Folkways* (1906), William G. Sunner wrote a chapter on "Popular Sports, Exhibitions, and Drama." But it was not until post-World War II that empirical interest in sport began to accelerate. In the 1950s studies such as Weinberg and Arond's (1952) report on the sub-culture of the boxer and Riesman and Denney's (1951) presentation of football as an avenue of cultural diffusion provided pioneer work in the sociology of sport in the United States. Subsequently Stone (1957) and Grusky (1963) offered interesting studies related to sport involvement and its relation to socio-economic status and the application of social organizational theory to sport teams.

Two books published in England in the post-World War II period have had a marked impact on the development of the study of the social aspects of sport in America. These books, *Sport in Society* (McIntosh, 1963) and *Sport and Society* (Natan, 1958), were basically descriptive accounts of the social dimensions of sport, but they were well-written and illuminated the potential for the study of sport.

Sports journalists have provided the most extensive literature on sports during the 20th century. Their contribution to sport has been considerable; although most have done reportorial work primarily, some have written on the sociological, historical, economic, and political aspects of sport. One professional sociologist said that "sports writers are among my favorite list of sociologists" [Page, 1969, p. 196]. While those who work in the social science of sport might agree with Professor Page, they would undoubtedly emphasize that there is need for exhaustive empirical research to support or refute the essay-type writing of the journalist.

One of the most significant events for the promotion and development of a sociology of sport occurred in the mid-1960s. In 1964, the International Committee for Sport Sociology was founded as an affiliate of two UNESCO organizations, the International Council of Sport and Physical Education and the International Sociological Association. This Committe sponsored its first conference in Cologne, Germany in 1966, with an invited group of around 50 participants. The second conference sponsored by this Committee was held in 1968 in Vienna, Austria, and several subsequent conferences have been held in the past decade. An outgrowth of the first conference held in Cologne was the establishment of the *International Review of Sport Sociology* which is published in Poland and which carries essays and research articles. One issue per year was published from 1966 to 1973, then it became a quarterly journal.

The future is promising. Undoubtedly physical educators and social scientists who are currently concentrating their efforts on the social dimensions of sport will attract others. Indeed events of the past few years in graduate schools of physical education give evidence that a "bandwagon" effect is occurring toward this subject, as students are electing to specialize in the sociology, or psychology, or history of sport instead of the old standbys of physiology and bio-mechanics. Sociology, psychology, history, and anthropology departments have already begun turning out Ph.D's with sport as their area of specialty. The prospects for the future are very exciting.

REFERENCE NOTE

1. Since the parent social science associations have not given much recognition to the study of sport, separate associations have been formed. The International Society of Sports Psychology was formed in 1965, the North American Society for the Psychology of Sport and Physical Activity, 1967, North American Society for Sport History, 1974, Association for the Anthropological Study of Play, 1974, North American Society for the Sociology of Sport, 1978.

REFERENCES

Burt, D. "A Helmeted Hero: The Football Player in Recent American Fiction," presented at the Convention of the Popular Culture Association, 1975.

Chapin, H. B., *Sports in Literature,* New York: David McKay, 1976.

Chapman, Brian, "East of the Wall," *Runner's World* (March 1978) pp. 60-67.

Coleman, J. S., "Athletics in High School," *Annals of the American Academy of Political Science,* 338 (November): 33-45, 1961.

Cowell, C. C. "Physical Education as Applied Social Science," *Educational Research Bulletin.* (Ohio State University), I: 147-155, 1937.

Cowell, C. C., "Validating an Index of Social Adjustment for High School Use," *Research Quarterly,* 29: 7-18, 1958.

Cozens, F., and Stumpf, F., *Sports in American Life,* Chicago: University of Chicago Press, 1953.

Deford, Frank, "Religion in Sport," *Sports Illustrated,* 44 (April 19, 26, May 3) 1976.

Gross, N., "The Sociology of Education," in R. K. Merton, *et al.* (eds), *Sociology Today,* New York: Basic Books, 1959, pp. 128-152.

Grusky, O., "Managerial Succession and Organizational Effectiveness," *American Journal of Sociology,* 69 (July): 21-31, 1963.

Higgs, R. J., and Isaacs, N., (eds.) *The Sporting Spirit: Athletics in Literature and Life,* New York: Harcourt Brace Jovanovich, 1977.

Kenyon, G. S., and Loy, J. W., "Toward a Sociology of Sport," *Journal of Health, Physical Education, and Recreation,* 36 (May): 24-25, 68-69, 1965.

Kirshenbaum, Jerry, "Assembly Line of Champions," *Sports Illustrated,* 45 (July 12, 1976), pp. 56-65.

Loy, J. W., "Toward a Sociology of Sport," in R. N. Singer, *et al., Physical Education: An Interdisciplinary Approach,* New York: The Macmillan Company, 1972, pp. 229-236.

Loy, J. W., "A Case for the Sociology of Sport," *Journal of Health, Physical Education, and Recreation,* 43 (June): 50-53, 1972.

Loy, John W., McPherson, B. D., and Kenyon, Gerald S., *The Sociology of Sport as an Academic Speciality: An Episodic Essay on the Development and Emergence of Hybrid Subfield in North America,* Canadian Association for Health, Physical Education, and Recreation, 1978.

McIntosh, P. C., *Sport in Society,* London: C. W. Watts Company, 1963.

Maheu, Rene, "Sport and Culture," *International Journal of Adult and Youth Education,* 14: 169-178, 1962.

Morton, H.W., *Soviet Sport,* New York: Collier Books, 1963.

Natan, A., *Sport and Society,* London: Bowers & Bowes Publishers, 1958.

National Federation of State High School Associations, "Sports Population Survey," 1978.

Page, C. H., "Symposium Summary, With Reflections Upon the Sociology of Sport as a Research Field," in G. S. Kenyon (ed.), *Aspects of Contemporary Sport Sociology,* Chicago: The Athletic Institute, 1969, pp. 189-209.

Palmer, M. D., "The Sports Novel: Mythic Heroes and Natural Men," *Quest,* Monograph XIX, January, 1973, pp. 49-58.

President's Commission on Olympic Sport, *Final Report,* Washington, D.C.: U.S. Government Printing Office, 1977.

Riley, M. W., "Membership in the ASA, 1950-1959," *American Sociological Review,* 25: 914-926, 1960.

Riesman, D., and Denney, R., "Football in America: A Study of Cultural Diffusion," *American Quarterly,* 3: 309-319, 1951.

Risse, H., *Soziologie des Sports,* Berlin, 1921.

Roberts, J. M., Arth, M. J., and Bush, R. R., "Games in Culture."

Roberts, J.M., and Sutton-Smith, B., "Child Training and Game Involvement," *Ethnology,* 1: 166-185, 1962.

Stehr, N., and Larson, L. E., "The Rise and Decline of Areas of Specialization," *The American Sociologist,* 7 (No. 7); 3, 5-6, 1972.

Steinitzer, H., *Sport and Kultur.* Munchen: 1910.

Stone, G., "Some Meanings of American Sport," *60th Proceedings of the College Physical Education Association,* Washington, D.C.: American Association for Health, Physical Education, and Recreation, 1957, pp. 6-29.

Sumner, William G., *Folkways,* Boston: Ginn, 1906.

Thoms, W. L., "The Gaming Instinct," *American Journal of Sociology,* 6, 750-763, 1901.

Weinberg, S. K., and Arond, H., "The Occupational Culture of the Boxer," *American Journal of Sociology,* 57 (March): 460-469, 1962.

Weiss, P., *Sport: A Philosophical Inquiry,* Carbondale, Ill.: Southern Illinois University Press, 1969.

SECTION II
HISTORY AND PHYSICAL ACTIVITY

WHAT IS HISTORY?

The man in the street would probably reply, "History is what happened in the past". Historians suggest that history is not quite so simple and they stress the fact that happenings do not occur in a vacuum. They point out that happenings have causes, happenings have results, and happenings have meanings. In other words, happenings can be linked to other happenings. Allan Nevins refers to history as a bridge which connects the past with the present and points out the road to the future.[1] This view suggests that by looking at the past one can better understand the present and possibly predict the future.

IS HISTORY A SCIENCE?

"The science of men in time".[2]

"The staunchest defender of the 'science of history' would not now contend that there is any real comparison between his subject and the sciences proper".[3]

Although Compte, J.S. Mill, Mark and Engels all agreed that scientific procedures could be applied to the study of human affairs, Teggart tells us that history remained as a branch of literature until the 1850's.[4] The historian would argue that, like any science, history is concerned with description, explanation and prediction. Classification, recognized as the backbone of description, is a way of life for the historian. The historian may not directly observe happenings but he does his best to verify the authenticity of the observations of others. Like any scientist, the historian, in his attempts to understand phenomena, suggests hypotheses and subjects these to testing. The increasing availability of quantitative data and the technical advances for verifying the validity of such data has caused historians to think of themselves not so much as humanists, but rather as scientists — social scientists.

HOW ARE HISTORY AND PHYSICAL ACTIVITY LINKED?

There is little evidence to indicate that historians have been or will ever be interested in describing and explaining the changes which occurred over time in the muscle twitch of the biceps or in the extension of the knee joint. However, historians have spent considerable time in examining the changes in the form and functions of the more structured forms of physical activity, such as games, sport and dance. For the most part, the historian has been more interested in learning what these activities could tell him about life in the time period examined than he was in learning about the evolution of the activities themselves. Today there are more and more sport historians who are examining the influences that historical happenings have had on physical activity.

ON WHAT BASIS WERE ARTICLES SELECTED FOR THIS SECTION?

The interrelationships between history and sport are introduced with two articles. The one a classic entitled "Toward a history of sport" by Dr. Max Howell appeared in the first issue of the Canadian Journal of The History of Sport and Physical Education. *The articles entitled "Some background influences on Nineteenth century Canadian sport and physical education" and "The technological revolution and the rise of sport 1850-1900" provide excellent examples of how changes in society resulted in changes in sport and other forms of physical activity. The last two articles dealing with women in sport and the Olympic games were included in order to exemplify persistent problems that have existed during the evolution of sport.*

1. A. Nevins, *The Gateway to History,* Garden City, N.Y.: Doubleday and Company, Inc., 1962.
2. M. Block, *The Historian's Craft,* Manchester: United Press, 1954, p. 2.
3. J. B. Black, *The Art of History,* New York: Russell and Russell, Inc., 1965, p. 14.
4. F. Teggart, *Theory and Processes of History,* Berkeley: University of California Press, 1962, p. 2.

Toward A History Of Sport — [1]*

Maxwell L. Howell
University of Alberta
Edmonton

It has long been recognized that physical educators have been neglecful in research in the humanities and social sciences. Their principal concentration to date has been in the physiology of exercise, though in recent years there has been an increase in research in such areas as "motor learning" and "sport psychology." Other divisions of our academic discipline are slowly emerging, such as the "sociology of sport."[2] Concentration in these areas has been, in the main, in the experimental sphere.

The very broad area of the history of games and sports in society has been particularly neglected. This, basically, though not necessarily, consists of non-experimental studies. The work is primarily inter-disciplinary and can embrace such disciplines as history, anthropology, art history, archaeology, and classics, in particular.

The sociology of sport according to Kenyon and Loy is "the study of the regularity, and departures from it, of human social behavior in a sports context," and the social psychology of sport is "the study of individuals in social and cultural settings associated with sport."[3]

And just, as pointed out by the authors, exercise physiology is somewhat less than the whole of physiology, and sociology of sport is somewhat less than the whole of sociology or social psychology, so likewise is the history of sport somewhat less than the whole of history, anthropology, archaeology, art history, and/or classics, yet adds a new dimension to such studies. The sport historian, similarly, need not be concerned with all of history, but rather those particular aspects that are unique to or indeed worthy of being added to the body of our knowledge.

THE HISTORY OF SPORT

The terms "sport history" and the "history of sport" are not precisely the same, and may perhaps be differentiated. Any isolated study is one in sport history, whereas the accumulation of the body of knowledge, the sub-

* Howell, Maxwell L. "Toward A History of Sport," *Canadian Journal of History of Sport and Physical Education*, Vol. I, No. 1 (May 1970), pp. 8-16. Reprinted by permission of the publisher.

discipline, is the history of sport.

Essentially, the subdiscipline, history of sport, must be concerned with a particular aspect of man's social activities — sports and games. The history of sport will ever be fragmentary and incomplete, but, indeed, history itself and human knowledge too must ever be incomplete.

While some historians assert that history is confined to the *written* record of the past or current events and thus preclude much of the work of archaeology, anthropology, and ethnology, the history of sport should not confine itself to such a definition. It should examine all that has happened in the past, concentrating on the dimension of sport and games in culture.

The main approaches of history that may be encompassed in the subdiscipline of the history of sport are: (a) *chronological* (the study of specific periods and sports in chronological sequence); (b) *geographical* (studies of the rise of certain games in geographical areas such as Micronesin, Australia, Mediterranean); (c) *political* (national systems of physical education, effects of nationalism on sport and games, effect of wars and militarism, influence of government); (d) *cultural* (role of sports and games in various societies); (e) *institutional* (influence of institutions on physical education, sport, and games — industrial sport, government decrees, institutional studies); (f) *biographical* (role of individual men and women). The dividing line is often thin between each approach to history.

Physical educators, it is asserted, have primarily concerned themselves with the political, institutional, and biographical approaches (a limited conception embracing systems of physical education and leaders) with a resultant neglect of the cultural approach in particular, though gaps are also evident chronologically and geographically.

Sport historians must examine the gaps in our knowledge and encourage studies to fill them. The essential processes of history must be rigidly adhered to: "the gathering of the data, the criticism of the data; the presentation of facts, interpretations, and conclusions in readable form."[4] The quantity and quality of the sources and the ability of the sport historian to evaluate those sources, will depend on the individual's training and knowledge of the historical method. As such studies accumulate, so will history of sport as a sub-discipline expand its body of knowledge.

The history of sport, then, is concerned with the evolution of sport and games in culture. It deals with the past and all that has happened in the past and is cognizant of movement and change. It deals with *evolution* of sports and games as well as their *role* in culture.

The sport historian eventually finds that, although he deals in the defined area of history, in effect the accumulation of the body of knowledge occasions excursions into disciplines other than history. The following are the main disciplines to command the attention of the sport historian, with suggested areas of study. The serious researcher, of necessity, makes use of more than one discipline in his study.

Anthropology

Cultural anthropology has emerged as a subdiscipline of anthropology and, in particular, has addressed itself to the study of nonliterate and other societies. The play and games of those societies have been examined but generally only as a minor aspect of the total society. There is an enormous literature awaiting the concentrated attention of the sport historian.[5] The few studies conducted to date have been academically rewarding.[6] They have necessitated a study of the total society under scrutiny, analyses in depth of the sports and games of that society, and finally attempts to place these physical activities in their true perspective in that society. They have necessitated detailed studies of current game theories and interesting innovations in this area. As such studies multiply, cross-cultural studies will be possible.

The range of possible anthropological studies is extensive: studies of the games of literate as well as nonliterate societies; of individual societies (e.g., New Hebrides, Solomon Islands) or total cultures (e.g., Indians, Micronesians); of the analysis and prevalence of certain activities, games, pastimes, team games, individual games, group pastimes, individual pastimes, and so on.

Archaeology

There is a considerable body of archaeological evidence of sport and games in societies,[7] which has only rarely attracted the attention of the physical educator.[8] The field is primarily concerned with the remains of sculpture, pottery, tablets, frescoes, ornaments, architecture, and seal stones.

Again the range of possible studies is broad: archaeological evidence of individual societies or cultures or civilizations (e.g., Hittite, Roman); archaeological evidence of certain activities, games, pastimes, or team games and their prevalence throughout the ages (e.g., wrestling, boxing).

Classics

Few physical educators have the background to translate for themselves in such languages as Greek and Latin, but scholars are appearing who are willing to devote themselves to such studies.[9] Even without command of a particular classical language, the translations of others need to be collated and interpreted. The ancient civilizations have been inadequately developed both in histories wirtten in our field and in lectures or courses of study.[10]

Studies are needed, utilizing available translations and the opinions of classicists, of sports and games in individual classical civilizations (e.g., Hittite, Egyptian); of individual activities (e.g., dance in ancient civilizations); of the coverage of sports activities by individual writers (e.g., athletics and Homer, athletics in Greek tragedies).

History

The broad category of history, being a record of the past, allows for a wide variety of studies,[11] but few to this point have been of sufficient depth. Physical educators need additional training to allow for better studies. Some promising efforts have been made but the gaps are considerable.

The range of studies includes: histories of sports, games, or physical education of individual countries (e.g., Canada, India); histories of individual and team sports (e.g., golf, football); biographies (e.g., Jay B. Nash, James Thorpe); effect of various social, political, and economic fac-

tors on sports and games (e.g., women's fashions, presidential efforts).[12]
Art History
The history of art has become, in recent years, a subdiscipline within art and affords much knowledge which has been neglected in our field. Much of the evidence of sports and games is in the art of a culture,[13] and a better understanding of art will assist the writing and the lecturing about specific periods. Analyses of the techniques of the ancient Greeks in athletics, for example, cannot basically be attempted without a knowledge of the limitations of the art and the artist in certain time periods and a knowledge of the comparative dating of the representations. Studies should encompass individual countries (e.g., sport and art in Turkey, sport and art in Etruria) and cross-cultural analyses (e.g., dance and art, tennis and art).[14]

PREPARING THE SPORT HISTORIAN

The body of knowledge is already considerable in the areas cited, but it has not been brought together and analyzed and it is primarily the work of scholars in other areas. Scholars are needed in the area of the history of sport, scholars who are willing to attain the levels accepted as necessary in the other disciplines and to approach the subject with the knowledges and background unique to our own field. A broad preparation is necessary in the humanities, with appropriate work in history, art history, archaeology, classics, and anthropology. A strong background in one of these disciplines would be of considerable advantage. Work in the historical method and the philosophy of history would also be advisable. The undergraduate and graduate student should also be given sufficient depth of training in those aspects unique to our body of knowledge and on which a body of literature is already available.

One such progressive offering, leading to the Ph.D., is suggested here. The individual background of professors must, of course, be taken into account, but it is submitted that preparation for the Ph.D. in the history of sport would be inadequate without a progressive scheme similar to this, covering the areas cited.

Undergraduate
History of Sport and Physical Education
Sports and games in various civilizations; systems of physical education; the place of sport in culture.

Master of Science, Master of Arts, and/or Doctor of Philosophy
Sports and Games in Ancient Civilizations
Archaeological and literary evidence; the Ancient Olympic games.
Comparative Sport and Physical Education
A cross-cultural comparison of the various systems of physical education and sport as viewed within a context of historical and sociological forces.
History of Physical Education
Growth of physical education in various cultures.
Cultural History of Dance
Development of dance forms in primitive to contemporary societies,

with emphasis on the relationship of dance to other societal and cultural forces.

Seminar in the History of Physical Education

Seminar in the History of Sport

Research Seminar

Sports in American Life
History and role of sports and games in American life from colonization to the present.

Sports and Games in Primitive Cultures
Comparison and analysis of sports and games in such cultures as: Polynesian, Micronesian, Melanesian, Indians of North America, game theories.

History of Sport from Roman Times
History of sports and games since Roman times the special emphasis on medieval renaissance influences, sport in Britain, and the industrial revolution; the history of individual games such as football, tennis, lacrosse, wrestling.

AUTHOR'S COMMENTS

The article "Toward a History of Sport" was a preliminary attempt to define the area we are endeavouring to work in, as well as to suggest possibilities of research in the various sub-areas. It was also written on request as a proposal for beginning studies in such an area at the University of Wisconsin. The latter explanation is necessary in explaining why the field of sociology was not mentioned in the list of disciplines in which students may wish to work. The area of sociology of sport is already well developed at the University of Wisconsin under the leadership of Dr. Gerald Kenyon, and including excursions into sociology would have demonstrated unnecessary overlapping. There is little doubt in my mind that sociology should be added to the list of disciplines.

For as I work in the area more and more and listen to graduate students discuss and debate the work we are doing, the more I feel that our work is demonstrating the role and continuing relevance of sport and physical education in society, or in culture. "Sport in culture" is our "bag", as the young ones say.

The other dilemma in writing the article was the title itself. It is not satisfactory, for it is not so restrictive as to be only "history" of sport. The field we are working in has been defined as the "humanitarian" bases by such logical thinkers as Gerald Glassford and Keith Lansley, but the term has never appealed to me; my mind turns to representatives of the Salvation Army dispensing soup, I have visions of starving young ones being helped by Rockefeller. We have toyed with the "humanities" and so on. My position at the moment is that the field may best be described by the terminology "Socio-Cultural Bases" and so, in reflection, perhaps the article should have been entitled "Toward Studies in the Socio-Cultural Bases" or some such. Perhaps next year I will recommend other changes. Whether this be so or not, the point is that the area that is encompassed is broader than what is traditionally thought of as history.

REFERENCE NOTES

1. Reprinted, with additions, from the *Journal of Health, Physical Education, Recreation,* March 1969. Copyright, 1969, by the American Association for Health, Physical Education, and Recreation, National Education Association, 1201-16th St., NW. Washington, D.C. 20036.
2. Gerald S. Kenyon and John W. Loy, "Toward a Sociology of Sport," *Journal of Health, Physical Education, Recreation,* May 1965, pp. 25-25.
3. *Ibid.,* p. 24.
4. H. C. Hockett, *The Critical Method in Historical Research and Writing* (New York: Macmillan Co., 1955), p. 9.
5. Examples are Elsdon Best, "Games and Pastimes of the Maori," *Dominion Museum Bulletin,* Vol. 8, 1925; Raymond Firth, "A Dart Match in Tikopia," *Oceania,* Vol. 1, 1930; Kathleen Haddon, *Artists in String* (London: Methuen, 1930); John Roberts, *et al.,* "Games in Culture," *American Anthropologist,* Vol. 61, August 1959; R. M. Berndt, "Some Aboriginal Children's Games," *Mankind,* October 1940, pp. 289-93; and so on.
6. Michael A. Salter, *Games and Pastimes of the Australian Aboriginal,* M. A. thesis, University of Alberta, 1967, pp. 203; Kevin G. Jones, *Games and Physical Activities of the Ancient Polynesians and Relationships to Culture,* M. A. thesis, University of Alberta, 1967, 226 pp.; Keith Lansley, *The Role of Recreational Activities in Maintaining Traditional Melanesian Culture,* M. A. thesis (in progress) University of Alberta.
7. Examples are A. J. Evans, *The Palace of Minos at Knossos* (London: Macmillan Co., 1921-1935); Frederick Poulsen, *Etruscan Tomb Paintings* (Oxford: Clarendon Press, 1922); G. E. Bean, "Victory in the Pentathlon," *American Journal of Archaeology,* 26; 361-68, 1956; A. E. Johnson, "A Ball Court at Point of Pines, Arizona," *American Antiquity,* Vol. 26, No. 4, 1961.
8. For example, Maxwell L. Howell and Denise Palmer, "Sports and Games in the Minoan Period," *Proceedings of the First International Symposium on the History of Sport and Physical Education* (Israel, 1968); Denise Palmer, "Sport and Games in the Art of Early Civilizations,"M. A. thesis, University of Alberta, 1967.
9. M. Lammer, "Der Diskos des Asklepiades aus Olympia und das Marmor Parium," *Zeitschrift Fur Papyrologie und Epigraphik,* Band 1, Heft 2, 1967, pp. 107-109; Peter Lindsay, *Literary Evidence of Physical Education Among the Ancient Romans,* M. A. thesis, University of Alberta, 1967.
10. However, there are excellent works by such classicists as R. S. Robinson, *Sources for the History of Greek Athletics* (338 Probasco St., Cincinnati Ohio); E. N. Gardiner, *Athletics of the Ancient World* (Oxford: Oxford University Press, 1931); H. A. Harris, *Greek Athletes and Athletics* (London: Hutchinson, 1964); K. J. Freeman, *Schools of Hellas* (London: Macmillan, 1912); and so on.
11. Examples are the comprehensive works of Alice Bertha Gomme, *A Dictionary of British Folklore — The Traditional Games of England, Scotland and Ireland,* Vol. II, London, 1898; Joseph Strutt, *The Sports and Pastimes of the People of England* (London: Chatts & Windus, 1898); Stewart Culin, *Games of the Orient* (Rutland, Vermont: Charles E. Tuttle, 1958); and so on.
12. Examples are the work of Marvin H. Eyler, *Origins of Some Modern Sports,* Ph.D. Dissertation, University of Illinois, 1956, 406 pp.; S. A. Davidson, *A History of Sports and Games in Eastern Canada Prior to World War I,* Ed. D. thesis, Teachers College, Columbia University, 1951; Uriel Simri, *The Religious and Magical Function of Ball Games in Various Cultures,* Ed. D. thesis, University of West Virginia, 1966; and so on.
13. This can be seen in such works as M. Pallottino, *The Great Centuries of Painting: Etruscan Painting* (Geneva, Switzerland: Skira, 1952); J. D. Beazley, *Attic Black-Figure Vase Painters* (Oxford: Clarendon Press, 1951); William D. Cox, *Boxing in Art and Literature* (New York: Reynal & Hitchcock, 1935); and so on.
14. Scholars in other countries would, of course, offer such a course related to their own society.

The Technological Revolution and the Rise of Sport, 1850-1900

John Rickards Betts

The roots of our sporting heritage lie in the horse racing and fox hunting of the colonial era, but the main features of modern sport appeared only in the middle years of the nineteenth century.[1] Organization, journalistic exploitation, commercialization, intercommunity competition, and sundry other developments increased rapidly after 1850 as the agrarian nature of sport gave way gradually to the influences of urbanization and industrialization. Just as the Industrial Revolution was to alter the interests, habits, and pursuits of all classes of society, it was to leave a distinct impression on the development of sport

Many other factors were responsible for the directions taken by sport in the half century from 1850 to 1900. Continuing rural influences, the decline of Puritan orthodoxy, the English athletic movement, the immigrant, frontier traditions of manliness and strength, and the contributions of energetic sportsmen were to have a significant effect on the sporting scene. Industrialization and urbanization, however, were more fundamentally responsible for the changes and developments in sport during the next generation than any other cause. Manufacturers, seeking cheap labor, encouraged immigration; factories were most efficiently run in larger towns and cities; urban masses, missing the rustic pleasures of hunting and fishing, were won to the support of commercialized entertainment and spectator sports; the emergence of a commercial aristocracy and a laboring class resulted in distinctions every bit as strong in sport as in other social matters; and the urgency of physical exercise as life became more sedentary was readily recognized.

The revolution in manufacturing methods, which had such profound social consequences for the American way of life, derived from a powerful inventive spirit which flourished throughout the nineteenth century. From England and western Europe we borrowed many mechanical innovations and most of our scientific theory, but Americans demonstrated a native ability soon recognized everywhere as "Yankee ingenuity." These inventions were to revolutionize transportation, communication, manufacturing, finance, and all the many facets of economic life. Although the tendency in

*Betts, J. R. "The Technological Revolution and the Rise of Sport, 1850-1900. *Mississippi Valley Historical Review, 40* (Sept. 1953), pp. 231-256. Reprinted by permission of the publisher.

narrating the history of sport has been to emphasize the role of individuals, the changing social scene was of equal importance in directing sport into the channels it eventually took in modern society. The impact of invention had a decisive influence on the rise of sport in the latter half of the century. By 1900 sport had attained an unprecedented prominence in the daily lives of millions of Americans, and this remarkable development had been achieved in great part through the steamboat, the railroad, the telegraph, the penny press, the electric light, the streetcar, the camera, the bicycle, the automobile, and the mass production of sporting goods.

The transformation of the United States from a rural-agrarian to an urban-industrial society, of course, affected the development of sport in other ways. Urbanization brought forth the need for commercialized spectator sports, while industrialization gradually provided the standard of living and leisure time so vital to the support of all forms of recreation. But it is the relationship of invention to sport, and that alone, which constitutes the theme of this study.

Early American interest in outdoor exercise was largely confined to hunting, fishing, horse racing, field sports, and the informal games of the local schoolyard. As the nation became more commercially minded in the decades after the War of 1812, many of those who lived in rapidly growing cities became concerned over the sedentary habits of clerks, office workers, and businessmen. In the years before 1850 there emerged a limited interest in rowing, running, prize fighting, cricket, fencing, and similar activities, but the only organized sport which excited the minds of most Americans was the turf. A more general interest in horse racing appeared in the 1820's and 1830's, and many jockey clubs held meetings attended by throngs of spectators in their carriages and barouches.[2]

From the early years of the century steamboat captains engaged in racing on the Hudson, Ohio, Mississippi, and other rivers, and the steamboat served as a common carrier of sports crowds. By the 1850's it became an indispensable means of transport to the races along the eastern seaboard and in the Mississippi Valley. As one of the first products of the age of steam it played a significant role in the rise of the turf and outdoor games.[3]

In the years preceding the Civil War the turf was also encouraged by the development of a railroad network. As early as 1838 Wade Hampton was transporting race horses to Charleston by rail;[4] in 1839 the Nashville Railroad was carrying New Orleans crowds to the Metairie Course;[5] in 1842 the Long Island Railroad was already suffering the abuse of irate passengers swarming to the races; and three years later it carried some 30,000 passengers to the Fashion-Peytona race at more than fifty cents each.[6] Kentucky became the leading breeding center for thoroughbreds and Louisville could announce in 1851: "Lexington, Georgetown, Frankfort, Paris and other towns in this State, are now but a short ride from our city by railroad conveyance. Horses can come from Lexington here in five hours."[7] The famous trotter Flora Temple began barn-storming tours; racing and trotting benefited from the cooperation of railroad lines; and "speed trials" at agricultural fairs during the 1850's were attended by excursionists.[8] Other outdoor sports also profited from the interest shown by certain lines. When excitement over rowing began to catch on in the late 1830's the first boat shipped west of the Appalachians went by way of the Erie Canal.[9] It was a railroad, however, which encouraged the holding of the first intercollegiate rowing race between Harvard and Yale in 1852.[10] Baseball clubs were organized throughout the East and Midwest during the decade and the National Association of Base Ball Players was founded in 1857, soon after both sections had been connected by rail. Chicago had its first baseball team in 1856, two years after it was linked by rail to Baltimore, Maryland, and Portland, Maine. In 1860 the Excelsior Club of Brooklyn made a tour of upper New York State. Most of the early prize fights were held along the rivers served by steamboats; the Harlem Railroad carried fight crowds in the early 1850's to the Awful Gardiner-William Hastings (*alias* Dublin Tricks) match sixty miles north of New York City and to a highly publicized championship fight at Boston Four Corners, New York;[11] and the John Morrissey-John Heanan match on the Canadian shore near Niagara Falls in 1858 was advertised by the Erie Railroad.[12]

The Civil War failed to halt turf meetings and outdoor recreation in the North. It was, however, only with the return of peace that the nation felt a new sporting impulse and began to give enthusiastic support to the turf, the diamond, the ring, and other outdoor activities. The game of baseball, spreading from cities to towns and villages, became a national fad, and matches were scheduled with distant communities. A tournament at Rockford, Illinois, in 1866 was attended by teams from Detroit, Milwaukee, Dubuque, and Chicago.[13] In 1869 Harry Wright's Cincinnati Red Stockings were able to make a memorable transcontinental tour from Maine to California; a New Orleans club visited Memphis, St. Louis, and Cincinnati; and eastern teams condescended to tavel as far west as the Queen City. The Erie line offered to convey a New Orleans club, then visiting Cincinnati, to New York and return at half-fare rates. When the Cincinnati Red Stockings made their tour by boat, local lines, and the Union Pacific in 1869 it was reported: "The boys have received every attention from the officers of the different roads. . . . At all the stations groups state us almost out of countenance, having heard of the successful exploits of the Club through telegrams of the Western Associated Press."[14]

Baseball clubs made use of the rapidly expanding network of the 1870's, and the organization of the National League in 1876 was only possible with the continued development of connecting lines. In the 1886 edition of *Spalding's Official Base Ball Guide* the Michigan Central advertised: "The cities that have representative clubs contesting for the championship pennant this year are—Chicago, Boston, New York, Washington, Kansas City, Detroit, St. Louis and Philadelphia. All of these cities are joined together by the MICHIGAN CENTRAL Railroad. This road has enjoyed almost a monopoly of Bass Ball travel in former years." Throughout the 1870's and 1880's the expanding railroad network played an indispensable role in the popularization of the "national game."[15]

A widespread interest in thoroughbred and trotting races also was in great part sustained by railroad expansion. In 1866 the Harlem, Rensselaer and Saratoga Railroad Company, realizing the advantage of encouraging the racing public, arranged to convey race horses at cost by express train from New York to Saratoga. *Turf, Field and Farm* pointed to the need for better transportation arrangements and predicted, "The completion of the Pacific Railroad will not be without effect upon the blood stock interests of the great West."[16] Jerome Park, Long Branch, and Gravesend catered to New York crowds, Baltimore attracted huge throngs of sportsmen, and in California racing was encouraged by the building of lines into the interior of the state. In the 1870's western turfmen began sending their horses by rail to eastern tracks, the Grand Circuit linked Hartford, Springfield, Poughkeepsie, and Utica with Rochester, Buffalo, and Cleveland, and racing associations formed in virtually every section. When Mollie McCarthy and Ten Broeck raced at Louisville in 1877, "Masses of strangers arrived by train, extra trains and steamboats." People from "all over the land" attended the Kentucky Derby in 1885, the City Council declared a holiday, and sixteen carloads of horses were sent from Nashville to Louisville.[17] Agricultural fairs, with the cooperation of numerous companies, drew thousands to their fairground tracks, and the railroads encouraged intersectional meetings by introducing special horse cars in the middle eighties.[18]

In the decades after the Civil War an apologetic but curious public acquired a "deplorable" interest in prize fighting, and railroad officials were not slow to capitalize on the crowd appeal of pugilism despite its illegality. When Mike McCoole met Aaron Jones in 1867 at Busenbark Station, Ohio, "Tickets were openly sold for excursion trains to the bout" and sporting men from the East were in attendance, while another McCoole fight in 1869 encouraged the lines to run specials from Cincinnati and other nearby cities.[19] After 1881 John L. Sullivan, the notorious "Boston Strong Boy," went on grand tours of the athletic clubs, opera houses, and theaters of the country, his fights in the New Orleans area with Paddy Ryan, Jake Kilrain, and James J. Corbett luring fans who jammed the passenger coaches. When the Great John L. met Kilrain near Richburg, Mississippi, in 1889, the Northeastern Railroad carried a tumultuous crowd from New Orleans to the site, even though Governor Robert Lowry of Mississippi issued a proclamation against the affair and called out armed guards to prevent any invasion of the state. After the brawl the Governor requested the attorney general "to begin proceedings to forfeit the charter of the Northeastern railroad."[20] Railroad companies expressed only a minor concern for such sporadic events, it is true, but the prize ring was greatly aided by their cooperation.[21]

Poor connections, uncomfortable cars, and the absence of lines in rural sections remained a problem for some years.[22] Many of the difficulties and inconveniences of travel remained throughout these expansive years of railroading, but all sports were encouraged by the improved transportation of the post-bellum era. Immediately after the war a New York crew visited Pittsburgh to participate in a regatta held on the Monongahela River.[23] The first intercollegiate football game between Rutgers and Princeton was attended by a group of students riding the train pulled by "the jerky little engine that steamed out of Princeton on that memorable morning of November 6, 1869."[24] Intercollegiate athletics depended on railroad service for carrying teams and supporters to football, baseball, and rowing, as well as track and field contests.

Harvard's crack baseball team made the first grand tour in 1870, "the most brilliant in the history of college baseball," according to Henry Chadwick almost two decades later. Playing both amateur and professional clubs, Harvard won a majority of the games played in New Haven, Troy, Utica, Syracuse, Oswego (Canada), Buffalo, Cleveland, Cincinnati, Lousiville, Chicago, Milwaukee, Indianapolis, Washington, Baltimore, Philadelphia, New York, and Brooklyn.[25] Amateur and professional cycling races were held throughout the country,[26] while rod and gun enthusiasts relied on branch lines into rural preserves.[27] By the closing years of the century virtually every realm of sport had shared in the powerful impact of the railroad on American life.

Almost contemporaneous with the development of a continental railroad system came the diffusion of telegraph lines throughout the nation. From its invention in 1844 the electric telegraph rapidly assumed a significant role in the dissemination of news.[28] When the Magnetic Telegraph Company's line reached New York, James Gordon Bennett's *Herald* and Horace Greeley's *Tribune* installed apparatus in 1846. Direct contact was made between the East and New Orleans two years later, largely to meet the urgent demand for quicker news from the Mexican War front. By 1861 San Francisco was connected by wire with the Atlantic coast, and throughout the war years use of the telegraph was extended in military operations.

During the pioneer years telegraphic messages were both costly and brief, and sports events were reported on a limited scale. One of the first reports by wire was that of the Tom Hyer-Yankee Sullivan brawl at Rock Point, Maryland, in 1849. A New York dispatch read, "We hope never to have to record a similar case of brutality in this country," and even Greeley, an inveterate foe of the prize ring, permitted the printing of dispatches of this brutal encounter. Interest was not confined to Baltimore, Philadelphia, and New York, for some newspapers in the West noticed it. In the next decade several fights were widely reported by telegraph. When Morrissey and Heanan fought for the American championship in Canada in 1858, anxious crowds waited at Western Union offices for the news; when Heanan met Tom Sayers in England two years later the news was spread by wire after it was brought to America by the *Vanderbilt*.[29] Horse racing and yachting news was less novel and less sensational, but Lady Suffolk's appearance on the course at the Rochester, New York, fair in 1851, the victory of Commodore John Cox Stevens' yacht *America* at Cowes in the same year, and the exciting trotting races of the decade were given extensive wire coverage.[30] When Lexington met Lecomte at New Orleans in 1855, however, there seems to have been little reporting of the race in the North. Newspapers of that section were primarily concerned in that year with the trouble in Kansas, the rise of the Republican party, the heat of the abolitionist crusade, and the public furor over the murder of pugilist William Poole.

The expansion of sporting news in ensuing years was directly related to the more general usage of telegraphy, which made possible instantaneous reporting of ball games, horse races, prize fights, yachting regattas, and other events. Box scores, betting odds, and all kinds of messages were relayed from one city to another, and by 1870 daily reports were published in many metropolitan papers. In that year the steamboat race of the *Natchez* and the *Robert E. Lee* was reported throughout the country in one of the most extensive telegraphic accounts of any nonpolitical event prior to that time.[31] Not only did the newspapers make a practice of publishing daily messages from all corners of the sporting world, but crowds formed around Western Union offices during any important contest.[33] When the Associated Press sent its representatives in 1889 to the Sullivan-Kilrain fight in New Orleans, reporters appeared from "every prominent journal in the Union," and Western Union was said to have employed 50 operators to handle 208,000 words of specials following the fight. Poolrooms and saloons were often equipped with receiving sets to keep customers and bettors posted on baseball scores and track results, while newspapers set up bulletin boards for the crowds to linger around.[33] And the business transactions of sporting clubs and associations were often carried on by wire.

Sport had emerged into such a popular topic of conversation that newspapers rapidly expanded their coverage in the 1880's and 1890's, relying in great part on messages sent over the lines from distant points. Among the leaders in this field during these formative years of "yellow journalism" were such New York papers as Bennett's *Herald,* Charles Dana's *Sun,* and Joseph Pulitzer's *World.* The sports page was not solely the result of improvements in telegraphy, however, for popular interest had encouraged the employment of specialists who were extremely quick, as were the publishers, to capitalize on the news value of sporting events. Chicago produced the pioneers in baseball writing in such masters of breezy slang and grotesque humor as Leonard Washburne, Charles Seymour, and Finley Peter Dunne. Cincinnati newspapers, staffed by experts like Harry Weldon, O. P. Caylor, and Byron (Ban) Johnson, were among the most authoritative journals in the diamond world. In 1895, when William Randolph Hearst invaded the New York field and bought the *Journal,* he immediately brought in western writers and, within a few years, developed the first sports section.[34] The telegraph retained its functional importance in recording daily box scores and racing statistics, but it was no longer the one indispensable factor it had been in earlier decades.

The Atlantic cable, successfully laid in 1866 by Cyrus Field, had overcome the mid-century handicap of reporting two- or three-weeks-old English sporting news. At the end of that year James Gordon Bennett, Jr., with the aid of the Associated Press, featured cable dispatches of the great ocean race. When the Harvard crew rowed against Oxford in a highly publized race in 1869, "the result was flashed through the Atlantic cable as to reach New York about a quarter past one, while the news reached the Pacific

Coast about nine o'clock, enabling many of the San Franciscans to discuss the subject at their breakfast-tables, and swallow the defeat with their coffee!''[35] The combination of cable and telegraph aroused a deeper interest in international sport. Nor must we ignore that forerunner of the modern radio, the wireless which was demonstrated publicly in America for the first time in the yacht races of 1899. From Samuel F. B. Morse to Guglielmo Marconi the revolution in communication had encouraged the rise of sport.

Public interest in sport was also aroused by the enlarged format and greater circulation achieved by numerous inventions which revolutionized the printing process. By 1830 the Napier double-cylinder press was imported from England and developed by R. Hoe and Company, printing those cheap and sensational papers which were the first to feature horse races, prize fights, and foot races—the New York *Sun,* the New York *Transcript,* and the Philadelphia *Public Ledger.* James Gordon Bennett, Sr., recognized the value of catering to the whims of the masses and occasionally featured turf reporting in the *Herald* of the 1840's.[37] In 1846 the Hoe type-revolving cylinder press was introduced by the *Public Ledger,* enabling newspaper publishers, after improvements were made in the machine, to print 20,000 sheets an hour.[38] Other inventions facilitated the mass publication of the daily paper, making possible the sensationalized editions of Bennett, Pulitzer, and Hearst.[39] With the arrival of the new journalism of the 1880's, sporting news rapidly became a featured part of the metropolitan press.[40]

Publishers also aided in the popularization of outdoor sport throughout this whole era. From the 1830's onward sporting books appeared, the most famous of prewar authors being Henry William Herbert, whose illustrious pseudonym was Frank Forester. After the Civil War cheap methods of publication gave a great stimulus to the dime novel and the athletic almanac. While the vast majority of the thrillers and shockers concerned the Wild West or city crime, athletic stories and manuals were put out by Beadle & Adams, the leading publisher of the paper-backed dime novel.[41] After the establishment of A. G. Spalding & Brothers the *Spalding Guide* developed into the leading authority on rules of play, and all sorts of handbooks were included in the *Spalding Library of Athletic Sports.* The *New York Clipper* began publishing a theatrical and sporting *Clipper Almanac* in the 1870's, while newspapers like the New York *World,* the New York *Tribune,* the Chicago *Daily News,* the Washington *Post,* and the Brooklyn *Daily Eagle* issued almanacs listing athletic and racing records and sporting news. Richard Kyle Fox of the *National Police Gazette* published *Fox's Athletic Library* and sporting annuals. By the end of the century book publication had grown to astronomic proportions when compared to the Civil War era, and the Outing Publishing Company issued more than a hundred titles on angling, canoeing, yachting, mountain climbing, hunting, shooting, trapping, camping, cycling, and athletics.

A few dime novels had taken up the athletic theme in the 1870's, but more mature stories like Mark Sibley Severance's *Hammersmith: His Harvard Days* (1878), Noah Brook's *Our Baseball Club* (1884), and, of course,

Thomas Hughe's English classics, *Tom Brown at Rugby* and *Tom Brown at Oxford*, were responsible for the rising desire for sports fiction. By the 1890's a demand for boys' athletic stories was met in the voluminous outpouring of the heroic sporting achievements of Gilbert Patten's "Frank Merriwell."[42] Along with the newspaper and the sporting journal the field of publishing, with its improved techniques and expanded output, did much to attract attention to athletics at the turn of the century.

Much of the angling and hunting equipment and horseman's supplies came from England in the colonial era, but in the years before and after the American Revolution several dealers in sporting wares appeared in Philadelphia, New York, and Boston. From the early years of the nineteenth century merchants and gunsmiths in Kentucky supplied the settlers west of the Appalachian range.[43] Field sports were still enjoyed mainly by schoolboys and sportsmen with their simple rods in the 1840's and 1850's, but from the 1830's onward fishing and hunting purely for recreation developed into a sporting fad, the end of which is not in sight. Charles Hallock, noted sportsman, conservationist, and journalist of the post-Civil War era recalled how the rural folk of Hampshire County, Massachusetts, responded to a visiting sportsman of the 1840's who brought with him a set of highly finished rods, reels, and fly-fishing equipment.

Ah! those were the halcyon days. No railroads disturbed the quiet seclusion of that mountain nook. . . Twice a week an oldfashioned coach dragged heavily up the hill into the hamlet and halted in front of the house which was at once post-office, tavern, and miscellaneous store. . . . One day it brought a passenger. . . . He carried a leather hand-bag and a handful of rods in a case. The village *quidnuncs* said he was a surveyor. He allowed he was from Troy and had "come to go a-fishing." From that stranger I took my first lesson in fly-fishing.[44]

By the 1850's the manufacture of cricket bats and stumps, billiard tables, archery equipment, guns, fishing tackle, and other sporting accessories was carried on by a host of individual craftsmen and by such concerns as J. W. Brunswick & Brothers of Cincinnati, Bassler of Boston, Conroy's of New York, and John Krider's "Sportsmen's Depot" in Philadelphia.

Mass-production methods of manufacture were still in their infancy in post-Civil War decades, but the factory system became ever more deeply entrenched. While the sporting goods business never attained any great economic importance in the nineteenth century,[45] much of the popularity for athletic games and outdoor recreation was due to standardized manufacturing of baseball equipment, bicycles, billiard tables, sporting rifles, fishing rods, and various other items.[46] Although most American youths played with restitched balls and a minimum of paraphernalia, college athletes, cycling enthusiasts, and professional ballplayers popularized the products of George B. Ellard of Cincinnati, Peck & Snyder of New York, and other concerns.[47]

By the end of the century A. G. Spalding & Brothers was the nationally recognized leader in this field. As a renowned pitcher for the Boston and Chicago clubs and then as the promoter of the latter, Albert Spalding had turned to the merchandizing of athletic goods in 1876.[48] One of the most avid sponsors of the national game, he branched out into varied sports in the 1880's, and acquired a virtual monopoly over athletic goods by absorbing A. J. Reach Company in 1885, Wright & Ditson in 1892, as well as Peck & Snyder and other firms. By 1887 the Spalding "Official League" baseball had been adopted by the National League, the Western League, the New England League, the International League, and various college conferences, and balls were offered to the public ranging in price from 5 cents to $1.50. To gain an even greater ascendancy over his rivals A. G. Spalding published a wide range of guides in *Spalding's Library of Athletic Sports,* in which his wares were not only advertised but those of rivals were derided as inferior.

The sewing machine was one of many inventions which made possible the more uniform equipment of the last decades of the century when local leagues and national associations took shape throughout the United States. Canoeing and camping were other diversions which gave rise to the manufacture of sporting goods on an ever larger scale. In the latter years of the century the mail-order house and the department store began to feature sporting goods. Macy's of New York began with ice skates, velocipedes, bathing suits, and beach equipment in 1872, although all sporting goods were sold by the toy department. By 1902, with the addition of numerous other items, a separate department was established. Sears Roebuck and Company, meanwhile, devoted more than eighty pages of its 1895 catalogue to weapons and fishing equipment, and within a decade not only hunting and fishing equipment but also bicycles, boxing gloves, baseball paraphernalia, and sleds were featured.[49]

When Thomas A. Edison developed the incandescent bulb in 1879 he inaugurated a new era in the social life of our cities. Although the first dynamo was built within two years, gas lighting did not give way immediately, and the crowds which jammed the old Madison Square Garden in New York in 1883 to see John L. Sullivan fight Herbert Slade still had to cope not only with the smoke-filled air but also with the blue gas fumes. The Garden had already installed some electric lights, however. At a six-day professional walking match in 1882 the cloud of tobacco smoke was so thick that "even the electric lights" had "a hard struggle to assert their superior brilliancy" over the gas jets. Even "the noisy yell of programme, candy, fruit and peanut vendors who filled the air with the vilest discord" failed to discourage the crowd, according to a philosophically minded reporter who wondered what Herbert Spencer would think of "the peculiar phase of idiocy in the American character" which drew thousands of men and women to midnight pedestrian contests.[50]

Within a few years electric lighting and more comfortable accommodations helped lure players and spectators alike to Y.M.C.A.'s, athletic clubs, regimental armories, school and college gymnasiums, as well as sports arenas. In 1885, at the third annual Horse Show in Madison Square Garden, handsomely dressed sportswomen reveled in the arena, "gaudy with festoons of racing flags and brilliant streamers, lighted at night by hundreds of electric lights," while visitors to the brilliantly lighted New York Athletic Club agreed that "fine surroundings will not do an athlete any harm."[51] The indoor prize fight, walking contest, wrestling match, and horse show were a far cry from the crude atmosphere of early indoor sport. In 1890 carnivals were held at the Massachusetts Mechanics' Association by the Boston Athletic Association and at the new Madison Square Garden in New York by the Staten Island Athletic Club; the horse show attracted fashionable New Yorkers to the Garden; and indoor baseball, already popular in Chicago, was taken up in New York's regimental armories.[52] A decade of electrification, paralleling improvements in transportation communication, had elevated and purified the atmosphere of sport. The saloon brawls of pugilists in the 1850's and 1860's were gradually abandoned for the organized matches of the 1880's and 1890's. At the time of the Sullivan-Corbett fight in the New Orleans Olympic Club in 1892, an observer wrote in the Chicago *Daily Tribune,* September 8, 1892: "Now men travel to great boxing contests in vestibule limited trains; they sleep at the best hotels . . . and when the time for the contest arrives they find themselves in a grand, brilliantly lighted arena."

Basketball and volleyball, originating in the Y.M.C.A. in 1892 and 1895, were both developed to meet the need for indoor sport on winter evenings. The rapid construction of college gymnasiums and the building of more luxurious clubhouses after the middle eighties stemmed in great part from the superior appointments and more brilliant lighting available for athletic games, and much of the urban appeal of indoor sport was directly attributable to the revolution which electric lighting made in the night life of the metropolis.

Electrification, which transformed everything from home gadgets and domestic lighting to power machinery and launches, exerted an influence on the course of sport through the development of rapid transit systems in cities from coast to coast. Horse-drawn cars had carried the burden of traffic since the 1850's, but the electric streetcar assumed an entirely new role in opening up suburban areas and the countryside to the pent-up city populace. Soon after the Richmond, Virginia, experiment of 1888, the streetcar began to acquaint large numbers of city dwellers with the race track and the ball diamond.[53] Experimental lines had been laid even earlier in the decade, and Chicago crowds going to the races at Washington Park in 1887 were jammed on "the grip," one reporter noting the "perpetual stream of track slang," the prodding and pushing, and the annoying delay when it was announced that "the cable has busted.[54] Trolley parks, many of which included baseball diamonds, were promoted by the transit companies; ball teams were encouraged by these same concerns through gifts of land or grandstands; and the crowds flocked to week-end games on the cars.[55] At the turn of the century the popular interest in athletic games in thousands of towns and cities was stimulated to a high degree by the extension of rapid transit systems, a development which may possibly have been as significant in the growth of local sport as the automobile was to be in the development of intercommunity rivalries.

Numerous inventions and improvements applied to sport were of varying importance: the stop watch, the percussion cap, the streamlined sulky, barbed wire, the safety cycle, ball bearings, and artificial ice for skating rinks, among others. Improved implements often popularized and revolutionized the style of a sport, as in the invention of the sliding seat of the rowing shell, the introduction of the rubber-wound gutta-percha ball which necessitated the lengthening of golf courses, and the universal acceptance of the catcher's mask.

Vulcanization of rubber by Charles Goodyear in the 1830's led to the development of elastic and resilient rubber balls in the following decade, and eventually influenced the development of golf and tennis balls as well as other sporting apparel and equipment. The pneumatic tire, developed by Dr. John Boyd Dunlop of Belfast, Ireland, in 1888, revolutionized cycling and harness racing in the next decade. Equipped with pneumatic tires, the sulky abandoned its old highwheel style, and the trotter and pacer found it made made for smoother movement on the track. Sulky drivers reduced the mile record of 2:08¾ by Maud S. with an old highwheeler to 1:58½ by Lou Dillion in 1903 with a "bicycle sulky." According to W. H. Gocher, a racing authority, the innovation of pneumatic tires and the streamlining of the sulky cut five to seven seconds from former records, which was "more than the breeding had done in a dozen years."[56] The pneumatic tire, introduced by racing cyclists and sulky drivers, went on to play a much more vital role in the rise of the automobile industry and the spectacular appeal of auto racing.

The camera also came to the aid of sport in the decades following the Civil War. Professional photography had developed rapidly in the middle period of the century, but nature lovers became devotees of the camera only when its bulkiness and weight were eliminated in the closing years of the century. Development of the Eastman Kodak after 1888 found a mass market as thousands of Americans put it to personal and commercial use. Pictorial and sporting magazines which had been printing woodcuts since the pre-war era began to introduce many pictures taken from photographs, and in the late 1880's and early 1890's actual photographic prints of athletes and outdoor sportsmen came into common usage. *Harper's Weekly, Leslie's Illustrated Weekly, Illustrated American,* and the *National Police Gazette* featured photography, and by the end of the century the vast majority of their pictures were camera studies.[57] Newspapers recognized the circulation value of half-tone prints, but because of paper and technical problems they were used sparsely until the New York *Times* published an illustrated Sunday supplement in 1896, soon to be imitated by the New York *Tribune* and the Chicago *Tribune.* The year 1897 saw the half-tone illustration become a regular feature of metropolitan newspapers, rapidly eliminating the age-old reliance on woodcuts. At the turn of the century sport was available in visual form to millions who heretofore had little knowledge of athletics and outdoor games.[58]

It was in 1872 that Eadweard Muybridge made the first successful attempt "to secure an illusion of motion by photography." With the help of Leland Stanford, already a noted turfman, he set out to prove whether "a trotting horse at one point in its gait left the ground entirely."[59] By establishing a battery of cameras the movements of the horse were successively photographed, and Muybridge later turned his technique to "the gallop of dogs, the flight of birds, and the performances of athletes." In his monumental study entitled *Animal Locomotion* (1887) he included thousands of pictures of horses, athletes, and other living subjects, demonstrating "the work and play of men, women and children of all ages; how pitchers throw the baseball, how batters hit it, and how athletes move their bodies in record-breaking contests."[60] Muybridge is considered only one among a number of the pioneers of the motion picture, but his pictures had presented possibly the best illusion of motion prior to the development of flexible celluloid film. A host of experiments gradually evolved principles and techniques in the late 1880's which gave birth to the true motion picture. Woodville Latham and his two sons made a four-minute film of the prize fight between Young Griffo and Battling Barnett in 1895, showing it on a large screen for an audience, an event which has been called "the first flickering, commercial motion picture."[61] When Bob Fitzsimmons won the heavyweight championship from James J. Corbett at Carson City, Nevada, in 1897, the fight was photographed for public distribution. With the increasing poularity in succeeding years of the newsreel, the short subject, and an occasional feature film, the motion picture came to rival the photograph in spreading the gospel of sport.[62]

When sport began to mature into a business of some importance and thousands of organizations throughout the country joined leagues, associations, racing circuits, and national administrative bodies, it became necessary to utilize on a large scale the telephone, the typewriter, and all the other instruments so vital to the commercial world. Even the phonograph, at first considered a business device but soon devoted to popular music, came to have an indirect influence, recording for public entertainment such songs as "Daisy Bell," "Casey at the Bat," "Slide, Kelly, Slide," and, early in the present century, the theme song of the national pastime, "Take Me Out to the Ball Game." All of these instruments created a great revolution in communication, and they contributed significantly to the expansion of sport on a national scale.

The bicycle, still an important means of transport in Europe but something of a casualty of the machine age in the United States, also had an important role. After its demonstration at the Philadelphiha Centennial, an interest was ignited which grew rapidly in the 1880's and flamed into an obsession in the 1890's.[83] Clubs, cycling associations, and racing meets were sponsored everywhere in these years, and the League of American Wheelmen served as a spearhead for many of the reforms in fashions, good roads, and outdoor exercise. Albert H. Pope was merely the foremost among many manufacturers of the "velocipede" which became so popular among women's clubs, temperance groups, professional men, and, at the turn of the century, in the business world and among the trades. Contemporary observers speculated on the social benefits to be derived from the cycle, especially in enticing women to the pleasures of outdoor exercise. Bicycling was discussed by ministers and physicians, it was considered as a weapon in future wars, police squads in some cities were mounted on wheels, mail carriers utilized it, and many thought it would revolutionize society.[64]

As a branch of American industry the bicycle was reputed to have developed into a $100,000,000 business in the 1890's. Mass-production techniques were introduced, Iver Johnson's Arms and Cycle Works advertising "Every part interchangeable and exact." The Indiana Bicycle Company, home of the Waverly cycle, maintained a huge factory in Indianapolis and claimed to be the most perfect and complete plant in the world: "We employ the highest mechanical skill and the best labor-saving machinery that ample capital can provide. Our methods of construction are along the latest and most approved lines of mechanical work."[65]

Much of the publicity given to competing manufacturers centered around the mechanical improvements and the speed records of their products. Between 1878 and 1896 the mile record was lowered from 3:57 to 1:55$^1/_5$. While recognizing the effect of better riding styles, methodical training, improved tracks, and the art of pacemaking, one critic contended. "The prime factor . . . is the improvement in the vehicle itself. The racing machine of 1878 was a heavy, crude, cumbersome affair, while the modern bicycle, less than one-sixth its weight, equipped with scientifically calculated gearing, pneumatic tires, and friction annihilators, represents much of the difference."[46] Roger Burlingame has pointed out the impact of the bicycle on the health, recreation, business, and the social life of the American people, and on the manufacture of the cycle claimed that "it introduced certain technical principles which were carried on into the motor car, notably ball bearings, hub-breaking and the tangential spoke."[47] Little did cycling enthusiasts realize that in these same years a much more revolutionary vehicle, destined to transform our way of life, was about to make its dramatic appearance on the national scene.

One of the last inventions which the nineteenth century brought forth for the conquest of time and distance was the automobile. During the 1890's the Haynes, Duryea, Ford, Stanely Steamer, Packard, and Locomobile came out in quick succession, and the Pierce Arrow, Cadillac, and Buick were to follow in the next several years.[68] Manufacturers of bicycles had already turned to the construction of the motor car in a number of instances. As early as 1895 Herman H. Kohlsaat, publisher of the Chicago Times-Herald, sponsored the first automobile race on American soil. One of the features of this contest, run through a snowstorm and won by Charles Duryea, was the enhanced reputation achieved for the gasoline motor, which had not yet been recognized as the proper source of motor power. A number of European races inspired American drivers to take to the racecourse, and the experimental value of endurance or speed contests was immediately recognized by pioneer manufacturers. Nor were they slow to see the publicity value of races featured by the newspapers.[69]

Henry Ford "was bewitched by Duryea's feat," and he "devoured reports on the subject which appeared in the newspapers and magazines of the day." When other leading carbuilders sought financial backing for their racers, Ford determined to win supremacy on the track. After defeating Alexander Winton in a race at Detroit in 1902, "Ford's powers as a 'speed demon' began to appear in the columns of the widely circulated trade journal *Horseless Age.*"[70] In later years he was to contend, "I never thought anything of racing, but the public refused to consider the automobile in any light other than as a fast toy. Therefore later we had to race. The industry was held back by his initial racing slant, for the attention of the makers was diverted to making fast rather than good cars." The victory over Winton was his frist race, "and it brought advertising of the only kind that people cared to read." Bowing to public opinion, he was determined "to make an automobile that would be known wherever speed was known," and he set to work installing four cylinders in his famous "999." Developing 80 horse power, this machine was so frightening, even to its builders, that the fearless Barney Oldfield was hired for the race. Oldfield had only a tiller with which to drive, since there were no steering wheels, but this professional cyclist who had never driven a car established a new record and helped put Ford back on his feet. The financial support of Alex Y. Malcomson, an admirer of "999," gave him a new start: "A week after the race I formed the Ford Motor Company."[71]

The next few years witnessed the establishment of Automobile Club of America races, sport clubs in the American Automobile Association, the Vanderbilt Cup, and the Glidden Tour. Reporting on the third annual Glidden Tour in 1906, *Scientific American* defended American cars, heretofore considered inferior to European models: "Above all else, the tour was demonstrated that American machines will stand fast driving on rough forest roads without serious damage to the cars or their mechanism. Engine and gear troubles have practically disappeared, and the only things that are to be feared are the breakage of springs and axles and the giving out of tires. Numerous shock-absorbers were tried out and found wanting in this test; and were it not for the pneumatic tires, which have been greatly improved during the past two years, such a tour would be impossible of accomplishment."[72]

The Newport social season featured racing, Daytona Beach soon became a center for speed trials, and tracks were built in various parts of the nation, the first of which may have been at Narragansett Park in 1896.[73] Not until the years just prior to World War I did auto racing attain a truly national popularity with the establishment of the Indianapolis Speedway, but the emphasis on speed and endurance in these early years spurred manufacturers to build ever faster models and advertisers to feature the record performances of each car. Henry Ford had long since lost interest, while the Buick racing team was discontinued in 1915. By then mass production had turned the emphasis toward design, comfort, and economy. Racing was not abandoned and manufacturers still featured endurance tests in later years, but the heated rivalry between pioneer builders had become a thing of the past.[74]

Technological developments in the latter half of the nineteenth century transformed the social habits of the Western World, and sport was but one of many institutions which felt their full impact. Fashions, foods, journalism, home appliances, commercialized entertainment, architecture, and city planning were only a few of the facets of life which underwent rapid change as transportation and communication were revolutionized and as new materials were made available. There are those who stress the thesis that sport is a direct recreation against the mechanization, the division of labor, and the standardization of life in a machine civilization,[75] and this may in part be true, but sport in nineteenth-century America was as much a product of industrialization as it was an antidote to it. While athletics and outdoor recreation were sought as a release from the confinements of city life, industrialization and the urban movement were the basic causes for the rise of organized sport. And the urban movement was, of course, greatly enhanced by the revolutionary transformation in communication, transportation, agriculture, and industrialization.[76]

The first symptoms of the impact of invention on nineteenth-century sports are to be found in the steamboat of the ante-bellum era. An intensification of interest in horse racing during the 1820's and 1830's was only a prelude to the sporting excitement over yachting, prize fighting, rowing, running, cricket, and baseball of the 1840's and 1850's. By this time the railroad was opening up new opportunities for hunters, anglers, and athletic teams, and it was the railroad, of all the inventions of the century, which gave the greatest impetus to the intercommunity rivalries in sport. The telegraph and the penny press opened the gates to a rising tide of sporting journalism; the sewing machine and the factory system revolutionized the manufacturing of sporting goods; the electric light and rapid transit further demonstrated the impact of electrification; inventions like the Kodak camera, the motion picture, and the pneumatic tire stimulated various fields of sport; and the bicycle and automobile gave additional evidence to the effect of the transportation revolution on the sporting impulse of the latter half of the century. Toward the end of the century the rapidity with which one invention followed another demonstrated the increasingly close relationship of technology and social change. No one can deny the significance of sportsmen, athletes, journalists, and pioneers in many organizations, and no one can disregard the multiple forces transforming the social scene. The technological revolution is not the sole determining factor in the rise of sport, but to ignore its influence would result only in a more or less superficial understanding of the history of one of the prominent social institutions of modern America.

REFERENCE NOTES

1. Among the most useful works to be consulted on early American sport are John A. Krout, *Annals of American Sport* (New Haven, 1929); Jeannie Holliman, *American Sports, 1785-1835* Durham, 1931); Foster R. Dulles, *America Learns To Play: A History of Popular Recreation, 1607-1940* (New York, 1940); Robert B. Weaver, *Amusements and Sports in American Life* (Chicago, 1939); and Herbert Manchester, *Four Centuries of*

Sport in America, 1490-1890 (New York, 1931). For certain aspects of ante-bellum sport, see Arthur M. Schlesinger and Dixon R. Fox (eds.), *A History of American Life*, 13 vols. (New York, 1927-1948).

2. See the New York *American*, May 27, 1823; New Orleans *Daily Picayune*, March 27, 1839; New York *Weekly Herald*, May 17, 1845, July 11, 1849; and accounts of many years in the *Spirit of the Times* (New York) for prewar years. In an era when bridges were more the exception than the rule the ferry was an indispensable means of transportation. See, for example, Kenneth Roberts and Anna M. Roberts (eds.), *Moreau de St. Mery's American Journey, 1793-1798* (Garden City, 1947), 173; New York *American*, May 27, 1823.

3. For examples of the steamboat in the early sport, see the New York *Herald*, June 17, 1829; *Wilkes' Spirit of the Times* (New York), XII (August 5, 1865), 380; New Orleans *Daily Picayune*, December 1, 1855, December 10, 1859; *Spirit of the Times*, XX (June 19, 1869), 276; New York *World*, June 19, 1869. When the passenger lines began converting to steam in the Civil War era, the development of international sport was facilitated to a considerable degree. In the latter decades of the century the steam yacht became the vogue among American millionaires.

4. John Hervey, *Racing in America, 1665-1865*, 2 vols. (New York, 1944), II, 101.

5. New Orleans *Daily Picayune*, March 27, 1839.

6. *American Turf Register and Sporting Magazine* (Baltimore), XIII (July, 1843), 367; New York *Daily Tribune*, May 14, 1845.

7. *Spirit of the Times*, XXI (July 12, 1851), 246.

8. Albert L. Demaree, *The American Agricultural Press, 1819-1860* (New York, 1941), 203-204. Specific instances of such aid can be found in the *Cultivator* (Albany), IX (March, 1842), 50; *American Agriculturist* (New York), II (October 16, 1843), 258; New York *Daily Tribune*, September 18, 1851; *Transactions of the Illinois State Agricultural Society* (Springfield), I, *1853-54* (1855), 6; II, *1856-57* (1857), 24-32; *Report and Proceedings of the Iowa State Agricultural Society . . . October, 1855* (Fairfield, 1856), 24; *Fifth Report of the Indiana State Board of Agriculture . . .* I (July, 1858), 12; *Wisconsin Farmer and North-Western Cultivator* (Madison), IX (October, 1857), 873; XI (October, 1859), 386-87; Springfield *Weekly Illinois State Journal*, September 5, 19, 1860. The "prolonging matches" of the ante-bellum era attracted large crowds seeking both entertainment and the latest improvements in agricultural implements.

9. Samuel Crowther and Arthur Ruhl, *Rowing and Track Athletics* (New York, 1905?), II.

10. James N. Elkins, superintendent of the Boston, Concord and Montreal Railroad, agreed to pay all transportation costs for the crews and their equipment to the New Hampshire lake where the race was to be held. Robert F. Kelley, *American Rowing: Its Background and Traditions* (New YOrk, 1932), 100-101.

11. New York *Daily Times*, October 13, 1853; Boston *Advertiser*, October 14, 1853.

12. New York *Herald*, October 23, 1858.

13. *Wilkes' Spirit of the Times*, XIV (July 7, 1866), 294. More rural areas felt the impact somewhat later, Warrenton, Mississippi, holding a tourney in 1885 to which special trains were sent. New Orleans *Daily Picayune*, July 19, 1885.

14. New York *World*, August 21, 1869; Cincinnati *Commercial*, September 22, 1869; San Francisco *Evening Bulletin*, October 5, 1869. Their use of Pullman cars set a precedent in sports circles. Advertising by local lines for an approaching game appeared in the Cincinnati *Commercial*, August 24, 1869.

15. See *Spalding's Offical Base Ball Guide* (New York, 1896), appendix. The Memphis Reds Base Ball Association sent a printed circular to Harry Wright of the Boston team in 1877 in which it stressed the reduced rates to any club visiting St. Louis of Louisville. Harry Wright Correspondence, 7 vols. I (1865-1877), 40, Spalding Baseball Collection (New York Public Library). In the 1880's enthusiastic crowds turned out to the railroad station to welcome home the victorious nines. *Frank Leslie's Boys' and Girls' Weekly* (New York), XXXV (October 6, 1883), 174; New York *Sun*, September 7, 1886.

16. *Turf, Field and Farm* (New York), I (September 2, 1865), 69; VIII (May 28, 1869), 344.

17. *Wilkes' Spirit of the Times*, XIV (May 19, 1866), 185; San Francisco *Evening Bulletin*, October 15, 1869; Baltimore *American and Commercial Advertiser*, October 25, 1877; New Orleans *Daily Picayune*, April 20, 1884, May 9, 15, 1885; Charles E. Trevathan, *The American Thoroughbred* (New York, 1935), 371.

18. New York *World,* April 29, 1884.

19. Alexander Johnston, *Ten—And Out! The Complete Story of the Prize Ring in America* (New York, 1947), 42-43.

20. Dunbar Rowland (ed.), *Encyclopedia of Mississippi History,* 2 vols. (Madison, 1907), II, 142; St. Paul and Minneapolis *Pioneer Press,* February 8, 1882; New Orleans *Daily Picayune,* August 6, 1885; New York *Sun,* May 12, 1886.

21. Railroad interest in sport was illustrated by the *New York Railroad Gazette:* "Horse-racing tracks of the violest *[sic]* character are encouraged (indirectly, it may be) in more than one case by railroads normally law-abiding. Sunday excursions patronized chiefly by roughs who conduct baseball games of a character condemned by all decent people are normally the same as prize fights in kind though not in degree." Quoted in the New Orleans *Daily Picayune,* August 6, 1885.

22. For illustrations of the difficulties of railroad travel, see the Walter Camp Correspondence, Box 64 (Yale University Library, New Haven).

23. *Wilkes' Spirit of the Times,* XIII (October 14, 1865), 102.

24. Parke H. Davis, *Football, The American Intercollegiate Game* (New York, 1911), 45.

25. *Outing* (New York), XII (August, 1888), 407-408.

26. By the 1890's many railroads carried bicycles as free freight and professional cyclists could tour their National Circuit in luxury cars. New York *Journal,* September 18, 1897.

27. Scores of railroads in every section of the country served those seeking to hunt or fish in the rustic countryside. See, particularly, Charles Hallock (ed.), *The Sportsman's Gazetteer and General Guide* (New York, 1877), Pt. II, 1-182. See also the Chicago and Northwestern Railway advdertisement in the *Spirit of the Times,* XCII (August 19, 1876), 53.

28. For the early development of the telegraph, see James D. Reid, *The Telegraph in America and Morse Memorial* (New York, 1887); Waldemar Kaempffert (ed.), *A Popular History of American Invention,* 2 vols. (New York, 1924); and Robert L. Thompson, *something a Continent: The History of the Telegraph Industry in the United States, 1832-1866* (Princeton, 1947).

29. Boston *Daily Journal,* February 7, 8, 9, 1849; New York *Daily Tribune,* February 8, 9, 1849; Milwaukee *Sentinel and Gazette,* February 10, 1849; Boston *Daily Courier,* October 21, 1858; New York *Times,* October 21, 1858; New Orleans *Daily Picayune,* May 6, 7, June 29, 1860; Nashville *Daily News,* April 29, 1860.

30. New York *Daily Tribune,* September 19, 1851; Natchez *Courier,* September 19, 1851.

31. New Orleans *Daily Picayune,* July 6, 1870.

32. *Ibid.* See also New York *Times,* October 21, 1858; *Harper's Weekly* (New York), XXVII (October 13, 1883), 654.

33. Oliver Grambling, *AP: The Story of News* (New York, 1940), 232; New Orleans *Daily Picayune,* July 10, 1889. For poolrooms, saloons, and bulletin boards, see the New York *Sun,* October 6, 1878; New York *Herald,* February 7, 1882; New Orleans *Daily Picayune,* May 17, 1884, July 6, 1885; New York *World,* September 8, 1892. Also see *Harper's Weekly,* XXVII (October 13, 1883), 654; XXXVI (April 2, December 17, 1892), 319, 324, 1210. Henry L. Mencken, in *Happy Days, 1880-1892* (New York, 1940), 225, nostalgically recalled how, since there were few sporting "extras" in Baltimore in the 1880's, "the high-toned saloons of the town catered to the [baseball] fans by putting in telegraph operators who wrote the scores on blackboards."

34. The New York *Transcript* and the *Sun* sensationalized the news as early as the 1830's and began reporting prize fights. James Gordon Bennett's *Herald* exploited sporting interest in pre-Civil War years and his son continued to do so in the period following the war. Magazines which capitalized on sport included the *American Turf Register and Sporting Magazine,* the *New York Clipper,* and the *National Police Gazette* (New York), as well as a host of fishing and hunting journals. Through the 1880's, and 1890's the New York *Sun* and the *World* competed for the sporting public, only to be outdone by the *Journal* at the end of the century. Among the prominent writers of the era were Henry Chadwick, Timothy Murname, Harry Weldon, Harry C. Palmer, Al Spink, Sam Crane, Walter Camp, Caspar Whitney, and Charles Dryden. See William H. Nugent, "The Sports Section," *American Mercury* (New York), XVI (February, 1929), 329-38; and Hugh Fullerton, "The Fellows Who Made the Game," *Saturday Evening Post* (Philadelphia), CC (April 21, 1928), 18 ff.

35. New York *Herald,* December 30, 31, 1866; Cincinnati *Commercial,* August 24, 28, 1869; *Frank Leslie's Illustrated Newspaper* (New York), XXIX (September 28, 1969), 2.

36. The origins of the penny press are ably discussed in Willard G. Bleyer, *Main Currents in the History of American Journalism* (Boston, 1927), 154-84; and in Frank L. Mott, *American Journalism, A History* (New York, 1941), 228-52.

37. Bleyer, *History of American Journalism,* 197, 209; Alfred M. Lee, *The Daily Newspaper in America* (New York, 1937), 611; New York *Weekly Herald,* May 15, 17, 1845, and *Herald* files for the 1840's.

38. Bleyer, *History of American Journalism,* 394.

39. *Ibid.,* 394-98.

40. Joseph Pulitzer's New York *World* began in intensive emploitation of sport as a front-page attraction almost immediately after its purchase in 1883, and by the following year first-page accounts of pedestrian matches, dog shows, and similar topics became regular features.

41. Albert Johannsen, *The House of Beadle and Adams and its Dime and Nickel Novel: The Story of a Vanished Literature,* 2 vols. (Norman, 1950), 1, 260, 377-79.

42. John L. Cutler, *Gilbert Patten and His Frank Merriwell Saga,* University of Maine *Studies* (Orono), Ser. II, No. 31 (1934).

43. Charles E. Goodspeed, *Angling in America: Its Early History and Literature* (Boston, 1939), 285 ff.

44. Charles Hallock, *The Fishing Tourist: Angler's Guide and Reference Book* (New York, 1873), 18.

45. In 1900 the value of sporting goods manufactured was only $2,628,496. United States Bureau of the Census, *Statistical Abstract of the United States* (Washington, 1909), 188.

46. See the *Spirit of the Times,* XX (May 4, 1850), 130; Natchez *Courier,* November 26, 1850; Madison *Daily State Journal,* March 26, 1855; New Orleans *Daily Picayune,* April 4, 1856. As midwestern merchants began to purchase large stocks from the East, John Krider advertised widely. Madison *Daily State Journal,* April 13, 1855. Michael Phelan, who in 1854 developed an indiarubber cushion permitting sharp edges on billiard tables, joined with Hugh W. Collender in forming Phelan and Collender, the leading billiards manufacturer until the organization of the Brunswick-Balke-Collender Company in 1884. Gymnastic apparatus, created by Dudley A. Sargent and other physical educators, was featured by many dealers, while the readers of *American Angler* (New York), *Forest and Stream* (New York), and other sporting journals were kept informed of the latest models of rifles, shotguns, and fishing rods and reels.

47. George B. Ellard, who sponsored the Red Stockings, advertised his score as "Base Ball Headquarters" and "Base Ball Depot," with the "Best Stock in the West." Cincinnati *Commerical,* August 24, 1869. Other merchandisers included Horseman's Base Ball and Croquet Emporium in New York and John H. Mann of the same city. Peck & Snyder began dealing in baseball equipment in 1865 and by the 1880's claimed to be the largest seller of sporting goods.

48. Moses King (ed.), *King's Handbook of the United States* (Buffalo, 1891), 232; Arthur Bartlett, *Baseball and Mr. Spalding: The History and Romance of Baseball* (New York, 1951), something (New York,), II (August, 1930), 62 ff; Arthur Bartlett, "They're Just Wild About Sports," *Saturday Evening Post,* CCXXII (December 24, 1949), 31 ff.; *Spalding's Official Base Ball Guide for 1887* (New York and Chicago, 1887), *passim.*

49. It was on mass manufacture of baseballs and uniforms that Spalding gained such a leading position in the sporting goods field. Since the business was restricted in these early years certain difficulties had to be overcome. To make the most out of manuracturing bats Spalding bought his own lumber mill in Michigan, while Albert Pope received little sympathy from the rolling mills in his first years of manufacturing bicycles. *Wheelman* (Boston), I (October, 1882), 71. For department and mailorder stores, see Ralph M. Hower, *History of Macy's of New York, 1858-1919* (Cambridge, 1946), 103, 162, 234-35, 239; Boris Emmet and John C. Jeuck, *Catalogues and Counters: A History of Sears, Roebuck and Company* (Chicago, 1950), 38; Cohn, David L.: The Good Old Days. New York 1940, 443-60.

50. New York *Herald,* October 23, 1882; New York *Sun,* August 7, 1883. The introduction of electric lighting in theatres was discussed, while the opposition of gas companies was

recognized. *Scientific American,* Supplement (New York), XVI (November 10, 1883), 6535-36.

51. *Harper's Weekly,* XXIX (February 14, November 14, 1885), 109, 743.

52. See *ibid.,* XXXIV (March 1, 8, 1890), 169, 171, 179. A new Madison Square Garden with the most modern facilities was built in the years 1887-1890; the California Athletic Club in San Francisco featured a "powerful electric arc light" over its ring; and electric lights in the Manhattan Athletic Club's new gymnasium in 1890 "shed a dazzling whiteness." *Ibid.,* XXXIV (April 5, 1890), 263-64; New York *Daily Tribune,* November 2, 30, 1890.

53. After the completion of the Richmond line rapid transit spread throughout the country. Although in 1890 there were only 144 electric railways in a national total of 789 street lines, by 1899 there were 50,600 electric cars in operation as contrasted to only 1,500 horse cars. Gilson Willets *et al., Workers of the Nation,* 2 vols. (New York, 1903), I, 498. For the suburban influence, see the *Street Railway Journal* (New York), XVIII (November 23, 1901), 760-61.

54. Chicago *Tribune,* July 5, 1887.

55. *Street Railway Journal,* XI (April, 1895), 232; XII (May, November, 1896), 317, 319, 708; *Cosmopolitan* (New York), XXXIII (July, 1902), 266; *Collier's* (New York). CXXV (May, 1953), 85; Oscar Handlin, *This Was America* (Cambridge, 1949); 374; New Orleans *Daily Picayune,* February 27, 1899.

56. Gocher, W. H. *Trotalong* (Hartford, 1928), 190.

57. Robert Taft, *Photography and the American Scene: A Social History, 1839-1889* (New York, 1938), 441.

58. Photography developed throughout the nineteenth century as an adjunct of the science of chemistry. Chemical and mechanical innovations were also responsible for the improvements of prints and all kinds of reproductions. Woodcuts were featured in the press, engravings were sold widely, and lithographs were found in the most rural home. Nathaniel Currier (later Currier & Ives) published hunting, fishing, pugilistic, baseball, rowing, yachting, sleighing, skating, trotting, and racing scenes for more than half a century. Cheap prints, calendars, and varied reproductions of sporting scenes did much to popularize the famous turf champions and sporting heroes of the era. See Harry T. Peters, *Currier & Ives: Printmakers to the American People* (Garden City, 1942).

59. Frank L. Dyer and Thomas C. Martin, *Edison: His Life and Inventions,* 2 vols. (New York, 1910), II, 534-35.

60. Kaempffert, *Popular History of American Inventions,* I, 425.

61. Lloyd Morris, *Not So Long Ago* (New York, 1949), 24.

62 The pioneer years of the motion picture industry are described by numerous other works, among them Deems Taylor, *A Pictorial History of the Movies* (New York, 1943), 1-6; Leslie Wood, *The Miracle of the Movies* (London, 1947), 66 ff.; George S. Bryan, *Edison: The Man and His Work* (Garden City, 1926), 184-94; Josef M. Eder, *History of Photography,* trans. by Edward Epstean (New York, 1945), 495 ff.; Taft, *Photography and the American Scene,* 405-12; Morris, *Not So Long Ago,* 1-35.

63. There was a brief craze in 1869, during which year, according to Albert H. Pope, "more than a thousand inventions were patented for the perfection and improvement of the velocipede." *Wheelman,* I (October, 1882), 70. Interest declined, however, until the Philadelphia celebration of 1876. Although race meetings and cycling clubs were widely reported in the 1880's, there were only 83 repair establishments in 1890 and the value of products in bicycle and tricycle repairs was only about $13,000,00. United States Bureau of the Census, *Statistical Abstract of the United States* (Washington, 1904), 516.

64. For summaries of the impact of the bicycle, see E. Benjamin Andrews, *History of the Last Quarter-Century in the United States, 1870-1895,* 2 vols. (New York, 1896), II, 289-90; Arthur M. Schlesinger, *The Rise of the City, 1878-1898* (New York, 1933), 312-14; Roger Burlingame, Roger, *Engines of Democracy: Inventions and Society in Mature America.* New York, 1940, 369-74.

65. *Harper's Weekly,* XL (April 11, 1896), 365. It is interesting that the "father of scientific management," Frederick W. Taylor, a tennis champion and golf devotee, was said to have learned through sport "the value of the minute analysis of motions, the importance of mechanical selection and training, the worth of time study and of standards based on rigorously exact observation." Charles De Freminville, "How Taylor Introduced the Scientific Method Into Management of the Shop," *Critical Essays are Scientific Manage-*

ment, Taylor Society *Bulletin* (New York), X (February, 1925), Pt. II, 32. Mass-production techniques, however, were only partially responsible for the outpouring of athletic goods which began to win wider markets at the turn of the century. The manufacture of baseball bats remained a highly specialized trade, while Scotch artisans who came to the United States maintained the personalized nature of their craft as makers of golf clubs. Despite the great improvements in gun manufacture, Elisha J. Lewis asserted in 1871 that there were thousands of miserable guns on the market: "The reason of this is that our mechanics have so many tastes and fancies to please, owing principally to the ignorance of those who order fowling-pieces, that they have adopted no generally-acknowledged standard of style to guide them in the getting up of guns suitable for certain kinds of sport." Elisha J. Lewis, *The American Sportsman* (Philadelphia, 1871), 435. Although numerous industries had taken up the principle of interchangeable parts, mass-production techniques were to come to the force only with the assembly lines of Henry Ford and the automobile industry in the years before World War I.

66. *Harper's Weekly,* XL (April 11, 1896), 366.

67. Burlingame, *Engines of Democracy: Inventions and Society in Mature America,* 3.

68. Herbert O. Duncan, *World on Wheels,* 2 vols. (Paris, 1927), II, 919 ff.

69. Lawrence H. Seltzer, *A Financial History of the American Automobile Industry* (Boston, 1928), 91; Pierre Sauvestre, *Histoire de L'Automobile* (Paris, 1907), *passim;* Ralph C. Epstein, *The Automobile Industry, Its Economic and Commercial Development* (Chicago, 1928), 154; Reginald M. Cleveland and S. T. Williamson, *The Road Is Yours* (New York, 1951), 175-76, 194-97.

70. Sward, Keith: *The Legend of Henry Ford.* New York, 1948, 14.

71. Henry Ford and Samuel Crowther, *My Life and Work* (Garden City, 1927), 36-37, 50-51.

72. *Scientific American,* XCV (August 11, 1906), 95.

73. G. F. Baright, "Automobiles and Automobile Races at Newport," *Independent* (New York), LIV (June 5, 1902), 1368.

74. In these years the motorcycle and the motorboat also created interest. Sir Alfred Harmsworth (later Lord Northcliffe) establishing the Harmsworth Trophy for international competition in 1903. Air races also won widespread publicity in the press from 1910 onward. Glenn H. Curtiss achieved an enviable reputation as an aviator, newspapers sponsored air meets, and considerable attention was given to the "new sport of the air." *Ibid.,* LXIX (November 3, 1910), 999.

75. Lewis Mumford, *Technics and Civilization* (New York, 1934), 303-305; Arnold J. Toynbee, *A Study of History,* 6 vols. (London, 1934-1939), IV, 242-43.

76. Technological developments throughout the business world transformed the pattern of city life. The electric elevator and improvements in the manufacture of steel made possible the skyscrapers of Chicago and New York in the late 1880's. Concentration of the business community in the central part of the city was increased also by the telephone switchboard and other instruments of communication. Less and less open land remained for the youth living in the heart of the metropolis, and it was to meet this challenge that the Y.M.C.A., the settlement house, the institutional church, and boys' club, and other agencies expanded their athletic facilities. The playground movement and the public park grew out of the necessity for recreational areas for city dwellers, and public authorities early in the twentieth century began to rope off streets for children at play. The subway, the streetcars, and the automobile made possible the accelerated trend toward suburban development, where the open lot or planned play area offered better opportunities to participate in sport. The more general implications of the impact of the technological revolution on society, already considered by several outstanding scholars, are not discussed here, the principal aim of this study being to describe the interrelationship of sport and invention in the latter half of the nineteenth century. Although the account of the auto slightly transgressed the limits of this study, it was felt necessary to give it an abbreviated treatment. The twentieth century, and the role of improved sporting equipment, racing and training devices, the radio, television, improved highways, and bus and air transport, would require an equally extensive study.

Some Background Influences On Nineteenth Century Canadian Sport And Education*

Alan Metcalfe
University of Windsor
Windsor, Ontario

A cursory examination of books, monographs, dissertations, and articles on Canadian history of sport and physical education discloses a lack of research and writing on societal variables which influence both the form and function of physical activity in any society. Most researchers of Canadian sport history have concerned themselves with the compilation of factual histories of sport and physical education.[1] The function of this brief analysis, therefore, is to discuss in a general sense some of the background influences on Canadian sport and physical education. In particular, the focus will be upon clusters of ideas that influenced middle class attitudes to life and society and thus to recreation, sport, and physical education. The important role played by the middle classes in the organization and administration of sport, the development of recreational facilities, and the growth of education make the basic values underlying middle class actions throughout the nineteenth century of critical importance.[2] Without an understanding of these attitudes and values it is difficult to go on to a more comprehensive analysis of the place of sport in Canadian society.

Although Canada became a semi-independent political entity in 1867, it is doubtful whether a particularly Canadian way of life or culture existed during the nineteenth century. Canadians were heavily dependent upon continental Europe. Britain and the United States for immigrants, financial resources, and attitudes and values. Therefore, any analysis of nineteenth century Canadian sport will include a consideration of sources lying outside of Canada itself. Because of the predominance of the British influence during the nineteenth century, many of the ideas can be traced to British sources and, thus, English speaking Canada assimilated many of the contemporary British viewpoints. However, it must be emphasized that within Canada there were two different trends of thought represented in the

* Metcalfe, A. "Some Background Influences on Nineteenth Century Canadian Sport and Physical Education," *Canadian Journal of History of Sport and Physical Education*, Vol. V, No. 1 (May 1974), pp. 62-73. Reprinted by permission of the author.

French and English speaking communities, and in this instance attention will only be paid to the ideas that gained acceptance, in the main, in the English communities.

Organized sport and regular physical education classes in the schools originated, for the most part, in the burgeoning urban areas of Ontario and Quebec.[3] This mirrored the changing Canadian society, from a frontier and rural environment to an increasingly urban and industrial society. Providing some stability in this era of change was the church, both as a social institution and as representative of an underlying set of beliefs, norms and values. Christianity in conjunction with liberalism provided the basic foundation stones of middle class Canadian attitudes and values about life and society, and, therefore, this analysis will focus on these central concepts before taking into account Darwinism and Marxism, sets of ideas which symbolize the changes of the second half of the nineteenth century.

CHRISTIANISM

Christianism is one of the cornerstones of western thought, action, and society. Thus, it is impossible to fully understand attitudes towards sport and physical education without comprehending the pervasive influence of Christian ideals. However, it is important to differentiate between the basic theology of Christianity and the church's concept of its role and function within society.[4] This function changed from a narrow concern with spiritual development to a wider concern with the social problems of an emerging industrial society. Although its societal function altered, the basic doctrine of the church remained unchanged and even the cataclysmic impact of industrialization and Darwinism did not radically affect the basic doctrine of the church as it pertained to sport and physical education. Bridging interdenominational disagreements was one common tenet — the dichotomization of a human being into a superior spirit and an inferior body.[5] This meant that no matter how the church conceptualized its role in society, the body was always inferior to the spirit; thus, sporting activities were a means to an end and never an end in themselves. In the more fundamental Baptist, Methodist, and Presbyterian denominations, this resulted in a complete repudiation of all recreation and frivolous activities and ultimately the rejection of sensual activities as being evil and sinful in themselves. Even in the liberal portions of the church, recreation and sport had to be justified on the grounds of the attainment of worthwhile ends. Unless recreation could be justified on moral and religious grounds, it was rejected as frivolous and unnecessary. Therefore, the church was essentially antagonistic towards the growth of sporting activities since, for the most part, they were equated with idleness, gambling, and wastage of time. However, it is just as apparent that by the end of the century the church had become involved in the promotion of recreational activities centres.[6] The acceptance of recreational physical activities as a function of the church's role in society did not imply a rejection of the dichotomization between the mind and body, but rather the implicit survival instinct of an institution which was rapidly losing its predominant position in society. The church found itself losing its ability to influence decisions pertaining to the total life of individuals in society. As the nature of society changed with increasing secularization, the acquisition of free time by an ever increasing proportion of the population, and an increase in the level of education, there was a parallel decline in the ability of the church to affect the behavior patterns of individuals in society. The church's focus upon the spiritual was antithetical to the increasingly materialistic nature of society. This was evidenced in a general decrease in the influence of the clergy in terms of their ability to influence societal variables; for instance, the universities which in several instances were instituted by religious denominations and administered and staffed by men of the cloth, became less religious and more secular in both course offerings and teaching staff.[7] The church's role in society was changing from that of the leading actor to that of a supporting player. However, it must be emphasized that the church in conjunction with the basic philosophy of liberalism exerted a very strong influence on Canadian society throughout the whole of the nineteenth century.

LIBERALISM

The other foundation stone of Victorian society was liberalism with its basic concepts of individualism, science, and progress. A religious like belief in the paramount importance of the individual was central to the optimism and progress of Victorian Canada. By allowing the individual to "do his own thing" the best of all possible worlds would result. The second feature was the emphasis upon science as the methodology to be used to solve the problems of life and society. It was only by using the scientific method that the problems of this society could and would be solved. Individualism plus science equalled progress — the third basic tenet of nineteenth century liberalism. It was this inherent belief in progress toward an ultimate good life and society that gave the Victorians their optimistic outlook on life and enabled them to justify the long hours of work and working conditions in the factories, and the slums of Montreal and Toronto. The Victorian Canadian firmly believed that by following the code of individualism and science inevitably progress would result, which would lead to the greatest happiness for the greatest number.

Liberalism as an ideology affected many aspects of Canadian life: political, social, economic, and moral.[8] In terms of physical activity and sport it was in the areas of politics and morals that liberalism had a significant impact. Politically, liberalism promulgated a set of attitudes pertaining to the relationship between government and individual Canadians. The emphasis upon individualism led logically to a *laissez faire* attitude which denied the right of government to interfere with the rights of individuals. Essentially, this meant that government was reluctant to legislate in areas such as trade, industry, hours of work and, more pertinently, the creation of public recreational facilities in the burgeoning urban areas. There was a great reluctance on the part of town councils to becoming involved in the creation of public baths, public parks, and public playgrounds.[9] This should not be seen as a criticism of the Victorian liberals but rather as the actuality that determined the norms that they brought to municipal and provincial government. It was difficult for middle class Canadians to conceive of the need to provide any sort of facility for the population of the growing towns, and it was not until well into the second half of the century that the conditions in such towns as Montreal and Toronto drew people's attention to the need for more local, provincial, and federal involvement in a variety of heretofore private concerns.[10] The result in terms of recreation was too little, too late.

More important in terms of the influences of ideas upon physical activity was the liberal morality which formed the foundation stone of middle class Canadian norms and values. The basic tenets of this moral code are classically illustrated in two best selling books, *Self Help* by Samuel Smiles and *Tom Brown's Schooldays* by Thomas Hughes. Samuel Smiles expressed very clearly the core of Victorian attitudes.

> Heaven helps those who help themselves, is a well worn maxim, embodying in small compass the results of vast human experience. The spirit of self help is the root of all genuine growth in the individual; and, exhibited in the lives of many, it constitutes the true source of national vigour and strength. Help from without is often enfeebling in its effects, but help from within invariably invigorates. Whatever is done for men or classes, to a certain extent, takes away the stimulus and necessity of doing for themselves; and where men are subjected to over guidance and over government, the inevitable tendency is to render them comparatively helpless.[11]

Self help was a moral justification of individualism as it related to individuals and classes, and was used to justify the competitive instincts of a developing industrial society. To Smiles "national progress is the sum of individual industry, energy, and uprightness".[12] However, self help alone did not ensure success in life; the individual had to possess certain basic characteristics before success could be guaranteed.

> It is not even eminent talent that is required to ensure success in any pursuit so much as purpose — not merely the power to achieve, but the will to labour energetically and perseverantly. Hence energy of will may be defined to be the very central power of character in a man, in a word, it is the man himself.[13]

In other words, dogged perseverance was the foundation of true greatness of character and, thus, an indispensable attribute for individual development.

When self help was combined with perseverance the logical outcome was work. Work was the cornerstone or bulwark of Victorian morality and society; it was espoused with a religious like fervour and proclaimed throughout the land by disciples who regarded it as the ultimate meaning of life itself. There was, in essence, a societal code based on the interlinked concepts of work, perseverance, and self help. It is obvious, therefore, that a society with these underlying foundations would have little time for such "frivolous" concerns as recreation, sport, and idle amusements. Only when these could be justified in the light of self help, perseverance, and work could they gain societal approval. Hence, when games were played they had to be seen as contributing to something beyond simple fun and enjoyment, and it was as a moral code or as a means of increasing the productivity of the work force that games and sports gained any acceptance within the boundaries or framework of the Victorian ethic. The work ethic, therefore, which has underlain capitalistic society for many centuries was central to the Victorian ethic.

Rampant individualism would logically lead to chaos or the Nietzschean overman; it was necessary, therefore, to develop some system which would hold to check the inherent evils of individualism while maintaining the sanctity of the individual. Politically and socially this was manifest in the idea of balance between the individual good and societal needs. In fact, a liberal morality developed which emphasized individual restraint and character while stressing the concept of group responsibility and societal needs. The inculcation of these beliefs was achieved in a variety of ways but the most important was on the playing fields of the private schools and clubs. It was felt that desirable personality and character traits could be developed through participation in team games and that these characteristics would then be transferred to individual actions in life. The playing fields provided a laboratory for the inculcation of moral principles and gentlemanly conduct; they also provided a learning experience for budding leaders and the creation of a group spirit more powerful than the needs or desires of any individual.

The basic tenets of muscular christianity or athleticism, as the movement was known, were most fully developed in Thomas Hughes' novel, *Tom Brown's Schooldays,* first published in 1857.[14] This highlights the ideals of athleticism and stresses the qualities that were thought to be developed through games; leadership, courage, honesty, fair play, endurance, and team spirit. Throughout *Tom Brown's Schooldays* these characteristics were emphasized repeatedly. The stress is placed upon individual performance within a team situation; a fight, a football game and a cricket match being the central incidents in the book. This clearly illustrates the contradictory concepts of the individual and the community. The individual had to exhibit certain individual characteristics but at all times remain true to the basic objectives of the group — never could individual aspirations be placed above those of the group. For instance, it was inconceivable for a pupil at Rugby School to report an incident involving other schoolboys to the school authorities, no matter how terrible the offense. For instance, when Tom Brown had been roasted over a fire by the bully, Flashman, he gained great status within the group by refusing to tell the authorities what had happened even though Flashman was universally despised. Status was gained, therefore, by adhering to group norms.

In many ways, the outcome of the game was unimportant; it was how the game was played that counted. If an individual exhibited undesirable behaviour, a win was nothing; it must be achieved within the norms established by the group. A player must exhibit endurance, courage, and fair play above skill. These ideals were transmitted to Canada by immigrants and espcially by graduates of the Public Schools of England who came out to teach in the private schools in Canada.[15] There is little doubt that this set of values underlay the justification for intra and inter school sport in tʰ. Canadian private schools and also formed the foundation of the morality underlying the amateur approach to sport in the late nineteenth century. Perhaps these ideas were most pertinent to Canada in the private schools, the training grounds of the Canadian elite, such as Upper Canada College, where the masters were, in many instances, trained at the English universities of Oxford and Cambridge and had themselves been exposed to the athletic system of the English Public Schools. There is little doubt, therefore, that the ideals expressed in muscular christianity and the morality involved have, throughout the last one hundred years, provided one of the basic rationales for the educational use of games in a school and within the inter-school competitive situation. The importance of this set of ideas to Canadian sport and physical education cannot be over emphasized.

The combination of a powerful conservative church and an individualistic liberal, political, social, and moral ethic provided a strong foundation for the norms and values of the Canadian middle classes. This set of ideas remained basic to the power groups in Canadian society throughout much of the nineteenth century. However, winds of change were blowing through the land which had a significant influence upon the ideas held about society and life and which in the end were to bring into question the validity of the liberal morality. These were the result of a change in the nature of society; particularly the growth of urban industrial towns in the second half of the nineteenth century.[16] As with the previous ideas, many of them were generated in England and Europe and were transmitted to Canada by immigrants. These changes heralded a growing storm of protest against the ideas of the Victorian middle classes and the changing conditions of life in urban society.

DARWINISM

The publication of Charles Darwin's *The Origin of the Species* in 1859 heralded the revolt against the traditional moral, religious, and social bases of Victorian society.[17] Darwinism had a cataclysmic impact upon society and perhaps has been the most influential set of ideas in the last hundred years, since it irrevocably changed man's attitudes about life and society. Although many other scientists were thinking along evolutionary lines, it was Darwin who crystalized and published these views which were to change society. The basic tenets are relatively simple. There were more individuals of every species born than could survive, and within each species, as well as between species, there was a constant struggle for survival. This battle for survival culminated in the survival of the fittest. These rather simple and, to the modern generation, rather obvious statements gave rise to a vigorous and sometimes violent analysis of society, religion, and morality. It led to the development of such widely differing views as the moral Darwinism of Thomas Huxley, the racial theories of De Gobineau and Chamberlain, and the social theories of Spencer and others. Evolutionary theory and survival of the fittest were used to justify imperialistic expansion, the subservience of certain social classes to others, and the superiority of one race over another.

Observations as to the effect of urban industrial life upon the human frame and upon human capabilities made it clear to factory owners and the middle classes that the capabilities and physical performance of the "factory fodder" were less than could be desired.[18] In terms of physical education, the noticeable effect of urban living upon the physical condition of children, in addition to the Darwinism emphasis upon the need to develop the physical animal, led to the inclusion of physical training in the curricula of schools throughout Canada in the second half of the century.[19] Physical training programmes were introduced to produce fit people either to work in the factories or to fight for the country. The first programmes included military drill, elementary calisthenics, and gymnastic systems aimed at maximizing the growth and development of the individual. It is not too much to say that the ideas generated by evolutionary theory were essential to the development of physical education as a curricular subject in Canada in the second half of the nineteenth century. This also helps explain the difference between the curricular and extra-curricular portions of the physical education programme. The physical training curriculum was grounded in Darwinism whereas the athletic programme was heavily indebted to the middle class ideals of muscular christianity and athleticism.

MARXISM

One of the critical changes which radically affected man's views about life and society was the process of industrialization. Although industrialization is generally recognized as starting in Montreal about 1854 with the creation of the Redpath Refinery, it was not until between 1860 and 1880 that the number of factories and factory workers increased significantly in Montreal and Toronto.[20] However, the industrial way of life was transmitted by immigrants from Britain and influenced by the United States. The impact of industrialization upon society was not analyzed in great depth by any Canadian intellectuals and it was achieved most clearly by Karl Marx who, although not necessarily applicable to Canada per se, developed concepts and ideas which were pertinent to everyone.[21] In terms of society, the Marxian concept of class was to have a significant effect upon social thinking because it attempted to differentiate between social groups solely on their relationship to the means of production. It is not necessary to decide upon the validity of Marx's concept of class but rather to recognize his valid assumption that an urban industrial society differentiated very clearly between different social strata. Although this concept was Marx's major theoretical contribution, in terms of physical activity and recreation, his most important idea was that of alienation. He claimed that the factory system alienated man from his labour and it was through labour, essentially physical, that man expressed himself and his individuality; therefore, it was through the creative process of his work that man found meaning in life. To

87

be meaningful, labour must take place within the productive process of man's work which was central to life. Capitalism, according to Marx, was the perversion of man's labour into meaningless activity. By doing this, by alienating man from his labour, life itself lost meaning and the working man was deprived of his selfhood and his existence, becoming in fact little more than an animal. This emphasized the fact that factory work brought significant changes to the work patterns of the labour force of any industrial society. Marx's analysis of the influence of factory work upon man's life seems to have been followed very closely by a growing awareness in the second half of the nineteenth century of the problems of monotony, discipline, and factory work in general and the resultant lack of meaning in life for the proletariat. Obviously, this was of critical concern to physical educators and recreationists because it was from the dehumanization of work that much of the thinking and concepts in recreation and physical education today have been developed. It is not too much to say that modern day physical education and recreation are offsprings of industrialization.

CONCLUSION

In conclusion, it is quite apparent that underlying Victorian middle class Canadian society were the basic principles of work, perseverance, and self help which were necessary conditions for an emerging industrial society. The liberal philosophy or gospel of work was, in fact, an intellectual justification for capitalistic industrial society; and while the middle class maintained its position of power as the effective purveyors of recreational facilities, school curricula, and work hours, this philosophy remained the basic foundation. However, the immense changes in society that took place as a result of industrialization created conditions which brought about the downfall or the dilution of the liberal Victorian ethic, which was epitomized most clearly in the cataclyomic change of thought wrought by Darwinism. This was the beginning of an immense process of change which was to make, in Canada, an essentially new society with a new set of values, norms, and ideals. It was also the era in which physical education became part of the school curriculum. These changes were closely linked to the basic societal trends and intellectual ideas that have been discussed above. Essentially, these can be divided into two main categories: (1) the physical education curriculum within the schools which focused heavily upon the survival of the individual and the nation, both in terms of military supremacy and industrial development (2) the growth of amateur sport, the intercollegiate athletic programmes and the development of physical education in the private schools were largely a reflection of the middle class beliefs in athleticism and muscular christianity.

It must be emphasized that the whole process was complex and that, in this instance, only the value structure of the middle classes is being considered. Underlying all this was a popular culture based upon values and assumptions possibly different from and, in many ways, antithetical to those of the middle classes. Little or no research has been undertaken in the identification and analysis of popular or mass culture in Canada.[22]

88

Fragmentary evidence, however, does suggest that the value structure, way of life, and ideology of a significant section of the population was different from the predominant work ethic of the middle classes. Yet, in terms of ability to influence decision making in affairs pertaining to recreation and physical education, they remained throughout the nineteenth century a completely ineffectual majority. Nineteenth century Canada was indeed a bourgeois century.

REFERENCE NOTES

1. In books, articles, theses, and dissertations pertaining to history of sport and physical education in Canada there are few which make more than a fleeting reference to societal variables. The notable exceptions are Ian Jobling, "Sport in Nineteenth Century Canada: The Effects of Technological Changes on its Development", unpublished Ph.D. dissertation, University of Alberta, 1970; Gerald Redmond, "The Scots and Sport in Nineteenth Century Canada", unpublished Ph.D. dissertation, University of Alberta, 1972; Howard A. Christie, "The Function of the Tavern in Toronto, 1834 to 1875 with Special Reference to Sport", unpublished M.P.E. thesis, University of Windsor, 1973; Henry Roxborough, One Hundred-Not Out: The Story of Nineteenth Century Canadian Sport (Toronto: The Ryerson Press, 1966).

2. Once again there is a paucity of research and writing on the power structures operating in nineteenth century Canada. However, the important role of the professional groups or middle classes in the governing of the larger towns is indisputable; for instance, the Montreal City Council which controlled financial expenditures on public education, recreation, and health, in 1871 consisted of 28 members of which all but 6 could accurately be classed middle or upper class. A theoretical frame work for the analysis of power is contained in John Porter, The Vertical Mosaic (Toronto: University of Toronto Press, 1970).

3. A brief history of physical education which gives support to this contention is given in Frank Cosentino and Maxwell L. Howell, A History of Physical Education in Canada (Toronto: General Publishing Co., 1971).

4. There is little or nothing written which pertains directly to the relationship between the church and ideas influencing attitudes to sport. However, there is a small collection of essays which provides a useful background and starting point. John Webster Grant (ed.), The Churches and the Canadian Experience (Toronto: The Ryerson Press, 1968).

5. For a provocative analysis of the concept of the mind-body dichotomy see J. Fairs, "When Was the Golden Age of the Body", CAHPER Journal, Vol. 37, No. 1 (September 1970 -October, 1970), p. 11-24.

6. This is evidenced most clearly by the involvement of Y.M.C.A. and Y.W.C.A. in the area of providing physical recreation. See Murray G. Ross, The Y.M.C.A. in Canada (Toronto: Ryerson Press, 1951).

7. The role of religion and religious institutions in the development of higher education in Canada is well documented. Any history of the universities indicates the diverse role played by the churches in creating them and by the ministers in administering and staffing them. For example, see D. D. Calvin, Queen's University at Kingston, Kingston 1941; Hugh MacLennan (ed.), McGill: The Story of a University, London: George Allen and Unwin Ltd., 1960; William F. Tamblyn, These Sixty Years, 1878-1938, London: University of Western Ontario, 1938.

8. A brief but excellent analysis of the genesis of liberalism in England is to be found in George L. Mosse, The Culture of Western Europe (Rand McNally and Co., 1962), p. 93-110. Because of the influence of British ideas upon Canadian thought, this serves as a useful introduction.

9. The development of public recreational facilities during the nineteenth century is discussed briefly in Elsie Marie McFarland, The Development of Public Recreation in Canada (Canadian Parks/Recreation Association, 1970), p. 7-16.

10. It is surprising that little work has been done on the changing Canadian society during the second half of the nineteenth century. The most outstanding exception to this is an excellent statistical analysis by Peter G. Goheen, Victorian Toronto: 1850-1900 (Chicago Department of Geography, University of Chicago, 1970).

11. Samuel Smiles, *Self Help* in Franklin LeVan Baumer, *Main Currents of Western Thought* (New York: Alfred Knopf, 1961), p. 496.

12. *Ibid.*

13. *Ibid.,* p. 498.

14. Thomas Hughes, *Tom Brown's Schooldays* (London: The Macmillan and Co., Limited, 1958).

15. For a brief account of the development of athleticism in some Canadian private schools see G. Watson. "The Founding and Major Features of the Sport and Games in the Little Big Four Canadian Private Schools," *CAHPER Journal,* Vol. 40, No. 1 (September - October 1973), p. 28-37.

16. These changes were reflected by the first example of provincial and federal government legislation and investigation into the impact of industrialization upon the lives of Canadians. These changes occurred in the 1880's.

17. The basic aspects of Darwin's thought as it pertains to society is contained in Van Baumer, *op. cit.,* p. 525-532.

18. These effects were fully documented in Canada by the Royal Commission on the Relations of Labor and Capital, 1889. For an abridged version of these proceedings see Greg Kealey (ed.), *Canada Investigates Industrialism* (Toronto: University of Toronto Press, 1973.

19. For a very brief account of the development of physical education in Ontario see A. Metcalfe, "Physical Recreation in Ontario During the Nineteenth Century", *CAHPER Journal,* Vol. 37, No. 1 (September - October 1970), p. 29-33.

20. The impact of the working classes was felt for the first time in a unified class action in the Nine Hour Movement that swept through the industrial centres of Ontario and Quebecc in 1872.

21. It must be emphasized that this is not an attempt to give a Marxian interpretation of Canadian history (although this could be done) but rather to use some of Marx's penetrating insights into the effects of industrialization to clarify some issues that are pertinent to Canada.

Woman's Place In Nineteenth Century Canadian Sport*

Peter L. Lindsay
Faculty of Physical Education
University of Alberta
Edmonton, Alberta

John Hudson,[1] former national track coach, was asked to name Canadian athletes most likely to succeed in winning Olympic medals in Munich in 1972. The first five potential medalists he mentioned were women. In both swimming and skiing, Canada recently had world champions in Elaine Tanner and Nancy Green, and the next Canadian champions to win international recognition in these respective sports again promise to be female. Today, the Canadian woman athlete has proved her pre-eminence in sporting competition, and the nation's pride in her achievements is reflected in public approval and encouragement. In the past, however, just as women encountered opposition to their demands for political rights through female franchise, and economic rights through female employment, so they encountered opposition in the exercise of their social rights to compete in the sports and games of the community. An examination of the emerging emancipation of women in sport in Canada is a parallel comment and embellishment upon the emancipation of women within the whole framework of Canadian society. The history of female participation in sporting activities has had a slow, critical progression.

The gentlewomen in British North America in pre-Confederation years had rigidly prescribed roles to play at athletic contests. These roles had remained virtually unchanged from those adopted by the ladies of the court of Aquitane who, under the codes of chivalry, inspired their knights to even greater feats of valour on the tourney fields. The passage of several centuries merely added the weight of tradition to the view that the participatory role of women in sport was a passive, rather than active, one.

Female attendance at horse races, regattas, cricket matches, and other such spectator sports was obviously encouraged, as most early nineteenth century newspaper reports of these events carried verbose tributes to the

* Lindsay, Peter L. "Woman's Place in Nineteenth Century Canadian Sport," *CAHPER Journal,* Vol. 37, No. 1 (Sept.-Oct. 1970), pp. 25-33.
Printed by permission of the Canadian Association for Health, Physical Education and Recreation.

ladies present, often to the exclusion of any mention of the results of the contests themselves. On reading these old newspapers, one receives the discinct impression that the whole success of the organized sports meeting depended entirely upon the number of ladies who could be encouraged to decorate the scene with their gay ensembles. Even at the mid-century, this societal attitude was still prevalent, as evidenced in the words of a *Montreal Gazette* journalist reporting on the forthcoming Montreal Snow Shoe Club Races:

> Very many of our lady friends, we doubt not, will be on the grounds, and, as in the knightly tournament of by-gone days, incite the friendly combatants to put forth still greater exertions to win their smiles and applause.[2]

Attempts by the gentlewoman of the town to indulge more actively in even mild physical exercise invariably met with censure, cloaked in concern for her frailty and delicate constitution. The ladies of Kingston, in 1811, discovered the fashionable pleasures of swinging, much to the distress of many a Kingston male, one of whom was driven to voice his concern in the *Kingston Gazette* on April 28, 1812. This gentleman, besides deploring the immodesty and indecorum of these swinging ladies, condemned as physically deleterious "an exercise which though allowably beneficial to the health when practised in a proper place, loses that merit when a delicate girl mounts a lofty and dangerous swing just after leaving a warm tea room and at that hour of all others when the chilly dew is more prejudicial to even a strong constitution."

There were a few recreational activities in which women were accepted as participants, though convention dictated that their participatory role be that of passenger rather than instigator of the activity. Carrioling was the favourite recreation of the fashionable elite during the winter, with many a young lady aspiring to be known as the season's most attractive "Miss Muffin," the colloquial name given to the lady companion who sat beside the dashing owner of the vehicle. Indeed, the officers of the garrisons and the gentlemen of society took great care and pains in the purchase and decoration of their expensive carrioles, motivated perhaps by the hope that such care would ensure them a winter of companionable "Muffinage." For the more venturesome ladies, ice-boating offered an exhilarating experience, but, again, they enjoyed the sport as mere passengers bundled up in furs which successfully hid any emotion or enthusiasm which might have been deemed improper.

Charges of impropriety were difficult to avoid, as some ladies of Quebec who engaged in innocent snowshoe treks were to discover:

> Small parties of ladies have lately taken to the exercise of snow-shoeing, and, accompanied with a protective male friend, may be seen occasionally striding (Oh! What a term!) along the plains or over the ice — in nice secluded localities, be it always understood. This same snowshoe practice is in itself splendid exercise, but not, we do humbly opine, of a kind exactly fitted to ladies, even as matter of healthful amusement, nor, as yet,

on the whole, affording the most advantageous display of the graces on their part. And their pretty ancles (sic) and delicate feet are so liable to twists and sprains from falls, and to be swollen by the rude pressure of the deer-skin tie, that we hold it scarcely to merit laudatory mention as a favourite exercise for the "gentle fair."[3]

This criticism must have seemed unjustified to the ladies concerned, in that French women of Lower Canada had long used the snowshoe to enable them to proceed with their daily errands in the winter,[4] and the English women of the province had followed their example. It would seem, then, that it was the recreational or sporting nature of the exercise rather than the exercise itself, which rendered it unsuitable and thus disturbed the complainant's sense of propriety.

Horseback riding, like snowshoeing, served a utilitarian purpose in that it provided an important method of transportation on the poorly made early roads of the provinces. In the pioneer settlements where the horse and canoe provided the inhabitants with vital means of communication with the urban centres, women, of necessity, were as proficient riders and canoeists as were the men, an eyewitness of the time reporting that country girls rode skilfully even without a saddle.[5] This sport, however, was conventionally permissible for pleasurable relaxation for ladies where snowshoeing was not. The incongruity may be explained by the fact that riding had been a well established British tradition since the days when ladies on horseback had joined their knights at falconry and the hunt, while the sport of snowshoeing had no such heraldic associations.

One of the earliest references to fox hunting in British North America reported the presence of both lady and gentlemen followers at a winter hunt arranged by William Jarvis on the ice of the bay at York.[6] References through the years establish that ladies not merely followed the hunt, but rode with the pack. Such sporting involvement, far from being censured, met with society's approval, as the ladies of the Montreal Hunt were commended for their "dashing riding" which caused them to finish well up in the field at the club's outing on September 30, 1866.[7]

Croquet was another activity deemed suitable for lady competitors, croquet parties being "all the rage" in leisured society by the 1860's. On the estate of the Lawson family of Hamilton, a guest described one of the "very fashionable" games played there with officers from the nearby garrison serving as willing partners for the ladies who enjoyed "a sense of exhilaration at being out in the air . . ."[8] This guest also experienced her first square dance which was held in the rural community adjacent to the estate, and found the "tremendous speed" of the dance quite breathtaking.[9]

Dancing was popular in both rural and urban localities, the round and square dances favoured in the country finding counterparts in the more sophisticated minuets, mazurkas, reels, quadrilles, and later, waltzes, of the towns. Entries in the diary of Mrs. Monck,[10] sister-in-law of the Governor General and wife of the Colonel of the 17th Regiment, contain constant reference to balls conducted by both garrison officers and the elite of town society. Dancing academies were in evidence throughout all the townships of the provinces, Halifax reportedly having such an establishment as early as 1752.[11] Though dancing met with opposition from the Calvinists and critics who deplored the frivolous nature of the activity, it remained the most universally popular of all recreations available to women.

By the latter half of the century, it was becoming apparent that there was a slight but definite favourable change in the attitude of society towards women's participation in physical activities and especially in competitive sport. Through no coincidence, this changing attitude occurred at a time when the structure of British North American society itself was experiencing dramatic change under such influences as advanced technology and social reform.

The greatest technological revolution of the time was wrought by the steam engine in its application to improved transportation and communication. As a direct result of these improvements, sport within communities experienced unprecedented popular support. Steam boats made excursion trips possible for inter-town sporting competition, luring both teams and supporters with offers of return trips to matches for the price of a single fare. Such generosity was tinged with self-interest, as the *Novascotian* pointed out on March 5, 1855: "The steamboat Company ought to be very much obliged to the curlers for increasing the travel across the Ferry." Whatever the material motives, greater community involvement in sporting competition was the result. Railway companies also offered the half price return excursion ticket to sporting travellers, the increasing number of inter-city matches played showing a close relationship to the expanding distance of laid track.

Whereas technology produced an upswing in inter-city, inter-provincial, and international sporting competition from the mid-nineteenth century onwards, it was the whimsical vagaries of fashion which allowed women to play an increasing part in the expansion of sporting activity. There had been rare occasions when that most restrictive article of fashionable female clothing, the crinoline, had actually been a benefit to women who suddenly found themselves immersed in water which, a few seconds earlier, they had been sailing upon:

> A lady in Saint John, New Brunswick, was recently saved from drowning by the much abused crinoline. She fell overboard and instead of going plump to the bottom, her expansive skirts acted as a life preserver, and she floated down the stream sitting like a duck upon the water.[12]

The crinoline was perhaps as much responsible as social pressure for the designation of croquet and dancing as acceptable female amusements. Encased in hoops with layer upon layer of petticoats, the gentlewoman found there were few, if any, alternate activities in which she might indulge with decorum. Mrs. Monck dared not try skating for fear, she said, of falling and breaking an arm or a leg. A fall in a crinoline would probably have wounded her dignity more than her person.

Prior to the 1850's, some inventive women had discovered for themselves the freedom afforded by trousers or pantaloons. So garbed, they were able to enjoy a wider range of exercises than those of their sex who wore conventional dress, but they failed to create a vogue for their unconventional attire. During the fifties, it was Amelia Bloomer, with the publicity she generated for her "bifurcated bags", who popularized a costume which allowed freedom of movement without loss of either dignity or modesty. Significantly, the reported participation of women in such sports as horse riding, snowshoeing, foot racing, rowing, and especially skating, increased greatly after 1860.

At this time, designs of the bicycle were being improved, and in 1885, with the advent of the "safety bicycle," cycling became the rage across the country. With cycle clubs to be found in all major towns and cities, women, indebted to Mrs. Bloomer, took up the sport as eagerly as did the men, in some centers even forming independent clubs.[13] By 1900, most recreational cycle clubs had long lists of female members who dressed for their sport in trouserettes that were "ample and full below the knee," where they met gaiters "so long that no stocking is shown," a figure fitting bodice, sailor hat, white veil and grey gloves completing the costume.[14]

Not all women adopted a mode of dress that, to a large section of the community, particularly fathers and husbands, appeared unfeminine. Tennis, which by the 1880's had become a popular sport amongst ladies from British Columbia to the Maritimes,[15] was socially acceptable as a decorous game for modestly attired females, although the modest attire certainly restricted play. Rather than urging drastic reform of dress, a typical male attitude recommended that females abandon the game for one more in keeping with the masculine ideal of ladylike recreation:

There are signs of a croquet revival. Lawn tennis is not altogether doomed, but young ladies are beginning to see that it is a game for men. If played by girls it should be played without corsets. Against a fellow in flannels, a girl in stays and a dress weighted with the cumbersome protruberances which are now in fashion, has no chance. . . . At croquet the fair player may wear what she pleases, strike picturesque attitudes, go through the game without hurry, and hold sweet confidential chats between hits.[16]

This gentleman pleaded for a return to a golden age, where men performed on the tourney fields of sport under the approving and admiring gaze of ladies, but alas, he pleaded in vain. Too many women were beginning to regard themselves as more than sweet, picturesque objects.

Despite being continually urged throughout the nineteenth century, to remain ladylike, decorative, and static, by 1900 women had experienced independence from the dictates of fashion and prescribed activities. No longer choosing to be encased and hobbled in sweeping skirts, no longer restricted to gentle games deemed by over-protective males as suitable to the delicate female constitution, no longer rebuked by society for seeking pleasure in physical exercise, the woman of the new century bicycled towards the goal of individual freedom, and emancipation from cultural taboos.

REFERENCE NOTES

1. Cited in Robert McKeown, "Canada's Big Nine for Munich," *Sports Canada* (January, 1970), pp. 12-14.
2. *Montreal Gazette,* February 23, 1861.
3. *Montreal Gazette,* March 12, 1842.
4. Isabel Foulche-Delbos, "The Women of New France," *Canadian Historical Review,* XXI (June, 1940), 133.
5. Cited in T. Radcliffe (ed.), *Authentic Letters From Upper Canada* Toronto: MacMillan Company of Canada Ltd., 1953, p. 180.
6. *Upper Canada Gazette,* February 14, 1801.
7. *Montreal Gazette,* October 1, 1866.
8. Isabella Moore, cited in Luella Creighton, *The Elegant Canadians* (Toronto: McClelland and Stewart Ltd., 1967), p. 155.
9. *Ibid.,* p. 50.
10. Frances E. Monck, *My Canadian Leaves* (Reprinted, Toronto: University Press, 1963), *passim.*
11. *Halifax Gazette,* April 25, 1752.
12. *Morning Chronicle,* Quebec, September 20, 1858.
13. Winnipeg *Free Press* reported the founding of such a club on July 17, 1896. The Imperial Bicycle Club of Petrolia, founded in 1893, had so many female members by 1894 that they formed their own branch (Charles Whipp and Edward Phelps, *Petrolia, 1866-1966* (Petrolia: Advertiser-Topic and the Petrolia Centennial Committee, 1966), pp. 52-53).
14. A Krout, *Annals of Ameican Sport* (New Haven: Yale University Press, Pageant of America Series, 1929), XV, 176.
15. A. E. Cox, *A History of Sports in Canada, 1868-1900* (Unpublished Doctoral thesis, University of Alberta, Edmonton, Alberta, 1969), pp. 175-176.
16. *Reporter,* Fredericton, July 9, 1884.

The Modern Olympic Games: Fanfare And Philosophy, 1896-1972 *

John A. Lucas

The modern international Olympic Games, no less than the ancient Greek quadrennial sporting festival, have involved more than extraordinary athletic performances. For nearly eighty years, Olympic events have occurred amidst a rich, contrived pageantry, and always under the mantle of heroic symbolism. Pierre Fredy, Baron de Coubertin (1863-1937), promotor and organizer of the modern Olympics, conceived of the games as an expression of the Greek philosophy that the harmonious discipline of body, intellect, and spirit in athletics can lead men and women to understand both themselves and the right way to live. Never for an instant during a half century of writing and activity did Coubertin deviate from his belief that preparation for and competition in joyful, challenging, scrupulously honorable non-professional sport could best accomplish such a happy human state. In practice, however, increasing chauvinism and commercialism have defeated the Olympics and taken away some of the idealism that Coubertin built into the games. This defect would erupt with sufficient frequency to give rise to a questioning of the Olympics as a viable force for enlightened cosmopolitanism.

Before the end of the nineteenth century, the aristocratic and brilliantly educated Coubertin became convinced that devotion to sport and physical education was one powerful denominator among the world's empire builders, Great Britain, Germany, and the United States. He saw in this commitment a formula for national greatness; and its absence in France, he believed, might spell her doom. Baron de Coubertin devoted many years of nearly fruitless work to the popularization of sport and physical education in his own country. At the same time, the visionary historian-educator consecrated his time and fortune to the reestablishment of the ancient Olympic Games in modern guise.

Dr. Thomas Arnold, an early nineteenth century Rugby School headmaster, held the greatest single influence on Coubertin's thinking. Arnold's sweeping academic and administrative changes acted as a catalyst for much needed reform in English public school education. Soon after Arnold's

*Lucas, John A. "The Modern Olympic Games: Fanfare and Philosophy, 1896-1972," *The Maryland Historian*, Vol. 4, No. 2, Fall 1973, pp. 71-88. Reprinted by permission of the publisher.
John A. Lucas is Professor of Physical Education and Sport Historian at the Pennsylvania State University.

97

death, England's best schools added competitive athletics as part of his sweeping "Muscular Christian" movement. The shadow of Arnold remained ever-present, and Coubertin would later pronounce that true education must deal with the muscular, the intellect, and with morality, all integrated in the same activity.[1]

Baron de Coubertin agreed with the dictum that "without athletics, Greek art and the Greek conception of beauty would have been inconceivable."[2] The ancient Greeks could not think any physical form beautiful unless it was also healthy. The Greek Olympics included manliness, rhythm, art, balance, and religious symbolism, all of which the idealistic Frenchman planned for in his modern games. The Greek poet Pindar had commemorated the success of athletic victors by acclaiming: "Blessed . . . is the man who by excellence of hand and speed in his feet takes by strength and daring the highest prizes."[3] Twenty centuries later the modern Olympic "Hymn to Sport" would sing "praise to the glory of sport, praise to sport! To beauty, to youth be praise, and to the victor's praise to sport."[4]

Eventually, Coubertin succeeded in his efforts to transcend centuries and create an athletic festival in the image of the Greek Ideal. The first Olympic Games of the modern era began in Athens, Greece, on Sunday, April 5, 1896. That year, by chance, the Orthodox Easter and the Catholic Easter coincided. Equally important to the success of the games, it was the 75th anniversary of the Greek War of Independence. The thirty-three year old Baron now saw his life-long dream fulfilled. The years ahead would be filled with crisis and halting progress, but on that day Coubertin was radiant with joy.

Three hundred and eleven athletes from thirteen countries assembled in the new and gleaming white marble stadium amidst a festive, patriotic population. Flags and shields gaily adorned Athens. Eighty thousand curious and animated Greeks accompanied the King and Queen, Crown Prince Constantine, and the royal family to the stadium. Spiridon Samora led the chorus in an Olympic cantata imploring the ancient muses to look down and give life to the restored noble games: "Throw wreaths of fadeless flowers to the victors in the race and in the strife! Create in our breasts, hearts of steel! . . . and form a vast temple to which all nations throng to adore thee, oh immortal spirit of antiquity!"[5]

Greek national pride, however, quickly overcame the spirit of Coubertin's internationalism. No victory was more remarkable than that of Spiridon Louis, winner of the marathon race. As he crossed the finish line in front of the nearly uncontrollable partisan crowd, the Crown Prince and Prince George rushed forward and embraced the Greek shepherd boy. The King of Greece presented the gold medal. Greek nationalism rose so high that the Frenchman Pierre de Couberton was thoroughly ignored. He was forced to remind all who would listen that he was "sole author of the whole project." Yet he remained filled with gratitude that his experiment had turned out so well. At the closing ceremonies, the royal family awarded olive and laurel wreathes. All prize winners received, in addition, diplomas and medals. The scene reminded art historian Charles Waldstein of a scene two thousand years earlier when "the victor approached the high priest of Zeus and received the prize before the great temple at Olympia."[6] A parade of athletes and the Greek National Anthem came next, followed by the recitation of a Pindaric ode. The place was "a scene of indescribable excitement."[7] Swept up by the concluding ceremonies, Timoleon J. Philemon, the hard-working General-Secretary of the Greek Olympic Committee, saw in the Greek triumph "sure proof that the blood of our glorious ancestors still flows in our veins." The city of Athens remained ablaze with electric lights all through the night, and the lone *New York Times* correspondent concluded that the future of the Olympic Games was decided, "and they will henceforth take their place among the noted events in the athletic world."[8]

Had that correspondent been present in Paris during the summer of 1900, he might have had some doubts. French authorities lacked sympathy for athletics, had little organizational skill in these matters, and presented the 1900 Olympic Games in Paris as an awkward appendage to the Great World's Fair.[9] As early as the spring of 1898, Coubertin grew uneasy at his countrymen's lack of diligence in gathering the world's best athletes at Paris' Bois de Boulogne. A tireless letterwriter, Coubertin invited many world leaders to come to Paris. One was addressed to Harvard President Charles Eliot, "welcoming many Harvard men" provided they be "good sports, first class athletes—also, of course, pure amateurs."[10] Some 1319 athletes from twenty-two countries arrived to contest seventeen sports. George Poage of the United States won two bronze medals in the 200 meter and 400 meter hurdles, becoming the first black sprinter to win a medal in the modern Olympic Games. In the informal atmosphere of Paris, Australian Frederick C. V. Lane broke the world's record in freestyle swimming, although the event took place in the River Seine where the current aided the contestants.[11] For all the fanfare, the Paris Olympics were a failure and Baron de Coubertin knew it. He lamented that "wherever public authorities undertake to meddle with any sports organization they introduce the fatal germs of impotence and mediocrity."[12]

Coubertin's warning proved again true for the sporting disaster of St. Louis in 1904. The St. Louis Exposition of that year celebrated the hundredth anniversary of the Louisiana Purchase. An aggressive games committee, aided by President Theodore Roosevelt, defeated Chicago as host for the Third Olympic Games. Only twelve countries were represented; most of the athletes were American. The idea of international sport had not yet taken hold. War between Russia and Japan plus the remoteness of St. Louis discouraged participation. Progress in many recognized competitions was muted by bizarre "Anthropology Days," pitting against one another African pygmies, Kaffirs, Moros and Igorots from the Philippeans, Ainus from Japan, Patagonians, and Mexican and American Indians.[13] The United States won almost everything. Coubertin moaned and saw the end of his beloved Olympic "bebe." His reaction was typical, and an interim or "local cycle" Olympic Games, out of sequence with ancient and recent quadrennial festivals, was organized for Athens in 1906. Through all this,

Coubertin persisted, saying that "honorable and amateur international athletics is the most viable and potentially rewarding form of cosmopolitanism the world has to offer."[14]

The Greek government, convinced that the games never should have left their birthplace, organized and carried out a most successful "intermediate" festival between April 22 and May 2, 1906. The King and Queen of Greece never missed a day at the stadium. Athletic performances reached new heights. James E. Sullivan, unabashed patriot and patriarch of American amateur athletics, pointed out that his team's brawn and muscle had "spread-eagled the field." American athletes, he said, were singular among the scientifically-trained athletes of the world. As if that were not enough, he pointed out "we go into athletic sports with an earnestness that other countries cannot understand."[15] The President of the United States, Theodore Roosevelt, cabled the American athletes: "Uncle Sam is all right."[16] Not only America's success but the positive reaction among the majority of athletes, officials, and spectators were significantly "right" for these unofficial Olympics. The Athens games probably saved the Olympics from a premature death. With them, the Baron de Coubertin had finally gained recognition as the world leader of amateur sport.

Despite diverse cultural mores, complex national sporting regulations that defied singular interpretations, and sometimes vigorous arguments, the games of the Fourth and Fifth Olympiads met with a generally favorable press. England accepted the Fourth Games with a grace and efficiency that befitted a country frequently called the mother lode of western sport. Twenty-two nations and, more importantly, 2000 athletes participated. Anglo-American athletes won the lion's share of medals. Early in the competition, the American tug-of-war team protested the special boots worn by the United Kingdom's Liverpool police team. A provoked American sports reporter noted that the steel-encased shoes were "so heavy in fact that it was only with great effort that they could lift their feet from the ground."[17] The Americans withdrew, defaulting the gold medal to the British. The royal family and English aristocracy filled the stands. Receptions and lawn parties abounded.[18] At the Grafton Galleries on July 24, 1908, an after-dinner speech by Coubertin focused on his synthesis of the Olympic athlete as graceful, strong, and chivalric. He quoted the Bishop of Pennsylvania at the service held in St. Paul's Cathedral in honor of the athletes, declaring that "the importance of the Olympic Games lies not so much in winning as in taking part."[19] Oppressive heat, the most formidable enemy of marathon runners, took a heavy toll during the classic final race. A tough little Italian, Dorando Pietri, struggled into the jammed stadium, turned in the wrong direction, staggered and fell, arose, headed for the finish line and fell again. The famous creator of Sherlock Holmes, Sir Arthur Conan Doyle, cried out: "Thank God, he is on his feet again, the little red legs going incoherently but drumming, hard driven by the supreme will within. . . . Will he fall again? No—he sways and balances; then he is through the tape into a score of friendly arms. He has gone to the extreme of human endurance. No Roman of prime ever has borne himself better; the great breed is not yet extinct.''[20] Pietri had been helped to his feet and was disqualified, but in so doing he had gained sporting immortality.

The Stockholm Olympic Games of 1912 were a dress rehearsal for extraordinary athletic performances in tune with twentieth century technology. In the pentathlon and decathlon, the competitors Jim Thorpe, George S. Patton, and Avery Brundage would be remembered longer than the marks they set. Ralph Craig, winner of both the 100 and 200 meter dashes, noted that the Olympic experience ''is more valuable than all the peace conferences in the world.''[21] In keeping with the Olympic ideal, art and cultural competitions (later changed to ''exhibitions'') were introduced at the Fifth Games, and still remain an integral part of the Olympics. Georg Hohrod and M. Eschback won the first literature award for an ''Ode to Sport,'' but the names were pseudonyms, for the author was later revealed to be the altogether human Baron de Coubertin.[22]

Cosmopolitanism on a large scale began emerging as a reality. The London *Times* reporter, walking through the streets of Stockholm, was amazed at the extraordinary mixture of races and kinds of men. The streetboy, he said, ''is getting a gratuitous education . . . of the most cosmopolitan sort.''[23] These 1912 Olympics were not concluded without a hitch, yet the uniqueness of the idea caused one young British competitor to note that the bringing together of the world's youth had immense implications and that the press had shown irresponsibility in accentuating the minor disharmonies. Beyond this immediate trial of strength, said Philip J. Baker, one must be impelled ''by devotion to the idea that lies behind it.''[24] Nearly a half-century later, Baker won the Nobel Peace Prize, in part for his book *The Arms Race: A Programme for World Disarmament* and also for a lifetime devotion to the idea of international athletics.[25]

The First World War cancelled the 1916 Olympics scheduled for Berlin. With the outbreak of the war, Baron de Coubertin joined the French army, but was discharged three months later because he was over-age. He returned to Lausanne and began plans for the next games. Antwerp, Belgium, ''the Cockpit of Europe'' during the war, was ill-prepared for the 1920 Olympics but succeeded in making the transition of eight years without international sport. Drawing an unholy but oft-repeated analogy, one eye-witness at the Seventh Olympic Games saw America's recent war victory and the need to win at Antwerp as a form of categorical imperative. ''When the American athlete begins to fail it will signify the decline of the country.''[26] The Americans did, in truth, perform well. The Belgium fencer, Victor Boin, on behalf of all the athletes, took the first Olympic Oath. National flag in his left hand, his right hand raised, he swore ''that we will take part in these Olympic Games in the true spirit of sportsmanship and that we will respect and abide by the rules which govern them for the glory of sport and the honour of our country.'' Coubertin's special kind of amateurism, which he called ''Olympism,'' had become a living sporting philosophy. The individual's part-time preparation for and involvement in competitive athletics, said the Baron, would enhance physical fitness and serve mankind through a sense of mutual respect and disinterestedness.

101

In 1924 the games of the Eighth Olympiad[27] again took place in Paris. Coubertin felt that his own countrymen might muster sufficient sporting "joie de vivre" to run a superior festival. Nearly 3000 athletes from forty-four nations arrived during Paris' hottest summer in decades. Americans won 99 medals, as Johnny Weissmuller, Dr. Benjamin Spock, and others added their names to the roster of gold medal winners. Some French intellectuals were puzzled at their country's lack of athletic success and called for, as had Coubertin a generation earlier, a vigorous national program of physical fitness.[28] The world press seized on minor disagreements, and the *Literary Digest* called for "No more Olympic Games," but *The Living Age* observed that "there is nothing so effectual as sport in making the mass of people in one country respect the people of another," and the two sides were drawn.[29]

On April 17, 1927, speaking from Olympia, Greece, Baron de Coubertin addressed the world's youth, calling for individual commitment to noble and uncommercial sport, and for a "sporting disinterestedness" that would inexorably enrich the total fabric of men and in so doing uplift humanity.[30] In the mind of Coubertin, the Amsterdam Games of 1928 continued to manifest universal brotherhood. The jaundiced view of Douglas McArthur, President of the American Olympic Committee, was more provincial. "If I were required to indicate today that element of American life which is most characteristic of our nationality, my finger would unerringly point to our athletic escutcheon," he wrote. "It arouses national pride and kindles anew the national spirit."[31] Less exuberantly, the London *Daily Express* noted that "the British nation, profoundly interested in sport, is intensely uninterested in the Olympic Games."[32] The inauspicious beginning of women's Olympic competition further strengthened this negative position. The 800 meter final for women met with near disaster. The half-dozen prostrate and violently ill girls on the infield grass horrified the sensibilities of the crowd. "The women's 800 meter final today," said Jesse Abramson," . . . proved that such events are not right for the Olympics."[33] He could not foresee the progress of women's competitive athletics in the next forty-five years.

In 1932 the Great Depression threatened the Los Angeles Tenth Olympics. The organizers of the games wisely reduced ticket prices to one dollar and less. A tenth of a million people jammed the new colosseum on the opening day, possibly seeking respite from reality and, in a vicarious way, the same search for excellence and joy so important to the assembled athletes. In what might have been the most cloquent speech ever delivered at an Olympic Games, Robert Gordon Sproul, President of the University of California, reminded all that the ancient games were not only physical contests, but "a solemn reunion in Greek energy, the totality of human activity, physical, mental, and spiritual." He said that the Olympic Games must be a social, intellectual, and athletic symposium where the individual, idealized competitive spirit penetrated and energized all elements of society. May these modern games, he continued, "promote the love of play, the reciprocity of good will, the solvent of sportsmanship in which shall be washed away by the immemorial feuds of mankind."[34]

By the Eleventh Olympiad, the games had become magnificent athletic achievements, set in an atmosphere saturated with pageantry, ritual, symbolism, and nationalism. In 1936 an Olympic torch relay, the creation of Carl Diem, began at Olympia and involved several thousand runners, ending inside the main Berlin stadium at the climax of the opening day ceremonies. Flags of all participating nations formed a colorful ribbon at the top of the arena and were dominated by the Olympic flag; white background with five interlocking rings. The colors represented all the world's flags, while the rings symbolized the unity of the continents. The parade of athletes, all splendidly dressed, began with Greece and ended some ninety minutes later with the host country, Nazi Germany. Local, national, and international dignitaries and Olympic officials rendered brief, brave, and idealized speeches. A fanfare of trumpets, the Olympic Anthem, the symbolic release of doves of peace all took place rapidly and impressively. The Olympic Flame arrived in the hand of an ideal German youth. The Sacred Flame was lighted, not being extinguished until the close of the games. Following the innovation, the athletes swore a solemn oath "in the true spirit of sportsmanship, for the glory of sport and the honour of our teams." The German national anthem was played and sung. The participants marched out through the nearest exits, with dancing, gymnastic displays, ceremonial exhibitions, and demonstrations as encores on center stage. Fifteen days later the closing ceremonies, some three hours long and equally impressive, ended the games.[35]

Coubertin, old and destitute in 1936, could not believe that Adolph Hitler had turned the Berlin Olympics into an aggressive instrument of nationalistic German propaganda. The Baron's unceasing rhapsodical tune continued to call the Olympic Games "not simply championships of the world but a dedication to noble youth—a universal and viable religion."[36] He never ceased to fear the spectre of nationalism-gone-mad. Coubertin was seventy-four in the fall of 1937. He appeared in good health as a result of a spartan life which included frequent mild rowing excursions. On September 2nd, while walking through La Grange Park in Geneva, the diminutive Baron, white-haired and moustached, suddenly stopped, dropped his cane, lost his balance, and fell dead on the gravel path. An era had come to an end.

At the time of Coubertin's death, the glorious and ominous Berlin Olympics had ended only a year before and the outbreak of the Second World War was but two years in the future. Maurice Capella for *LeFigaro* felt that a life of idealism had failed to find fertile ground, that "his idea had been deformed."[37] Dr. F. M. Messerli, a life-long friend, explained that in accordance with Coubertin's wishes his body was buried in the cemetery of Bois-de-Vaux in Lausanne while his heart, placed in an urn, was transported to Olympia, Greece. "A great and noble figure disappeared," he said; "it was an incalculable loss for olympism and for humanity."[38] On Olga saw the splendor of the Olympic movement "in its offer of hope that if men will summon the courage to find one another, despite the barriers between them, they will discover they can compete with honor and live in peace."[46] Avery Brundage put it differently. Idealized sport participation, he said, can afford the individual an unrivaled opportunity to develop "inner worth," something "that cannot be equalled in any classroom."[47]

The Olympics became a nearly uncontrollable sports festival at the 1960 Rome games of the Seventeenth Olympiad. A disquieting movement towards gigantism had continued acceleration. Nearly ten thousand athletes and officials from eighty-four countries, plus a tenth of a million visitors poured into the ancient capital that had failed to receive the games in 1904 and 1908. Vestal virgins illuminated the sacred torch of Olympia and the relay made its way to the sea and aboard the *Amerigo Vespucci,* across the Mediterranean to Syracuse, following the route of the Grecian city-states' culture westward, then northward along the Italian peninsula. Teams of runners carried the flame through historic Taormina, Pastum, Monte Circeo, Castelgondolfo, and into Rome. Awards were widely spread with twenty-three countries gaining at least one gold medal. "Mostly it has been good, clean fun," exclaimed the English publication *Economist.* What a sad, psychological nemesis it is, said the writer, that the British were beginning to behave in a manner they used to deplore in others so long ago "when Britain did not depend on its sportsmen for the figure it cut in the world. This year, for sport or sportsmanship, the old lady had precious few medals to show."[48]

Athletes from ninety-four nations participated in the Tokyo Olympics of 1964, which cost several million dollars over a five-year period. The games had been awarded to the city of Tokyo, but they had become so large that all Japan became their venue. National fervor was rewarded by a remarkable, although awesomely complex games. A Japanese official called the Olympic movement the "largest world-wide peace movement based on humanism and moral justice."[49] A British editorial titled "Can it ever be a temple again?" reflected the ancient dichotomy regarding the Olympic Games. With rare insight, the writer demanded of the Olympic fathers that they immediately decide what they wanted: a colossal athletic circus or a smaler, idealized sporting jewel, a Fair or a Temple?[50] The London *Times* called them the "Science Fiction" Olympics, an immense athletic ceremony, the apotheosis of individual physical skill, all with a heavy quality of unrealness about them.[51]

Preparations for the high-altitude Mexico City games of the Nineteenth Olympiad cost nearly 200 million dollars. For a poor country without a tradition of international athletic involvement, Mexico did well. Excellent facilities, the spiralling reservoir of athletic talent, technological advancement, and good weather combined to create new Olympic records in wholesale lots. The rarified air acted as a two-edged sword, helping some and suffocating others. Controversy and confrontation appeared as they had at every single Olympics. The other side of the ledger was heavy with athletic achievements and exhilarating cosmopolitanism. International sport could be viewed as a means of working off national antagonisms, or as a means of promoting them. For some, it was a "war without weapons,"

104

for others it was one of the most important experiments in the world. Nearly 5000 athletes from one hundred twelve countries, all races, colors, and creeds, tested themselves in the fall of 1968. And though frictions, ineptitudes, displays of authoritarianism, and painful rumors abounded, these young people tested one another, displayed their strength, beauty, and courage, and returned home probably better men and women for it. "That is what the Olympics are intended to do; to show that valor is a personal virtue and that superlative achievement knows no color or flag."[52]

If one includes the permanent municipal improvements, then the 630 million dollars spent preparing Munich for the 1982 Olympic games might appear not a bad bargain. It did transform a wasteland into a wonderland. Significantly, in the past twenty years, fewer and fewer cities had bid for the honor of hosting the games. The Munich festival celebrating the beginning March 26, 1938, the world press took note that Coubertin's heart was interred in a column of marble adorned with a head of Zeus. The Greek and International Olympic Committees gathered there, as did Crown Prince Paul, scores of dignitaries, and thousands of spectators. It was a scene similar to those with which the Baron had lived for half a century. The Greek Minister of Education eulogized the Olympic founder in lavish language so dear to Coubertin himself; "You achieved the great aim of your life; may you sleep in peace! Your great soul will be satisfied to have a set of high goal before humanity."[39]

The cancelled games of 1940 and 1944 left a chasm of twelve years from Berlin to London in 1948. The post-war Olympics, as a pageant, in no way compared to the neopagan grandeur of the 1936 games. The London affair was simple, dignified, and rainy. At the opening ceremonies of the Fourteenth Olympiad, Lord Burghley, athlete and Olympic aficionado, pointed out that critics of the movement had acted as a spur to increase the speed of its advance. "The secret of its success," he explained, "lies in the certain knowledge of its rightness bedded in the very being of its adherents."[40] The British organizers felt the Berlin games had gone beyond themselves, they hoped for a reversal, shorn of spectacular irrelevancies, "rescued from under-cover exploitation, restored to simplicity and integrity."[41] This desire for a pleasurable rather than a grandiose affair continued through 1956, but became buried in pageantry and gigantism at the Rome, Tokyo, Mexico City, and Munich games. The Olympics were in business again, their principles unchanged. The president of the International Olympic Committee, J. Sigfrid Edstrom, warned, however, that "the Olympic Games cannot enforce peace in the world . . . but they give the opportunity to all the youth of the world to find out that all men on earth are brothers."[42]

Avery Brundage, for two decades the president of the Olympic movement, often called the games of the Fifteenth Olympiad in 1952 the "perfect Olympics." It was all very tasteful, unostentatious, and supported magnificently by the Finnish people. President Paasikivi declared the Helsinki games open. The name of the final torch-bearer had been kept secret, but the 70,000 spectators cheered when they saw the "Flying Finn," Paavo Nurmi, enter the stadium and race 350 meters with the Olympic torch in his right hand. The assembled athletes broke ranks and cheered as Nurmi ignited the Olympic beacon and turned the torch over to another great distance star, Hannes Kolehmainen, who climbed the 252 foot tower. As the final notes of the Olympic Hymn died away in the Helsinki arena, a second flame burst from atop the tower.[43] Another game had begun in measured solemnity touched with joy and youthful anticipation. *Pravda's* correspondent noted Russia's impressive entry into the games and hoped the universal language of sport might contribute "to the struggle for peace throughout the world."[44]

The electric quality among the citizens of a host Olympic city was never so manifest as that of Melbourne, Australia, in 1956. Nearly 3000 athletes from 67 countries assembled during November and December, catching up much of that nation's population in a wave of pacific nationalism. The tiny Australian city of Avalon saw no reason why Melbourne should monopolize the Olympic games. The sea-side town held its own games, with a torch made of a syrup tin can jammed on a piece of pipe, with a kerosene-fed flame. Girls tossed four pound ball-bearings, the local physician carved javelins, and all the town children competed in foot-races. School headmaster T. E. L. McGuire explained how all activities for four weeks had been linked with the Olympic games project. "We've even managed to get the children interested in arithmetic by letting them work out just how fast John Landy runs," he said.[45] Ugly manifestations of the Soviet invasion of Hungary erupted half-way round the world in an Olympic water polo match between the two teams. Soviet and American athletes won the largest share of honors, but athletes from thirty-five nations won medals. Olga Fikotova, who won the discus throw, fell in love with hammer champion Harold Connolly. They were united in a celebrated marriage shortly after the games. Olga saw the splendor of the Olympic movement "in its offer of hope that if men will summon the courage to find one another, despite the barriers between them, they will discover they can compete with honor and live in peace."[46] Avery Brundage put it differently. Idealized sport participation, he said, can afford the individual an unrivaled opportunity to develop "inner worth," something "that cannot be equalled in any classroom."[47]

The Olympics became a nearly uncontrollable sports festival at the 1960 Rome games of the Seventeenth Olympiad. A disquieting movement towards gigantism had continued acceleration. Nearly ten thousand athletes and officials from eighty-four countries, plus a tenth of a million visitors poured into the ancient capital that had failed to receive the games in 1904 and 1908. Vestal virgins illuminated the sacred torch of Olympia and the relay made its way to the sea and aboard the *Amerigo Vespucci,* across the Mediterranean to Syracuse, following the route of the Grecian city-states' culture westward, then northward along the Italian peninsula. Teams of runners carried the flame through historic Taormina, Pastum, Monte Circeo, Castelgondolfo, and into Rome. Awards were widely spread with twenty-three countries gaining at least one gold medal. "Mostly it has been good, clean fun," exclaimed the English publication *Economist.* What a sad, psychological nemesis it is, said the writer, that the British were beginning to behave in a manner they used to deplore in others so long ago "when Britain did not depend on its sportsmen for the figure it cut in the world. This year, for sport or sportsmanship, the old lady had precious few medals to show."[48]

Athletes from ninety-four nations participated in the Tokyo Olympics of 1964, which cost several million dollars over a five-year period. The games had been awarded to the city of Tokyo, but they had become so large that all Japan became their venue. National fervor was rewarded by a remarkable, although awesomely complex games. A Japanese official called the Olympic movement the "largest world-wide peace movement based on humanism and moral justice."[49] A British editorial titled "Can it ever be a temple again?" reflected the ancient dichotomy regarding the Olympic Games. With rare insight, the writer demanded of the Olympic fathers that they immediately decide what they wanted: a colossal athletic circus or a smaler, idealized sporting jewel, a Fair or a Temple?[50] The London *Times* called them the "Science Fiction" Olympics, an immense athletic ceremony, the apotheosis of individual physical skill, all with a heavy quality of unrealness about them.[51]

Preparations for the high-altitude Mexico City games of the Nineteenth Olympiad cost nearly 200 million dollars. For a poor country without a tradition of international athletic involvement, Mexico did well. Excellent facilities, the spiralling reservoir of athletic talent, technological advancement, and good weather combined to create new Olympic records in wholesale lots. The rarified air acted as a two-edged sword, helping some and suffocating others. Controversy and confrontation appeared as they had at every single Olympics. The other side of the ledger was heavy with athletic achievements and exhilarating cosmopolitanism. International sport could be viewed as a means of working off national antagonisms, or as a means of promoting them. For some, it was a "war without weapons," for others it was one of the most important experiments in the world. Nearly 5000 athletes from one hundred twelve countries, all races, colors, and creeds, tested themselves in the fall of 1968. And though frictions, ineptitudes, displays of authoritarianism, and painful rumors abounded, these young people tested one another, displayed their strength, beauty, and courage, and returned home probably better men and women for it. "That is what the Olympics are intended to do; to show that valor is a personal virtue and that superlative achievement knows no color or flag."[52]

If one includes the permanent municipal improvements, then the 630 million dollars spent preparing Munich for the 1982 Olympic games might appear not a bad bargain. It did transform a wasteland into a wonderland. Significantly, in the past twenty years, fewer and fewer cities had bid for the honor of hosting the games. The Munich festival celebrating the beginning of the Twentieth Olympiad was the most brillant and controversal of all. A towering 8500 athletes from almost every nation in the world gathered in the Bavarian capital. But the Olympian dream of the world's youth gathering together without reservation and without resentment remained unfulfilled. Absolutely no sporting event had ever received such coverage as did the

Munich games, but the drama of Arab terrorists and Israeli hostages stole away much of the world's attention from the games. When it was over, press opinion split down the middle, as usual. One writer called it "a disaster—a hoodoo Olympics."[53] But Jerry Nason of the *Boston Globe,* another eye-witness, refused to join the cry of "Doomsday" and saw in the Olympic philosophy something "too precious, too splendid, to be thus abandoned without a mighty struggle."[54] Again, another correspondent concluded that despite everything that had gone wrong, it would be a grievous mistake if these were the last Olympics. The Olympic ideals of sportsmanship and brotherhood "are stronger than political murder," John Dixon wrote. "In an age which has few ideals to offer, the Olympics symbolize human yearnings for competition, human contacts, peace."[55]

No Olympic games have yet lived up to Coubertin's high expectations. Oblique criticisms persist that mere sport has no right to such awesome claims. Others find incongruities in the squabbles and displays of chauvinism at these games. Some find in their growing gigantism a danger rather than a sign of health. Commercialism, the unbearable financial burden inflicted on the host city and nation, the size of the games, and the universal disorientation regarding the spirit and the letter of amateurism jeopardize the continuance of the games into the next century. Yet their demise would be a great loss, and the resulting vacuum hard to fill. Much of the writings about the games has been negative, but then the essence of news is strife, and marketable print thrives on controversies. Only drastic means can arrest the present collision course of the Olympic movement. The aftermath of every one of the seventeen games held found no lack of suggestions.

The following abbreviated suggestions for improving and saving the Olympics represent a synthesis of many people's ideas together with several unique and even radical courses of action: (1) Future Olympic games should be held at a single site. (2) An "International Olympics Site" should be located in Switzerland. (3) During the Olympics games year, the events should be spread over four distinct ten-day periods. (4) During the remaining three year period, the site should be used on a continual basis for amateur, professional, and recreational sports. (5) A full staff of experts, on permanent assignment, should operate the site, collecting income for services rendered. (6) The site should continually undergo change and growth until ready for the 1992 games of the Twenty-fifth Olympiad. (7) A mandatory quadrennial fee of 1/300,000th of a member nation's gross national product would not burden any nation more than another. (8) The method of selecting International Olympic Committee members should not be changed, but more recent Olympic athletes should be selected for membership. (9) Five roving ambassadors, one for each continent, might be chosen and put to work; some members of the International Olympic Committee as well as ambassadors should be permanent, professional, and well-paid. (10) The laudable but incendiary phrase concerning banishment for countries displaying racial discrimination on their teams should be eliminated from the Olympic "Principles." (11) National anthems and flag raising at Olympic victory ceremonies should be terminated. (12) Participation in the opening ceremonies parade should be by sport or event rather than by nation states.[56]

The Olympic philosophy is a precious commodity. It can function as a viable idea in these modern and materialistic times. It is the central expression of a Greek idea that the body has a glory second only to that of the intellect and spirit. It is by the harmonious discipline of all three in experiences such as the Olympic games that men and women may be led to understand their chief and proper concern, knowledge of themselves and the right way to live. The Baron de Coubertin's dream of speaking a common language through the medium of cosmopolitan and honorable sport was a grandiose and unique idea. The Olympics have fulfilled some of his visionary plans, yet fallen short of full potential. Hopefully these failings can act as a catalyst for today's sports' leaders to reaffirm Coubertin's faith in beauty, peace, athletics, fair play, and the Olympic ideal.

REFERENCE NOTES

1. Pierre de Coubertin, "A Forgotten Side of the Question," *Bulletin du Bureau international de pedagogie sportive,* No. 7 (1931). 7.

2. Walter W. Hyde, *Olympic Victor Monuments and Greek Athletic Art* (Washington, 1921), 57.

3. Richard Lattimore, trans., *The Odes of Pindar* (Chicago, 1959), 87.

4. Hymn to Sport, *Mexico Llama a tos XIX Juegos Olympico 1968* (Frankfort, 1968), 35.

5. Official Report Olympic Games 776 B.C.-1896 A.D. (New York, 1896), 81.

6. Charles Waldstein, "The Olympian Games at Athens, *"Harper's Weekly,* 10. (16 May 1896). 490.

7. "The Olympic Games," *The Times* [London]. 16 Apr. 1896.

8. "The Americans Ahead," *The New York Times,* 8 Apr. 1896.

9. James P. Boyd, *The Paris Exposition of 1900* (N.p., 1900). In a revealing chapter, entitled "Supplemental Palaces and Side Shows," there is tucked away brief mention of "The Olympian Games." See also Richard D. Mandell, *Paris 1900, The Great World's Fair* (Toronto, 1967).

10. Pierre de Coubertin to Charles Eliot, 9 Mar. 1898, Box 133, Folder 905, Charles Eliot Papers, Harvard University.

11. Erich Kamper, *Encyclopedia of the Olympic Games* (New York, 1972). 332 n.158.

12. Pierre de Coubertin, *Une Campagne de Vingt-et-un ans (1887-1908)* (Paris, 1908). 152.

13. See M. R. Werner, "More Fun Than at the Games," *Sports Illustrated,* 13 (15 Aug. 1960), EM5-EM8.

14. Pierre de Coubertin in the *Congres International de sport et d'education physique* (Paris, 1905), 16.

15. James E. Sullivan, "American Athletes in Ancient Athens," *American Review of Reviews,* 34 (July 1906), 44.

16. See James E. Sullivan, "American Athletes Champions of the World." *Outing,* 48 (Aug. 1906), 625.

17. "Yankees Make Protest," *New York Tribune,* 18 July 1908.

18. One fourth of all the money spent at the 1908 Olympics was for "entertainment." But before any "captious critic" objected, said Theodore Andrea Cook, one must remember that "the knowledge of one author's habits, the possibilities of mutual friendships, the opportunity of mutual courtesy are among the greatest assets which the modern Olympic Movement can posess." See *Official Report—The Fourth Olympiad London 1908* (London, 1908), 394.

19. Pierre de Coubertin, "Les 'trustees' de l'idee olympique," *Revue olympique* (July 1908), 110, and *The Times* [London], 25 July 1908.

20 Sir Arthur Conan Doyle, "Yankee Runner Wins Marathon," *New York Tribune,* 25 July 1908.

21. Ralph Craig quoted in Paul Withington, *The Book of Athletics* (Boston, 1914), 247.

22. Kamper, *Encyclopedia of Olympic Games,* 355 n.677.

23. "The Olympic Games," *The Times* [London], 5 July 1912.

24. Philip J. [Noel] Baker, "Olympiads and Liars," *The Outlook,* 102 (19 Oct. 1912), 355.

25. "Novel Prize for Briton," *The Times* [London], 6 Nov. 1959.

26. Martin T. Durkin, "Memories of the Last Olympics," *The Literary Digest,* 66 (3 July 1920), 101.

27. An Olympiad is a chronological span of time. In Greek antiquity it was 48 lunar months; in modern times it is approximately four years. The games must occur during the first year of the Olympiad.

28. See *La Revue de France,* 4 (July 1924), 217-24; *Mercure de France,* 173 (1 Aug. 1924), 753-7, 174 (1 Sept. 1924), 311-26.

29. "Olympic Discords," *The Living Age,* 322 (23 Aug. 1921), 313.

30. "Twenty Years Ago," *Bulletin du comite international olympique,* 9 (15 Mar. 1948), 30.

31. Douglas MacArthur, "Report to the President," *American Olympic Committee Report,* 1928 (New York, 1928), 7.

32. John Tunis, "The Olympic Games," *Harper's Monthly Magazine,* 157 (Aug. 1928), 314.

33. Jese Abramson in *New York Herald-Tribune,* 3 Aug. 1928.

34. Robert Gordon Sproul, quoted in *Riverside* [California] *Press-Enterprise,* 1 Aug. 1932.

35. See Chapter V, "Olympic Protocol," in *The Olympic Games* (Lausanne, Switzerland, 1967), 41-5, for details of opening and closing ceremony procedures. Two particularly good histories of the 1932 and 1936 Olympics (other than the official national reports) are Bill Henry, *An Approved History of the Olympic Games* (New York, 1918), and Richard Mandell, *The Nazi Olympics* (New York, 1971).

36. Pierre de Coubertin in Maurice Pottecher, "L'olympisme et son renovateur Pierre de Coubertin," *Revue Hebdomadaire,* 8 Aug. 1936, 154.

37. Maurice Capella, "La mort du Baron de Coubertin," *Le Figaro,* 3 Sept. 1937.

38. Fr. M. Messerli, *Histoire des Sports et de L'Olympisme* (Lausanne, 1950), 22.

39. M. Georgacopoulos in *Olympische Flamme,* 1 (Berlin, 1942), 261-3, as found in *The Olympic Idea* (Cologne, 1970), 10.

40. David Burghley in "Lord Burghley's Speech," *The National Review,* 131 (Sept. 1948), 248-9.

41. Ronald Stead, "A Spartan Torch: Postwar England Proudly Carries Olympic Torch," *Christian Science Monitor,* 10 July 1948.

42. J. S. Edstrom in "Last Ceremonies of Olympiad," *The Times* [London], 16 Aug. 1948.

43. "Paavo Nurmi Lights the Helsinki Beacon," *The Illustrated London News,* 221 (26 July 1952), 139-41.

44. V. Novoskoltev in *The Current Digest of the Soviet Press,* 4 (Sept. 1952), 27.

45. "Just Fun and Games," Sydney *Sun-Herald,* 9 Dec. 1956.

46. Olga Connolly, *The Rings of Destiny* (New York, 1968), 311.

47. Avery Brundage in Robert Creamer, "The Embattled World of Avery Brundage," *Sports Illustrated,* 4 (6 Feb. 1956), 43.

48. "La Dolce Vita," *Economist,* 196 (10 Sept. 1960), 974.

49. Kenkichi Ohshima, "Olympic Movement and Its Influence on Physical Education,' in *Proceedings of International Congress of Sports Sciences, 1964* (Tokyo, 1964), 224.

50. Doug Gardner, "Can It Every Be A Temple Again?" *World Sports,* 31 (Jan. 1965), 5.

51. "Sour End to 'Science Fiction' Olympics," *The Times* [London], 26 Oct. 1964.

52. "Adios' to the Olympics," *Nation,* 207 (11 Nov. 1968), 484.

53. Vernon Morgan, "The Disastrous Munich Olympics," in *1972 United States Olympic Book* (New York, 1972), 74.

54. Jerry Nason, "The Future Rests With the Athletes," in *ibid.*, 88.
55. John Dixon, "Olympics: Mankind's Hope," in *ibid.*, 88.
56. A certain marshalling of ideas on Olympic changes can be found in John A. Lucas, "Olympism and the Genesis of the Modern International Olympic Games Philosophy," in 75th *Proceedings,* National College Physical Education Association for Men, 1972, 26-30, and "Open Letter to Lord Killanin," *Journal of Health, Physical Education and Recreation,* 44 (Feb. 1973), 8-10.

SECTION III
GEOGRAPHY AND PHYSICAL ACTIVITY

WHAT IS GEOGRAPHY?

Geography is a discipline which examines the character of place, as well as the spatial arrangement and organization of phenomena on the earth's surface. Geography resembles the natural sciences in that it is interested in climate, vegetation, topography and the habitats of animals. However, Geography's concern for the distribution of population, economic conditions, and routes of communication allows this discipline to be classified also as a social science.

HOW ARE GEOGRAPHY AND PHYSICAL ACTIVITY RELATED?

Only recently has there been any formalization of a geography of physical activity. The development of this youthful sub-field can be attributed primarily to the work of Professor John F. Rooney of Oklahoma State University. Indeed his text **A Geography of American Sport** *is the first to synthesize and organize what is known on the topic.[1] Dr. Rooney suggests that the major conceptual subdivisions of a geography of sport include:*

1. *The spatial variation in sports, that is to say the place-to-place differences in the games which people play and with which they identify;*
2. *The spatial organization of sport at different competitive levels;*
3. *The origin and diffusion of sports and athletes;*
4. *The social and symbolic impact of the spatial organization of sport;*
5. *The effect of sport on the landscape;*
6. *The relationship between the spatial organization of sport and national character.*

With such a scope this sub-field should attract scholars for years to come. It is hoped that the geography of Canadian Sport will soon be examined.

---

1. Rooney, J. F. *A Geography of American Sport.* Reading, Mass.: Addison-Wesley, 1974.

Geography, Sport and Geographical Education**

J. R. Bale*

Abstract. Both recreational and spectator sports are of great importance in modern life but have been relatively ignored in academic studies. A conceptual framework for geographic studies of sport and examples of sports — geographical approaches are provided. It is suggested that a geography of sport ought to be given greater prominence in both geography and sports studies courses.

INTRODUCTION

The geography of leisure has become a well developed sub-discipline both at school and at the research levels. The *Man, Land and Leisure* theme of the "Geography for the Young School Leaver" (GYSL) project is testimony to the perceived importance of recreational and leisure studies in school geography (Beddis, Bowen, Dalton and Higginbottom, 1974). At the post-graduate level the variety of research interests ranges from highly quantitative approaches to modelling travel patterns to the countryside (Baxter, 1979), to more cognitive-behavioural analyses of spatial choice of rural recreation (Elson, 1979). Of course, a major part of leisure activity involves participation in many kinds of sports. Of all the words in the English language, "sport" is one of the most difficult to define, but for the purposes of the present paper it will be interpreted as institutionalised types of physical contests between individual or teams of human beings (Guttman, 1978). Geographies of leisure do not entirely ignore sport but they do not give it very much emphasis either. The aim of this paper is to draw attention to the emerging geography of sport and to suggest how courses in sports geography might be structured. At the same time the paper illustrates the ways in which geographical concepts and techniques may be exemplified in a variety of sports contexts.

Few would deny that sport has major relevance and importance in life and leisure patterns. Sport is a growth industry. After expenditure on television, radio and audio equipment, sport is the most rapidly growing sector of the leisure industries, spending having increased at a rate of 8•1 per cent per annum between 1970 and 1977 (Martin and Mason, 1979). Sport receives saturation coverage on television and takes up about three pages of each of the 'quality" newspapers and nearer five pages of the tabloids. Attendances

* J. R. Bale is Lecturer in Education at the University of Keele. This paper was read at the Annual Conference of the Geographical Association. 9th April 1980.
**Bale, J. R., "Geography, Sport and Geographical Education." *Geography*, 1981, 66, pp. 104.115. Reprinted by permission of the publisher.

at a declining spectator sport such as association football still totalled over 24,500,000 for the English Football league season, 1978-9 (Rollin, 1979). The Wimbledon tennis tournament alone paid out 260,000 in prize money in 1979 (*The Economist,* 1979, pp. 120-1). Fortunes are made and lost through sport. About half the adult population staked 233 millions on the football pools in 1978, though this figure appears extremely modest compared with the 1868 millions staked on off-course betting (Central Statisitcal Office, 1979). Britain's three major recreational sports, soccer, cricket and table tennis, claim about a million, half a million and a quarter of a million active participants respectively. At the international scale it has been suggested that "next to a national airline, countries see success in sport as a prime objective — and they will pay anthing to get it" (Tomasson, 1980).

Lawson and Morford have identified various ideal type models for sport, the first of which they term "recreational — participatory", the second "commercial — consumer" and the third "educational — instructional" (Lawson and Morford, 1979). In this paper it is the first two which provide the principal foci of attention, being recreational activities for participant and spectator respectively. The third is hardly recreational for anybody, being part of the school curriculum. Whereas recreational sport possesses an egalitarian idealogical base, commercial—consumer sport is essentially meritocratic. In recreational sport the aim is to experience fun and the joy of playing while in commercial sport, the objective is to win, to maximise profits or to propagate national interests. It is the spectators who experience recreation and not the "players". Modern consumer sport, which is often professional, "has ceased being a recreation intended as a relaxation from fatigue or relief from the monotony of oppressive and exhausting work" (Callois, 1962). Indeed, some observers see in modern sport certain residuals of exploitive capitalism with its child labour (e.g. teenage swimming champions), the ruthless sacking of workers (e.g. football "managers"), the risk of damage to the body (e.g. rugby and boxing) and the constant increase in the time spent working (i.e. training) (Goldbach, 1979). Others refer to sport as the new opiate of the masses. Trotsky noted that working class fervour for revolution has been "drawn off into artificial channels with the aid of boxing, football, racing and other forms of sport" (Trotsky, 1926). Alternatively, we may observe the ubiquitous nature of sport and prefer to view it simply as the most fun people can have with their bodies in public! (Lipsyte, 1977).

These examples should be sufficient to demonstrate that sport is a subject of major importance which is amenable to academic study. Yet apart from a growing sociology of sport and a longstanding historical interest, it remains something of an academic blindspot. Not suprisingly, therefore, sport failed to attract the attention of the GYSL curriculum innovators. Even for recreational sports, which have received slightly more attention from geographers than have spectator sports, a large number of questions need to be answered. At the national scale, we do not know very much about the degree of provision for our principal recreational sports. We know little about regional differences in tastes for recreational sports beyond the anecdotal and apocryphal. Do working class industrial areas really identify with different sports from leafy southern suburbs? Are minority recreational sports localised geographically as well as numerically? How equitable is the degree of provision of opportunities for various sports? Can sport provide clues which aid the identification of regional cultures? These kinds of questions indicate only a few of the areas of inquiry facing the sports geographer.

It is true that several geographers have utilised sport in the teaching of geographical concepts and techniques (e.g. Sas and Jones, 1976). This approach is adopted on the assumption (usually correct) that students are more interested in sport than in geography. Yet in a sense, sport is being relegated to the status of a teaching gimmick when used in this way. A subject of such economic, social and cultural importance deserves to be studied in its own right. If education is concerned with creating a population which is better informed about the contents of both the world and the media, then sport ought to be studied by others besides physical educationalists. There is no further need to justify a geography of sport; it justifies itself. The purpose of the remainder of this paper is to exemplify the nature of sports geography and its component parts.

A FRAMEWORK FOR GEOGRAPHICAL STUDIES OF SPORTS

The geographical study of sport, as opposed to leisure, is almost entirely the creation of Professor John Rooney of Oklahoma State University. His work, and that of some of his students, is contained in the only tex-

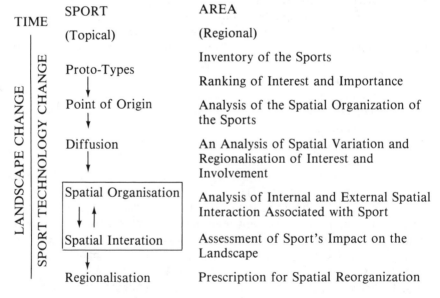

Source: J. Rooney. Sport from a geographic perspective, in D. W. Ball and J. Loy (eds.) *Sport and Social Order*. Addison Wesley, 1975. p. 56.

Figure 1. A conceptual framework for the geographic analysis of sport.

116

book on the subject (Rooney, 1974), but this work is set in an American context and sports studies by geographers in other countries have been slow in developing (Paratore, 1976). A potential course on the geography of sport might be based on Rooney's "conceptual framework" (Fig. 1) for sports geography (Rooney, 1975). It might commence by examining sports prototypes, origins and diffusion in both time and space. Innovations in sports as well as sports as innovations would need to be studied. This would be followed by a consideration of the spatial organisation of sport and the concomitant spatial interaction. Such an approach would be basically nomothetic, searhing for generalisations and models of the spatial organisation of sport. A complementary part of the course would focus more explicitly on regional differentiation in sport. Sports regions might be identified and the different degrees of localisation of individual sports explored. Such is the interest in sport that such a course might be taught at different levels of the educational hierarchy, developing *a la* Bruner at increasing degrees of sophistication. In the space available in the present paper, only a limited number of examples can be provided to illustrate the different elements of the conceptual framework described above.

PROTOTYPES, ORIGINS AND DIFFUSION

All present-day sports possess prototypes and origins in both time and space. In most cases sports diffused away from their original locations to embrace regions, nations and in some cases the world. Most historical studies of sport, both popular and academic, contain much implicitly geographical material, especially with respect to the early localisation of sport. For the quintessentially English game of cricket, for example, numerous descriptions refer to its early geographical localisation in south-east England. "Kent and Sussex are the ancestral home of cricket", wrote Ditchfield (Ditchfield, 1891). "The spreading of the game in the southern counties may be attributed to the meeting of the hop-growers at the annual fairs", speculated Gale (Gale 1871). By 1800, "cricket had become the common practice of the common people in Hampshire, Surrey, Sussex and Kent", noted Pycroft in his classic book, *The Cricket Field,* (Pycroft, 1922).

A more precise indication of the localisation of cricket in pre-Victorian times may be made by analysing the entries in Buckley's monumental works on eighteenth and nineteenth century cricket (Buckley, 1935 and 1937). It would appear that three fairly distinct bands of cricketing activity existed in the geography of eighteenth century cricket and it is difficult to avoid drawing the analogy with Meinig's "culture region" (Meinig, 1967). A cricket "core" existed in the counties of the south-east (excepting the metropolis) where between two and seven times the national average per capita number of clubs were found. A "domain" stretched from Norfolk to Wiltshire, this area possessing above average but not spectacular numbers of clubs per capita. To the north-west an area of well below average emphasis existed though "peripheral acculturations" were found in places like Nottinghamshire, Cornwall and Flint. The industrial and urban revolutions of the nineteenth century saw cricket diffuse "even to the northern counties" (Pycroft, 1922). Yet as late as the first quarter of the nineteenth century both anecdotal and statistical evidence suggest a remarkable degree of localisation, prior to the diffusion and widespread adoption of a form of popular culture.

The nineteenth century witnessed the growth of popular sports on a vast scale. Furthermore, innovations in sport were common and have continued to occur with alarming frequency (e.g. synthetic running tracks, fibre-glass vaulting poles, anabolic steroids). Yet the geographical analysis of the diffusion of both sport as an innovation and of innovations in sport remains limited in number. Hagerstrand included among the numerous phenomena which he studied diffusing across Sweden, the sports facilities of swimming pools and sports halls (Hagerstrand, 1966); Pillsbury has noted the spread of stock car racing in the USA, away from its "culture hearth" in the Deep South (Pillsbury, 1974); and Bale has interpreted the adoption of professionalism in football in England and Wales as a form of innovation diffusion (Bale, 1978). But the spread of sport at both national and international scales presents a vast field of research for those interested in applying geographical ideas to a data-rich subject.

SPATIAL ORGANISATION OF SPORT

Following the diffusion and adoption of sport, a pattern of spatial organisation emerged. The distribution of sports facilities can be usefully analysed according to the tenets of central place theory. Sport ought to be arranged hierarchically, certain activities being found only above a certain threshold size with other low order activities being ubiquitous. The Olympic Games possess such stringent locational requirements that only a few cities in the world can even begin to entertain hosting them. A recreational football pitch, on the other hand, is found within a mile of over 90 percent of the British population (Sillitoe, 1969). In American professional baseball, a common rule of thumb is that a franchise needs to attract about 1 million fan-visits per annum to its home games in order to break even (Aldini, 1981). Large cities are therefore at an obvious advantage. The number of outlets for a given sport might be expected to be related positively to size of town. In fact, many gaps exist in the sports hierarchy, at all levels of scale. Many places which, according to normative theory ought to have sports facilities, in reality do not. In Edinburgh, for example, aggregate travel to the present public swimming pools in the city is 42 per cent greater than would be the case if the pools were optimally located (Hodgart, 1978). In London, the borough of Southwark possesses one football pitch for every 6317 of its population, whereas more suburban Greenwich has one per 1497 (Bale 1979a). At the national scale, Toyne has highlighted the spatial inequality in the supply of first class cricket matches (Toyne, 1974), while in the case of the Football League the present location pattern of clubs is explained more by locational inertia then equality in regional provision. The new city of Milton Keynes, for example, is anxious to attract a football league club to serve a future market area of over 250,000 people.

118

There is considerable evidence to suggest that big-time sport is becoming increasingly primate in its location pattern. For example, in 1951 two-fifths of the population attending football matches in Lancashire went to watch Liverpool, Everton, Manchester City and Manchester United. In 1971 the proportion had risen to two-thirds (Rivett, 1975). Wiseman predicts that the football industry will go the same way as the cinema with fewer local outlets being able to survive at the present scale of operations (Wiseman, 1977). In North America, where profit maximisation is a principal motivation operating consumer sports clubs, considerable numbers of inter-regional moves occur as clubs seek more optimal locations. Yet given the uneven revenue potential, some clubs seem permanently doomed to only short term success and Demmert has shown how there will be a long run tendency for clubs located in the strong markets to be both economically and sportingly superior to those located in weak markets (Demmert, 1973).

Predicting the best location for sport is a subject which has not attracted the attention it deserves. Yet it is vital that if an equitable distribution of recreational and spectator sport is to be achieved, greater effort needs to be directed towards this end.

SPATIAL INTERACTION IN SPORT

Sports nodes generate various forms of spatial interaction. Stadiums create spheres of influence which will naturally vary in size according to the quality of service being offered and to the presence of intervening sporting (and other) opportunities. The most obvious kind of sphere of influence in sport is the "fan region". "There are as many fan regions as there are teams. Some are small and embrace only a few people, while others associated with the professional teams include millions of followers" (Rooney, 1975). Such fan regions have been delimited empirically and can be expressed as distance decay functions (Bale and Gowing, 1976). People living inside "fan regions" benefit from accessibility to the sports node in question. People living inside a second sphere of influence, however, consume more of the effects of a given sport than they would freely choose. Whereas the fan region might be described as a positive sphere of influence, a negative sphere is identifed when a sports node generates nuisances in the neighbourhood around it. Low order sports facilities, such as village cricket grounds, probably fail to generate any negative spillovers, but the impact on the local area of international sports events or professional clubs can be very serious indeed. The increased development and added congestion associated with the Winter Olympics was perceived by the State of Colorado as being so serious that a decision was made not to bid for the hosting of the games in 1976 (Cox, 1979). On a local scale, "nuisance fields" around football grounds, though limited in geographical extent, nevertheless present serious hazards to local residents. Such nuisance fields could be minimised spatially in suburban locations where the absence of residential development would internalise many of the nuisances generated in existing inner city locations (Bale, 1980). Hence, sports activities need to maximise one kind of sphere of influence and minimise the other.

Another kind of spatial interaction is the movement necessary for a sports club to fulfil its fixture list. Though transport costs do not account for a major cost item in operating professional sports clubs, minimising the costs of a season's fixtures is obviously desirable. Two possible solutions are used in sport to solve the problem. First, regionalisation of the league in which the club plays prevents long-distance travel. This is the solution adopted in most sports. In table tennis in England, for example, about 300 leagues exist. In semi-professional football the leagues cover larger areas and in professional football the league embraces the whole of England and Wales. Until 1958, however, the lower divisions of the Football League were regionalised and a return to this arrangement is widely advocated today (Department of Education and Science, 1968). Fourth division clubs (as a result of their more decentralised locations) have to travel greater distances than the more wealthy first division clubs in order to complete their league fixtures. A second solution to the problem of distance minimisation is to combine several matches on a tour. This approach is applied in North America where Campbell and Chen have demonstrated that for a ten team basketball league the application of a minimum distance scheduling algorithm reduced the total travelling distance for all teams by 29•3 per cent (Campbell and Chen, 1976).

A final form of spatial interation involves the movement of sports employees between places during the course of their careers. The recruitment of players by professional clubs in Britain and by colleges in America displays a well pronounced distance decay effect. Players are more likely to be playing near their place of birth than at some distance from it (Rooney, 1974). The movement of transferred footballers between clubs exemplifies another kind of player movement. Complex patterns of criss-crossing lines joining clubs between which players have been transferred, can be generalised by using the Nystuen-Dacey method in order to reveal the dominant flows. For Britain, this technique reveals that the dominant directon of movement is towards the south-east (Bale, 1979a).

REGIONAL DIFFERENTIATION IN SPORTS

A more ideographic approach to sport focuses on differences between places with respect to some sports attribute. It is diffuclt to establish accurately the sporting idiosyncracies of British regions because of the absence of comparable data for all sports. The pioneering study by Rodgers which tried to identify regional differences in interest in recreational sports is frustrating for the sports geographer because several of the most popular pursuits were aggregated as "team sports" (Rodgers, 1967 and 1969). More recently, Veal has drawn attention to the more disaggregated data found in the General Household Survey (GHS) of 1977 (Veal, 1979). The GHS asked respondents to indicate in which sports they had participated, either actively or as a spectator, in the four weeks prior to interview. Although the samples participating in sport are quite small, it is possible to recognise regions in which particular sports are represented disproportionately to their population. For example, Wales possesses 6 per cent of the population but 8 per cent of the sample participants in rugby. The south east possesses 20 per cent of the population but 29 per cent of the sample playing tennis. By using location quotients it is possible to identify those regions which emphasise particular recreational sports, though the caveat about the likely existence of quite wide confidence intervals needs to be stressed.

Data have been published which reveal regional differences in the consumption of a number of spectator sports. These are summarised in Table 1 and show, among other things, that Scotland is dominated by football and Wales is the nation's only two-sport region, when measured by spectator interest. The disadvantage of these data is that they do not indicate frequency of attendance at spectator sports. The GHS data are an improvement in this respect but cover far fewer sports than those shown in Table 1.

Table 1. Percentage of Adults Who Paid to Watch Various Sports, 1974

	Soccer	Cricket	Horse racing	Speed-way racing	Motor racing	Motor cycle racing	Rugby Union	Show jumping	Rugby League
All adults	19:6	5:4	5:1	4:7	4:3	2:8	2:8	2:8	2:5
Greater London	17:9	4:2	5:4	4:4	4:8	2:6	2:5	2:9	1:0
South east/EA	17:6	5:5	4:3	6:4	6:3	3:6	1:8	2:8	0:9
South west	17:3	6:3	3:7	5:0	4:6	3:0	4:4	2:9	1:1
Wales	15:3	5:1	3:9	1:9	2:8	2:2	12:9	3:3	2:5
W and E Midlands	21:3	6:5	5:0	5:1	4:9	2:6	2:1	3:0	1:0
North west	22:6	6:4	6:1	3:9	3:3	3:2	2:4	2:4	7:1
Yorks & Humberside	17:8	7:0	5:7	3:9	2:3	1:7	2:2	2:8	7:8
North	20:0	5:0	5:7	3:3	2:2	2:3	2:0	2:2	1:3
Scotland	26:2	1:5	5:3	3:2	3:4	1:5	3:0	2:4	0:8

Source: IPC *Sociological Monographs,* 12, "Leisure", IPC Marketing Services, 1975, p. 49

For the study of regional differentiation of individual sports, various approaches may be adopted. For a *geography of opportunity,* data would be required on the number of playing facilities or number of clubs per head of the population. Because clubs vary in size, *a geography of emphasis* would be best obtained by analysing the number of teams or active participants per head. In a commerical-consumer sport, the birthplaces of participants provide the raw material for a *geography of "production"* of sportsmen and women. Each of these geographies may now be briefly illustrated, a different sport being used to exemplify each approach. In each of the case studies which follow, the country is used as the areal unit for identifying differences in per capita opportunity, emphasis and production and it is recognised that subtle differences in each will occur at the intra-county scale.

(a) Cycling Clubs in England and Wales

The geographical distribution of cycling clubs per head of the population il-

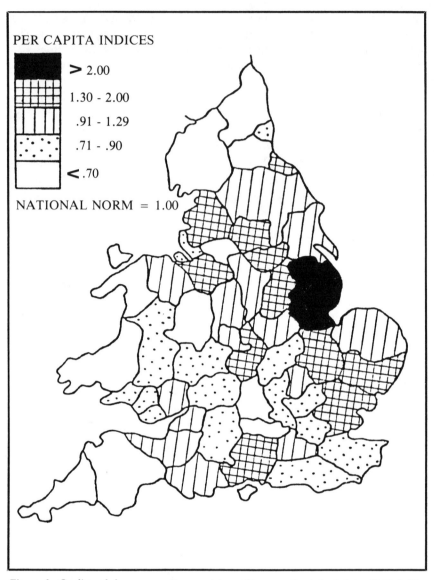

PER CAPITA INDICES

> 2.00

1.30 - 2.00

.91 - 1.29

.71 - .90

< .70

NATIONAL NORM = 1.00

Figure 2. Cycling clubs: per capita provision. (Source of original data: British Cycling Federation Handbook, 1979.)

lustrates the geography of opportunity for serious participation in one of our major sports. In 1979 there were 636 cycling clubs in England and Wales, one club per 77,200 of the population. This figure may be represented as an index of 1•00 against which individual county indices may be readily compared. County indices range from 2•04 in Lincolnshire to zero in Northumberland. Broadly speaking, a "bicycling belt" extends across England from Lancashire to Essex, where a contiguous band of counties possess indices of over 1•30 (Fig. 2). Notably deficient in cycling clubs are the northern and western peripheries. The main urban centres differ considerably. Greater Manchester (index 0•29) is grossly deficient in cycling clubs, Merseyside (0•99) is almost exactly the same as the nation, while West Yorkshire (1•64) provides opportunities for cycling well above the national norm.

Several other studies of this type have been undertaken, most frequently at the sub-national scale. The Sports Council has been responsible for initiating much research into the provision of playing pitches, swimming pools and other facilities, in several regions (e.g. Horn, 1975). Yet surpris-

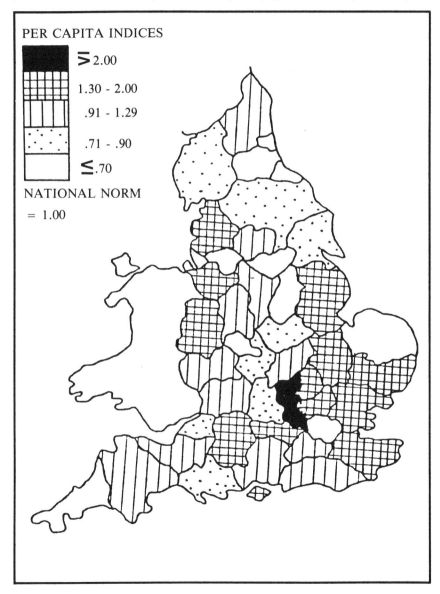

Figure 3. Per capita involvement in table tennis. (Source of data: English Table Tennis Association, Table Tennis Address List, 1978-9, E.T.A., Hastings, 1979.)

123

ingly, *national* coverage of opportunities for participating in many sports has yet to be undertaken. It is not known, for example, how many football pitches or running tracks exist in Britain and it is therefore impossible to plan provision adequately at a national scale.

(b) Table Tennis Teams in England

The geography of opportunities is important for the planning of sports facility provision but the number of clubs or the number of pitches may not be particularly a sensitive indication of the degree of participation in the sport in question. The geography of *emphasis* on various sports is best examined by comparing the number of active participants or the number of teams, rather than the number of clubs *per se*. Clubs can obviously vary considerably in the number of active participants and teams which they can support. The degree of participation in particular sports may be a reflection of regional culture. "The cultural geographer would be well rewarded", wrote Zelinsky, "by attending to all of the many forms of recreation" including sports (Zelinsky, 1973). The emphasis placed on one major British sport, table tennis, exemplifies this approach.

Table tennis is Britain's third most popular sport, and is easily the major indoor sport. In 1979 there were 8539 clubs and 200,000 players. The clubs support 21,514 teams, one team for every 2024 of the population of England. This figure is represented as an index of 1•00 against which county emphases can be compared. Fig. 3 illustrates regional differences in the emphasis on table tennis in England. It is very obviously a suburban sport. The top counties in southern England are Bucks (index of 2•09), Essex (1•90) and Kent (1•80). Greater London (0•53) is an island of relative inactivity. In the north, the urban areas of Merseyside (0•34) and Greater Manchester (0•35) are sandwiched between Lancashire (1•84) and Cheshire (1•35). The Midlands are flanked by Shropshire (1•55) and Lincoln (1•74). The pattern displayed in Fig. 3 is not unlike that for badminton, squash and tennis—sports which might be termed suburban-southern in orientation.

Studies of the emphasis placed on particular sports might well contribute to a geography of popular culture. To date, little is known about variations in participation rates in different sports at the national scale. Yet for a better understanding of the relationship between people, place and recreation it is essential that work in this intriguing subject continues.

(c) Professional Boxer "Production" in Britain

The third case study focuses on the production of participants in a declining professional sport, namely boxing. Boxing is a sport which has been traditionally associated with areas of limited economic opportunity, professional pugilism being seen as a "way out of the ghetto" when alternatives are few in number. The "hungry fighter" is as much fact as folk-lore. In 1979 there were 495 professional boxers registered in Britain. Of these, 10 per cent were first generation immigrants. The remainder exhibit an extreme form of localisation in the pattern of their birthplaces. In this case, our per capita index of 1-00 represents one professional boxer per 125,000 of the population. Fig. 4 reveals high indices in South Glamorgan, where one professional box-

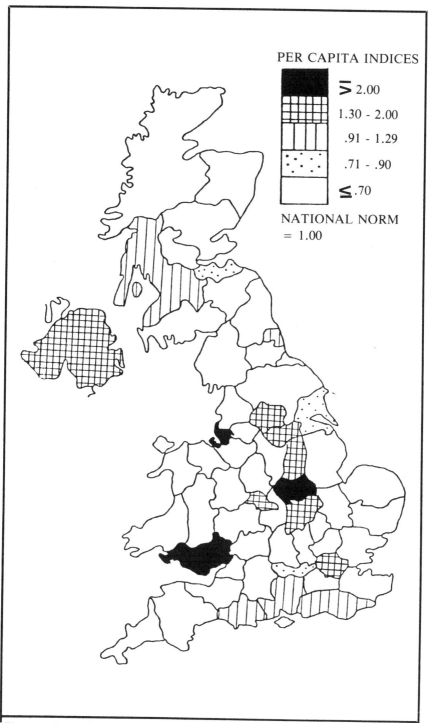

PER CAPITA INDICES

≥ 2.00
1.30 - 2.00
.91 - 1.29
.71 - .90
≤ .70

NATIONAL NORM
= 1.00

Figure 4. Per capita "production" of professional boxers. (Source of original data: Boxing News Annual, By Ibos Publications, 1979).

125

er is produced per 29,550 of the population (index 4•23) and in the contiguous counties of Gwent (3•43) Mid Glamorgan (2•79) and West Glamorgan (2•73). This confirms South Wales as having the dubious distinction of being the principal focus of professional boxer "production" in Britain. In England, Merseyside and Leicester (both 2•41) are the main centres, though a belt of contiguous counties stretching from West Yorkshire to Northampton all produce boxers at over one-and-a-third the national norm. The West Midlands (1•52) and Greater London (1•66) are other principal foci—indeed professional boxing is one of the few sports which the metropolis appears to emphasise above the national rate. Northern Ireland (1•71) is the final focus of boxer production, though the figure for Glasgow would certainly be above the national average if more disaggregated areal units had been used in Scotland.

Several other studies of the geography of top class sports participants have been undertaken. Extensive analyses of baseball, basketball and football player production in the USA are the best examples (Rooney, 1974). The production of professional footballers in Britain (Bale, 1979a) and of world class track and field athletes at a continental and global scale (Bale, 1981), are other examples. A more objective view of the relative strengths of east-west sport than is provided by the popular media was obtained by applying point biserial correlation to the association between per capita production of world class track and field athletes and whether they were from Eastern or Western Europe. No significant relationship was found to exist (Bale, 1979b). Elsewhere Weaver's method of combination analysis has been used to classify the nations of Europe into the categories of track and field events which best describe their athletic output (Bale, 1979c), In an Olympic Year which has been fraught with international conflict, it seems apposite to plead for greater involvement by geographers in the study of international sports. Indeed, the Olympic Games seem "to reflect the best and worst of the people-place tie which makes sport such a geographical phenomenon" (Rooney, 1974).

CONCLUSION

This paper has suggested that both recreational-participatory and commercial-consumer sports are of sufficient importance in modern society and of sufficient interest to students to justify inclusion in a geography curriculum. There can be few more widespread phenomena than sport which geographers have taken so long to start studying in depth. There is no particular paradigm or methodology for sports geography. Rather, the geographal interest in place, regions, movement, location, landscape and spatial injustice can all be applied in the context of sport. As such, fresh insights can be obtained into a subject which to date in academia, has been principally studied by those in disciplines other than ours.

Geographic studies of sport might contribute towards a more balanced curriculum and could be undertaken at all levels of the educational hierarchy. Alerting children to the geographical imbalance in one of their principal interests might be undertaken in the early years of schooling by focusing initially on sport in the local area and later adopting a national or even global perspective. The more subtle relationships between sports and regional culture, attempts to develop inductively derived generalisations about the spatial patterns in sport, and prescriptions for more geographically equitable allocation of sports facilities and resources, might complement such approaches. The growing number of Sports Studies courses (as parts of degree or diploma programmes in physical education or sports science) also need to include the geographical as well as other disciplinary approaches. Sport is a data-rich subject. Indeed, quantification may be regarded as one of the basic characteristics of modern sports (Guttman, 1978), and popular reference sources such as *Wisden, Rothman's Football Yearbook* and the annual handbooks of national sports organisations are mines of geographical information. As such, they provide sources for the illustration of numerous geographical principles and data for the exemplification of quantitative techniques in geography. A number of these have been referred to in this paper. Fieldwork and project work in the geography of sport also possess great potential. It is to be regretted that space has not permitted any consideration of the equally great potential in the physical geography of sport, a direction in which Thornes has begun to show the way (Thornes, 1977).

Pressure for an education for leisure is likely to increase in the nineteen-eighties and beyond. Where better to start developing teaching interests in leisure than in one of the most rapidly growing of the leisure industries—sport. As Loy put it, "studying sport is often as much fun as playing sport and on occasion just as serious" (Loy, 1975).

REFERENCES

Aldini, C. 1981 "A regression model for baseball franchise location forecasting," in J. Bale (ed.), *Geographical Perspectives on Sport*. London: Lepus Books.

Bale, J. R. 1978 "Geographical diffusion and the adoption of baseball in England and Wales'',
Geography, 63, pp. 138-97.

Bale, J. 1979a "The development of soccer as a participant and spectator sport: geographical aspects", *State of the Art Review*. London: Sports Council/SSRC.

Bale J. (1979b) "The Geography of European Athletics", *Sports Exchange World*, 3.

Bale, J. (1979c) "Track and field regions of Europe", *Physical Education Review*, 2, p. 2.

Bale, J. (1980) "Football clubs as neighbours", *Town and Country Planning*, 49, pp. 93-4.

Bale, J. (1981) "A geography of world class track and field athletes with special reference to the Third World," in Bale, J. (ed.), *Geographical Perspectives on Sport*. London: Lepus Books.

Bale, J. and Gowing, D. (1976) "Geography and football', *Teaching Geography Occasional Paper*, 28.

Baxter, M. J. (1979) "Measuring the benefits of recreational site provision", *State of the Art Review*. London Sports Council/SSRC.

Beddis, R. et al. (1974) *Geography for the Young School Leaver, 2, Man, Land and Leisure*. Sunbury-on-Thames: Nelson.

127

Buckley, G. B. (1935) *Fresh Light on Eighteenth Century Cricket.* Birmingham: Cotterell; and (1937) *Fresh Light on Pre-Victorian Cricket.* Birmingham: Cotterell. In compiling these inventories Buckley researched in no fewer than 29 museums, libraries or newspaper files from Carlisle to Maidstone. Buckley's findings are described and mapped in Bale, J., (1981) "Cricket in pre-Victorian England and Wales", *Area* (in press).

Caillois R. (1962) *Man, Play and Games.* London: Thames and Hudson.

Campbell, K. T. and Chen. D. S. (1976) "A minimum distance basketball scheduling problem," in Ladany, S. P., Machol, R. E. and Morrison, D. G. (eds.), *Management Science in Sports.* Amsterdam: North Holland Publishing House, pp. 15-25.

Central Statistical Office (1979) *Social Trends.* London: HMSO.

Cox, K. (1979) *Location and Public Problems.* Oxford: Blackwell, p. 213.

Demmert, H. G. (1973) *The Economics of Professional Team Sports.* Lexington, Mass.: Lexington Books.

Department of Education and Science (1968) *Report of the Committee on Football.* London: HMSO.

Ditchfield, P. H. (1891) *Old English Sports, Pastimes and Customs,* London: Methuen

Elson, M. J. (1979) "Countryside trip-making", *State of the Art Review.* London: Sports Council/SSRC.

Gale, F. (1871) *Echoes of Old Cricket Fields.* London: Simpkin Marshall, p. 14.

Goldbach, E. (1977) "Protestantism — Capitalism — Sports", *Journal for Sports History,* 4, pp. 285-94.

Guttmann, A. (1978) *From Ritual to Record: The Nature of Modern Sports.* New York: Columbia University Press.

Hagerstrand, T. (1966) "Quantitative techniques for the analysis of the spread of information and technology", in Anderson, C. A. and Bowman, M. J. (eds.), *Education and Economic Development.* London: Cass, pp. 244-80.

Hodgart, R. L. (1978) "Optimizing access to public services", *Progress in Human Geography,* 2, 1, p. 42.

Horn, C. J. (1975) *Playing Pitches in the Northern Region.* Durham: Northern Sports Council.

Lawson, H. A. and Morford, W. R. (1979) "Ideal typical models for sport", *Journal of Physical Education and Recreation,* 50, pp. 52-4.

Lipstyle, R. (1977) "Sportsworld revisited", *Journal of Sport and Social Issues,* 1, pp. 5-15.

Loy, J. (1975) "Foreword", in Ball, D. W. and Loy, J. (eds.). *Sport and Social Order: Contributions to the Sociology of Sport.* Reading, Mass.: Addison-Wesley, p. vii.

Martin, W. H. and Mason, S. (1979) "Broad patterns of leisure expenditure", *State of the Art Review.* London: Sports Council/SSRC.

Meinig, D. (1967) "Cultural geography", in *Introductory Geography: Viewpoints and Themes.* Association of American Geographers. Commission on College Geography. Publication 5, p. 97-103.

Paratore, E. (1976) "Pour une geographie du sport; aspects geographiques du football en Italie", in *23rd International Geographical Congress,* 6. Moscow: General Economic Geography.

Pillsbury, R. (1974) "Carolina Thunder: a geography of Southern stock car racing". *Journal of Geography, 73,* pp. 39-47.

Pycroft, J. (1922) *The Cricket Field.* London: St. James's Press, pp. 23 and 24. (First edition published in 1851.)

Rodgers, H. B. (1967 and 1969) *The Pilot National Recreation Survey.* British Travel Association, Keele University.

Rivett, P. (1975) "The structure of league football", *Operational Research Quarterly,* 26.

Rollin, J. (ed. 1979) *Rothman's Football Yearbook.* London: Queen Anne Press.

Rooney, J. (1974) *A Geography of American Sport: From Cabin Creek to Anaheim.* Reading, Mass.: Addison-Wesley. For migration patterns of other sports personnel see Loy, J. and Sage, G. (1978) "Georgaphical mobility patterns of college coaches", *Urban Life,* 7. pp. 253-74.

Rooney, J. (1975) "Sports from a geographic perspective", in Ball, D. W. and Loy, J. (eds.), *Sport and Social Order: Contributions to the Sociology of Sport.* Reading, Mass.: Addison-Wesley.

Sas, A. and Jones, J. (1976) "Mapping the action", *Journal of Geography, 75.* See also Bale and Gowing 1976, *op. cit.;* Darby, H. (1978) "An introduction to accessibility and leisure through local swimming pool provision", *Classroom Geographer.* March, pp. 22-24.

Sillitoe, K. (1969) *Planning for Leisure.* London: HMSO, pp. 243-44.

Thornes, J. (1977) "The effect of weather on sport", *Weather, 32,* pp. 258-69.

Tomasson, H. (1980) quoted in Price. C. "What makes Coe run?" *Sunday Times Magazine.* 10 February , p. 64.

Toyne, P. (1974) *Recreation and Environment.* London: Macmillan.

Trotsky, L. (1926) *Where is Britain Going?* London: Communist Party of Great Britain, quoted in Allison, L. (1975) "Association football and the urban ethos", *Stanford Journal of International Studies.* 13, pp. 203-28.

Veal, A. J. (1979) "Sport and recreation in England and Wales: an analysis of adult participation patterns in 1977", *Research Memorandum.* 74. University of Birmingham. Centre for Urban and Regional Studies.

"Wimbledon's money machine", *The Economist.* 271, 23rd June 1979, pp. 120-21.

Wiseman, N. (1977) "The economics of football', *Lloyd's Bank Review.* 123, pp. 29-43.

Zelinsky, W. (1973) *The Cultural Geography of the United States,* Englewood Cliffs: Prentice-Hall.

SECTION IV
ANTHROPOLOGY AND PHYSICAL ACTIVITY

WHAT IS ANTHROPOLOGY?

Anthropology has been broadly defined as "The Study of Man". The discipline is recognized as having four major subfields, namely: physical anthropology, archeology, cultural anthropology, and linguistic anthropology. Of these subfields, only cultural anthropology is regarded purely as a social science. In fact, cultural anthropology is often referred to as social anthropology. Cultural anthropology seeks to understand man's adaptation to, and his control of his social environment. Traditionally cultural anthropologists studied only non-literate and non-western societies, today however, these scientists are also investigating modern western society. Cultural anthropologists not only examine single cultures in depth (i.e., the intra-cultural approach), but also compare different cultures (i.e., the cross-cultural approach). In any case, anthropologists do not tamper (i.e., experiment) with the universe for fear that they might distort reality.

HOW ARE ANTHROPOLOGY AND PHYSICAL ACTIVITY RELATED?

For many years anthropologists have been very interested in such physical activities as play, games, sport and dance. For the most part this interest has been due more to a desire to learn about the culture in which the physical activities existed than to learn about the activities themselves. It appears inevitable that as interest increases in the latter relationship, such sub-disciplines as the anthropology of dance, the anthropology of play and the anthropology of sport will become more prominent. University courses dealing with topics within these sub-disciplines have existed since the late 1960s, however it wasn't until 1974 that a formal organization devoted to the scholarly study of the anthropological aspects of physical activity was established. This organization known as TAASP, The Association for the Anthropological Study of Play meets annually to present research papers relating anthropology to physical activity.

HOW WERE THE READINGS SELECTED FOR THIS SECTION?

The first article in this section which was written by Sutton-Smith was included in order to give the reader an overview of the relationships that exist between anthropology and physical activity. The article by Ager dealing with the Tununak Eskimos was included in order to provide an example of the intra-cultural method of study whereas the article by Roberts, Arth and Bush demonstrates the cross-cultural approach.

131

The Study of Games *

AN ANTHROPOLOGICAL APPROACH

Brian Sutton-Smith
Columbia University
New York — U.S.A.

At the 1973 meeting of the American Anthropological Association, in a symposium on play and games, Margaret Mead presented the opinion that from any worthwhile scientific point of view, anthropologists had never really studied the subject. There were a few records here and there of high quality, there were the many accounts in the Human Relations Area Files, but in general, these records did not tell you how play and games were functioning in the lives of the players. The data was too cursory to allow of any very clear interpretations in most cases.

Unfortunately, although there has been more activity on this subject, in psychology, the interpretation might well be the same. For both cases, I think there are at least two reasons. First, there has been the general neglect in social science of the expressive and non serious subject-matters, a neglect there is now some signs will be remedied. Secondly, there is the inherent difficulty in studying these subject matters. They tend to be ephemeral. They tend more easily to freeze under observations. Thirdly, they are related to the rest of life in ways we are not easily able to understand. Because of our work oriented way of life which makes us see the world in characteristic ways, it seems particularly difficult for us to generate a theoretical framework which is appropriate to play. In the face of play we are like anthropologists in a strange place, with a strange group and in a state of culture shock.

In our book, *The Study of Games,* Eliot Avedon and I reviewed the major work of the early anthropologists (Avedon & Sutton-Smith, 1971), in particular the work of Tylor and Culin who used games as a part of their larger arguments over cultural diffusion versus the independent invention of cultural traits. In the same book we demonstrated that early folklorists also used games in a similar tendentious way believing that through games scientists could reconstruct the character of early history. The names of the

Opening address to the 4th International HISPA Seminar, Leuven, Belgium, April 1, 1975. Prepared with the support of a grant from the National Institute of Education, "The Enculturation of the Imagination in Early Childhood," = NE - 9 - 00 -3 - 0133.

*Sutton-Smith, B. The study of games: An Anthropological approach in R. Renson et al (Ed's.). Proceedings of the 4th International Seminar on the History of Sport and Physical Education, Leuven, Belgium, 1976. Reprinted by permission of the publisher.

American Scholar, William Newall, and the British folklorist Gomme, are remembered in this light. Even the more recent British folklorists Peter and Iona Opie, give us a version of the same notion, when they say that although games may not be used to reconstruct the past, they can at least be used to show the continuity with the past. They say. "From this point of view the study of games remains important, not for the purpose of reconstructing history, but for the purpose of illustrating the continuity of human nature" (Avedon & Sutton-Smith, 1971, p. 161). Let me say of the Opies that their interest in what they term "Child Life and Literature" to which they devote almost every day of both their lives is a totally admirable preoccupation. Their home in England is a most impressive library of everything associated with children in the history of recent centuries. More than anyone else I know they seem to realize that the changing treatment of children is a focal point for understanding the history of civilization.

But, my point here, is that like Tylor and Gomme, they perpetuate the notion that there is one language of play and games, and that we can understand what that language is, simply by putting those plays and games on record. If we could actually achieve such a goal, then Margaret Mead's skeptical review of the facts, would be out of order. But, of course, she is right. All these esteemed scholars, were not really concerned with play and games, they were concerned with other more important and serious subject-matters (such as diffusion). They were neglecting play at the very moment it was being studied. While this is a less fair charge to bring against the Opies, it still holds true. Although their focus is more completely on play and games, their functional assumptions lead to the same result. Because they take their human nature for granted, they, in effect, always study text without also studying context. So we never really do know how or what these plays mean to those that use them. We have the record of play and games they provide, but little insight into what they mean to the players, which is Mead's point about the anthropological literature on the subject.

It is not my business here to deal with The Psychology of Play, but in the book *Child's Play* (with R. E. Herron, Wiley, 1971), I came to very similar conclusions. The collections of children's play and games in the early part of this century were meant to be illustrations of the necessary stages through which children must go. They were meant to indicate facts about human evolution. In the nineteen thirties, most of the study of play had to do with the management of the kindergarten. Who plays with blocks, who plays with sand? Do children fight more or less when they have play apparatus? In the psychoanalytic studies of play, which constitute the largest body (if we take doll play therapy and diagnosis into account) of play studies in any subject-matter, play is conceived of as a projection of those other more important human subjects, aggression, eroticism, dependency, anality and the like. Here we have context without text. The play is studied to tell us once again only about human nature that is not play. This time not about diffusion, evolution, nor management, but about human conflict. Actually, there is probably more information about the way play functions in human nature in this body of material than there is anywhere else. But the problem is, one cannot always tell with those who write about play diagnosis and therapy, which of their intuitions are brilliant insights and which are simply their own projections. When the theory of play as projection is confused with the projections of the theorist as player, the rest of us must necessarily be a little uncertain about the conclusions that are offered. In the more recent studies of play as a cognitive or a voluntary behavior, there continues (I have argued) to be a reduction of play to cognitive structures on the one hand or exploratory behaviors on the other (care of Child's Play, Wiley 1971, Section 8). Once again, we are not able to focus on play without using it as an illustration of something else that is more important, although I would hasten to point out that I think the increasing intensity of this circumjacent activity is having a cumulative effect on our knowledge. When you look at those who give us only text (like the Opies and the folklorists) and those who give us only context, (like most psychologists) some glimmering of the relations between both begins to emerge.

In *The Study of Games,* Avedon and I suggested that the new studies of Roberts and others, that is, the cross cultural studies of games represented a new start in the anthropology of play. And while this was certainly true on an empirical level, because much new information was added, one has to question whether any real breakthrough was accomplished on a theoretical level, or whether Roberts, myself and others, didn't simply serve once more to reduce games to some other more important functions and in so doing have the subject-matter elude us once more. Let me briefly review what we did achieve in our studies (Sutton-Smith, 1973).

The Roberts-Sutton Smith Studies. These studies show:

1. That in cross-cultural studies there are hundreds of statistically significant associations between the presence of games and other cultural variables.

2. Different types of games (strategy, chance, physical skill and central person) have different patterns of association. There are also patterns associated with the absence of games and with the presence of more types of games.

3. The cultural variables with which associations have been made include child training variables, economic, technological, political and sociological variables.

These are, in brief, the major cross cultural findings. The interpretations from the more simple to the more complex are as follows:

1. That games are in some way functionally related to culture. They are not trivial or unessential or random.

2. That more complex cultures have more complex games and more types of games and that these various associations are merely an index of general complexity (cultures with no competitive games are very simple, cultures with all types are the most complex). This argument has been amplified by Don Ball of the University of British Columbia, Vancouver (Ball, 1971).

3. That there are meaningful structural relationships between each type of game and its patterns of association. Thus chance is linked with responsibility, divination, nomadic habits and economic uncertainty; physical skill is linked with the tropics and hunting; central person games are linked with independence training and marriage.

4. That the way to explain the linkages both with child training variables and cultural variables is in terms of the conflict enculturation hypothesis, which says, that conflict engendered by child training procedures (one is both rewarded and punished for interest in certain behaviors) leads to a readiness to be aroused by symbolic systems (games) which configure the conflict (in their role reversals). Involvement over times in these rewarding game patterns, leads to mastery of behaviors which have functional value (that is, transfer) to culturally useful behavior.

5. That the way to prove this pattern of hypotheses is to show that the same patterns hold within our own culture as were to be found cross-culturally in the original studies (sub-system replication). Studies of adult preferences for games, and of children's play appear to provide support for the original patterns of relationships. See, in particular, the studies of Tick Tack Toe in *The Folkgames of Children*. (Sutton-Smith, 1973).

6. That the way the enculturation aspect of this thesis occurs, is through the games acting as models of cultural power relationships, that is, those involving strategy, chance, force or arbitrary status. Studies of the character of power in games when compared with the exercise of power in the family, suggest that there is no simple parallel between the two spheres, although factor analytic studies of such family power do yield some factors that are interpretable as strategy, force and chance (These studies are described in Sutton-Smith and Rosenberg, 1971, chapter 4).

Now let me return to my original point about most of the work in anthropology, and psychology, that it is a study of context without much reference to text. These studies of mine with Roberts are susceptible to the same criticism. What is textual here, are the determinants of outcome (strategy, chance, etc.). That is all we have to say about games. What is contextual are the asserted relationships about psychogenic and sociogenic correlates. We are saying like Durkheim or Malinowski, that games don't exist randomly in the structural fabric, they are there for a cultural purpose. As models of power, they replicate the larger systems of power of which they are a part and serve their purpose within these, as buffered training systems, to use our phrase. To say this, is to subordinate the game to the larger system. Granted we make it more than the sort of ephemera that the word "projection" implies. Our acquaintance with the vigour of play in the cross cultural materials saves us from that. We put more life into play as the notions of miniature power systems and buffered models suggest, and we do imply that they are larger systems for learning. But still, even so, we make them an echo of the larger systems. Our games are systems for the socialization of conflict, as I have recently argued, and the socialization of power, as we argued earlier (Sutton-Smith, 1974).

What has been occurring recently within sociology and anthropology, and has existed for a long time within literature, is the realization that these minor cultural systems such as games, and more obviously novels, do not exist simply to socialize members into the normative systems of the culture of which they are a part. On the contrary, the very nature of many of these systems is to challenge, even to reverse the systems of which they are a part. This thesis was taken up in a two part seminar of the American Anthropological Association in 1973 entitled "Forms of Symbolic Aversion." (Babcock-Abrahams, in press). Here there was a study of the role of the trickster in folklore, of the fool at court, of the role of festivals such as the Mardi Gras, of inversion within ritual in simple cultures, of reversals in the alienated groups of hippies. addicts and communes, of reversals in sex groups in all their current variety and finally, of reversals in leisure, including a study of my of my own of what I have called games of order and disorder (Sutton-Smith, in press).

GAMES OF ORDER AND DISORDER

What all the investigators were concerned with within these papers was to attempt to understand the role of such inversions in culture. By and large these phenomena were pictured as anti-structure set off in a compensatory or cathartic relationship to the rest of the culture, a point of view originally (but no longer) taken by Victor Turner in his outstanding work on these problems *Ritual Process* (1969). I took the view that these phenomena could also be considered as proto structure (that is, as a source of new culture. To quote: "The normative structure represents the working equilibrium, the anti-structure represents the latest system of potential alternatives from which novelty will arise when contingencies in the normative system require it. We might more correctly call this second system the proto cultural system because it is the precursor of innovative-normative forms. It is the source of new culture."

To briefly summarize my argument there, it was that the anomalous class of pastimes if considered in conflict terms, could be viewed as a set of oppositions between order and disorder, between anarchy and chaos. That these pastimes were in effect games, in which the players did not compete with each other, but with the forces of chaos. That children between the ages of three and six years are preoccupied with such games. That there are four stages in their development (1) games in which all act in concert and then collapse (Ring-a-Ring-a-Roses; Hand holding and winding up and out amongst the Trobrianders) (Malinowski, 1929). (2) One or more players has a central role in bringing about the collapse (Poor Pussy; Jack-a-Balan) usually by causing them to laugh by absurd mimicry, etc. (3) There is a co-ordinated series of actions leading to a climax of chaos (Consequences, My Aunt Went to Paris). (4) Actions are co-ordinated towards the downfall of a central figure (King of the Golden Sword; Queen of Sheba). This series 1-4 covers the age levels in order from about four years to fourteen. There are many examples in the Human Relaions Area Files from all culture areas, but insufficient to use in any statistical sense. They have been, by and large, just too ephemeral for anthropologists and others to note seriously. They are, however, just one part of a more general concern with chaos, tumult, and vertigo in mankind's leisure, first focussed for us, I believe by Roger Callois is his *Man, Play and Games* (1961), and exampled by all the arts of clowning, acrobatics, fun fair vertigo, danger, hazard, and dizziness with which we are familiar in the worlds of play and entertainments.

In my analysis of these and other games I suggested various ways in which role inversions could occur, and thus provide the player with a novel experience (rather than simply with a replication of cultural experience). First, each player gets a turn at roles he may not get usually. Most cultural relationships are asymmetrical. Most game relationships are symmetrical. They model equality of turn taking, where life does not. There is more reversibility of roles in games than is to be found in the normative structure. Dominant persons tend to hold on to their dominance in everyday affairs. What is usually inverted, therefore, is not the cultural dimensions (success or failure) but access to the roles within them. At least that is true for competitive games which both model power relationships as we said, but give leeway of access to these where that does not always exist elsewhere. Secondly, however, games of order and disorder are a special case, because they model the system only to destroy it. Their ambivalence is much more fundamental. They are both the most fundamental form of games (establishing for the young the roots of co-operation) and the most radical (upsetting the orders of motor, conventional impulse and social hierarchical control). Thirdly, all games provide a great deal of leeway within any given role, for tactical variations and innovation. There are always new ways to be more strategic, to deceive or to cheat. These may be minuscule in the larger scale of the game, but they are indeed often reversals of the usual procedures for life and not unsuggestive of the way things might be done differently.

So in sum we have in games behavior in which conventional roles are mocked (the games of order and disorder), we have in games an unconventional access to roles, and we have in games access to novelty within role. All of which I would contend could be seeds of potential novelty for the larger society, which is a thesis in the interpretation of play to which I will return shortly.

THE SIX CULTURES STUDIES

It was always my hope that the extensive work of John and Beatrice Whiting would ultimately provide us with sufficiently convincing evidence on children's play and games that we might finally begin to get some idea of how we might resolve the various issues of cultural replication and reversal in play and games. It does not look as if it will do this, although there are some important relationships to be found there. The work on the Nyansongo of Kenya, for example, shows that in cultures where the children are an important cog in a fragile economic machine, there is little scope for them to play. The major job for these children is herding the cattle. It is reported that "fantasy play is almost non existent among these children"

137

(1963, p. 173). All that was observed was some fairly desultory physical play such as blocking streams and swimming, climbing trees, shooting birds with slings, fighting with each other, tussling, chasing and exchanging blows, watching cars on the roads. This is consistent with the studies of Dina Feitelson who reports that in the carpet weaving cultures of the Middle East where children are an economic asset, they also begin early in direct imitation of adult activity and do not indulge greatly in what you or I might call play (1974). The studies of Sarah Smilansky of hierarchical cultural groups in Israel are of similar importance (1967). This does not mean that all relatively simple cultures do not play, because the records of play amongst Australian aboriginal groups are very extensive. What seems to be critical is whether or not the adults have a direct economic need to train the children in highly normalized means of survival. In such cultures the "work ethic" makes real sense. The adults know what must be done to survive and they cannot afford the wasted time of child play. Children are an important cog in the machine. The same position prevailed in England in the early half of the nineteenth century when pauperism was widespread and young children were exploited in mines and factories as a necessary way of helping each family to survive. The Australian aborigines have an open ended environment for their children. There is much they can teach but much also the child must learn through self reliance, including the fact that he must deal with novel circumstances. Play seems to be most relevant in such "open" societies, and much less relevant in "closed" ones. It has more value for foragers than for tillers.

Even within complex societies when there is more leeway for the children to roam about and choose their own companions, then there seems to be more play activity. In the Whiting's study when the Taira of Okinawa are compared with the even more culturally complex Rajputs of India whose children are restricted to sibling play in backyards, the former show much more activity. The Taira have tag, marbles, rope jumping, races, team chasing, houses, robbers and peddlers, kick the can, hopscotch, ball bouncing, tip cat, marbles, wrestling and prisoner's base; whereas the Rajputs have much less: the imitation of parent cooking or farming, dolls, small toy models, bows and arrows, hoops, wagon grinders and scales, plus some chasing and seesaw.

Nevertheless, as a society gets to be more complex, there are more problems, more novel contingencies which must be managed, so not surprisingly the more complex cultural groups in the Whiting sudy (USA, India, Okinawa), exhibit more types of play than the less complex groups (Mexico, Philippine and African). One can manage this in the simplistic terms of arousal theory and say, that novelty prompts exploratory activity. And then add the recent findings that more exploratory activity is usually followed by more play. Or we can break it down as we did in the cross cultural studies, showing what sorts of games go with what sorts of complexity; or suggest as I have more recently that there are certain varieties of play which are relevant to certain types of cultural problems. Thus there is exploratory play, imitative play, testing play and constructive play and there are the social

138

forms of sociodrama, contesting, and make-believe (1971). It is possible to look at, say, the aborigines and see that most of their play involves exploration and testing; whereas in a symbolic and achievement oriented civilization like ours, most play involves make-believe and contesting. It is my opinion that future research in the anthropology of play will go further along these lines into the careful specification of types of play and the type or subset of the cultural system to which it is related either directly or inversely.

There are some other possible differences between the society with the most observed play in the Whiting study (the Taira of Okinawa) and the society with the least observed play (the Nyansongo of Kenya), and these are worth mentioning as leads to future research. The family unit in Taira is nuclear, there are private courtyards (so privacy is possible), children can wander in an open and friendly society of other children, they meet more children who are not their kin, there is a school and there are competitive games at the school, there is more interaction with the father, there are more outsiders in the playgroups, children under five are seldom given chores, they do not have to look after younger children to any extent, there are various specialized buildings such as shops, etc., children are self assertive. In the Nyansongo by contrast where subsistence agriculture prevails the children must help with the work, they must help with the care of the younger children. Under the mother's control they help with many chores, getting fuel, cooking. They are members of an extended family and they are discouraged from leaving their immediate home environment. There is no school and no organized play (there is some dirt throwing and roughhousing by boys). There is little interaction with the father. They are very much under the mother's control and dominance. These are all interesting contrasts. It is simply not possible yet for us to know which of these variables is intrinsic to the difference in play, and which merely an accidental associate. Intuition suggests the complexity, the play groups, the privacy, the father stimulation, the lack of chores might all be important contributors.

TEXT AND CONTEXT IN THE STUDY OF GAMES

What I have been leading to in all this is an attempt to rethink the questions of text and context that were raised in the introduction. The Roberts cross-cultural studies provided empirical evidence of a relationship between a conflict in context (specifically in child training) and the character of the text (strategy, chance). The study of games of order and disorder was meant to show that it is possible to see a direct relationship between the character of the conflict in context (anarchy and chaos) and the character of the dialectic in the game itself (order and disorder). The Whiting studies were reviewed to show that games replicate society (complexity in one is matched by complexity in the other), but also that more games occur where there is more leeway and less stringent control within that society. That is games require both the stimulus of complexity to expand but also the scope of protected freedom.

By and large interpretations of these relationships in this society have been of an integrative character. Theorists have been concerned to show that games played a socializing role in society. They contributed to co-operation, character, achievement etc. One can see this "conservative" interpretation as an historically important rehabilitation of games after centuries of ideological neglect. But it would be wrong to see games only in this contextual way. What I am implying is that while it may well be true that the conflicts in games mirror those in the larger society, they permit a flexibility about those conflicts which is not a typical part of the larger society. That is, there is conflict, or dialectics or reversibility which are all different ways of talking about the matter, both in text and context, but each functions differently in its own system.

Conflicts in context, such as achievement conflicts have a very definite functional end in view in the larger society. But conflicts in text, as in the game, aim to reproduce, buffer, model and abstract those other conflicts while conferring on the players a new flexibility, versatility of leeway with respect even to those conflicts. My suggestion for future research therefore is that we try to specify more explicitly the forms of reversibility to be found in each type of game (text) and in the process of game life interaction (intersect), as well as the parallel irreversibilities within life itself (context) with the aim of studying these patterns of interrelationships more explicitly.

SUMMARY
The Study of Games: an anthropological approach.

B. SUTTON-SMITH

Historical approaches to the study of games are reviewed and their attention to game structure (text) or causal influences (context) is evaluated. It is contended that attention to text alone (folklore and recreation) has oversimplified their diversity of human play and games, and that attention to context alone (psychology and anthropology) has devalued the phenomena itself. The empirical cross cultural studies of Roberts and Sutton-Smith are reviewed as they allow for both diversity of text and causal setting. The concept of "reversibility" is presented as a key conceptual term for understanding these text and context relationships and this is illustrated through an analyis of games of order and disorder. Varieties of reversal within games are discussed and the cross cultural materials of Whiting et al. are examined for indications of context relationships. (Author's summary.)

ZUSAMMENFASSUNG
Das Studium der Spiele: Eine anthropologische Betrachtung.

B SUTTON-SMITH

Historische Annaherungen uber das Studium der Spiele wurden uberarbeitet und man lenkte die aufmerksamkeit auf die Struktur (Text) der Spiele oder auf die kausalen Einflusse (Zusammenhang). Die Aufmerksamkeit auf den Text allein (in de Folklore und Entspannung) hat die Mannigfaltigkeit menschlicher Spiele zu sehr vereinfacht und die Aufmerksamkeit nur auf den Zusammenhang (in der Psychologie und Anthropologie) hat das Phanomen selbst entwertet. Das empirische cross-kulturelle Studium von Roberts und Sutton-Smith ist heir in Betracht genommen da sie es elauben die Manigfaltigkeit des Textes wie auch den Kausalen Zusammenhang zu betonen. Der Begriff der "Umkehrbarkeit" ist als ein Schlosselbegriff fur das Verstandnis dieser Relation zwischen Text und Zusammenhang dargestellt was anhand einer Analyse der Spiele veranschaulicht wird. Mannigfaltigkeit und Umkehrbarkeit innerhalb der Spiele werden diskutiert und die cross-kulturellen Materialien von Whiting und anderen wurden auf Anweisungen des Zusammenhangverhaltnisses hin untersucht.

REFERENCES

Avedon, E. & Sutton-Smith, B. (Eds.), *The study of games,* New York, John Wiley & Sons, 1971.

Babcock-Abrahams, B. (Ed.), *The reversible world-essays on symbolic inversion,* Cornell University, in press.

Ball, D., *Skills, Strategy and Chance: The scaling of gaming.* (University of Victoria, British Columbia) Paper presented to the 3rd International Symposium on the Sociology of Sport, Waterloo, Ontario, August, 1971.

Caillois, R., *Man, Play and Games,* Glencoe, Free Press, 1961.

Culin, S., A review of his work is presented in: Avedon, E M. & B. Sutton-Smith (Eds.), *o.c.,* 55-62.

Feitelson, D., & Ross, G. S., The neglected facts — Play. *Human Development,* XVI (1973), 202-223.

Gomme, A. B., *Traditional games of England, Scotland and Ireland,* London, Nutt, 1894 & 1898, 2 vol. — Cit. in: Avedon, M. E. & B. Sutton-Smith (Eds.), *o.c.,* 159-166.

Herron, R. E. & Sutton-Smith, B., *Childs Play,* New York, John Wiley & Sons, 1971.

Malinowski, B., *The sexual life of savages,* New York, Harcourt, Brace & World, 1929.

Newell, W. W., *Games and songs of American children,* New York, Harper Brothers, 1883. Republished with an introduction by Carl Withers, New York, Dover Publications, Inc. 1963. — Cit. in: Avedon, E. M. & B. Sutton-Smith (Eds.), *o.c.,* 159-166.

Opie, P. & Opie, I., The tentacles of tradition. *The advancement of science,* XX (1963-1964), p. 10 — Cit. in: Avedon, E. M. & B. Sutton-Smith (Eds.), *o.c.,* 159-166.

Opie, P. & Opie, I., *The languages and lore of schoolchildren,* London, Oxford, University Press, 1959. — Cit. in: Avedon, E. M. & B. Sutton-Smith (Eds.), *o.c.,* 159-166.

Smilansky, S., *The effect of sociodramatic play on disadvantaged preschool children,* New York, John Wiley & Sons, 1968.

Salter, M. A., *Games and Pastimes of the Australian Aboriginal,* Eugene Oregon, Microcard Publications, 1967.

Sutton-Smith, B., *The Folkgames of Children,* Austin, University of Texas, 1972.

Sutton-Smith, B., Children at Play. *Natural History,* LXXX (1971), 54-59.

Sutton-Smith, B., Play as the mediation of novelty (pp. 557-561) and "Games as the socialization of conflict" (pp. 70-75). In: Ommo Grupe (Ed.), Sport in the modern world. *Chances and problems,* Berlin, Springer, 1973.

Sutton-Smith, B., Play as adaptive potentiation. *Sportwissenschaft,* V (1975), 103-118.

Sutton-Smith, B., Games of Order and Disorder, a chapter in: *The Dialectics of Play,* Munich (in press).

Turner, V., *Ritual Process,* New York, Aldine, 1969.

Games in Culture*

John M. Roberts
Cornell University
Malcolm J. Arth
Harvard University
Robert R. Bush
University of Pennsylvania

Recreational activities have been classic ethnographic concerns, and sophisticated questions about the distributions of games were asked early in the history of anthropology.[1] Still, the science has yet to produce a general theory which deals with such anthropological problems as the description and explanation of the historical development of games, their world distribution, and their functional significance in various societies. This paper suggests a line of inquiry which might lead to the construction of such a theory.

In the extensive ethnographic literature on the subject, a wide range of recreational activites has been called "games," but this general category is too broad for the purposes of this article. Here, a game is defined as a recreational activity characterized by: (1) organized play, (2) competition, (3) two or more sides, (4) criteria for determining the winner, and (5) agreed-upon rules. Other recreational activities which do not satisfy this definition, such as noncompetitive swimming, top-spining, and string-figure making, are considered "amusements". It is relevant to note that most games reported in the ethnographies are activites in which adults can particpate.

The games of the world may be classified in terms of distinctive patterns of play. Some outcomes are determined primarily by the physical abilities of the players, some by a series of moves, each of which represents a player's choice among alternatives, and others either by nonrational guesses or by reliance on the operation of some mechanical chance device such as a die; some are determined by combinations of these patterns. All these ways of determining outcomes are widely distributed among the societies of the world, and it is therefore possible to offer the following general classification of games: (1) physical skill, (2) strategy, and (3) chance.

Each of these three categories requires further definition. Games of

* Roberts, J. M., Arth, M. J., and Bush, R. R. "Games in Culture," *American Anthropologist,* Vol. 61, 1959, pp. 597-605. Reprinted by permission of the publisher.

physical skill as herein defined must involve the use of physical skill, but may or may not involve strategy or chance; examples are marathon races, prize fights, hockey, and the hoop and pole games. In games of strategy, physical skill must be absent and a strategy must be used; chance may or may not be involved. Chess, go, poker, and the Ashanti game of *wari* are examples. Finally, games of chance are so defined that chance must be present and both physical skill and strategy must be absent; examples are high card wins, dice games, and the moccasin games. We should note that there are three defining attributes for games of chance (chance, strategy, and physical skill), two for games of strategy (strategy and physical skill) and one for games of physical skill (physical skill).

Games of each type are widely but unevenly distributed. Although we did not conduct a comprehensive survey, data on games were sought both from the literature and from the Cross-Cultural Survey files[2] on approximately 100 tribes. These tribes displayed a wide geographical distribution and great cultural variability, but they did not represent either a stratified sample or a random sample of the tribes of the world; the recorded materials on games were so uneven that this was impossible.

In 82 instances the tribal literature contained some information on games. In the literature on 19 tribes explicit statements were found that either a complete description of the games was being given or that no games existed. We refer to these tribes as well-covered: Baiga, Chagga, Chukchee, Copper Eskimo, Hopi, Kababish, Lepcha, Lesu, Macheyenga, Menomini, Murngin, Nauru, Siriono, Siwa, Tanala, Wapishana, Warrau, Yaruro, and Zuni. With 31 additional societies, it was inferred either from similar reports by independent observers or from the extensive treatment by a single writer that the descriptions were intended to be complete. We refer to these tribes as apparently well-covered: Achewa, Ainu, Aleut, Alor, Arikara, BaVenda, Bena, Buka, Dahomey, Euahlayi, Gros Ventre, Jukun, Kansa, Kiwai, Korea, Kwakiutl, Lakher, Lamba, Malekula, Maricopa, Masai, Mbundu, Navaho, Papago, Rwala Bedouin, Sema Naga, Vietnam, Witoto, Woleaian, Yap, and Yungar. The materials on the remaining societies were inadequate; although games were noted in some of them, there was no reason to infer that the descriptions were complete. It is plain that while widespread interest in games can be easily documented, the systematic description of all the games played by the members of a tribe is by no means common in the ethnographic literature.

Among the 50 tribes that were either well-covered or apparently well-covered, 19 had games of strategy, 19 had games of chance, and 44 had games of physical skill. Five were reported as having no games at all. It is clear that games, as here defined, are widely distributed, but that no single type is universal.

Games occur so widely that it is an easy inference that they meet general human needs. They are integrated into tribal cultures in many ways. For example, in some societies games are linked with religion; elsewhere, they are associated with hunting or war. The relationships between games and needs of any single society must be complex and generalizations about

143

them cannot be made easily, but consideration of two general characteristics of all games points the way toward further inquiry. These are the expressive and the model characteristics.

The expressive character of games is plain. They do not directly satisfy the biological need associated with survival. There are few obvious environmental and technological limitations on them. Indeed, the artifacts for most games can be made by people with quite simple technologies. Go, a Japanese game of strategy, requires only two sets of "stones" and a rectangular board on which 19 equidistant lines are drawn parallel to one edge and 19 lines at right angles to them. This simple equipment could easily be duplicated by almost any group, but the game itself is equal in complexity to any in the world. Everything suggests that games are expressive, much as are folk tales, dramatic productions, music, and paintings. If such is the case, games should be related to other expressive behavior, some of which has already been explored cross-culturally.

Table 1. Distribution of Game Types in Fifty Societies

Societies	Number of Societies	Physical Skill	Chance	Strategy
Achewa, Aleut, Chagga, Hopi, Korea, Nauru, Vietnam, Zuni	8	+	+	+
BaVenda, Jukun, Lakher, Lamba, Masai, Mbundu, Tanala, Woleaian, Yap	9	+	−	+
Dahomey	1	−	+	+
Siwa	1	−	−	+
Baiga, Chukchee, Copper Eskimo, Gros Ventre, Kansa, Kwakiutl, Maricopa, Menomini, Navaho, Papago	10	+	+	−
Ainu, Alor, Arikara, Bena, Buka, Euahlayi, Kiwai, Lesu, Macheyenga, Malekula, Rwala Bedouin, Sema Naga, Siriono, Wapishana, Witoto, Yungar	16	+	−	−
Kababish, Lepcha, Murngin, Warrau, Yaruro	5	−	−	−

It is also evident that most games are models of various cultural activities. Many games of physical skill simulate combat or hunting, as in boxing and competitive trap shooting. Games of strategy may simulate chase, hunt, or war activities, as in backgammon, fox and geese, or chess. The relationship between games of chance and divining (ultimately a religious activity) is well known. In instances where a game does not simulate a current cultural activity, it will be found that the games ancestral to it were more clearly models. The characteristics of such models have not been systematically studied, but they are related to problems in abstract thought and cognitive mapping.

If games are expressive models, they should be related to other aspects of culture and to the variables which figure in expressive or projective mechanisms. More specifically, games of strategy which are models of social interaction should be related to the complexity of the social system; games of chance which are models of interaction with the supernatural should be linked with other expressive views of the supernatural; and there is a possibility that games of physical skill may be related to aspects of the natural environment. This paper examines these possibilities in the hope of stimulating further inquiry.

GAMES OF STRATEGY

Games of strategy do appear to be models of social interactive systems. Chess, for example, as described in an early classic,

. . . must be classed as a game of war. Two players direct a conflict between two armies of equal strength upon a field of battle, circumscribed in extent, and offering no advantage of ground to either side (Murray 1913: 25).

The role structure of the two "armies" is quite complex. Both the structure and the terminology of such a game of strategy may offer clues to the nature of the interactive system it represents. Pieces are called "men"; they capture or kill, they attact or defend, they race, and so on.

Table 2. System Complexity and Games of Strategy

		Games of Strategy Present	Games of Strategy Absent
Low Political Integration	Social Classes Absent	3 (Hopi, Woleaian, Zuni)	13 (Baiga, Copper Eskimo, Kiwai, Lesu, Murngin, Navaho, Papago, Siriono, Wapishana, Warrau, Witoto, Yaruro, Yungar)
	Social Classes Present	2 (Aleut, Nauru)	5 (Alor, Buka, Chukchee, Kwakiutl, Malekula)
High Political Integration	Social Classes Absent	2 (Achewa, Masai)	4 (Ainu, Gros Ventre, Maricopa, Menomini)
	Social Classes Present	12 (BaVenda, Chagga, Dahomey, Jukun, Korea, Lakher, Lamba, Mbundu, Siwa, Tanala, Vietnam, Yap)	2 (Kababish, Rwala Bedouin)

145

Let us consider the hypothesis, then, that since games of strategy simulate social systems, those systems should be complex enough to generate such needs for expression. Simple societies should not possess games of strategy and should resist borrowing them.

In his world sample, G.P. Murdock provided various ratings on 565 tribes (Murdock 1957). Two of his ratings — on levels of political integration, and on levels of social stratification — may be used as indices of social system complexity. Some of Murdock's ratings were combined to produce the breakdown shown on Table 2. The ratings "No political integration" and "Autonomous local communties" were classed as low political integration; "Minimal states," "Little states," and "States" were classed as high political integration. The categories "Absent," "Formal age groups," and "Wealth distinctions," were classed as social stratification absent. "Hereditary aristocracy" and "Complex stratification" were classed as social stratification present. Forty-three of the 50 tribes found to be adequately covered in our study received ratings on these two dimensions. The results given below confirm the expected relationship between games of strategy and social complexity, but this relationship does not hold for games of chance and physical skill.

With political integration, 52 tribes supported the hypothesis while 11 did not. With social classes, 31 tribes fitted the hypothesis and 12 did not. Among societies with either low political integration and no social classes or high political integration and social classes, 25 societies supported the hypothesis and five did not.

The association between games of strategy and complexity of social organization is supported also by the fact that among the adequately-covered tribes, the four hunting and gathering groups lacked games of strategy, only one out of five fishing groups had such a game, and only one out of three pastoral groups. On the other hand, no truly complex society appears to have lacked them.

Table 2 does not list the most complex American tribes, but among the inadequately-covered tribes, games of strategy were reported for the Aztec, Inca, Ashanti, and Tiv. According to Murdock, three of these tribes were politically integrated and socially stratified, but the Tiv had local autonomy and incipient social stratification with slavery. The presence of the Aztec and Inca in this group would indicate that the hypothesis also holds for the New World.

A few cases are worthy of special note. In Africa, the Bushmen do not have a game of strategy and the Hottentot do. The Tanala may be divided into two distinct groups, one of which is hierarchically organized while the other is not, and of these only the first has a game of strategy.[3]

GAMES OF CHANCE

Unlike games of strategy, games of chance appear to be associated with religious activities. It is commonly thought by many peoples that the winners of games of chance have received supernatural or magical aid. Even in the European tradition, religious beliefs conditioned views of games of chance:

The Greeks and the Romans (so far as one can make summary statements about races whose members held such differing views) seem, on the whole, to have regarded the world as partly determined by chance. Gods and goddesses had influence over the course of events and, in particular, could interfere with the throwing of dice; but they were only higher beings with superhuman powers, not omnipotent entities who controlled everything. And the vaguer deities — Fortuna, the Fates, and Fate itself — appear to modern eyes more in the retributive role of a personified guilty conscience than as masters of the universe. The situation was radically changed by Christianity. For the early fathers of the Church, the finger of God was everywhere. Some causes were overt and some were hidden, but nothing happened without cause. In that sense, nothing was random and there was no chance . . . Thomas Aquinas, arguing that everything is subject to the providence of God, mentions explicitly the objection that, if such were the case, hazard and luck would disappear . . . He reflected the spirit of his age, wherein God and an elaborate hierarchy of His ministers controlled and foreordained the minutest happening; if anything seemed to be due to chance that was our ignorance, not the nature of things (Kendall 1956: 11).

Although games of chance, as found over the world, are "fair" games, perhaps as a result of long trial and error, explicit theories of chance do not appear in primitive cultures. Again and again, outcomes are attributed to the intervention of magical or supernatural forces.

Table 3. Frequency of Benevolence and Aggression by Gods, and Games of Chance

		Games of Chance Absent	Games of Chance Present
Benevolent less than 50%	*Aggressive more than 50%*	7 (Alor, BaVenda, Buka, Lakher, Lamba, Lepcha, Siriono)	1 (Kwakiutl)
	Aggressive less than 50%	1 (Lesu)	
Benevolent more than 50%	*Aggressive more than 50%*	1 (Bena)	1 (Navaho)
	Aggressive less than 50%	1 (Mbundu)	6 (Baiga, Chagga, Dahomey, Hopi, Papago, Zuni)

It is plausible, then, to argue that games of chance should be linked to the larger expressive system of religious beliefs and that they are exercises in relationships with the supernatural. These hypotheses were not tested extensively, but the use of three scales developed by Lambert, Triandis, and Wolf[4] provided some interesting results. Here a sample of tribes was scaled in terms of (1) the frequency of benevolent actions by gods or spirits, (2) the frequency of aggression by gods or spirits, and (3) the frequency of coercion of gods or spirits. The first two scales had seven points ranging from "always benevolent or aggressive" to "never benevolent or aggressive." The mid-points were defined as being "benevolent or aggressive about one-half of the time." Table 3 combines these two independent scales. The coercion scale ran from "continuous, every day or more often" to "never," and the midpoint was "once a month." The hypothesis that games of chance will occur in societies high in benevolence, low in aggression, or high in coercion is supported by Table 3 and Table 4 (only tribes appearing on the Lambert scale are cited). However, the relationships shown did not hold either for games of strategy or for games of physical skill.

Table 4. Frequency of Coercion of Gods or Spirits, and Games of Chance

Frequency of Coercion	Games of Chance Absent	Game of Chance Present
Low	9 (Alor, BaVenda, Bena, Buka, Lakher, Lamba, Lesu, Siriono, Tanala)	1 (Hopi)
High		5 (Baiga, Dahomey, Navaho, Papago, Zuni)

In the case of the benevolence measure, 16 out of 19 cases supported the hypothesis; with aggression, 15 out of 19 supported the hypothesis; and with coercion, 14 out of 15 cases supported the hypothesis. In keeping with the hypothesis, it might be conjectured from the lack of reference to gambling games in the latest concordance of the Bible that the God of the ancient Hebrews was neither benevolent more than 50 percent of the time nor was he easily coerced.

GAMES OF PHYSICAL SKILL

There is no apparent relationship between the presence or absence of games of strategy and the number of games of physical skill, but there does appear to be relationship between the presence or absence of games of chance and the number of games of physical skill (see Table 5 below). Societies having five or more games of physical skill frequently have games of chance but this may be a consequence of the varying conpleteness of descriptions in the literature.

There was also a relationship between geographical location and the number of games of physical skill in a society. Of 23 tribes living within 20 degrees latitude of the equator, 18 had fewer than five games of physical skill, while of 24 tribes living more than 20 degrees north or south, only nine had fewer than five games of physical skill. Tentative work with mean annual temperature and protein and fat in the diet suggests some correlation.

Table 5. Number of Games of Physical Skill and Games of Chance

Number of Games of Physical Skill Present	Games of Chance Present	Games of Chance Absent
0 to 4	4 (Achewa, Baiga, Dahomey, Kansa)	26 (Alor, Ainu, BaVenda, Bena, Buka, Jukun, Kababish, Kiwai, Lakher, Lamba, Lepcha, Lesu, Macheyenga, Malekula, Masai, Mbundu, Murngin, Sema Naga, Siriono, Siwa, Tanala, Wapishana, Warrau, Witoto, Yaruro, Yungar)
5 to 20	15 (Aleut, Chagga, Chukchee, Copper Eskimo, Gros Ventre, Hopi, Korea, Kwakiutl, Maricopa, Menomini, Nauru, Navaho, Papago, Vietnam, Zuni)	4 (Arikara, Euahlayi, Rwala Bedouin, Yap)

There may be a relationship between environment and activity as expressed in numbers of games of physical skill, but the data were inadequate for an extensive analysis.

DISCUSSION

The foregoing suggests that games of strategy are related to social systems, games of chance are related to religious beliefs, and that games of physical skill may be related to environmental conditions. The social system, the religion, and the environment are three important foci of anthropological interest, and further study of these relationships appears to be warranted.

Psychological inquiries are also indicated. In general, this paper supports the psychoanalytic notion that games are exercises in mastery. Certainly the area of child socialization, which has often been linked with expressive phenomena, should be considered. Exploratory work with unpublished data provided by Whiting, Lambert, and Child suggests that the presence of games of strategy is positively associated with low permissiveness in child training, high severity of bowel training, and high reward for obedience behavior. Games of chance appear to be related to none of the foregoing, but rather to high frequency of responsible behavior and high frequency of achievement behavior. Games of physical skill seem to be positively associated with low permissiveness and high conflict over nurturant and self-reliant behavior. Thus, we can speculate that further inquiry will show that games of strategy are linked with the learning of social roles, games of chance with responsibility and achievement, and games of physical skill with self-reliance. Alternatively stated, games of strategy may be related to mastery of the social system; games of chance may be linked with mastery of the supernatural; and games of physical skill are possibly associated with the mastery both of self and of environment.

This paper has advanced a three-category classification of games and has reviewed the distribution of these game types in 50 societies. It has suggested that games may be exercises in the mastery of environment or self, social system, and of the supernatural. We have not intended to say that the already well-recognized functions of games should be ignored, but rather have intended to suggest some new ways in which such expressive behavior might be viewed. If all the relationships suggested in this paper do not ultimately hold, it is still hoped that enough evidence has been presented to warrant further comparative studies of games. An anthropological theory of games could be the result.

REFERENCE NOTES

1. Cf. Tylor's famous articles on patolli and American lot-games (Tylor 1879:116-129; 1896:55-67). The patolli problem stated by Tylor has continued to intrigue anthropologists and interest in this problem provided the initial impetus for the present investigation.
2. The authors are indebted to the Laboratory of Social Relations, Harvard University, for the support of this research and to the Cross-Cultural Survey, Institute of Human Relations, Yale University, and the Center for Advanced Study in the Behavioral Sciences for auxiliary aid. The authors are also grateful to John Champe, Franklin Fenenga, William Lambert, Kimball Romney, Richard Savage, Elizabeth Tooker, Leigh Minturn Triandis, Gene Weltfish, John M. Whiting, Margery Wolf, and others, for useful suggestions and comments.
3. Personal communication from Elizabeth Tooker.
4. Use was made of the Lambert, Triandis and Wolf unpublished data which were subsequently reported in revised form in the Journal of Abnormal and Social Psychology.

REFERENCES

Kendall, M. G., 1956. Studies in the history of probability and statistics. II. The beginnings of a probability calculus. Biometrika 43:1-14.

Lambert, William W., Leigh Minturn Triandis, and Margery Wolf, 1959. Some correlates of beliefs in the malevolence and benevolence of supernatural beings — A cross-societal study. Journal of Abnormal and Social Psychology, 58:162-169.

Murdock, George Peter, 1957. World ethnographic sample. American Anthropologist, 59:664-687.

Murray, H. J. R., 1913. A history of chess. Oxford, Clarendon Press.

Tylor, E. B., 1879. On the game of patolli in ancient Mexico and its probable Asiatic origin. Journal of the Royal Anthropological Institute 8:116-129. 1896. On American lot-games as evidence of Asiatic intercourse before the time of Columbus. Internationales Archiv für Ethnographie 9:55-67.

Whiting, John W. M., and Irving L. Child, 1953. Child training and personality: A cross-cultural study. New Haven, Yale University Press.

The Reflection Of Cultural Values In Eskimo Children's Games *

Lynn Price Ager
The Ohio State University

In recent years there has been a surge of interest and research focused on the relationship of games and culture. One major result of cross-cultural surveys and culture-specific studies of games has been the discovery that in any society, games are integrally related to major cultural institutions such as religion (Lambert, Triandes, and Wolf 1959), levels of subsistence activity and social complexity (Roberts, Arth, and Bush 1959), and child-rearing customs (Roberts and Sutton-Smith 1962). Games are an important part of children's activities in many societies, and it is therefore of interest to study the roles and values of a society as they are perceived by children and acted out in games and play. Also, since games are viewed as mechanisms of socialization by many scholars, we may be able to learn *which* norms and values are learned in games or expressed in games. This paper is based on my research into the relationship of games and values in an Eskimo village,[1] but I believe the hypothesis that games are an expression of cultural values is a generally applicable one and can apply both to traditional societies and those undergoing acculturation.

I define a game as a play activity which has explicit rules, specified or understood goals (winning is not necessarily one of them), the element of opposition or contest, recognizable boundaries in time and sometimes in space, and a sequence of actions which is essentially "repeatable" every time the game is played. (I do not consider "competition" and "two or more sides" necessary for a definition of game.)

Games have been classified into four primary categories, based on the dominant or characteristic mode of contest present: games of physical skill, of chance, of strategy (Roberts, Arth and Bush 1959), and memory-attention (Eifermann 1971).

Values are used here as Clyde Kluckhohn defined them:

In the broadest sense . . . (one) may usefully think of values as abstract and enduring standards which are held by an individual and/or a specified group to transcend the impulses of the moment and ephemeral situa-

*Ager, Lynn P. "The Reflection of Cultural Values in Eskimo Children's Games," in D. Lancy & A. Tindall (Eds.). *The Anthropological Study of Play: Problems and Prospects,* New York: Leisure Press, 1976, pp. 79-86. Reprinted by permission of the publisher.

tions. From the psychological point of view, a value may be defined as that aspect of motivation which is referable to standards, personal or cultural, that do not arise solely out of an immediate situation and the satisfaction of needs and primary drives.

A value is a selective orientation toward experience, implying deep commitment or repudiation, which influences the 'choice' between possible alternatives in action. These orientations may be cognitive and expressed or merely inferable from recurrent trends in behavior. A value, though conditioned by biological and social necessity, is in its specific form arbitrary or conventional.

Values then, are images formulating positive or negative action commitments. They take distinctive forms in different cultures, tend to persist tenaciously through time, and are not mere random outcomes of conflicting human desires. (Kluckhohn 1958, quoted in Lantis 1959, p. 37).

My research into children's games took place during eight months in Tununak, an Eskimo village on Nelson Island, along the Bering Sea coast of Alaska. This area of southwestern Alaska has been one of the last to be exposed to the outside world, primarily, I think, because of its lack of commerically exploitable resources. No gold prospectors, whalers, or fur trappers have descended on this area in hoards as they have in so many other Eskimo communities in the past. Itinerant Catholic missionaries have been in varying degrees of contact with Nelson Islanders since the 1890s, but their influence was a gradual one, as evidenced by the fact that shamanism as a viable religious practice has disappeared only within the memory of middle-aged informants. Anglo-American school teachers have been teaching in Tununak since the 1920s, and earlier in the century a Northern Commercial Company store was operating for awhile. But compared to many other Alaskan Eskimo coastal communities, Tununak has been pretty much left alone by the outside world until the past two decades. Here, men still hunt and fish to supply the staples of their family's diet; and the people still all speak Yupik, their native tongue, as their first, and sometimes only, language. Dog teams were replaced by snow machines within the past nine years, and the last semi-subterranean house was abandoned for a "modern" plywood frame dwelling only about six years ago. Electricity was brought to the community four years ago, but there is still no indoor plumbing or running water. After completing 8th grade in the village Bureau of Indian Affairs school, some students leave to attend regional high schools, but higher education is a relatively new goal, still rarely fulfilled. Even the young people who do graduate from high school often return to live in Tununak rather than move to metropolitan areas in the state where they can find jobs.

What the culture of Tununak was like prior to contact I can only surmise from ethnographies of other southwestern Alaskan communities, since I am the first anthropologist to carry out ethnographic research on Nelson Island. The closest communities for which we have good information are on Nunivak Island, about 20 miles across the Etolin Strait from Nelson Island, where Margaret Lantis conducted ethnographic fieldwork beginning in 1939 (Lantis, 1946). My discussion of Eskimo values is based on my own observations in Tununak as well as on published reports of other ethnographers, particularly those of Lantis (1959). Games mentioned are those I saw played or ones informants told me used to be played, and these were all classified according to the categories mentioned on page 80. The relationship between games and values is one I perceived through analysis. An emic approach to this subject was not possible under the particular field conditions I encountered.

The Eskimos of Nelson Island are classified as Bering Sea hunters and fishermen (Oswalt 1967). They derive most of their subsistence from the ocean — primarily fish (salmon and herring) and seals, with walrus, white whale, and sea lion from time to time. As hunters, they place a high value on hunting, hunting skill, and hunting achievements. This overwhelming fact of their lives, that their very survival depended on a hunter's ability to find, kill, and retrieve game, has dominated every aspect of their culture and cannot be overstressed. It has been only recently that a cash economy has affected in any major way the subsistence patterns of these people, and government aid of various kinds now provides them with economic security should their traditional means of getting food fail. A man's prestige, however, is still measured to a great extent in terms of his hunting skill. It is no surprise, therefore, that we find games of physical skill to be overwhelmingly preferred to other types. Of 39 games recorded for the village, 25 were games of physical skill. Games which require dexterity, strength and endurance are quite obviously functional in a society so dependent upon these qualities in its members, both male and female. The significance of this type of game is further apparent when we discover that games of physical skill and games of memory-attention were the *only* kinds played in the traditional culture. None of my informants reported "old time" games of chance or strategy, and Lantis (1946) reports that there were none on Nunivak Island, although games of chance have been reported for aboriginal groups of Eskimos from other areas. Success in games depended exclusively on one's own skills. This was true in real life as well. Economic pursuits were individual for the most part (Oswalt 1963: 100,121), although sometimes partners might hunt or set fish nets together and divide the spoils. Self reliance and independence were valued personal traits (Lantis 1959). Individual self testing games are far the most popular among Eskimos today, and so far as I can determine, have always been. Old games such as dart throwing, juggling, tag, and contests of strength, such as broad jumping, wrestling, and foot racing, tested the ability of the individual. Many new games which have been adopted by the Eskimos are also essentially individual tests — marbles and jacks are two examples. A good memory was also a valuable personal asset in a hunting culture (Nelson 1969), for it is of positive survival value to remember one's own experiences in emergencies, the experiences of others in similar situations, to remember landmarks on an almost featureless terrain, to remember animal habits which help one predict their behavior. *Remembering* helps the hunter and

153

may even save his life. Two games which test children's memory are story-knifing (Oswalt 1964; Ager 1974), and string figures.

Emphasis on individuality in achievement, both in real life and in games, has fostered a spirit of competition among Eskimos. But mitigating the disruptive aspects of aggressive competition is the social morality of the group. It is realized, or at least used to be, that the group was the only insurance an individual had. If one man had a run of bad luck in hunting, his family would not go hungry if he had relatives and friends to provide for him in emergencies. Thus, there was a high value on group survival (Lantis 1959; Nelson 1899: 294), which led, in the most extreme situations, to sacrifice of individuals for the good of the group (e.g. infanticide and elimination of the old and infirm in periods of starvation). The kind of competition in games I saw was the one in which everyone tried to do his best but not at anyone else's expense. (Senengutuk 1971: 145). Consistent with the idea that one man's gain is not necessarily another's loss is the custom of giving prizes. In the old days, the winner of one game put up the prize for the next, so the only real winner, materially, was the winner of the last game played. Today in Tununak, when games are held on the 4th of July, *everyone* who plays receives a prize. On a game night organized for the children in the community hall, no prizes were given at all. In addition, there are games of individual skill which have no element of real competition, such as storyknifing and string figures, and thus have no criteria for winning. These two games may be played in groups in which each participant tries to tell her best stories or make many string figures and be able to make them very quickly (so contest is present but minimal), or they may be played alone and are therefore sometimes only amusements because the element of opposition is lacking. The lengths to which we go, in our own society, to encourage a winning spirit in players can be seen on any summer Saturday afternoon at little league baseball games. Parents and players boo ''bad'' calls by the umpire; those who strike out sometimes cry; and the losing team goes home depressed. Coaches admonish the players to be good sports because ''winning isn't everything,'' but the very fact that we feel it necessary to verbalize such a concept is some indication that it is not ingrained.

The high value placed on non-aggression within the group is reflected in the lack of malice in games and sports among the Eskimos. Even in the most painful contests of endurance and strength (such as mouth pulling, finger pulling, and other trials between two individuals), participants do not become angry at one another because of the discomfort each is inflicting on the other. (Contrast this with our own sports, such as boxing and hockey). Eskimo losers are good sports. They leave laughing; the audience laughs when someone loses or looks funny or makes a mistake; and participants in many games derive much amusement from playing. (I should mention here that laughter is not *always* an indication of amusement. In some instances, laughter in Eskimo culture is a means of concealing shame or hurt feelings.) Humor is greatly valued among all Eskimos reported in the literature (Lantis, 1959; Nelson 1969). The children show this when they play, too. Even cheaters do not evoke an angry response but an amused one. The other

154

players yell "cheater" good naturedly and laugh; in fact, the cheating is blatant when it occurs, as if done to amuse oneself and the others. Although the subject of this paper is children's games, I might note here that nearly all adult games I witnessed were also occasions for humor.

Another value in Eskimo society is what Lantis calls the "devaluation of possessiveness" (1959). In general, there is very little, if any, emphasis in games upon equipment. One of the favorite games in Tununak is called "Lapp game." It resembles baseball in that a ball is hit with a bat, but the bat need only be a handy piece of wood. In another popular game which has been introduced, marbles, the children bring one marble to the game and leave with that same marble. The game they play has no provisions for winning another player's marble. They do know a game in which the object is gain possession of others' marbles, but they rarely play it. In all my months there, I saw the "winning game" of marbles played only once; a novice player who had lost his marble sat off to the side waiting for the game to end so his marble would be returned. When it was explained that it would not be returned, he was incredulous. It appeared to me that since this game was so rarely played, the children (who played marbles in little groups throughout the village almost every day for the entire summer of 1974) were indeed expressing a preference for the non-winning game. They enjoyed the contest of skill, but did not seem to enjoy taking each others' marbles as prizes.

What I have said so far applies to the traditional cultural values which survive today. But what about the changes taking place in Eskomo society as a result of contact with Anglo-Americans? As I see it, many values are just now beginning to change in Tununak, and the full effect of modernization will be felt there within the next decade (it has been felt already in other, less isolated, villages). Because of the changes Eskimo culture is making to adapt to modern technology, economy, and life-styles, many individuals now find that it is becoming increasingly important to be well educated in order to cope with the complexities of Anglo-American culture. What we see now in the game repertoire is still a preponderance of games of physical skill, but these, along with memory-attention games, are no longer the only kinds played. Games of strategy (chess, checkers), games combining chance and stategy (board games, card games), and sports such as basketball and football which combine physical skill and strategy have been adopted by the children and the adults. The relationship of games of strategy to cultural complexity has been discussed by Roberts, Arth, and Bush (1959). Following their line of thinking, we can say that acceptance of games of strategy is consistent with new values regarding competence in coping with the complexities of modern life, particularly since the recent settlement of the Native Land Claims with its complicated legal and economic significance for the natives and the new demands on community leaders to formulate long range plans and goals for the group.

A final point I wish to make with regard to the games is that children actually play very few formal games in their total play activity (Oswalt 1963). Sutton-Smith and Rosenberg (1971: 44-45) have suggested that the trend away from formal games to informal play activities among Anglo-American children may be explained by the changes in the society they live in — a society increasingly permissive and more informal in social relationships, particularly in relationships with parents. If this is true, we could suggest that it may apply cross-culturally as well: one reason for the relative scarcity of formal games compared to informal play activities among Eskimo children may be the value of equality in their society (Senungetuk 1971: 45). Eskimo culture is noted for its lack of rigid, formal, hierarchically ordered social relationships, which is consistent with their emphasis on essentially equal standards of living for everyone and lack of formal authority in leaders. Their preference for the unstructured and the permissive may help to explain the children's preference for informal play. Interestingly, if they adapt completely to modern western civilization, they will have to introduce *more* formal organization and structure in their social organization, so perhaps we will see an increase in the number of formal games played in the future.

In summary, I think we can see that the traditional hunting complex requiring individual initiative, memory, and physical strength fosters values which are expressed in the *types* of games traditionally played by Eskimo children, i.e. those games of physical skill, particularly the self-testing variety, and games requiring both dexterity and memory-attention, such as string figures. The cultural value placed on individuality and self-reliance but without disruption of group unity and solidarity is expressed in *attitudes* in games, that is, pleasurable competition in some games but absence of humiliation for the losers and the humor which envelops game playing. The general lack of emphasis on material possessions is reflected in players' careless attitude toward game equipment and in minimal emphasis on prizes in competitions. New values associated with competence in the complex modern world may be related to increasing interest in games of strategy, where the emphasis is on testing the mind rather than the body. Finally, infrequency of formal games can tell us something about values as well. In Tununak, formal games are less frequent than informal play activities, and this may be a reflection of the high value placed on informal, permissive relationships in social relations.

The hypothesis that important cultural values will be reflected in children's games has been shown to be a workable one in the community I studied. It remains for other investigators to discover if cultural values find such clear expression in the games of other societies.

REFERENCES

Ager, L. P. 1974 *Storyknifing: An Alaskan Eskimo Girls' Game.* Journal of the Folklore Institute XI: 3. Indiana University.

Eifermann, R. 1971 *Determinants of Children's Game Styles.* Israel Academy of Sciences and Humanities, Jerusalem.

Kluckhohn, C. 1958 The Scientific Study of Values. In *3 Lectures.* University of Toronto Installation Lectures, pp. 25-54.

Lambert, W., L. M. Triandis, and M. Wolf. 1959 *Some Correlates of Beliefs in the Malevolence and Benevolence of Super-natural Beings: A Cross Cultural Study.* Journal of Abnormal Psychology 58: 162-169.

Lantis, M. 1946 *The Social Culture of the Nunivak Eskimo.* Transactions of the American Philosophical Society 35: 3: 155-323. 1959 *Alaskan Eskimo Cultural Values.* Polar Notes 1: 35-48.

Nelson, E. W. 1899 *The Eskimo About Bering Strait.* Bureau of American Ethnology, Eighteenth Annual Report. Washington, D.C.

REFERENCE NOTE

1. This research was supported in full by the National Institute of Education grant number NEG-00-3-0104. Drafts of this paper were read by Daniel Hughes, Ojo Arewa, Allan Tindall, and Margaret Landis. Their reactions were appreciated.

157

SECTION V
SOCIOLOGY AND PHYSICAL ACTIVITY

WHAT IS SOCIOLOGY?

According to Inkles (1964), sociology seeks to explain the nature of the order and disorder in the social life of man. Kenyon says that sociology deals with social units, social attributes and social processes. To this list one could add the area of social problems.

HOW ARE SOCIOLOGY AND PHYSICAL ACTIVITY LINKED?

As was the case with history and anthropology, sociology is not interested in minute muscle movement but rather it attempts to explain the order and disorder which occur in the grosser and more structured forms of movement, such as play, games, dance and sport. Several sub-disciplines have developed which relate sociology to physical activity. The most notable of these are the sociology of dance and the sociology of sport. The pervasiveness of the latter is evidenced by the existence of (a) national and international organizations, (b) a great number of publications including several text books and an international journal, and (c) courses and even entire programmes that are being offered in this sub-discipline at universities throughout the world. It appears that the sociology of sport has taken under its wing the less developed sub-fields of the political science of physical activity and the economics of physical activity as literature in these areas is usually lumped with that of the sociology of sport.

WHAT READINGS IN THE SOCIOLOGY OF PHYSICAL ACTIVITY ARE INCLUDED IN THIS COLLECTION?

In an attempt to give students an overview of the relationships that exist between sociology and physical activity the present collection of readings includes:

1. *Articles depicting **social units** i.e., the institutions of education and religion.*
2. *Articles dealing with a **social attribute** i.e., being female.*
3. *Articles outlining certain **social processes** namely socialization, social change and social stratification.*
4. *Articles identifying the **social problems** of discrimination and deviancy.*

In addition this section contains articles linking politics to sport and economics to sport.

159

The Sociology Of Sport*

Barry D. McPherson

Unlike many of the other sub-disciplines described in this volume, the sociology of sport is a relatively new field of scholarly interest. That this field as a recent development is somewhat surprising in that sport has been an integral facet of social life in most societies throughout history. On the other hand, the late development of this subfield is understandable since sociology itself is a relatively new discipline compared to philosophy, anthropology, physiology, biology, or psychology. Nevertheless, it has been increasingly recognized that most forms of sport involvement occur in a social context, that sport has become a significant social institution in most modernized and developing nations, and that, to some extent, the degree of involvement and success in sport is accounted for by the social characteristics of individuals, and, by the social structure, cultural system, and social processes unique to a given society. As result, scholars have sought to describe and explain various facets of the phenomenon by utilizing the concepts, theories, and methods unique to the discipline of sociology. In the following subsections the standard who, what, when, where, why and how questions will be addressed as they pertain to the sociology of sport.

PURPOSE OF THE FIELD (WHY)?

Scholars in the sociology of sport seek to identify, describe and explain regular patterns and processes associated with individual and group behavior in a sport context. More specifically, sport sociologists are interested in understanding basic social units (i.e., individuals, groups, institutions, cultures, societies) and fundamental social processes (e.g., socialization, stratification and mobility, social conflict, social change) that are present in a variety of sport milieux. In addition, they are interested in social problems, in cultural and subcultural variations in social phenomena unique to sport, and in the relationship between sport and other social institutions (e.g., the family, the economic system, the educational system, the political system, religion, and the mass media).

Furthermore, unlike some elements of psychology, sociologists are not primarily interested in explaining the behaviour of a specific individual (e.g., "Tiger" Williams—or group, e.g., the Vancouver Canucks). Rather, they are motivated by the desire to refute myths (e.g., women have equal opportunity in sport), and to understand the social structure, social patterns, social processes and social organization of various groups engaged in sport. To illustrate, the group may well be a small social system (e.g., a

*McPherson B. D., "The Sociology of Sport", in J. Jackson and H. Wenger (Eds.), *The Sport Sciences*, University of Victoria, 1982, pp. 73-80. Reproduced with permission of the publisher and the author.

hockey team), a group of athletes or spectators with a common social characteristic (e.g., Francophones, females, the upper class), a large organization (e.g., the National Hockey League), a particular subculture (e.g., surfers), or a society (e.g., Canada's involvement in the Olympic Games). Finally, sport sociologists are increasingly being requested by sport administrators and government personnel to provide valid information about sport systems through applied systems or policy analysis (e.g., McPherson *et al.,* 1977; MePherson and Davidson, 1980).

THE HISTORICAL AND CONTEMPORARY DEVELOPMENT OF THE SOCIOLOGY OF SPORT (WHEN AND WHERE?)

Perhaps more than any other subfield represented in this volume, the sociology of sport has been subjected to an extensive historical analysis.[1] Although sport had been noted as a sociological phenomenon as early as the 1920s in Germany, the field did not really begin to develop until the mid 1960s. Prior to this time, most of the scholarly interest in sport by social scientists was concerned with defining the function and meaning of play and games (i.e., philosophy), with examining the interpersonal dynamics of small sport groups (i.e., social psychology), and with describing individual traits of athletes (i.e., psychology).

The sociology of sport emerged as a distinct field of study when a group of scholars founded the International Committee for the Sociology of Sport (ICSS) in 1964; when Kenyon and Loy (1965) proposed that a sub-discipline be created within the sport sciences to examine sport from a sociological perspective; and, when the *International Review of Sport Sociology* (IRSS) was published, first as an annual publication in 1966, and later as a quarterly in 1973. In North America, the first book in the field was a collection of edited papers published in 1969 (cf., Loy and Kenyon, 1969). Subsequently, over sixty texts or readers have appeared throughout the world. Moreover, undergraduate and graduate courses and programs were initiated throughout the 1970s, and a computerized information retrieval system (SIRLS) was established as a repository of scholarly work in the area.[2] At the present time, many universities in the United States, and most in Canada, employ a sport socilologist who is located within either a department of sociology or a sport-related department such as kinesiology, sport studies, or physical education. A recent significant development has been the formation of the North American Society for the Sociology of Sport (NASSS). This organization has approximately 200 members in Canada, Europe and the United States.

Employing a more analytical perspective, McPherson (1975) suggests why and how three generations of sport sociologists have been trained, while Loy *et al.* (1978a) argue that the field has evolved through the first three of the four common stages that subfields often pass through in their process of evolution.[3] To date, many reasons have been suggested as to why the most advanced stage has not been attained, and why the establishment of this field has not been as rapid as some other subfields within the sport sciences. Many of these reason reflect the difficulties encountered in the development of a new subfield within any well-established field, whether it be medicine (e.g., geriatrics), physiology (e.g., exercise physiology) or engineering (e.g., biomechanics). The following represent some of the subjective and objective explanations for the relatively slow evolution of the sociology of sport (cf., Loy *et al.,* 1978a):

1. A critical mass of scholars who regularly and creatively contribute to the body of knowledge has not been available.[4]

2. Sociology of sport, until recently, has been viewed by sociologists as a trivial social phenomenon (the toy shop of the world!), despite the fact that a large percentage of the population in most countries are active participants or spectators. In fact, in many countries more people may be involved in sport than in religion.

3. Within departments of physical education and athletics, sport sociologists have often been perceived as a threat to the status quo because they seek to refute myths, to identify social problems, and to ask questions which have heretofore not been asked about the world of sport (e.g., do Blacks or women experience unequal opportunity in sport? do athletes fail to meet admission or graduation requirements?)

4. Like the early stages of development in many subfields, the quality of research has been inferior to that in the major discipline. One reason for this lack of quality has been the failure to utilize sociological concepts and theories to guide the research. Fortunately, current research is increasingly being grounded in the basic theories, concepts and methods of sociology.

5. Within university departments, and within the sport sciences, a majority of faculty have been trained in the "hard" rather than the "soft" sciences. This has sometimes created intra-departmental conflict. That is, sociology of sport is viewed by those in physiology, motor learning, medicine, and biomechanics as unscientific, nonquantitative and nothing more than "common sense"; whereas "cousins" in history, philosophy, and administration view sociology of sport as too scientific, too abstract and too quantitative.

6. The sociology of sport has been criticized by "outsiders" as irrelevant because it lacks immediate practical application, because it lacks a technological basis, because it does not contribute to readily observable and pragmatic occupational skills, or because it does not directly lead to a specific occupation (e.g., teacher, fitness leader). These subjective opinions continue despite the fact that almost any occupation pertaining to sport or physical activity requires an understanding of the social context in which the exercise, learning, or competition occurs.

7. To date, some of the higher quality work in this field has been completed by sociologists who publish in sociology journals. Hence, their work, including that of an applied nature, may not be known by sport scientists in other subdisciplines.

In summary, despite growing pains and a failure to attain legitimacy and acceptance within some sectors of the sport sciences, as well as within sociology, the field is alive and well. Evidence to support this statement includes active associations (ICSS and NASSS), a large body of literature, numerous courses and programs within sociology and sport science departments (especially in Canada), and, the increasing awareness by sport administrators and government personnel that sport sociologists can contribute to problem-solving and policy analysis within the system of institutionalized sport at the local, regional, national, or international level.

CURRENT CONTENT AND QUESTIONS OF SOCIOLOGY OF SPORT (WHAT?)

Although the field is less than twenty years old, a vast amount of information has been presented at professional meetings or published in books or journals. Not surprisingly, the content and quality of this work varies considerably from author to author, and from topic to topic. In fact, much of the early work was descriptive, atheoretical, ahistorical, asociological, and indeed, at an intellectually low level of conceptualization.

Despite these criticisms, which are likely typical of most evolving fields of study, a large body of quality work has been produced. However, it is beyond the scope of this brief article to identify all the topics of inquiry that have been addressed by scholars in this field. Therefore, the interested reader should refer to the text by Coakley (1982), which illustrates the issues, problems, or controversies approach to sociology of sport; or, to the text by Loy *et al.* (1978b), which illustrates a social systems analysis of the structure and social processes inherent within institutionalized sport. In addition, there are a variety of handbooks and readers that include discrete research papers or review articles on particular social phenomena within sport systems (cf. Gruneau and Albinson, 1976; Loy *et al.,* 1981; Luschen and Sage, 1981b).

By way of summary and overview, some of the more frequent topics have included: social differentiation and social mobility as a result of involvement in sport; the process of socialization into sport; racial, ethnic, and gender discrimmination within sport; the relationship between sport and other social institutions (e.g., the family, education, politics, economics, the mass media); player and spectator aggression and violence in sport especially in hockey and soccer; the relationship between the structure and dynamics of sport groups and team success; sport as an occupation; social problems in children's sport; and, cross-cultural and subcultural variation in the meaning, function, and structure of sport.

As for the future, ideally studies will address more fundamental, yet generalizable questions, will be based on sociological concepts and theories; will seek creative, alternative explanations; will focus more on explanation than description, especially from a cultural, institutional or historical perspective (cf., Gruneau, 1976); will broaden the sample in research studies from the local level to the regional, national or cross-national level in order to enhance the generalizability of findings; and, will move beyond the individual level of analysis to the institutional, structural or cultural level of analysis. If these principles for improved scholarship are accepted and incorporated, the quality of knowledge in the field will be enhanced considerably.

METHODS OF SOCIOLOGICAL INQUIRY (HOW?)

In order to answer general sociological questions pertaining to sport as a social phenomenon, and to more specifically discover, describe, confirm, and explain relationships unique to individuals and social systems within institutionalized sport, a variety of quantitative and qualitative methods are utilized. For the most part, research is conducted in the real world (i.e., the field) rather than in laboratory settings. While this can create problems with respect to the control of extraneous factors and with respect to collecting information, the findings from a "natural" social setting are usually considered more valid, despite the lack of complete experimental control.

The particular research method utilized in the specific study is ideally related to the theoretical question that is being addressed. However, in reality, much of the research is guided by the practical matter of gaining access to a particular sport group in a particular social milieu. Notwithstanding this caveat, the following represent the major approaches to the search for knowledge in the sociology of sport. First, most research is based on the use of mailed questionnaires or interview schedules to survey large or small samples that represent larger populations. Second, because of the cost of survey research, scholars have increasingly initiated content analyses of existing materials stored in archives, or secondary analyses of data sets housed in data banks. Both of these techniques utilize information that has been collected at an earlier point in time, and which contains information needed to verify an hypothesized relationship (e.g., between chronological age and frequency of involvement in sport).

More recently, an increasingly popular method is that of participant observation. Here, the investigator is directly or indirectly involved in watching and participating in the activities of a particular social group over a period of time. This procedure also involves formal and informal interviewing of the participants. These interviews seek to determine the meaning and function of the activity or group, as interpreted by members who occupy different social positions. Thus, by way of summary, a variety of methods and theoretical perspectives have been utilized in the search for knowledge within the sociology of sport. Since it is beyond the scope of this paper to provide more detailed information about research methods, the interested reader should consult articles by Loy and Segrave (1974), McPherson (1975), and Loy et al. (1978b).

SUMMARY AND CONCLUSIONS

In summary, this paper has briefly described the purpose, historical development, content, methods and leading scholars of the subfield known as the sociology of sport. Throughout, in addition to critiquing the field, it has been noted that this relatively new area of study is still evolving. Hence, there is a need for young, creative scholars to increase the critical mass that is necessary to produce a more complete and valid knowledge base for use by both research personnel and policy-makers.

REFERENCE NOTES

1. Some of these analyses include: Kenyon and Loy (1965), McPherson (1975, 1978), Loy *et al.* (1978a), Loy (1979), 1980), Snyder and Spreitzer (1979), Luschen (1980), Spreitzer *et al.* (1980), and Luschen and Sage (1981a).

2. This system is housed within the Faculty of Human Kinetics and Leisure Studies at the University of Waterloo and presently includes over 10,000 documents.

3. Specifically, Loy *et al.* (1978a) note that sociology of sport passed through the "Normal" stage between 1951 and 1964 and the "Network" stage between 1965 and 1972. Since 1973 the field had remained at the "Cluster" stage and has yet to move into the "Speciality" stage.

4. For example, McPherson (1975, 1978), Loy *et al.* (1978a); Loy (1979, 1980), Snyder and Spreitzer (1979) and Spreitzer *et al.* (1980) all document and lament the fact that there are somewhat less than 100 active, productive scholars in the field. Moreover, Loy (1979) found that a core of 10 scholars accounted for over 40 percent of the published work in the field. Some of those who have continuously produced a significant amount of original work in the field, and/or who have played a leading role in the development of the field include:

   Canada: P. Donnelly, R. Gruneau, A. Hall, G. Kenyon, B. McPherson, M. Smith, N. Theberge.

   United States: S. Birrell, J. Coakley, S. Eitzen, S. Greendorfer, A. Ingham, J. Loy, G. Luschen, H. Nixon, E. Snyder, E. Spreitzer.

   Europe:, Japan, Australia: E. Dunning (Great Britain), K. Kageyama (Japan), M. Klein (German Federal Republic), Z. Krawczyck (Poland), H. Lenk (German Federal Republic), K. Pearson (Australia), R. Renson (Belgium), P. Seppanen (Finland), R. Sugawara (Japan), A. Wohl (Poland).

REFERENCES

Forscher, B. Chaos in the brickyard. *Science,* 1963, *142,* 3590.

Gruneau, R. Sport as an area of sociological study: An introduction to major themes and perspectives. Pp. 8-43 in R. Gruneau and J. Albinson (Eds.), *Canadian sport: Sociological perspectives.* Don Mills, Ontario: Addison-Wesley, 1976.

_____, and J. Albinson (Eds.). *Canadian sport: Sociological perspectives.* Don Mills, Ontario: Addison-Wesley, 1976.

Kenyon, G., and J. Loy. Toward a sociology of sport. *JOHPER,* 1965, *36,* 24-25, 68-69.

Loy, J. An exploratory analysis of the scholarly productivity of North American based sport sociologists. *International Review of Sport Sociology,* 1979, *14,* 97-113.

_____. The emergence and development of the sociology of sport as an academic speciality. *Research Quarterly,* 1980, *51,* 91-109.

_____, and G. S. Kenyon. *Sport, culture, and society.* New York: Macmillan, 1969.

_____, and J. Segrave. Research methodology in the sociology of sport. Pp. 289-333 in J. Wilmore (Ed.), *Exercise and Sport Sciences Reviews.* Volume 2, New York: Academic Press, 1974.

_____, *et al. The sociology of sport as an academic speciality.* CAHPER Monograph Series. Ottawa: Canadian Association for Health, Physical Education and Recreation, 1978a.

_____, *et al. Sport and social systems.* Reading, Mass.: Addison-Wesley, 1978b.

_____, *et al.* (Eds.). *Sport, culture and society.* 2nd Edition. Philadelphia: Lea & Febiger, 1981.

Luschen, G. Sociology of sport: Development, present state, and prospects. *Annual Review of Sociology,* 1980, *6,* 315-347.

_____, and G. Sage. Sport in sociological perspective. Pp. 3-21 in G. Luschen and G. Sage (Eds.), *Handbook of social science of sport. Champaign, Illinois: Stipes, 1981a.*

_____, and _____. *(Eds.), Handbook of social science of sport.* Champaign, Illinois: Stipes, 1981b.

McPherson, B. Past, present and future perspectives for research in sport sociology. *International Review of Sport Sociology*, 1975, *10*, 55-72.

_____. Avoiding chaos in the sociology of sport brickyard. *Quest*, 1978, *30*, 72-79.

_____, and L. Davidson. *Minor hockey in Ontario: Toward a positive learning environment for children in the 1980's*. Toronto: Province of Ontario Government Bookstore, 1980.

_____, *et al*. *A study of age-group swimmers in Ontario*. Toronto: Canadian Amateur Swimming Association (Ontario Section), 1977.

Snyder, E., and E. Spreitzer. Sport sociology and the discipline of sociology: Present status and speculations about the future. *Review of Sport and Leisure*, 1979, *4*, 11-29.

Spretizer, E., *et al*. Reflections on the integration of sport sociology into the larter discipline. *Sociological Symposium*, 1980, *30*, 1-17.

Women In Sport: Cooptation Or Liberation?*

George H. Sage

Liberation movements have a way of promising more than they deliver. The underlying idealism and optimism produces an aura of excitement and anticipation. People expect that justice is about to prevail and that social oppression is about to be eliminated for another group of people. It turns out, however, that the liberationists were only after a piece of the existing pie rather than striving for truly alternative modes of living for large blocks of humanity. Never mind that the pie has many ingredients that are spoiled, sour, or downright hazardous to health. The important thing is "getting a piece of the action," "getting what's coming to one." The idealism and the potential for "real" change—change that promotes human growth throughout the broad spectrum of human life—gets blunted and diffused as the libberationists get absorbed into the mainstream of the social system; they are co-opted.[1]

Granted, the mainstreamers may have to make some accommodations and concessions to the liberationists, but gradually, as the latter begin to obtain the "goodies" of the mainstream, they adopt and internalize most mainstream orientations, thus becoming a "new class" of powerful persons with limited perspectives of equalitarianism and very protective of the power and influence they now hold.

What does this have to do with women's sports? Well, I think that it is obvious that the field of sport has witnessed a liberation movement within the past eight years — women's sports liberation. The women's sports movement has been one of the most significant liberation activities of the century. We really must applaud it. God knows that females need the same opportunities as males to engage in healthful sports. The female sex stereotyping which has discouraged female sports involvement has been an integral part of Western Civilization for over 2,000 years, and the need to break this cultural bondage was long overdue.

What have been its consequences? Well, surely it has opened up unprecedented opportunities for girls and women to engage in sports. While social attitudes do not change overnight, or even in a decade, female achievements in sport have produced new attitudes among both males and females about females' potential as athletes and as human beings. In many ways, it

* Sage, George H., "Women in Sport: Cooptation or Liberation?" *Colorado Journal of Health, Physical Education and Recreation*, 1. No. 2 (March) 1975. Reprinted by permission of the author.

has given females a new respect for themselves.

Like most liberation movements, the women's sports movement has not achieved some of the outcomes that many had hoped and wished for. When it began a few years ago, there was an excitement and an anticipation that women were not only going to move into greater sport involvement but that they were going to develop a new model for interscholastic and inter-collegiate sports. A model that would contain the best features of the male programs but that would exclude the worst features, a model that would add new, exciting, humane features.

It was reasoned that for over 50 years women had the opportunity to observe, sometimes with horror, as male high school and collegiate athletics, in the process of fostering healthful, educational sports, entered the field of professional entertainment. For the male coaches, marketplace criteria became virtually the only measure of coaching ability, and "win" became synonymous with success, and "lose" became associated with failure. Prestige in coaching was based upon won-loss records. This system tended to emphasize the treatment of athletes for what they could do for the coach—win—rather than the treatment of athletes based upon what coaches could do for the personal-social growth of athletes as persons.

Surely, many thought, leaders of female inter-school sports programs would, in their wisdom and with their years of observing male sports programs, advance an alternative educational sports model. It is now clear that there is no intention on the part of women physical educators and coaches of doing this at all. The main thrust of the women's sports movement is to mirror the men's programs in virtually every respect in the name of equality of opportunity. The opportunity to observe the strengths and weaknesses of male programs over the past half century and to select the strengths for emulation and reject the weaknesses as unwanted has been sacrificed in the quest to have exactly what the males have, regardless of the consequences (and historians say we learn from history!).

I am being facetious now, but it almost makes one wonder if the women's sports movement has not been a very subtle and clever scheme of male chauvinists. If male chauvinists in sports had intentionally set out to co-opt females into the mainstream orientations of the sport social system they could not have been more successful. Their grand strategy would have gone like this:

Give them (female sports leaders) a piece of the action. Of course, we will have to make some concessions, but basically we will continue to operate as usual. But once the females are in the business, there will be at least two benefits for male sports programs. First, the females will have to stop bellyaching about the enormous sums of money and human resouces that are expended in male programs because the females will now be part of the problem—that is, they'll be spending large sums too. Second, in order to protect their own newly won empires, the females will be supportive of male programs because they know that their programs depend on the health of male programs. Neat, the entire effect is to reinforce the existing main-stream school sports system, the one that has serious problems which are acknowledged by coaches such as Joe Paterno and Frank Broyles, football coaches at Penn State and Arkansas, as well as by thoughtful educators throughout the country.

Earlier in this essay, I mentioned that once a liberation group secured its immediate demands and became co-opted by the mainstream of the social system, its members tend to adopt a rather narrow perspective of equalitarianism. Let me use one example of how this notion is related to the women's sports movement. It quickly became evident that when women sports leaders spoke of equality of women's intercollegiate sports with men's collegiate sports they included the granting of athletic scholarships. Oh, there was a brief show by the AIAW denying the desire for athletic scholarships, but few really took this seriously, and many women physical educators and coaches did not agree with this position. Besides, it was clear that this policy would be tested in court rather quickly. And so it was.

Now, the stage was set. If men give athletic scholarships, women could too. But surely a stronger argument than that is needed, and sure enough, it was available; the men have been using it for years. It goes like this: Athletic scholarships can be justified on the basis that they are "talent" scholarships. Athletes have a special talent and one way of rewarding talent is to give some monetary reward—it's the All-American way. Female sports leaders had their justification. Female athletes, like male athletes, possess a talent—a talent that has been developed through years of practice. Why shouldn't colleges award scholarships to these talented athletes—females as well as males?

Fine, but, and here is where we get into the limited perspectives of liberationists' notions, if we are going to award "talent" scholarships to football, field hockey, basketball and track athletes, why not soccer, table tennis, billiards, judo, figure skating and sky diving athletes? Are not skilled performers in these latter sports, and many others, as "talented" as those in the former group? How about modern and contemporary dancers? Are they not skilled? Athletic? Dedicated? Talented? Why are not the dance teachers at collegiate institutions given a specific number of athletic scholarships just as the coaches of football, field hockey, basketball, etc.?

Let's face it, at every college in the country there are many students who possess talents for which they receive no financial renumeration from the institution. Why are they less worthy to receive talent scholarships? My guess is that most coaches would say that their talent is not marketable; that is, it cannot be used to entertain or amuse. Or it might be contended that the scholarship group practices long hours to maintain the award. Thus, athletic scholarships are justified on the moral basis of rewarding the talented, but the exclusive nature of the awards is based upon financial, entertainment, and public relations considerations. I wonder if this is consistent with a real liberation, or equalitarian, perspective? I hope you will give it some thought.

I want to note, in concluding this essay, that I don't want to seem to be overcritical of the emerging women's sports program. Men have lived with a number of serious programs in their inter-school sports programs for the past half century and have made little effort to correct these problems. It may be too much to expect that women will be able to develop an ideal sports model in the first decade of intensive interschool sports involvement. But we can hope for better things because an alternative sports structure which stresses cooperation, participation, expressiveness, fun, intrinsic motivation, and self-actualization would be a refreshing substitute for the current emphasis in interscholastic and intercollegiate programs. What is needed is a better model for these sports programs to make them truly "educational."

REFERENCE NOTES

1. Phillip Selznick: defines cooptation as "the process of absorbing new elements into the leadership or policy-determining structure of an organization as a means of averting threats to its stability or existence." (Selznick, P., *TVA and the Grass Roots,* New York: Harper Torchbook, 1966).

FOR FURTHER STUDY

Beisser, Arnold. *The Madness in Sports.* New York: Appleton-Century-Crofts, 1967.

Boslooper, Thomas, and Marcia Hayes. *The Femininity Game.* New York: Stein and Day, 1973.

Butt, Dorcas Susan. "New Horizons for Women in Sport." *Sport Psychology: An Analysis of Athletic Behavior.* Edited by William Straub. Ithaca, N.Y.: Mouvement Publications, 1978, pp. 189-194.

Coakley, Jay J. *Sport in Society: Issues and Controversies.* St. Louis: C. V. Mosby, 1978, chapter 10.

"Comes the Revolution: Joining the Game at Last, Women are Transforming American Athletics." *Time* (June 26, 1978), 51-60

Creamer, Robert. "Women's Worth." *Sports Illustrated* (January 17, 1977), p. 6.

Davenport, Joanna. "The Women's Movement into the Olympic Games." *JOPER,* 39 (March 1978), 58-60.

De Beauvoir, Simonte. *The Second Sex.* New York: Alfred A. Knopf, 1952.

Dunkle, M. C. "What Constitutes Equality for Women in Sport?" *Newsletter for the Project on the Status and Education of Women,* Association of American Colleges, Washington, D.C., 1974.

Edwards, Harry. "Desegregating Sexist Sport." *Intellectual Digest,* 3 (1972), 82-83.

Fasteau, Brenda Feigen. "Giving Women a Sporting Chance." *Ms.,* 2 (July 1973), 56-58, 103.

Felshin, Jan. "The Triple Option . . . For Women in Sport." *Quest,* 21 (January 1974), 36-40.

Feltz, Deborah L. "Athletics in the Status System of Female Adolescents." *Review of Sport & Leisure,* 3 (Fall 1978), 98-108.

Fields, Cheryl M. "July 31: Title IX Deadline." *The Chronicle of Higher Education* (November 14, 1977), pp. 9-11.

Fields, Cheryl M. "Women's Athletics: Struggling with Success." *The Chronicle of Higher Education* (May 22, 1978), pp. 5-6.

Gerber, E. R., J. Felshin, P. Berlin, and W. Wyrick. *The American Woman in Sport.* Reading. Mass.: Addison-Wesley. 2974.

Gilbert, Bill, and Nancy Williamson. "Women in Sport." *Sports Illustrated* (May 28, 1973, June 4, 1973, and June 11, 1973); and a progress report (July 29, 1974).

Griffith, Patricia S. "What's a Nice Girl Like You Doing in a Profession Like This?" *Quest.* 19 (January 1973), 96-101.

Hamon, Kent. "Too Far, Too Fast." *Sports Illustrated* (March 20, 1978), 34-15.

Harding, Carol, ed. "Women in Sport." Special issue of *Arena Newsletter* (April/June 1977).

Harris, Dorothy V. "The Sportswoman in Our Society." *Women in Sport.* Edited by Dorothy V. Harris, Washington, D.C.: American Association for Health, Physical Education, and Recreation, 1971, 1-4.

Harris, Dorothy V., ed. *Women and Sport: A National Research Conference.* Penn State HPER Series No. 2, The Pennsylvania State University, 1972.

Hart, M. Marie. "Women Sit in the Back of the Bus." *Psychology Today,* 5 (1971), 64-66.

Hart, M. Marie. "On Being a Female in Sport." *Sport in the Socio-Cultural Process.* 2nd ed. Edited by M. Marie Hart. Dubuque, Iowa: Wm. C. Brown, 1976, pp. 438-447.

Huckle, Patricia. "Back to the Starting Line." *American Behavioral Scientist,* 21 (January/February: 1978), 279-392.

Klafs, C. E., and J. J. Lyon. *The Female Athlete.* 2nd ed. St. Louis: C. V. Mosby, 1978.

Ley, Katherine. "Women in Sports: Where Do We Go From Here, Boys?" *Phi Delta Kappan,* 56 (October 1974), 129-131.

Loggia, Morjorie. "On the Playing Fields of History." *ms.,* 2 (July 1973), 62-64.

Malmisur, Michael C. "Title IX Dilemma: Meritocratic and Egalitarian Tension," *Journal of Sport Behavior,* 1 (August 1978), 130-138.

Metheny, Eleanor. "Symbolic Forms of Movement: The Feminine Image in Sports." *Sport American Society.* 2nd ed. Edited by George H. Sage. Reading, Mass.: Addison-Wesley, 1974, 289-301.

Michener, James A., *Sports in America.* New York: Random House, 1976, chapter 5.

Novak, Michael. "Football for Feminists." *Commonweal,* 101 (1974), 104, 110.

Roark, Anne C. "Count Rejects NCAA Challenge to Ban on Sex Bias in Sports." *The Chronicle of Higher Education* (January 16, 1978), p. 1.

Schafer, Walter E. "Sport and Male Sex-Role Socialization." *Sport Sociology Bulletin,* 4 (Fall 1975), 47-54.

Scott, Jack. "Making Athletics a Masculinity Rite." *Ramparts,* 10 (January 1973), 64.

Scott, Jack. "The Masculine Obsession in Sports." *Women's Athletics: Coping with Controversy.* Edited by B. J. Hoepner. Washington, D.C.: American Association for Health, Physical Education and Recreation, 1974.

Sherriff, Marie C. "The Status of Female Athletes as Viewed by Selected Peers and Parents in Certain High Schools of Central California." Master's thesis, California State College, Chico, 1969.

Snyder, Eldon E., and Joseph E. Kivlin. "Women Athletes and Aspects of Psychological Well-Being and Body Image." *Research Quarterly,* 46 (May 1975), 191-199.

Snyder, Eldon E., and Joseph E. Kivlin. "Perceptions of the Sex Role Among Female and Nonathletes." *Adolescence,* 12 (Spring 1977), 23-29.

Snyder, Eldon E., Joseph E. Kivlin, and Elmer Spreitzer. "The Female Athlete: An Analysis of Objective and Subjective Role Conflict." *Psychology of Sport and Motor Behavior.* Edited by Daniel M. Landers. University Park: Pennsylvania State University Press, 1975, 165-180.

Snyder, Eldon E., and Elmer Spreitzer. "Correlates of Sport Participation Among Adolescent Girls." *Research Quarterly,* 47 (December 1976), 804-809.

Athletics In High School*

James S. Coleman

Abstract: Research—based on the visibility of athletic stars, on most desired achievement, on the composition of the leading-crowd, on status criteria in leading-crowd membership, on popularity—demonstrates conclusively that athletics is far and away more important as a value among high school students than intellectual achievement. And the school itself seems to encourage rather than to discourage this relative evaluation. There must be basic reasons for these phenomena, and these may be discerned in the functions performed by athletics not only in the school but also in the community. Among boys, for example, it has been found that athletics has a democratizing effect, breaking up organization based on background and reconstituting it on the basis of common activity or achievement. Athletics serves an important function in motivating students. It generates strong positive identification with the school; without athletics the school would be lifeless for the student, deficient in collective goals. With athletics, it is possible for all students to identify with their school through their teams. Not only schools but whole communities depend upon the collective enthusiasm generated by their local high school athletic teams. The problem for the school is to find a way to have the functions now performed by athletic teams performed in ways more conducive to the intellectual aims of the school. Debate used to serve this function, music contests may also, as well as drama contests, and mathematics tournaments. It is possible that social and economic games played by means of complex computers may come to perform, on a far more intellectual level, the integrating function now performed almost exclusively by athletics.

The role of interscholastic athletics in high schools is a controversial one. Athletics is castigated as the antithesis of scholastic activity by intellectuals—many of whom have never taken part in interscholastic sports. It is defended and praised as the builder of men by coaches and athletes—most of whom have a vested interest in this proposition.

It is characteristic of athletics to provoke violent and lasting controversies, for it occupies a very special position in high schools. The amount of attention devoted to athletics would be most striking to an innocent visitor to a high school. A visitor entering a school would likely to be confronted, first of all, with a trophy case. His examination of the trophies would reveal

* James S. Coleman, Ph.D., Baltimore, Maryland, is Professor of Sociology at John Hopkins University. He was a fellow at the Center for Advanced Study in Behavioral Sciences, 1955-1956. He has engaged in extensive research on the values of high school students and on community conflict. He is author of *The Adolescent Society* (1961).

Coleman, James S. "Athletics in High School," *American Academy of Political and Social Science Annals,* Vol. 338, Nov. 1961, pp. 33-43. Reprinted by permission of the publisher and author.

a curious fact: The gold and silver cups, with rare exception, symbolize victory in athletic contests, not scholastic ones. The figures adorning these trophies represent men passing footballs, shooting basketballs, holding out batons;they are not replicas of "The Thinker." The concrete symbols of victory are old footballs, basketballs, and baseballs, not works of art or first editions of books won as literary prizes. Altogether, the trophy case would suggest to the innocent visitor that he was entering an athletic club, not an educational institution.

Walking further, this visitor would encounter teen-agers bursting from classrooms. Listening to their conversations, he would hear both casual and serious discussions of the Friday football game, confirming his initial impression. Attending a school assembly that morning, he would probably find a large segment of the program devoted to a practice of school yells for the athletic game and the announcement of a pep rally before the game. At lunch hour, he would be likely to find more boys shooting baskets in the gymnasium than reading in the library. Browsing through a school yearbook, he would be impressed, in his innocence, with the number of pages devoted to athletics.

Altogether, this visitor would find, wherever he turned, a great deal of attention devoted to athletics. As an impressionable stranger, this visitor might well suppose that more attention is paid to athletics by teen-agers, both as athletes and as spectators, than to scholastic matters. He might even conclude, with good reason, that the school was essentially organized around athletic contests and that scholastic matters were of lesser importance to all involved.

To be sure, his impression would vary from school to school—but, perhaps surprising to him, it would vary little by the social origins and destinations of the adolescents served by the schools. In ten schools recently studied by the author, athletics was about as dominant, by any of several criteria, in middle class schools with a high proportion of their graduates going to college as in working class schools.[1]

Considering his impressions, such a visitor to American high schools might ask himself two questions: First of all, why is it this way? He had assumed, naively, that schools were for learning, yet his impressions led to a different conclusion. He had talked with educators about curriculum, new academic programs, and scholastic standards. Yet, upon visiting the schools, he found the adolescents' attention on athletics, and all the excitement and enthusiasm he found was focused around athletic contests. Why the discrepancy?

The visitor might ask another question: What are the consequences of the attention devoted to athletics? What are the consequences within the school itself, and what are the long-term consequences for these adolescents when they have become adults?

It is to these two questions, the question of consequences and the question of sources, that this paper is directed. The examination will be based upon evidence collected during a study of ten high schools in 1957-1958. These high schools are located in the Middle West. Five were small-town schools with 500 or fewer students; one was a parochial school of 750 boys in a large city; there was a working class, suburban school of 1,000 students; two small-city comprehensive schools were included of 1,400 and 2,000 students respectively; there was an upper middle class, suburban school of 2,000 students. Unless otherwise noted, the generalizations mentioned below apply to all schools.[2] In fact, a striking discovery in this study was the similarity of all schools in the importance attached to athletics. Greater similarity among schools was found in this than in any other dimension of the research.

CONSEQUENCES

The more difficult question concerns the long-term consequences of at tention to athletics. On this question, the study has no evidence, since adolescents were studied only during one year in high school, and there seems to be no systematic evidence on the matter available elsewhere. However, evidence from the research does show some of the short-term consequences, those manifest in the school itself.

Impact on freshmen

The attention focused upon athletics in high schools directly affects the impact of the schools upon their incoming freshmen. Football, which is played in the fall as school begins, is especially important. A major element in the impact of athletics is the visibility of athletic stars. A boy who achieves something, however creditable his achievement, can be a model to emulate only if that achievement is made visible by the structure of activities in the school.

Some idea of the relative visibility of scholastic achievement and athletic achievement can be gained through a finding from the survey of the ten schools. About six weeks after school opened in the fall, each boy in every school was asked to name the boy whom he saw as the best student in his grade and the boy who was the best athlete. This can be a difficult task for freshmen, but it is less difficult in those areas for which school activities focus attention on achievement. Thus, a comparison of the proportions of boys able to answer the questions provides some guide to the relative visibility of scholastic and athletic achievements in each of the four years of school.

Table 1 shows this comparison. The data indicate, in general, that the best athletes are more visible than the best scholars. The difference is greatest for the freshmen—the best athlete is known 10 percent more often than the best scholar in the small schools and 14 percent more often in the large schools. Only in the junior and senior years does the visibility of the best scholars catch up with that of the best athletes. Thus, for the impressionable freshmen, the achievements that stand out most are those of the athlete, not those of the scholar.[3]

Assuming adolescents desire to be successful, known, and recognized, one consequence of the visibility of achievement in athletics or scholarship would be the desire to achieve in these particular areas. Does the environment and climate of opinion in the school affect these desires? Boys were

Table 1. —Comparative Visibility of Best Athletes and Best Scholars
to Their Classmates

	Freshmen	Sophomores	Juniors	Seniors
Small Schools				
Percent naming best athlete	68%	75%	88%	85%
Percent naming best scholar	58%	66%	83%	88%
Number of cases	317 .	292	214	205
Large Schools				
Percent naming best athlete	54%	56%	48%	72%
Percent naming best scholar	40%	47%	57%	68%
Number of cases	635	1,049	749	557

Note: Percentages are based on the nine public schools.

asked, in the fall shortly after school had started and again in the spring
toward the end of the school year, how they would most like to be remembered at school—as a brilliant student, an athletic star, or most popular.
One would suppose, if schools focus attention on scholastic endeavors, that
the effect of the school year would be to increase the strength of the
brilliant-student image relative to that of the athletic-star image. Yet, for
the freshmen and sophomores of the schools surveyed, matters are quite
different. Of all those responding either "brilliant student" or "athletic
star," 44 percent in each grade responded "brilliant student" in the fall and
only 37 percent gave this reponse in the spring.[4] Rather than increasing in
strength over the school year, the brilliant-student image declined in strength
relative to that of the athlete. It appears, then, that the very functioning of
the school itself tends to reduce the initial interest of the adolescent in being
seen as a brilliant student, or tends differentially to increase his interest in
being seen as an athletic star.

Another effect of athletics upon the incoming freshmen concerns the
"leading crowd" in school. Most high schools, other than the very smallest,
have a leading crowd in each grade, though schools larger than about 2,000
in enrollment may have more than one. This crowd is recognized by other
students and by its own members, and most students can name members of
the leading crowd in their grade. This, in fact, was what they were asked to
do in the research discussed above. In addition, all boys were asked to name
their friends, so that it was possible to reconstruct the actual crowds or
cliques in the school. Then, by identifying which of the cliques had as members boys frequently named as members of the leading crowd, it was possible to identify objectively the leading clique or crowd in each grade of each
school. Having done this, the question then was asked: What do these boys,
who constitute the leading crowds in their grades, have in common?[5]

Among the freshmen in each of the four schools studied for leading
cliques, the one attribute shared by every boy in every leading clique—
twenty-three boys in all—was being out for either football or basketball.
Most of the twenty-three were out for both. No other attribute—in back-

ground, activities, or attitudes—so sharply distinguished the leading cliques. In the later years of school, the leading cliques were found to be less uniformly athletic, but, among freshmen, they were found to be totally so.

Athletic participation as a basis for membership in the leading clique is not, of course, characteristic of every freshman class in the country, but it seems likely that the general tendency is widespread. Athletic teams provide a basis for intensive and prolonged association, more than any other activity in school. Thus, the foundation is laid, from the very beginning of high school, for a cohesive, tightly knit group. This, together with the attention directed toward athletic contests and athletic stars in high school, makes it very likely that the athletes will constitute the leading crowd among freshmen. Later, when other activities develop in school and groups form on other bases, there is less dominance of the athletic crowd. But, in the crucial first year, when a boy's aims and aspirations in high school are established, the athletic crowd dominates.

Altogether, then, athletics is a particularly important factor in the impact of the high school upon its freshmen. Through the several mechanisms discussed above, the freshmen get a picture of the school focused even more toward athletic achievement than it actually is.

Athletics in the status system

One of the most important aspects of any social system is its distribution of status: the way status attaches to different persons and to different activities. The importance of the distribution of status lies partly in its effect as a motivating device, for it motivates people toward those activities which confer status upon them. To the extent that adolescents are concerned with status among their peers—and every indication suggests that the great majority of them are so motivated—their motivations and aspirations in various activities are shaped by the distribution of status.

It is important, then, in assessing the consequences of the attention to athletics in high schools, to examine the position of athletics in the adolescent status system. In the present research, this was done by several means.

Each boy was asked to assess what was required in his school to be a member of the leading crowd, and he was asked to rank various attributes for making a boy popular.

In response to the first question, the two attributes most often mentioned were personality—mentioned by 23 percent of the boys—and a good reputation—mentioned by 17 percent. Next in order, however, was athletic ability—mentioned by 16 percent. This was followed by good looks and success with girls—mentioned by 14 percent—and good grades or "brains' —mentioned by 12 percent.

In ranking attributes for their effect in making a boy popular, six attributes were available to be ranked from first to sixth. These attributes, with their average rank in all schools, were the following:"[6]

Being an athletic star	2.2	High grades, honor roll	3.5
Being in the leading crowd	2.6	Having a nice car	3.9
Leader in activities	2.9	Coming from the right family	4.5

176

Table 2. —Average Numbers of Choices Received by Athletes, Scholars, and All Other Boys on Status Criteria

	Be Friends With or Be Like	Members of Leading Crowd	Number of Cases
Athletes	5.6	7.8	272
Scholars	3.4	4.9	278
All Other Boys	0.4	0.8	3,598

Note: "Athletes" and "scholars" are those named two or more times as best athlete or best scholar in their respective grades by other boys. Percentages are based on the nine public schools.

These answers show the great value that boys attribute to athletic achievement in gaining popularity. It is ranked considerably above any other item and far above good grades, which is fourth among the six.

In addition to these subjective estimates, it is also possible to determine which boys have highest status. In this research, it was done by asking each boy to name another boy he would like to be like, one he would like to be friends with, and who were members of the leading crowd. The status of a boy was determined by the number of such choices he received. Another question had made it possible to identify the boys seen as the best athletes and the best scholars. By comparing the likelihood of the best athletes to receive the status choices with the likelihood of the best scholars to receive such choices, it is possible to examine the objective status of athletic achievement. Table 2 shows the average number of choices on these criteria received by the best athletes, the best scholars, and all other boys in the schools studied.

As in various other tests, athletics scored higher than scholarship, although both athletes and scholars far out-distanced other boys. Stated another way, the star athletes, only 6.6 percent of the schools' male enrollment, received 47.4 percent of the "be friends with" and "be like" choices and 36.5 percent of all the leading crowd nominations.

According to all evidence, then, the status of athletic achievement in the schools surveyed is exceedingly high, considerably higher than that of scholastic achievement. Thus, the attention paid to athletics in American high schools, which would so puzzle an innocent visitor, is paralleled by the status of athletic achievement among adolescents.

Other studies

Other research shows that these facts are not limited to the ten schools surveyed nor even to high schools in the Middle West.

In a large, predominantly Jewish, middle class high school in New York City, Abraham Tannenbaum studies evaluations of stereotyped, fictitious students.[7] These fictitious students were distinguished in short descriptive statements on the bases of intelligence, athletic ability, and studiousness. Juniors in the high school were then asked to ascribe traits—some desirable, some undesirable—to each of the eight fictitious characters. Tannenbaum devised a mean acceptability rating from the ascribed traits, and the fictitious students fell in the following order of acceptability, from high to low:

(1) Brilliant nonstudious athlete
(2) Average nonstudious athlete
(3) Average studious athlete
(4) Brilliant studious athlete
(5) Brilliant nonstudious athlete
(6) Average nonstudious nonathlete
(7) Average studious nonathlete
(8) Brilliant studious nonathlete

As the order shows, all athletes had higher acceptability ratings than any nonathlete. Brilliance apparently had little effect in increasing acceptability, and studiousness reduced acceptability. Thus, in a school in which, because of its location and student body, one would expect to find brilliance or studiousness outdistancing athletics, the results are otherwise—and consistent with the results in the ten midwestern high schools.

These data on the status of athletic achievement in schools of widely varying types raise even more insistently the question of why there is such a dominance of athletics. Athletics is wholly outside the focus of attention of many educators in schools of education, for whom curriculum variations have overriding importance. Yet athletics is central to the attention of adolescents, far more so than curriculum variations. And, despite educators' professional disinterest, athletics is an activity promoted by the schools themselves—not an outside interest like cars and dates. These inconsistencies and paradoxes all lead to the question: Why does athletics hold a place of such high importance in the high schools?

Athletics, democracy, and legitimacy of the system

The effect of athletics in forming leading crowds among freshmen was examined earlier; the formation of leading crowds among girls was left unexamined. The cliques of girls among freshmen reflect, much more than for boys, associations from earlier grades. Girls who travel together in the lower grades maintain their cliques in high school and often present an impregnable front to outsiders. Presumably as a result, the leading crowds for girls among freshmen are more completely middle class in background than for boys.

In effect, athletics provides for boys an interruption of this pattern, breaking down the organization based on common background and replacing it with organization based on common activity or achievement. Perhaps as a consequence, boys are more willing than girls to accept the status system of the school and view it as more legitimate. When asked to agree or to disagree that "There are a few who could control things in this school, and the rest of us are out in the cold," 43 percent of the girls agreed with the statement in the fall, and the number increased to 48 percent by the next spring.

Only 34 percent of the boys agreed that the statement was true in the fall, and their number decreased to 32 percent by spring.

Such a democratizing mechanism is particularly important for boys, who, to begin with, are less involved in school than girls and get poorer grades. If it were not for interscholastic athletics or something like it, the rebellion against school, the rate of dropout, and the delinquency of boys might be far worse than they presently are. This can only be a matter of conjecture. It does seem clear, however, that athletics introduces an important democratizing factor in the status system for boys in high school by undercutting social background as a basis for status.

SOURCES

Clearly, a part of the importance of athletics for adolescents lies in its compatibility with teen-age energy, enthusiasm, and explosive spirits. Were it not for this basic compatibility, the avidity with which teen-agers follow sports contests would be difficult to explain.

But the compatibility does not explain the special place that athletics holds in the activities of a school. As an innocent visitor might observe, the institution itself often seems more oriented toward athletic goals than academic ones. This can hardly be explained by the interests of teen-agers alone, for teen-agers are interested in many things—popular music, cars, dates—which have relatively little place in the high school structure of activities. Nor can the interests of teen-agers explain the fact that, in the ten schools surveyed, the strength of the athletic-star image increased during the school year and, apparently, decreased over the summer.[8]

Athletic contests in schools seem to serve an important function for the institution. Every institution depends for its survival upon capturing a certain portion of the energies of its members. In business organizations, this is done by pay, including incentive pay, and by opportunity for promotion. Among some members of an organization, identification with the achievements of the organization provides additional motivation. In unions, motivation derives from the common goals of the members, which can only be gained through concerted, collective effort.[9]

Schools, however, provide no comparable motivating devices for their students. Students are forced by family and by law to attend school, but this insures only their physical presence, not their involvement in school activities. The necessary motivation for the expenditure of effort in school arises naturally only for those students whose backgrounds and aspirations make good grades important for them. For some students, that is, grades are comparable to pay for workers in a factory. The crucial difference is that grades are important only for a part of the school population. For many adolescents, high school only delays their access to adult freedoms and pleasures and does not offer any unique and necessary benefits.

But, even for students with the right backgrounds, grades are a poor motivating mechanism, because they are unique to the school and useful only in comparison with grades of fellow students. This generates invidious comparisons, sets each student in competition with his fellows, and is a powerfully divisive force among the students. Direct incentive pay, or price work, in factories produces the same effect and has sometimes been consciously used by employers to keep employees divided against each other.[10]

In the long run, this is a dangerous mechanism, as the history of incentive pay has shown. Under many conditions, it encourages informal norms restricting production —against the "rate-buster"—just as grade systems in high schools promote informal action against too much studiousness— against "the curve-breaker" or the "D.A.R.," Damned Average Raiser. Finally, piece work systems in factories have led to organized collective activity against the companies, unless the workers feel strongly identified with their companies.[11]

A much more successful mechanism of control in an institution is one which generates strong positive identification with the institution. Churches employ such mechanisms with their revival meetings and special holy day services. Associations and groups of all sorts do the same with rallies and collective events. But schools—apart from their athletic contests and similar activities—are peculiar institutions. There are no collective goals which the students share, and the institution is lifeless. There are only individual goals, individual scholastic achievements, made largely at the expense of other students.

Athletic contests with other schools provide, for these otherwise lifeless institutions, the collective goals that they lack. The common goals shared by all makes the institution part of its members and them part of it, rather than an organization outside them and superimposed upon them. The results are evident to any observer: The adolescent social system is centered at the school, not at the drugstore; the name by which the teen-agers identify themselves is that of the school ("Those are East High kids; I'm from Tech."); the teen-agers think of the school, the team, and the student body as one and use the pronoun "we" in referring to this entity ("We're playing Parkville Friday.").

Such effects are evident as well in the bases of alumni loyalty to many private preparatory schools and colleges. Athletic competition as a basis of loyalty is so dominant that the stereotypical alumnus is a man cheering wildly at a football game, waving a school banner in his hand. Colleges which dropped interscholastic athletics, like University of Chicago, or which never depended on them, like John Hopkins, thereby sacrificed the attention and support of many alumni.[12] Historians have noted that colleges in the United States, before the introduction of organized sports, were beset by student violence directed at both the college and other students. Sports seemed to transform the disorganized and explosive student body into a close-knit community with strong common goals.

Thus, the importance of athletic contests in both high schools and colleges, at least in part, in the way the contests solve a difficult problem for the institution—the problem of generating enthusiasm for and identification with the school and drawing the energies of adolescents into the school.

In the study of the ten high schools upon which much of this paper is based, all students were asked, "If school were not compulsory and it were completely up to you, would you stay in school until graduation, leave school before graduation, or are you undecided? Very few students, only 3.6 percent, responded that they would leave, and only 9.3 percent were undecided. It is hard to imagine that the great body of adolescents in our society which has been brought into high school in such a short period could be so positively oriented to school without some mechanism such as athletic contests for providing common goals.[13]

Lack of common commuinity goals

A force which strengthens the emphasis upon athletics in the high schools comes from outside the schools themselves. Except in the very largest cities, a high school is a community or neighborhood institution. Many communities have only a single high school, whose name is the name of the town. In those cities with several high schools, each school usually represents a community area within the city and often carries the name of that community.

Communities, like schools without interscholastic games, have few common goals. They fight no wars, seldom engage in community rallies, and are rarely faced with such crises as floods or tornadoes that can endanger a communal spirit and make members feel close to one another by creating collective goals. One of the few mechanisms by means of which this can occur is that of games or contests between communities. Sometimes these games are between professional teams representing the communities.[14] More often, there are high school games, and these contests serve the purpose admirably. The community supports the team, and the team rewards the community when it wins. The team is a community enterprise, and its successes are shared by the community, its losses mourned in concert.

The results of this are evident in many ways. One striking evidence is teacher salaries. The school board characteristically pays more to athletic coaches than to other teachers and, occasionally, to keep a winning coach, may pay more than to the principal. When a new principal is to be found among the ranks of teachers, the pattern is common for the athletic coach to be promoted to the job.[15]

Another indicator is buildings. It is often easier to obtain funds for a new gymnasium—especially in "basketball territory'—than for other buildings. In Paris, Illinois, for example, where the high school team won the state basketball tournament a few years ago, the community voted funds for a large new gymnasium, while the high school remained without a library. In one of the ten schools included in the survey, the author found, returning in 1961, that a new gymnasium and a new reading room had been built. Funds for the gymnasium had been donated by a member of the community; the reading room had been added by means of school building funds.

SUBSTITUTES FOR ATHLETICS

It is indisputable that the interscholastic sports function to give the school and the community a collective identity. Few principals would seriously consider dispensing with these games. Yet, it is also indisputable that athletic contests create serious problems for schools. Perhaps the most serious problem is the change they engender in the institution itself. Their very importance to the life of the school transforms the school from an institution devoted to learning into an institution focused, at least partly, on athletics.

It is useful to wonder whether another mechanism might not give the school collective goals without effecting this transformation. Completely to replace athletic contests between schools with something else would possibly have ill effects. To reduce the dominance of athletics in high schools, however, clearly would be desirable. The most obvious course is to keep the game but to change the contest in the direction of educational goals. Although it is true that athletics fits especially well with the interests and energies of adolescents, other games could fit equally well.

There is some experience with games and contests other than athletics, the most extensive being with debate. In a number of areas where debate leagues have flourished, these contests have generated some of the same community and school enthusiasm and involvement that is evident with athletic games. In a few states, interscholastic leagues promote competition in other fields than athletics: music, drama, mathematics. Although the effects of these contests have not been adequately evaluated, they do provide examples of what might be done.

There has very recently been another development which promises to make games truly educational in many areas. These are social and economic games which use a complex environment provided by electronic computers. The first to be developed were management games which involve teams of decision-makers representing competing firms. These games have been used by business and are coming to be used in graduate business schools. A political game, with teams representing political candidates in competition for votes, has been programed for a computer and is used in a college course at Johns Hopkins. At least one economic game has been developed—at Washington University in St. Louis—for teaching the course in principles of economics. Experience with these games shows that they generate a high degree of involvement and interest among players and spectators. It is possible that the most valuable use of machines in education will come to be their use for games, rather than programed learning.

These examples indicate that it is possible to change the content of games in an educational direction yet to maintain some of the values athletics provides for school. To do this, however, would require more than sporadic contests. To gain attention and involvement, leagues, schedules, and tournaments would be necessary. Through such means, it might be possible to transform schools back into the educational institutions they were intended to be. An innocent visitor to such an institution, upon examining the trophy case, listening to student conversation, and examining a yearbook, might well conclude that the institution was one devoted to learning.

182

REFERENCE NOTES

1. See James S. Coleman, *The Adolescent Society* (Glencoe: The Free Press, 1961), pp. 70-71, 88-90.

2. In certain cases, random variation due to the small number of students in the smallest school prevents separate conclusions about it.

3. Other areas of achievement were included in the questionnaire, for example, knowing about cars and being most attractive to the girls. The visibility for both of these was far below that for athletes or scholars.

4. The number of cases was over 800 in each grade, so the difference reported is significant beyond the .001 level.

5. This question was studied only in four of the five smallest schools; technical problems prevented it in the large schools, and the smallest school had no distinct crowds.

6. The ranks average to 3.3 rather than 3.5 as they should, because not every boy assigned all ranks.

7. Abraham J. Tannenbaum, ''Adolescents' Attitudes Toward Academic Brilliance'' (unpublished Ph.D. dissertation, New York University, 1960).

8. For further discussion of this point, see Coleman, *op. cit.,* p. 303.

9. When a union becomes merely a business union, no longer actively fighting for collective worker benefits, it survives in name, but it can no longer depend upon its members for active support. This, in fact, is the fundamental problem of many unions at the present time.

10. This can be illustrated by the story, perhaps apocryphal, of the employer who paid every second worker on an assembly line a higher rate, so that every worker's neighbors received rates different from his own. A similar mechanism has been documented in department stores, where clerks are given marginal differentiations in title and pay to keep them divided. See Carl Dreyfuss, ''Prestige Grading: A Mechanism of Control,'' in R. K. Merton and Others, *Reader in Bureaucracy* (Glencoe: The Free Press, 1952), pp. 258-264.

11. One of the important reasons that incentive pay, in the form of commissions, has always worked well for salesmen is that their active work in selling the company products to doubtful customers generates in them a positive identification with the company. Another reason, of course, is that they are usually dispersed, not in contact with one another.

12. This is not to say that the absence of athletic emphasis in these institutions has principally had consequences. Many colleges have, rather, compromised their original goal's through the power and interest of their athletically involved alumni. But the withdrawal from interscholastic athletics without the substitution of other bases for institution-inspired pride and identification leaves the institution worker and less likely to survive.

13. Thus suggests that high schools in Europe, which are coming to enroll larger and larger proportions of adolescents, will increase the emphasis upon athletic contests, unless they find another mechanism to accomplish the same end.

14. The sense of shock and disbelief in Brooklyn when the Dodgers moved to Los Angeles is a measure of Broooklynites' identification of the team with their community. On the other side, it has been said that Los Angeles ceased to be a collection of suburbs and became a city for the first time when ''their'' Dodgers won a pennant.

15. This pattern is being replaced by a pattern of promoting assistant principals or guidance counselors, who have administrative training in schools of education. There is no evidence that they make better principals than coaches do.

The Relationship Between Academic Achievement And Interscholastic Participation: A Comparison Of Canadian And American High Schools *

Wendy C. Jerome
John C. Phillips

Interscholastic athletics have been considered an anti-intellectual influence by some authors (Henry, 1963; Coleman, 1961, 1965) who argue that school athletic programs encourage a diversion of school resources, parental support, and student energies away from the mission of scholastic excellence. Recent studies of American high school athletic programs, however, provide compelling evidence that participation in athletics is associated with better grades, higher aspiration levels, and a more positive attitude towards school.

A variety of plausible explanations for this phenomenon have been suggested which center around three basic themes: (1) selection—the better, more pro-school students try out for, and are selected to membership on school teams; (2) "spill-over"—there is a transfer of positive work habits, attitudes, and values from sports to school work; and (3) differential school experiences—athletes are more visible, acquire increased status, and receive more encouragement from school personnel than do non-athletes.

This paper will review some of the evidence concerning athletic participation and scholastic achievement in American and Canadian high schools and discuss certain cultural differences which may explain the variation noted in the relationships between sports and studies.

Schafer and Armer (1968) found that high school athletes achieved slightly better grades than their non athletes matches and that this advan-

* Wendy C. Jerome and John C. Phillips, "The Relationship Between Academic Achievement and Interscholastic Participation: A Comparison of Canadian and American High Schools," *Journal of the Canadian Association for Health, Physical Education and Recreation*. January-February 1971, Volume 37, pp. 18-21. Reprinted by permission of the publisher.

tage increased among boys from blue-collar homes and boys who were not in a college-preparatory program. Bend (1968), in a nationwide study of American high school athletes, found substantially the same pattern. Athletes got slightly better grades and the advantage of the athletes was most pronounced among "low endowment" (low IQ, blue-collar) boys. Buhrmann's (1968) study of junior high school boys in Oregon also found that participation seemed to encourage students from poor and disadvantaged groups to achieve scholastically at a much higher level than their non-participating peers.

There is strong evidence to indicate that athletes aspire to attend college and succeed in attending college more than do non-athletes. Bend (1968) found that 81.8% of his superior athletes aspired to at least some college work compared to 56.1% of his non-athletes. The figures for low-endowment superior athletes were 39.8% and 13.3% respectively. Of the superior athletes, 71.4% actually attended college while 50% of the non-athletes attended. Figures for the low-endowment athletes and non-athletes were 14.8% and 6.9%. Rehberg and Schafer (1968; 1970) found similar patterns in aspirations and expectations for college attendance.

In a recent study of one American high school, Phillips and Schafer (1970) found that athletes, when compared to non-athletes, shared attitudes which were somewhat more favourable toward the school and its traditions. They concluded that the better academic performance by athletes could be explained by the greater pressures toward conformity to school rules and traditions expected of athletes, as well as a more positive attitude toward the school among athletes. Since athletic's, to a greater degree than scholarship, also provides entry to elite school status in American schools (Coleman, 1960; Clark, 1957; Horowitz, 1967), we should not be surprised at the athletes' relatively strong support for school rules and traditions.

It should be noted that there is some support for the concept of the "all-round" individual. Both Coleman and Horowitz found that the "athlete-scholar" rated highest on measures of interpersonal popularity. In comparisons between the "pure" athlete and the "pure" scholar, however, both found that the athlete was accorded much higher status. Explaining this phenomenon, Coleman presents the view that because members of the school and community identify strongly with the success and failure of "their" team, the athlete gains status because he is doing something for the community. Success in scholastic matters, on the other hand, is obtained at the expense of classmates and often results ridicule and rejection of the achiever, unless balanced by athletic contributions.

These, and other recent studies, have provided some insight into the relationship of high school athletic participation to scholastic achievement. However, the results of these studies conducted in American high schools are often applied to the Canadian high school, perhaps because of the apparent similarities between the two countries and the fact that little research has been conducted on the Canadian high school athlete.

It would appear from the results of the few studies that have been conducted that a difference does exist. Jerome, in a study currently underway in Sudbury, Ontario finds that while the majority of students would aspire to be "athlete-scholars," in comparisons between the "pure" athlete and the "pure" scholar, the athlete was far down the line. This attitude among Canadian students is further supported by Zentner and Parr (1968) whose study of social status among high school students in Calgary led them to conclude that high academic performance was a positive factor in the student status structure. In that study, students with high academic achievement were overrepresented in the leading crowds.

As for the relationship between academic achievement and athletic participation, Jerome found that when final grade averages obtained by students prior to opportunity for interscholastic competition were compared to those achieved after this opportunity was available, the non-participants' grades changed in an upward direction while those of the athletes became lower. The differences between the two groups were significant at the .05 level. Further, when socio-economic status and academic program were considered, it was found that non-participant's grades improved to a greater degree than did those of athletes of the same social class and academic program. Again the differences were significant.

A further study by King and Angi (1968) of the hockey playing student in Ontario found that in Grade 9 hockey playing students achieved similar marks to non-hockey playing students, were slightly lower on achievement and aptitude tests, and had higher academic and vocational goals. However, by the time these hockey players had reached Grade 12 they had significantly lower school marks than the non-players, significantly lower achievement and aptitude scores, and had lowered their academic and vocational goals. It should be noted that these hockey players were not involved in interscholastic hockey, but in highly organized Junior A, B, C, and D hockey programs in the community which are not conducted to fit around the students' academic repsonsibilities as are interscholastic sports.

Why these differences between school athletes in the two countries? On the surface it would appear that the interscholastic programs in Canada and the United States are similar. A wide range of activities, competitive leagues, school awards, state and provincial championships are common to both. Certified teachers coach the teams. The local news media cover the competitions and report on the results.

Returning to the three explanations posed earlier, if the better, more motivated students tend to go out for, and be selected to athletic teams, we could expect the positive relationship between athletic participation and academics to hold in both American and Canadian schools. Also, if as Schafer and Armer (1968) have suggested, good habits and application to sports carry over to academic matters, we would expect athletes from both cultures to do better in school. If we accept this reasoning, we can expect students to do better in studies as a result of participation in athletics regardless of whether they receive special attention from the school. This does not appear to be so in Canadian schools. It would seem then, that the third explanation offered, differential school experiences, would be the most plausible.

186

It is clear that in the American secondary school high recognition and accompanying status are achieved directly through athletic activities. Athletes are more likely to be members of the leading crowds than are scholars. Coleman (1960) showed that athletic success was clearly and consistently the most important means to achievement of status in every school he studied. Schafer and Armer (1968) feel that for the blue-collar boy the most certain means of entry into the "leading crowd" is athletics. This does not appear to be the case in the Canadian school. The athlete is visible, but not to the same degree, and his acceptance into the leading crowd appears to be dependent to a greater degree on his scholastic aptitude.

Downey's (1960) study of cultural differences between various regions of the United States and Canada sheds some light on why this situation may be present. He found that Canadians placed a greater emphasis on the pursuit of knowledge and scholarly attitudes as an outcome of schooling than did Americans. The American schools tended to emphasize physical development, citizenship, and social skills. The reward structures of the schools would tend to reflect these emphases. Spady (1970) has suggested that many students may view athletics as an alternative to, rather than complementary to, the academic mission of the school. Canadian schools, by increasing rewards available to participants in academic areas may encourage the less interested students to use athletics as an alternative.

Schafer and Armer (1968) reason that another positive effect participation in athletics may have upon the grades of American students is the "lure" of a college career in sports provided through athletic scholarships. This financial assistance available in almost every post-high school institution in the United States is not common in Canadian institutions of higher learning. The availability of these scholarships to American students might well encourage them to maintain their grades at a level which would assure them of consideration by college coaches.

In addition, the degree of emphasis and support from the American community for the high school athletic program is much greater than that found in Canada. American communities identify with "their" team. It is not uncommon to see a large number of adults mixed with students at high school athletic contests. In most Canadian schools, it is uncommon to see a large number of students in attendance. Local news media in both countries provide coverage for high school sports; however, in the United States this coverage extends to national sports magazines. These periodicals carry results of high school competitions, they publicize all-stars, and carry articles on high school athletes of national calibre. Rarely does one see a Canadian high school athlete mentioned outside the high school column of the local newspaper.

The findings suggest that the positive relationship between athletic participation and academic achievement in American high schools can probably best be explained by special rewarding experiences in and from the school and community. Athletes, like all other creatures, appear to become positively attached to sources of rewarding experiences, in this case the school. Perhaps, too, as Schafer and Armer (1968) suggest, the high prestige that American students obtain from sports participation gives them a better self-concept resulting in a more positive attitude towards themselves and their abilities—both athletic and scholastic. In the absence of a differential reward structure favouring athletics, one cannot expect athletes, as a group, to excel in their school work to a greater degree than other students.

REFERENCE NOTES

1. Bend, Emil. *The Impact of Athletic Participation on Academic and Career Aspiration and Achievement.* (New Brunswick, New Jersey: The National Football Foundation and Hall of Fame, 1968).

2. Buhrmann, Hans G. "Longitudinal Study of the Relationship Between Athletic Participation, Various Social-Psychological Variables, and Academic Achievement of Junior High School Boys' (Microcarded Ph.D. dissertation, University of Oregon, 1968).

3. Clark, B. R. *Educating the Expert Society.* (San Francisco: Chandler, 1962), pp. 244-258.

4. Coleman, James S. "Adolescent Subculture and Academic Achievement," *American Journal of Sociology,* Vol. LXV (January, 1960), pp. 337-347.

5. _____. *The Adolescent Society.* (New York: The Free Press, 1961).

6. _____. "Peer Cultures and Education in Modern Society." In Theodore M. Newcomb and Everett K. Wilson (eds.), *College Peer Groups: Problems and Prospects for Research.* (Chicago: Aldine, 1966), pp. 244-269.

7. Downey, L. W. "Regional Variations in Educational Viewpoint," *Alberta Journal of Educational Research,* Vol. VI, No. 4 (December, 1960), pp. 195-199.

8. Hargreaves, David H. *Social Relation in a Secondary School.* (London: Routledge and Kegan Paul, 1967).

9. Henry, Jules. *Culture Against Man.* (New York: John Wiley and Sons, 1963).

10. Horowitz, Herbert. "Prediction of Adolescent Popularity and Rejection from Achievement and Interest Tests," *Journal of Educational Psychology,* Volume 58, No. 3 (1967), pp. 170-174.

11. Jerome, Wendy C. "A Study to Determine the Relationships Between Participation in Organized Interscholastic and Community Sports and Academic Achievement," (Unfinished Ph.D. dissertation, University of Oregon).

12. King, A. J. C., and Carol E. Angi. "The Hockey Playing Student," *CAHPER Journal,* Vol. 35, No. 1 (October-November, 1968), pp. 25-28.

13. Phillips, John C., and Walter E. Schafer. "The Athletic Subculture: A Preliminary Study." Paper presented at the annual meeting of the American Sociological Association, Washington, D.C., 1970.

14. Rehberg, Richard A. and Walter E. Schafer. "Participation in Interscholastic Athletics and College Expectations," *American Journal of Sociology,* 73 (May, 1968), pp. 732-740.

15. Schafer, Walter E., and J. Michael Armer. "Athletes are Not Inferior Students," *Transaction,* (November, 1968), pp. 21-26. 61-62.

16. _____ and Richard A. Rehberg. "Athletic Participation, College Aspirations and College Encouragement." *Pacific Sociological Review,* 13 (Summer, 1970), pp. 182-186.

17. Spady, William G. "Lament for the Letterman: Effects of Peer Status and Extracurricular Activities on Goals and Achievement," *American Journal of Sociology,* 75 (January, 1970), pp. 680-702.

18. Zentner, Henry, and Arnold R. Parr. "Social Status in the High School: An Analysis of Some Related Variables," *Alberta Journal of Educational Research,* Vol. XIV, No. 4 (December, 1968).

DISCUSSION QUESTIONS

D. Wendy C. Jerome and John C. Phillips

1. How do American and Canadian student-athletes compare in terms of academic achievement?

2. What accounts for the differences in academic achievement between American and Canadian student-athletes?

3. Do you feel that another type of reward system could successfully replace athletics in the American school system? Explain your answer.

Socialization Into And Through Sport Involvement*

Barry D. McPherson

INTRODUCTION

Socialization is a complex social process designed to produce as an end product an individual who is prepared (i.e., socialized) for the requirements of participation in society in general, and for the performance of a variety of social roles in specific sub-groups within that society.

While the socialization process has functioned in both primitive and modern societies, it is only since the early 1900s that the phenomenon has been the subject of scholarly investigation. Initially, the findings and explanations were based on the insights and observations of philosophers and psychologists who were intrigued with the problem of how the human animal became a human social being. With the advent of experimental psychology, interest in child development was initiated, including the study of child rearing-techniques. More recently, a third stage has suggested that individuals are involved in the socialization process throughout the life-cycle, and hence, studies related to adolescent and adult socialization have appeared in the literature (Brim and Wheeler 1966; Goslin 1969: 821-1002; Mortimer and Simmons 1978).

This article describes conceptual frames of reference and outlines the process of socialization in general; reviews recent findings which seek to describe socialization "into" a variety of sport roles; and, reviews the general socialization effects resulting from participation in sport.

THE SOCIALIZATION PROCESS

Theories and Conceptual Approaches

In recent years a vast amount of literature pertaining to the process of socialization has appeared, including four major publications (Clausen 1968; Goslin 1969; Sewell 1963; Zigler and Child 1969). A review of this literature indicates that several conceptual and theoretical approaches have been utilized, including psychoanalysis, psychoanalytically-oriented social anthropology, a normative-maturational approach, a developmental-cognitive approach, a genetic and constitutional approach, and various learning theory approaches. To date, the social learning orientations have been

*In Luschen, Gunther R. F. and Sage, George H. (eds.). *Handbook of Social Science of Sport*. Champaign, Ill.: Stipes Pub. Co. 1981, pp. 246-273. Reprinted by permission of the publisher.

the most productive in terms of both theoretical development and empirical findings (Bandura and Walters 1963; Brim and Wheeler 1966; Clausen 1968). Furthermore, an understanding of the process has been facilitated by the contributions of role theory (Sarbin and Allen 1968) and reference group theory (Kemper 1968).

Social learning theory is based on the concepts of "modeling," "immitation," and "vicarious learning." Bandura and Walters (1963) and Bandura (1969) argued that most social behavior, including the learning of specific social roles, is acquired by observing the behavior of significant others (role models or reference groups), without the observer reproducing the observed behavior at that point in time. That is, unlike traditional stimulus-response learning, the novice does not immediately practice the behavior and receive feedback or direct reinforcement. Rather, the behaviors are observed, assimilated and subsequently exhibited in appropriate situations. The models for this imitation process can be real (e.g., adults, peers) or symbolic (e.g., observing television characters whereby the individual does not have direct face-to-face interaction with the role model).

Role theory recognizes that a child is born into an ongoing society with common symbols, established patterns of behavior in recognized social positions, and, it is through others that the child learns these elements of the social world. This theory seeks to explain the process by which an individual becomes a functioning member of the group, and does not seek to account for the unique expression in interpersonal relationships of particular attitudes, opinions and traits. According to role theory the learning process consists of the role of socializer, occupied by established members of the system (i.e., significant others), and the role of socializer, occupied by the newcomers (Jones 1965).

Reference group theory is a third paradigm which has some utility in helping us to understand the socialization process. According to this model "a person orients himself to groups and other individuals and uses them as significant means of reference for his own behavior, attitudes or feelings" (Deutsch and Kraus 1965: 193). The importance of reference groups in the socialization process was first noted by Kemper (1968) who suggested that reference groups have different functions as socializing agents in that they can serve as normative groups, role models, or audience groups. Thus, the normative group (e.g., the family) interacts with the individual and provides guides to action by establishing norms and espousing values; the role model demonstrates how something is done in a technical sense; and, the audience group, which does not take notice of the individual, is recognized by the individual who attributes certain values and attitudes to this group and attempts to behave in accordance with these values.

In summary, a great deal of social learning occurs through observation, immitation, role-playing, interaction with significant others and identification. However, it must be remembered that individual patterns of learning may vary because of sex, social class, community or ethnic differences within the same society; or, because of individual differences in lifestyle for exposure to social learning agents.

191

The Process of Socialization

Although an extensive review of the parameters influencing the process of socialization (cf. McPherson 1972) is not possible here the following is a synopsis of the "social role-social system approach" advocated by Sewell (1963). The three main elements of the socialization process include: *Significant others* (Woelfel and Haller 1971) or socializing agents who serve as role models; *social situations* (e.g., the home, school, gymnasium, neighborhood) and, *role learners* who are characterized by a wide variety of relevant ascribed and achieved personal attributes (e.g., personality traits, attitudes, motivations, values, attitudes, motor ability, race, ethnicity, gender). More specifically, the learning of a social role takes place when a role aspirant is exposed to a variety of stimuli and reinforcements provided by significant others (e.g., parents, peers, coaches, teachers, professional athletes, etc.) who are within one or more norm-encumbered social systems such as the family, school, church, peer group, sport group, or the mass media. Furthermore, within each social system these significant others have the potential to facilitate or inhibit role learning depending on the unique values, norms, sanctions and opportunity sets (Smelser 1962) they provide at any given point in time.

It must be recognized that a given social system (e.g., the school) may be supportive, indifferent or in direct opposition to the learning of a role, and that the influence of a given system may vary over time depending on the role aspirant's stage in the life-cycle. For example, while parents and siblings may be important, if not essential, in the socialization process during childhood, they become of less importance, or of no importance, when considering the learning of specific roles during young adulthood.

To illustrate the foregoing, the following digression provides an example of how and to what extent an individual is socialized into the role of elite hockey player (Clark 1977; McPherson 1977). Although a certain amount of trial-and-error learning occurs, especially with respect to the learning of sport skills, much of the learning occurs through imitation and modeling of significant others including: parents and siblings within the family system; coaches, peers and other players in the hockey milieu; teachers and peers within the schools; and, those who appear in the mass media, including reporters, telecasters, and professional athletes (Goldstein and Bredemeier 1977; Smith and Blackman 1978). Each significant other has the potential to facilitate or inhibit a child's development depending on the values, norms, sanctions and opportunity set provided at a given point in time. For example, if hockey, and especially the attainment of a high level of success, does not rank high in the leisure or career hierarchy of values held by parents, peers and teachers; if positive reinforcement for achieving in hockey is not received from these significant others; and, if an opportunity set is not provided so that equipment, ice-time and coaching are available, then it is highly unlikely tht an individual exposed to this type of socialization setting would ever become involved in hockey, or become an elite hockey player, regardless of how much natural ability they may have.

On the other hand, an individual with parents, friends, coaches and teachers who encourage and reinforce their interest and success in hockey; who learns that professional or Olympic hockey is a legitimate career path; and, who receives good equipment and coaching; is likely to continue in the game and establish aspirations to attain the highest level of success that his physical skills permit. In fact, this latter social milieu often permits an individual with marginal physical skills to attain high levels of success, whereas in the former environment he may drop out of competitive hockey because he does not receive sufficient social support from his significant others.

Factors Influencing Role Acquisition

The nature of the role dictates to some extent the socialization process, and therefore an understanding of the characteristics of a particular role is an essential prerequisite to the study of the process whereby that role is learned. Thus, the first problem for an investigator involves identifying and classifying the many roles within a given social system. Kenyon (1969) presented a conceptual framework outlining a number of primary and secondary roles, such as participant, consumer and producer which are found within a sport system. These three categories can be further delineated to include specific participant (e.g., hockey, football, tennis players), consumer (direct or indirect), or producer (e.g., team, owner, manufacturer, official) roles. Moreover, each of the specific roles includes a behavioral, cognitive and affective component which may vary in importance depending on the role. For example, whereas the role of sport consumer may demand higher levels of involvement in the cognitive and affective dimensions, the role of official would require more skill in the behavioral and cognitive dimensions (McPherson 1976b).

Although it is not possible in this paper to delineate the role expectancies associated with a variety of sport roles, as an example, those who play the role of sport consumer may be expected to: (1) invest varying amounts of time and money in numerous forms of direct and indirect secondary sport involvement; (2) have varying degrees of knowledge concerning sport performers, sport statistics, and sport strategies; (3) have an effective (emotive) involvement with one or more individuals or groups in the sport system; (4) experience, and either internalize or verbalize feelings and mood states while consuming a sport event; (5) employ sport as a major topic of conversation with peers and strangers; and, (6) arrange their leisure-time life-style around professional and amateur sport events.

Regardless of the role, there appear to be four stages which a role incumbent must pass through in order to be socialized into that role (Thornton and Nardi 1975). Each stage is characterized by an increasing awareness of implicit or explicit expectations encompassing: how they should behave in that social position; the appropriate attitudes and values they should hold; and, the specific knowledges or skills they should require. Thus, each stage involves interaction between individuals and externally induced expectations.

The first stage is anticipatory wherein the role aspirant, not yet in the position, holds a number of stereotyped expectations. These are often incomplete representations of reality in that only the overt, positive facets of the role are known and recognized. For example, for the role of professional athlete, the job insecurity, the fatigue of travelling, and the possibility of a short career with an involuntary retirement are seldom recognized by children or adolescents.

Thornton and Nardi (1975: 876) describe the second stage as the "formal" period wherein the individual enters the social position and encounters official and formal expectations concerning behavior and abilities. This stage is characterized by a high degree of consensus between the significant others and the role aspirant which results in conformity. This would be characteristic of a first year professional or college athlete (i.e., a rookie).

The "informal" third stage involves the learning of unofficial and informal expectations pertaining to the attitudinal and cognitive features of the role which are transmitted through interaction with individuals. Much of this learning for the professional athlete takes place in the "backstage" area (Goffman 1959) such as, restaurants, locker rooms and hotel rooms. It is in this stage that the individual begins to shape the role to "fit" himself, his past experiences and future objectives, and to work out an individual style of role performance (Thornton and Nardi 1975: 879).

The "personal" stage occurs last and is an extension of the previous stage. Individuals now are able to impose their own expectations and conceptions on roles and thereby modify role expectations according to their own personalities. By this stage in the process they are able to influence the expectations others hold for them and thereby merge the "self" with the "role." Thus, we see similar roles played with different "style," both on and off the field.

The process is also influenced by a number of macro and microsystem factors and by ascribed social categories. At the macro level, within a given society, there is often a dominant ideology which reflects the social values and norms and which influences the behavioral patterns in that country or community, including those related to sport. Thus, there tend to be both intra-societal regional differences and cross-national differences in the socialization process.

Within both macro and micro social systems, readily identifiable social categories influence the socialization process. These categories, most of which are ascribed rather than achieved, include: social class background, ethnicity, religion, gender, place and type of residence, ordinal position and age. Since it is possible to group people into social categories, rights, expectations and opportunities in a variety of domains are allocated according to prevailing values or beliefs. These ascribed attributes often dictate an individual's life chances. For example, these categories may influence whether the individual has access to certain sport opportunities or sport organizations. Interestingly, most of these attributes derive from the family system but remain as influential factors throughout the life-cycle and operate in most social systems. If an individual is situated in two or more of these categories (e.g., a lower class black female) they may experience discrimination and therefore the possibility of their becoming involved in certain leisure

194

phenomena may be highly restricted. Other categories such as social class background, ethnicity, and religion influence the socialization process by virtue of both the opportunity set that members of certain groups can provide, and by the prevailing values, attitudes and norms which derive from these specific sub-cultures.

Further, although changes are occurring, there are unique sex differences in the socialization process (Hall 1978; Greendorfer 1978b; Loy, McPherson and Kenyon 1978; 225-225; Lever 1978). This occurs because there are different expectations for the "female" and the "male" role in most societies as a result of differing values, norms and sanctions which are considered appropriate with respect to involvement in sport and physical activity (Lever 1976).

An individual's ordinal position also influences the socialization process in that a first born does not have the same opportunity to imitate siblings as does the later born. For example, Nisbett (1968) suggested that first borns, compared to later borns, are more psychologically dependent upon adults, have less freedom selecting activities, are more vulnerable to stress, and are less capable of enduring pain. Furthermore, both Nisbett (1968) and Gould and Landers (1972) found that the first born child is much less likely than later borns to participate in more dangerous sports such as hockey, football, and wrestling. Similar findings have been reported by Yiannakis (1976) and Casher (1977). More specifically, Casher studied individual sports of a low-harm and high-harm nature and found that the proportion of athletes in the more dangerous sports increased directly with birth order from first born (41%) to second born (45%) to third born (75%).

Age is another social category which influences the process. That is, there are age-related norms which are unique to particular cultures or subcultures and which determine appropriate or inappropriate behavior at particular points in the life-cycle. Thus, whereas a female may be permitted to participate in sport and physical activity during childhood, she may receive negative sanctions for continuing this type of behavior as she approaches early adolescence. Age, alone and in conjunction with gender can greatly influence the process of socialization into sport roles (McPherson 1978b).

The geographical area where an individual spends the first ten or fifteen years of life also influences the process. It is this location within the country and within a community (whether one lives in a rural or urban environment, in an apartment or a house, or in the suburbs versus the urban core) which determines the opportunity set that is provided to become involved in specific leisure activities (Rooney 1974).

To summarize, the socialization process is a complex phenomenon which is highly dependent upon formal and informal learning, imitation of significant others, and the influence of a variety of system-induced factors and ascribed social categories. The remaining sections discuss these parameters as they pertain to socialization and sport.

SOCIALIZATION INTO SPORT ROLES
Introduction
Despite the importance of understanding how and why some people

become involved in sport while others do not, relatively little research has been undertaken in this area. However, some recent efforts have been directed toward this problem and findings are presented for two major models of sport involvement: primary involvement, including the role of elite (Olympic calibre) athlete and college athlete; and, secondary involvement, including the role of sport consumer, coach and sport executive. In addition, related information is presented to indicate the impact of macro and micro systems and social categories on the process of becoming socialized into sport roles. Throughout, the reader should note that the social systems exert varying degrees of influence according to the sport, the stage in the life-cycle, the gender of the role aspirant, and, the particular component of the role being considered (i.e., the behavioral, affective or cognitive domain).

Socialization Into Primary Sport Roles

Kenyon and McPherson (1973) and Kenyon (1977) considered the factors which influence an individual to achieve the role of Olympic track and field athlete. For most, involvement in sport began early in life with 96 percent indicating that they participated in football, basketball or baseball in elementary school. Moreover, over 65 percent indicated that they participated in football, basketball or baseball in elementary school. Furthermore, over 65 percent reported that they were "winners" the first time they competed in a sport event, thereby suggesting that a high degree of sport aptitude was present at an early age. However, ability alone does not totally account for their involvement and later success in the role of track and field athlete since 50 percent of the subjects did not participate or compete in track and field until after they entered high school. That is, the learning of the role was situationally influenced by significant others who either competed themselves and served as role models or taught and reinforced the role behavior within a specific social setting, namely, the school. For example, over 75 percent of the respondents indicated that their interest in the activity was first aroused in school. In addition, over 80 percent of the athletes reported that they attended a school where the students and teachers valued track and field and considered it to be an important extra-curricular activity. Thus, a social situation which values certain patterns of behavior and provides opportunities for the learning of that behavior influences which roles will be learned.

In addition to the social situation, significant others with whom the respondents interacted also contributed to the socialization process. This influence appeared to be sport specific. For example, a peer group (e.g., track athletes) and school personnel (teachers and coaches) were reported as the agents who were most responsible for arousing an initial interest in track and field. This contrasts with the response to a similar question concerning involvement in the traditional team sports of baseball, basketball and football where the parents were found to be considerably more important than school personnel. In general, it appears that the elite track and field athlete receives encouragement and reinforcement from many sources, several of which act simultaneously.

McPherson (in Kenyon and McPherson 1973) examined the psycho social factors influencing college tennis and ice hockey players to become involved in sport. He found that interest in sport was initially aroused within the family, mainly by the father. In many cases the parents were still actively involved in sport as a participant, and thus served as role models. However, during the high school years family influence decreased and any new interest in physical activity was aroused mainly by peers, coaches and physical education teachers. Thus the source of influence changes at different periods in the life-cycle. It was interesting to note that approximately 75 percent of the respondents reported that they were secondarily involved via the mass media (e.g., television, radio and newspapers) prior to their participation in sport. In summary, it appears that college athletes receive a stimulus to compete from involved peers and from a home environment which considers sport to be an important facet of life. This latter finding is supported by Pudelkiewicz (1970: 93) who found that a positive evaluation of sport by Polish parents gives rise to sport interests among the children. Similarly, Snyder and Spreitzer (1973) found a positive relationship between parent's interest in sport and the respondent's sport involvement. This held for both sexes and all three dimensions of sport involvement (i.e., the behavioral, affective and cognitive domains).

Family support may be even more essential for female athletes as noted by Malumphy (1970) who found that the family was a major factor in college women continuing to compete. Furthermore, the influence of the mother may be more important for some sports than for others. For example, the study reported by McPherson (in Kenyon and McPherson 1973) indicated that mothers were more influential in arousing interest and providing reinforcement for the tennis players than for the hockey players.

A final significant other for college athletes is the professional athlete. Almost all respondents reported they had an "idol" and, since a Canadian sample was utilized, it is not surprising that most of the idols listed by both hockey and tennis players were outstanding professional hockey players. However, as the tennis respondents reached college age, a highly ranked tennis player often replaced the hockey idol. It was interesting to note that for the hockey players there was a positive relationship, which increased with age, between the position played by the respondent and that played by the idol.

In a related study by Kenyon and Grogg (in Kenyon and McPherson 1973) eighty-seven intercollegiate athletes in a variety of sports at the University of Wisconsin were interviewed. The social situation in which interest in a specific sport was first generated varied by sport. For example, interest in baseball was initiated about equally in the home and the school; for fencing and crew the school was most important; for football and hockey the home and neighborhood; for swimming, the home and club or recreation agency; and, for track the home and the school. Finally, the data suggested "opportunity set" differences. For example, the athlete's place of residence during high school varied among sports in that none of the hockey players, swimmers, or tennis players grew up in the open country or on a farm, indicating, as one might expect, that specific facilities and a motivational climate necessary for learning and perfecting certain sport roles are not readily available in rural areas.

Vaz (1972), in a study of the culture of young hockey players, found that certain criteria were essential for initiation into the role of professional hockey player. He reported that aggressive fighting behavior is normative, institutionalized conduct and as such is an essential facet in socializing future professional hockey players. This behavior, because it is institutionalized, becomes an integral part of the role obligation of young hockey players and is learned by subsequent novices via formal and informal socialization. A similar but more detailed analysis of professional hockey players was provided by Faulkner (1975).

More recently, Clark (1977) sampled 116 Junior A and 133 College hockey players in Ontario to determine whether patterns of early socialization vary for those who were about the same age. (e.g., 18-20) but who competed at different levels of competition. To illustrate, most professional hockey players are drafted from Junior A teams and hence this level of competition represents pre-professional training. This was clearly illustrated by the motives reported for being still involved in hockey at this age. Whereas the college players reported pursuing hockey mainly for fun and enjoyment, the Junior A players reported that they were training for a career in professional hockey. While the early socialization experiences were relatively similar, the Junior A players appeared to receive significantly more encouragement, both material and non-material, to pursue a hockey career as they grew older. Not surprisingly, the college players are superior students at all stages in the life-cycle. Thus, inherent in the socialization process may be unique values and inherent skills which channel those who have similar life-chances in childhood into different career paths in the later adolescent years.

Similarly, McPherson (1977) administered a questionnaire to 109 players in the National Hockey League. Again, the players recalled that most social reinforcement was received from the family, especially the father during early childhood and adolescence. Not surprisingly, during the high school years, 21% indicated that teachers discouraged their participation, most likely because of inferior academic performance. The mean age at which the players report that they first realized that they had the ability, interest and motivation to attempt a professional hockey career was 17.3 years. A firm decision was made for most 1 year later and hockey became a full-time occupation for most at a mean age of 19.7 years.

In one of the first attempts to utilize path analysis in the study of sport phenomena, Kenyon (1970) examined the factors influencing college students to become involved in sport at two stages in the life-cycle, namely, high school and college. An examination of the path coefficients indicated that a male who has a high level of sport aptitude, who lives in a large community which has adequate facilities and instructors (i.e., a good opportunity set), and who receives encouragement from significant others from

198

within and outside the school will have a greater chance of being socialized into a primary sport role.

While most of the early studies of sport role socialization concentrated exclusively on male athletes, more recent studies have demonstrated that while the general model holds (Greendorfer 1978a; Hall 1976, 1978) for females, there are sex differences in the process which appear to focus on opportunity set and significant others. For example, Theberge (1977), in a study of 82 women professional golfers, found that the most significant others in their career socialization were parents, peers and a teaching professional. Moreover a form of social differentiation was present in their occupational socialization process in that 66% became increasingly dependent with age on access to private golf clubs for playing privileges and lessons. In fact, by 13 years of age most were receiving private lessons from teaching professionals at private clubs. Again, this indicates the extent to which the sport role socialization process is somewhat sport specific.

A number of studies in recent years have examined the influence of a variety of significant others on the sport role socialization process for females (Bohren 1977; Greendorfer 1977, 1978b; Greendorfer and Lewko 1978; Smith 1978; Snyder and Spreitzer 1976). Generally, these studies have found that a high value climate which encourages sport involvement must be present in the family, often in the form of actual participation by both parents (especially the mother) and overt encouragement for their daughter's involvement. Moreover, while the family and peer group, especially male athletes, appear to be the most influential significant others for women, regardless of sport, there appears to be a need for a greater number and variety of significant others for females as opposed to males, if they are to continue being involved into the high school and college years.

Finally, since involvement in sport during adulthood is of recent concern, some mention should be made of the importance of childhood socialization for later participation during the adult years of the life-cycle. Studies by Spreitzer and Snyder (1976), Kelly (1977), Laakso (1978) and McPherson (1978b) have all found that involvement as an adult is greatly influenced by whether sport became part of one's life-style during childhood. This is consistent with the continuity theory of aging (Atchley, 1977) which suggests that behaviors, attitudes and values acquired at one stage in the life-cycle predispose an individual to similar patterns of social participation at later stages. Thus, although longitudinal studies are not present, it might be predicted that a favourable sport role socialization process initiated within a nuclear family will have pronounced cumulative effects upon subsequent generations, assuming opportunity sets are reasonably comparable.

In summary, it appears that college athletes and Olympic aspirants become interested and involved in sport by age 8 or 9; that they participate, usually with a great deal of success, in a number of sports before they begin to specialize in one sport; that they receive positive sanctions to become involved and to compete from a number of significant others, of which the family, peer group and coaches appear to be the most influential. Although the general socialization process has a number of common elements, there are differences in the process between sports, for each sex and at different stages in the life-cycle.

Socialization Into Secondary Sport Roles

In comparison to the study of primary sport roles, relatively few studies have been concerned with socialization into such secondary roles as sport consumer, coach and sport leader. In one of the earliest studies of the sport consumer, Stone (1957) found that the formation of loyalty to a team occurred prior to formation of loyalty to a specific player. He also noted that men form these loyalties at an earlier age than women, and that there are class differences as to when these loyalties are initiated.

In a paper primarily designed to test the utility of path analysis for sport sociology, Kenyon (1970) investigated the causal factors influencing college students to consume major league baseball and the 1964 Summer Olympic Games. Although most of the variance in the two models remained unexplained, this initial attempt indicated that the most influential factors leading to baseball consumption were, in order of importance: sport aptitude, general sport interest in high school, involvement by same-sex peers in sport consumption, and secondary involvement in baseball during high school. The most important factors accounting for the consumption of the Mexico Olympic Games included: secondary involvement in the previous Olympic Games, and knowledge about the athletes who participated in the Tokyo Olympics.

In a secondary analysis of factors hypothesized to be important in the sport socialization of male adolescents in Canada, the United States and England, Kelly (1970) found that frequency of attendance at sport events was directly related to family size and indirectly related to age. He also noted that the frequency of attendance at winter sport events was positively associated with social class background in Canada and the United States, but negatively associated in England.

McPherson (1976b) constructed and tested an axiomatic theory to explain the process whereby urban-dwelling adolescents were socialized into the role of sport consumer. It was hypothesized that the degree of consumer role socialization is a function of the collective influence of significant others and the opportunity set found in the family, peer group, school, and community social systems. This study employed multiple regression analyses to test an additive and a multiplicative model for both a male and a female cohort. The results indicated, that for the male cohort, the peer group, the family, and the school were the most influential social systems in order of importance. For the female cohort, the family, the peer group and the community were most important. This study suggested that social systems vary in their degree of influence in the process of learning a specific leisure role and that the process varies by sex. Furthermore, it appears that adolescents are socialized into a specific role by being exposed to significant others who engage in consummatory behavior, and thereby serve as role models and reinforcing agents for role aspirants who subsequently imitate and interact with them.

200

In a more detailed analysis (McPherson 1976a) the specific factors operating within each system were analyzed. It was found that, for males, if there is a high frequency of interaction concerning sport phenomena with significant others in the family and peer group, and if there is a high degree of sport consumption by the peer group, then socialization into the role of sport consumer is facilitated. Similarly, for females, if there is a high frequency of sport-oriented interaction with significant others in the family and in the community, if the family and peer groups have a high degree of sport consumption, and if the family places a high value on sport participation and sport consumption, then socialization into the role of sport consumer is likely to occur more readily.

Although many leadership roles are found within sport, few have been the subject of empirical inquiry. Bratton (1971) investigated the demographic characteristics of executive (e.g., president, vice-president, treasurer, regional representatives, etc.) members of two Canadian amateur sport associations and found sport differences. For example, the volleyball executives were ten years younger than the swimming executives, and a majority played the role of player as well as that of executive. Furthermore, Catholics were under-represented and people of British origin held a large proportion of the executive positions.

In a more comprehensive study of sport executives, Beamish (1978) compiled a socio-economic and demographic profile of 146 volunteer executives in 22 national amateur sport associations in Canada. He found that 68 percent were drawn from high status white collar occupations, 66 percent had a university degree and most were in the highest quintile in terms of annual income. Furthermore, most were involved in sport themselves, with 50 percent having competed at the provincial level at least, and 25 percent having been a competitor at the international level. Other background factors indicated that most were from large urban centres and most of their fathers were located in high status white collar occupations. Thus, a selected sample of elites within Canada are responsible for developing and administering amateur sport policies. In terms of socialization into this position of influence it would appear that an upper-middle class background, a university education and participation as an elite athlete are important opportunity factors in the process. Similar findings have been reported by Kiviaho (1973) for Finnish sport executives. In fact, he found that as executives move up the organizational hierarchy from the local to the district to the national level, a higher occupational position and greater success in sport as an athlete become increasingly important criteria for advancement.

Finally, two other studies have provided descriptive information about the background characteristics of college and youth league coaches. Loy and Sage (1972) analyzed the social background of college football and basketball coaches and found that they came from lower socioeconomic backgrounds. Similarly, McPherson (1974) found that most of the volunteer Canadian (N = 852) and American (N = 88) minor hockey coaches were originally from blue-collar backgrounds. However, the present occupational prestige of the coaches was found to be equally distributed across the

Blishen (1967) Socioeconomic Index, thereby suggesting that volunteer leaders from all socioeconomic strata are involved in minor hockey today.

Societal Factors and Social Attributes
Influencing Socialization Into Sport Roles

As noted earlier, within a given society there is usually a dominant ideology which reflects the social values and norms of that society, including those related to sport.

Recent studies have provided some empirical support that there is a relationship between both ideology (values, norms, beliefs, social expectations) and social structure (division of labor, power structure, class differences) and degree of sport involvement and level of sport performance. Seppanen (1972) examined the relationship between ideology and Olympic success and found that where either Protestant or socialist values predominate a high level of success (i.e., medals) has been attained. In both types of societies achievement via hard work and mastery over others is highly valued. However, he further noted that in recent years the socialist countries have made the greatest improvement because they promote these values more and promote them in all facets of life, not just in the sport milieu. Thus, sport success seems to be a reflection of dominant societal values. In a similar study, Ball (1972) found that Olympic success was related to the possession of human and economic resources, along with a centralized form of political decision-making and authority which maximizes the allocation of these resources.

Similar findings were reported by Novikov and Maksimenko (1972) and Grimes, Kelly and Rubin (1974). They noted that a nation's social structure is related to successful performance, and that in recent years the socialist countries have shown a more consistant increase in performance than the capitalist countries. Levine (1975), based on an examination of the 1972 Summer Olympic Games, found that the following four factors correlated highly with the number of Olympic medals won: gross domestic product, area of the country, having a socialist economy, and newspaper circulation.

Most recently, Kiviaho and Makela (1978) compared the influence of non-material (social and cultural) and material (economic) factors on both absolute success (total number of medals won or points received) and relative success (number of victories in proportion to the population). They found that the non-material factors were less useful in explaining Olympic success. Moreover, more of the variance in absolute success was explained, particularly by per capita income, population size and socialism. Thus, absolute success may reflect the amount of resources which are utilized, whereas relative success may reflect the effectiveness with which resources (even if limited) are used.

Within both the macro and micro social systems a number of ascribed social categories dictate an individual's life chances in sport and determine whether they have access to sport opportunities or sport organizations. For example, the importance of class background as it relates to opportunity set

202

has been noted by a number of investigators (Eggleston 1965; Luschen 1969; Gruneau 1971; Loy 1972; Crawford 1977). In many countries the lower classes are less involved than the middle or upper classes in most sports, and are virtually excluded from many elite sport roles. For example Gruneau (1972), in an analysis of the athletes of the 1971 Canada Winter games, found that most came from the upper-middle or upper socioeconomic groups.

Other social categories influencing involvement in sport are ethnicity and race. For example, studies by Landry *et al.* (1971), Gruneau (1972) and Marple (1974) have shown that Francophones in Canada are under-represented on Provincial, National and International teams, despite out-performing Anglophones in certain skills (Marple 1974). Similarly, Roy (1974) found that Francophones do not have equal access to the positions of coach and general manager within professional hockey after their playing career is terminated, while McPherson (1978c) found that the process of sport role socialization for both primary and secondary involvement varies for Anglophone and Francophone adults.

In the United States, studies by Loy and McElvogue (1970), Yetman and Eitzen (1972), Pascal and Rapping (1972), Scully (1974), and Eitzen and Sanford (1975) have reported that blacks are under-represented at certain playing positions, thereby indicating that through the socialization process they do not receive the opportunity or encouragement to occupy certain sport roles. More specifically, McPherson (1975) has suggested that blacks may be differentially socialized into specific sport roles.

In addition to class background, race, and ethnicity, religion may also influence the process. Again, this variable is linked to the family of origin. The evidence suggests that Catholics are under-represented while Protestants are over-represented among elite athletes and executives (Seppanen 1972). However, to date no definitive explanation for this finding has been presented although it has been suggested that it is related to the "Protestant Work Ethic."

Another social category which influences the degree of involvement in specific sport roles is the geographical area where an aspirant spends the first ten to fifteen years of life. As noted by Rooney (1974) and Sage and Loy (1978) certain countries and regions of a country produce significantly higher proportions of athletes and coaches, respectively.

Gender is also an important variable in socialization into sport roles. As noted earlier, role learning is facilitated when significant others within each social system provide and reinforce common values and norms. Unfortunately, this is not always the situation experienced by young women during childhood and adolescence.

For example, within a given community a female may see her mother and older female siblings participating and competing in a sport and thus desire to imitate this behavioral pattern. However, she may receive negative sanctions from the school or the peer group (who do not receive this reinforcement in their home). Even within the school system there may be conflicts. For example, whereas a physical education teacher may provide support and encouragement for involvement in sport, a teacher of another subject may provide discouragement. Similarly, there are wide between-community (rural vs. urban) and between-nation differences in values and norms concerning female involvement in sport. For example, in the socialist countries of Eastern Europe boys and girls have equal rights and access to sport activities; sport is a way of life for both males and females; and, equality of rights for women is a norm which has been attained in almost all facets of life.

Because of social system differences it is difficult to establish common values and norms concerning the role of women in sport. This makes social change that much more difficult to attain and may create role conflict for females who get interested in physical activity. Thus women are faced with the dilemma as to whether they should behave according to what is expected of them in their ascribed role as female (whatever that may be in the local community) or whether they should follow their interests and strive to achieve and learn new roles such as that of athlete, business person, politician, etc. For example, in a recent study by Sage and Loudermilk (1979) 26% of the 268 collegiate female athletes reported perceiving role conflict to a great or very great extent. Moreover, athletes who participated in sports which were not traditionally socially approved for women experienced significantly greater role conflict. In this situation they are in a doublebind; they have to worry not only about failure, but also about the reaction of others if they are successful.

This role conflict for females could be resolved in a number of ways. First, they might engage in instrumental acts to modify the external ecology such as attempting to prove their femininity in dress or action (e.g., verbal reactions to the "sex" test at the Olympic Games); by separating the conflicting roles in time and space so that they do not compete in school sport, but only in the community so that they are known as a "female" at school; or, by playing the two roles in a Jekyl and Hyde routine whereby they are highly competitive while playing the sport role and then refuse to discuss or acknowledge their sport roles while playing other social roles. A second way to resolve the conflict might be to attempt to change the beliefs of others and convince them that the "athlete" role is compatible with the "female" role; or they might try to change their own beliefs by arguing that others don't have the right to accept the traditional female stereotype and follow an alternative life-style. The third way to resolve the role conflict could be the most serious and yet the most common as females reach the adolescent years. That is, they drop out of sport as a participant.

A final category influencing the socialization process is the subculture in which some individuals have been socialized. For example, if one is a member of a particular ethnic, religious or racial group they are often faced with norms and values which differ from those of mainstream society. These differences may have an impact on the socialization process, including the learning of sport roles. For example, McPherson (1975) argued that involvement in specific sport roles by blacks is self-induced rather than due to overt or subtle discrimination by white leaders with the sport system.

Based on a descriptive analysis of 96 white athletes and 17 black athletes who competed in the Olympic track and field trials in 1968, it was noted that the opportunity set, the value orientations, and the type of role models present early in life may account for involvement in a particular sport by members of a minority group. More specifically, it was hypothesized that members of a minority group may segregate themselves into specific sport positions due to imitation of members of the minority group who have previously been highly successful in a specific sport role. Some support for this modeling hypothesis was presented by Castine and Roberts (1974). Based on a questionnaire administered to 129 black college athletes attending both predominantly black and predominantly white universities, they reported that 57 percent of the sample who admitted to having a sport idol before high school played the same position as their idol while at high school. Similarly, 48 percent played the same playing position as their sport idol while they were in college.

In summary, the process whereby primary and secondary sport roles are learned seems to vary by sport, by specific roles within a sport, by nation, by sex, and by stage in the life-cycle. Moreover, the process is influenced by both macro and micro system parameters, including ascribed attributes of the socializee. In short, the learning of specific sport roles is a complex phenomenon which is not adequately understood at this point in time.

SOCIALIZATION VIA SPORT

Since sport involves role-playing it is frequently considered to be a basic contributor to the socialization process. For example, since the attitudes and beliefs of individuals have their origins in primary social interaction, it is argued that games and sport provide a milieu for this interaction so that the child can internalize the complexities of the adult world.

Turning to an analysis of the socialization effects which result from playing sport roles, it must be noted that little empirical evidence exists to substantiate the many claims that have been made for the contribution of sport, physical education and physical activity to the general socialization process (Stevenson 1975). As Loy and Ingham (1973: 298) conclude in their review of the relationship between play, games and sport and the psychosocial development of children and youth:

Socialization via play, games and sport is a complex process having both manifest and latent functions, and involving functional and dysfunctional, intended and unintended consequences. Since research on the topic is limited, one must regard with caution many present empirical findings and most tentative theoretical interpretations of these findings.

The variety of socialization outcomes that have been predicted to result from participation in sport and physical activity can be classified into three types: the development of individual traits and skills; behavioral and attitudinal learning about the environment; and, learning to interact with the environment. Although it is beyond the scope of this paper to extensively review the literature in each of these areas, a brief overview follows. Groos

205

(1898) noted the saliency of play and games during infancy and childhood in both lower vertebrate and superior primates. The work of Harlow (1964) with young monkeys further demonstrated that the playpen is as important as natural mothering for some facets of the socializing process. This suggests that the dimension of playing games versus non-playing has far reaching consequences for socialization.

Anthropologists have frequently suggested that play and game experiences are structurally isomorphic to experiences in a larger society. For example, in many societies it is largely through imitative play that the individual is patterned for the culture he lives in. As children develop, play behavior becomes more highly structured and may take the form of more complex games. For example, Roberts and Sutton-Smith (1962) in a cross-cultural study of 56 societies related prevalent game forms to cultural configurations. They reported that games of strategy are more likely to be found in structurally-complex societies and are linked directly with obedience training; that games of chance are found where a culture's religious beliefs emphasize the benevolence or coerciveness of supernatural beings and are linked with training for responsibility; and that games of physical skill are salient whenever the culture places a high value on the mastery of the environment and on personal achievement. In their development of the conflict-enculturation hypothesis of game involvement, Roberts and Sutton-Smith suggested that conflicts induced by child-training processes and subsequent learning lead to involvement in games, which in turn provide buffered learning or enculturation important both to the player and to their societies. Such observations certainly emphasize the inter-relatedness of game behavior, variations in child-training practices, and general cultural demands.

Sociologists and psychologists have also examined the importance of play and games in the socialization process. Levy (1952) stated that childhood participation in competitive sports is one of the most important educational elements in society, and although they may not be of the real world, they have essential functions for socialization, integration, and as a general reinforcement of the social structure. To illustrate, although causality can not be established, Landers and Landers (1978) reported that among high school males, lower rates of delinquency were found for those involved in extra-curricular activities. More specifically, those who were involved in both sport and non-sport activities had the lowest rates, while those not involved in any extra-curricular activities had the highest rates.

Ritchie and Koller (1964) reported that sport is functional in the socialization process in that the play orientation and play experience gained in childhood is carried over into adulthood. Specifically they noted that play and games involve attitudes, values, norms, roles and skills that are similar to those found in adult work activities (Bailey 1977). Similarly, Lindesmith and Strauss (1964-209) noted that participation in play and game activities enable a child to gain a repertoire of social skills necessary for participation in the adult world. More recently, Larson *et al.* (1975) considered the short-term and long-term consequences of participation in youth sport. They concluded that participation has a socialization effect which continues into adulthood. Helanko (1960) stated that sport is a significant factor in socialization to the basic rules of social behavior in a group; while Webb (1969) reported that sport and games provide the medium for socializing individuals into the values of society.

Kenyon (1968) challenged this belief when he suggested that there was little, if any, evidence to indicate that experiences in such diffuse roles as "democratic citizen" or "responsible individual" are provided through sport or physical education programs. He suggested that through physical education an individual may be socialized into specific roles such as that of athlete, spectator, or official. Snyder (1970) concluded, without presenting data, that some physical activity results in the development of role-specific characteristics, while other activity contributes to the learning of diffuse roles.

If socialization via sport occurs, the nuclear family appears to play a prominent role and the influence varies by social class (Watson 1977). Moreover, very clear sex differences in the process emerge during the early childhood years. For example, Lever (1976, 1978) and Duquin (1977) report sex differences in the early sporting experiences of children. More specifically, Duquin (1977) found that young girls are seldom exposed in children's literature to female role models who are involved in sport or physical activity. Similarly, Lever (1976, 1978) found that boys play different types of games and more complex games during early childood. She suggests that girls may therefore learn fewer skills which are essential for success in occupations based on organizational skills such as, interpersonal competition, leadership, interacting in large groups and strategic thinking.

While many have considered participation in sport and physical activity to be functional for socialization, others have considered it to be dysfunctional. Spencer (1896) believed that games and sport were essentially useless for society. Soule (1955) noted that many considered the frivolity of games to be damaging since adult life requires the performance of many serious and unpleasant duties, whereas play and games over-emphasize pleasure-seeking pursuits. Similarly, Aries (1962) stated that tennis, bowling and the like are essentially quasi-criminal activities, no less serious in their deleterious social effects than drunkeness or prostitution. More specifically, Bend (1971) reported that participation in sport can be dysfunctional from at least two perspectives. First, it may lead to personality problems in that individuals develop unrealistic perceptions of the self, they become extremely narrow individuals in terms of interest, and they may become over-aggressive in their pursuit of excellence (Bailey 1977; Tyler and Duthie 1979). Secondly, he suggested that participation in organized sport may lead to the learning of deviant norms such as, cheating, violence, and a win at all costs philosophy. In fact, Goldstein and Bredemeier (1977) conclude that the media, and particularly television, has led to an increase in the professionalization and formalization of sport at all age levels. They argue that television has influenced children to learn that the outcome is more important than the process. Hence, the effects of televised sport are dysfunctional in that children learn that violence, illegal strategies and extrinsic motivation are highly valued and essential to success. Thus, if socially acceptable norms and values can be generalized from sport experiences, it can similarly be argued that deviant values and norms may also be generalized to other situations.

In summary, there are many beliefs and hypotheses concerning the role of play and physical activity in the general socialization process. However, to date, there is little empirical data to support the beliefs and hence little is really known about the relationship between sport participation and general social learning. Thus, parents, coaches, physical educators and administrators should moderate their attempts to proselytize the value of sport as a socializing medium until more evidence is available.

SUMMARY

Socialization is a learning process wherein a novice, through observation, imitation and interaction with significant others (role models) within social systems such as the family, school, peer group, mass media and sport team, acquires the affective, cognitive and behavioral components of a social role. This process applies to the learning of specific roles within sport. Moreover, the role acquisition appears to occur in four stages and is influenced by ascribed personal attributes which an individual brings to a learning situation, and by the dominant values and ideology present in the community or society where they reside.

An analysis of the learning of sport roles indicated that the process varies by sport, by stage in the life-cycle, and by sex. More specifically, social systems exert varying degrees of influence depending on the sport role and the particular component of the role being considered (i.e., the behavioral, cognitive or affective domain), and that the process varies cross-nationally and intra-nationally where unique subcultures exist. As with other social roles, such factors as the dominant societal ideology and such ascribed attributes as social class, ethnicity, race, religion, sex and ordinal position influences who does or does not learn a specific sport role, and who is not given the opportunity to attain elite levels of performance.

The final section of this paper indicated that while many have claimed that participation in play, games and sport enhances the socialization process for children and adolescents, there is little empirical evidence to substantiate the beliefs or hypotheses. Furthermore, statements concerning the dysfunctional outcomes of involvement in sport have recently been made, but similarly lack empirical support at this time. In short, role-specific expectations are situationally determined and may not carry over to other social roles unless the situational and role expectations are similar.

Based on the limited knowledge concerning socialization and sport to date, educators and administrators must realize that they do not operate in a vacuum as they initiate and operate programs to get people involved in sport and physical activity. Rather each social system has the capacity to support or hinder the efforts of other systems. Thus, to encourage the development of physical activity as an integral facet of life-styles, social systems must reinforce each other. For example, the school, the family, the peer group, community recreation agencies, amateur sport organizations within community and federal or state agencies must support each other. Of all these systems, the school probably has the greatest potential to provide leadership in efforts to change the socialization process concerning sport roles since it already interacts in a variety of ways with such systems as, the family, the peer group, government agencies and community agencies.

Based on the findings to date, it appears that there are sex differences in the process of learning sport roles and that the process varies depending on the sport and the specific role within that sport. Furthermore, since socialization occurs throughout the life-cycle it must be recognized that individuals can be socialized into sport roles beyond the adolescent years and therefore greater efforts should be directed to socializing or re-socializing adults into sport roles. While elite status may never be attained, participation in a wide variety of sport roles is possible until late in life. Thus, different socialization practices must be utilized depending on the sport role, the sex of the socializee and the stage of the life-cycle. Furthermore, programming should also consider class, racial, ethnic and religious differences since it will be of little long term use to introduce individuals to a sport role if their sub-cultural heritage, life-chances or opportunity set mitigates against them ever being involved or playing the role later in life. Finally, those involved in sport and physical activity must show restraint as they attempt to justify or legitimate new or existing programs, since, to date, there is little empirical evidence to support the belief that what is learned on the playing field is transfered to other social contexts.

REFERENCES

Aries, P. 1962. *Centuries of Childhood.* New York: Vintage Books.

Atchley, R.C. 1977. *The Social Forces in Later Life.* 2nd edition. Belmont, Cal.

Bailey, I.C. 1977. Socialization in play, games and sport. *Physical Education.* 34, 4: 183-187.

Ball, D.W. 1972. Olympic games competition: structural correlates of national success. *Intern. Journal Comp. Sociology.* 15, 2: 186-200.

Bandura, A. 1969. Social-learning theory of identificatory process. Pp. 213-262 in D.A. Goslin, ed. *Handbook of Socialization Theory and Research.* Chicago: Rand McNally.

Bandura, A. and R.H. Walters, 1963. *Social Learning and Personality Development.* New York: Holt. Rinehart and Winston.

Beamish, R. 1978. Socioeconomic and demographic characteristics of the national executives of selected amateur sports in Canada (1975). *Working Papers in the Sociological Study of Sport and Leisure.* (Kingston, Ont.), 1. Queen's University.

Becker, H.S. et al. 1961. *Boys in White: Student Culture in Medical School.* Chicago: University of Chicago Press.

Becker, H.A. and B. Geer. 1967. The Fates of Idealism in Medical School. Pp. 163-173 in P.I. Rose, ed. *The Study of Society.* New York: Random House.

Bend, E. 1971. Some Potential Dysfunctional Effects of Sport Upon Socialization. Paper. *Third International Symposium on the Sociology of Sport.* Waterloo, Ont.

Blishen, B.K. 1967. A socioeconomic index for occupations in Canada. *Canadian Review of Sociology and Anthropology.* 4 February: 41-53.

Bohren, J. 1977. *The Rate of the Family in the Socialization of Female Intercollegiate Athletes.* Ph.D. Thesis. University of Maryland.

209

Bratton, R. 1970. Demographic characteristics of executive members of two Canadian sport associations. *Journal Canadian Association of Health, Physical Education and Recreation.* 37, Jan.-Feb.: 20-28.

Brim, O.G. and S. Wheeler, eds. 1966. *Socialization After Childhood.* New York: Wiley.

Casher, B. 1977. Relationship between birth order and participation in dangerous sports. *Research Quarterly.* 48, March: 33-40.

Castine, S.C. and G.C. Roberts, 1974. Modelling in the socialization process of the black athlete. *IRSS.* 9, 3-4: 58-73.

Clark, W. 1977. *Socialization into the Role of College and Junior A Hockey Player.* Masters Thesis. University of Waterloo.

Clausen, J.W., ed. 1968. *Socialization and Society.* Boston: Little, Brown and Company.

Crawford, S. 1977. Occupational prestige rankings and the New Zealand Olympic athlete. *IRSS.* 12: 5-15.

Deutsch, M. and R.M. Kraus. 1965. *Theories in Social Psychology.* New York: Basic Books.

Duquin, M. 1977. Differential sex role socialization toward amplitude appropriation. *Research Quarterly.* 48, May: 288-292.

Eggleston, J. Secondary schools and Oxbridge blues. *Brit. J. Sociology.* 16, 21: 232-242.

Eitzen, D.S. and D.C. Sanford. 1975. The segregation of blacks by playing position in football: accident or design? *Social Science Quarterly.* 55, March: 849-959.

Faulkner, R.R. 1975. Coming of age in organizations: a comparative study of career contingencies of musicians and hockey players. Pp. 525-558 in D.W. Ball and J.W. Loy, eds. *Sport and Social Order.* Reading, Mass.: Addison-Wesley.

Goffman, E. 1959. *The Presentation of Self in Everyday Life.* Garden City, N.Y.: Anchor Doubleday.

Goldstein, J. and B. Bredemeier. 1977. Socialization: some basic issues. *Journal of Communication.* 27: 154-159.

Goslin, D., ed. 1969. *Handbook of Socialization Theory and Research.* Chicago: Rand McNally.

Gould, D. and D. Landers. 1972. Dangerous sport participation: a replication of Nisbetts' birth order findings. Paper. *North American Society for the Psychology of Sport.* Houston.

Greendorfer, S. 1977. Role of socializing agents in female sport involvement. *Research Quarterly.* 48, May: 304-310.

Greendorfer, S. 1978a. Socialization into sport. Pp. 115-140 in C.A. Oglesby, ed. *Women and Sport: From Myth to Reality.* Philadelphia: Lea and Febiger.

Greendorfer, S. 1978b. Differences in childhood socialization influences of women involved in sport and women not involved in sport. Pp. 59-72 in M. Krotee, ed. *Dimensions of Sport Sociology.* West Point: Leisure Press.

Greendorfer, S. and J. Lewko. 1978c. Children's socialization into sport: a conceptual and empirical analysis. Paper. *World Congress of Sociology.* Uppsala.

Greendorfer, S. 1979. Childhood sport socialization influences of male and female track athletes. *Arena Review.* 3: 39-53.

Grimes, A., W. Kelly and P. Rubin. 1974. A socioeconomic model of national Olympic performances. *Social Science Quarterly.* 55, Dec.: 777-783.

Groos, K. 1898. *The Play of Animals.* New York: Appleton.

Gruneau, R. 1972. *A Socioeconomic Analysis of the Competitors of the 1971 Canada Winter Games.* Masters Thesis. University of Calgary.

Hall, A. 1976. Sport and physical activity in the lives of Canadian women. Pp. 170-199. in R. Gruneau and J. Albinson, eds. *Canadian Sport: Sociological Perspectives.* Don Mills, Ont.: Addison-Wesley.

Hall, A. 1978. *Sport and Gender: A Feminist Perspective on the Sociology of Sport.* CAHPER Sociology of Sport Monograph Series. Calgary: University of Calgary.

Harlow, H.F. 1964. The heterosexual affectional system in monkeys. In W.G. Bennis et al., eds. *Interpersonal Dynamics.* Homewood, Ill.: Dorsey.

Helanko, R. 1960. Sports and socialization. *Acta Sociologica.* 8, April: 229-241.

Jones, F.E. 1965. The socialization of the infantry recruit. Pp. 258-279. in B.R. Blishen et al., eds. *Canadian Society: Sociological Perspectives.* Toronto: MacMillan.

Kelly, J.R. 1977. Leisure socialization: replication and extension. *Journal of Leisure Research.* 9, 1: 121-132.

Kemper, T.D. 1968. Reference groups, socialization, and achievement. *ASR.* 33, FEb.: 31-45.

Kenyon, G.S. 1968. Sociological considerations. *Journal American Association of Health, Physical Education and Recreation.* 39, Nov.-Dec.: 31-33.

Kenyon, G.S. 1969. Sport involvement: a conceptual go and some consequences thereof. Pp. 77-84 in G.S. Kenyon, ed. *Sociology of Sport.* Chicago: Athletic Institute.

Kenyon, G.S. 1970. The use of path analysis in sport sociology. *IRSS.* 5, 1: 191-203.

Kenyon, G.S. 1977. The process of becoming an elite track and field athlete in Canada. Pp. 163-169 in J. Taylor, ed. *Post-Olympic Games Symposium.* Ottawa: Coaching Association.

Kenyon, G.S. and B.D. McPherson. 1973. Becoming involved in physical activity and sport: a process of socialization. Pp. 303-332 in G.L. Rarick, ed. *Physical Activity: Human Growth and Development.* New York: Academic Press.

Kiviaho, P. 1973. The recruitment of sport leaders at different organizational levels in Finland. Pp. 368 in O. Grupe et al., eds. *Sport in the Modern World.* New York: Springer.

Kiviaho, P. and P. Makela, 1978. Olympic success: a sum of non-material and material factors. *IRSS.* 13, 2: 5-17.

Laakso, L. 1973. Characteristics of the socialization environment as the determinant of adult sport interests in Finland. Pp. 103-112 in F. Landry and W. Orban, eds. *Sociology of Sport.* Miami: Symposia Specialists.

Landers, D. and D. Landers. 1978. Socialization via interscholastic athletics: its effects on delinquency. *Soc. Education.* 51, oct.: 299-303.

Landry, F. et al. 1971. Les Canadiens-Francais et Les Grands Jeux Internationaux. Paper. *International Symposium Sociology of Sport.* Waterloo.

Larson, D. et al. 1975. Youth sport programs. *Sport Sociology Bulletin.* 4, 2: 55-63.

Lever, J. 1976. Sex differences in the games children play. *Social Problems.* 23, April: 478-487.

Lever, J. 1978. Sex differences in the complexity of children's play and games. *ASR.* 43, 3: 471-483.

Levine, N. 1975. Why do countries win Olympic medals? Some structural correlates of Olympic games success: 1972. *Sociology Social Research,* 59, 2: 353-360.

Levy, M.J. 1952. *The Structure of Society.* Princeton: Princeton University Press.

Lindesmith, A.R. and A.L. Strauss. 1964. The social self. Pp. 206-209 in R.W. O'Brien et al., eds. *Readings in General Sociology.* Boston: Houghton-Mifflin.

Loy, J.W. 1969. The study of sport and social mobility. Pp. 101-110 in G.S. Kenyon, ed. *Sociology of Sport.* Chicago: Athletic Institute.

Loy, J.W. 1972. Social origins and occupational mobility patterns of a selected sample of American athletes. *IRSS.* 7, 1: 5-23.

Loy, J.W. and J.F. McElvogue. 1970. Racial segregation in American sport. *IRSS.* 5, 1: 5-23.

Loy, J.W. and G. Sage. 1972. Social origins, academic achievement, athletic achievement, and career mobility patterns of college coaches. Paper. *American Sociological Association Meetings.* New Orleans.

Loy, J.W. and A. Ingham, 1973. Play, games, and sport in the psychosocial development of children and youth. Pp. 257-302 in G.L. Rarick, ed. *Physical Activity: Human Growth and Development.* New York: Academic Press.

Loy, J.W., B.D. McPherson and G.S. Kenyon. 1978. *Sport and Social Systems.* Reading, Mass.: Addison-Wesley.

Luschen, G. 1969. Social stratification and social mobility among young sportsmen. Pp. 258-176 in J.W. Loy and G.S. Kenyon, eds. *Sport, Culture and Society.* New York: MacMillan.

Malumphy, T.M. 1970. The college women athlete — questions and tentative answers. *Quest.* 14, June: 18-27.

Marple, D.P. 1974. An analysis of the discrimination against the French Canadians in ice hockey. Paper. *Canadian Sociology Anthropology Meetings.* Toronto.

Maukson, H.O. 1963. Becoming a nurse: a selective view. *Annuals* AAPSS 346, March: 88-94.

McPherson, B.D. 1972. Socialization into the role of sport consumer: the construction and testing of a theory and causal model. Ph.D. Dissertation. University of Wisconsin.

McPherson, B.D. 1974. Career patterns of a voluntary role: the minor hockey coach. Paper.

Canadian Sociology and Anthropology Meetings. Toronto.

McPherson, B.D. 1975. The segregation by playing position hypothesis in sport: an alternative explanation. *Social Science Quarterly.* 55, March: 960-966.

McPherson, B.D. 1976a. Consumer role socialization: a within-system model. *Sportwissenschaft.* 6, 2: 144-154.

McPherson, B.D. 1976b. Socialization into the role of sport consumer: a theory and causal model. *Canadian Review Sociology Anthropology.* May: 165-177.

McPherson, B.D. 1977. The process of becoming an elite hockey player in Canada. Pp. 170-179 in J. Taylor, ed. *Post-Olympic Games Symposium.* Ottawa: Coaching Association.

McPherson, B.D. 1978a. Success in sport: the influence of sociological parameters. *Canadian Journal Applied Sport Sciences.* 3, March: 51-59.

McPherson, B.D. 1978b. Aging and involvement in physical activity: a sociological perspective. Pp. 111-125 in F. Landry and W. Orban, eds. *Physical Activity and Human Well-Being.* Vol. 1. Miami: Symposia Specialists.

McPherson, B.D. 1978c. The sport role socialization process for Anglophone and Francophone adults in Canada: accounting for present patterns of involvement. Pp. 41-52 in F. Landry and W. Orban, ed.. *Sociology of Sport.* Miami: Symposia Specialists.

McPherson, B.D., L.W. Guppy and J.P. McKay. 1976. The social world of children's games and sport: a review in J. Albinson and G. Andrews, eds. *The Child in Sport and Physical Activity.* Baltimore: University Park Press.

Mortimer, J.T. and R.G. Simmons. 1978. Adult socialization. In A. Inkeles, J. Coleman and N. Smelser, eds. *Annual Review of Sociology.* Volume 4. Palo Alto, Cal.: Annual Reviews.

Nash, D.J. 1968. The socialization of an artist: the American composer. *Journal of Personality and Social Psychology.* 8, 2: 351-353.

Niemi, R. and B. Sobieszek. 1977. Political socialization. In A. Inkeles, J. Coleman and N. Smelser, eds. *Annual Review of Sociology.* Volume 3. Palo Alto, Cal.: Annual Reviews.

Nisbett, R.F. Birth order and participation in dangerous sports. *Journal of Personality and Social Psychology.* 8, 2: 351-353.

Nixon, H. 1976. Sport socialization and youth: some proposed research directions. *Review Sport Leisure.* 1, 1: 45-61.

Novikov, A.D. and M. Maksimenko. 1972. Sociale und okonomische Faktoren und das Niveau sportlicher Leistungen. *Sportwissenschaft.* 2: 156-167.

Pascal, A.H. and L.A. Rapping. 1972. The economics of racial discrimination in organized baseball. Pp. 119-156 in A.H. Pascal, ed. *Racial Discrimination in Economic Life.* Lexington, Mass.: Health.

Pooley, J.C. 1971. *The Professional Socialization of Physical Education Students in the United States and England.* P.h.D. Thesis. University of Wisconsin, Madison.

Pudelkiewicz, E. 1970. Sociological problems of sports in housing estates. *IRSS.* 5: 73-103.

Redmond, G. 1978. *Sport and Ethnic Groups in Canada.* CAHPER Sociology of Sport Monograph Series. Calgary: University of Calgary.

Ritchie, O.W. and M. Koller. 1964. *Sociology of Childhood.* New York: Appleton-Century-Crofts.

Roberts, J. and B. Sutton-Smith. 1962. Child training and game involvement. *Ethnology.* 1, 1: 166-185.

Rooney, J.F. 1974. *A Geography of American Sport: From Cabin Creek to Anaheim.* Reading, Mass: Addison-Wesley.

Rostow, W.W. 1971. *The Stages of Economic Growth.* Cambridge: Cambridge University Press.

Roy, G. 1974. The Relationship Between Centrality and Mobility: The Case of the National Hockey League. Masters Thesis. University of Waterloo.

Sage, G.H. and S. Loudermilk. 1979. The female athlete and role conflict. *Research Quarterly.* 50, 1: 88-96.

Sage, G.H. and J.W. Loy. 1978. Geographical mobility patterns of college coaches. *Urban Life.* 7, July: 253-274.

Sarbin, T. and V. Allen. 1968. Role theory. *Handbook of Social Psychology.* Volume one. Pp. 488-567 in G. Lindzey and E. Aronson, eds. Reading, Mass.: Addison-Wesley.

Scully, G.W. 1974. Discrimination: the case of baseball. *Government and the Sports Business.* Pp. 221-273 in R.G. Noll, ed. Washington, D.C.: The Brookings Institute.

Seppanen, P. 1972. Die Rolle des Leistungssports in den Gesellschaften des Welt. *Sportwissenschaft.* 2: 133-155.

Sewell, W.H. 1963. Some recent developments in socialization theory and research. *Annals AAPSS.* 349, September: 163-181.

Smelser, J.J. 1962. *Theory of Collective Behavior.* New York: The Free Press.

Smith, G. and C. Blackman. 1978. *Sport in the Mass Media.* CAHPER Sociology of Sport Monograph Series. Calgary: University of Calgary.

Smith, M.D. 1978. Getting involved in sport: sex differences. *Sociology of Sport.* Pp. 113-120 in F. Landry and W. Orban, eds. Miami: Symposia Specialists.

Snyder, E. 1970. Aspects of socialization in sports and physical education. *Quest.* 14, June: 1-7.

Snyder, E.F. and E. Spreitzer. 1976. Family influence and involvement in sports. *Research Quarterly.* 44, Oct.: 249-255.

Snyder E. and E. Spreitzer. 1973. Correlates of sport participation among adolescent girls. *Research Quarterly.* 47, Dec.: 804-809.

Soule, G.H. 1955. *Time for Living.* New York: Viking Press.

Spencer, H. 1896. *The Principles of Psychology.* New York: Appleton.

Spreitzer, E. and E. Snyder. 1976. Socialization into sport: an exploratory path analysis. *Research Quarterly.* 47, 2: 238-245.

Staniford, D.J. 1978. *Play and Physical Activity in Early Childhood Socialization.* CAHPER Sociology of Sport Monograph Series. Calgary: University of Calgary.

Stevenson, C.L. 1975. Socialization effects of participation in sport: a critical review of the research. *Research Quarterly.* 46. Oct.: 287-301.

Stone, G.P. 1957. Some meanings of American sport. *Proceedings National College of Physical Education Association for Men.* 60: 6-29.

Sutton-Smith, B. 1972. *The Folk Games of Children.* Austin: University of Texas Press.

Theberge, N. 1977. Some Factors Associated With Socialization Into the Role of Professional Women Golfers. Paper. *Canadian Psycho-Motor Performance Symposium.* Banff, Alberta.

Thornton, R. and P.M. Nardi. 1975. The dynamics of role acquisition. *AJS* 80, Jan.: 870-885.

Tyler, J.K. and J.H. Duthie. 1979. The effect of ice hockey on social development. *Journal of Sport Behavior.* 2, Feb.: 49-59.

Vaz, E. 1972. The culture of young hockey players: some initial observations. *Training: Scientific Basis and Application.* Pp. 222-234 in A. Taylor, ed. Springfield, Ill.: Thomas.

Watson, G. 1977. Games, socialization and parental values: social class differences in parental evaluation of Little League Baseball. *IRSS.* 12, 1: 17-48.

Webb, H. 1969. Professionalization of attitudes toward play among adolescents. *Sociology of Sport.* Pp. 161-179 in G.S. Kenyon, ed. Chicago: Athletic Institute.

Westby, D.L. 1960. The career experience of the Symphony musician. *Social Forces.* 38, March: 223-224.

Woelfel, J. and A.O. Haller, 1971. Significant others, the self-reflexive act and the attitude formation process. *ASR.* 26, Feb.: 74-87.

Yetman, N.R. and D.S. Eitzen. 1972. Black Americans in sports: unequal opportunity for equal ability. *Civil Rights Digest.* 5, Aug.: 21-34.

Yiannakis, A. 1976. Birth order and preference for dangerous sports among males. *Research Quarterly.* 47, March.: 62-67.

Zigler, E. and I.L. Child. 1969. Socialization. *A Handbook of Social Psychology.* Volume 3, G. Lindzey and E. Aronson, eds. Reading, Mass.: Addison-Wesley.

Summary of the Final Report

Parent Survey To Examine The Quality Of Minor Hockey*

In March and April 1979, this survey was conducted by the Parent Education Committe of the Ontario Hockey Council, sponsored by the Ministry of Culture and Recreation. In total, 78,754 questionnaires were mailed out to parents of competitive players, with the purpose of examining the quality of minor hockey. The response was simply amazing. Just under 40% filled in the questionnarie and returned it. It has taken some time to tabulate the responses and determine the survey findings, but Parent Education Committee Chairman Barry McPherson and OHC Chairman Lloyd Davidson, who also teamed up to conduct many public forums around the province, have done a most commendable job. We are pleased to present a summary of their final report in this special issue of Hockey Scope.

Hon. Reuben C. Baetz, Minister, Culture and Recreation.
Barry McPherson, Chairman, OHC Parent Education Committee.
Lloyd Davidson, Chairman, Ontario Hockey Council.
Ron Smith, Executive Director, Ontario Hockey Council.

MINOR HOCKEY IN ONTARIO

Toward a Postive Learning Environment for Children in the 1980s

Dedication

This study was undertaken so that future generations of children in Ontario could have the opportunity to participate in hockey (at whatever level of involvement they choose) in an environment which fosters learning, enjoyment and healthy competition, in that order of importance. Furthermore, they should have the opportunity to learn to play as well as possible and to learn that enjoying the game is more important than winning any single game or tournament.

This study was initiated in 1979, The International Year of the Child. Where children's sport is concerned, every day of every year should be dedicated to the child.

*Ontario Hockey Council, "Ontario Hockey Council Parents Survey — Summary of the Final Report," *Hockey Scope*, Volume 2, Issue 3, 1980. Permission granted by Ontario Hockey Council.

This report is further dedicated to the volunteer parents, coaches, officials and executives who, for the most part, are genuinely interested in assisting children to mature and realize their potential, and who recognize that hockey is but one avenue, and not the only avenue, to attain this goal.

Definitions

Minor hockey includes all players up to 18 years of age, excluding those playing junior hockey. Minor hockey is for children — it is not and should not be professional hockey. A child's world involves play, fun, learning, participation. The adult world of work often involves an emphasis on achievement, performance, pressure to win, etc.

"Organized", **"Competitive"**, **"Select"**, **"Representative"**, **"All-Star"** hockey are relatively similar terms for the minor hockey organized by the following Branches within Ontario: Thunder Bay Amateur Hockey Association; Ottawa District Minor Hockey Association; Northern Ontario Hockey Association; Ontario Minor Hockey Association and the Metropolitan Toronto Hockey League. This level of hockey is generally more competitive and usually involves more travel, more games, and results in regional and provincial play-offs. All players playing at this level must be "registered" with the Branch, and therefore with the CAHA. In 1978-79 there were an estimated 61,000 players at this level in Ontario.

House league hockey is organized and operated by the hockey association in each community. These associations are not required to affiliate with one of the Branches unless they wish to compete in regional or provincial playdowns. This type of hockey usually involves less time and travel since the teams generally get fewer practice times and play fewer games than those involved in Branch play. This hockey, on the ice, is just as "competitive" as so-called "organized" hockey. The players on these teams are not required to register with the Branch or CAHA. In 1978-79 there were approximately 150,000 players involved at this level in Ontario.

Areas of Concern

This report does not focus on "violence" but rather on the over-all quality of the environment in which hockey is taught, played and organized in Ontario. As a result, this report is concerned with:

1. the aims and objectives of minor hockey and the extent to which they are being attained.

2. the quality of leadership (coaches, referees, executives, parents).

3. the rules and structure of the game at the child's level.

4. the philosophy of minor hockey.

5. the perceived problem areas within children's hockey.

6. the need for better communication and sharing of ideas and concerns by those most directly involved — that is players, parents, coaches, referees and executives.

Why Survey Parents?

There are many ways in which this study could have been undertaken and there are many groups which could have been consulted exclusively, or to a greater extent. However, it was decided to focus on the adults, and particularly the parents, for two reasons. First, some of those within organized hockey (eg. coaches, referees, executives) claim that "parents are the biggest problem" in minor hockey. On the other hand, the parents often claim that whenever they have complaints (real or imagined) or positive suggestions to make, the either don't know whom to talk to, or if they get a chance to express their opinion, it is often ignored. Therefore, it was decided to consult the "clients who pay the bills" by conducting a survey of parents of children playing at the competitive level.

How do you view Minor Hockey?

Do you see minor hockey as a child's activity where the game is primarily for the players, not for the adult volunteers? Basically this attitude is essential, and it represents quite a shift for some adults in their view of minor hockey.

Hockey should be part of the educational process of children and therefore should be operated as an educational experience so that all children have the right to learn and participate in an enjoyable, positive, pressure-less environment.

The basic aim of any hockey experience should be to maximize the development of the potential of every child who decides to become involved. This means that adults should strive to develop the essential skills of the game to the highest level possible for every child, and to ensure that the hockey experience promotes values and objectives similar to that found within the schools. Learning to play hockey should be no different than learning to colour, print, write and read.

SYNOPSIS OF SURVEY RESULTS

Here are the highlights of the survey findings:

On Skills Development:

Parents say more time should be spent on developing hockey skills. The vast majority, 94.3 percent, believe children under ten should be learning skating, passing and shooting rather than be travelling and playing in a competitive schedule.

Parents also indicated they want more emphasis on skating and puck control rather than body contact.

To make way for this new emphasis, parents say they would support a reorganization of minor hockey so their children would have at least one practice for every game.

Parents were asked if they would support a ban on body-checking for Pee-Wee (12 years) or younger. Fifty-four percent thought it would be a good idea for associations across Ontario, including their own. More than 65 percent felt it would be a positive move for minor hockey across Canada.

On Parent's Behaviour

Most parents, 82.3 percent, feel parents create problems by pushing their

216

children too hard.

Seventy-nine percent feel parents create problems by their behaviour at games.

Parents expressed a desire for some form of publication, such as a parents minor-hockey newsletter, which would provide more information about the sport and the role they can play in it.

On Money and Time Invested in Minor Hockey

Most parents feel their youngsters have the time to play competitive minor hockey and still be involved in other activities.

Approximately 75 percent feel their child is not required to travel too far for games or practices, but 57 percent said the cost of hockey equipment was too high.

On Coaches

A majority, 71 percent, supported certification programs for minor hockey coaches.

On Referees

While most parents think referees do a good job, many feel this job has become more difficult. Specifically, parents believe that verbal abuse of officials is increasing and they rate parents as the prime offenders. Players and coaches rank second and third.

Most parents also want "stick-abuse" penalties, such as slashing and high-sticking, called more often.

On Violence in Minor Hockey

On the average, 76.1 percent of parents said there is too much violence in minor hockey. But only 41.6 percent thought there was too much violence in their own child's league.

On Improving Minor Hockey

Parents were presented with twenty potential problem areas in minor hockey. They ranked the following five as their top concerns:

• the amount of intimidation and violent acts by players of all ages.
• the education of parents about minor hockey.
• knowledge of the rules by parents.
• parent behaviour at games.
• time spent in practicing hockey skills.

When asked if minor hockey could be improved parents said yes, and the majority felt that currently minor hockey places more stress on winning than on recreation.

HIGHLIGHTS OF REPORT RECOMMENDATIONS
Recommendations

The findings from the survey become a challenge for the 1980s. Namely, every adult, child, or adolescent who is involved in minor hockey must dedicate himself to creating an environment in which:

1. Basic skills can be learned.

2. Competition can be safe and fun.

3. Respect for and understanding of officials and opponents is present.

4. Parents are interested observers rather than active and verbal distractions.

5. Officials consistently and strictly enforce the playing rules.

6. Executives are more open to suggestions and work together to make decisions for the benefit of the player and the game.

It is in this type of environment that the game will develop and that the players will seek excellence and remain in the game.

The Aims, Objectives and Philosophy of Minor Hockey

1. Development is as important as Competition and should occur first.

2. There should be at least two practice hours for every game hour that is played.

3. A maximum number of games per year, including tournaments and playoffs, should be established for each age level.

4. The Fair Play Codes should be distributed to all players, parents, officials and executives, and they should be framed and mounted in a prominent place in every arena in the Province.

5. Winning and competition are important and necessary ingredients for minor hockey but, they are not the same and should not become the only, or the most important ingredients.

6. There should be no "all-star" hockey for atom (ten years old) and younger players. Rather, an instructional Skills Program, combined with house league or recreational games, should be offered for all players. At eleven years of age, players should be streamed, according to ability, into competitive or house league teams, and offered programs to meet their particular needs.

7. The amount of community prestige attached to a novice, atom, Pee-Wee, etc., team defeating a team from another community must be eliminated. Is it really important in the long run whether a group of ten year olds from one town defeat a team of ten year olds from another town?

8. There is too much specialization too early. A player should be encouraged or required to play all positions, including goaltender, in the early years of hockey involvement.

The Organization (Structure and Executives) of Minor Hockey

1. Local and Branch Associations need to devote more time and expertise to the development and philosophical aspects of minor hockey.

2. Coaches, referees, players and parents should be represented on the Executive of Local Hockey Associations.

3. Leadership seminars should be held in every community or region to enable volunteer executives to develop management, public relations and decision-making skills.

218

4. The right to be a leader (e.g. President) in minor hockey should be earned by demonstrating skills and competence in leadership.

5. Each Association should publish a Parent's Handbook of information about the game.

6. Local Associations should host an Annual Forum for Parents, Players, Officials, etc., to express concerns and ideas for improving minor hockey.

7. More efficient use of the ice is needed at all age groups.

8. Local Associations must demonstrate greater responsibility in actively recruiting coaches, executives and officials, evaluating the job they are doing, and providing support so that quality leaders do not get frustrated and leave the association.

9. There needs to be developed a better spirit of cooperation and communication among all adults involved in minor hockey, whether they be executive, coach, manager official or parents.

10. There should only be one hockey association per community.

Coaching

1. All coaches should be required to obtain at least Level Two certification.

2. Each coach should be evaluated during games and practices by a Head Coach/Instructor. This evaluation should be a positive experience in that the purpose is to make the coach a better teacher.

3. Regional Development Coordinators should be appointed on a fulltime basis to develop the coaching and referee skills, and to serve as consultants to local minor hockey associations.

4. Every local hockey Association should appoint a Head Coach/Instructor to recruit and train new coaches, assign coaches to teams, train and evaluate all coaches. This position should be a part-time salaried position.

5. Coaches should play each player on an equal basis.

6. Coaches must stress the teaching of skills, sportsmanship, how to accept defeat and the spirit of competition, rather than stressing "winning".

Officiating

1. Referees should be required to visit the dressing room of each team prior to every game, to introduce themselves by name, teach and review certain rules, and to answer questions about rule interpretations.

2. Local Associations need to actively recruit and train officials from among the more mature midget and juvenile players. The Association should provide them with a helmet, sweater and whistle, and pay their registration fee for Level One and Two of the National Referees Certification Program.

3. Referees must be more strict, uniform, and consistent in calling stick-related infractions.

4. Supervision and Evaluation of Officials must be expanded and improved.

Parents

1. Parents must cease the abuse they direct toward officials.

2. Parents must have the right to discuss their concerns with coaches or executives.

3. Parents should ask how they can contribute in a positive way to the Association and to their child's team.

4. Every parent, as part of the registration fee, should receive an annual subscription to Hockey Scope.

5. Parents should be more interested in seeing the players improve their skills over a season than in expressing concern or disappointment at a loss in a single game. Learning can occur even when the score reflects a loss.

Players

1. The decision to play "house-league" or "all-star" hockey should be made by the player, not the parent.

2. Players should be consulted about how minor hockey is taught and played.

3. More practice time (optional) should be made available for house league players who wish to improve their skills.

4. Midget and Juvenile players should be encouraged to get involved as assistant coaches or as referees, and to go to the Certification courses.

Teaching and Development of Fundamental Skills

1. Communities must take a more active role in development by providing ongoing instructional programs for coaches, referees, players and parents.

2. A program of supervision and positive constructive evaluation of coaches must be initiated at the local and provincial level by local or regional Development Coordinators.

3. Each community should have an assigned goaltender instructor who works with all goalies, in a one- or two-hour per week practice session only for goalies.

4. Each community should allocate at least one hour per week per age group for voluntary instructional sessions, taught by the head instructor and other coaches.

5. The Department of Education should stress the teaching of hockey skills in the elementary school physical education curriculum.

6. Every community should have a salaried part-time Head Coach/ Instructor to coordinate the development of hockey.

7. Regional Development Coordinators should be appointed to provide leadership and to provide on-going supervision and evaluation of coaches.

8. A special instructional program for 6-12 year olds must be available in all communities.

Playing Rules for Minor Hockey

1. Modification of hockey rules should be given priority for research.

2. Body Checking should be prohibited for PeeWee-and-under age groups.

3. Local Associations should eliminate body checking in all age groups of the House Leagues.

4. All two-minute penalties should be served to duration, no matter how many goals are scored.

5. A larger, semi-circular crease should be created, with a time limit of five seconds for the attacking player to stand in it.

6. On blueline offsides, do not have a faceoff, but give the non-offending team a free breakout (from behind its goal-line) with five seconds to advance the puck over its own blueline, unchecked by the offending team.

The Financing of Minor Hockey

1. Provincial lotteries should not be used to assist teams for travel but rather for development purposes.

2. Shorten the length of the season and reduce the number of games played.

Local and Provincial Governments

1. Other than providing resource personnel and financial assistance for development, government bodies should serve minor hockey in an advisory capacity rather than in a controlling way.

2. Regional and District offices of the Ministry of Culture and Recreation should be supplied with copies of all educational materials pertaining to minor hockey. The regional sport consultants should be more readily available to assist local hockey associations with administrative matters.

3. The government should utilize lottery funds, or other funds, to provide each region or local community with a set of educational material and instructional films.

Professional and Junior Hockey

1. These groups must contribute to the development of hockey by providing financial assistance and by providing a better model.

CONCLUSION

Children's hockey is a game, not a business to entertain adults. As such, children should have the opportunity to learn the essential skills of the game so that it can be played in a safe, enjoyable atmosphere. In recent years, some adults have perceived the game more as a form of entertainment, as a business and as a means to enhance community or personal prestige.

As we enter the 1980s, minor hockey must be given back to the children and adolescents. Adults must re-direct and limit their involvement to providing, in order of priority, excellent instruction in the essential skills (skating, shooting, puck control, positional play), and then, organizational and leadership skills so that children can compete at a level suitable to their skills and their needs.

In order to achieve these objectives, the following corrective measures must be initiated lest hockey, similar to lacrosse, become virtually extinct in Canadian society:

- Because of the need for a greater emphasis on development (skills, atmosphere, leadership and attitudes), the Ontario Hockey Council should play a major leadership role in the future development of minor hockey. This could be accomplished by a restructuring of the Ontario Hockey Council to provide unified leadership for the development of minor hockey in terms of new programs, directions and activities. In short, the mandate of the Council needs to be more concerned with the development of hockey than with the operation (administration) of hockey.
- Every local Association must have a Constitution which clearly states the philosophy, and the aims and objectives of the Association. These statements are more important than by-laws or administrative guidelines. Moreover, every Constitution must include procedures whereby the degree to which the aims and objectives are being met for every player and can be evaluated annually.
- Minor hockey needs to recruit volunteer coaches, officials and executives who are motivated by a genuine desire to work for the child and who will make decisions based on current knowledge obtained from wide consultation with parents, players, educators, coaches, officials and executives.
- Politics in minor hockey within communities and within or between Associations and teams must be eliminated.
- Competition is necessary and desirable for children and should be continued, provided the social atmosphere in which it occurs is improved.
- Minor hockey should not be such a "serious" activity, for so many people, for so much of the year.
- There must be more open and honest communication, and a willingness to listen and consider alternative ideas, by all those involved in minor hockey. The minor hockey expert has yet to appear!
- Development is a prerequisite for competition. In order for this to take place, full or part-time Regional Development Co-ordinators must be hired to provide highly-qualified leadership for the volunteer coach and executive.
- A reduction in travel, the number of games and in the length of the season must take place.
- The number of practices per year should exceed the number of games.
- Players, coaches and parents must show, at all times, respect for opponents and officials.
- Parents should "be seen but not heard" in the arenas.
- A continuing program of education for parents and children (i.e. future parents) should provide knowledge about rules, the philosophy of minor hockey, skill development, behaviour at games, the structure and organization of minor hockey, how to buy and fit equipment, etc.

- A more active recruitment and training program for qualified adult volunteers must be initiated by local Associations.
- All coaches should be certified and evaluated.
- Every community or region should have a part-time or full-time head hockey instructor to co-ordinate the development of hockey.
- Referees must communicate more with coaches, parents and players in order to explain and interpret the rules.
- Referees must strive for consistency, strictness and uniformity in their performance, at all age levels and in both "House League" and "Competitive" hockey.
- The playing rules should be modified for minor hockey. Different modifications, suggested in the Recommendations, are necessary at different age levels.
- In minor hockey, a penalty for highsticking should be called whenever the stick is raised above the waist, except in the act of shooting. The puck is on the ice, not around the shoulders!
- The cost of ice time, travel and equipment must not increase or hockey will become an elite sport — only the rich will be able to have their children become involved.
- Hockey must reduce its dependency on play-off gate-receipts as a major source of revenue.
- The media can contribute to the growth and development of minor hockey by providing positive and constructive coverage of ideas and events. The media can also serve as a continuing forum (e.g. through talk shows, feature interviews, letters to the editor, etc.) to promote the introduction of new ideas in the future.
- Local and provincial governments should limit their involvement to providing resource personnel and to providing funds for developmental purposes and for research.
- Professional and Junior hockey must demonstrate greater leadership and social responsibility in the type of product they present to the public. If improving the calibre of Canadian hockey is a goal of professional hockey, then they must make greater financial and leadership contributions to the devleopment of minor hockey.

In conclusion, if minor hockey is to achieve its goal as a game whereby children can have fun, and maximize their potential to become both a skilled player and a good citizen, then high-quality leadership needs to be provided by adult volunteers. However, for volunteer leaders to be successful in this endeavour, they need to draw upon the expertise and resources that can best be provided by full-time hockey development co-ordinators located throughout the province.

Levels of Occupational Prestige and Leisure Activity*

Rabel J. Burdge

Many sociological variables are related to leisure participation. For instance, people in high income brackets, young age categories, high educational levels, and having positions with paid vacations generally have been found to be the most active participants in structured leisure activity.[1]

For the purposes of this paper, leisure is defined as activity occurring during periods free from obvious and formal duties of a paid job or other obligatory occupation.[2] Occupational prestige is the variable here used to explain differences in the use of leisure. Membership in an occupation provides social recognition in the form of status. Society assigns higher status to individuals who are willing to acquire the necessary skill and education for complex occupations. The work experience also provides an opportunity for identity and meaningful life experience. Many of the experiences and associations gained during preparation for work and participation in it carry over to leisure time.

The general proposition guiding this study, then, is that a person's position in the occupational prestige structure is a determinant of how leisure is used. In short, the accrument of rewards — monetary and status — will determine the variety of leisure outlets.[3] Participation in leisure is designated as the dependent variable and occupational prestige as the independent variable. In keeping with previous research studies dealing with status evaluations the North-Hatt Occupational Prestige Scale was used as the empirical method of assigning prestige evaluations to specific occupations.

PREVIOUS RESEARCH

The most influential study relating occupational prestige levels and leisure activity was completed by Clarke (1956). This researcher studied the relationship between social status levels as measured by the North-Hatt Occupational Prestige Scale and participation in specific leisure activities. Clarke mailed questionnaires so as to obtain at least 100 completed sched-

* Rabel J. Burdge, "Levels of Occupational Prestige and Leisure Activity," *Journal of Leisure Research,* 1(3):262-274, 1969. Reprinted by permission of the National Recreation and Park Association.

ules in each of the five occupational prestige categories. He found that most of the relationships were linear or near linear; that is, participation in specific forms of leisure were common to persons in either the highest or lowest occupational prestige level. Watching television, fishing, playing poker, attending drive-in movies, spending time in a tavern, and attending baseball games were activities common to persons in the lowest occupational prestige level. Working on automobiles was associated with level IV, playing golf with level III, and weekend trips, football games, and attending parties associated with persons in level II. Most other forms of leisure such as attending concerts, playing bridge, reading books, and working in a flower garden were found to be common to persons in prestige level I. Leisure activities found to be distributed among all prestige levels include hunting, bowling, gardening, listening to the radio, and picnicking. Reissman also found differences between occupational prestige groups on such items as reading and watching television (1965).

Other investigations, which include the research of Outdoor Recreation Resources Review Commission (1962), White (1955), Havighurst and Fiegenbaum (1959), Burdge (1962), and Hollingshead (1949), have found differences in the use of leisure time among occupational prestige groups and social class levels.

METHODOLOGICAL PROCEDURES

Data for use in this study come from a random, stratified sample of persons living in Allegheny County, Pennsylvania (which includes the city of Pittsburgh). This county typifies most metropolitan areas in that it is characterized by a large central city with a declining population, an expanding suburban area, and a hinterland of mixed rural and urban influences. The employment patterns of Pittsburgh may be classed as industrial, devoted predominantly to basic metal manufacturing.

A representative sample of 1,635 individuals was drawn from the 1,628,587 people in Allegheny County. The investigation was limited to individuals eighteen or older. Thus, for the age group selected, the sample includes about one in approximately 700 people eighteen and older living in Allegheny County. The sample was stratified utilizing a series of social, income, ethnic, racial, and residential variables taken from census data. From the 1,635 persons in Allegheny County selected for personal interview, 1,562 completed schedules were obtained. This represents a completion rate of 95.3 percent. Seventy-three people, including three persons who discontinued the interview, would not cooperate in completing the scheduled list of questions. No substitutions were permitted for those who refused to answer or were not at home.

In sampling validity checks reported in detail elsewhere, it was found that the sample of respondents obtained adequately reflected the racial, age, and occupational characteristics of Allegheny County (Burdge 1963). It therefore appears reasonably safe to generalize the findings of this study to Allegheny County and perhaps to similar metropolitan areas in the Northeast. Although the inland Ohio Valley location of Allegheny County de-

225

presses the amount of participation in both deep water and mountaineering types of recreation, it is not anticipated that the basic relationships uncovered would be altered greatly at more favored locations.

North-Hatt Occupational Prestige Categories

The North-Hatt Scale was used as a measure of occupational prestige. This scale ranks occupations according to their relative prestige in relation to other occupations. The initial rating of occupational prestige was done by a nationwide sample of adults interviewed by the National Opinion Research Center (1947). Respondents were instructed to assign scores from zero to one hundred to a series of occupations. The higher scores were to be assigned to the higher prestige occupations. The list of occupational prestige scores from the original study has been expanded to include most common occupations.

For purposes of analysis, the North-Hatt occupational prestige scale was divided into four broad categories — functionally labeled as levels of occupational prestige. Class I includes professional and high-level management; Class II includes other white-collar workers; Class III includes skilled workers; and Class IV includes unskilled workers. These levels of occupational prestige are similar to categories developed by Clark from the North-Hatt Occupational Prestige Scale.[4]

In selecting occupational prestige as the measure of social class, such variables as income and education are explicitly excluded. Occupation, however, generally quite accurately reflects levels of income and education. There may be some deviant cases such as the high-status college professor drawing a low salary or the blue-collar truck driver making $17,000 a year, but the normative pattern suggests that occupation is a defensible choice.

Leisure Activity

The respondents were asked if they had participated in certain leisure activities within the past year. The responses were categorized as "participation" or "no participation.' Information on annual frequency of participation was obtained for certain outdoor and urban recreation activities, but this analysis is not included in the present paper.

Outdoor recreation is here referred to as that activity taking place in an outdoor setting. Urban activities refer to types of leisure that generally are done at home or in an organized commercial setting.

ANALYSIS

Two important questions are explored in this section:

Are specific leisure activities associated with a particular occupational prestige level?

What, if any, clustering of leisure activities exists for a particular occupational prestige level?

The chi-square test for significant differences was used to determine if any significant disproportionality exists between participation in a specific leisure activity and levels of occupational prestige. The analysis examines six categories of leisure activity: outdoor recreation, urban recreation, playing sports, attending sports events, hobbies, and a collection of other recreation and activity orientations of interest to planners, developers, and administrators of recreation areas.

Outdoor Recreation Activities

Table 1 shows which occupational prestige level participated most frequently in sixteen types of outdoor recreation. With the exception of picnicking, canoeing, and hiking the analysis indicates that all the relationships were significant and that persons in prestige levels I and II were the most active in the listed sixteen forms of outdoor recreation. No outdoor recreation activities were found to be most common to persons in the class III and IV prestige levels. These data also indicate that winter sports and most water-related activities were more common to persons in prestige level I, while activities such as hunting and fishing were more common to prestige level II.

These findings disagree somewhat with those of other researchers. Fishing was found to be associated more with persons in the middle prestige groups than with the lower prestige groups as reported previously by Clarke

Table 1 Outdoor Recreation Activities by Prestige Level Participating Most Frequently*

| Activity | Prestige level participating most frequently | | | | Level of significance |
	I (N = 157)	II (N = 586)	III (N = 519)	IV (N = 254)	
Picnicking	X				.10
Swimming or to the beach	X				.01
Camping	X				.05
Sailing	X				.01
Water skiing	X				.01
Nature walks	X				.05
Snow skiing	X				.01
Ice skating	X				.01
Tobogganing or coasting	X				.01
Fishing		X			.01
Hunting		X			.05
Bicycling		X			.05
Horseback riding		X			.05
Canoeing		X			NS
Other boating		X			.01
Hiking		X			.NS

* The Chi-Square test of significance was used to test for disproportionality between leisure activity and the four levels of occupational prestige. In all cases a 2 x 4 table resulted with a level of significance of .10 or less being reported. The X shown in the analysis tables indicates which prestige level had the highest percentage of persons participating in the particular leisure activity. Persons in other prestige levels also participate to a lesser degree. For example, all four groupings went picnicking, but Class I's went most often. This format for analysis and presentation follows also for Tables 2 through 6.

(1956) and Burdge (1965). Hunting, which was previously reported to be associated with the lowest prestige category, was found to be more common among persons in Class II. Picnicking appears to be common to all prestige levels. Clarke and Burdge may have reached different conclusions due to the nature of their sampling procedures. Both used mailed questionnaires which yielded low return rates and required extensive remailings. It is suggested that persons responding to a mailed questionnaire about leisure might be more active in leisure. Nonrespondents in the present study tended to be older and unemployed.

Except for certain activities, such as canoeing which showed little response, and hiking, which was sometimes taken by respondents to mean simply walking around the block, the statistical evidence strongly suggests that persons in the highest social classes are the major users of outdoor activities. Almost 60 percent of the sample households reported participation at least once during the year, although the percentage was most frequent for Class I persons.

The significant finding for the outdoor recreation activities, with the exception of the large amount of nonparticipation by the two lower occupational prestige classes, is the syndrome of activities associated with the two upper prestige classes. There appears to be a difference based on routinely available and moderately priced versus the more exclusive and expensive. Activities that might be classed as more expensive and less generally available include camping, sailing, snow skiing, water skiing, and tobogganing. Activities which are generally accessible include fishing, hunting, bicycling, and boating.

Urban Activities

Twelve types of urban recreation activity in relation to occupational prestige level are shown in Table 2. With the exception of driving for pleasure, all chi-square relationships were significant.

Urban leisure activities were most common to persons in prestige level I, with the exception of bowling and working in a vegetable garden, which were characteristic of persons in Class II and Class III, respectively. For persons in prestige level IV, no urban recreation activities were the most popular.

Another term for urban activities might well be after-work activities. Most are readily available within the immediate living environs of urban dwellers. Skill is a limitation only for the golfer and the bowler, although for the casual participant this is not a problem. A more realistic block to participation in some urban activities such as golf might be lack of money or perhaps lack of prior socialization in the activity. As an activity becomes more popular, it would be expected that appeal would increase for persons in all class levels. Bowling seems to be undergoing such a transition, but golf continues to be the exclusive domain of persons in the higher-status occupations.

The findings shown in Table 2 are rather consistent with status expectations. We expected and found that persons in the highest prestige category

Table 2 Urban Recreation Activities by Prestige Level Participating Most Frequently

Activity	Prestige level participating most frequently				Level of significance
	I	**II**	**III**	**IV**	
Driving for pleasure	X				.10
Walking for pleasure	X				.01
Work in flower garden	X				.01
Play golf	X				.01
Go dancing	X				.01
Attend the movies	X				.01
Attend concerts and plays	X				.01
Play cards	X				.01
Spend time in a tavern, bar, club	X				.01
Attend parties	X				.01
Go bowling		X			.01
Work in vegetable garden			X		.01

played golf, went dancing, attended concerts and plays, drank at cocktail lounges and clubs, and attended parties.[5] Some of these activities, such as golfing, spending time in a bar or club, and parties might well be dictated by occupational demands. The surprising finding is that activities such as flower gardening, dancing, attending the movies, and card playing were most common to a greater percentage of persons in the upper prestige levels. This finding appears to indicate that participation in a variety of even the more mundane leisure activities is most common among the higher prestige groups.

The activities of bowling and working in a vegetable garden were found to be common for persons in prestige levels II and III, respectively. Bowling certainly has the connotation of middle class or lower-middle class. While recreational bowling is quite popular, this sport has been sustained by bowling leagues that keep the alleys full during otherwise slack recreational periods. Working in a vegetable garden, while undeniably a relaxing activity, has certain economic value to families on a limited budget. The conclusion that status differences affect the type of gardening and that the importance of gardening for production would increase for lower-status persons appears reasonable.

Sports Activity

Table 3 shows the results of the chi-square analysis between playing certain sports and games and occupational prestige levels. Many of the results are not statistically significant, due to the small number of people who reported participation in some of the sports activities.

The results indicate that playing sports was generally most common to

Table 3 Sports Activity by Prestige Level Participating Most Frequently

Activity	Prestige level participating most frequently				Level of significance
	I	II	III	IV	
Played soccer	X				NS
Played tennis	X				.01
Played badminton	X				.01
Played croquet	X				.01
Played chess	X				.01
Played checkers	X				NS
Target shooting or variation	X				NS
Played baseball		X			NS
Played volleyball		X			NS
Played archery		X			NS
Played miniature golf		X			.01
Played at the driving range		X			.01
Played wrestling		X			NS
Played softball			X		NS
Played basketball			X		NS
Played touch football			X		NS

the two highest occupational prestige levels. Playing softball, basketball, and touch football were common to Class III, with no participation in sports common to level IV.

Although most of the statistical relationships were not significant, a general clustering of sports activity around different prestige levels appears to exist. The sports requiring individual skill and execution appear to be popular for persons in the highest prestige level. Team sports appear to be generally more popular with persons in prestige level III. This relationship, however, is not statistically significant. Persons in prestige level II have an interest in a mixture of team as well as individual sports, although only in the case of miniature golf and the driving range was the relationship significant. The finding that playing miniature golf or frequenting the driving range is a middle class to lower-middle class activity supports the earlier finding that golf — actually playing on a course — is predominantly the domain of higher-income persons.

Attending Sports Events

Attendance at sporting events was compared with occupational prestige levels using chi-square analysis as shown in Table 4. Most of the relationships were significant and indicate that persons in the highest prestige level were the most likely to attend sporting events.

Attendance at sports events follows the popular conception of high and low prestige activities. For example, high-status persons reported minimal attendance at stock car races, or boxing and wrestling matches (with the possible exception of amateur wrestling), but were most likely to watch

230

Table 4 Attendance at Sporting Events by Prestige Level Participating Most Frequently

Sporting event	I	II	III	IV	Level of significance
Football games	X				.01
Baseball games	X				.01
Hockey games	X				.01
Zoo	X				.01
Soccer matches	X				NS
Golf matches	X				.01
Horse races	X				.01
Go-cart races	X				NS
Basketball games		X			.01
Stock car races			X		NS
Boxing matches			X		NS
Wrestling matches				X	NS

(The header "Prestige level participating most frequently" spans columns I–IV.)

football, soccer, or golf. Watching basketball was found to be most comon to persons in prestige level II. Since the sample area was without a professional basketball team, it can be assumed that attendance was at secondary and collegiate level games.

These results differ radically, but not unexpectedly, from those of other researchers. Clarke found attendance at baseball games and the zoo common to the lowest prestige level, while the present study found these activities to be characteristic of persons in the highest prestige level (Clarke 1956). The syndrome of upper middle class activity includes football games, hockey, golf, and betting on the horse races. Most of these sporting events are expensive and admission charges, with the exception of horse races, are enough to exclude lower income groups. Attendance at the zoo could very likely be part of the socialization process of upper middle and middle class persons. Attendance at soccer matches and go-cart races was so small for the entire sample to make comparison almost impossible. The general finding is that persons in the higher prestige categories tend to be the greater participants in spectator sports.

A major finding in this study that runs counter to popular conception regards baseball. Most people have thought, and popular literature supports the notion, that baseball is the working man-laborer sport. According to this study most frequent attendance, and significantly so, is for the highest prestige categories. Data on the number of times respondents attended baseball games was not obtained in the questionnaire. It may be that certain members of the working class attend many games throughout the year and that many persons in the higher prestige classes attend only once a year.

Hobbies

Table 5 shows the results of the chi-square analysis between levels of

Table 5 Hobbies by Prestige Level Participating Most Frequently

Activity	Prestige level participating most frequently I	II	III	IV	Level of significance
Sketching	X				.05
Decorating	X				.01
Refinishing furniture	X				NS
Painting	X				NS
Flower arranging	X				NS
Photography	X				.01
Music	X				.01
Reading books	X				.01
Collections	X				.01
Ceramics		X			NS
Carving		X			NS
Woodworking			X		NS
Home improvement			X		NS
Automobiles			X		NS
Motorcycles			X		NS
Cooking				X	.01
Sewing				X	NS

occupational prestige and participation in hobbies. The results provide many instances of nonsignificance, although this was due in part to the small numbers of persons reporting activity in hobbies. More than half of the respondents did not report even one hobby. Persons in prestige level I generally had the greatest variety of hobbies.

Respondents in Class IV indicated cooking and sewing as hobbies. Unfortunately, the analysis did not determine if the cooking was recreational or done from necessity. Gourmet cooking, which is generally classed as a hobby, is popularly thought to be the exclusive domain of the highest prestige individuals. Woodworking, home improvement, automobiles, and motorcycles were found to be common as hobbies to persons in prestige level III. The occupations in this category mostly include persons with some technical skills that were being transferred to leisure use. The hobbies common to persons in Class I require some special talent as well as financial support and educational background.

Other Recreation Activities and Activity Orientations

Table 6 shows the relationship between levels of occupational prestige and certain forms of leisure which are of special interest to persons concerned with the future development of outdoor recreation facilities.

Persons in the higher prestige occupations appear to be among those most interested in private recreation facilities. Those who have fished at a fee fishing lake, would like to fish at a fee fishing lake, would like to hunt at a commercial hunting area, would like to and do rent cottages or cabins, would like to go on a farm vacation, and would like to camp at a private campground, are more likely to come from the highest prestige occupa-

Table 6 Other Recreation Activities and Activity Orientations by Prestige Level

Activity	Prestige level participating most frequently				Level of significance
	I	II	III	IV	
Fished at fee fishing lake	X				NS
Would like to visit fee fishing lake	X				NS
Would like to hunt at commercial area	X				NS
Would like to rent a cabin or cottage	X				NS
Would like to go on a farm vacation	X				NS
Would like to camp at private campgrounds	X				.01
Took vacation	X				.01
Took overnight trip	X				.01
Took vacation at home			X		NS
No hobbies				X	.01
Played no sports				X	.01
Attended no sports events				X	.01

tions. These are the same people who took the most vacations and weekend trips. Those in prestige level III, however, were the most likely to have taken a paid vacation at home. Persons in prestige level IV did not have any hobbies, did not participate in sports, and did not attend sporting events.

The analysis indicates that persons in the highest prestige level would be a potential market for any type of private recreation. These persons, however, represent only about 10 percent of the families. Also, it should be remembered that verbalizing a desire and actual participation are quite different; but since persons in Classes I and II, which make up about half of the sample, were the most active in other forms of outdoor recreation, they seem to offer the best prospect for any future private development.

CONCLUSIONS

This paper has examined the relationship between specific leisure activities and levels of occupational prestige as measured by the North-Hatt Occupational Prestige Scale. It was found that persons in the highest occupational prestige level were the most active in all major types of structured leisure. Of the 82 specific forms of leisure activity here reported, persons in the highest prestige level were the most active in 57, followed by 17 for level II, 11 for level III, and 3 for level IV. Although some class differences in types of leisure behavior were found, the persons in the highest prestige classes were found to participate in the greatest variety of leisure activities.

For the outdoor recreation activities, winter and water sports, such as snow skiing, water skiing, and sailing, were significantly associated with persons in Class I. Persons in Class II were more likely to be active in such forms of outdoor recreation as fishing, hunting, and bicycling. None of the outdoor activities were related statistically to persons in Classes III and IV.

Urban recreation, with the exception of bowling and working in a vegetable garden, was found to be most common to persons in prestige level I. Bowling was common to persons in level II and working in a vegetable garden common to level III.

Participating in sports activities was found to have occupational prestige differences based on whether the sport was of an individual or team nature. The higher the occupational prestige, the more likely the person was to engage in individual sports. The finding that golfing (on a golf course) was common to Class I persons with miniature golf and the driving range common to Class II persons suggests that one of the ways people prepare for entrance into a higher social class is to imitate the leisure behavior of that group.

Attendance at sports events followed a rather common-sense pattern. Events such as stock car races, boxing and wrestling matches, which have not enjoyed widespread popularity, were found to be attended most frequently by individuals in the lower prestige occupations. Most other sports events included in this study were attended by persons in the higher prestige occupations.

Hobbies were found to vary by prestige levels. Hobbies that require aesthetic and educational background were common to persons in Class I. Hobbies that require a special occupational skill, such as woodworking and automobiles, were common to the prestige levels that include skilled workers. Finally, hobbies that have a daily, functional application were common to persons in the lowest prestige groups.

Questions concerning the desire to utilize private recreation facilities were analyzed in relation to levels of occupational prestige. Persons in the highest occupational prestige level were the most likely immediate prospects for future participation in private outdoor recreation.

This study indicates that the concept that various forms of leisure or free-time activity are associated with specific social classes should be re-examined. The data presented here show that for almost every type of leisure activity the probability is that, proportionately, the participants will come from the middle or upper classes. Persons in these occupations, while not generally experiencing a decline in the length of the work week, are afforded sufficient income to pursue leisure in their free moments. Another reason for greater participation by the upper prestige occupations is that their life experience opens up a variety of opportunities. Education tends to broaden one's perspective and the income from better-paying jobs allows opportunity to explore a variety of leisure pursuits. Persons in the working or lower occupational groupings tend to have limited education and life experience.

234

They tend to interact with other persons of limited perspective, and they may also feel that many forms of leisure are not open to them simply because of their class position.

By including only "structured" forms of leisure activity in the interview schedule certain types of free-time activity common to persons in lower prestige occupations may have been excluded. It may be that unstructured activity such as "sitting" and "talking" is more common to persons in this prestige level. A detailed investigation focusing on this particular group would be helpful in better understanding their leisure styles.

This paper does not suggest that most structured forms of leisure activity are the exclusive domain of the two highest class levels. Except for the activities of snow skiing, sailing, attending golf matches, and ceramics, some frequency of participation was noted in each activity for each class. The normative styles of persons in Classes I and II suggest, however, that they are the present participants in leisure activity. The long-term trend in American society is for professional, business, and white-collar occupations to increase, and for blue-collar and semi-skilled occupations to decline. It is suggested that the leisure styles found to be associated with Class I and II persons will become more widespread as the occupational composition of American society becomes more like persons represented in this study by Class I and II persons. As the general level of affluency increases, however, leisure and recreation styles may diffuse more rapidly from upper to lower classes.

REFERENCE NOTES

1. Structured leisure refers to that activity which is specifically named and has societal recognition to the extent that persons derive status from the social structure for participating in the activity. Structured leisure is the opposite of activity that is nondescript and provides no specific status for the participant.

2. This definition, with some slight rewording, is similar to that proposed by Lundberg, et al. These researchers noted that "leisure is popularly defined as the time we are free from the more obvious and formal duties which a paid job or other obligatory occupation imposes upon us." George A. Lundberg, Mirra Komarovsky, and Mary Alice McInery, *Leisure: A Suburban Study* (New York: Columbia University Press, 1934), p. 2.

3. The effect of work or occupation on other types of nonwork behavior has not been ignored in sociological thought. Sorokin points out that in a society with a complex division of labor, the occupation exerts influence in the form of occupational selection and in "molding the body, mind, and behavior of its members." On this last position he notes that "the occupation group is one of the most indispensable coordinates for a definition of the sociocultural position in an individual. . . ." See Pitirim A. Sorokin, *Society, Culture, and Personality* (New York: Cooper Square Publishers, Inc., 1962), pp. 211 and 215.

3. See Alfred C. Clarke, "The Use of Leisure and Its Relation to Levels of Occupational Prestige," *American Sociological Review,* Vol. 21 (September, 1956), pp. 301-312. The present study utilized the following ranges in the North-Hatt scores for the four levels of occupation prestige: Class I 93-75; Class II, 74-65; Class III, 64-65; and Class IV, 53-55. These categories were developed on the basis of the normal curve which ideally places 16 percent of all respondents in Class I, 34 percent in Class II, 34 percent in Class III, and 16 percent in Class IV. However, due to frequent cases of many persons receiving the same score (107 steel workers received the North-Hatt score of 60) it was not possible to achieve these ideal divisions. The empirical categories yielded 10.4 percent of the sample in Class I

(N=157), 38.7 percent in Class II (N=586), 34.3 percent in Class III (N=519), and 16.6 percent in Class IV (N=253). This measure of occupational prestige was found to correlate with education +.470, family income +.468, and with a measure of social class—based on social and economic data from census tracts—of +.374.

5. Unfortunately, these data did not distinguish between the separate establishments of taverns, cocktail lounges, and clubs. It might be expected that different status groupings would frequent different surroundings. However, most of the responses to this question came from persons in Class I.

REFERENCES

Burdge, Rabel J., "Occupational Influences on the Use of Outdoor Recreation," Ph.D. dissertation, The Pennsylvania State University, 1965.

Burdge, Rabel J., and others, 1962, *Outdoor recreation research: a pilot study of the economic, sociological and physical aspects of private and public outdoor recreation in a selected Ohio county,* Columbus: The Natural Resources Institute, The Ohio State University.

Clarke, Alfred C., 1956, "The use of leisure and its relation to levels of occupational prestige," *American Sociological Review,* 21:301-7.

Department of Agricultural Economics and Rural Sociology, The Pennsylvania State University, 1963, "The North-Hatt Scale," mimeographed.

Havighurst, R. J., and Fiegenbaum, K., 1959, "Leisure and life style," *American Journal of Sociology,* 64: 396-404.

Hollingshead, A. B., 1949, *Elmtown's Youth,* New York: Wiley.

Lundberg, George A., Komarovsky, Mirra, and McInery, Mary Alice, 1934, *Leisure: A Suburban Study,* New York: Columbia University Press.

North, Cecil C. and Hatt, Paul K., 1947, "Jobs and occupations: A popular evaluation," *Opinion News* (September).

Outdoor Recreation Resources Review Commission, 1962, *National Recreation Survey,* Study Report No. 19, Washington, D.C.: Government Printing Office.

_____, 1962, *Outdoor Recreation for America,* Washington, D.C.: Government Printing Office.

_____, 1962, *Participation in outdoor recreation: Factors affecting demand among American adults,* Study Report No. 20, Washington, D.C.: Government Printing Office.

Reissman, Leonard, 1954, "Class, leisure, and social participation," *American Sociological Review,* 19: 76-84.

Sorokin, Pitirim A., 1962, *Society, Culture, and Personality,* New York: Cooper Square Publishers.

White, R. C., 1955, "Social class differences in the use of leisure," *American Journal of Sociology,* 61: 145-50.

Blacks in Sport: Prejudice and Discrimination *

INTRODUCTION

Prejudice, an unfavorable feeling or attitude toward a person or group, and *discrimination,* the unfavorable treatment of a person or group, are not new phenomena. These social processes have existed in most societies, and in American society, *minority groups,* a term limited to racial and ethnic groups (principally blacks and Spanish-speaking), have occupied socially subordinate positions. Sport, being a mirror of the larger society, tends to perpetuate these same patterns despite wishful thinking to the contrary. In this chapter we will consider the manner in which prejudice and discrimination have existed and continue to exist in the world of sport. Our focus will be upon blacks — the most visible and discriminated-against ethnic group in sport — although reference will also be made to Latin[1] professional baseball players.

A Brief History of Blacks' Involvement in Professional and Amateur Sport

Boxing was one of the first sports in which blacks participated and excelled. Tom Molyneux became the first recognized heavyweight boxing champion around 1800. A black jockey won three Kentucky Derbies in the last quarter of the nineteenth century.[2] Prior to the turn of the twentieth century (circa 1883) two blacks, Weldy and Moses Fleetwood Walker, were members of the professional Toledo baseball club.[3] Toward the end of the 1800s blacks were forced out of pro baseball (and were excluded from other sports as well) and formed their own baseball league in 1920.[4] From the late 1800s to the mid-1940s there was only a handful of black professional athletes. Henry McDonald was the first black professional football player in 1911 although it was not until 1946 that Marion Motley became the first black in the All-American Football Conference when he played for the Cleveland Browns.[5]

In 1950 three blacks broke the racial barrier in the National Basketball Association. Other blacks first include: Althea Gibson became the first black female professional tennis player in 1959; Bill Russell became the first black head coach of pro basketball's Boston Celtics in 1966; Emmit Ashford became the first black umpire (in the American League) in 1968; Wayne

*Leonard, W. M. *A Sociological Perspective of Sport,* Burgess Publishing Co., 1980. Reprinted by permission of the publisher.

Embry became the first black NBA general manager in 1971; and James Harris became the first black starting quarterback (for the season) in 1975. In short, blacks' participation in professional sport was virtually nonexistent during the first half of the present century.

On the amateur level blacks' involvement tended to parallel their professional involvement. A spate of blacks who attended Eastern schools (Rutgers, Brown, Harvard, and Amherst) early in this century did participate in football, baseball, and track and field.[6] With the emergence of black colleges, blacks were also afforded an opportunity for playing sports. Fletcher reported that blacks enjoyed opportunities to participate in athletics in the U.S. Army between 1890 and 1916.[7] In Olympic competition blacks won bronze and gold medals in 1904 and 1908, respectively.

Paul Robeson of Rutgers was one of the most celebrated black athletes in the first quarter of the twentieth century and was elected to Walter Camp's All-American team in 1918. Historically, blacks played at black colleges until fairly recently. Among football conferences, it was the South Eastern Conference (SEC) that was the last one to integrate when Tennessee signed a black defensive back in 1966.[8]

In summarizing the history of black involvement in sport, McPherson wrote:

. . . black athletes were excluded from most professional sports until the "color bar" was broken by Jackie Robinson. From the early 1900s until 1947 the color line was prevalent in most professional sports just as it was in most other social institutions. Thus, except for the few amateur athletes who competed in track and field in the Olympics or who competed in college or in the Army, integrated organized sport was not available to most blacks until the late 1940s.[9]

DISCRIMINATION IN SPORT

One of the first blatant forms of overt discrimination in sport began as early as the late 1800s. Boyle suggested the "feet-first" slide was a deliberate ploy to injure black second basemen.[10] In a similar vein, Fleischer reported that editorials in papers during the late 1800s and early 1900s warned of black supremacy in sports.[11] Vignette 8.1 demonstrates the strategy Branch Rickey employed in signing Jackie Robinson to a professional baseball contract. Today, however, the form of racism appears to have taken a more subtle cast, and even sportcasting has been judged to be racially prejudiced (see Vignette 8.2). Three aspects of sport that appear to be racially biased are: (1) *position allocation,* (2) *performance differentials,* and (3) *rewards and authority structures.*[12] Each of these will be considered.

Position Allocation

One of the recurring patterns of discrimination in collegiate and professional athletics is known as *stacking,* a term coined by Harry Edwards in 1967. It is a common form of *spatial segregation* and refers to the disproportionate concentration (i.e., stacking) of ethnic minorities — particularly blacks — in specific team positions. In effect, it denies them access to other team roles.[13] Consequently, intra-team competition is between members of the same ethnic status. For example, in baseball those competing for starting pitching positions tend to be white while those vying for the outfield slots tend to be black; in football, players competing for quarterback positions tend to be white while those competing for running back positions tend to be black.

VIGNETTE 8.1
BRANCH RICKEY'S STRATEGY FOR SIGNING JACKIE ROBINSON TO A PROFESSIONAL BASEBALL CONTRACT

Branch Rickey, the president of the Brooklyn Dodgers, worked out deliberate tactics to see that the first black baseball player had special personal qualities as well as outstanding baseball ability. Rickey saw his task as a long-term campaign to

1. secure the backing and sympathy of the Dodgers' directors and stockholders;
2. select a Negro who would be the right man *off* the field;
3. select a Negro who would be the right man *on* the field;
4. elicit good press and public reaction;
5. secure backing and understanding from Negroes in order to avoid misinterpretation and abuse of the project; and
6. gain acceptance of the player by his teammates.

(Leonard Broom and Philip Selznick, *Sociology,* New York, NY: Harper and Row, 1963 pp. 529-532.)

Like any social action program this one met with social friction. For example, ex-baseball star Rogers Hornsby stated flatly, "Ball players on the road live (close) together. It won't work. . . ." Furthermore, the National League executives issued a report which included this statement: "However well-intentioned, the use of Negro players would hazard all the physical proprieties of baseball." (Seven club owners tacitly accepted this statement.)

Rosenblatt was among the first to notice this form of discrimination in the social organization of baseball when he observed that between 1953 and 1965 the distribution of positions on a team varied for whites and blacks.[14] For example, he pointed out that there were twice as many pitchers on a team as outfielders but there were three times as many black outfielders as black pitchers.

A more theoretical formulation of this social phenomenon combines the organizational principles of Grusky and Blalock. What is significant to the present discussion is that:

All else being equal, the more central one's spatial location: (1) the greater the likelihood dependent or coordinative tasks will be performed, (2) the greater the rate of interaction with the occupants of other positions . . ., (3) performance of dependent tasks is positively related to frequency of interaction.[15]

Blalock maintained:

(1) The lower the degree of purely social interaction on the job . . ., the lower the degree of racial discrimination. (2) To the extent that performance is relatively independent of skill in interpersonal relations, the lower the degree of racial discrimination. (3) To the extent that an individual's success depends primarily on his own performance, rather than on limiting or restricting the performance of specific other individuals, the lower the degree of discrimination by group members.[16]

The thrust of this formulation according to sport sociologists Loy and McElvogue is that central positions increase the likelihood that coordinating and dependent tasks will be performed, as well as increase the likelihood of social interaction with other position incumbents. Loy and McElvogue forwarded the concept of *centrality*. To them it "designates how close a member is to the 'center' of the group's interaction network and thus refers simultaneously to the frequency with which a member participates in interaction with other members and the number and range of other members with whom he interacts and the degree to which he must coordinate his tasks and activities with other members."[17] They hypothesized that "racial segregation in professional team sports is positively related to centrality."

Hence, one of the hypothesized forms of discrimination in organized athletics is spatial segregation, or what is called "stacking" in the sport literature. In brief, the hypothesis that "racial segregation in professional team sports is positively related to centrality" has been advanced. Loy and McElvogue noted that:

. . . baseball teams have a well-defined social structure consisting of the repetitive and regulated interaction among a set of nine positions combined into three major substructures or interaction units: (1) the battery, consisting of pitcher and catcher; (2) the infield, consisting of 1st base, 2nd base, shortstop, and 3rd base; and (3) the outfield, consisting of leftfield, centerfield, and rightfield positions.[18]

VIGNETTE 8.2
ARE WHITE ANNOUNCERS PREJUDICED AGAINST BLACKS?

Howard Cosell is steaming at claims that white football announcers like himself are unconsciously prejudiced against black football players. The charges came from a blind psychologist, Raymond Rainville of the State University of New York. Rainville taped NFL games on all three TV networks, featuring sportcasters like Cosell, Don Meredith, Curt Gowdy, Frank Gifford, Pat Summerall. Rainville compared their remarks about black and white players. He concluded blacks received much less praise than whites for doing the same thing. He feels the announcers are unaware of their biased attitudes. Here's Cosell's reaction: "It's garbage," said Cosell of Rainville's survey. "My whole life has been spent fighting for minority causes. I spent 3½ years fighting all alone for Muhammad Ali when he was stripped of his title. Who started the Jackie Robinson Foundation in America? . . . I go out of my way the other way when it comes to black athletes because of my beliefs. And now some guy picks out a phrase here or there, which goes against the whole fabric of one's life."

Source: *Chicago Daily News,* November 11, 1977.

Baseball

Table 8.1 (column labeled "L&M") shows the distribution of white and black players by position in major league baseball between 1956 and 1967. Notice that the percentage of blacks was very small at the catcher position (5½%), moderate at the infield positions (ranging between 9 and 19%), and greatest in the outfield (32%). Since blacks comprised 19 percent of the total, those percentages (at the various positions) less than 19 percent reveal an under-representation of blacks, while those equal to and greater than 19 percent show an equal proportion or greater proportion, respectively.

When the positions were classified for a single year, 1967, Loy and McElvogue found that 83 percent of the infielders were white and 49 percent of the outfielders were black. The largest percentages of whites were reported in the catcher (96%) and pitcher (94%) positions. Eitzen and Yetman found little change in these figures for 1975.[19] The percentage of infielders who were white dropped from 83 to 76 percent, but the outfield positions held by blacks remained at 49 percent. Furthermore, pitchers (96%) and catchers (95%) remained predominantly white.

Leonard examined the distribution of starters, not all players on the roster, for the 1977 season. Tables 8.1 presents the results. Of all the starters, 55 percent were white, 32 percent were black, and 12 percent were Latin. The number and percentage of white, blacks, and Latins can be garnered from examining Table 8.1. When the individual positions were grouped into central (catcher and infield) and noncentral (outfield) positions — see Table 8.2 — it was discovered that 79 percent of white players occupied central positions in contrast to 69 percent of Latins and 35 percent of blacks who did the same. Furthermore, all comparisons revealed statistically significant differences as determined by the chi square statistic.

Football

Turning from baseball to football, we also note a well-defined social organization. Whereas the position alignments in baseball are for defensive categories, football possesses both an offensive and a defensive alignment. The central positions for the offensive formation include center, right and left guard, and quarterback; the central defensive positions include the linebacker slots. Loy and McElvogue studied the distribution of white and black athletes in the American and National Football Leagues in 1968.[20] They discovered the majority of black athletes occupied defensive slots

Table 8.1 Distribution of White, Black and Latin Starters by Position in Major League Baseball 1956-1967 and 1977.

Position	L&M*** %	White** N (%)	Black** N (%)	Latin** N (%)	Total	White % (55)	Black % (32)	Latin % (12)	Rank Order of Whites
Catcher	.056	25(18)	0(0)	1(3½)	26	96	0	4	1
Pitcher		22(16)	3(4)	1(3½)	26	84½	11½	4	3
1B	.194	11(8)	12(16)	3(10)	26	42	46	11½	5.5
2B	.103	11(8)	7(9)	8(27½)	26	42	27	31	5.5
3B	.180	22(16)	3(4)	1(3½)	26	85	11½	4	2
SS	.093	19(14)	2(2½)	5(17)	26	73	8	19	4
LF	.321	9(6½)	16(21)	1(3½)	26	35	61½	4	8.5
*CF	.321	5(4)	15(19)	5(17)	25	19	58	19	10
*RF	.321	9(6½)	13(17)	2(7)	24	35	50	8	8.5
DH		5(4)	6(8)	2(7)	13	38½	46	15	7
*Totals	N = 99	N = 138	N = 77	N = 29	N = 244				

*% does not total 100 because all players' ethnicity was not determined.

**This column represents the % of the ethnic group's occupancy of the particular position, e.g., 16% of all white starters were pitchers.

***This column represents the proportion of blacks found by Loy and McElvogue at the designatied positions. The .321 figure represents the observation that 32.1% of all blacks were outfielders.

X^2 (total table) = 84.41, $18d_f$; p   .001; V = .42
X^2 (white vs. black) = 64.21, $9d_f$; p   .001; V = .36
X^2 (white vs. Latin) = 25.63, $9d_f$; p   .01; V = .23
X^2 (black vs. Latin) = 20.53, $9d_f$; p   .02; V = .20

Source: Wilbert M. Leonard II, "Stacking and Performance Differentials of Whites, Blacks, and Latins in Professional Baseball," paper presented at the annual meeting of American Sociological Association, Chicago, Ill. (September, 1977).

Table 8.2 Position of Players by Ethnicity (Excluding Pitchers and Designated Hitters)

		White		Black		latin	
		N	%	N	%	N	%
Central	Catcher	25	22 ⎱ 79%	0	0 ⎱ 35%	1	4 ⎱ 69%
	Infield	63	57 ⎰	24	35 ⎰	17	65 ⎰
Noncentral	Outfield	23	21	44	65	8	31
		111	100%	68	100%	26	100%

X^2 (total table) = 46.36, d_f = 4, p < .001; V = .34, G = .52
X^2 (white vs. black) = 9.78, d_f = 2, p < .01; V = .15
X^2 (white vs. Latin) = 5.08, d_f = 2, p < .10; V = .21
X^2 (black vs. Latin) = 10.44, 2d_f, p < .01; V = .22

Source: Wilbert M. Leonard, II, "Stacking and Performance Differentials of Whites, Blacks, and Latins in Professional Baseball," paper presented at the annual meeting of American Sociological Association, Chicago, Ill. (September, 1977).

(59%) rather than offensive ones (41%). More specifically, blacks within the offensive alignments comprised 4 percent of the players at central positions and 34 percent at the non-central ones. For the defensive alignments blacks occupied 8 percent of the playing personnel at central positions and 42 percent at peripheral ones.

Dougherty replicated Loy and McElvogue's study using 1974 data.[21] He found a continuation, for the most part, of the earlier patterns. On offensive teams, 9 and 42 percent of central and noncentral positions, respectively, were manned by blacks. Defensively, 10 and 56 percent of the central and peripheral positions, respectively, were manned by blacks. Hence, several years later a similar position distribution was generally found, although there were some changes.

Brower also found that the situation in pro football resembled that of pro baseball.[22] He found that blacks were statistically more likely than whites to be on starting teams. More specifically, for 1970, 63 percent of black players started in comparison to 51 percent of white players. These findings lead Brower to write: "Black . . . players must be superior in athletic performance to their white counterparts if they are to be accepted into professional football. . . . mediocrity is a white luxury."[23]

Brower also provided longitudinal data for examining stacking in football.[24] Table 8.3 shows the distribution of white and black athletes by position for 1960 and 1975. Several observations are noteworthy. First, blacks' contribution, numerically speaking, has risen from 12.3 to 41.6 percent. Second, central positions continued to be disproportionately occupied by whites, Third, blacks have increasingly replaced whites at non-central positions.

In interpreting these data Eitzen and Yetman wrote:

Blacks appear to have made some inroads in the central offensive positions — for example, a shift from 97 percent white to 87 percent white from 1960 to 1975. But when length of time in the league is held constant, the overwhelming proportion of whites in these positions remains. Among those players in the league 1 to 3 years, 79 percent were white in 1975; 4-6 years, 80 percent white; and 10 or more years, 96 percent white. (The latter may be a consequence of the league's having a small proportion of blacks in the past.)[25]

Basketball

Research on stacking in basketball has been somewhat neglected. This is due, in part, to Edwards' declaration:

In basketball there is no positional centrality as in the case in football and baseball, because there are no fixed zones of role responsibility attached to specific positions. . . . Nevertheless, one does find evidence of discrimination against black athletes on integrated basketball teams. Rather than stacking black athletes in positions involving relatively less control, since this is a logistical impossibility, the number of black athletes directly involved in the action at any one time is simply limited.[26]

Table 8.3 Distribution of White and Black Players in Major League Football 1960 and 1975 (in percentages)

Playing position	1960*			1975		
	% of all whites	% of all blacks	Percent black by position**	% of whites	% of blacks	Percent black by position
Kicker/Punter	1.2	0	0	9.0	.2	1.3
Quarterback	6.3	0	0	9.7	.5	3.5
Center	5.3	0	0	6.7	.5	4.9
Linebacker	11.5	3.6	4.2	17.4	8.6	26.0
Off. Guard	8.0	1.8	3.0	8.7	4.5	26.9
Off. Tackle	8.3	23.2	28.3	8.6	5.7	31.8
Def. Front Four	11.0	14.3	15.4	12.3	15.7	47.6
End/Flanker	22.6	7.1	4.6	11.6	20.2	55.3
Running Back	16.5	25.0	17.5	8.1	21.1	65.2
Def. Back	9.3	25.0	27.5	8.1	23.2	67.3
Total number	100.0	100.0	12.3	100.2	100.2	41.6
	(199½)	(27)		(870)	(620)	

*The 1960 data were compiled by Jonathan Brower, who obtained them from the media guides published annually by each team. Whenever a player was listed at two positions, Brower credited him as one-half at each position. 1975 data are taken from 1975 *Football Register* published annually by *The Sporting News*. Since both the media guides and the *Football Register* are published before each season, they include only information on veterans. The total N for 1960 is smaller than one would expect, presumably because Brower was unable to obtain media guides for all teams.

**Since blacks wer 12.3 percent of the player population in 1960, those playing positons with a black percentage less than 12.3 were under-represented. In 1975 those positions less than 41.6 percent black were under-represented.

Source: D. Stanley Eitzen and Norman R. Yetman, "Immune from Racism," *Civil Rights Digest* IX (Winter, 1977), p. 5. Reprinted by permission.

Eitzen and Tessendorf reasoned differently.[27] The astute basketball observer knows that basketball positions vary in responsibility, leadership, an in such mental abilities as judgment and decision making, and outcome control. To substantiate this the researchers content-analyzed instruction manuals to determine whether specific responsibilities were associated with guard, forward, and center positions. They found general consensus regarding the requirements for these different positions. Guards were seen as the team's quarterback or "floor general" and were to have such characteristics as good judgment, leadership, and dependability. The center was viewed as possessing the greatest amount of outcome control because of his location relative to the basket and his serving as the team's pivot man. Forwards' desired traits included speed, quickness, physical strength, and rebounding ability, the latter two characteristics give credence to the notion of "glass eater."

On the basis of this information Eitzen and Tessendorf hypothesized that blacks would be disproportionately found — *stacked* — at forward and under-represented at center and guard. Their empirical findings were mixed. For 274 NCAA basketball teams (1970-71 season) they confirmed their hypothesis. Whereas 32 percent of the entire sample was black, 41 percent of the forwards were black, but 26 and 25 percent of guards and centers, respectively, were black. This distributional pattern held for starters as well as the "bench" and for Division I and II teams. On the other hand, their hypothesis was not substantiated in professional basketball. Nearly two-thirds of pro basketball players were black, and in professional basketball, unlike football and baseball, stacking did not appear to be operative.

CONSEQUENCES OF STACKING AND THEORETICAL EXPLANATIONS

In the three major team sports alluded to above (with the exception of *pro* basketball), stacking exists. What are its consequences? There appear to be several ramifications of stacking:[28]

1. Nearly 75 percent of radio, TV, and newspaper advertising slots were allotted to players from central positions (as a result of surveying 65 percent of pro football teams).

2. Because non-central playing positions in baseball and football depend to a considerable extent on speed and quickness (attributes which diminish with age), playing careers appear to be shorter for those occupying these positions than for those occupying central positions. This is supported by noting that in 1975, 4.1 percent of the players listed in the *Football Register* in the predominately black positions — defensive back, running back, and wide receiver (65 percent of all black players) — had been playing professionally for 10 or more years, in contrast to nearly 15 percent of whites in their predominant positions of quarterback, center, and offensive guard.

3. Shortened careers are a harbinger of less lifetime earnings.

4. Shorter careers reduce players' pension benefits since remuneration

from these problems is dependent upon the duration of one's career.

5. The paucity of black coaches and managers can be traced to earlier position occupancy.[29] In baseball between 1871 and 1958, 75+ percent of all managers had been former infielders or catchers. Since blacks are "stacked" in the outfield, it may be that they do not acquire and cultivate the necessary skills required for these "executive" positions.

We have presented the theoretical rationales advanced by Grusky, Blalock, and Loy and McElvogue to account for stacking. A host of other explanations exist. For convenience's sake, we will subsume the various accounts under three categories: (1) *sociological/social psychological,* (2) *psychological,* and (3) *biological.*[30]

Sociological/Social Psychological Explanations

Since most investigations of stacking have been undertaken by sociologists, it should not be surprising that their explanations predominate. These include the following (Curtis and Loy, 1979):

1. The Stereotyping Hypothesis

According to this school of thought, stacking is a consequence of management's perceptions regarding the physical, social, and personality skills of minority and majority group members coupled with their perceptions of the different physical, social, and personality skills required for occupants of different playing positions. Our earlier example whereby coaching manuals indicated agreement regarding the skills of basketball guards, centers, and forwards dovetails with this contention. In football, too, we have seen that central positions call for certain traits and non-central positions demand others, and the fact that blacks and whites are disproportionately distributed among these positions further supports this hypothesis. On the matter Brower wrote:

> The combined function of centrality in terms of responsibility and interaction provides a frame for exclusion of blacks and constitutes a definition of the situation for coaches and management. People in the world of professional football believe that various football positions require specific types of physically- and intellectually-endowed athletes. When these beliefs are combined with the stereotypes of blacks and whites, blacks are excluded from certain positions. Normal organizational processes when interlaced with racist conceptions of the world spell out an important consequence, namely, the racial basis of the division of labor in professional football.[31]

While Brower wrote exclusively for football, the same *stereotyping* process applies to other sports as well.

Tutko provided some evidence for the stereotyping hypothesis.[32] He presented 300 coaches — those persons who should be able to identify characteristics of black and white athletes because of their direct personal experience with them — with a list of traits or characteristics and asked them, "would you expect black or white athletes to be high or low on each of these items?": (1) orderliness, (2) exhibitionism, (3) impulsivity, (4) understanding, and (5) abasement (humility). The majority of the coaches expected blacks to be "low" on orderliness, understanding, and abasement and "high" on exhibitionism and impulsivity. In terms of the actual results on a scale of items measuring these traits, blacks scored "high" on orderliness, understanding, and abasement and "low" on exhibitionism and impulsivity. In short, expectations and empirical results were polar opposites. The moral is simple: coaches held conceptions of black athletes that were not scientifically verified. The unfortunate side effect is that people think and act toward social categories in terms of their conceptions even when their expectations are fallacious.

2. The Interaction and Discrimination Hypothesis

This explanatory notion is permised on the idea that management and players perceive intimate interaction between minority and majority members in negative terms and, consequently, work to exclude the minority members from central (with high interaction potential) positions. Underlying this hypothesis is probably the majority group's belief that minority group members possess undesirable characteristics.

3. The Outcome Control Hypothesis

This account views management and players as preferring to keep minority members out of positions of control, leadership, and authority because of prejudice or the belief that ethnic minorities are not capable of adequately executing such responsibilities. Edwards has argued for this interpretation:

> Centrality of position is an *incidental* factor in the explanation of positional segregation of race in sports. The factors which really should be considered have to do with the degree of relative outcome control or leadership responsibilities institutionalized into the various positions. . . . Centrality . . . is significant only in so far as greater outcome control and leadership . . . are typically invested in centrally located positions since actors holding these positions have a better perspective on the total field of activity.[33]

To Edwards, this explanation coupled with the myth of black intellectual incompetence is the real culprit.

4. The Prohibitive Cost Hypothesis

Medoff advanced an economic argument for stacking.[34] To him, the high cost of training athletes for certain positions coupled with the low socioeconomic standing of minorities is responsible for differential position occupancy. Due to their "inferior" socioeconomic status, blacks will be relegated to non-central positions because they lack access to training, instruction, equipment, facilities, and coaching. Under stuch situational contingencies blacks choose those positions with relatively little "cost." Medoff provided a modicum of support by showing a positive correlation between the rising socioeconomic status of blacks and their increase in central positions between 1960 and 1968. Such a conclusion assumes all other conditions (such as prejudice and discrimination) have remained constant, an assumption not empirically verified.

5. The Differential Attractiveness of Positions Hypothesis

This explana‘ion assumes minority members perceive positions differently and make choices on the basis of these perceptions. There are, however, two variants of this hypothesis. *First,* minority group athletes select those playing positions that provide the greatest opportunity for individual success, recognition, achievement, popularity, prestige, and monetary rewards. When former all-pro wide receiver Gene Washington was at Stanford, he played quarterback his first two years and switched to flanker his junior year. Washington himself, not his coaches, desired the change. "It was strictly a matter of economics. I knew a black quarterback would have little chance in pro ball unless he was absolutely superb."[35] Outfield positions in baseball and wide receivers, cornerbacks, and running backs in football require independent task activity and receive much visibility and publicity; generally these positions are correlated with high salaries. This formulation does not, however, account for blacks' under-representation at other lucrative and socially significant positions, such as quarterbacks, pitchers, and catchers, as well as their absence from professional sports like hockey, tennis, golf, auto racing, and horse racing.

The *second* variation of this hypothesis contends that blacks shy away from those positions that are perceived to be unattainable at higher levels of sport competition. Eitzen and Sanford found a significant shift by blacks from central to non-central positions for a sample of 387 pro football players who formerly played in high school and college.[36] Eitzen and Yetman wrote:

. . . given discrimination in the allocation of playing positions (or at least the belief in its existence), young blacks will consciously avoid those positions for which opportunities appear to be low (pitcher, quarterback), and will select instead those positions where they are most likely to succeed (the outfield, running and defensive back).[37]

6. The Role Modeling Hypothesis

According to this thesis young blacks emulate and seek to play the positions in which black stars have been successful. In other words, black youths *model* themselves after those blacks who have attained success and recognition, and those visible blacks have played at non-central positions. McPherson argued that the first black baseball players were predominantly outfielders, and the first black football players were in the offensive and defensive backfield and the defensive line.[38] It is precisely in these non-central slots that blacks are over-represented today.

There has been a spate of indirect evidence supporting this hypothesis. Brower interviewed 23 white and 20 black athletes and found that 70 percent of the black athletes had only black role models (while white athletes had role models from both races) and the majority of these role models played traditional black positions.[39] Castine and Roberts reported that, among black college players, 57 percent had a black idol and played the same position as the idol when they were in high school, and 48 percent played the same position as the idol while in college.

The present hypothesis does not explain the initial playing positions of blacks when the "color bar" was lifted nor the fact that blacks shift from central high school and college playing positions to non-central ones in the pros. This formulation implies the operation of irrationality, too. "It assumes that as black athletes become older and are in more keenly competitive conditions, they will be more likely to seek positions because of their identification with a black star rather than because of a rational assessment of their own athletic skills."[40]

In summarizing these sociological/social psychological explanations, we find the first three — the *stereotyping hypothesis*, the *interaction and discrimination hypothesis*, and the *outcome control hypothesis* — maintaining that prejudicial and discriminatory social processes are operating. The principal discriminatory agents are majority group players and management. Each of these hypotheses also implies the operation of social psychological mechanisms; that is, they involve assumptions about differential perceptions regarding minority and majority players by both players and management. The remaining four are to some extent premised on early socialization experiences whereby minority and majority group members self-select themselves out of certain positions and into others. Then, the perceptions and subsequent actions based upon these definitions channel their behavior accordingly.

Psychological Explanations

There are currently two "psychological" interpretations for the stacking phenomenon.

1. The Hypothesis That Blacks Excel at Reactive Tasks

Worthy and Markle contend that blacks excel at *reactive* activities (those in which the individual must respond appropriately at the right time to changes in the stimulus situations) whereas whites excel at *self-paced* ones (those in which the individual responds whenever he chooses to a relatively static and unchanging stimulus).[41] To test their hypothesis, they reasoned that blacks should excel at hitting, a reactive task, whereas whites should excel at pitching, a self-paced task. As support for this claim, they demonstrated that whereas 7 percent of pitchers were black, 24 percent of nonpitchers were black. Another test of their contention applied to basketball. They suggested free throw shooting is essentially self-paced while field goal shooting is reactive. They found that whites excelled at free throw shooting (a self-paced activity) and blacks at field goal shooting (a reactive activity).

Worthy and Markle's data were criticized by Jones and Hochner on methodological grounds.[42] The latter researchers claimed that the former's data were frequently counts and not performance factors, and that the data analysis did not demonstrate white superiority at free throws and black excellence at field goals. In re-analyzing and replicating Worthy and Markle's study, Jones and Hochner found support for superior black performance at hitting and superior white performance at free throw shooting. The other contentions — racial differences in field goal percentages and white superiority at pitching — were not upheld.

Dunn and Lupfer studied 55 white and 122 black fourth-grade boys playing a modified game of soccer and discovered that, consistent with Worthy and Markle's hypothesis, self-paced activities were superior for whites and reactive activities were superior for blacks.[43]

The present hypothesis may account for blacks' over-representation at "reactive" playing positions, e.g., outfield (baseball), wide receivers, cornerback, running back (football), and their under-representation in such "self-paced" sports as bowling, golf, and swimming. Just the same, the hypothesis does not explain blacks' under-representation in such reactive individual sports as auto racing, fencing, skiing, squash, and tennis.

2. The Hypothesis That Blacks and Whites Have Personality Differences

Jones and Hochner wrote:

The manner in which an individual is socialized into sports activities will have a significant effect on his sports personality. . . . Further, this sports personality will have a significant effect on sports preference and performance.[44]

According to them, black athletes in comparison to whites "(1) emphasize an individualistic rather than a team orientation, (2) stress style or expressive performance over success or technical performance, and (3) reflect a personalized power orientation associated with individual winning instead of a power orientation correlated with team winning." The researchers cite evidence in support of their hypothesis, but the overall evidence is at present quite meager.

Biological Explanations

Several investigators have discovered statistically significant differences between select samples of white and black athletes on a variety of *anthropometric* (measurements of the body) measures.[45] These studies have shown that blacks have (1) longer arms and lower legs, (2) greater hand and forearm length, (3) less body fat, (4) shorter trunks, (5) narrower hips, (6) greater muscle mass, (7) greater skeletal weight, (8) wider bones in the upper arm, (9) more muscle tissue in the upper arm and thigh, (10) less muscle mass in the calf, (11) a higher degree of mesomorphy, (12) a lower vital lung capacity, (13) a different heel structure, (14) more muscle fibers needed for speed and power and fewer of those needed for endurance, and (15) a higher specific gravity. Additionally, there is evidence that black bodies function differently from white bodies. They mature more quickly, they are more likely to have hyper-extensibility ("double-jointedness"), dissipate heat more efficiently, become chilled more easily in cold temperatures, and possess superiority in rhythmic abilities.[46]

These biological-physiological differences have been used by some to explain blacks' dominance in numbers and performance in certain sports as well as their under- or over-representation in some sports and at particular playing positions. For example, blacks' arm and leg lengths have been cited

251

as explanations for their outstanding performances in certain running and jumping events (track and field), over-representation in some sport niches — outfield (baseball), defensive backs, running backs, and wide receivers (football). Their greater mesomorphy, lower vital lung capacity, and higher specific gravity have been advanced as reasons for their paucity in swimming and endurance events.

Several criticisms of these bio-physiological explanations for racial variations in sport demand our attention. First, most of these differences are average (mean) differences and fail to account for variations within particular races as well as the overlap between members of different races. Second, just how such differences affect athletic performance in interaction with each other is not fully known. For example, there is little evidence that buoyancy is related to swimming ability. Third, some of the advantages of black athletes may offset one another. Malina wrote:

> The greater weight and density of the Negro skeleton, might possibly offset the advantage suggested by mechanical principles relative to body proportions; . . . further, since strength of muscle is physiologically related to its cross-sectional area, it is difficult to assume that the Negro calf musculature produces more power, enabling him to excel in the sprints and jumps.[47]

Fourth, the samples of performers, particularly top-level performers, have not been randomly selected.

PERFORMANCE DIFFERENTIALS

The empirical data suggest that blacks and whites (as well as Latins in baseball) do *not* perform at the same level. It appears that blacks must perform better if they are to transit from the minor leagues to the majors, as well as to maintain their positions in a specific sport. This form of discrimination is called "unequal opportunity for equal ability" by Yetman and Eitzen (1972).

Baseball

Rosenblatt observed that between 1953 and 1957 the mean batting average for blacks was 20.6 points higher than that for whites.[48] Between 1958 and 1961 this mean difference was 20.1, while from 1962 to 1965 it was 21.2. More recent studies have discovered a continuation of this gap at around 21 percentage points.[49] It seemed that:

> . . . discriminatory hiring practices are still in effect in the major leagues. The superior Negro is not subject to discrimination because he is more likely to help win games than fair to poor players. Discrimination is aimed, whether by design or not, against the substar Negro ball player. The findings clearly indicate that the undistinguished Negro player is less likely to play regularly in the major leagues than the generally undistinguished white player.[50]

Pascal and Rapping studied whether black minor leaguers must be better than whites to be promoted to the major leagues.[51] Based upon a sample of 784 major league players, dichotomized into veterans (n = 453) and non-veterans (n = 331), they found that regardless of position, blacks' mean lifetime average was higher than whites'.[52] Furthermore, for pitchers who appeared in 10 or more games, black pitchers won 10.2 games in comparison to 7.5 for whites. These findings led them to conclude:

On the average a black player must be better than a white player if he is to have an equal chance of transiting from the minor leagues to the major.[53]

Edwards claimed that it was generally conceded that black athletes are superior to whites.[54] To support this statement, he uses "evidence" from research in sports other than baseball. Leonard confined his study to pro baseball and made all possible *pair* comparisons among white, black, and Latin players.[55] Statistical comparisons were made in the following categories: (1) batting averages (for 1973 and 1974), (2) slugging, (3) home run averages, (4) runs batted in, (5) fielding averages, (6) earned run averages (1973 and 1974), (7) number of strike outs, and (8) number of bases on balls. Notice that categories 6, 7, and 8 are components of pitching performance, 5 is a "defensive" category, and 1, 2, 3, and 4 are "offensive" categories.

In general, Edwards' assertion that blacks were superior athletes received empirical corroboration. For both 1973 and 1974 there were statistically significant differences between black and white batting averages. In 1973 black averages were 17 points higher and in 1974, 14 points higher. Although these batting average differentials were slightly lower than Rosenblatt's and Yetman and Eitzen's, they indicated the same trend. Also interesting was the finding that Latin averages were significantly higer than whites'. Although the black batting average was higher than Latins', the difference was not significant.

There were also significant differences — in favor of blacks — in slugging, home run production, and runs batted in. Blacks were the best performers on all these variables. White averages on these dimensions were higher than Latins', but the differences were not statistically significant. On the pitching performance factors, there were some slight differences, but none were statistically significant. The same was true of fielding averages.

When Leonard's data were compared with more extensive data,[56] the same rank ordering of performances was, in general, revealed. Neft et al. categorized ethnic groups into black, Latin, and white and compared performance differentials for three time periods: (1) 1947-60, (2) 1961-68, and (3) 1969-73. On batting, slugging, home runs, ERA's, and bases on balls, the same order of performance, generally favoring blacks and Latins over wites, was discovered.

Leonard constructed the following "ideal types" for Latin, black, and white professional baseball players on the basis of aggregate minor and major league statistics:

Latins have spent about 4½ years in the minors and during that time have played in 470 games, come to the plate nearly 1700 times, scored about 270 runs, made 470 hits, banged nearly 40 homers, driven in 220 runs, and maintained a .276 batting average.

Latin players have spent more than 6 years in the majors and during that time have participated in 775 games, come to the plate 2800 times, scored almost 350 runs, produced 760, 50, and 755-plus hits, home runs, and RBI's, respectively, while maintaining a .270 batting average. In addition, they earn about $96,000 per annum, were born outside the United States, tend to be infielders and are about 29 years old.

Blacks have spent approximately 4 years in the minors and during that time have played in slightly less than 400 games, come to the plate about 1400 times, scored 250 runs, produced 425 hits, banged a little more than 40 home runs, drove in slightly more than 200 runs, and maintained a batting average of .283.

Black players have spent about 5½ years in the majors and during that time have played in hearly 700 games, come to the plate 2400 times, scored more than 350 runs, produced 670, 77, and 400 hits, home runs, and RBI's, respectively, while maintaining a .279 batting average. They earn about $103,000 a year, tend to be outfielders and are about 29 years old.

Whites have spent about 3½ years in the minors and during that time have played in approximately 360 games, come to the plate nearly 1300 times, scored almost 200 runs, made a little more than 350 hits, banged 33 home runs, knocked in 180 runs, and maintained a .270 batting average.

White players have spent slightly more than 4½ years in the majors and during that time have played in 550 games, stood at the plate almost 1900 times, scored 240 runs, produced 500, 44, and 498 hits, home runs, and RBI's, respectively, while maintaining a .264 batting average. They average $90,000 a year and tens to concentrate at the infield positions with a disproportionate number manning one of the battery positions and are about 28 years old.[57]

Football

Demonstrating performance differentials in football is strained by the fact that the outcome of the game is heavily based upon team performance coupled with the fact that offensive statistics are more extensive and more frequently published than defensive ones. At present, the most complete data for which comparisons between whites and blacks can be made are for running backs and wide receivers. A significant performance factor in football is average yards gained. Black runners have gained a little more than one-half yard per carry over their white counterparts, and wide receivers have gained nearly two more yards per pass reception. Black backs score nearly twice as often as white backs. Furthermore, black receivers score more than whites by a 1.78 factor. Black players were also used more than white players. Scully wrote:

Among running backs, blacks will have about 33 more rushing attempts per season, a differential of about 56 percent over white running backs, and they will have 4.4 more pass receptions per season, a 41 percent differential. Among wide receivers blacks will complete nearly 8 more passes per season, a differential of some 50 percent in comparison to white wide receivers.[58]

Basketball

Three indices of scoring — field goal and free throw percentages and points scored — will be compared.[59] The findings are mixed with respect to race as well as statistical significance in the two professional leagues. For example, blacks had higher field goal and free throw percentages in the ABA (but not significantly higher), whereas whites had higher field goal (not significant) and free throw percentages (p .05)[60] in the NBA. With regard to scoring, blacks' performance was superior to whites' in total points per person (101.41 in the ABA and 35.50 in the NBA), points per game (1.42 in the ABA and 1.15 in the NBA), and points per minute (.05 in the ABA and .03 in the NBA), but only the last variable was statistically significant.

Some researchers believe points scored per minute is the best single indicator of performance because of the fast pace of basketball. Using this indicant, blacks significantly outperformed whites by a 12.5 percent margin in the ABA and by 7.3 percent in the NBA.

Blacks out-rebounded whites in both leagues, but the data were significant only in the ABA. In both leagues whites had more assists, but these differences were not significant. In basketball, unlike football where blacks appear to be used more intensively, blacks in the ABA did play in more games and record more total "floor" time, but in neither case was the difference significant.

Leonard and Schmidt compared black/white performances (among the top 25 NBA and ABA scorers) in eight categories: (1) average point production for 1972-73, (2) games played, (3) minutes played, (4) number of field goals made, (5) number of free throws made, (6) number of rebounds, (7) number of assists and (8) total number of points scored.[61] None of the sixteen comparisons (eight in both leagues) produced statistically significant differences between blacks and whites although there were directional differences generally favoring blacks. Table 8.4 contains the summary statistical data.

Several researchers have explored the "unequal opportunity for equal ability" notion in pro and collegiate basketball. Yetman and Eitzen analyzed the performance of players on 246 integrated NCAA basketball teams in 1970.[62] They found 67 percent of the blacks and 44 percent of the whites occupied starting positions. These results applied regardless of region of the country, size, or type of school. The researchers suggested this may be due to discriminatory recruitment practices in which only "star" blacks were granted scholarships.

In a more encompassing study, Yetman and Eitzen surveyed black participation in *college* basketball from 1954 to 1970.[63] They found blacks disproportionately under-represented in the second five (the "bench"). On *pro* teams blacks were found to be slightly over-represented in starting roles, but the differences diminished from 1958 to 1970. For the 1975 season Eitzen and Yetman discovered that while blacks continued to be over-

Table 8.4 Summary Table of X's , S's and t Values for Comparing White and Black Performances of Top 25 Players in the NBA and ABA for 1973

	NBA					ABA				
	White (n = 8)		Black (n = 17)			White (n = 8)		Black (n = 17)		
	X̄	S	X̄	S	t Value	X̄	S	X̄	S	t Value
Average Point Production	22.00	2.41	23.92	4.13	-1.21 N.S.	19.56	4.03	20.57	4.19	-0.56 N.S.
Games Played	80.00	2.00	78.52	3.46	1.10 N.S.	79.37	6.54	80.23	4.65	-0.37 N.S.
Minutes Played	3,024.25	322.21	3,152.29	208.94	1.19 N.S.	2,958.25	437.57	2,895.11	302.56	0.42 N.S.
Field Goals Made	714.00	64.69	765.82	123.58	-1.10 N.S.	610.62	152.60	604.94	135.80	0.09 N.S.
Free Throws Made	329.50	8.00	347.70	120.24	0.38 N.S.	323.75	105.50	399.88	109.93	-1.62 N.S.
Number of Rebounds	696.50	372.94	599.58	353.29	0.62 N.S.	737.00	306.21	619.58	363.32	0.78 N.S.
Number of Assists	347.87	139.50	385.00	207.34	-0.45 N.S.	304.62	173.45	305.76	129.47	-0.01 N.S.
Total Number of Points	1,757.50	176.28	1,879.35	333.43	-0.96 N.S.	1,576.12	392.10	1,641.88	294.23	-0.46 N.S.

Souce: Wilbert M. Leonard, II and Susan Schmidt, "Observations on the Changing Social Organization of Collegiate and Professional Basketball, *Sport Sociology Bulletin* 4 (Fall, 1975) p. 34.

represented as starters, a decline from 76 percent in 1962 to 61 percent in 1975 had been witnessed. Johnson and Marple, considering the first eight *pro* players on pro basketball teams, discovered 60 percent of the top eight were black in comparison to 52 percent in the lower four positions.[64]

Johnson and Marple provide evidence that in *pro* basketball less productive black players appear to be "dropped" earlier than less productive white players.[65] In testing this hypothesis the researchers trichotomized years in pro basketball into: (1) rookies, (2) 2-4 years' expreience, (3) 5 or more years' experience. They found a reduction of white players from 46.5 to 37.7 percent between the first two categories, whereas blacks increased from 53.5 to 62.3 percent between the rookie and 2-4 years' experience categories. To Johnson and Marple, this suggested that marginally skilled whites are provided with more of an opportunity to make the team than less skilled blacks. For players with five or more years' experience, there was an increase (over the percentage in the 2-4 year category) from 37.7 to 46.3 percent whites and a decline from 62.3 to 53.7 percent blacks. They interpreted this to mean that blacks are "let go" earlier (when their performances begin to become suspect) than whites. To test this contention, they examined the correspondence between race and experience while holding constant *points per game* (trichotomized into less than 10 *ppg*, 10-19 *ppg*, and 20 and more *ppg*). Regardless of experience, blacks were in the majority. For marginal players who scored less than 10 *ppg* but were at least in their fifth year of experience, 43 percent were black as opposed to 57 percent white in the same category. This cannot be attributed to the unavailability of blacks since they were in the majority among those with five or more years of experience and scoring 10-19 *ppg* (59%) and 20 or more *ppg* (63%). These data were consistent with other nonempirical contentions claiming blacks must be better to be given a chance to play in professional sport.[66]

EXPLAINING THE SUPERIORITY OF THE BLACK ATHLETE

The data reported herein generally attest to superior performances on the part of black athletes (see pp. 139-141 also). Several attempts to explain why this is the case have been advanced.

Matriarchal Explanation

One scheme for explaining superior black performance is attributed to the historically dominant *matriarchal* black family structure (a form of family organization in which power and authority are invested in the female.)[67] The argument is that a black male reared in the absence of a father compensates for this "social/emotional void" by developing very positive, meaningful, and intense relationships with the coach, a surrogate father figure. As a consequence, his identification with the coach as a father figure leads him to outperform whites who have been socialized in the statistically dominant *patriarchal* (male dominated) family structure. As interesting and appealing as the matriarchal explanation seems, it does not cohere with other empirical findings. For example, about one-third of black families are structured this way, but in *absolute numbers,* there are more

257

whites who come from matriarchal families. Further, the past and present protests of black athletes against the dominant group — even white coaches — denies the compensatory role the coach father-figure may have on athletic prowess.

Race-Linked Characteristics Explanation

Kane has invoked three major race-linked categories to explain black athletic superiority. One of these is that there exist *racially linked physical and physiological characteristics.*[68] The limitation of this approach surrounds the scientific ineptness of the concept of "race." Race seems to be more meaningfully understood as a social rather than a biological designation. Furthermore, the black population and the black athlete manifest significant variability in body physiques, body proportions, and other anatomical and physiological features. Coakley wrote:

> To say that Kareem Abdul-Jabbar, Julius Erving, George McGinnis, David Thompson, Lenny Wilkins, and Calvin Murphy are successful in professional basketball because of some similar physical trait is absurd. Even if they all had similar bones in their heels and double-jointed hips, such characteristics would be insignificant compared to the dramatic differences between them. Indeed Calvin Murphy and George McGinnis have more in common with white players such as Ernie DiGregorio and Dave Cowens, respectively, than with any of the other black players mentioned.[69]

A second explanation of black athletic superiority advanced by Kane is a *race-linked psychological* one. Here, black athletes are conceived to be "calm, cool, and collected," particularly under pressure. This conclusion was reached using case studies but is inconsistent with the survey data of Ogilvie.[70] On the IPAT (Institute for Personality and Ability Test), it was found that black athletes were significantly ($p <$ .05) more "uptight," concerned, and serious than their white counterparts. However, on another IPAT item — "casual-controlled" — successful black athletes scored significantly ($p <$ .01) higher than white athletes, suggesting a more controlled orientation. These data are attitudinal in nature, and there may exist discrepancies between responses to verbal items and actual behavior. One possibility Edwards raises is that the myth of black athletes' "coolness" may become self-fulfilling.

The third category Kane advanced to explain black athletic superiority revolved around *unique, racially specific, historical experiences* stemming from slavery. In brief, he contended that survival of blacks demanded and required an excessive degree of physical-physiological skill. Calvin Hill, a black graduate of Yale and a former stalwart on the Dallas Cowboys, summed up the essence of this position:

> I have a theory about why so many sports stars are Black. I think it boils down to the survival of the fittest. Think of what African slaves were forced to endure in this country merely to survive. Well, Black athletes

are their descendents. They are the offspring of those who are physically tough enough to survive.[71]

As a consequence of this natural selection and survival of the fittest argument, the potential for superior athletic performances accrued to black athletes. As with the other explanations, this one suffers from scientifically unacceptable assumptions. The implication that blacks are a "pure" race is not supported by demographic data regarding inbreeding among human populations.

A Sociological Explanation

Our own thinking leads us to cautiously disregard these three explanations. In their place we find the ideas of Edwards[72] and Eitzen and Sage[73] most appealing. Edwards' reasoning is sociological in nature: "different *value orientations* and *a lack of opportunity to participate* offer the greatest promise as explanatory factors." We believe that the rationale applies to the historical paucity of Asian-Americans, Mexicans/Mexican-Americans, Puerto Ricans, and Native Americans (Indians) in American athletics. The fact that there are perfromance differentials attests not to the fact that there are inherent superiorities but that the role models available for blacks and the closed occupational doors in other areas have led minority group members to participate and excel in areas that have not been barred to them.[74] Edwards said:

With the channeling of black males disproportionately into sports, the outcome is the same as it would be at Berkeley if we taught and studied nothing but English. Suppose that everyone who got here arrived as a result of some ruthless recruitment process where everyone who couldn't write well was eliminated at every level from age six all the way through junior college. It would only be a short time before the greatest prose — the greatest innovations in teaching, learning, and writing English — came out of Berkeley. It is the inevitable result of all this talent channeled into a single area. The white athlete who might be an O. J. Simpson is probably sitting somewhere behind a desk.[75]

Eitzen and Sage argue that black dominance in sport can be plausibly explained by *structural constraints* on blacks in American society.[76] These constraints are of two types: (1) *occupational discrimination,* and (2) *the sports opportunity structure.* Since blacks have historically been denied job opportunities in various sectors of American society, they have channeled themselves into other socially acceptable outlets, one of which is sport. However, occupational discrimination does not explain why blacks have gravitated to some sports (football, basketball, baseball, boxing, and track) and not to others (swimming, golf, tennis, skiing, and polo).

According to Phillips this selectivity can be explained by the sport *opportunity structure.*[77] This is reminiscent of Medoff's "prohibitive cost" hypothesis. Eitzen and Sage wrote:

Blacks tend to excel in those sports where facilities, coaching, and competition are available to them (i.e., in the schools and community recreation programs). Those sports where blacks are rarely found have facilities, coaching, and competition provided in private clubs. There are few excellent black golfers, . . . and they had to overcome the disadvantages of being self-taught and being limited to play at municipal courses. Few blacks are competitive skiers for the obvious reasons that most blacks live far removed from snow and mountains, and because skiing is very expensive.[78]

It seems fair to say that, ironically, racist ideologies in the larger society are at least partially responsible for black athletic superiority. This may also prove to be the case with other ethnic minorities. The continued existence of ethnic athletic superiority may be a barometer of the lack of equal opportunity in other work-related realms in American society. As these barriers are broken — and legislation has moved in that direction — we may witness an "equalization" of ethnic performances in the sports world as well as in the occupational world at large.

REWARDS AND AUTHORITY STRUCTURES

We have seen that black performances are superior to those of whites. Is this fact a predicator of higher financial remuneration? Black athletes in professional sports has commanded gigantic yearly salaries. In 1978 football players O. J. Simpson and John Riggins were earning $733,358 and $250,000, respectively; basketball players Julius Erving ($600,000), George McGinnis ($3.2 million in six years), Kareem Abdul-Jabbar ($625,000), David Thompson ($400,000 per year for five years plus $200,000 in deferred compensation), and Bob Lanier ($350,000 per year) were also commanding huge sums; baseball players Gary Matthews and Joe Morgan were making $400,000 yearly, and Reggie Jackson was earning $580,000.

When *average* salaries (arithmetic means) of whites and blacks are compared, there is *no* evidence to support the charge of discriminatory practices. Since data for sports other than baseball are not readily available, the comments regarding financial rewards apply exclusively to this sport. Scully compiled Table 8.5 (upper tier) showing the *average* salary of whites and blacks by position for the 1968-69 season.[79] In all cases blacks earned larger salaries, exceeding those of whites from a minimum of $9,100 (outfield) to a maximum of $21,500 (pitchers).

Leonard's study of the 1977 baseball "elite" (starters) discovered mean salaries of $103,000, $96,000, and $90,000 for blacks, Latins, and white players, respectively.[80] When these mean figures were "broken down" by race and position, it was discovered that (lower tier Table 8.5) whites had the highest salaries at pitcher, 3B, CF, and RF; blacks had the highest at catcher, 2B, and designated hitter (DH); and Latins had the highest at 1B, SS, and LF.

When average salary differentials exist but performance differentials also exist, one cannot easily establish salary discrimination. To tap this dimension, it is necessary to examine the interrelationships among race, performance, and salary. Scully studied this question and concluded that, by holding performance levels constant, blacks experienced salary discrimination because they received less pay than whites for equivalent performance.[81] He argued that salary differences favoring blacks were due to equal pay for superior performance. For example, in employing regression analysis, he contended that to earn $30,000 black outfielders had to out-perform whites by about 65 points in their slugging averages.

Data on salary differentials for ethnic groups in sports besides baseball are meager. Nevertheless, Mogrell reported no significant differences in bonuses[82] and starting salaries among black and white professional *football* players. He did, however, find higher salaries for white veterans than blacks, but this difference was not significant. One important caveat is in-order: namely, little can be made of the data unless adjustments for position and performance are considered in the analysis. Since Scully has demonstrated performance differentials favoring blacks, the equal black/white salaries would be indicative of salary discrimination, all other things being equal.

Another area of unequal opportunity resides in the lucrative business of endorsing or promoting commercial products. In 1968, the Equal Employment Opportunity Commission revealed that in 1966 only 5 percent

Table 8.5. Average Racial Salary Differentials in Major League Baseball, 1968-1969*, 1977**

	1968-1969		
Position	Black	White	Difference
Outfield	$66,000	$56,900	$ 9,100
Infield	$53,100	$40,800	$12,300
Pitchers	$59,900	$38,400	$21,500

	1977			
Position	White	Black	Latin	Entire Group
Pitcher	$121,227 (n = 22)	$100,000 (n = 3)	$ 50,000 (n = 1)	$116,038 (n = 26)
Catcher	84,800 (n = 25)	145,000 (n = 1)	— (n = 0)	87,115 (n = 26)
1B	91,091 (n = 11)	124,583 (n = 12)	211,667 (n = 3)	120,462 (n = 26)
2B	48,909 (n = 11)	124,857 (n = 7)	62,250 (n = 8)	73,462 (n = 26)
SS	83,368 (n = 19)	65,000 (n = 2)	106,400 (n = 5)	86,385 (n = 26)
3B	103,409 (n = 22)	101,667 (n = 3)	75,000 (n = 1)	102,115 (n = 26)
LF	64,778 (n = 9)	127,750 (n = 16)	150,000 (n = 1)	106,808 (n = 26)
CF	131,000 (n = 5)	68,267 (n = 15)	88,000 (n = 5)	84,760 (n = 25)
RF	109,222 (n = 9)	101,923 (n = 13)	50,000 (n = 2)	100,333 (n = 24)
DH	74,400 (n = 5)	84,833 (n = 6)	60,000 (n = 2)	77,000 (n = 13)

*1968-1969 data are from Gerald W. Scully, "Economic Discrimination in Professional Sports," *Law and Contemporary Problems* 38 (Winter-Spring, 1973), p. 76.
**1977 data are from Wilbert M. Leonard, II, "Social and Performance Characteristics of the Pro Baseball Elite: A Study of th 1977 Starting Lineups, *International Review of Sport Sociology* (forthcoming).

of 351 commercials associated with New York sport events featured blacks. Similarly, Yetman and Eitzen found that of the starters for one professional football team in 1971, 8 of 11 whites (73%) in comparison to 2 of 13 blacks (15%) appeared in advertising and media slots.[83] The difference may reflect the dearth of blacks in central playing positions since 75 percent of all advertising opportunities were given to football players who occupied central playing positions.

Once one's direct athletic involvement in sport has terminated, there is evidence that discrimination continues to exist. This observation is reflected in several areas:[84]

1. *Sportcasting.* No black has had a job other than providing the "color" in radio and television sport broadcasting.

2. *Officiating.* Most game officials are disproportionately white. In the history of baseball there have been only two black umpires; professional basketball has only recently broken the "color line", and most blacks in football are head linesmen.

3. *Managers and Owners.* Black ownership is nonexistent. Data for the 1976 baseball and football season showed that, in 24 baseball clubs and 26 football franchises, only one coach was black.

In the black-dominated pro basketball, 5 of the 17 (29%) head NBA coaches were black. In the college circles, again for 1976, not a single major college had a black head coach and only a spattering of colleges (Illinois State, Arizona, Georgetown, Harvard, Eastern Michigan, and Washington State) had a black head coach in basketball or track.

Leonard and Schmidt reported that black head coaches increased from 2 to 21 between 1970 and 1973, but this tabulation included both major (NCAA Division I) and smaller schools.[85] In major colleges the percentage of black head basketball coaches increased from .64 to 5.1 percent and the percentage of major colleges with blacks on their coaching staffs increased from 20 percent (1971) to 45 percent (1975) (Berghorn and Yetman, "Black American in Sport," 1976).

In the minor baseball leagues there is also a paucity of blacks. In 1973 there were only two black managers in 100-plus minor league teams. In the NFL for 1973 there were only 12 blacks — 7 percent among the 180 assistant coaches.

Frank Robinson broke the "color bar" in managing a professional baseball team when he became the "field general" of the Cleveland Indians in 1974. Oly three coaches in major league baseball (less than 3 percent) were black that year. Furthermore, Frank Robinson has been quoted as saying: "You hardly see any black third base or pitching coaches. And those are the most important coaching jobs. The only place you see blacks coaching is at first base, where most anybody can do the job."[86] In the summer of 1978 Larry Doby (the first black baseball player in the American League) became the second black baseball manager when he took over the helm of the Chicago White Sox.

4. *Executive Positions.* In 1976, only one major college, Southern Il-

linois University, had a black athletic director (Gayle Sayres). In professional circles there were no black owners of sport franchises. No black held a high executive position in baseball and there was only one black assistant to Commissioner Bowie Kuhn. In pro basketball 2 of the 17 (12%) NBA clubs had black general managers in 1971 (Wayne Embry, a former NBA star, was the first black to occupy such a position in professional sports).

SUMMARY

In this chapter we have reviewed the existence of *prejudice* and *discrimination* — forms of *racism* — in sport. *Prejudice,* an unfavorable feeling of attitude toward a person or group, and *discrimination,* the unfavorable treatment of a person or group, have been pervasive phenomena in sport from antiquity to today. However, our thrust has been to examine these social processes in *contemporary* times.

Three modern forms of racism revolve around: (1) *position allocation* ("stacking"), (2) *performance differentials* ("unequal opportunity for equal ability"), and (3) *rewards and authority structures. Stacking* refers to the disporportionate concentration of ethnic minorities, especially blacks, in specific team positions and is a common form of spatial segregation. For example, in baseball blacks tend to be over-represented in the outfield positions while whites tend to be over-represented at the positions of pitcher, catcher, and infield. In football, blacks tend to be disproportionately found in running back positions while whites tend to be more likely to occupy quarterback and other positions like center and guard. In basketball there is a tendency for blacks to be concentrated at the forward positions rather than at the center and guard positions (in collegiate basketball but not in pro basketball where over two-thirds of all players are black). In general, blacks tend to occupy non-central positions (in the major team sports of baseball, football, and basketball) while whites tend to occupy central position.

Stacking appears to have important consequences as well. Advertising slots tend to go to those occupying central positions, black positions such as defensive back, running back, and wide receiver are associated with shorter careers and shorter careers mean less lifetime earnings and fewer pension benefits.

A host of *sociological/social psychological, psychological,* and *biological* reasons have been advanced for explaining these differences.

Regarding performance, empirical evidence suggests that blacks and whites (and Latins in pro baseball) do *not* perform at the same level. Generally speaking, black performance in the team sports of baseball, football, and basketball is superior on most specific indices of performance (such as batting average, home run production, field goal and free throw percentages, points scored per minute, touchdowns scored, number of pass receptions, etc.).

The author contends that the superior performance of black athletes is probably due to *occupational discrimination* in the larger society whereby blacks have been channeled into only a few socially acceptable outlets —

such as sport — and the sports opportunity structure whereby blacks take to those sports which have not been barred to them for various reasons.

With respect to rewards and opportunity structures, there is evidence that while black superstars are recipients of handsome salaries and other benefits, blacks may have to outperform whites to receive such sums. Furthermore, they are not readily found in sportscasting, officiating, management, and ownership and executive positions. In short, although strides toward equality have been made, racism continues to exist in American sport.

IMPORTANT CONCEPTS DISCUSSED IN THIS CHAPTER

Prejudice
Discrimination
Racism
Stacking (Position Allocation)
Centrality
The Stereotyping Hypothesis
The Interaction and Discrimination
 Hypothesis
The Outcome Control Hypothesis
The Prohibitive Cost Hypothesis
The Differential Attractiveness of
 Positions Hypothesis
The Role Modeling Hypothesis

The Hypothesis that Blacks Excel at
 Reactive Tasks
The Hypothesis that Blacks and
 Whites have Personality Differences
Biological Explanations
Performance Differentials
Matriarchal Explanation
Race-Linked Characteristics
 Explanation
A Sociological Explanation
Structural Constraints
Occupational Discrimination
Sports Opportunity Structure
Rewards and Authority Structures

REFERENCE NOTES

1. "Latin" refers to those parts of America colonized by the Spanish and Portugese and includes, geographically, Central and South America, Cuba, Puerto Rico, and the Dominican Republic.

2. R. E. Clement, "Racial Integration in the Field of Sports," *Journal of Negro Education* 23 (1954), pp. 222-230; B. Quaries, *The Negro in the Making of America* (New York: Collier, 1961).

3. Robert Boyle, *Sport-Mirror of American Life* (Boston, Mass.: Little, Brown, 1963); David Q. Voight, "Reflections on Diamonds: American Baseball and American Culture," *Journal of Sport History* 1 (May, 1974), pp. 3-25; Robert W. Peterson, *Only the Ball Was White* (Englewood Cliffs, N.J.: Prentice Hall, 1970).

4. Peterson, *Only the Ball Was White.*

5. D. Stanely Eitzen and George H. Sage, *Sociology of American Sport* (Dubuque, Iowa: Wm. C. Brown, 1978), p. 236.

6. E. B. Henderson, *The Black Athlete—Emergence Arrival* (New York: Publishers Co., 1968).

7. M. E. Fletcher, "The Black Soldier Athlete in the United States Army, 1890-1916," *Canadian Journal of History and Sport Physical Education* 3 (December, 1972), pp. 16-26.

8. Eitzen and Sage, *Sociology of American Sport,* p. 238.

9. Barry D. McPherson, "Minority Group Involvement in Sport: The Black Athlete," *Sport Sociology,* ed. A. Yiannakis et al. (Dubuque, Iowa: Kendall/Hunt, 1976), pp. 153-166.

10. Boyle, *Sport—Mirror of American Life,* pp. 103-105.

11. McPherson, "Minority Group Involvement in Sport: The Black Athlete," p. 158.

12. Eitzen and Sage, *Sociology of American Sport,* pp. 244-255; D. S. Eitzen and N. R. Yetman, "Immune From Racism?" (see endnote 19). Used with permission.

13. One researcher defines stacking as the assignment "to a playing position, an achieved status, on the basis of an ascribed status." See Donald W. Ball, "Ascription and Position: A Comparative Analysis of 'Stacking' in Professional Football," *Canadian Review of Sociology and Anthropology* 10 (May, 1973), pp. 97-113.

14. Aaron Rosenblatt, "Negroes in Baseball: The Failure of Success," *Transaction* 4 (September, 1967), pp. 51-53.

15. Oscar Grusky, "The Effects of Formal Structure on Managerial Recruitment: A Study of Baseball Organization," *Sociometry* 26 (1963), pp. 345-353.

16. Hubert M. Blalock, Jr., "Occupational Discrimination: Some Theoretical Propositions," *Social Problems* 9 (Winter, 1962), pp. 240-247.

17. John W. Loy and Joseph F. McElvogue, "Racial Segregation in American Sport," *International Review of Sport Sociology* 5 (1970), pp. 5-23.

18. Ibid., p. 8.

19. D. Stanley Eitzen and Norman R. Yetman, "Immune From Racism?" *Civil Rights Digest* 9 (Winter, 1977), pp. 3-13.

20. Loy and McElvogue, "Racil Segregation in American Sport."

21. Joseph Dougherty, "Race and Sport: A Follow-up Study," *Sport Sociology Bulletin* 5 (Spring, 1976), pp. 1-12.

22. Jonathan J. Brower, "The Quota System: The White Gatekeeper's Regulation of Professional Football's Black Community" (Paper presented at the Annual Meeting of the American Sociological Association, New York, August, 1973).

23. Ibid., p. 3.

24. Eitzen and Sage, *Sociology of American Sport.*

25. Eitzen and Yetman, "Immune From Racism?" p. 4.

26. Harry Edwards, *Sociology of Sport* (Homewood, Ill.: The Dorsey Press, 1973), p. 213.

27. Eitzen and Irl Tessendorf (cited in Eitzen and Sage, *Sociology of American Sport).*

28. Eitzen and Yetman, "Immune From Racism?"

29. Another possible reason for their paucity in these circles could be overt discrimination on the owners' parts, whereby competent blacks are eschewed because of owners' prejudices and/or because they fear the negative reaction of fans to having blacks in leadership positons.

30. James E. Curtis and John W. Loy, "Race/Ethnicity and Relative Centrality of Playing Positions in Team Sport," *Exercise and Sport Sciences Reviews* 6 (1978), pp. 285-313, Philadelphia, Penn.: The Franklin Institute Press, 1979. Used with permission.

31. Jonathan J. Brower, "The Racial Basis of the Division of Labor Among Players in the National Football League as a Function of Stereotypes" (Paper presented at the Annual Meeting of the Pacific Sociological Association, Portland, Ore., 1972).

32. Tutko (cited in Edwards, *Sociology of Sport).*

33. Edwards, *Sociology of Sport,* p. 209.

34. M. H. Medoff, "Positional Segregation and Professional Baseball," *International Review of Sport Sociology* 12 (1977), pp. 49-54.

35. Jack Olsen, "The Black Athlete—A Shameful Story," *Time* (August 8, 1968).

36. D. Stanley Eitzen and David C. Sanford, "The Segregation of Blacks by Playing Position in Football: Accident or Design?" *Social Science Quarterly* 55 (March, 1975), pp. 948-959.

37. Eitzen and Yetman, "Immune From Racism?", p. 6.

38. McPherson, "Minority Group Involvement in Sport: The Black Athelte."

39. S. Castine and G. C. Roberts, "Modeling in the Socialization Process of the Black Athlete," *International Review of Sport Sociology* 3-4 (1974), pp. 59-73.

40. Eitzen and Yetman, "Immune From Racism?", p. 6.

41. M. Worthy and A. Markle, "Racial Differences in Reactive versus Self-Paced Sports Activities," *Journal of Personality and Social Psychology* 16 (1970), pp. 439-443.

42. J. Jones and A. Hochner, "Racial Differences in Sports Activities: A Look at the Self-Paced versus Reactive Hypothesis," *Journal of Personality and Social Psychology* 27 (1973), pp. 86-95.

43. J. Dunn and M. Lupfer, "A Comparison of Black and White Boys' Performance in Self-

Paced and Reactive Sports Activities," *Journal of Applied Social Psychology* 4 (1974), pp. 24-35.

44. Jones and Hochner, "Racial Differences in Sport Activities: A Look at the Self-Paced versus Reactive Hypothesis," p. 92.

45. S. L. Norman, "Collation of Anthropmetric Research Comparing American Males: Negro and Caucasian" (Master's thesis, University of Oregon, 1968). J. Jordon, "Physiological and Anthropometrical Comparisons of Negroes and Whites," *Journal of Health, Physical Education and Recreation* 40 (November/December, 1969), pp. 93-99. R. M. Malina, "Anthropology, Growth and Physical Education," *Physical Education: An Interdisciplinary Approach,* ed. R. Singer et al. (New York: Macmillan, 1972), pp. 237-309.

46. Jay J. Coakley, *Sport in Society: Issues and Controversies* (St. Louis, Mo.: The C. V. Mosby Co., 1978), p. 304.

47. Malina, "Anthropology, Growth and Physical Education," p. 300.

48. Rosenblatt, "Negroes in Baseball: The Failure of Success."

49. Eitzen and Yetman, "Immune From Racism?"

50. Rosenblatt, "Negroes in Baseball: The Failure of Success," p. 53.

51. Anthony Pascal and Leonard A. Rapping, *Racial Discrimination in Organized Baseball* (Santa Monica, Calif.: The Rand Corporation, 1970).

52. This study has been criticized on the grounds that other factors besides hitting average are important (such as bunting ability and defensive skills).

53. Pascal and Rapping, *Racial Discrimination in Organized Baseball,* p. 36.

54. Edwards, *Sociology of Sport,* pp. 190-191.

55. Wilbert M. Leonard, II, "Spatial Separation and Performance Differentials of White, Black, and Latin Pro Baseball Players" (Paper presented at the Annual Meeting of the American Sociological Association, Chicago, Ill., September, 1977).

56. David S. Neft, Roland T. Johnson, Richard M. Cohen, and Jordan A. Deutsch, "The Black, Latin, White, Report," *The Sports Encyclopedia: Baseball* (New York: Grosset and Dunlap, 1974).

57. Wilbert M. Leonard, II, "Social and Performance Characteristics of the Pro Baseball Elite: A Study of the 1977 Starting Lineups," *International Review of Sport Sociology* (forthcoming).

58. Gerald W. Scully, "Economic Discrimination in Professional Sports," *Law and Contemporary Problems* 38 (Winter-Spring, 1973), p. 73.

59. Ibid., pp. 73-75.

60. Designations like "$p < .05$" mean that less than 5 times in 100 could chance produce the outcomes. Hence, the reader can be reasonably confident that these differences are "real" and not "spurious."

61. Wilbert M. Leonard, II and Susan Schmidt, "Observations on the Changing Social Organization of Collegiate and Professional Basketball," *Sport Sociology Bulletin* 4 (Fall, 1975), pp. 13-35.

62. Norman R. Yetman and D. Stanley Eitzen, "Black Americans in Sports: Unequal Opportunity for Equal Ability," *Civil Rights Digest* 5 (August, 1972), pp. 20-34.

63. Ibid.

64. Norris, R. Johnson and David P. Marple, "Racial Discrimination in Professional Basketball," *Sociological Focus* 6 (Fall, 1973), pp. 6-18.

65. Ibid.

66. Boyle, *Sport-Mirror of American Life;* Jim Bouton, *Ball Four* (New York: World, 1970); Harry Edwards, *The Revolt of the Black Athlete* (New York: Free Press, 1969); D. C. Boulding, "Participation of the Negro in Selected Amateur and Professional Athletics from 1935 to 1955" (Master's thesis, University of Wisconsin-Madison, 1957); Johnny Sample, *Confessions of a Dirty Ballplayer* (New York: Dial, 1970).

67. Edwards, *Sociology of Sport,* pp. 191-192.

68. Martin Kane, "An Assessment of Black is Best," *Sports Illustrated* 34 (January 18, 1971), pp. 72-83.

69. Coakley, *Sports in Society: Issues and Controversies,* p. 305.

70. Bruce C. Ogilvie, *Problem Athletes and How to Handle Them* (London, England: Pelham Books, Ltd., 1966).

71. Edwards, *Sociology of Sport,* p. 197.

72. Ibid., pp. 175-176.

73. Eitzen and Sage, *Sociology of American Sport,* pp. 241-243.

74. Terry Bledsoe, "Black Dominance of Sports: Strictly from Hunger," *The Progressive* 37 (June, 1973), pp. 16-19.

75. "The Black Dominance," *Time* (May 9, 1977), pp. 58-59.

76. Eitzen and Sage, *Sociology of American Sport.*

77. John C. Phillips, 'Toward an Explanation of Racial Variations in Top-Level Sports Participation," *International Review of Sport Sociology* (November, 1976), pp. 39-55.

78. Eitzen and Sage, *Sociology of American Sport,* p. 242.

79. Scully, "Economic Discrimination in Professional Sports," p. 76.

80. Leonard, "Social and Performance Characteristics of the Pro Baseball Elite: A Study of the 1977 Starting Lineups."

81. Scully, "Economic Discrimination in Professional Sports."

82. Robert Mogrell, *Wall Street Journal* (May 1, 1973). Pascal and Rapping, "The Economics of Racial Discrimination in Organized Baseball," found significant differences in bonuses for whites and blacks *prior* to 1958. This difference decreased over the years so that by 1965-67 it was virtually eliminated.

83. Yetman and Eitzen, "Black Americans in Sports: Unequal Opportunity for Equal Ability."

84. Eitzen and Yetman, "Immune from Racism?", p. 8.

85. Leonard and Schmidt, "Observation on the Changing Social Organization of Collegiate and Professional Basketball."

86. Pete Axthelm, "Black Out,' *Newsweek* (July 15, 1974), p. 57.

Sport and Religion *

D. S. Eitzen
G. H. Sage

On the one hand, there may seem to be little in common between sport and religion; going to church on Sunday, singing hymns, studying the Bible, worshiping God all seem quite alien to the activities that we associate with sport. On the other hand, it has been contended that contemporary sport has all the trappings of formal religion. It has its gods (superstar athletes); its saints (those who have passed to the great beyond, such as Vince Lombardi, Knute Rockne, Jim Thorpe, George Gipp, etc.); its scribes (the sports journalists and sportscasters who disseminte the "word" of sports deeds and glories); its houses of worship (the Astrodome, Yankee Stadium); and masses of highly vocal "true believers." Sociologist Harry Edwards has argued that "if there is a universal popular religion in America, it is to be found within the institution of sport."[1]

While it may be too superficial to suggest that sport equates with the complex phenomenon known as religion, it is nevertheless true that the two have become increasingly intertwined and that each is making inroads into the traditional activities and prerogatives of the other. In previous generations, Sunday was the day reserved for church and worship, but with the increase in opportunity for recreational pursuits — both for participants and spectators — and the virtual explosion in televised sports, worship on weekends has been replaced by worship of weekends.[2] As a result, sport has captured Sunday, and churches have had to revise their schedules to oblige sport. At most Roman Catholic churches, convenient Saturday late-afternoon and evening services are now featured in addition to traditional Sunday masses, and other denominations frequently schedule services to accommodate the viewing of professional sports events. In a series on "Religion in Sport" for *Sports Illustrated,* Frank Deford noted that "the churches have ceded Sunday to sports. . . . Sport owns Sunday now, and religion is content to lease a few minutes before the big games."[3]

At the same time that sports seem to be usurping religion's traditional time for worship and services, many churches and religious leaders are attempting to weld a link between the two activities by sponsoring sports events under religious auspices and/or proselytizing athletes to religion and then using them as missionaries to spread the Word and recruit new members. Thus, contemporary religion uses sport for the promotion of its causes.

* Eitzen, D. S. and G. H. Sage, *Sociology of American Sport,* Second Edition, Wm. C. Brown Company Publishers, 1978. Reprinted by permission of the publisher.

Sport uses religion as well and in more ways than just seizing the traditional day of worship. For those involved in sports — as participants or as spectators — numerous activities with religious connotations are employed in connection with the contests. Ceremonies, rituals, taboos, festishes, and so forth, all of which are part of religious practices, are standard observances in the world of sport.

In this chapter, we shall examine the multidimensional relationship between two universal social institutions — religion and sport.

RELIGION AND SOCIETY

Religion is the belief that supernatural forces influence human lives. According to J. Milton Yinger, a leading scholar in the sociology of religion, religion is "a system of beliefs and practices by means of which a group of people struggle with those ultimate problems of human life. It is the refusal to capitulate to death, to give up in the face of frustration, to allow hostility to tear apart one's human association."[4] As a social institution, religion is a system that functions to maintain and transmit beliefs about forces considered to be supernatural and sacred. It provides codified guides for moral conduct and prescribes symbolic practices deemed to be in harmony with beliefs about the supernatural.[5] For all practical purposes, the universality of religious behavior among human beings may be assumed, since ethnologists and anthropologists have not yet discovered a human group without traces of the behavior we call "religious."[6]

Societies have a wide range of forms and activities associated with religion, including special officials (priests), ceremonies, rituals, sacred objects, places of worship, pilgrimages, and so forth. In modern societies, religious leaders have developed elaborate theories or theologies to explain the place of humans in the universe. Moreover, the world religions — Christianity, Hindusism, Buddhism, Confucianism, Judaism, and Muhammadanism — are cores of elaborate cultural systems that have dominated world societies for centuries.

Social Functions of Religion

The term "social functions" as used here refers to the contribution that religion makes to the maintenance of human societies.* The focus is on what religion does, and what it contributes to the survival and maintenance of societies and groups.

Religions exist because they perform important functions for society and the individual. At the individual level, psychic needs are met by religious experience. The unpredictable and sometimes dangerous world produces personal fears and general anxiety that reverence for the powers of nature or seeking cooperation through religious faith and ritual may

---

* Functionalism as used in the social sciences involves applying to social systems the biological notion that every organism has a structure made up of relatively stable interrelationships of parts. Each of these parts performs a specialized task, or function, that permits the organism to survive and to act. With respect to societies, the notion assumes they consist of elements that perform specific functions contributing to the overall survival and actions of the society.

alleviate. Fears of death are also made bearable by beliefs in a supernatural realm into which a believer passes.

Religion also assigns moral meaning and makes comprehensive human experiences that might seem otherwise a "tale told by an idiot, full of sound and fury, signifying nothing." If one can believe in a God-given scheme of things, the universal quest for ultimate meaning is validated, and human strivings and sufferings seem to make some sense. Finally, the need to celebrate human abilities and achievements and the sense of transcendence are met and indeed fostered by many religions through ceremonies and rituals that celebrate humans and their activities.[7]

For society, one function of religion is so crucial that it almost includes all the others — social integration. Religion promotes a binding together, both of the members of a society and of the social obligations that help to unite them. August Comte, considered by many as the founder of sociology, believed that a common belief system held people together. Comte summarized the function of religion as an integrative tool in this way:

> Our being is thus knit together, within and without, by a complete convergence both of the feelings and of the thoughts towards that Supreme Power which controls our acts. At this point there arises Religion in its true sense, that is, a complete unity, whereby all the motives of conduct within us are reduced to a common object, whilst our conduct as a whole submits with freedom to the necessity imposed by a power without.[8]

Religion is an important integrative force in society because it organizes the individual's experience in terms of ultimate meanings that include but also transcend the individual. When many people share this ordering principle, they can deal with each other in meaningful ways and can even transcend themselves and their individual egotisms, sometimes even to the point of self-sacrifice.[9]

Since all human social relationships are dependent on symbols of one kind or another, religion supplies the ultimate symbols, the comprehensive ones, the ones through which all other ones make sense. As Neil J. Smelser said: "Religion is a symbolic canopy stretched out over the network of social institutions, giving them an appearance of stability and 'rightness' that they would otherwise lack. In this manner, religion functions to maintain and perpetuate social institutions."[10]

Religious ceremonies and rituals also promote integration, since they serve to reaffirm some of the basic customs and values of society. Emile Durkheim, in his classic study of religion, noted that "before all, [religion is] a means by which the social group reaffirms itself periodically."[11] here, the societal customs, folkways, and observances are symbolically elevated to the realm of the sacred. In Ronald J. Johnstone's words: "In expressing common beliefs about the nature of reality and the supernatural, in engaging in joint ritual and worship activities, in retelling the sagas and myths of the past, the group (society) is brought closer together and linked with the ancestral past."[12]

Another important integrative function that religion performs is to bring persons with diverse backgrounds into meaningful relationships with each other. To the extent that religious groups can reach people who feel isolated and abandoned and are not being relieved of their problems elsewhere, to that extent religion is serving society.

Religion also serves as a vehicle for social control; that is, religious tenets constrain the behavior of the community to keep them in line with the norms, values, and beliefs of society. In all the major religions, there is an intertwining of religion and morals, and schemes of otherworldly rewards or punishments for behavior, such as those found in Christianity, become powerful forces for morality. The fear of hell fire and damnation has been a powerful deterrent in the control of Christian societies. The virtues of honesty, conformity to sexual codes, and all the details of acceptable, moral, behavior in a society become merged with religious beliefs and practices.

A third social function of religion is what Smelser calls "social structuration," which means that religion tends to legitimize the secular social structures within a society. There is a strong tendency for religious ideology to become united with the norms and values of secular structures, producing, as a consequence, religious support for the values and institutions of society.[13]

From its earliest existence, religion has provided rationales that serve the needs and actions of a society's leaders. It has legitimized as "God-given" such disparate ideologies as absolute monarchies and democratic forms of government. Moreover, when obedience to the social agents of control is interpreted as a religious duty and disobedience is interpreted as sinful, religion serves well this social function.

THE RELATIONSHIP OF RELIGION AND SPORT

Primitive Societies

According to Rudolph Brasch, sport began as a religious rite: "Its roots were in man's desire to gain victory over foes seen and unseen, to influence the forces of nature, and to promote fertility among his crops and cattle."[14] The Zuni Indians of New Mexico played games that they believed would bring rain and thus enable their crops to grow. In southern Nigeria, wrestling matches were held to encourage the growth of crops, and various games were played in the winter to hasten the return of spring and to ensure a bountiful season. One Eskimo tribe, at the end of the harvest season, played a cup-and-ball game to "catch the sun" and thus delay its departure. In his monumental work on the Plains Indians, Stewart Culin wrote: "In general, games appear to be played ceremonially, as pleasing to the gods, with the objective of securing fertility, causing rain, giving and prolonging life, expelling demons, or curing sickness."[15]

Ancient Greece

The ancient Greeks worshipped beauty and entwined religious observance with their athletic demonstrations in such a way that it is difficult to define where one left off and the other began. Greek gods were anthropomorphic, and sculptors portrayed the gods as perfect physical specimens, who were to be both admired and emulated by their worshipers. The strong anthropomorphic conceptions of gods held by the Greeks led to their belief that gods took pleasure in the same things as mortals — music, drama, and displays of physical excellence. The gymnasia located in every city-state for all male adults provided facilities and places for sports training as well as for the discussion of intellectual topics. Furthermore, there were facilities for religious worship — an altar and a chapel were located in the center of each gymnasium.

The most important athletic meetings of the Greeks were part of religious festivals. According to one scholar of Greek athletics:

> The Olympic Games were sacred games, staged in a sacred place and at a sacred festival; they were a religious act in honor of the deity. Those who took part did so in order to serve god and the prizes which they won came from the god."[16]

The Olympic Games were held in honor of Zeus, king of the gods; the Pythian Games took place at a festival in honor of Apollo; the Isthmian Games were dedicated to the god Poseidon; and the Nemean Games were held in honor of Zeus. Victorious athletes presented their gifts of thanks upon the altar of the god or gods whom they thought to be responsible for their victory. The end of the ancient Olympic Games was a result of the religious conviction of Theodosius, the Roman emperor of A.D. 392-95. He was a Christian and decreed the end of the games as part of his suppression of paganism in favor of Christianity.[17]

The Early Christian Church

Religious support for sport found no counterpart to the Greeks in Western societies until the beginning of the twentieth century. The Roman Catholic church came to dominate society in Western Europe from A.D. 400 until the Reformation in the sixteenth century, and since then Roman Catholicism has shared religious power with Protestant goups.

At first opposing Roman sport spectacles, such as chariot racing and gladiator shows because of their paganism and brutality, eventually Christians came to regard the human body as an instrument of sin. The early Christians did not view sports as evil per se, for the Apostle Paul wrote approvingly of the benefits of physical activity.[18] But the paganism prominent in the Roman sports events was abhorrent to the Christians. Moreover, early Christianity gradually built a foundation based on asceticism, which is a belief that evil exists in the body and, therefore, the body should be subordinate to the pure spirit. As a result, church dogma and education sought to subordinate all desires and demands of the body in order to exalt the spiritual life. Saint Bernard argued: "Always in a robust and active body the mind lies soft and more lukewarm; and, on the other hand, the spirit flourishes more strongly and more actively in an infirm and weakly body."[19] Nothing could have been more damning for the promotion of active recreation and sport.

Spiritual salvation was the dominant feature of the Christian faith. Accordingly, the cultivation of the body was to be subordinated to the salvation of the spirit, especially since the body, it was believed, could obstruct the realization of this aim. An otherwise enlightened Renaissance scholar, Desiderius Erasmus, while a monk at a monastery (before he became a critic of Roman Catholicism), wrote an essay "On the Contempt of the World," which articulately characterized the Christian attitude of his time toward body and soul:

> The monks do not choose to become like cattle; they know that there is something sublime and divine within man which they prefer to develop rather than cater for the body. . . . Our body, except for a few details, differs not from an animal's body but our soul reaches out after things divine and eternal. The body is earthly, wild, slow, mortal, diseased, ignoble; the soul on the other hands is heavenly, subtle, divine, immortal, noble. Who is so blind that he cannot tell the difference between body and soul? And so the happiness of the soul surpasses that of the body.[20]

The Reformation and the Rise of Protestantism

The Reformation of the early sixteenth century signaled the end of the vicelike grip that Roman Catholicism had on the minds and habits of the people of Europe and England. With the Reformation, the pejorative view of sports might have perished where the teachings of Martin Luther and John Calvin prevailed. But Protestantism had within it the seeds of a new asceticism, and the Calvinism imported to England, in its Puritan form, became a greater enemy to sport than Roman Catholicism had been.

Puritan influence grew throughout the sixteenth century, and by the early seventeenth century had come to have considerable influence on English life. Moreover, since Puritans were some of the earliest English immigrants to America, they had considerable influence on the social life of the colonies. Perhaps no Christian group exercised a greater opposition to sports than the Puritans. Dennis Brailsford asserted that "the Puritans saw their mission to erase all sport and play from men's lives."[21] They gave England the "English Sunday" and its equivalent in the United States, the blue laws, which, until a few decades ago, managed to debar sports on the Sabbath and severely limit the kinds of sports that were considered appropriate for a Christian. As a means of realizing amusement and unrestrained impulses, sport was suspect for the Puritan, and as it approached mere pleasure or involved physical harm to participants or to animals (boxing, cockfighting) or involved gambling, sport was, of course, altogether evil. The English historian Thomas B. Macaulay claimed that the Puritans opposed bearbaiting not so much because it was painful for the bear but because the bear's pain gave pleasure to the spectators.[22]

The Colonial Period to the Twentieth Century

The principal relationship between the church and sport in the American colonies was one of restriction and probation, especially with regard to sports on the Sabbath. Legislation prohibiting sports participation on Sunday began soon after the first English settlement in the colonies and was enacted by a group of Virginia ministers. But such repressive acts are more commonly associated with the Puritans in New England who also enacted legislation of this type. Actually, most of the colonies passed laws against play and sport on the Sabbath, and it was not until the mid-twentieth century that industrial and economic conditions brought about the repeal of most of these laws, although most had been annulled by custom.[23]

There were a number of reasons for Protestant prejudice against play and sport in the colonies. One prominent objection was that participation would divert attention from spiritual matters. There was also the belief that play and its resultant pleasure might become addictive because of the inherent weakness of human nature. There was, of course, the practical matter that survival in the colonies and on the frontier required hard work from everyone; thus, time spent in play and games was typically considered time wasted. Finally, the associations formed and the enviroment in which play and sport occurred conspired to cast these activities in a bad light. The tavern was the center for gambling and table sports, dancing and obvious sexual overtones, and field sports often involved gambling and cruelty to animals.

Churchly opposition to leisure pursuits was firmly maintained in the first few decades of the new republic, and each effort to liberalize attitudes toward leisure pursuits was met with a new attack on sport as "sinful." Sports were still widely regarded by the powerful Protestant religious groups as snares of the devil himself. But in the 1830s, social problems became prominent concerns of social reformers, many of whom were clergy and intellectual leaders. There were crusades against slavery, intemperance, and poor industrial working conditions; widespread support for the emancipation of women, public education, and industrial reform; indeed, every facet of American life came under scrutiny. One aspect of this comprehensive social-reform movement was the concern for numan health and physical fitness.

Social conditions had begun to change rapidly under the aegis of industrialization — the population shifted from rural to urban residence, labor changed from agricultural toil to toil for wages in squalid working and living conditions. The physical health of the population became a major problem, leading a number of reformers to propose that people would be happier, more productive, and have better health if they engaged in vigorous sports activities. Surprisingly, some of the leading advocates of play and sport were clerics, and from their pulpits they presented forceful arguments that physical prowess and sanctity were not incompatible. Intellectual leaders joined the movement, Ralph Waldo Emerson said: "out upon the scholars . . . with their pale, sickly, etiolated indoor thought! Give me the out-of-door thoughts of sound men, thoughts all fresh and blooming."[24] The esteemed poet and novelist Oliver Wendell Holmes joined the attack on the physical condition of the youth. He wrote:

> I am satisfied that such a set of black-coated, stiff-jointed, soft-muscled, paste-complextioned youth as we can boast in our Atlantic cities never before sprang from the lions of Anglo-Saxon lineage.[25]

Holmes argued that widespread participation in sports would make for a more physically fit citizenry, as well as create a more exciting environment. The proposals of support for physical fitness and wholesome leisure had a profound effect on the church. Responding to the temporal needs of the people, the clergy began to shed much of the otherworldly emphasis and seek to alleviate immediate human problems. Recognizing the need for play and the health benefits of leisure amusements, the church began to soften its attitude toward play and sports. In summarizing the change that occurred, sports historian Guy Lewis said:

Sport, within a few decades of the 1836 to 1860 period, became an integral part of the life in the nation. Its emergence began with the concern of a few intellectuals for the health and well-being of their fellow countrymen. Although the "Muscular Christianity" phase of social reform directly affected only a small segment of the population, its total impact must be measured in terms of the end result — the establishment of a new American institution.[26]

Although the development of a more liberal attitude by church leaders toward sport began to appear in the antebellum period, not all church authorities subscribed to the trend. The staid Congregationalist magazine, the New Englander, vigorously attacked sport:

Let our readers, one and all, remember that we were sent into this world, not for sport and amusement, but for labor; not to enjoy and please ourselves, but to serve and glorify God, and be useful to our fellow men. That is the great object and end in life. In pursuing this end, God had indeed permitted us all needful diversion and recreation. . . . But the great end of life after all is work . . . It is a true saying . . . We come into this world, not for sports." We were sent here for a higher and nobler object.[27]

In official publications and public speeches, some church leaders fought the encroaching sport and leisure mania throughout the later nineteenth century. Militant organizations, such as the American Sabbath Union, the Sunday League of America, and the Lord's Day Alliance, were visible proof of the vitality of the strong forces still mobilized in support of this phase of Protestant doctrine.[28] But there was a growing awareness that churches were fighting a losing war. Churchmen gradually began to reconcile play and religion as medical, educational, and political leaders emphasized that physical, mental, and, indeed, moral health was developed through games and sports. City churches began to minister to the social, physical, and economic needs of their members and residents in the neighborhood, extending their role beyond just preaching salvation of the soul. To meet the social needs of rural and city members, churches adopted sports and sponsored recreations to draw people together, and church leadership played an important role in the promotion of community recreation and school physical education in the latter nineteenth century. Many clergy used their church halls and grounds as recreation centers for the neighborhood. Clarence E. Rainwater proposed that the beginning of the playground movement in America began in 1885, when the sand gardens were opened in the yards of the West End Nursery and the Parmenter Street Chapel in Boston.[29] The New York City Society for Parks and Playgrounds was begun in 1890 with the support of clergymen, who delivered sermons to their congregations on children's need for playgrounds.[30]

Support for physical education found its way into denominational journals and meetings, and religious support for physical education played an important role in its acceptance into colleges and its eventual adoption by public school boards across the country. The Young Men's Christian College (now Springfield College) at Springfield, Massachusetts, made sport and physical fitness one of the cornerstones of a proper Christian education and life-style.

Increasingly, churches broadened their commitment to play and sport endeavors as means of drawing people together. Bowling leagues, softball leagues, and youth groups, such as the Catholic Youth Organization (CYO), were sponsored by churches for their young members. The church's prejudice against pleasure through play had broken down almost completely by the beginning of the twentieth century.

Twentieth-Century America

Churches have been confronted with ever-increasing changes in the twentieth century; economic pressures, political tendencies, and social conditions have been the chief forces responsible for the drastically changed relationship between religion and sport. Increased industrialization turned the population into a nation of urban dwellers, while higher wages were responsible for an unprecedented affluence. The gospel of work (the Protestant work ethic) has become no longer acceptable to everyone, and increased leisure has enhanced the popularity of sports. The story of changes in the attitudes of religionists in the twentieth century "is largely one of accelerating accommodation." Much of Protestant America has come "to view sport as a positive force for good and even as an effective tool to promote the Lord's work."[31] Sports and leisure activities have become an increasingly conspicuous part of the recreation program of thousands of churches and many church colleges. Richard A. Swanson summarized the new role of the church:

> Throughout the twentieth century, the church has moved steadily further into recreation. Camping programs, athletic leagues, organized game periods at various group meetings, and even full-time recreation directors are all evidences of a posititive relationship between religion and play.[32]

Perhaps the best example of the change in the symbolic relationship between religion and sport within the last century occurred at the dedication of a Sports Bay in the Cathedral of St. John the Divine in New York in 1929. At the ceremony, Bishop William T. Manning said:

> Clean, wholesome well-regulated sport is a most powerful agency for true and upright living. . . . True sport and true religion should be in the closest touch and sympathy. . . . A well played game of polo or of football is in its own way as pleasing to God as a beautiful service of worship in the Cathedral.[33]

276

The Roman Catholic and Protestant clergymen who over the centuries had preached that sport was a handmaiden of the devil must have shifted uneasily in their graves at such an oration. Times have certainly changed, the church as well, and reconciliation between sports and organized religion has approached finality. Perhaps the change in church attitude toward sports was best described by Frederick W. Cozens and Florence S. Stumpf: "If you can't lick 'em, join 'em.' "[34]

Sport as Religion

In the past two decades, the power and influence of sport has increased enormously, while at the same time formalized religion and the institutional church have suffered a decline of interest and commitment. Sport has taken on so many of the characteristics of religion that some have argued that sport has emerged as a new religion, supplementing, and in some cases even supplementing, the traditional religious expressions.[35] Howard S. Slusher noted that "ceremony and rituals of religious life have traditionally given *order* to man's existence," but, since religion and the associated rituals are playing a less significant role in our lives, "it is not surprising man turns to other 'rites' to again see some form of quasi-order to his life. For many, sport fulfills this function."[36] Cornish Rogers contended that "sports are rapidly becoming the dominant ritualistic expression of the reification of established religion in America."[37]

A few examples will illustrate how organized sports have taken on the trappings of religion. Every religion has its idols (or saints or high priests) who are venerated by its members. Likewise, sports fans have persons whom they worship: the saints who are now dead — such as Knute Rockne, Babe Ruth, and, of course, Vince Lombardi, who earned a place among the saints for his fierce discipline and the articulation of the basic commandment of contemporary sport. "Winning is the only thing:"* The high priests of contemporary sports, such as Joe Paterno and "Bear" Bryant (whom some have claimed can "walk on water") direct the destinies of large masses of followers.

In addition to the fundamental commandment of sport according to Saint Vince, numerous proverbs fill the world of sport: "Nice guys finish last"; "When the going gets tough, the tough get going"; "Lose is a four-letter word"; and so forth. These proverbs are frequently written on posters and hung in locker rooms for athletes to memorize.[38]

The achievements of athletes and teams are celebrated in numerous shrines built throughout the country to commemorate and glorify sporting figures. These "halls of fame" have been built for virtually every sport played in America, and some sports have several halls of fame devoted to them. According to Gerald Redmond:

Athletes become "immortal heroes" as they are "enshrined" in a sports

---

* The "canonization" of Lombardi in itself is an interesting commentary on sport in American society. Somehow his brutal methods were overshadowed by his success at winning football games.

277

hall of fame, when "devoted admirers" gaze at their "revered figures" or read plaques "graven in marble" before departing "often very moved" (or even "teary-eyed") from the many "hushed rooms, filled with nostaligia." This is the jargon of the churches of sport in the twentieth century.[39]

Symbols of fidelity abound in sports. The athletes are expected to give total commitment to the cause, including abstinence from smoking, alcohol, and, in some cases, even sex. The devout followers who witness and invoke traditional and hallowed chants show their devotion to the team and add "spirit" to its cause. It is not unusual for these pilgrims to travel hundreds of miles, sometimes braving terrible weather conditions, to witness a game, as a display of their fidelity.

Like religious institutions, sport has become a function of communal involvement. Perhaps the most salient role that sport-as-religion plays for its followers is in the sense of belonging and of community that it evokes. One cheers for the Green Bay Packers, the New York Yankees, or the Denver Nuggets. The emotional attachment of some fans to their teams verges on the religious fanaticism previously seen in holy wars against heretics and pagans. Opposing teams and their fans, as well as officials, are occasionally attacked and brutally beaten.

RELIGION USES SPORT

Churches

From a position of strong opposition to recreation and sport activities, the church has made a complete reversal within the past century and now heartily supports these activities as effective tools to promote "the Lord's work." Social service is a major purpose behind religious leaders' providing play and receation under the auspices of their churches. Church-sponsored recreation and sport programs provide services to members and sometimes the entire community that are often unavailable in acceptable forms anywhere else. Church playgrounds and recreation centers in urban areas have facilities, equipment, and instruction that municipal governments often cannot provide. YMCA, Young Women's Christian Association (YWCA), CYO, and other church-related organizations have performed a variety of social services for old and young alike, one of which is the sponsorship of sports leagues.

Churches also promote sport to strengthen and increase fellowship in the congregations, which has been beneficial to the churches as well as to their members. At a time when churches were just beginning their extensive support for recreational and sports programs, one clergyman said: " . . . there is a selfish reason why the church should offer recreation of some sort — because it aids the church and enlivens the people."[40] In a time of increasing secularization, such as the United States has witnessed in the past fifty years, it is understandable why churches would accommodate activities that solidify and integrate church membership.

Religious Leaders

Not to merely provide recreational and sports opportunities under the sponsorsip of the church, some religious leaders outwardlly avow the association between religion and sport in their preaching. Bob Richards, an Olympic pole-vault champion and a minister said: "I motivate people with sports stories and witness to my Christian faith. . . . Pastors should get out of the pulpits and into sports."[41]

One of the most popular contemporary evangelists, Billy Graham, enthusiastically supports the virtues of sports competition and the sanctity of Christian coaches and athletes. He has made sports a basic metaphor in his ministry. According to Graham, the basic source of Christianity, the Bible, legitimates sport involvement. He said: "The Bible says leisure and lying around are morally dangerous for us. . . . Sports keep us busy."[42]

Church Colleges

Intercollegiate sports programs were originally organized and administered by the students merely for their own recreation and amusement. But by the early years of the twentieth century the programs gradually changed form and character, and one of the new features that emerged was the use of the collegiate sports teams to publicize the school and bind alumni to their alma mater. Church-supported colleges and universities — both Roman Catholic and Protestant — began to use their athletic teams to attract students, funds, and public attention to improverished and often academically inferior institutions. The classic, but by no means the only, example is Notre Dame.* Recently, the chaplain of the Notre Dame athletic department acknowledged that the athletic program had been used to promote the university. He said: "Of course Catholic schools used athletics for prestige. Notre Dame would not be the great school it is today, the great academic institution, were it not for football."[43]

The most recent example of a religious university deliberately using intercollegiate athletics for its promotion is Oral Roberts University in Tulsa, Oklahoma. When evangelist Oral Roberts founded this university in 1965, one of his first actions was the establishment of an athletic program to bring recognition and prestige to the university. With respect to the program, Roberts said:

Athletics is part of our Christian witness. . . . Nearly every man in America reads the sports pages, and a Christian school cannot ignore these people. . . . Sports are becoming the No. 1 interest of people in America. For us to be relevant, we had to gain the attention of millions of people in a way that they could understand.[44]

Religious Organizations for Athletes

One of the most notable outgrowths of religion's use of sport has been

---

* Many Roman Catholic colleges and universities have used football and basketball to publicize the institutions. Protestant institutions have followed the same pattern (Brigham Young University and Southern Methodist University are among the most visible).

279

the nondenominational religious organizations composed of coaches and athletes that provide a variety of programs designed to serve current members and recruit new members to religion. There are at least six, major, incorporated organizations that offer everything from national conferences to services before games. The most well known of the organizations are Fellowship of Christian Athletes (FCA), Athletes in Action (AIA), Pro Athletes Outreach (PAO), Sports Ambassadors Overseas, Sports World Ministries, and Baseball Chapel.

The oldest and largest of these organizations is the Fellowship of Christian Athletes (FCA), which was founded in 1954. The avowed purpose of the FCA — which appears on most of the Fellowship of Christian Athletes official publications and appears on the title page of each issue of *The Christian Athlete* — is "to confront athletes and coaches and through them the youth of the nation, with the challenge and adventure of following Christ and serving him through the fellowship of the church. . . ." It attempts "to combat juvenile delinquency, to elevate the moral and spiritual standards of sports in an unprincipled secular culture; to challenge Americans to stand up and be counted for or against God and to appeal to sports enthusiasts and American youth through hero worship harnessed."[45]

The FCA uses older athletes and coaches to recruit younger ones to Christ. It has a mailing list of more than fifty-five thousand persons and a staff of more than thirty-five. Its most important single activity is the sponsoring of annual, week-long, summer conferences attended by more than ten thousand participants, where coaches and athletes mix religious and inspirational sessions with sports instruction and competition. With regard to the activity at these conferences, the executive director of the FCA said: "It's 50 percent inspirational and 50 percent perspirational."[46] Another important facet of the FCA is the high school and college group session programs known as the "huddle-fellowship program" .n which high school and college athletes in a community or a campus get together to talk about their faith, engage in Bible study, and pray. They also engage in projects such as serving as "big brothers" for delinquent or needy children, visiting nursing homes, and serving as playground instructors. There are now some 1,600 high school huddles in the United States and more than 200 college fellowships, the bulk of which are found in the South, Southwest, and Midwest. Most of the members are white, middleclass boys; however, in recent years, female athletes have been admitted to the FCA, and their membership in the organization is growing rapidly. In addition to these activities, the FCA sponsors state and regional retreats; provides various informational materials such as films, records, tapes; and publishes a monthly periodical *The Christian Athlete*.

Another religious group formed mostly by former athletes is a division of the Campus Crusade for Christ and is called Athletes in Action (AIA). With a special dispensation from the NCAA, the AIA fields several athletic teams made up of former college athletes. These teams compete against amateur teams throughout the country each year and, as part of each appearance, the AIA athletes make brief evangelical speeches and testimonials

280

to the crowds and distribute free religious materials.[47]

Other organizations also enlist the assistance of athletes in spreading the gospel. The Pro Athletes Outreach (PAO) was founded largely as an intramural peacekeeping force because the AIA and FCA were squabbling over enlisting the best missionary athletes for their programs. The PAO sends phalanxes of professional athletes on what it calls "speaking blitzes" of the country. The athletes deliver religious and testimonial speeches to groups largely of young people.

Missionaries

Of all the purposes and/or consequences of religion's association with sport, certainly one of the most important is the use of athletes, coaches, and the play environment to recruit new members to the Church. The use of play as a drawing card has been a major consideration of many religious leaders. An often-used slogan nicely sums up this principle: "There are many a one who comes to play and remains to pray." Getting persons into church recreation and sports programs is often viewed as a first step into the Church and into Christian life. Playgrounds and recreation centers in or near churches, and the supervision of these facilities by clergy or lay persons with a strong religious commitment, provide a convenient setting for converting the non-church-going participant. A great deal of informal missionary work is done in these settings, often resulting in conversions to religion. However, due to the prominence and prestige of famous athletes and coaches, religious leaders have realized that they could be used as effective missionaries, and virtually every religious group has used coaches and athletes to recruit new members.

In his series for *Sports Illustrated,* Deford reported that "the use of athletes as amateur evangelists is so widespread that it might be fairly described as a growth industry." He observed that it "is almost as if a new denomination has been created: Sportianity."[48] *The Wittenburg Door,* a contemporary religious journal, derisively labeled this movement "Jocks for Jesus."[49]

The practice of using "jock evangelists" was explained by one of the directors of the FCA in this way: "Athletes and coaches . . . have a platform in this country. Athletes have power, a voice."[50] Billy Zeioli, one of Sportianity's leading evangelists, said: ". . . the fact is the people view athletes . . . as stars, and we can't change that. So we say: let's . . . teach them to be right and moral, and then take them to the people."[51] Another advantage of using athletes to reach other athletes is access. As one former AAU wrestling champion and AIA assistant athletic director noted: ". . . I can get into a fraternity, a locker room, where nobody else would be permitted."[52] Ira Lee Eshleman, head of Sports World Ministries, said "The committed athlete who understands the basis of his faith can reach more people — and especially young people — than I could ever hope to reach."[53]

Athletes and coaches are used to sell religion. The technique is fairly straightforward and simple: those who are already committed to religion convert the athletes. Since athletes are among the most visible and prestigious persons in our society, they may be used for missionary work in spreading the Gospel to their teammates and others with whom they interact.[54] As Deford observed: "Jesus has been transformed, emerging anew as a holler guy, hustler, a give-it-100-percenter."[55] Combining the popular appeal they have as celebrities with the metaphors of the sports world, athletes are able to catch and hold the attention of large groups of people. Some pro teams have a "God Squad," a group of teammates who pray together and make public appearances on behalf of the Christian cause. Roger Staubach, former Dallas Cowboy quarterback and God Squader, in a pep talk on "the game of life" at the International Student Congress on Evangelism, said: "The goal we must get across is our salvation . . . [and] God has given us a good field position."[56]

Sportianity and Social Issues

There is little inclination on the part of religious leaders and the various organizations that make up Sportianity to confront the pressing social issues of sport or the larger society. Virtually all of the leaders in the Sportianity movement are fundamentalists who preach a conservative theology. They are generally reluctant to take a stand on moral issues within sports or within the wider society. According to Deford: "In the process of dozens of interviews with people in Sportianity, not one even remotely suggested any direct effort was being considered to improve the morality of athletics."[57]

In an interview with the directors of the communications department of the FCA, the editor for *The Wittenburg Door* asked: "Your magazine is the mouthpiece of FCA. Do you see your role as trying to change athletics?" The response was: "The FCA board and officers would not see that. . . . Stick with the positive, don't deal with the evils in athletics . . . the board would rather have us not stir the waters. Just print the good story about the good ole' boy who does good things."[58]

The various Sportianity organizations and their members have not spoken out against racism, sexism, cheating in sport, the evils of recruiting, or any of the other well-known unethical practices, excesses, and abuses in the sports world. Deford articulately described this indifference to sports problems:

Sportianity does not question the casual brutality — spearing, clotheslining, gouging — that sends players . . . to the hospital every year. It does not censure the intemperate behavior of coaches like Woody Hayes and Bobby Knight.[59]

According to psychologist Thomas Tutko, "It would be healthy if some of the leading religious figures and churches would come out and say, 'Look, let's face it, a large part of sports is corrupt and we will no longer help sanction it. . . . By remaining on the sidelines, so to speak, religion is contributing to the problem."[60]

In the final analysis, sports mortality does not appear to have been improved by the Sportianity movement. Instead, Sportianity seems willing to accept sport as is, more devoted to maintaining the status quo than resolving the many problems in sport today.

The Value Orientations of Religion and Sport

The value orientations underlying competitive sports in America may seem remotely connected with religion, but most of those that are central to sports are, more or less, secularized versions of the core values of Protestantism, which has been the dominant religious belief system throughout American history.

The Protestant Ethic

The classic treatise on the Protestant ethic and its relationship to other spheres of social life is Max Weber's *The Protestant Ethic and the Spirit of Capitalism,* originally published near the turn of the century.[61] The essence of Weber's thesis is that there is a relationship — a parallel — between the Calvinist doctrine of Protestantism as a theological belief system and the growth of capitalism as a mode of economic organization. Weber understood the relationship between Protestantism and capitalism as one of mutual influence; he used the term "elective affinity."[62] The relationship existed in this way: for John Calvin, God could foresee and, therefore, know the future; thus, the future was predestined. In a world whose future was foreordained, the fate of every person was preestablished. Each person was, then, saved or doomed from birth by a kind of divine decree; nothing the individual did could change what God had done. Although each person's fate was sealed, the individual craved for some visible sign of his or her fate; and since Calvin taught that those elected by God acted in a godly manner, the elected could exhibit their salvation by glorifying God, especially by their work in this world. According to Weber, "the only way of living acceptably to God . . . was through the fulfillment of obligations imposed upon the individual by . . . his calling."[63] Thus, the best available sign of being among the chosen was to do one's job, to follow one's profession, to succeed in one's chosen career. According to Weber, "In practice this means that God helps those who help themselves."[64] Work per se was exalted; indeed, it was sacred. The clearest manifestation of being chosen by God was success in one's work. Whoever enjoyed grace could not fail, since success at work was visible evidence of election. Thus, successful persons could think of themselves, and be thought of by others, as the righteous persons. The upshot was that this produced an extreme drive toward individual achievement, resulting in what Weber called "ascetic Protestantism" — a life of strict discipline and hard work as the best means of glorifying God.

Although the Protestant ethic gave divine sanction to the drive to excel and encouraged success in business, industry, and science, it condemned the material enjoyment of success. The chosen person merely used success to document salvation. Persons who used success for personal gratification and luxury merely showed that they were doomed by God. To avoid the accumulation of vast personal wealth, Calvinism promoted the reinvestment of profits to produce more goods, which created more profits and, in turn, represented more capital for investment ad infinitum — the essence of entrepreneurial capitalism. In addition, the avoidance of waste, distractions, and pleasure, the reliance on technical knowledge and functional rationality were advocated as means of demonstrating salvation.

Weber's study of the relationship between religious beliefs and capitalism investigated the religious principles that provided a rationale for the ideology of capitalism and for the authority of the capitalist. The spirit of capitalism, according to Weber, consisted of several principles, each of which was compatible to Protestant principles. Collectively, they constituted a clear, elective affinity between Calvinist Protestantism and the spirit of capitalism. Weber made it quite clear that he was not suggesting that one social process was a *causal* agent for the other. In his final paragraph, he said: "It is . . . not my aim to substitute for a one-sided materialistic an equally one-sided spiritualistic causal interpretation of culture and history."[65]

What does this have to do with sports? Sociologist Gunther R. F. Luschen noted that "Max Weber's findings about the relationship between the Protestant ethic and the spirit of Capitalism may . . . well be extended to the 'spirit' of sport."[66] Anyone who is familiar with contemporary sports and the Protestant ethic cannot overlook the unmistakable link between them (there is, of course, also a correspondence between capitalistic ideology and modern sports, but that will not be examined here). The emergence of sport as a pervasive feature of American life undoubtedly owes it development to various social forces, one of which may be Protestant Christianity, the value orientations of which form the basis of the fundamental doctrine of the American sports creed. The notion of a sports creed in American sports was proposed by sociologist Harry Edwards, who suggested that persons involved with sports, especially coaches and athletes, adhere to a particular kind of institutional ideology, the overriding orientation of which is individual achievement through competition.[67] The phrase "ideology of sport" is used as a generic designation for all ideas espoused by or for those who participate in and exercise authority in sports as they seek to explain and justify their beliefs.

If we place the values inherent in the Protestant ethic and the sports creed side by side, it immediately becomes apparent that the two are congruent; that is, they share a significant equivalence. Without attempting to claim a causal link between the two belief systems, it does seem possible to suggest an elective affinity between them.

Success

The Protestant stress on successful, individual achievement is in keeping with the values of sport. The notion that achievement separates the chosen from the doomed is seen in the winning-is-everything ideology in sports. Winners are the good people; personal worth, both in this and the other world, is equated with winning. The loser is obviously not one of God's chosen people; failure in one's occupation stamps the Protestant-ethic believer as doomed to hell.

In the final analysis, the sports creed mirrors the core values of the Protestant ethic and vice versa. Success, self-discipline, and hard work — the original tenets of the ethic — are the most valued qualities of an athlete. The characteristics of the good Christian are also those needed by the successful athlete. The temper of organized sports is competitive, with an overriding sense of wins and losses. In describing the intercollegiate athletic program at Oral Roberts University, its founder Oral Roberts said: "Just playing the game is not enough. It's all right to lose some but I'm not much for losing. We're geared up for winning here."[68] The founder of AIA aspires that the teams representing that organization become the best amateur teams in America because he believes that they cannot be effective missionaries if they are losers.[69] The notion that nothing converts like success was confirmed by the former Dallas Cowboy quarterback, Roger Staubach, who said: "When the Cowboys played Miami in the Super Bowl, I had promised that it would be for God's honor and glory, whether we won or lost. Of course, the glory was better for God and me since we won, because victory gave me a greater platform from which to speak."[70]

Self-discipline

The notion that dedication, self-discipline and sports participation may be an occupational calling is central to the theology of Sportianity. God is glorified best when athletes give totally of themselves in striving for success and victory. As one spokesman for Sportianity puts it, no athlete "can afford to discredit Jesus by giving anything less than total involvement with those talents that he has been given in this training and competition."[71] One NFL football player echoed this sentiment: "The Christian athlete's talents are a gift of God. And the worst thing for a Christian to do is to waste his talents, to cheat God."[72]

Hard Work

Just as the businessman is responsible to God to develop his talents to the fullest, so is the athlete equally responsible. If God has granted one athletic abilities, then one is obligated to use these abilities to glorify and honor God; anything less than total dedication to the task is insufficient.[73] Discipline, sacrifice, training, and unremitting work by athletes may only lead to success ("workers are winners"), but they are seen as ways of using God-given ability as a way of glorifying God, an important Protestant requirement. Success can be considered as the justly deserved reward of a person's purposeful, self-denying, God-guided activity.

Any belief system that can help provide athletes and coaches with a rationale for their deep commitment to athletics provides a means of expressing the essence of their striving and is most welcome. Protestant theology does help give expression to the essence and striving of athletes and coaches. In short, it is a belief system to which the athlete and coach can hold an elective affinity. Whether they actually hold such an elective Protestantism certainly is not responsible for the creation of the sports creed, it does provide religious reinforcement for it. According to Edwards, "There are strong indications that the predominant emphasis upon this orientation in sport does not stem solely from Protestant religious traditions . . . thought the latter undoubtedly heightens and legitimizes the achievement value."[74]

Perhaps it is not coincidental that the belief systems of fundamentalist

Protestantism and modern sports are so congruent. The two institutions use similar means to respond to their members' needs. They try to enforce and maintain, through a strict code of behavior and ritual, a strict belief system that is typically adopted and internationalized by all involved in the particular institution. They serve cohesive, integrative, and social control functions for their members, giving them meaningful ways to organize their world. Because of the sacredness nurtured by these systems, both religion and sport resist social change, and, in this way, support the status quo.

Sport Uses Religion

Religious observances and competitive sports constantly impinge on each other, and magico-religious practices of various kinds are found wherever one finds athletics. Religion can be viewed from one point of view as an important means of coping with situations of stress. There are two main categories of stress situations, both of which involve situations in which persons have a great deal of emotional investment in a successful outcome. The first category includes situations in which individuals or groups suffer the death of other persons who are important to them. In the second category are those situations in which largely uncontrolled and unpredictable natural forces may imperil the vital personal and social concerns of an individual or group. Athletic competition falls into the latter category of stress, since competition involves a great deal of uncertainty about the typically important outcome.

Coaches and athletes are well aware of and have great respect for the technical knowledge required for successful performance, but they are also aware of its limitations. As a supplement to the practical techniques, sports participants often employ magico-religious practices in conjunction with sports competition. The coaches and athletes do not believe that these practices make up for their failure to acquire necessary skills or to employ appropriate stragegy. However, these practices help them to adjust to stress by providing opportunities to dramatize their psychological anxieties, thus, reinforcing their self-confidence. Religion invokes a sense of "doing something about it" in undertakings of uncertainty in which practical techniques alone cannot guarantee success. The noted anthropologist Bronislaw Malinowski concluded from his research that when the outcome of vital social activities is greatly uncertain, magico-religious or other comparable techniques are inevitably used as a means of allaying tension and promoting adjustment.[75]

The Use of Prayer

Prayer is perhaps the most frequently employed use of religion by athletes — prayer for protection in competition, prayer for good performance, and prayer for victory are three examples. Sometimes the act of prayer is observed as a Roman Catholic crosses himself before shooting a free throw in basketball or in a team at prayer in the huddle before a football game. The first historical example of prayer and the direct intervention of gods in sports competition is described by Homer in the *Iliad*. During the funeral games held in honor of Patroclus, who was killed in battle, one of the events was a footrace in which three men competed. Ajax took the lead from the start, followed closely by Odysseus:

> Thus Odysseus ran close behind him and trod in his footsteps before the dust could settle in them, and on the head of Ajax fell the breath of the godlike hero running lightly and relentlessly on.

As they neared the finish line, Odysseus prayed for divine assistance and his prayer was answered by Athene, who not only inspired Odysseus to make a last minute dash but caused Ajax to slip and fall in a mass of cow dung, and Odysseus won the race. Ajax received an ox as second prize:

> He stood holding the horns of the ox and spitting out dung, and exclaimed: "Curse it, that goddess tripped me up. She always stands by Odysseus like a mother and helps him."[77]

Very little is known about the actual extent to which individual athletes use prayer in conjunction with their participation, but it seems probable that if some athletes are seen praying, others may be doing so without outward, observable signs. In some cases, coaches arrange to have religious services on the Sabbath or on game days. At present, almost every major league baseball and football team — more than fifty of them — hold Sunday chapel services, at home and away, and Sunday services are also held in sports as varied as stock-car racing and golf.[78] One of the claims for this type of service is that the sharing of rituals and beliefs strengthens a group's sense of its own identity and accentuates its "we" feeling. The chaplain for Notre Dame athletics said about the game-day mass, "it provides unity."[79] There are probably other reasons why coaches sanction locker-room prayers. Sportswriter Larry Merchant suggested that prayer may be used simply because it cannot do any harm: "It might not help, but how much can it hurt? The other coach does it an you can't let him get the edge."[80]

Many sports contests are started with two ceremonies: the playing of the national anthem and a religious invocation. Some invocations are brief and to the point, while in others, clergy use the invocation to conduct a religious service or attempt to dramatize metaphorically the relationship between athletics and religion. An example of the latter was the following invocation delivered at a dinner before a hockey All Star game:

> Heavenly Father, Divine Goalie, we come before You this evening to seek Your blessing. . . . Keep us free from actions that would put us in the Sin Bin of Hell. . . . Help us to stay within the blue line of Your commandments and the red line of Your grace. Protect us from being injured by the puck of pride. May we ever be delivered from the high stick of dishonesty. May the wings of Your angels play at the right and left of our teammates. May You always be the divine Center of our team, and when our summons comes for eternal retirement to the heavenly grandstand, may we find You ready to give us the everlasting bonus of a permanent seat in Your coliseum. Finally, grant us the courage to skate without tripping, to run without icing, and to score the goal that really counts — the one that makes each of us a winner, a champion, and All-Star in the hectic Hockey Game of Life. Amen."[81]

Although there is little empirical work on the use of prayer by athletes and coaches, Joseph A. Marbeto, Jr. collected data on male baseball, basketball, football, and tennis athletes and coaches from twenty-three colleges and universities in California. Fifty-five percent of the coaches and athletes indicated that they pray at least sometimes in connection with athletic contests.[82] They pray for a variety of specific reasons, for personal excellence and a winning performance are the most frequently expressed reasons. Most who prayed did so before the contest, fewer did so during the contest, and even fewer did so after the contest.

Marbeto reported that those who pray in athletics are likely to be regular churchgoers with a strong religious upbringing. His data on church attendance and the use of prayer suggested that the prayers for assistance in the game are said primarily out of habit. According to Marbeto:

> Quite often the person who goes to church regularly prays in numerous phases of his daily living. Thus, the athlete who prays at game time probably does it because of his past conditioning, not because the contest elicits such prayers any more than other stressful episodes in his life.[83]

Marbeto further divided his respondents into those at church-affiliated colleges and those at public institutions and found that athletes and coaches at church-affiliated schools indicated that they feel more dependent on a spiritual power or ultimate being than their counterparts at public colleges. There was also considerable difference between the two types of institutions with respect to team prayers. Eighty-two percent of the coaches at church colleges had team prayers in connection with the contest, while only 10 percent of the coaches from the public schools encouraged or set aside time for team prayer.[84]

Marbeto reported that 51 percent of the respondents who prayed believe that the use of prayer might indirectly affect the outcome of the game. One athlete responded: "I never play my best if I haven't recited the Lord's Prayer first." Another said: "My experience tells me that sincere prayer can be the winning factor."[85]

The religiosity of college athletes and nonathletes was the subject of a study by David M. Turnball. Using a multidimensional instrument that assessed thirteen aspects of religious involvement, he found that athletes were significantly more religious than nonathletes on creedal assent (fundamental belief in God), devotionalism (personal prayer, feelings of closeness to and communication with God), and salience, or cognition (belief in the importance of religion for thought and feeling). There were no statistical differences between the two groups on the other dimensions of religiosity, although the athletes expressed somewhat greater religiosity on most of them.[86]

There is a growing resistance to the use of prayers in the locker room before games and the use of prayers in the sideline huddle preceding sports events, especially when they are a part of public school events. One clergyman who objected to team prayers said: "God was never intended to be used as a blessing for a particular competitor, or for a particular sport

288

event."[87] In Tennessee, a high school football player's father objected to team prayers. He said: "It bothered me that children who were participating in athletics be required to participate in prayer. . . . There are a lot of pressures on kids at school to conform to things. To be required to participate in a religious ceremony or prayer is contrary to the First Amendment."[88] The state attorney general's office agreed that the practice was unconstitutional, and, if challenged in court, a ban probably would be issued against it.

The Use of Magic

Religion supplies an important means by which humans meet situations of stress. In practice, religion and magic are closely entwined, but there are important distinctions between the two. Both magic and religion are alike in assuming the existence of supernatural powers, but there is a significant difference between the ends that they seek. Religion's goals are oriented to the otherworldly, toward a supreme supernatural god, and religion typically centers on overarching issues, such as salvation and the meaning of life and death. While the physical and social welfare of humans is often a concern of religion, it always has a transcendental point of reference; this is not true of magic. The practitioner of magic seeks ends that are in the everyday world of events. Religion is concerned with ultimate issues; magic is oriented toward immediate, practical goals. Moreover, religious worshipers possess an attitude of awe and reverence toward the sacred ends they pursue, but the users of magic are in business for practical and arbitrarily chosen ends. The latter are manipulators of the supernatural for their own private ends rather than worshipers of it; the attitude of magic users is likely to be utilitarian. In this respect, Malinowski noted that magic has an end, in pursuit of which the magical ritual is performed. The religious ritual has no purpose — that is, the ritual is not a means to an end but an end in itself. Malinowski said: "While in the magical act the underlying idea and aim is always clear, straightforward and definite, in religious ceremony there is no purpose directed toward a subsequent event." Furthermore, the content of magic and religion differ. The content of magic has no unified inclusive theory but instead tends to be atomistic, somewhat like a book of recipes. On the other hand, religion tends to encompass the whole of life; it often provides the comprehensive theory of both the supernatural and human society.[89]

The Malinowski Thesis

Magic flourishes in situations of uncertainty and threat; it is most commonly invoked in situations of high anxiety about accomplishing desired ends. The origin of most magical rites can be traced to fears experienced individually or collectively. They are associated with human helplessness in the face of dangers and unpredictability, which gives rise to superstitious beliefs and overt practices to ward off impending danger or failure and bring good luck. According to Malinowski:

We find magic wherever the elements of chance and accident, and the emotional play between hope and fear have a wide and extensive range. We do not find magic wherever the pursuit is certain, reliable, and well under control of rational methods. . . . [90]

In support of this contention, Malinowski comapred two forms of fishing among natives of the Trobriand Islands of Melanesia: lagoon and open-sea fishing.

> It is most significant that in the lagoon fishing, where man can rely completely upon his knowledge and skill, magic does not exist, while in the open-sea fishing, full of danger and uncertainty, there is extensive magical ritual to secure safety and good results. [91]

Malinowski's thesis about the conditions under which magic appears is applicable to the world of sport. Athletes and coaches are engaged in an activity of uncertain outcome and in which they have a great deal of emotional investment. Even dedicated conditioning and practice and the acquisition of high-level skill do not guarantee victory because opponents are often evenly matched and player injury and other dangers are often present. Thus, "getting the breaks" or "lucking out" may be the determining factor in the outcome of a contest. Having a weakly hit baseball fall in for a base hit or a deflected football pass caught by an unintended receiver are examples of luck or "getting the breaks" in sports. Although the cliche "the best team always wins" is part of the folk wisdom of sports, athletes and coaches commonly believe that this is not always so and indeed believe that factors leading to a win or a loss are somewhat out of their control.

Drawing on Malinowski's theory, it appears that athletes and coaches might use magic to bring them luck and to assure that they "get the breaks," thus supplying them with beliefs that serve to bridge over uncertainty and threat in their pursuit of victories. It would also enable them to carry out their actions with a sense of assurance and confidence and to maintain poise and mental integrity in the face of opponents. In Malinowski's words:

> The function of magic is to ritualize man's optimism, to enhance his faith in the victory of hope over fear. Magic expresses the greater value for man of confidence over doubt, of steadfastness over vacillation, of optimism over pessimism. [92]

It is difficult to assess just how extensive the uses of magic are in sport. Stories about athletes and coaches in newspapers and magazines leave little doubt, however, that magical beliefs and practices play a prominent role in the lives of athletes and coaches. They tend to employ almost anything imaginable that might ensure "getting the breaks," and this often involves some form of ritualistic, superstitious behavior. (Superstition is "a belief that one's fate is in the hands of unknown external powers governed by forces over which one has no control." [93] Superstition is a form of magical belief.) Indeed, stories about the magical rites that pervade sports make witch doctors look like supersophisticates.

Empirical study of magic in sport is virtually nonexistent, but C. Jane Gregory and Brian M. Petrie investigated magical practices among members of six intercollegiate athletic teams at a Canadian university and found that the ranking for sport superstitions were similar between team and individual-sport athletes. They also reported that team athletes indicated greater support for superstitions related to equipment and its use, to the order of entering the sports arena, to dressing-room rituals, to repetitive rituals, and to sports personalities. Individual-sport athletes showed greater support for superstitions related to wearing charms, to lucky lane numbers, to team cheers, and to crossing oneself before participation (see table 6.1). They concluded that magical practices were prevalent among athletes of their sample, and "that 137 respondents endorsed 904 superstitions (with repetition) which could be grouped into 40 categories clearly indicating the strength of superstition in sport."[94]

Various forms of magic are practiced in sports — ritual, taboo, fetishism, witchcraft — that coaches and athletes employ to enhance their chances of victory or to protect them from injury.

Ritual

Rituals are standardized actions directed toward entreating or controlling the supernatural powers in regard to some particular situation. There is an almost infinite variety of rituals practiced in sport, since all athletes are free to ritualize any activity they consider important for successful performance. Typically, rituals arise from successful performances. When an athlete plays well, the successful outcome frequently leads to the idea that something must have been done in addition to the actual skill or strategy to have produced the successful outcome; thus successful performance becomes associated with a certain type of behavior. An NHL hockey player explained how a victory affects his pregame rituals:

When you win, you try not to change anything — nothing. You do everything exactly as you did the whole day of your win. Beginning from the time you get up, was your window or door open? Get up on the same side of the bed. Eat the same meals, at the same places — home or at the same restaurant — nothing extra. If your salad was dry, order it dry again; if you had a large milk, then again; if your steak was ordered medium, then again; no dessert; and so on. You leave at the same time, take the same route, park in the same place, enter through the same door and prepare for the finale — game time — with the accent on precision.[95]

Table 6.1 Frequency of Endorsements of Sport Superstitions Among Athletes

Sport Superstition Category	Athletes (N = 137)		
	Male (N = 66)	Female (N = 71)	Overall f
Uniform	77	117	194
Equipment	81	25	106
Clothes	52	32	84
Routines	46	27	73
Charms	14	23	37
Food	19	14	33

Table 6.1 Frequency of Endorsements of Sport Superstitions Among Athletes (Cont'd.)

Sport Superstition Category	Athletes (N = 137)		
	Male (N = 66)	Female (N = 71)	Overall f
Numbers	8	17	25
Order or playing position	20	12	32
Balls	12	11	23
Coaches beliefs	11	8	19
Religion	14	5	19
Respective actions	14	5	19
Spectators' beliefs	14	3	17
Sports persons	9	3	12
Speaking	2	10	12
Hair	1	19	20
Dressing room	15	4	19
Team cheers	2	11	13
Crossing self	7	3	10
Personal beliefs	6	4	10
Jewelry	9	4	13
Coins	10	3	13
Colors	3	3	6
Facilities	4	4	8
Travel	7	0	7
Hands	2	4	6
Date toss of coin	5	3	8
Pregame night	1	6	7
Scoring	0	5	5
Whites	6	1	7
Time	5	1	6
Good Samaritan	5	0	5
Rabbits' feet	2	0	2
Shaving	2	3	5
Rules	1	2	3
Sex	1	0	1
Weather	2	1	3
Injury	2	0	2
Concentration	0	1	1
Horseheads	0	1	1
Touching wood	0	1	1

Source: Adapted from C. Jane Gregory and Brian M. Petrie, "Superstitions of Canadian Intercollegiate Athletes: An Intersport Comparison." *International Review of Sport Sociology* 10 (No. 2, 1975), p. 63.

In a study of the uses of ritual by college students, the investigators reported that one "linebacker on a varsity football team vomited and was the last player to come on the field before a game in which he made many tackles. Before each game during the remainder of the season, he forced himself to vomit and made certain he was the last to leave the locker room.''[96] Former professional baseball player and anthropologist George Gmelch related how he attempted to prolong a batting streak through ritual:

I . . . ate fried chicken every day at 4 p.m., kept my eyes closed during the national anthem and changed sweat shirts at the end of the fourth inning each night for seven consecutive nights until the streak ended.[97]

He also told of one baseball pitcher who had the complex ritual of touching a crucifix in his back pocket, straightening his cap, and then clutching his genitals before each pitch.[98]

In addition to individual rituals, there are a number of team rituals. In basketball, the ritual of stacking hands is frequently employed just before the team takes the floor to begin the game and after time-outs. The most universal hockey ritual occurs just before the start of a game when players skate in front of their goal and tap the goalie on the pads for good luck. Green Bay Packer coach Vince Lombardi had his players pat a small Buddha statue for luck.[99] Gmelch reported that one major league baseball team wore the same uniforms in every game during a sixteen-game winning streak and refused to let them be washed because they feared that their good luck might be washed away with the dirt.[100]

Taboo

A taboo is a strong social norm prohibiting certain actions that are punishable by the group or by magical consequences. There are numerous institutional taboos in each sport and, of course, many personal taboos. Two of the strongest taboos in baseball are crossing the handles of bats and mentioning a no-hitter that the pitcher has in progress. Crossing bats is believed to bring bad luck and mentioning a no-hitter to the pitcher is believed to break the spell the pitcher has on the hitters, ending his chances to complete a no-hit game.

Some athletes develop taboos about touching portions of the playing surface, such as not stepping on the chalk foul lines (just as children avoid stepping on sidewalk cracks) or as not wearing certain parts of the uniform.

Festishism

Fetishes are revered objects believed to have magical power to attain the desired ends for the person who possesses or uses them. Fetishes are standard equipment for coaches and athletes. They include a bewildering assortment of objects: rabbits' feet, pictures of heroes or loved ones, pins, coins, remnants of old equipment, certain numbered uniforms, and so forth. Typically, these objects obtain their power through association with successful performances. For example, if the athlete or coach happens to be wearing or using the object during a victory, the individual attributes the good fortune to the object; it then becomes a fetish embodied with supernatural power. The seriousness with which some athletes take fetishes was described by Gmelch:

I once saw a fight caused by the desecration of a fetish. Before the game, one player stole the fetish, a horsehide baseball cover, out of a teammate's back pocket. The prankster did not return the fetish until after the game, in which the owner of the fetish went hitless, breaking a batting streak. The owner, blaming his inability to hit on the loss of the fetish, lashed out at the thief when the latter tried to return it.[101]

Judy Becker described the numerous rituals, taboos, and fetishes employed by athletes at that bastion of intellect and rationality, Yale University. For example, in hockey, the use of the word "shut-out," as in "let's protect the shut-out," was taboo. Once, in a game in which Yale went into the locker room with a 4-0 lead and someone violated this rule, it disturbed the entire team. Within ten minutes after the teams returned to the ice, the opponents had tied the score. One of the most common magical practices involved clothes fetishes, such as the wearing a particular article of clothing. One track athlete believed that "new shoes go fast," so he got new spikes before each meet. Becker reported that uniform numbers had magical connotations for many athletes, and they would go to great lengths to obtain their lucky number.[102]

Applying the Malinowski thesis to baseball players, Gmelch hypothesized that magical practices would be associated more with hitting and pitching than with fielding, since the first two involve a high degree of chance and unpredictability whereas the average fielding percentage or success rate is about 97 percent, reflecting almost complete control over the outcome. From his observations as a participant in professional baseball, Gmelch reported that there was indeed a greater incidence and variety of rituals, taboos, and use of fetishes related to hitting and pitching than to fielding. He concluded:

. . . nearly all of the magical practices that I participated in, observed, or elicited, support Malinowski's hypothesis that magic appears in situations of chance and uncertainty. The large amount of uncertainty in pitching and hitting best explains the elaborate magical practices used for these activities. Conversely, the high success rate of fielding . . . involving much less uncertainty, offers the best explanation for the absence of magic in this realm.[103]

Witchcraft

Magical practices harmful in intent, or whose intent is to bring misfortune on others, are known as black magic or witchcraft. In sport, those who employ this form of magic believe that supernatural powers are being employed to harm or bring misfortune on opponents. In Africa, witchcraft dominates some sports. Medicine men who claim they can make the ball disappear or cast a spell on opposing players are especially active in soccer. It is estimated that about 95 percent of Kenyan soccer teams hire witch doctors to help them win matches, and matches have been marred by witchcraft-inspired riots.[104]

We may laugh when reading about African soccer teams traveling with a witch doctor but not give a second thought to a clergyman traveling with one of our teams. In discussing this issue, one observer noted:

In Nairobi, Kenya, one team spent $3,000 on witch doctors last year. Sports leaders there have tried to discourage witchcraft as well as the practice of players painting their bodies with pig fat to ward off evil spirits. Athletic teams in our country, of course, are much too sophisticated to travel with witch doctors and wear pig fat. Our teams travel with clergymen and wear medals.[105]

Actually, witchcraft is not confined to African sports. During the 1975 ABA championship playoff between the Indiana Pacers and the Denver Nuggets, the Pacers employed a witch doctor by the name of Dancing Harry to cast hexes on the Denver players. Denver counteracted with The Wicked Witch of the West, equipped with a cauldron, to mix up evil spirits designed to reduce the Pacers' effectiveness.

Summary

In this chapter, we have examined the reciprocal relationship between sport and religion. Although sport and religion may seem to have little in common, we have attempted to demonstrate that contemporary sport and contemporary religion are related in a variety of ways. For many centuries, Christian church dogma was antithetical to play and sport activities, but over the past century, with the enormous growth of organized sport, churches and religious leaders have welded a link between these two institutions by sponsoring sports events under religious auspices and/or proselytizing athletes to religion and then using them as missionaries to convert new members.

While contemporary religion uses sport for the promotion of its causes, sport uses religion as well. Numerous activities with a religious connotation — ceremonies, rituals, and so forth — are employed in connection with sports contests.

REFERENCE NOTES

1. Harry Edwards, "Desegregating Sexist Sport," *Intellectural Digest* 3 (November 1972), p. 82.
2. Editorial, "Sport: Are We Overdoing It?" *Christianity Today* 20, 20 February 1976, p. 22.
3. Frank Deford, "Religion in Sport," *Sports Illustrated* 44, 19 April 1976, pp. 92, 102, © 1976 Time, Inc.
4. J. Milton Yinger, *Religion, Society and the Individual* (New York: Macmillan 1957).
5. David Dressler, *Sociology: The Study of Human Interaction* (New York: Alfred Knopf, 1969), p. 658.
6. Elizabeth K. Nottingham, *Religion: A Sociological View* (New York: Random House, 1971), pp. 7-9.
7. Leonard Broom and Philip Selznick, *Sociology,* 5th ed. (New York: Harper and Row, 1973), pp. 393-95.
8. August Comte, *System of Positive Policy,* trans. Frederick Harrison (New York: Burt Franklin, 1875), pp. 16-17.
9. Emile Durkheim, *Suicide,* trans. John Spaulding and George Simpson (Glencoe, Ill.: The Free Press, 1951), p. 159. *See also* Emile Durkheim, *The Elementary Forms of the Religious Life* (New York: Collier Books, 1961). This book is one of the classics in the sociology of religion.

10. Neil J. Smelser, ed., *Sociology: An Introduction* (New York: John Wiley and Sons, 1967), p. 340.

11. Emile Durkheim, *The Elementary Forms of Religious Life,* trans. Joseph W. Swain (Glencoe, Ill.: The Free Press, 1954), p. 387.

12. Ronald L. Johnstone, *Religion and Society in Interaction* (Englewood Cliffs, N.J.: Preintice-Hall, 1975), p. 143.

13. Smelser, *Sociology,* pp. 343-44.

14. Rudolph Brasch, *How Did Sports Begin?* (New York: David McKay, 1970), p. 1.

15. Stewart Culin, *Games of the North American Indians,* (Washington, D.C.: U.S. Government Printing Office, 1907), p. 34.

16. Ludwig Deubner quoted in Ludwig Drees, *Olympia: Gods, Artists, and Athletes,* trans. Gerald Onn (New York: Praeger, 1968), p. 24.

17. P. C. McIntosh, *Sports in Society* (London: C. A. Watts, 1963) pp. 3-4.

18. *See,* for example, I Cor. 6:12-20, 9:24-26; I Tim. 4:8.

19. Quoted in G. G. Coulton, *Five Centuries of Religion,* vol. 5 (Cambridge: Cambridge University Press, 1923), p. 532.

20. Quoted in Albert Hyma, *The Youth of Erasmus* (Ann Arbor: University of Michigan Press, 1930), p. 178.

21. Dennis Brailsford, *Sport and Society* (London: Routledge and Kegan Paul, 1969), p. 141. For a more sympathetic but not altogether convincing argument about the Puritan attitude toward sport, *see* J. Thomas Jable, "The English Puritans—Suppressors of Sport and Amusement?" *Canadian Journal of the History of Sport and Physical Education* 7 (May 1976): 33-40.

22. Thomas B. Macaulay, *The History of England,* vol. 1 (London: Longman, Green, Longman, and Roberts, 1861), p. 162.

23. John Scollard, "Birth of the Blue Laws," *Mentor* 18 (May 1930), pp. 46-49, 58-60; William C. White, "Bye, Bye Blue Laws," *Scribners* 94 (August 1933), pp. 107-9; J. Thomas Jable, "Sunday Sport Comes to Pennsylvania: Professional Baseball and Football Triumph Over the Commonwealth's Archaic Blue Laws, 1919-1933," *Research Quarterly* 47 (October 1976): 357-65.

24. Quoted in Van Wyck Brooks, *The Flowering of New England, 1815-65* (New York: Random House, The Modern Library, 1936), p. 253.

25. Oliver Wendell Holmes "The Autocrat of the Breakfast Table," *Atlantic Monthly* 1 (May 1858), p. 881.

26. Guy Lewis, "The Muscular Christianity Movement," *Journal of Health, Physical Education, and Recreation* 37 (May 1966): 42.

27. "Amusements," *New Englander* 9 (1851), p. 358. Cited in Ralph Slovenko and James A. Knight, eds., *Motivation in Play, Games, and Sports* (Springfield, Ill.: Charles C. Thomas, 1967), pp. 124-25.

28. Arthur M. Schlesinger, *The Rise of the City, 1878-1898* (New York: Macmillan, 1933), p. 335.

29. Clarence E. Rainwater, *The Play Movement in the United States* (Chicago: University of Chicago Press, 1922), pp. 22-23.

30. Ibid., p. 5.

31. William R. Hogan, "Sin and Sports," in *Motivations in Play, Games and Sports,* ed., Ralph Slovenko and James A. Knight (Springfield, Ill.: Charles C. Thomas, 1967), pp. 133-34.

32. Richard A. Swanson, "The Acceptance and Influence of Play in American Protestantism," *Quest* 11 (December 1968), p. 58.

33. Quoted in "Modern Sport Symbolized," *Sportsmanship* 1 (January 1929), p. 9; cited in Frederick W. Cozens and Florence S. Stumpf, *Sports in American Life* (Chicago: University of Chicago Press, 1953), p. 104.

34. Cozens and Stumpf, *Sports in America,* p. 93.

35. A James Rudin, "America's New Religion," *Christian Century* 89, 5 April 1972, p. 384; Cornish Rogers, "Sports, Religion and Politics; The Renewal of an Alliance," *Christian Century* 89, 5 April 1972, pp. 9-94; Michael Novak, *The Joy of Sports* (New York: Basic Books, 1976).

36. Howard S. Slusher, *Man, Sport and Existence,* (Philadelphia: Lea & Febiger, 1967), p. 130.

37. Rogers, "Sports, Religion, and Politics," pp. 392-94.

38. Eldon E. Snyder, "Athletic Dressing Room Slogans as Folklore: A Means of Socialization," *International Review of Sport Sociology* 7 (1972): 89-102.

39. Gerald Redmond, "A Plethora of Shrines: Sport in the Museum and Hall of Fame," *Quest* 19 (January 1973), pp. 41-48.

40. Quoted in Fred Eastman, "Rural Recreation Through the Church," *The Playground* 6 (October 1912), p. 234.

41. Quoted in Cozens and Stumpf, *Sports in America,* p. 106.

42. Quoted in "Are Sports Good for the Soul?" *Newsweek,* 11 January 1976, p. 51.

43. Quoted in Deford, "Religion in Sport," p. 96.

44. Quoted in Robert H. Boyle, "Oral Roberts: Small BUT OH, MY," *Sports Illustrated* 33, 30 November 1970, p. 64, © 1970 Time, Inc.

45. *Fellowship of Christian Athletes Summer Conference Guide,* Kansas City, Missouri, 1975, p. 2.

46. Quoted in Joe McGuff, "Sporting Comment," *Kansas City Star,* 24 May 1970.

47. Joe Jares, "Hallelujah, What a Team!" *Sports Illustrated* 46, 7 February 1977, pp. 41-42.

48. Deford, "Religion in Sport," p. 92.

49. *The Wittenburg Door* 24 (April/May/June/July 1975).

50. Quoted in Frank Deford, "The Word According to Tom," *Sports Illustrated* 44, 26 April 1976, p. 69, © 1976 Time, Inc.

51. Ibid.

52. Quoted in Deford, "Religion in Sport, p. 92.

53. Quoted in Teri Thompson, "Athletes Seek Support in Much Different Game," *Rocky Mountain News,* 4 February 1979, p. 74.

54. Deford, "The Word According to Tom," pp. 65-66.

55. Deford, "Religion in Sport," p. 98.

56. Quoted in "The Christian Woodstock," *Newsweek,* 26 June 1972, p. 52. *See also* George Vecsey, "Religion Becomes an Important Part of Baseball Scene" *New York Times,* 10 May 1981, pp. 421-22.

57. Deford, "Religion in Sport," p. 100.

58. Quoted in *The Wittenburg Door* 24 (April/May, June/July 1975), pp. 19-20.

59. Deford, "The Word According to Tom," p. 67.

60. Thomas Tutko and William Bruns, *Winning is Everything and Other American Myths,* (New York: Macmillan, 1976), p. 23.

61. Max Weber, *The Protestant Ethic and the Spirit of Capitalism,* trans. Talcott Parsons (New York: Charles Scribner's, 1958). This essay is probably the most famous work in the sociology of religion. It has aroused a great deal of controversy among sociologists and historians. The whole notion of a relationship between Protestantism and capitalism is called into serious question by Kurt Samuelsson in *Religion and Economic Action: The Protestant Ethic, the Rise of Capitalism, and the Abuses of Scholarship* (New York: Basic Books, 1961). For an excellent collection of the views of Weber's critics, *see* Robert W. Green, ed., *Protestantism and Capitalism: The Weber Thesis and Its Critics* (Boston: D.C. Health, 1959).

62. Reinhard Bendix, *Work and Authority in Industry* (New York: John Wiley and Sons, 1956), p. 63. Bendix observed that "Weber stated . . . that he was investigating whether and at what points certain 'elective affinities' are discernible between particular types of religious beliefs and the ethics of work-a-day life." Werner Stark, "the Theory of Elective Affinity," in *The Sociology of Knowledge* (Glencoe, Ill.: The Free Press, 1958) p. 257. Stark notes that the term "elective affinities" implies that "human groupings of whatever kind will, for their part, always be on the lookout for appropriate ideas to give expressions to their essence and their striving." In the Talcott Parsons translation of Weber's study, the word "correlation" is substituted for "elective affinity."

63. Weber, *The Protestant Ethic,* p. 80.

64. Ibid., p. 115.

65. Ibid., p. 183.

66. Gunther Luschen, "The Interdependence of Sport and Culture," *The Cross-Cultural Analysis of Sport and Games,* ed., Gunther Luschen (Champaign, Ill.: Stipes Publishing Co., 1970), p. 89.

67. Harry Edwards, *Sociology of Sport,* (Homewood, Ill.: Dorsey Press, 1973), pp. 64, 334.

68. Quoted in Boyle, "Oral Roberts" p. 65.

69. Deford, "Religion in Sport," p. 90.

70. Quoted in Michael Roberts, *Fans!* (Washington, D.C.: New Republic, 1976), pp. 117-18.

71. Jay Dirkson, "The Place of Athletics in the Life of the Christian," *Sport Sociology Bulletin* 4 (Spring 1975), p. 54.

72. Quoted in Thompson, "Athletes Seek Support in Much Different Game" p. 74.

73. Ibid.

74. Edwards, *Sociology of Sport,* p. 335.

75. Bronislaw Malinowski, *Magic, Science, and Religion and Other Essays* (Glencoe: Ill.: The Free Press, 1948).

76. Louise R. Loomis, ed., *The Iliad of Homer,* trns. Samuel Butler (Roslyn, N.Y.: Walter J. Block, 1942), pp. 368-69.

77. Ibid.

78. Deford, "Religion in Sport," p. 92.

79. Quoted in Frank Deford, "Reaching for the Stars," *Sports Illustrated* 44, 3 May 1976, p. 60, © 1976 Time, Inc.

80. Larry Merchant, *And Every Day You Take Another Bite* (New York: Doubleday, 1971), p. 36.

81. Quoted in Deford, "The Word According to Tom," p. 65.

82. Joseph A. Marbeto, Jr., "The Incidence of Prayer in Athletics as Indicated by Selected California Collegiate Athletes and Coaches" (Master's thesis, University of California, Santa Barbara, 1967).

83. Ibid, p. 68.

84. Ibid., p. 72.

85. Ibid., p. 87-88.

86. David M. Turnball, "Comparison of the Religiosity of Athletes and Non-Athletes," (Master's thesis, Northeast Missouri State University, Kirksville, 1978).

87. Don R. Laue, "The 'Athletic' Jesus" (Sermon delivered at the Congregational Church, Greeley, Colorado, 10 February 1980).

88. Quoted in *Denver Post,* 27 November 1980.

89. Malinowski, *Magic, Science, and Religion,* pp. 12-30.

90. Malinowski, *Magic, Science, and Religion,* p. 116.

91. Ibid., p. 14. *See also* A. R. Radcliffe-Brown, *Structure and Function in Primitive Societies* (New York: The Free Press, 1965) and G. Homans, *The Human Group* (New York: Harcourt, Brace, World, 1950) for alternative explanations of magic.

92. Malinowski, *Magic, Science, and Religion,* p. 70.

93. G. Johoda, *The Psychology of Superstition* (London: Penguin Press, 1969), p. 139.

94. C. Jane Gregory and Brian M. Petrie, "Superstitions of Canadian Intercollegiate Athletes: An Inter-Sport Comparison," *International Review of Sport Sociology* 10, no. 2 (1975).

95. Mari Womack, "Sports Magic," *Human Behavior* 7 (September 1978): 43.

96. George Gmelch and Richard Felson, "Can a Lucky Charm Get You Through Organic Chemistry?" *Psychology Today* 14, December 1980, p. 76.

97. George Gmelch, "Baseball Magic," *Trans-Action* 8 (June 1971), p. 40. A number of rituals, taboos, and fetishes employed in baseball are described in the chapter "The Folklore of Baseball" by Tristram P. Coffin, *The Old Ball Game* (New York: Herder and Herder, 1971).

98. Ibid. For a discussion of some bizarre rituals of hockey goalies, *see* Jerry Kirshenbaum, "Reincarnation and 13 Pairs of Socks," *Sports Illustrated* 46, 28 March 1977, pp. 30-33.

99. Jerry Kramer, *Instant Replay* (New York: Signet Books, 1969), p. 193.

100. Gmelch, "Baseball Magic," p. 40.

101. Ibid., p. 54.

102. Judy Becker, "Superstition in Sport," *International Journal of Sports Psychology* 6, no. 3 (1975), pp, 148-52.

103. Gmelch, "Baseball Magic," p. 54.

104. "Soccer Witchcraft Anything But Charming," *Rockey Mountain News,* 2 July 1975, p. 38. *See also* Douglas Hill, et al., *Witchcraft, Magic and the Supernatural* (London: Octopas, 1974), pp. 20, 150, for a discussion of the Italian sorcerer who puts the "evil eye" on the opponents of his favorite soccer team.

105. Cited in Merchant, *And Every Day You Take Another Bite,* p. 37.

Sport and the Polity*

In an interview for the student newspaper at the University of Kansas, the school's director of athletics said: "I don't think athletics has a thing to do with politics. They shouldn't even be mentioned together. There's no relationship between the two. They're entirely different subjects."[1] This type of statement is often made by sports officials of universities, professional leagues, and the United States Olympic Committee. The argument of this chapter, however, is just the converse—that sport and politics are very closely intertwined. Several characteristics inherent to sport serve to guarantee this strong relationship.

First, sports participants typically represent and have an allegiance to some social organization (e.g., school, factory, neighborhood, community, region, or nation). Much of the ritual accompanying sporting events (slogans, chants, music, wearing of special clothing, and so forth) is aimed at symbolically reaffirming fidelity to the sponsoring organization. Phillip Goodhart and Christopher Chataway argued that there are four kinds of sport: sport as exercise, sport as gambling, sport as spectacle, and representative sport.

[The latter] is a limited conflict with clearly defined rules, in which representatives of towns, regions, or nations are pitted against each other. It is primarily an affair for the spectators: they are drawn to it not so much by the mere spectacle, by the ritual, or by an appreciation of the skills involved, but because they identify themselves with their representatives. . .

Most people will watch [the Olympic Games] for one reason only: there will be a competitor who, they feel, is representing them. That figure in the striped singlet will be their man—running, jumping, or boxing for their country. For a matter of minutes at least, their own estimation of themselves will be bound up with his performance. He will be the embodiment of their nation's strength or weakness. Victory for him will be victory for them; defeat for him, defeat for them.[2]

This last point is worthy of emphasis. Evidence from any recent Olympics or from other international competition shows that for many nations and their citizens, victory is an index of that nation's superiority (in its military might, its politico-economic system, and its culture). Clearly, the outcomes of international contests are very often interpreted politically.

A second basis for a close relationship between sports and politics is inherent in the process of organization itself. As sport has become increasing-

*Eitzen, D. S. and G. H. Sage *Sociology of American Sport*, Second Edition, Wm. C. Brown Company Publishers, 1978. Reprinted by permission of the publisher.

ly organized, a plethora of teams, leagues, players' associations, and ruling bodies has been created. These groups acquire certain powers that by their very creation are distributed unequally.[3] Thus, there may be a power struggle between players and owners (e.g., the major league player strike in 1981), or between competing leagues (e.g., NBA vs. ABA in professional basketball), or between various sanctioning bodies (AAU vs. NCAA in amateur athletics).[4]

The linkage between sport and politics is quite obvious when the impact of the federal government on sports is considered. Several illustrations make this point: (1) legislation has been passed exempting professional sports from antitrust laws; (2) tax laws give special concessions to owners of professional teams; (3) the blackouts of televised home games have been lifted for professional football despite the protests of the league commissioner and the owners; (4) the Congress decides which sport organization will have the exclusive right to select and train athletes for the Olympic Games.[5]

Another indication of the close relationship between sports and politics is that sports events and political situations have reciprocal effects on each other. A famous example of a sports event affecting politics was the tour of China in 1971 by the American table-tennis contingent. This tour proved to be the prelude to political exchanges between the two nations. Other examples were the wars that erupted between El Salvador and Honduras and between Gabon and the Congo after soccer matches. There are also many examples of political situations that have affected sports. The apartheid policies of South Africa have resulted many times in that nation being barred from sports competition.[6] In the early 1970s, a United States-Russia track meet was cancelled because of increased tensions between the two countries. And, as a final example, Russia boycotted the Twenty-Second Chess Olympics in 1976 because it was held in Israel.

The United States boycott of the 1980 Olympics provides an example of another way in which sport and politics are related. It demonstrates clearly that sport is a tool of foreign policy.[7] Sport is used to achieve legitimacy for a political regime. Sport can be used as a prelude to formal relations between countries. Conversely, refusal by one country to compete against another is a way of pressuring that country. By boycotting the 1980 Olympics, the United States and many other nations attempted to embarras Russia, the host country, in the hope that Russia would withdraw its troops from Afghanistan.

The institutional character of sport is a final source of the strong relationship between sport and politics. Sport, as are the institutions of the polity and of religion, is conservative; it serves as a preserver and ligitimator of the existing order. The patriotic pageants that accompany sporting events reinforce the political system. Moreover, sport perpetuates many myths, such as anyone with talent regardless of race or social station has an equal chance to succeed. Sport also legitimizes ideas such as "winning is not everything, it is the only thing."[8] Sport is a model of law and order. As former Texas football coach Darrell Royal said, "Football is the last bastion of traditional American values. It's the last institution where you have rules to obey—in bed at ten, lights out at eleven, breakfast at seven."[9]

We have seen that the very nature of sport makes politics endemic to it. The remainder of this chapter will demonstrate this relationship further by examining in greater detail the various political uses of sport. The final section will focus on the political attitudes of persons in sport (especially coaches and athletes).

THE POLITICAL USES OF SPORT

Sport as a Propaganda Vehicle

Success in international competition frequently serves as a mechanism by which a society's ruling elite unites its citizens and attempts to impress the citizens of other countries. A classical example of this was Adolf Hitler's use of the 1936 Olympic Games to strengthen his control over the German people and to introduce Nazi culture to the entire world. According to Richard D. Mandell in his book *The Nazi Olympics,* the festival planned for these games was a shrewdly propagandistic and brilliantly conceived charade that reinforced and mobilized the hysterical patriotism of the German masses.[10]

More recently the communist nations have used sport for promoting their common cause. During the 1972 Olympics, 600 medals were awarded. Since about 10 percent of the athletes at that Olympics, were representatives of communist countries, on a proportional basis one would expect that they would have won about 60 medals. Instead, they won an astounding 285 medals, or 47.5 percent of the total. This, the communists argued, was evidence of the superiority of the communist politico-economic system. Similarly, when Cuba won twenty times more gold medals than did the United States on a per capita basis at the 1971 Pan American Games, Cuban Premier Castro proclaimed to Latin America that this was proof of the superiority of the Cuban people and the Cuban system.

The most striking example of success in the 1976 Olympics came from East Germany. Although it is a nation smaller in population than California (17 million), East Germany placed third with a total of 90 in the overall number of medals awarded whereas the United States won 94 and the Soviet Union won 125. East Germany spends an estimatd $300 million annually on its massive sports program. From the age of seven, children are tested, and the most promising athletes are enrolled in sixteen special schools where they receive special training and expert coaching in addition to their normal schooling. After their formal education is completed, the star athletes are given special jobs, permanent military deferments, and new apartments.[11] But why would a nation devote so much money, time, and talent to sport? One reason is the competition between East and West Germany. A second reason is the goal of international acceptance of East Germany as a sovereign state. A third reason is the desire to demonstrate the superiority of the communist way of life. East Germany is not unlike the other communist countries in using sport for the accomplishment of political goals. The emphasis on sport by the Eastern bloc countries — the Soviet Union,

East Germany, Poland, Yugoslavia, Rumania, Hungary, Czechoslovakia, and Bulgaria — is seen by their winning 53 percent of all the medals awarded at the 1976 Olympics.

But the use of sport internationally as a propaganda vehicle is not limited to communist countries. International sports victories as just as important to the United States. After the 1972 Olympics when the Americans fared worse than was expected (especially in track and basketball), many editorial writers and politicians advocated plans whereby American athletes would be subsidized and receive the best coaching and facilities to regain athletic supremacy. This did not happen and the cry arose again after the 1976 Olympics. As a result, Congress then appropriated funds for the United States Olympic Committee and for the establishment of permanent training sites for the Winter and Summer Games.

The clear assumption behind these plans was that if Americans were allowed to devote as much time and money to athletics as the communists, Americans would prevail — proving the superiority of the free enterprise system.

The United States government uses athletes to promote international goodwill and enhance the American image abroad. The State Department, for example, sponsors tours of athletes to foreign countries for these purposes. Arthur Ashe, the black American tennis star, toured Africa for eighteen days in 1971 under the sponsorship of the United States Informaton Agency. He gave exhibitions, clinics, and interviews. The tour cost $12,000 plus $60,000 for film. The film was then offered to schools, clubs, and public theaters around the world (except in the United States), especially in Africa.[12]

Sport as an instrument of national policy is not limited to the industrialized nations of the world. The developing countries use sport even more for this purpose. A study of the 133 members of the United Nations in 1973 showed that while 26 percent of the nations had a cabinet-level post related to sport, 87 percent of the nations classified as developing had such a position.[13] The probable reason for this keen interest in sport by developing nations is that sport provides a relatively cheap political tool to accomplish national objectives of prestige abroad and unity at home.

Sport and Nationalism

Success in international sports competition tends to trigger pride among a nation's citizens. As mentioned previously, the Olympics and other international games, tend to promote an "us vs. them" feeling among athletes, coaches, politicians, the press, and fans. It can be argued, then, that the Olympic games represent a political contest, a symbolic world war in which nations win or lose. Because this interpretation is commonly held, citizens of the nations involved unite behind their flag and their athletes.[14]

The integral interrelationship of sport and nationalism is easily seen in the blatantly militaristic pageantry that surrounds sports contests. The playing of the national anthem, the presentation of the colors, the jet-aircraft flyovers, the band forming a flag or a liberty bell, are all political acts supportive of the existing political system.

The irony, however, is that nationalistic displays are not generally interpreted politically. Recognition of the explicit acceptance of the political content of these festival rituals was manifested in 1970 by the refusal of the American Broadcasting Company (ABC) to televise a halftime program in which the University of Buffalo band presentation featured three themes: antiwar, antiracism, and antipollution. The network refused because the halftime show was a "political demonstration." But later in that same season, ABC televised the halftime of the Army-Navy game where several Green Berets who had staged a raid on a prisoner of war camp in North Vietnam were honored. That one of these halftimes was labeled political while the other was not is revealing. Clearly, both were political, but only those demonstrations or ceremonies that were controversial and antiestablishment were so labeled and frowned upon.[15]

In this vein, sport columnist Jerry Isenberg speculated:

I wonder, for example, if just once during that long string of half-time shows someone had called for a minute of silence for all the cancer victims who did not benefit from research because the funds were spent on the space program, whether or not the management might not have judged that to be political, with no place in the sports arena. I wonder how many airplanes in what kind of formation the government would have agreed to send over for that one.[16]

An interesting question is, Why are patriotic displays commonplace at sports contests, but not at most other public events (e.g., plays, lectures, concerts, and movies)? The support for these patriotic rituals is so strong, that when an administrator decided not to play the national anthem at a track meet, as was the case at Madison Square Garden in early 1973, he was forced by public opinion and politicians to reverse hi aself. Typically, a bill was introduced before the New York City Council that would make it unlawful "to commence any sporting event, open to the public and for which admission is charged, without first playing the national anthem, either by live musicians or by mechanical reproductions."[17] Similarly, when the Baltimore Orioles decided to limit the playing of the anthem to special occasions, fans were outraged, and the city council passed a resolution suggesting that the song be played before *every* Baltimore baseball game.[18]

Athletes who do not show proper respect for the flag or for the national anthem are subject to stiff penalties. When Tommie Smith and John Carlos raised gloved, clenched fists and bowed their heads during the national anthem at the 1968 Olympics, the Olympic Committee stripped them of their medals and banned them from further Olympic competition. Vince Matthews and Wayne Collett received a similar penalty for their alleged disrespect for the United States national anthem at the 1972 Olympics. The Olympic Committee made such decisions even though they claimed the Olympics are nonpolitical events; a claim that could not be further from the truth. The playing of the winner's national anthem, athletes representing nations, and decisions made as to where the Olympics will be held, and which nations may or may not compete are just some of the more overt examples of the political nature of the Olympic Games.

Why are athletic events so overladen with patriotic themes? Tom Wicker, of the *New York Times,* made the following speculation:

What is the correlation, if any, between patriotism and people battering one another in the boxing ring or in football games — or for that matter between patriotism and track meets, baseball games and other athletic events that are not so violent?

The explanation probably is that symbols like the flag and the anthem, appropriate as they are to the warlike spirit, are equally appropriate to sports events, with their displays of the instinct to combat and the will to win. Even the so-called "noncontact" sports exalt competition and the pursuit of victory, including the kind of individual heroism and team spirit that are evoked in wartime.[19]

For whatever reason, sport competition and nationalism are closely intertwined. When American athletes compete against those of another country, national unity is the result (for both sides, unless one's athletes do poorly). Citizens take pride in their representatives' accomplishments, viewing them as collective achievements. This identification with athletes and their cause of winning for the nation's glory tends to unite the citizenry regardless of social class, race, and regional differences. Thus, sport can be used by political leaders whose nations have problems with divisiveness.

Sport as an Opiate of the Masses

We have shown that sport success can unite a nation through pride. After Brazil won the World Cup in soccer (*futebol)* for the third time in succession, one observer noted:

The current *futebol* success has promoted a pride in being Brazilian and a unifying symbol without precedent. Even the lower classes of the cities, thanks to television, felt a sense of participation in something representing national life. They know that Brazil is now internationally significant, not necessarily for reasons of interest to the scholar or public figure, but of importance to the common man. It is estimated that over 700 million soccer fans throughout the world watched Brazil defeat England and Italy. The Englishman in his pub, the French worker, the German with a Volkswagen all know that Brazil is not just another large "tropical country," but the homeland of the world's best *futebol* and a legend named Pele.[20]

This pride in a nation's success, because it transcends the social classes, serves as an opiate of the masses. Sanders asserted that *futebol* in Brazil enables the poor to forget partially the harshness of their life. It serves also as a safety valve for releasing tensions that might otherwise be directed toward disrupting the existing social order.[21]

The same situation appears to be true of the United States. Virtually all homes have television sets, making it possible for almost everyone to participate vicariously in and identify with local and national sports teams. Because

305

of this, the minds and energies of many persons are deflected away from the hunger and misery that is disproportionately the lot of the lower classes in American society. Bill Bradley — former Rhodes scholar and professional basketball player and now senator from New Jersey — has pointed out that sport deflects us from seeking solutions to the problems of war and racism.

> Life is full of ironies . . . It's really ironic the way the fans come out to cheer the Big Game when there's a war on; people being bombed to death; racism, and all the rest of it . . . It's also ironic that when 100,000 people will be at tomorrow's rally [a New York peace rally], the Knicks and me will be going over tonight's game films . . . And Bill Bradley wonders hard about the morality of providing what he calls a "fix," a temporary escape from the problems of the world to a sports dreamworld; an escape that is really no escape because it permits those problems to go on just as before.[22]

Sport also acts as an opiate by perpetuating the belief that persons from the lowest classes can be upwardly mobile through success in sports. Chapter 10 will deal with this topic more fully, but, meanwhile, it is enough to say that for every major leaguer who came up from poverty, tens of thousands did not. The point, however, is that most Americans *believe* that sport is a mobility escalator and that it is merely a reflection of the opportunity structure of the society in general. Again, poor youth who might otherwise invest their energies in changing the system, work instead on a jump shot. The potential for change is thus impeded by sport.[23]

The Exploitation of Sport by Politicians

Politicians may use athletics and athletes in several ways. First, an athlete can use his fame and free publicity as an aid to getting elected or appointed to office. Of course, these persons may have had the political skills to win anyway, but athletic fame undoubtedly helps.

Politicians also find it beneficial to get the approval and active campaign support of athletes. Athletes, because they are well known and admired, can get votes for either themselves or for candidates whom they support. But sport itself is so popular in American society that politicians may use examples of sport or sport metaphors to communicate with the public.[24] Moreover, they find it useful to identify with teams, to attend sports events, and to talk with coaches and athletic heroes. Richard Nixon, more than any recent president, identified with sports. But governors, congressmen, mayors, and other officials tend more and more to identify with sports.

Politicians capitalize on the popularity of athletes by using them to support the system. In the United States, for example, athletes are often sent overseas to maintain the morale of servicemen. Athletes are also used in advertisements that urge the veiwer or reader to join the army or ROTC, to vote, and to avoid drugs. They are also asked to give patriotic speeches on holidays and other occasions.

Use of athletes for the maintenance of the status quo is used in other countries as well. In communist countries, the avowed goal of sports is to

306

aid in the socialist revolution. Subsidized by the state, athletes visit factories and villages to hold demonstrations and make political speeches. These activities spread the philosophy of the rulers and bolster the morale of the factory and farm workers to increase production.[25]

A final way that sport can be exploited by politicians is related to the manipulation of sports audiences. As noted before, militaristic displays and patriotic pageants can be used to promote nationalism among the spectators. Moreover, this captive audience can be manipulated by politicians to win votes. The sporting crowd is viewed by many politicians as a type of ethnic or regional group worthy of courting for votes.[26]

Sport as a Socializing Agent

We have frequently pointed out that sport is a vehicle by which the American values of success in competition, hard work, perseverance, discipline, and order are transmitted.[27] This is the explicit reason given for the existence of Little League programs for youngsters and the tremendous emphasis on sports in American schools. While vice president, Spiro Agnew voiced the prevailing view well in a speech delivered to the Touchdown Club of Birmingham, Alabama. The following are some excerpts:

Not the least of these values is the American competitive ethic which motivates young Americans . . . to strive toward excellence in everything they undertake. For such young Americans — whether on the athletic field, in the classroom, or on the job — the importance of our competitive ethic lies in the fact that it is only by trial of their abilities — by testing and challenging — can they discover their strengths, and, yes, their weaknesses. Out of this process of self-discovery, painful though it may be at times, those young Americans who compete to excel learn to cope with whatever challenges lie ahead in life. And having given their best, they also emerge from the competitive test with greater ability to determine for themselves where their individual talents lie. Life is a great competition. In my judgment it will remain so despite the efforts of the social architects to make it a bland experience, controlled by their providing what they think is best for us. Success is sweet but it entails always the risk of failure. It is very, very important to learn how to lose a contest without being destroyed by the experience. For a man who has not known failure cannot fully appreciate success. A person cannot know pleasure to any greater degree than he has known pain. And from defeat, from failure, from hardship, something builds within a person. If a person can throw off disappointment and come back and try again, he develops a personal cohesiveness that holds him together as a man throughout his life — and that gives him the durability to convert temporary defeat into ultimate victory.

And so, to me, that is the messsage of competitive sports: not simply trying to win, and to achieve, but learning how to cope with a failure—and to come back. In this regard, let me say something about my personal philosophy concerning the meaning of success and failure in sports for young Americans.

307

First, I believe that sports—all sports—is one of the few bits of glue that holds society together, one of the few activities in which young people can proceed along avenues where objectives are clear and the desire to win is not only permissible but encouraged.

Opponents of the free-enterprise system tell our young people that to try for material success and personal status is bad; that the only thing worthwhile is to find something to wring your hands about; that the ultimate accomplishment is to make everybody feel better.

I, for one, would not want to live in a society that did not include winning in its philosophy; that would have us live our lives as identical lemmings, never trying to best anybody at anything, all headed in the same direction, departing not from the appointed route, striving not for individual excellence. In short, I would rather be a failure in a competitive society which is our inheritance than to live in a waveless sea of nonachievers.[28]

Agnew, of course, overlooked the noncompetitive aspects of corporate sport—e.g., professional teams are exempt from the Sherman Antitrust Act, team owners receive a special statutory tax break, professional teams play in tax-subsidized stadiums. In short, he neglected to say that team owners do not compete. He did voice, however, what most people believe.[29]

Whether sport actually transmits those values or whether only the most competitive individuals survive are empirical questions. We do know that societies differ in the sports they emphasize and that these correlate with the values of the society (or those values that the leaders desire to promote). As an example of a society that uses sport to promote quite different values than those enumerated by Agnew, let us look briefly at China.

Sport in China, as reported by Americans, has a very different emphasis than that found in America.[30] Sport is found throughout the country—in factories, communes, and schools—but winning in a competitive situation is not the major objective. The goals, rather, are teamwork, cooperation, working for a group goal, friendship, and physical fitness. American schools and communities shower great rewards on their athletes. Winners receive ribbons, medals, and trophies—all prominently displayed. This is in sharp contrast to what is found in China. After a tour there, William Johnson noted that he had not seen a single sports trophy or pennant in all the schools and universities he had visited. He asked a school coach about this, whose response was:

It is true that sometimes we are awarded modest banners for winning, but I do not know where they are. Perhaps in a desk drawer. We consider friendship first, learning good technique second, victory banners third or perhaps even less.[31]

Johnson received similar replies from other coaches, athletes, and factory workers. Clearly, a socialist system is better served if its citizens learn cooperation and teamwork, while a capitalist society is best served by encouraging one to strive to outdo one's fellows—and sport can be organized to achieve either of these goals.

Sport as a Vehicle to Change Society

A recurring theme of this book is that sport reflects the dynanmics of the larger society. So, with the social and political turmoil in American society in the 1960s, one would expect that the sports world would be similarly affected.

Sport and sporting events have been used by revolutionaries and reformers to attack two major problems—racism and the recent American involvement in the Vietnam war. Racism has been attacked in a number of ways. Most dramatic was the proposed boycott of the 1968 Olympics by black athletes. Harry Edwards, a black sociologist and former athlete, was a leader of this boycott. His rationale for the protest was as follows:

> The roots of the revolt of the black athlete spring from the same seed that produced the sit-ins, the freedom rides, and the rebellions in Watts, Detroit, and Newark. The athletic revolt springs from a disgust and dissatisfaction with the racism prevalent in American society—including the sports world.[32]

Another boycott was directed against the New York Athletic Club's annual indoor track meet. The goal of this action was to dramatize and change the club's policy of excluding Jews, blacks, and other minorities from membership. And, black athletes at schools such as San Jose State and the University of Wyoming participated in a symbolic protest against Brigham Young University, a Mormon-supported university. These athletes wore arm bands to symbolize their contempt for the racial policies of the Mormon Church.

These examples show once again how sport and politics are intertwined. The world-wide popularity of sport and the importance attached to it by fans and politicians alike make sport an ideal platform for political protest. However, it should be noted that the use of sport for protest, although an important means of dramatizing social problems, is generally successful in effecting a meaningful change. This is a tribute to the institutional character of sport, with its built-in bias for preserving and legitimizing the status quo.

THE POLITICAL-ECONOMIC OLYMPICS

The motto of the Olympic Games—"Citius, Altius, Fortius" ("Faster, Higher, Stronger")—implies that athletic performance is to supersede all other concerns. Ever since the revival of the Olympics in 1896, however, there has been an erosion of the prominence of athletic accomplishments and the corresponding ascendance of political, economic, and bureaucratic considerations. The move by the United States in 1980 to use the Olympics as a political weapon against an enemy was just one more example of how political the Olympics really are.

The problems with the Olympics are legion. They can be divided into political, economic, and bureaucratic problems, each of which diminishes the importance of athletic competition for its own sake.

Political Problems

Politics overshadowing the joy of participation is not a new phenomenon in the Olympics. A brief history will illustrate just how political the Olympics have been:

1936—Hitler turned the Games in Berlin into a propaganda show for Nazi Germany. As a concession to the Nazis, the United States dropped two Jewish sprinters from the 400-meter relay.

1940—44—World War II interrupted the Games.

1948—Israel was excluded from participation after a threat of an Abrab boycott.

1952—Taiwan boycotted the Games when Communist China was admitted to the International Olympic Committee (IOC). East Germany was denied admittance because it was not a "recognized state." East Germany refused, in turn, to compete as one team with the West Germans.

1956—Egypt, Lebanon, and Iraq boycotted the Olympics because of the Anglo-French seizure of the Suez Canal. The Communist Chinese team walked out when the Nationalist Chinese Flag was hoisted in the Olympic village. Spain, Switzerland, and the Netherlands withdrew from the Olympics in protest after the Soviet Union invaded Hungary. As a direct consequence of Russia's invasion, a riot broke out during their water polo match with Hungary.

1960—The IOC decreed that North and South Korea should compete as one team, using the same flag, emblem, and uniform. North Korea refused to participate under these conditions. Nationalist China was forced to compete under the name of Taiwan. As the Chinese placard-bearer passed the reviewing stand in the opening ceremonies, he showed a sign saying "Under Protest."

1964—South Africa was banned from the Olymp:cs for its apartheid policies.

1968—South Africa was again banned from participation. American black athletes threatened a boycott to protest racism in the United States. Tommie Smith and John Carlos raised a black-power salute during the American national anthem and were banned for life from Olympic competition. The Mexican government shot and killed students protesting the Games in Mexico City.

1972—Eleven Israeli athletes were murdered by Palestinian terrorists. Prior to the Games, the IOC ruled that Rhodesia would be allowed to participate. Many African nations were incensed because of the racist policies of the ruling elite in Rhodesia and threatened to boycott the Games unless Rhodesia was barred. The IOC ultimately bowed to this pressure and rescinded its earlier action.

1976—Athletes from twenty-eight African nations boycotted the Games because New Zealand, whose rugby team had toured South Africa, was allowed to compete. The host country Canada refused to grant visas to athletes from Nationalist China unless they agreed to compete under the designation of Taiwan instead of the Republic of China.

310

1980—Some sixty nations— including the United States, West Germany, Canada, and Japan—boycotted the Games in protest of Russia's invasion of Afghanistan. Sixteen of the nations that participated refused to march or show their flags in the opening and closing ceremonies.[33]

In addition to these corruptions of the Olympics ideals, the very ways that the Games are organized are political. Nations select which athletes will perform (no athlete can perform without national sponsorhsip). The IOC provides ceremonies where athletes march behind their country's flag. The winner's national anthem is played at the awards ceremony. The IOC also considers political criteria in the selection of the site of the Olympics and in the choice of judges, ensuring in the latter case a balance between East and West, especially in the judging of events such as boxing, ice skating, and gymnastics.

Economic Problems

The cost of producing the Olympics every four years has become very expensive for the International Olympic Committee, the host nation, and each competing country.[34] These high costs have, for example, encouraged the United States Olympic Committee to sell the rights to the Olympic symbol to a variety of advertisers, which allows a corporation to claim that their product is the official beer, chewing tobacco, snow tire, mattress, jeans, tooth paste, or whatever of the Olympics. The 1980 Winter Games in Lake Placid were sponsored, for example, by almost 100 American corporations paying fees ranging from $50,000 to $1.5 million for the right to use the logo of the Lake Placid Olympic Organizing Committee in corporate advertising. Corporations were even allowed to use athletes in their commercial activities to sell their products as long as the USOC benefited rather than the athletes, who had to retain their amateur standing.

The cost to the host country and host city to provide the facilities and ancillary activities exceeded $1 billion for the 1976 Summer Games in Montreal and are predicted to surpass $2.1 billion for the 1988 Games in London. The high cost encourages the host country and host city to exploit visiting athletes, officials, and spectators to recover costs and garner a profit with excessive charges for housing, food, entertainment, transportation, and the like. The commercialization of the Games reached its zenith when ABC agreed to pay $225 million for the rights to televise the 1984 Olympics in Los Angeles. The ultimate irony of all of the big-business enterprises that surround the Games is that so many of these benefit economically from the gathering of the world's great athletes, yet the athletes cannot be tainted by economics or they will lose their eligibility. The resulting hypocrisy is monumental.

Bureaucratic Problems

The IOC, composed of the wealthy elite from around the world, has tried unsuccessfully to maintain a standard for amateurs based on the nineteeth-century ideal that sport should be done for enjoyment during leisure time. If strictly applied, this ideal would mean that only the affluent could participate. In practice, each nation has been allowed to establish its own rules for amateur standing. This has meant that fully subsidized Russian athletes have been allowed to compete, as have American college-scholarship athletes or those Americans now subsidized by corporations to further their athletic prowess. Yet occasionally the Olympic Committee has ruled some athletes ineligible for accepting money from a corporation. The inconsistencies, hypocrisies, and inequities involved in who is and who is not an amateur provide ever fuller meaning to the derisive term "shamnateurism."

The political problems already mentioned provide further testimony to the impotence of the Olympic hierarchy. Despite the rhetoric of the leadership, they have not been able to transcend national, political, and economic considerations. Obviously, these considerations continually shape and guide their actions.

The Olympic Revolutions

The problems surrounding the Olympics continue to escalate, raising serious questions about the future of the Games. As presently structured, the Olympics are a sham because the athletes' pursuit of excellence has become secondary. The time has come for dismantling the Olympics as we know them and the establishment of Olympics organized to eliminate or at least drastically minimize the problems endemic to the current system. The following are several proposals that would help to accomplish the aim of neutralizing the crippling political and economic problems that presently work to negate the Olympic ideals.

1. *Establish two permanent sites for the Games.* The summer Olympics should always be held in Greece and the Winter Games in Switzerland. Greece is a natural choice because the ancient Olympic Games were held there. Both Greece and Switzerland would be ideal because they are small, independent countries that are not considered vital in the political struggles between the East and West.

2. *Restrict the events to competition among individuals.* All team sports should be eliminated because each team represents a country, which makes political considerations inevitable. A second reason for eliminating team sports is that they are inherently unfair; the larger the population base of a nation, the more likely that country will be able to field a superior team.

3. *Allow athletes to represent only themselves.* Athletes, in actuality and symobolically, should not represent their country. The nation-state should not be represented by uniforms, flags, national anthems, or political leaders. When an athlete is awarded his or her medal for winning an event, only the Olympic Hymn should be played. Athletes also should be randomly assigned to housing and eating arrangements at the Games to reduce national identification and to maximize cross-cultural interaction.

4. *Allow all athletes (amateur and professional) of the world to compete.* The nation-state should not be involved in the selection process because this encourages nationalistic feelings. To ensure that the best athletes of the world are able to compete, a minimum standard for each

312

event should be set by the governing board. Athletes meeting this standard would have all expenses paid to meet in regional competition. At the regionals, another and higher standard of excellence would be set for athletes to qualify for the Olympics. Again, for those athletes qualifying for the Olympics, all expenses for travel and per diem would be paid by the Olympic committee.

5. *Subsidize the cost of the Olympics by revenues generated from admissions to the regionals and the Games and television.* By establishing permanent sites and eliminating team events, the cost of the Olympics would be reduced dramatically. The costs would still be considerable, however, especially during the initial stages of preparing the permanent sites. Revenues from admissions and from television should pay for the costs after the Games are established. During the building of the permanent sites, though, the Games may need a subsidy from the United Nations. Television revenues present a particularly thorny problem because the revenue potential is great and this lends itself to threats of overcommercialization, the intrusion of corporations into the decision-making arena, and jingoism by chauvinistic television commentators. To reduce these potential problems the events could be televised and reported by a company strictly controlled by the Olympic committee. The televising of the Olympics would be provided to each country at a cost determined by the existing number of television sets in that country. Each nation would decide how that fee would be paid, but the important point is that no country would have any control over what would be shown or the commentary emanating from the Games.

6. *Establish an Olympic Committee and a Secretary-General to prepare for and oversee the Games.* The composition of the committee would be crucial. Currently the members of the IOC are taken from national committees, with an important criterion being the maintenance of a political balance between opposing factions. The concept of a ruling body is important, but the committee should be reorganized to ensure that the intent of the changes suggested here would be implemented. This is a baffling problem because the selection will always involve political considerations. One possibility would be to incorporate the selection procedures used in the United Nations to select its Secretary-General. These procedures have worked, even during the darkest days of the Cold War, toward the selection of a competent, objective, and nonaligned (of neither a pro-West or a pro-Eastern bloc) arbitrator. In addition to an Olympic Secretary-General, a governing board and a permanent staff would also have to be selected.

These proposals are not complete. They are a beginning. As they are amended and others added the reorganization of the Olympics should be guided by three goals: (1) to encourage individual athletic excellence; (2) to eliminate politics; and (3) to maximize interaction among athletes across national boundaries. The task is challenging, but not impossible. The Olympics movement is important—that is why it must be altered radically from its present form if its lofty goals are to be realized.

THE POLITICAL ATTITUDES OF COACHES AND ATHLETES

Sociologists are interested in the political attitudes of various social categories, such as social classes, occupations, and religious groups. This interest is based on the assumption that individuals in similar social situations are constrained to view the world and evaluate events and ideas from the same perspective. The remainder of this chapter will focus on the political attitudes of two categories—coaches and athletes—that face somewhat similar pressures and therefore have congruent attitudes.

Liberalism—conservatism is a multidimensional phenomenon. Some of the many dimensions involved are attitudes about welfare, foreign aid, racial integration, the free-enterprise system, morality, and social change. Few persons, therefore, hold a consistent pattern of thought across these dimensions. Nevertheless, the discussion that follows will consider political conservatives to be persons who support the existing socio-economic-political system. This means that they have a great respect for tradition, authority, law and order, the free-enterprise system, patriotism, and the tired-and-true values of hard work, goal orientation, and Christian morality. This implies, further, that they tend to be tolerant of challenges against these traditional values.

Despite an occasional political protest, athletes as a group are politically conservative. Although former pro athletes such as Dave Meggyesy, George Sauer, and Bernie Parrish have been critical of sport in American society, they are clearly exceptions to the rule. The response of the vast majority of athletes, coaches, reporters, and others in the sports world to critiques of contemporary sport is indicative of this conservative tendency. We will attempt to examine and explain this conservatism, focusing particularly on the political attitudes of coaches and athletes. Two caveats before we begin. First there is little empirical research in this area. We will supply what information is available, but much additional research is needed. Second, the available data are limited to males.

Coaches

Generalizations about any social category are always difficult because few such groups are homogeneous. The coaching profession is no exception. There are harsh and lenient coaches, bigoted and nonbigoted coaches, and hawks and doves on America's military policies. Despite these differences, however, coaches as a category can be characterized as politically conservative. Let us examine the available evidence from three sources: anecdotes, surveys, and scientific research.

A good deal of anecdotal evidence supports the contention that coaches tend to be politically conservative. As David Nelson, athletic director at the University of Delaware and formerly its head football coach, summarized: "Having been a coach . . . I know that most of us are almost Harding Republicans and three degrees to the right of Genghis Khan."[35]

Item: When one of his players sat down during the playing of the national anthem, Coach Ellis of Adelbert College suspended him, saying, "[There are] no rules about standing for the national anthem, but no rules

314

about dropping a player who doesn't do it, either."[36]

Item: When social activists and sports critics Jack Scott and Dave Meggyesy were scheduled to speak at the University of Kansas, athletes were told not to attend. Assistant coaches observed each entrance to the auditorium to determine which athletes attended.

Item: A college recruiter was questioning a high school coach about a black athlete. After asking the standard questions about height, weight, speed, test scores, and class rank, the recruiter found it necessary to ask, "Is he militant?"[37]

Item: F. Melvin Cratsley, basketball coach at Carnegie Tech for seventeen years, said, "I object to players telling me they want beards, long hair and all the rest, because the next thing they want to do is run the team. More important than the beard is what it represents—rebellion. If you can't tell them what to do, they don't need a coach."[38]

Item: Tony Simpson, coach of a Houston junior high school, said: "It is time that American coaches stopped allowing themselves to be personally represented by male athletic teams and individuals who look like females. It is time that American coaches realized that a male's hair is not just an American tradition but an issue involving biblical principles; time that coaches stopped rationalizing and compromising their common sense; time to show the American athlete that his most valuable characteristic is not physical ability but respect for authority."[39]

These extreme examples may not be representative of coaches and certainly should not be taken as proof of the basic conservatism of this occupational category. They may indicate, however, the tendency of coaches to support the existing political and social order. Let us examine some more reliable evidence.

One source of such evidence are questionnaires distributed to coaches. The two examples given below illustrate the policy of coaches regarding changing norms:

Item: Of the 1,098 respondent coaches in Florida, 82 percent disagreed with this statement in a questionnaire: "A member of an athletic squad should be able to dress (hair, beard, sideburns, clothes) any way he wishes."[40]

Item: A study of fifty southern California high school basketball coaches revealed that 42 percent controlled their athletes' off-court activities.[41]

Several studies indicate that physical education teachers (and most coaches are trained in this field) tend to be more conservative than teachers in other fields. One study compared prospective high school physical education teachers with prospective high school liberal arts teachers at a large midwestern university. The researcher found the physical educators to be more traditional, dogmatic, authoritarian, and more conservative in political and religious values.[42]

Physical education teachers at the college level have also been found to be more conservative than professors in other fields. A survey by the Carnegie Commission on Higher Education of the political opinions of over sixty thousand full-time college faculty members found that physical educa-

315

tion faculty ranked second out of thirty fields in percentage of respondents who characterized themselves as strongly and moderately conservative (only agriculture faculty members were found to be more conservative).[43]

Unfortunately, there has been little research on the political attitudes of coaches to support the impressionistic observations and indirect evidence we have cited but existent research tends to support these notions. One study by sport psychologists Bruce C. Ogilvie and Thomas A. Tutko concluded:

We know that coaches are aggressive people, self-assertive; we know that they are highly organized and ordered; . . . they are also inflexible in their profession as coaches; they dislike change and experimentation; and they are extremely conservative—politically, socially and attitudinally. . . .[44]

In a comparison of high school football coaches with government teachers in Kansas, the former were found to be more conservative on political attitudes and more willing to impose patriotic attitudes on students. This second finding is especially interesting since the coaches were more inclined to do the government teacher's job than the government teacher. Apparently, government teachers felt that it was their duty to pass on the facts and let the students decide, while the coaches felt a responsibility to impose their values on their students.[45]

George H. Sage, in a study comparing college head coaches (football, basketball, and track) with college students and businessmen, found the coaches to be more conservative than the students but somewhat less so than the businessmen.[46] Using the Polyphasic Values Inventory, Sage found the coaches to be significantly more conservative than the college students on fourteen of the twenty items. Of special interest were items of greatest conservatism: the value of obedience to authority and the value of good conduct. Sage concluded:

The total response profile of the college coaches showed them to possess moderate-conservative values. . . . Although conservatism is not extreme among coaches, it is more pronounced than it is among college students. . . . The findings of this study support the notion that coaches possess a greater conservatism than college students. But an item-by-item analysis of the response choices certainly does not support the assertions which have been made recently that coaches are extremely conservative—even reactionary—in value orientation.[47]

The available but sketchy evidence suggests that coaches tend to be conservative. Research has shown, moreover, that coaches, regardless of their sport and of their age, tend to have similar political and social outlooks.[48] The question remains, then, why is there a tendency for coaches to be politically conservative?

The first of at least six reasons for this relationship has to do with the particular lifelong socialization of coaches.[49] There is considerable evidence that coaches, when compared to other faculty members, come from markedly lower socioeconomic backgrounds.[50] For example, while 22 percent of the fathers of college professors in general held high-status jobs, only 6 percent of the fathers of college football and basketball coaches had high-status occupations. Moreover, 58 percent of the fathers of basketball coaches and 54 percent of the fathers of football coaches had jobs in the low or very low occupational prestige categories. There are two related reasons why this is significant for our discussion. Considerable social-sicence research shows that child-rearing practices differ by social class. Working-class parents, for instance, are much more likely than middle-class parents to use physical punishment, to be more authoritarian, and to be more rigidly conventional.[51] In addition, working-class parents tend to hold particular values; law and order, obedience to authority, and political conservatism.[52] Because parental values are transmitted to their offspring and then internalized, it follows that persons growing up in working-class families will themselves tend to possess values stressing political and social conservatism.

The second reason for the propensity for conservatism among coaches is that almost invariably they are former athletes. As we will see in the next section, athletics is a ruthless selection process that encourages certain traits and discourages others. Coaches are products of the American athletic system, and the thesis of this chapter is that this system is conservatism.

Third, coaching is an occupational subculture, and socialization theory suggests that members of a group tend to possess similar value orientations. There are two reasons for this: selection and assimilation. Occupational choice is often made on the basis of compatible values; that is, the individual is attracted to a particular occupation because he or she is in agreement with the values of that occupation. Typically, too, an individual who aspires to a particular occupation will internalize the values, attitudes, and behaviors characteristic of persons in that occupation, especially the characteristics of the most successful ones (this process is called "anticipatory socialization").[53]

Fourth, in addition to selection and assimiliation, the individual will also feel overt pressure to adopt the attitudes, values, and behaviors of those supporting him in his occupation. Communities, school boards, and fans demand that their coaches support the traditional values because coaches are hired to mold the character of youth. Thus, those coaches or potential coaches who harbor political and social views outside the mainstream will have great difficulty in finding or in retaining a job, thereby leaving the vast majority of the jobs to those considered politically safe.

Fifth, the subcultural character of the coaching profession is maintained by the open opposition from the academic community. This hostility strengthens the isolation of coaches by creating alienation and polarization. This opposition stems from the belief that coaches are anti-intellectual, dehumanizing, and insensitive to the individuality of their athletes. Whether these beliefs are accurate or not, the result of an antagonistic relationship that develops solidarity among coaches and tends to reinforce their unity around specific beliefs.[54]

Sixth, and perhaps the most crucial reason, is that the success or failure of a team depends almost entirely on whether the coach is considered competent (in other words, whether his or her team wins more than it loses). Thus, there is a strong tendency for coaches to control the situation as much as possible. Since they will be held responsible for the outcome, they will make the decisions (who will play, what plays will be called, and what strategy will be used). Moreover, they will control as much of the players' lives as possible because what the players eat, when they sleep, whom they date, and whether they have long hair may make a difference in the coaches' uncertain world.

The rationale for controlling the lives of players off the field is summed up in this statement given by a coach to the players on his team: "Our school, our team, our coaches, and our community are judged by your behavior. It is very important that you be gentlemen in all your actions."[55] Apparently, this coach felt the need to control an area that is more certain than the outcome of a game and that also has a bearing on whether he keeps his job or not. For all these reasons, coaches find it difficult to be tolerant of behavior outside of community norms. As Harry Edwards put it, "the apparent inflexibility of coaches then derives at least in part from the institutionalized demand that they be totally liable for outcomes in a situation wrought with uncertainties."[56] In short, the behaviors of coaches are likely not the results of personality but rather are products of their unique social situation.,

Athletes

Existing research that contrasts athletes with nonathletes consistently finds that the former are the more politically conservative. Walter E. Schafer examined this relationship, especially among high school students, and concluded:

Interscholastic athletics serve first and foremost as a social device for steering young people—participants and spectators alike—into the mainstream of American life through the overt and covert teaching of "appropriate" attitudes, values, norms and behavior patterns. As a result school sports tend to exert more of a conservatizing and integrating influence in the society than an innovative or progressive influence.[57]

Two studies support Schafer's contention. The first was a study of 937 male seniors from eight high schools in New York. The researchers found: (1) the greater the participation in extracurricular activities (athletics and others), the greater the acceptance of authority; (2) athletes were more likely than nonathletes to believe that the American way of life is superior to that of any other country; (3) athletes were less likely than nonathletes to endorse a statement calling for fundamental structural change in American society; (4) athletes, more than nonathletes, believed that resistance to the draft was basically wrong.[58]

Research on college students has produced essentially the same findings. When compared with college nonathletes, college athletes were found to be more conservative, less interested and active in politics, more tolerant of violations of civil liberties, and more tolerant of repressive reactions to campus unrest.[59]

However, one qualification exists to the generalization that athletes tend to be conservative. Brian M. Petrie and Elizabeth L. Reid studied the political attitudes of Canadian athletes and found them to be generally liberal.[60] This may mean that the conservatism of sport is situationally specific, i.e., specific to a particular culture. If true, this would reconfirm the thesis that sport mirrors society.

Why do American athletes tend to be politically conservative? A number of reasons have been advanced. First, athletes are the prestige leaders in their school and community. Because they benefit from the way things are, they rarely criticize the status quo. Second, since athletes devote substantial time and energy to sports activities, they have less time than nonathletes to become involved in or even consider social criticism. Third, athletes are more likely to have grown accustomed to accepting, rather than questioning, authority.[61] Fourth, it is almost impossible to remain radical in the sports world. Athletes whose views and behavior are nonconventional will soon be weeded out from the regimented world most coaches insist on.[62]

No research has yet been undertaken contrasting the political attitudes of professional athletes and nonathletes with similar educational backgrounds. Presumably, two factors should operate to make professional athletes especially conservative: (1) they have been successful school athletes with all the attendant pressures by the schools and the communities on athletes to be conventional; (2) they are successful in both monetary and prestige dimensions, making it difficult to question the system.

A most important reason why athletes at all levels are politically more conservative than nonathletes is that most persons who wield authority in the sports world are conservative. Athletes, then, hear a consistent viewpoint and feel a consistent set of constraints on their behavior from powerful others. Let us examine who these powerful persons are, first at the school level and then at the professional level.

Athletes in school are affected most by their coaches and school administrators. We have already noted that coaches tend to be very conventional, politically conservative, and resistant to change. School administrators, too, tend to be politically conservative. Their significant reference groups are the school boards or the boards of regents, which represent the schools' constituencies. These groups do not want school representatives deviating from community expectations.

At the college level, a most significant reference group is the college's alumni, especially those who are likely to be the biggest financial contributors. We can assume that as persons become wealthier, they will tend to be more conservative. These persons pressure college administrators, at least indirectly, to keep their college's representatives in line. According to Jack Scott:

The conservatism that engulfs the American sporting scene to this day stems in no small measure from the alumni groups that control intercollegiate athletic programs throughout the country. Not surprisingly, alumni who have the time, finances, and inclination to involve themselves in, and contribute to the financing of, a professionalized athletic program for college students are conservative men. Despite the existence at nearly all colleges of athletic advisory boards comprised of faculty, administrators, and students, it is these wealthy alumni who play the most influential role in the hiring and firing of college coaches and athletic directors. Berny Wagner, the head track and field coach at Oregon State, openly admits that coaches are not hired primarily to serve college athletes, but to please "alumni and other interested private parties" who finance the athletic programs.

Just how do Mr. Wagner and other coaches please "alumni and other interested private parties"? The most obvious way is by producing winning teams that the alumni can proudly and vicariously identify with. Another less obvious but perhaps more important way is by molding young boys into clean-cut, obedient, yet competitive, acquisitive adults who will take their "proper" place in American society.[63]

Another set of persons who exert a powerful influence on amateur athletes are those running the various leagues or sanctioning bodies (e.g., State High School Activities Association, the Big Eight, the National Collegiate Athletic Association, the Amateur Athletic Union). Decision makers in these organizations have great power over athletes and athletic programs. They decide on matters of eligibility, investigate cases of alleged violations of rules, negotiate television contracts, sanction postseason play, and so forth. These leaders, like school administrators, are image conscious. To obtain television contracts or favorable treatment from Congress, one must not condone nonconventional politics. So, Walter Byers, the executive director of the NCAA, insisted that the decision by the American Broadcasting Company not to show the peace-oriented halftime show at the previously described Buffalo-Holy Cross football game was correct. Moreover, his editorials in the *NCAA News* praised Vice President Spiro Agnew (before Agnew's resignation from office) and condemned Harry Edwards, leader of the black boycott of the 1968 Olympics. Ironically, however, Byers insisted that "college athletics are not political and he regularly condemns anyone who attempts to inject 'politics' into the intercollegiate athletic arena."[64]

Professional athletes, in addition to the conservative pressures exerted on them during their school days, experience constraints on their behavior from several additional sources. Foremost of these are the owners of professional teams. By definition, these owners are wealthy persons who have benefited from the existing system. Moreover, their teams can exist only with community support. Hence, there is a strong tendency among owners to promote patriotic pageantry at games and to expect their athletes to conform to community norms.

Sports announcers and sports writers also tend to be biased toward the conservative end of the political spectrum. Sports announcers are controlled totally by the team owners or by the networks. Thus, the attitudes they express are those of powerful (and conservative) others. To a lesser extent, this is also true of sports writers. These persons, if they travel with the team, receive all kinds of consideration — from meals and travel to permission to interview—if they are in the good graces of the team owners. Leonard Shecter described it this way:

George Weiss, recently retired president of the New York Mets, once put it this way: "To hell with the newspapermen. You can buy them with a steak." This might be overstatement. Sports reporters who like their jobs so much have a tendency to *want* to please the management of the sporting organizations. They easily become what are called "house men." The man who covers a baseball team year after year spends a good deal more time with the management of the ball club than with his own editors; indeed, with his own wife. He becomes, if he is interested enough in his job to want to keep it, more involved with the fortunes of the team than that of his newspaper.[65]

In addition to the owners and the media, professional athletes are constrained to be conservative by their coaches and their league sanctioning body. A classic example of the latter was the action taken by the persons who control boxing in the United States to strip Muhammad Ali of his world title because of his stand as a conscientious objector. The concern of league officials is exemplified in the efforts of Pete Rozelle, commissioner of the National Football League, to have all players show proper respect for the national anthem (the athletes are told how to stand, how to hold their helmets, and so forth). The NFL is also responsible for the patriotic festivals that accompany the Super Bowl (perhaps the best example being the re-creation of the Battle of New Orleans in the War of 1812 during the halftime of the 1971 Super Bowl).

SUMMARY

Two themes have dominated this chapter: sport is political in character, and persons connected with sport in almost any capacity tend to be conservative. The basic conservatism of sport has two important implications for American society. First, the athletic programs of American schools, to which most persons are exposed, support and reinforce a view of the world and society that perpetuates the status quo. This is accomplished through the promotion of American values and the support of the American politico-economic system.

A second implication, given the institutional character of sport, is that efforts to change sport will not come from those who control sport. Moreover, any attack on sport will be defined as an attack on society itself. Thus, change in sport will be slow and more likely than not, the result of a real struggle.

REFERENCE NOTES

1. *University Daily Kansan,* 12 December 1971.

2. Phillip Goodhart and Christopher Chataway. *War Without Weapons* (London: W. H. Allen, 1968), p. 3.

3. See Ralf Dahrendorf, *Class and Class Conflict in Industrial Society* (Palo Alto: Stanford University Press, 1959); and Robert Michels, *Political Parties* (New York: Dover, 1959, first published in 1914).

4. Frederick C. Klein, "Power and Politics Muddle Amateur Athletics," *Wall Street Journal,* 31 October 1979, p. 22.

5. See Arthur T. Johnson, "Public Sports Policy," *American Behavioral Scientist* 21 (January/February 1978); 319-43; Arthur T. Johnson, "Congress and Professional Sports," *The Annals* 445 (September 1979); 102-15.

6. See Richard E. Lapchick, *The Politics of Race and International Sport: The Case of South Africa* (Westport, Conn.: Greenwood Press, 1975); idem, "South Africa: Sport and Apartheid Politics," *The Annals* 445 (September 1979): 155-65.

7. See Benjamin Lowe, David B. Kanin, and Andrew Strenk, eds., *Sport and International Relations* (Champaign, Ill.: Stipes Publishing, 1978), pp. 297-470; Andrew Strenk, "The Thrill of Victory and the Agony of Defeat: Sport and International Politics," *Orbis: A Journal of World Affairs* 22 (Summer 1978): 453-69.

8. Jerry Isenberg, *How Many Miles to Camelot?* (New York: Holt, Rinehart and Winston, 1972) p. ix.

9. Quoted in James Toback, "Longhorns and Longhairs," *Harpers Magazine,* November 1970, p. 72.

10. Richard D. Mandell, *The Nazi Olympics* (New York: Macmillan, 1971).

11. See "Diplomacy Through Sports," *Newsweek,* 4 September 1972, p. 42; Jerry Kirshenbaum, "Assembly Line for Champions," *Sports Illustrated* 45, 12 July 1976, pp. 56-65; Michael Novak, "War Games: Facts and Coverage,' *National Review,* 3 September 1976, pp. 953-54; Lynn Baker, "The Communist Assembly Line for Olympic Champions," *National Review,* 32, 16 May 1980, pp. 584-87. For a similar study of the Soviet Union's emphasis on sport, *see* Robin Herman, "The Soviet Union Views Sports Strength as a Power Tool," *New York Times,* 11 July 1976, p. 15S. *See also* Andrew Strenk, "Sport as an International Political and Diplomatic Tool," *Arena Newsletter* 1 (August 1977): 3-9.

12. Frank Deford, "The Once and Future Diplomat," *Sports Illustrated* 34, 1 March 1971, pp. 63-75.

13. Robert M. Goodhue, "The Politics of Sport: An Institutional Focus," *Proceedings of the North American Society for Sport History* (1974): 34-35.

14. See Donald W. Ball, "Olympic Games Competition: Structural Correlates of National Success," *International Journal of Comparative Sociology* 13 (September/December 1972): 186-99; Goodhart and Chataway, *War Without Weapons.*

15. Sandy Padwe, "Sports and Politics Must be Separate—At Least Some Politics, That is," *Philadelphia Inquirer,* 14 December 1971, p. 35.

16. Jerry Isenberg, *How Many Miles to Camelot?* p. 197.

17. Neil Amdur, "Garden to Hear Anthem at Track Meet, After All," *New York Times,* 14 January 1973, p. 29.

18. See J. D. Reed, "Gallantly Screaming," *Sports Illustrated* 46, 3 January 1977, pp. 52-60.

19. Tom Wicker, "Patriotism for the Wrong Ends," *New York Times,* 19 January 1973.

20. Thomas G. Sanders, "The Social Functions of Futebol," *American Universities Field Staff Reports,* East Coast South America Series, vol. XIV, no. 2, (July 1970): 7.

21. Ibid.; 8-9. *See also* Janet Lever, "Soccer: Opium of the Brazilian People," *Trans Action* 7 (December 1969): 36-43.

22. Paul Hoch, "The World of Playtime, USA," *Daily World,* 27 April 1972, p. 12.

23. For greater depth on the theme of sport as an opiate, *see* Paul Hoch, *Rip Off the Big Game* (New York: Doubleday, 1972); Jean-Marie Brohm, *Sport—A Prison of Measured Time,* trans. Ian Fraser (London: Ink Links, 1978); Jay J. Coakley, *Sport in Society* (St. Louis: C. V. Mosby, 1978), pp. 26-30.

24. See Ike Balbus, "Politics as Sports: The Political Ascendancy of the Sports Metaphor in

America," *Monthly Review* 26 (March 1975): 26-39.

25. *See* John N. Washburn, "Sport as a Soviet Tool, *Foreign Affairs* 34 (April 1956): 490-99.

26. *See* Brian M. Petrie, "Sport and Politics," in *Sport and Social Order,* ed., Donald W. Ball and John W. Loy, Jr. (Reading, Mass.: Addison-Wesley, 1975), pp. 199-207.

27. *See* Richard Lipsky, "Toward a Political Theory of American Sports Symbolism," *American Behavioral Scientist* 21 (January/February 1978): 345-60.

28. Excerpts from the press release of the address by the Vice President of the United States, Spiro Agnew, Birmingham, Alabama, 18 January 1972, pp. 5-6.

29. For a critique of the Agnew position, *see* Nicholas von Hoffman, "The Sport of Politicians," *Washington Post,* 24 January 1972, p. B1.

30. *See* William Johnson, "And Smile, Smile, Smile," *Sports Illustrated* 38, 4 June 1973, pp. 76-78; idem, "Courting Time in Peking," *Sports Illustrated* 39, 2 July 1973, pp. 12-15; idem, "Sport in China," *Sports Illustrated,* 39, 24 September 1973, part I, pp. 82-100, and 1 October 1973, part 2, pp. 42-53; Jonathan Kolatch, *Sport, Politics and Ideology in China* (Middle Village, N.Y.: Jonathan David, 1972).

31. William Johnson, "Faces on a New China Scroll," *Sports Illustrated* 39, 24 September 1973, p. 86.

32. Harry Edwards, *The Revolt of the Black Athlete* (New York: The Free Press, 1969), p. xv. *See also* Jack Scott and Harry Edwards, "After the Olympics: Buying Off Protest," *Ramparts* (November 1969): 16-21; Joel Thirer. "The Olympic Games as a Medium of Black Activism and Protest," *Review of Sport and Leisure* 1 (Fall 1976): 15-31; Neil Amdur, "Politics Was Force That Had To Be Reckoned With," *New York Times,* 30 December 1979, p. S7.

33. For a sample of the sources dealing with the political aspects of the Olympics, *see* Richard D. Mandell, *The Nazi Olympics* (New York: Macmillan, 1971); Richard Espy, *The Politics of the Olympic Games* (Berkeley: University of California Press, 1979); James A. Baley, "Suggestions for Removing Politics from the Olympic Games," *JOPER* 39 (March 1978): 73; the entire issue of *Journal of Sport and Social Issues* 2 (Spring/Summer 1978); Roger M. Williams, "Troubled Olympics," *Saturday Review,* 1 September 1979, pp. 12-16; Jonathan Evan Maslow, "Forty Years of Strife," *Saturday Review,* 1 September 1979; WNET/WETA. "The Olympics and Politics," *The Robert MacNeil Report,* show no. 1140, library no. 209, 16 July 1976; John Cheffers, "The Foolishness of Boycott and Exclusion in the Olympic Movement," *JOPER* 40 (February 1979): 44-51; "An Olympic Boycott?" *Newsweek,* 28 January 1980, pp. 20-28; Harry Edwards, *The Revolt of the Black Athlete* (New York: The Free Press, 1970); and Joel Thirer, "The Olympic Games as a Medium of Black Activism and Protest," *Review of Sport & Leisure* 1 (Fall 1976): 15-31.

34. For a selection of writing, on the economics of the Olympics, *see* Frank Swertlow, "TV Buys the Games," *Saturday Review,* 1 September 1979, pp. 20-21; J. Cicarelli and D. Kowarsky, "The Economics of the Olympic Games," *Business and Economic Dimensions* 9 (1973): 1-5; M. Auf der Maur, *The Billion-Dollar Game: Jean Drapeau and the 1976 Olympics* (Toronto: James, Lorimer, 1976); George Wright, "The Political Economy of the Montreal Olympics Games," *Journal of Sport and Social Issues* 2 (Spring/Summer 1978): 13-18; Paul Good, "The Selling of Our Olympic Teams," *Sport* 69 (July 1979): 30-36; and "A Small U.S. Town Takes on a Big Job—the Winter Olympics," *U.S. News & World Report,* 20 November 1978, pp. 89-91.

35. David Nelson, quoted in the sports section of *The Oregonian,* 28 December 1970, p. 1.

36. Quoted in John Underwood, "The Desperate Coach," *Sports Illustrated* 31, 24 August 1969, p. 71, © 1969 Time, Inc.

37. Rod Paige, "Racial Empathy and the White Coach," *Scholastic Coach* 41 (October 1971): 62; *see also* "Black Athletes Stir Campuses at Risk of Careers," *New York Times,* 16 November 1969, p. 1.

38. F. Melvin Cratsley, quoted in Underwood, "The Desperate Coach," pp. 70-71.

39. Tony Simpson, "Real Men, Short Hair," *Intellectual Digest* 4 (November 1973): 76, excerpted from *Texas Coach* (May 1973).

40. Don Viller, "Survey '71," *The Athletic Journal* (October 1971): 58.

41. Gordon L. James, "The Changing Nature of the Coaching Challenge," *Scholastic Coach* 41 (February 1972): 57.

323

42. Gerald S. Kenyon, "Certain Psychological and Cultural Characteristics Unique to Prospective Teachers of Physical Education," *The Research Quarterly* 36 (March 1965): 105-12.

43. S. M. Lipset, M. A. Trow, and E. C. Ladd, *Faculty Opinion Survey* (Carnegie Commission on Higher Education, n.d.).

44. Bruce C. Ogilvie and Thomas A. Tutko, "Self-Perception as Compared with Measured Personality of Male Physical Educators" in *Contemporary Psychology of Sport,* ed. Gerald S. Kenyon (Chicago: The Athletic Institute, 1970), pp. 73-77; *see also* Eldon E. Snyder, "Aspects of Social and Political Values of High School Coaches," *International Review of Sport Sociology* 8 (1973), pp. 73-87.

45. Michael Boman and D. Stanley Eitzen, "The Political Attitudes of Football Coaches," paper, (University of Kansas, 1973).

46. George H. Sage, "Value Orientation of American College Coaches Compared to Those of Male College Students and Businessmen." *Sport and American Society,* 2nd ed., ed. George H. Sage (Reading, Mass.: Addison-Wesley, 1974), pp. 207-28.

47. Ibid., pp. 222-23.

48. George H. Sage, "Occupational Socialization and Value Orientations of Athletic Coaches," *The Research Quarterly* 44 (October 1973): 269-77.

49. Many of the insights that follow come from George H. Sage," An Occupational Analysis of the College Coach," in *Sport and Social Order,* ed. Donald W. Ball and John W. Loy, Jr. (Reading, Mass.: Addison-Wesley, 1975), pp. 395-455; John D. Massengale, "Coaching as an Occupational Subculture," *Phi Delta Kappan* 61 (October 1974): 140-42; idem, "Occupational Role Conflict and the Teacher/Coach" (Paper presented at the Western Social Science Association meeting, Denver, 2 May 1975); George H. Sage, "Sociology of Physical Educator/Coaches: Personal Attributes Controversy," *Research Quarterly* 51 (March 1980): 110-21; idem, "Socialization of Coaches: Antecedents to Coaches' Beliefs and Behaviors," in *Sport and American Society,* 3rd ed., ed. George H. Sage, (Reading, Mass.: Addison-Wesley, 1980), pp. 160-69.

50. John W. Loy, Jr. and George H. Sage, "Social Origins, Academic Achievement, Athletic Achievement, and Career Mobility Patterns of College Coaches" (Paper presented at the Annual Meeting of the American Sociological Association, New Orleans, August 1972).

51. For a summary of the research findings, *see* D. Stanley Eitzen, *Social Structure and Social Problems (Boston: Allyn and Bacon, 1974), pp. 255-61.*

52. M. L. Kohn and C. Schooler, "Class, Occupation, and Orientation," *American Sociological Review* 34 (October 1969): 659-78.

53. *See* Morris Rosenberg, *Occupations and Values* (Glencoe, Ill.: The Free Press, 1967).

54. Massengale, "Coaching as an Occupational Subculture," p. 141.

55. From a statement on the policies concerning individual conduct, Shawnee Mission, East High School, Shawnee Mission, Kansas, 1973.

56. Harry Edwards, *Sociology of Sport* (Homewood, Ill.: Dorsey Press, 1973). p. 140.

57. Walter E. Schafer, "Sport, Socialization and the School: Toward Maturity or Enculturation?" (Paper presented at the Third International Symposium on the Sociology of Sport, Waterloo, Ont., August 1971), p. 6.

58. Richard A. Rehberg and Michael Cohen, "Political Attitudes and Participation in Extra-Curricular Activities with Special Emphasis on Interscholastic Activities," mimeographed (New York: State University of New York at Binghamton, n.d.).

59. Derrick J. Norton, "A Comparison of Political Attitudes and Political Participation of Athletes and Non-Athletes," (Master's thesis, University of Oregon, 1971).

60. Brian M. Petrie and Elizabeth L. Reid, "The Political Attitudes of Canadian Athletes," *Proceedings of the Fourth Canadian Psycho Motor Learning and Sports Psychology Symposium* (Waterloo, Ont.: University of Waterloo, 1972), pp. 514-30.

61. These first three reasons are taken from Walter E. Schafer, "Sport and Youth Counterculture: Contrasting Socialization Themes" in *Social Problems in Athletics,* ed. Daniel M. Landers (Urbana, Ill.: University of Illinois Press, 1976), pp. 183-200.

62. Bruce C. Ogilvie and Thomas A. Tutko, "Sport: If You Want to Build Character, Try Something Else," *Psychology Today* 5, 5 October 1971, pp. 61-63; *see also* Terry Nau, "The Games People Play," *The Daily Collegian* (Pennsylvania State University). 6 May 1971.

63. Jack Scott, *The Athletic Revolution* (New York: The Free Press, 1971), pp. 187-88. Reprinted with permission of Macmillan Publishing Co., Inc., from *The Athletic Revolution* by Jack Scott. Copyright © 1971 by The Free Press, a Division of Macmillan Publishing Co., Inc.

64. Ibid. *See also* "Out of Right Field," *Newsweek,* 5 January 1970, p. 35.

65. Leonard Shecter, *The Jocks* (New York: Paperback Library, 1969), p. 23.

The Myth Of Canada's National Sport

Kevin G. Jones, Ph.D.

T. George Vellathottam, M.A.

York University, Toronto

In 1867 Dr. George Beers, a Montreal dentist, and Secretary of the newly formed Canadian Lacrosse Association,[1] formulated the first uniform code of playing rules of the game.[2] Two years later he published *Lacrosse: The National Game of Canada,*[3] which gave a brief description of the game's fundamentals as well as the up-dated rules. This was the start of the "great Canadian myth" which has mislead millions of people over the past century or so into believing that this country had an official National Game* and that it was Lacrosse.

In the past, many theories were advanced as to the origin of this game but it is now almost beyond dispute that it developed among some Indian tribes of North America. "Baggataway" was the name most widely used by the natives for this activity. As early as 1636 the game, as played by the Indians, was described by Jean de Brebeuf, a Jesuit Missionary, who witnessed the play of the Hurons at the southern part of Georgian Bay in Ontario.[4] In his description Brebeuf used the term "crosse" which may have resulted from its similarities to a French game played with a "crosse" or stick[4] or because the curved playing stick resembled the bishop's crozier,[5] also spelled "crosse" in French.

Baggataway, according to E. J. Dopp, is the "oldest known athletic contest played on the North American Continent"[6] and was probably the most popular game of the aborigines, it being played in no less than forty eight North American tribes.[7] It was probably initiated for deriving fun, for developing the body and for training youth in close combat,[8] but there is also evidence that it was performed for medicinal purposes and as a religious rite.[9] In addition to its recreational value, many tribes used it to train their warriors while others used it in settling major conflicts between communities or tribes as an alternative to armed conflict.[10] Father Paul le Jeune reported in 1638 that the game was "played among Hurons to influence the weather and favourable weather depended upon the spirit with which the game was played."[11]

Baggataway was played in a number of different forms but basically

* Jones, K. G. and Vellathottam, T. G. "The Myth of Canada's National Sport," *CAHPER Journal, 41,* No. 1 (Sept.-Oct., 1974) 33-36. Printed by permission of the Canadian Association for Health, Physical education and Recreation.

the game was contested between tribes or villages. In the earlier days, the teams consisted of up to 1000 players and the goals usually were up to half a mile apart with no boundaries.[12] The game was started by either placing the ball on the ground with players running to it at a given signal[13] or more commonly by throwing the ball into the air while the players fought to catch it.[14] The aim of the game was to pass or carry the ball to or beyond the goal as often as possible and a "presiding chief" usually marked these goals.[15] The medicine men of the tribes acted as officials of the game, and it was played until sunset with a single contest sometimes lasting two or three days.[16]

One of the most important historical events associated with baggataway occurred during the time of the Pontiac Conspiracy. Pontiac, Chief of the Ottawas, went to Fort Michilimackinac (Michigan) with his men to help the English celebrate the birthday of King George III, on June 4, 1763. Part of the celebrations was to be a game of baggataway between the Ojibway and Sac Indians, played outside the fort walls, with the soldiers and squaws as spectators. Alexander Henry,[17] a famous fur trader of the time, reported the events of the game as follows:

In the ardour of the contest, the ball as has been suggested, if it cannot be thrown to the goal desired, is struck in any direction by the adversary. At such a moment, therefore nothing could be less liable to excite premature alarm, that the ball should be tossed over the pickets of the fort, not that having fallen there it should be followed on the instant, by all engaged in the game, as well as the one party as the other, all eager, all struggling, all shouting, all in the unrestrained pursuit of the rude athletic exercise. Nothing could be less fitted to excite premature alarm — nothing, therefore could be more happily devised under the circumstances, than a strategem like this and this was, in fact, the strategem which the Indians had employed, by which they had obtained possession of the fort.

After the ball has been tossed over the wall, the Indians ran after it and seized the tomahawks that had been hidden under the blankets of their squaws. The English were defeated and "the score of that game was an officer, twenty-four enlisted men and one civilian trader killed."[18] The remainder of the soldiers were taken prisoner.

By 1790 the game had become more of a sport than a religious rite or warrior training. The number of players was reduced to sixty a side and the goals to thirty feet wide and five hundred feet apart.[19] This of course reduced the incidence of rough play. Although the game had been witnessed by Europeans at very early times, it was not played by whites until the early eighteen forties when the Montreal Olympic Athletic Club, formed in 1842, played its first lacrosse match in 1844, under the patronage of the Governor General, Sir Charles Metcalfe.[20] On August 29, 1844, a match was reported between five Indian and seven Montrealer's during the Montreal Olympic Games, but the latter, despite their numerical strength and the fact that they supposedly were "ahead in agility and swiftness,"[21] were easily defeated by the Indians.[22]

Lacrosse steadily gained popularity and in 1856 the members of the Old

Olympic Club formed the Montreal Lacrosse Club, which was probably the first lacrosse club ever formed in the world.[23] Enthusiasm for the game continued to grow in Montreal resulting in the formation of the Hochelaga Club in 1858 and the Beaver Club in 1859.[24] By 1862 the Ottawa Lacrosse Club had been formed[25] and the following year Cornwall became the first town in Ontario to establish a club.[26]

By 1866 lacrosse had become popular in many parts of Quebec and Ontario both at the city and rural level. Matches between white and Indian teams were frequent, with the natives maintaining supremacy during this period.

Dr. William George Beers can rightfully be called the 'Father of Lacrosse'.[27] The following quote will indicate his passion for the game and give the reader an insight into his intentions to try and create for lacrosse the title of Canada's "official national game".[28]

I believe that I was the first to propose the game of Lacrosse as the National Game of Canada in 1859; and a few months preceding the Proclamation of Her Majesty, uniting the provinces of Canada, Nova Scotia and New Brunswick into one Dominion, a letter headed "Lacrosse — our National Field Game", published by me in the MONTREAL DAILY NEWS in April 1867, was printed off and distributed throughout the whole Dominion, and was copied into many of the public papers.

Beers was probably Canada's first sports writer, when as early as October 17, 1860, he wrote in the Montreal Gazette under the pseudonym of "Goal-Keeper". In 1860, he produced a brochure on lacrosse and also wrote several letters to the press to gain popularity for the game.[29] In June, 1867 he formulated the first Uniform Code of Playing Rules[30] which was officially adopted first by the Montreal Lacrosse Club[31] the most prominent lacrosse club during that period. Later it was used with slight modifications by the National Lacrosse Association of the National Convention held in Kingston, Ontario on September 26 of the same year.[32] Dr. Beers played a very prominent role in the formation of the National Lacrosse Association and was consequently elected Secretary of that organization.[33] In 1869, he published his book, "Lacrosse, the National Game of Canada", the first book ever written on the game.[34]

Dr. Beers never missed an opportunity to popularize the game. In 1876 he selected two teams, one from the Montreal Lacrosse Club and another from the Caughnawaga Indians and toured the British Isles.[35] The tour proved very successful to his ideals and gave tremendous impetus to the game in Canada. On a second trip to the British Isles in 1883, again, under the leadership of Dr. Beers, as many as sixty games were played during a period of ten weeks.[36] An interesting feature of this trip was the distribution of "50,000 illustrated papers and 800,000 fly sheets"[37] with most of the information contained in these papers being written by Dr. Beers.[38]

An excellent writer, a gifted organizer and an outstanding player with abilities to teach, coach and officiate the game, he won great respect among lacrosse enthusiasts in the country. He also enjoyed a high status in society, being a prominent citizen of Montreal and a dentist by profession. Last but not least, he was also friendly with Sir John A. Macdonald,[39] Canada's Prime Minister during that period.

In short, Dr. Beers was in an excellent position to effectively publicize the myth that lacrosse was the national game of Canada and this, he did with remarkable success. The popularity of lacrosse during the confederation year, 1867, must have also helped in the acceptance of this idea.

The myth went mostly undisputed for nearly a century until Douglas Fisher, a journalist who made a thorough research on the topic reported:[40]

You have a new twist on the lacrosse myth. There was no Confederation Conference in 1867 at Charlottetown, or anywhere else. About 15 years ago I covered all available sources on this subject — The Montreal Gazette of 1860-70, The Globe, Kingston Whig, The Montreal Witness, plus Ottawa papers and The Canada Gazette. Conclusion — no political gathering with legislative or declatory powers ever said anything about lacrosse in this period. My explanation on the origin of the myth about lacrosse being our National Game by Act of Parliament leads to Dr. George Beers.

Again, about ten years ago, Jack Roxburgh, a Liberal Member of Parliament also became curious about the issue, examined the parliamentary records and "found no record of legislation, orders-in-council, or even debate on the subject of lacrosse."[41] Being a former president of the Canadian Hockey Association, he wished to see hockey as the national game of Canada and consequently, introduced a private member's bill to this effect. This bill brought strong opposition from a lacrosse fan who introduced a similar bill to designate lacrosse as the national sport. However, neither bill was voted on and thus, Canada has no official national game to this day.[42]

BIBLIOGRAPHY

1. The Montreal Gazette, October 3, 1867.
2. Alexander M. Weyand and Milton R. Roberts, The Lacrosse Story, Baltimore, Maryland: H. and A. Herman, 1865, p. 17.
3. W. G. Beers, Lacrosse, The National Game of Canada, Montreal: Dawson Brother, 1869.
4. Alexander M. Weyand and Milton R. Roberts, op. cit., p. 5.
5. R. W. Henderson, Ball, Bat and Biship, New York: Rockport Press Inc., 1947, p. 201.
6. E. J. Dopp, Short History of Lacrosse, Spalding's Official Box Lacrosse Guide, n.p., n.d., p. 41.
7. A. M. Weyand and M. R. Roberts, op. cit., p. 4.
8. W. G. Beers, op. cit., p. 8.
9. R. W. Henderson, op. cit., p. 198.
10. Ibid., p. 8.
11. Ibid., p. 9.
12. Tad Stanwick, Lacrosse, New York: A. S. Barnes and Co., Inc., 1940, p. 1.
13. W. G. Beers, op. cit., p. 23.
14 George Catlin, Letters and Notes on the Manners, Customs and Condition of the North American Indians, Vol. 2 (London: The Egyptian Hall, Piccadily, 1871), p. 125.
15. W. G. Beers, op. cit., p. 15.
16. A. M. Weyand and M. R. Roberts, op. cit., p. 7.
17. Alexander Henry, Travels and Adventures in Canada and the Indian Territories 1760-76, Toronto: Geo. N. Morang and Co. Ltd., 1901, p. 77.
18. A. M. Weyand and M. R. Roberts, op. cit., p. 10.
19. Ibid., p. 11.

20. T. G. Vellathottam, A History of Lacrosse in Canada Prior to 1914, Unpublished Master's Thesis, University of Alberta, 1968, p. 27.

21. The Montreal Gazette, August 29, 1844.

22. P. L. Lindsay, A History of Sport in Canada, 1807-1867, Unpublished Ph.D. Thesis, University of Alberta, 1969, p. 116.

23. A. M. Weyand and M. R. Roberts, op. cit., pp. 14-15.

24. Ibid.

25. Ibid., p. 16.

26. Michael A. Salter, "The History of Lacrosse", unpublished paper, University of Alberta, Edmonton, 1966, p. 10.

27. The Globe and Mail, December 27, 1900.

28. W. G. Beers, op. cit., p. 57.

29. A. M. Weyand and M. R. Roberts, op. cit., p. 17.

30. T. G. Vellathottam, op. cit., p. 31.

31. The Montreal Gazette, July 17, 1867.

32. T. G. Vellathottam, op. cit., p. 31.

33. Ibid., p. 35.

34. A. M. Weyand and M. R. Roberts, op. cit., p. 17.

35. The Montreal Gazette, June 27, 1876.

36. T. G. Vellathottam, op. cit., pp. 73-74.

37. A. M. Weyand and M. R. Roberts, op. cit., p. 41.

38. Ibid.

39. 'By Dick Beddoes', The Globe and Mail, December 20, 1968.

40. Ibid.

41. Mike Law, The Development of Lacrosse in Canada, Unpublished paper, University of Alberta, Edmonton, 1969, p. 47.

42. Ibid.

Reference Group Theory And The Economics Of Professional Sport*

Steve Lerch
Radford University

The recent drastic escalation of salaries paid to upper-echelon (i.e., "major league") professional athletes has been decried by nearly all connected with sports. Owners of professional franchises are nearly unanimous in condemning athletes as "selfish," "greedy," unconcerned about the "good of the game," etc. They express fears that increased payrolls will have to be met through increasing ticket prices; such increases, they say, will drive fans from stadiums and arenas and will eventually "kill the sport." (Obviously, they are less likely to note that they are in large part responsible for the increases themselves — or that their ultimate desire is to minimize salaries in order to maximize team profits.) Sportswriters often question the necessity of rewarding so handsomely the athletes they watch perform — athletes who are sometimes viewed, after all, as "only playing a game." Fans hear and read the lamentations of owners and sportswriters that high salaries are pricing them out of the ticket-buying market and that "it isn't sport anymore, it's business." Even certain athletes are asking themselves whether they may (in conjunction with the owners) be "killing the goose that lays the golden egg."

Most observers of professional sports in the United States have a rudimentary understanding of and appreciation for the salaries paid to "star" athletes. The mid-1970s court decisions which provided athletes with new negotiating freedoms — especially the right of "free agency" (or the threat of same, to use as a bargaining lever with one's present team) — led to a near immediate salary windfall for many professional athletes. Top athletes — those proclaimed most "valuable" on and off the field — earn whatever the sports market will bear. Questions are asked, however, about the "non-star" athletes: how is it that many with only moderately successful careers have asked for (and been rewarded with) multi-year, multi-million dollar contracts? In baseball alone, for example, recent years have seen the Giants

*Lerch, S. "Reference Group Theory and the Economics of Professional Sport," in A. Dunleavy, A. Miracle, and R. Rees (Eds.), *Study in the Sociology of Sport*, Texas Christian University Press, 1981, pp. 221-235. Reprinted by permission of the publisher.

give a virtually-lame Rennie Stennett $3 million over five years, the Braves pay a no-longer-fierce Al Hrabosky $2.2 million over five years, and the Angels give nearly $2.5 million in a five year contract to a sore-armed Bruce Kison (Chass, 1980:52). What has driven the salaries of even mediocre athletes to such an astonishingly high level?

REFERENCE GROUP THEORY AND SPORT

Both the upward salary spiral (e.g., baseball's average salary up 511% since 1970, basketball's up 450% over the same period, according to *Inside Sports* July, 1980) and the reactions to the increase can be at least partially explained in terms of reference group theory. This theory, which is basically an extension of Mead's notion of the "generalized other," was given substance by Merton, who applied the theory to the data of *The American Soldier*. Merton summarizes reference group theory as follows (1967:234):

> In general, then, reference group theory aims to systematize the determinants and consequence of those processes of evaluation and self-appraisal in which the individual takes the values or standards of other individuals and groups as a comparative frame of reference.

Phrased more succinctly, reference groups are those against which we evaluate ourselves — groups which we utilize as standards to tell ourselves how well (or how poorly) we are doing. Reference groups may also serve a normative function through setting norms for behavior.

Although the authors of *The American Soldier* do not use the term "reference group," reference group concepts play an important part in the interpretative apparatus they utilize (Merton, 1967:225). Specifically, the authors found that the soldier's evaluation of his own situation depended in large part upon comparisons he made between himself and others. For example, compared with their unmarried friends, married men felt they were making a great sacrifice by becoming soldiers; compared with black civilians they saw in local towns, black soldiers in the South felt that they enjoyed wealth and dignity (Bassis, Gelles, and Levine, 1980:140). In effect, says Merton (1967:229-230), status attributes such as race, marital status, educational achievement and age are utilized as independent variables. The situation of the soldier (e.g., attitude toward induction or appraisal of chances for promotion) is the dependent variable, and the frame of reference becomes the intervening variable.

One finding from *The American Soldier* which is noteworthy for our analysis of the situation in professional sport is that there are at least three different frames of reference which can be utilized. In some cases, the attitudes of the soldiers with regard to their own situation depended upon comparison with other soldiers with whom they were in *actual association*. A second basis of comparison was with others of the *same status or same social category;* a third frame of reference was those of a *different status or social category*. In more general terms, our reference groups may be "in-groups," either narrowly (actual association) or more broadly (same status or social category) defined, or "out-groups," in which we compare ourselves to those to whom we are dissimilar.

In this paper, of course, we are concerned with explaining reactions toward increasing salaries in professional sports. (We shall deal below with the reasons for such increases.) The thrust of our contention is that the differing attitudes on the part of athletes, fans, sportswriters, and owners (i.e., the dependent variable) can be partially explained through status as an athlete or a non-athlete (the independent variable) with one's frame of reference as the intervening variable. Specifically, the argument is this: athletes tend to use in-groups as their frame of reference in judging whether or not their salaries are equitable. These in-groups are sometimes other athletes with whom they are in actual association; e.g., the athlete who compares himself to teammates who earn more/less than he. Other times athletes compare themselves to those of the same status or social category. These terms can be broadly or narrowly defined, ranging from those playing the same position on one's team to all other professional athletes in the same sport. Clearly, such in-group comparisons will yield very different attitudes toward salaries than non-athletes' frames of reference; these individuals utilize out-group comparisons. Those in disparate social positions are likely to take a negative view of the high salaries in professional sports — since they are comparing them to their own salaries which are almost inevitably less extravagant.

There is, of course, another way to analyze the attitudes athletes and non-athletes have toward salaries in professional sports. Non-athletes, it can be argued, have the tendency to view salaries in an *absolute* sense; i.e., by looking only at the monetary figures involved. A five year contract for $4.5 million seems outrageous because the numbers involved are staggering. The athlete himself, however, is more likely to evaluate his salary *relative* to other members of his reference group — other professional athletes making equally large (as objectively measured) salaries, especially those in the same sport, on the same team, with the same abilities, having the same amount of experience, playing the same position, etc. Comparing the income of the average professional athlete to that of the average assistant professor, for example — and coming to the conclusion that the former is over- and the latter underpaid — is as useless as comparing the assistant professor's salary to that of the average cook at a fast-food restaurant and reaching the same conclusion. Only within group salary comparisons are truly useful.

RELATIVE DEPRIVATION AND SPORT SALARIES

The use of these in-group comparisons, it is argued, is in large part responsible for the upward spiral of salaries in professional sports. Athletes expressing displeasure with their salaries do so not by utilizing absolute dollar figures involved in contracts, but rather by examining their salaries relative to other members of their reference groups. In sociological parlance, the athletes are experiencing relative deprivation.

According to Merton, relative deprivation can provisionally be regarded as a special concept in reference group theory (1967:235). Although Merton does not state a formal definition of the concept, it has been variously defined as "a sense of deprivation in relation to some standard" (Lauer,

1978:250), "actors' perception of discrepancy between their value expectations and their value capabilities" (Gurr, 1970:24), or "feeling you have
gotten a bad deal in comparison with other people, especially in comparison
with your reference group" (Babbie, 1977:526). Basically, then, the concept
suggests that the important determinant of satisfaction or discontent is not
the absolute or "objective" level of achievement or deprivation but is rather
the level of achievement *relative* to some standard employed by the individual as a basis of comparison or self-evaluation (Crawford and
Naditch, 1970:208).

For example, de Tocqueville (1955:175-77) noted that just prior to the
French Revolution, the economic situation in France was actually improving (the objective situation). However, the French were apparently comparing their situation to some other standard than their past, and relative to
this standard, there was widespread dissatisfaction. In more modern times,
the concept of relative deprivation has frequently been utilized to explain
the situation of poverty-stricken Americans, especially members of minority groups. Robertson (1980:182), for example, has noted that people are
poor not only in relation to their needs but also in relation to those who are
not poor. Thus, the poor in America can see the affluent all around them,
and they evaluate their poverty not only in relation to their basic needs but
also in relation to the surfeit of wealth in the surrounding society (Miller,
1968:182-83).

Professional athletes, of course, are by no means deprived in any objective sense. However, they may perceive deprivation as they compare
themselves to other athletes. In Merton's terms, "'deprivation' is the incidental and particularized component of the concept of relative deprivation, whereas the more significant nucleus of the concept is its stress upon
social and psychological experience as 'relative'" (1967:235). Thus,
although fans and sportswriters may be astounded that an athlete can claim
he is underpaid at $100,000 or more per season, from the athlete's point of
view, he may very well be experiencing relative deprivation.

Here, again, we see the importance of one's frame of reference in the
explanation of variations in attitudes. Davis (1959: 283) discusses in-group/
out-group comparisons and their impact upon attitudes. His assumptions
(made with reference to *The American Soldier* data), are no less valuable as
applied to the situation of professional sports. First is an in-group comparison:

If a person (ego) compares himself with a person (alter) when ego
and alter differ in their deprivation, ego experiences a subjective feeling
opposite in direction to the evaluation of alter's condition.

a. When a deprived person compares himself with a non-deprived,
the resulting state will be called "relative deprivation."

b. When a non-deprived person compares himself with a deprived
person, the resulting state will be called "relative gratification."

The first case, of course, is the one which most concerns us here. The
shortstop who enters negotiation with the desire to become the "highest
paid shortstop in baseball" or the defensive end who complains that his

334

salary is lower than that of other ends of his ability and experience are both experiencing relative deprivation.

Importantly, for the present discussion, players are now privy to detailed and accurate information regarding what other players are making. This fact is responsible for a major part of the escalation in salaries. Kaplan (1981:36) explains how this occurs, using baseball as an example:

Before salary figures were published, a player had to take an owner's word that his income measured up well with that of his teammates. In the mid-'60s Dodger player representative Ron Fairly was a satisfied customer. The Dodgers had assured him that among his teammates only Sandy Koufax and Don Drysdale made more than he. But when the Players Association asked Fairly to poll the players, he discovered he was in 12th place. Fairly had been had.

Today all figures are known, and players can spot lesser performers who are making more. It's an irresistible argument for an increase. No wonder almost all major leaguers are well-paid.

It only takes one owner, therefore, desperate to fill a need on his team and willing to go to any expense to do so, to "raise the scale" for all athletes in the sport. One of the most obvious recent examples of this phenomenon occurred when owner Ted Turner of The Atlanta Braves signed free agent outfielder Claudell Washington, a career .279 hitter, to a five year, $3.5 million contract. Other ballplayers' frame of reference was changed before the ink dried on Washington's contract. Similarly, ever-increasing calls by athletes for contract renegotiation — words that are anathema to owners — are based upon athletes comparing their contracts (with which they were once evidently pleased) to those more recently signed by their counterparts.

Examples of "relative gratification" in sport are far more difficult to come by. Theoretically, this is because only the highest paid will ever feel "gratified"; all others have the potential to compare themselves to those better rewarded economically. Such expressions of "gratification" are most likely to emanate from player agents — sometimes, as they inflate the contracts of the athletes they represent in an effort to make themselves appear better negotiators.

Davis also postulates an assumption about out-group comparisons (1959:283):

If a person (ego) compares himself with a person (alter) in an out-group when ego and alter differ in their deprivation, ego will experience a feeling toward alter's group opposite in direction to the evaluation of alter's condition.

a. When a deprived person compares himself with a non-deprived out-group member, the resulting attitude toward the out-group will be called "relative subordination."

b. When a non-deprived person compares himself with a deprived out-group member, the resulting attitude toward the out-group will be called "relative superiority."

Given the present nature of the economics of sport, the deprived person is almost invariably the non-athlete. Thus, the first case is one we have mentioned above — the non-athlete (fan, sportswriter, etc.) who compares his salary to the athlete's. He experiences "subordination" because he almost inevitably comes up on the short end of such a comparison. Furthermore, the feelings of subordination may be heightened by his evaluation of the importance of the task given the size of the remuneration: the social service performed by the $15,000 per year high school teacher is by most objective measures more vital than that performed by the $150,000 per year middle linebacker.

The latter case is the reverse — the non-deprived athlete comparing his situation to that of the deprived non-athlete. Although this may actually occur frequently, the public is alerted to it only occasionally, as when athletes remark "I realize how lucky I am" or "I really don't deserve this kind of money." Too many expressions of "relative superiority," of course, may have the consequence of alienating sports fans and diminishing their interest in the sport.

THE ECONOMIC FUTURE OF SPORT: IS REVOLUTION IN THE OFFING?

One of the more interesting applications of the concept of relative deprivation has been as an explanatory factor in revolutions; Davies (1962), among others, has discussed this phenomenon. First, he notes that Marx's most famous thesis — that progressive degradation of the industrial working class would finally reach the point of despair and inevitable revolt — is not the only one Marx fathered. Marx also described, as a precondition of widespread unrest, not progressive degradation of the proletariat but rather an improvement in workers' economic condition which did not keep pace with the growing welfare of capitalists and therefore produced social tension (Davies, 1962:5). Likewise, de Tocqueville utilizes this latter thesis in his study of the French Revolution:

Revolutions are not always brought about by a gradual decline from bad to worse. Nations that have endured patiently and almost unconsciously the most overwhelming oppression often burst into rebellion against the yoke the moment it begins to grow lighter. The regime which is destroyed by a revolution is almost always an improvement on its immediate predecessor . . . Evils which are patiently endured when they seem inevitable become intolerable when once the idea of escape from them is suggested (de Tocqueville, 1955:176-77).

Davies, then, concludes that revolutions are more likely to occur when a prolonged period of objective economic and social development is followed by a short period of sharp reversal (1962:6). This situation is diagrammed in Figure 1. Davies explains Dorr's Rebellion of 1842, the Russian Revolution of 1917, and the Egyptian Revolution of 1952 with his "J-curve" theory of revolutions; others have utilized the theory to explain the urban riots in the United States in the 1960s.

The J-curve theory is also applicable to the economics of professional sport. Actually, the theory may be implemented to speculate on the econ-

336

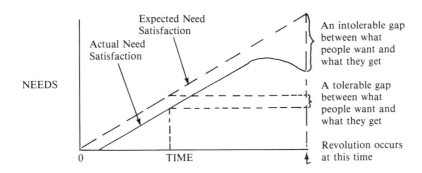

omic future of sport from the perspective of both athletes (individually and in groups) and non-athletes.

Individual athletes, for example, comparing their salaries to those of their peers, may come to the conclusion that their salaries (actual need satisfaction) are not keeping pace with those of their contemporaries of equal or lesser abilities, experience, etc. Thus, their actual needs satisfaction is falling short of their expected needs satisfaction. Although the actual need satisfaction may not resemble a "J" — since salaries in sport rarely decline — there is still the potential for an ever-widening gap between what the individual feels he deserves and what he actually receives. Typically, the "revolution" that occurs by individual athletes when an intolerable gap is reached is the walkout, holdout, or "retirement" until the gap is closed. (See Figure 2.)

From the group perspective, the theory can be utilized to explain recent "job actions" taken in various sports; e.g., the baseball strike of the summer of 1981. In the past 15 years, the players have grown accustomed to a series of successes both at the bargaining table and in the courtroom. In the most recent negotiations over baseball's "Basic Agreement," the owners apparently decided to take a hard line approach and refuse to make further concessions. Thus the previous successes had raised the expectations for continued victories; when the owners decided not to "give in" (and, indeed, actually attempted to recover from past "losses"), an intolerable gap between expectations and reality resulted, and the players went on strike. (See Figure 3.)

Far more vital to the future of professional sport is the potential for a revolution by non-athletes, especially fans. One of the by-products of increasing salaries paid to athletes is the expectation by fans of higher quality performances on the part of both individual athletes and the teams for which they participate. These expectations, of course, are heightened by owners and sportswriters; athletes receiving large salaries continually are asked to "prove" they are deserving of such huge monetary rewards. If the

337

Figure 2: *Expectations and Actual Salaries, Individual Athletes*

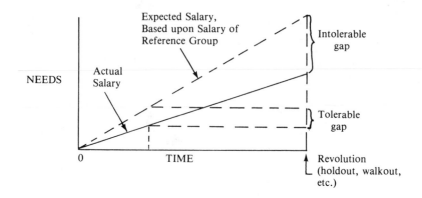

fans' expectations are not met — if an intolerable gap develops between what people want (in terms of winning percentage, championships, etc.) and what they get, the potential for a revolution is present. Furthermore, since salaries have more than outstripped performances, the potential for such a revolution is ever-increasing. (See Figure 4.)

We can speculate that the revolution may take one of two forms: first, dissatisfied fans may simply refuse to attend sports contests, causing severe financial problems for sports franchises. The most obvious recent example of this type of revolution may be the situation of the Philadelphia 76ers of the National Basketball Association. Since 1975, team management has acquired a variety of superstars; we can assume that they are being paid accordingly. (We know for a fact that the average NBA salary has risen from $93,000 in 1975 to $180,000 in 1980. The 76ers surely are among the highest paid teams in the sport.) Over this period, the team has met some expectations: winning percentage for the regular season has increased steadily (with one season's exception) from .110 in 1972-73 to .756 in 1980-81. However, the ultimate goal — an NBA championship — has eluded the 76ers. Meanwhile, attendance increased through the 1977-78 season; that year, the highly regarded 76ers finished first in their division but lost in the conference finals in post-season play. Apparently, this, combined with a small decline in winning percentage in 1978-79, produced the intolerable gap between expectations and performance: attendance has declined steadily since 1977-78, and the franchise changed ownership in 1980.

The second form of revolution is more serious: violence directed at individual athletes who fail to meet expectations. We must note, of course, that the violent fan may be no more than the intoxicated lout who indiscriminately directs violence at any player, or who sees violent acts (e.g., hurling objects at athletes) as a type of recreation (e.g., see how close to hitting him one can come). Thus, our theory by no means explains all sports violence. However, we can speculate that certain instances of violence are likely to be directed against those players deemed responsible for team fail-

338

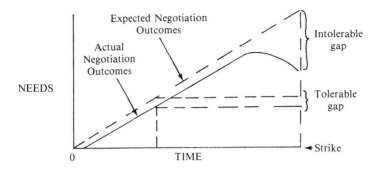

ures — again, sportswriters and owners are at least partially responsible for determining culpability. At any rate, fans are most likely to vent their frustrations over losses at athletes they think should be able to do the most to prevent them — those receiving the highest salaries, of whom the most is expected. For example, Dave Parker, outfielder of the Pittsburgh Pirates, has been the target of batteries, bolts, and bullets thrown from the stands in Pittsburgh as a result of his failure to meet the expectations that attend to a $1 million annual salary.

Figure 4: *Fan Expectations and Rewards*

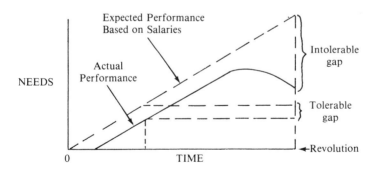

IMPLICATIONS

Although reference group theory and relative deprivation have some utility in explaining increasing salaries in sports and the reaction to them, as many questions are raised by this discussion as are answered. For example, why does one choose a particular reference group? In the present context,

339

which in-groups are chosen as reference groups by athletes — teammates, holders of the same position, those of similar ability, experience, etc.? Does the athlete always choose the reference group in which he appears to fare the worst — so he can plead "deprivation" and increase his salary? These and other questions remain to be answered.

Similarly, we may predict revolutions of fans and athletes based upon felt relative deprivation. However, we cannot pinpoint a time at which the gap becomes intolerable, nor predict with any accuracy the form of the revolution. Neither can we distinguish a quantifiable relationship between athletes' salaries and fans' performance expectations. Moreover, large-scale fan revolutions, though they may plague individual teams (e.g., attendance declines) or athletes (e.g., violence), may not be on the horizon for professional sports in general. On the other hand, declining attendance following the baseball strike may be an indication that some fans have reached an intolerable gap between their expectations of athletes and realities delivered. At any rate, the sports establishment would be wise to pay heed to the widening gap between salaries and the expectations they engender — which are theoretically limitless — and the performances which are limited by man's athletic abilities.

REFERENCES

Babbie, E. G., 1977 Society by Agreement. Belmont, California: Wadsworth.

Bassis, M. S., R. J. Gelles and A. Levine, 1980 Sociology, An Introduction. New York: Random House.

Chass, M., 1980 "Baseball's consumer guide to free agents." Inside Sports 2 (November 30): 51-54.

Crawford, T. J. and M. Naditch, 1970 "Relative deprivation, powerlessness, and militancy: the psychology of social protest." Psychiatry 33: 208-223.

Davies, J. C., 1962 "Toward a theory of revolution." American Sociological Review 27: 5-19.

Davis, J. A., 1959 "A formal interpretation of the theory of relative deprivation." Sociometry 22: 282-298.

de Tocqueville, A., 1955 The Old Regime and the French Revolution. New York: Anchor Books.

Gurr, T. R., 1970 Why Men Rebel. Princeton: Princeton University Press.

Inside Sports Magazine, 1980 "What the average player makes." Inside Sports 2 (July 31) 19.

Kaplan, J., 1981 "Is there a ceiling?" Sports Illustrated 54 (January 5): 35-38.

Lauer, R. H., 1978 Social Problems and the Quality of Life. Dubuque: Wm. C. Brown.

Merton, R. K., 1967 Social Theory and Social Structure. New York: The Free Press.

Miller, H., 1968 "Changes in the number and composition of the poor." In E. C. Budd (ed.), Inequality and Poverty. New York: Norton.

Robertson, I., 1980 Social Problems. New York: Random House.

SECTION VI
PSYCHOLOGY AND PHYSICAL ACTIVITY
WHAT IS PSYCHOLOGY?

In 1890 William James referred to psychology as the science of mental life. During the twentieth century, psychologists began to realize that they could never be certain as to what went on inside of a person's mind and that mental events could only be studied by listening to reports given by the individuals who experienced them. Recognition of the fact that no two persons perceive things in exactly the same way led to the conclusion that scientific study of the mind was impossible. Thus by the 1950s psychology was being defined as "the scientific study of individual behaviour". An individual's behaviour could be viewed objectively and described fairly consistently by others. Although some psychologists (known as "behaviourists") were content to "explain" such behaviour by simply pointing to visible antecedent conditions, others felt that adequate explanations required inferences about what was taking place inside the individual's mind. This latter group of scholars, known as cognitive psychologists defined psychology as "the scientific study of individual behaviour in terms of underlying mental processes". A comparison of the models developed by each of these schools of thought is presented below.

The model of psychology advanced by behaviourists

STIMULUS	$\longrightarrow$	RESPONSE
(antecedent condition)	$\longrightarrow$	*(consequent behaviour)*
e.g., the presence		*tennis performance*
of an audience	$\longrightarrow$	*improves*

On the other hand, cognitive psychologists would advance the following model:

I	*II*	*III*
STIMULUS $\longrightarrow$	INTERVENING $\longrightarrow$ VARIABLES(S)	RESPONSE
antecedent $\longrightarrow$ *condition*	*e.g., underlying* $\longrightarrow$ *attributes and processes* *"In the head"* *variables*	*consequent* *behaviour*
e.g., presence of $\longrightarrow$ *an audience*	*e.g., arousal increases* $\longrightarrow$	*tennis performance* *improves*

This latter group of scientists attempts to explain why Class I variables produce Class III responses by suggesting the presence of Class II variables. Some studies are devoted to segments of this chain e.g., I $\longrightarrow$ II relationships, I $\longrightarrow$ III relationships or II $\longrightarrow$ III relationships.

Psychology is often referred to as a hybrid science since part of this disci-

pline is biological in nature (e.g., physiological psychology) and part of it is social in nature (e.g., social psychology). There are however several other "branches" of psychology. Some of the more often cited are developmental, comparative, abnormal, applied and humanistic.

WHAT IS SOCIAL PSYCHOLOGY?

"The scientific study of individual behavior as a function of social stimuli" (Shaw and Costanzo, 1970).

"The scientific study of the experience and behavior of individuals in relation to social stimulus situations" (Sherif and Sherif, 1969).

"An attempt to understand and explain how the thoughts, feelings, and behavior of individuals are influenced by the actual, imagined or implied presence of others" (Allport, 1968).

These three definitions, indicate that in order for psychology to be social the stimulus (i.e., antecedent condition) must be social in nature. Although one could "cut the pie" of social psychology in many ways the traditional divisions advanced by Shaw and Costanzo (1970) are:

1. Social Influence Processes (e.g., the influence of onlookers)
2. Shared Influence Processes (e.g., attitudes)
and
3. Group Interaction (e.g., group cohesion)

HOW ARE PSYCHOLOGY AND PHYSICAL ACTIVITY RELATED?

For the most part, the association between psychology and physical activity has developed out of a desire on the part of practitioners in various areas of physical activity to know how to influence participation and performance in physical activity. Two major exceptions to this generalization exist. The first is in regard to an area known as motor learning where interest on the part of psychologists has matched or exceeded that of physical activity practitioners. Similarly, social psychologists for many years have been interested in the social influence process of competition.

Out of these interests developed a sub-discipline known as the psychology of physical activity. Some would refer to this field as the "psychology of sport". However, this author would point to studies dealing with attitudes toward exercise and the influence of an audience on treadmill performance and conclude that the sub-discipline cannot be restricted to only highly organized, competitive sport, but instead must be associated with the broader term "physical activity".

The psychology of physical activity is therefore "the scientific study of individual behaviour leading to, occurring during or resulting from involvement in physical activity". Those of us who label ourselves as cognitive psychologists would tack on the end "in terms of underlying mental attributes and/or processes". The scope of this field is extremely broad and in-

342

cludes (a) motor learning, (b) motor development, (c) motor control, (d) social psychology of physical activity, and (e) "other non-social" psychology of physical activity. The first three of these areas are subsumed in a field a field known in many circles as psycho-motor behaviour (PMB) whereas the latter two areas are often inappropriately referred to as sports psychology.

WHAT READINGS IN PSYCHOLOGY OF PHYSICAL ACTIVITY ARE INCLUDED IN THIS COLLECTION?

The last five readings in the text deal with social psychology of physical activity topics.

1. There is an article dealing with a social influence process (i.e., the influence of an individual simultaneously performing the same task as another person).

2. There are two articles related to a shared individual process (i.e., one dealing with attitudes while the other is about attitude change).

3. Finally there are two articles which examine group interaction. The first deals with the development of group motivation while the second examines the relationship between group cohesion and group performance in sport.

Aside from an introduction to the psychology of physical activity the remaining articles included in Section VI deal with psychological variables and processes in which the antecedent conditions are not necessarily social. Specifically these variables and processes are: (a) personality, (b) motivation, (c) arousal, (d) aggression, and (e) perception.

Psychology and Sport: Fear of Applying

John H. Salmela

The psychologist and the athlete or coach have always been uneasy partners. Neither the psychologist or the athlete/coach has had much understanding of the long-term concerns of the other, and hence they have had little respect for each other. Too often in the past psychological researchers (perhaps concentrating on graduate thesis or academic advancement) have borrowed inappropriate tools from experimental psychology and applied them indiscriminately to problems in sport. The coach and athlete have legitimately complained that psychologists have made use of them with no concern for their long-range needs. But before laying all the blame on the psychological researchers it must be said that until recently a clear statement of the needs of coach and athlete was wanting.

In working with the Canadian Gymnastic Federation I have learned that this sport federation, along with many others, has a genuine desire to know more about the psychological parameters of the problems of human well-being and excellence in performance. As noted in chapter 1, the National Sport Governing Bodies in Ottawa have expressed a strong desire for collaboration in the area of sport psychology. Researchers in the areas of skill acquisition and sport psychology are also, I believe, becoming more concerned with the problems of sportspeople.

In this chapter it is my aim to analyze the potential utility of the research that has already been done in the psychology of sport and physical activity by North American scientists, to attempt to evaluate the possibility of a successful partnership between the coach and/or athlete and the researcher, and to propose some ways of bringing the academic disciplines and the field of application closer together. To do so I have examined the legacy of the research published by the Canadian Society for Psychomotor Learning and Sport Psychology in its proceedings and by its American counterpart, the North American Society for the Psychology of Sport and Physical Activity. Brent Rushall, former president of the Canadian society, did a similar survey of the literature and reported on the sport psychology area at the society's fifth symposium in Montreal in 1973; at that time he indicated that there were only a few sport psychologists working in the applied area in Canada.

I have analyzed the content of the research articles of the Canadian

*Salmela, J. H. "Psychology and Sport: Fear of Applying", pp. 13-21 in P. Klavoia and J. Daniel (Eds.), *Coach, Athlete, and the Sport Psychologist*. Toronto: School of Physical and Health Education, University of Toronto, 1979. Reprinted by permission of the publisher.

proceedings (Williams and Wankel, 1973; Rushall, 1975; Bard *et al.,* 1975; Kerr, 1977; Landry and Orban, 1978), as well as those of the American society (Wade and Martens, 1974; Landers, 1975; Christina and Landers, 1978; Landers and Christina, 1978; Roberts and Newell, 1979) so that this information can be compared with the projected needs of coaches and athletes. The content of the ten publications within the broad categories of motor learning and motor performance is outlined in Table 1 and within the areas of sport psychology and social psychology of physical activity in Table 2.

RESULTS

Overall, there are 1.8 times as many studies in motor performance as in motor learning. The motor performance research has mainly been in the area of information processing in motor skills in which man's perceptual, decision-making, and response capacities have been evaluated experimentally. For the most part, attention has been on the execution of the response, using short-term motor memory and motor control paradigms. Whiting (1978), in a recent paper, questioned the disproportionate attention directed towards response execution, when in reality a great deal of the variance in motor skill results from perceptual and intellectual processes. In publications surveyed here, 54.5 percent of the performance research was in either motor memory or control. Only a small number of papers were directly related to the application of skill learning in sport, although it could be said that some of the non-applied papers would contribute to the eventual understanding of the theory underlying these phenomena. Finally, it should be noted that the predominant research vehicle in both the motor learning area (feedback theory and practice of simple tasks) and the research in motor performance (motor short-term memory and motor control) was a simple motor task, often involving a movement of only a few centimeters.

Papers in sport psychology and the social psychology of physical activity are analyzed in Table 2. The total number of papers in these two disciplines (144) is slightly lower than in the motor learning and performance field (188). However, the field of study is related to sport activity to a greater degree, by definition perhaps. The topics of personality of athletes, sport attitudes, competitive anxiety, achievement, motivation, and aggression make up 60.4 percent of the total. The area of personality was studied most frequently, a finding that was also reported by Groves, Heekin, and Banks (1978) for articles published in the *International Journal of Sport Psychology.* The great majority of these articles were experimental in nature and dealt with issues related to human well-being; a smaller number were concerned with the application of research and the pursuit of athletic excellence. Rushall (1973) pointed out a similar finding in his earlier survey of this research in Canada. The research in these areas was predominantly concerned with sport activity, however, an orientation found only in isolated instances in the motor learning and performance research.

Research in the social psychology of physical activity was not as abun-

345

dant as in sport psychology. The topic of social facilitation was most common, accounting for 39.4 percent of the total production. Again, sport is the focus of attention of most of these studies.

Table 1. Distribution of motor learning and motor performance research papers in recent North American sport psychology proceedings.

Subject Category	Frequency
Motor Learning	
Feedback theory for discrete movements	15
Practice for simple tasks	10
Learning of complex tasks	9
Transfer of training	4
Long-term practice	3
Fatigue effects on learning	2
Movement organization	2
Performance decrements	2
Schema theory of learning	2
Total	50
Motor Performance	
Motor short-term memory	50
Motor control	25
Motor reactivity	12
Long-term memory and motor programs	11
Motor abilities	8
Attention demands of motor tasks	8
Velocity prediction in sport	7
Measurement	6
Decision-making in sport	5
Sport taxonomies	6
Total	138

Most of the research undertaken in the area of motor learning and performance has not used sport as a focal point; the reverse is true for the areas of sport psychology and the social psychology of physical activity. Probably because of the concern of the two latter with sport, athletes and coaches have cooperated in advanced study in this area. Although we have not seen a concerted thrust in terms of athlete preparation and training as occurs in Europe (Groves *et al.*, 1978), researchers in these areas put considerable emphasis on attitudes, feelings, self-control, and other pehnomena related to sport and performance. It is probably because of this emphasis on what are some of the essential issues in sport that the directors of the different sport governing bodies indicated that sport psychology was the area of greatest importance to their programs.

At the same time the sport governing bodies ranked motor learning fifth in importance to their programs, behind sport psychology, physiology, and biomechanics, and sports medicine. This low ranking of motor learning may be due in part to the fact that little of the published research can be remotely related to sport or learning but is concerned with the testing of performance models of a theoretical nature. Defending this approach, Jack Adams (1971, p. 112) justified the search for broad general principles of skill acquisition when he stated: "The villain that has robbed skills of its precision is applied research that investigates an activity to solve a particular problem, like kicking a football, flying an airplane or operating a lathe. . . ." Such a viewpoint has helped to keep motor skill researchers in their comfor-

Table 2. Distribution of sport psychology and social psychology of physical activity research papers in recent North American sport psychology proceedings.

Subject Category	Frequency
Sport Psychology	
Personality of athletes	16
Attitudes toward sport	14
Competitive anxiety	14
Achievement and motivation in sport	10
Aggression in sport	9
Satisfaction in sport	6
Behavioral assessment in sport	6
Coping in sport	6
Intrinsic motivation	4
Roles and attitudes of women in sport	4
Competition	4
Self-control in physical activity	4
Meaning in sport	3
Cooperation in sport	3
Cognitive styles	3
Leadership in sport	2
Preparation for excellence	2
Superstition in sport	1
Total	111
Social Psychology of Physical Activity	
Social facilitation	13
Group structure and performance	6
Attributions for success and failure	5
Stereotypes in sport	4
Socialization in sport	3
Social motives	2
Total	33

table labs studying their subjects pushing buttons, moving levers, and pursuing rotors. Adams does, however, continue to say that "the task centered approach is justified when practical reasons require us to know about tasks and efficiency in them, but it is a limited way of achieving the larger scientific goals of law and theory. The question now becomes, whether it is more important at this moment in time to pursue applied solutions to specific sport problems, or continue to search for theory until all variables are understood?

A recent analysis of motor skill practices in mainland China demonstrated that much of the gymnastic skill that the Chinese have recently developed was not due to secret procedures or innovative theoretical development but to the application of principles that we have known for years, such as specificity of practice, matching task demands to performer ability, and the overlearning of motor skills.

sport problems, or continue to search for theory until all variables are understood?

Certain indicators in Canada suggest that energies should be applied to the resolution of specific sport problems. The first is the strong leadership role that the Coaching Association of Canada has taken towards "bridging the gap" between theory and practice by its recent hiring of an individual to try to do just that. Another indication is the ambitious research program initiated by the federal government in conjunction with the sport governing bodies and directed towards the search for performance excellence. It seems that the amount may now be ripe for applied research in order to understand better "tasks and efficiency in them," as Adams suggested.

It is my personal opinion that there already exists an abundance of usable information on motor learning that can be applied to specific sport problems. A recent analysis of motor skill practices in mainland China (Salmela, 1979) demonstrated that much of the gymnastic skill that the Chinese have recently developed was not due to secret procedures or innovative theoretical development but to the application of principles that we have known for years, such as the specificity of practice, matching task demands to performer ability, and the overlearning of motor skills.

It seems that there is but Crossman's classic study (1959) on cigar rolling that can be referred to when performance is considered across years of practice. Are the apparently constant increments of learning of cigar rolling across a ten-year period similar to those found in sport? Can the voluminous quantity of literature on performance decrements based on Hullian theory remain buried forever, or can parts of it be resurrected for application in practical situations?

CONCLUSION

Although I am by no means attempting to be exhaustive in outlining the projected needs of Canadian coaches and athletes, it seems apparent that research endeavors being undertaken at present may not be related even to their major preoccupations. Yet, there seems to be an abundance of areas to which sport scientists could turn their attention. The needs of the specific sport federations should provide the direction, if researchers decide to commit themselves to sport.

In summary, it seems that sport researchers, especially in the area of motor learning and performance, must change their attitudes if an attempt to bridge the gap between theory and practice is to succeed. The sports bodies also must actively search out the information they need to improve their programs, and when such information is unavailable they must be ready to identify their most urgent needs and to secure research funding. The sport psychology researcher, whether in the psycho-social or motor skill area, must also be willing to shift his priorities and look at research areas that they not be in fashion in the higher circles of the American Psychological Association, but may be of utmost importance to the athlete or coach. It goes without saying that the active support of government in funding applied research would help many scientists overcome the stigma attached to these endeavors. Only through this type of collaboration of athlete, coach, and researcher can we be confident of the development of performance excellence and personal development based upon sound psychological principles.

Research in sport psychology seems to be serving the needs of sport technicians in Canada to a certain extent. However, if a projection of the needs of the majority of Canada's coaches in the motor skill area was made at this moment, I do not think it would resemble the profile of published research that I have presented in Table 1. It is my belief that many of the old "chestnut" topics that were studied in the past regarding learning would surface and might read like the following.

Practice schedules. The research on massed versus distributed practice was beaten to death in the 1950s and 1960s in psychomotor learning research. Nevertheless, it is still an essential question for coaches and athletes in relation to the efficient distribution of their time. What can now be added to the age-old findings is how to dissect a motor task in terms of its information processing demands, so that more appropriate means of skill acquisition can be used. Given that high level performances are attained only after long periods of time, it would appear that more research on the learning of skills over extended practice periods is essential. Of course, such projects are not favored by graduate students who are looking for studies that are "fast and dirty."

Most of the research undertaken in the area of motor learning and performance has not used sport as a focal point.

Modes of learning. The incredible complexity of the motor skills that occur in sport has for the most part been ignored as a focus of interest in research, possibly because of the lack of conceptual models to deal with this variability (Salmela, 1976). Only recently has the work of such individuals as Nideffer in *The Inner Athlete* suggested that there may be different attention styles and, therefore, various means of learning tasks. This individualization of learning can be related back to whether the athlete conceptualizes the skill in whole or parts, and then related to the manner in which he attempts to acquire the skill. The information processing demands of the specific tasks could then be matched with the preferred mode of learning of the individual, whether it be visual, auditive, or kinesthetic.

Amount of learning. Like practice schedules, the issue of amount of learning is an area believed to be important to athletes and coaches but no longer to researchers. The studies that are at present being done on the attention demands of motor tasks could well be directed towards the question of overlearning and the automation of task components. When can attention be directed to new dimensions and when should efforts be sustained on previously, partially acquired ones?

350

Personality Research: The Current Controversy and Implications for Sports Studies *

John E. Kane, Ph.D.
West London Institute of
Higher Education

Not withstanding the growth of knowledge and understanding about aptitude, abilities and skills, the explanation of performance differences is acknowledged as depending to a crucial extent on the individual's unique personal and behavioural dispositions. Such dispositions as an individual brings to a performance situation, while clearly important with respect to the outcome, are not yet well understood, neither as to their nature and source, their quantification nor their predictive value. This is not surprising, since this area of psychology — essentially personality psychology — is necessarily complex and currently imprecise embracing such issues as, for example, the relative permanence/impermanence of personality states, the effects of cognitive and perceptual styles, the nature of intrinsic motivation, the person's modes of construing and the effects of learning and experience. Nevertheless the study of the person in the context of behaving and performing is not without a sound pedigree in psychology, and there are current signs of a new and healthy increase of interest in this area which promises to establish stronger theoretical bases for sounder experimental work.

No group of professional workers will be more sensitive to new explanations and findings which make operational sense than those involved in teaching and advising in physical education and sport, where it has long been held that performance, especially in competitive situations, ultimately rests on the psychological dispositions which the individual brings to the event, and that in turn the nature of the event may affect subsequent dispositions. The bases for these assumptions are not hard to find. The physical education literature is, for example, heavy with implied and stated links between personality development and involvement in appropriately conducted programmes of planned physical activities, games, dance and sport. Most recently and interestingly the argument for the existence of these links has focused attention on the possible effects of physical activity on body image and self concept (Kane 1972). Additionally, some recent literature

* Kane, J. E., Personality Research: The Current Controversy and Implications of Sports Studies, in W. Straub (Ed.), *Sport Psychology: An Analysis of Athlete Behaviour,* 2nd Edition, 1981, Ithaca, N.Y.: Mouvement Publications, 340-352. Reprinted by permission of the publisher.

of a psychological nature has tended to strengthen the hopes and expectations of coaches and advisers that the selection, training and performance of talented athletes could benefit from psychological insights (e.g. Cofer and Johnson 1960; Ogilvie and Tutko 1966; Vanek and Cratty 1969; Rushall and Siedentop 1975; Ponsonby and Yaffe 1976).

The research undertaken (mostly by physical educationists) to investigate the validity of these assumptions has not been inconsiderable since about 1960, but on the whole it has not produced coherent and unequivocal findings on which to rely for predictive purposes. It has, however, produced a great deal of useful descriptive information about the nature and extent of the relationship between personality and physical (athletics) ability and performance on which more sophisticated research may be based. The main criticisms levelled at much of this body of research have focused atention on methodological inadequacies (e.g. Cooper 1969 and Rushall 1973), and more recently on the virtual absence of any sound theoretical reference base (e.g. Kroll 1970 and Kane 1976). However, the real cause of the slow progress since 1960 or thereabouts from descriptive to analytical and experimental approaches lies in the conflict and confusion which has characterized the mainstream of research and theory in personality psychology. As a result, the research aimed at accounting for the personality variables in motor and sports performance has had to rely on inappropriate and insensitive tools and models and it is therefore not surprising that the search for enlightenment has been slow. In the last few years, however, a new urgent awakening in the field of personality psychology is apparent, focusing to a great extent on the search for alternatives or extensions of trait theory. Trait 'theory' is under attack not so much because it is an unsound *theory* but because ipso facto personality traits emphasize only the personal dispositions in explaining behaviour and minimize the role of situational factors. The result is that a number of alternative models and approaches have been proposed in an effort to explain a more vital and dynamic concept of personality sensitive to situational factors in behaviour. In these recent developments there appear to be the kinds of explanations, theories and models that may be particularly attractive and appropriate for research in physical education and sport. In particular the current efforts to develop an *interactional* model of personality emphasizing the cognitive interpretations of the person in a given situation deserve special attention, if only to make clearer the nature of the current objections to the traditional *trait* model. It is not quite clear, incidentally, what writers mean by the 'traditional trait model' nor precisely what there is about traits that make them unsuitable or defective (Alston 1976). It depends to a large extent what you mean by 'traits' and certainly the current psychological literature is anything but clear on this point. What is reasonably clear from the present controversy is a serious questioning of the *emphasis* of person factors as the main determinants of human behaviour. My first task must, therefore, be to give a brief and admittedly personalized account of the present state of knowledge to which the trait approach has brought us in the personality/performance area. I shall then consider the theoretical possibilities of the interaction approach before adding a final suggestion about alternative perspectives.

1. *The trait approach.* A number of very useful reviews are available (e.g. Hendry 1970, Harris 1972, Hardman 1976, Kane 1976) which, while not totally in agreement, give a useful indication of the present understanding of the link between personality and physical abilities and also point up many of the possibilities for clarifying the nature of this link. The studies included in these reviews tend to fall into two categories; those attempting a relatively simple personality (via Cattell or Eysenck) description and/or comparison of selected groups of athletes and a few correlational studies demonstrating the relationship between personality and physical ability variables. While reviewers have found difficulty in coming to unequivocal or generalized conclusions there is a tendency for the male athlete to be described in terms of extraverted and stable dispositions (such as high dominance, social aggression, leadership, tough-mindedness and emotional control) and for women athletes to be shown as relatively anxious extraverts. If, for example, we were to find that certain personality variables are related to outstanding goalkeeping ability in soccer, it would be surprising to find that all the same variables are linked with high level performance in javelin throwing, cross-country running or rifle shooting. A few illustrations and examples may serve best to summarize the kinds of analyses that have been undertaken.

DESCRIPTIVE PROFILES AND COMPARISONS

Figure 1 typifies the profile description. This early and classic account

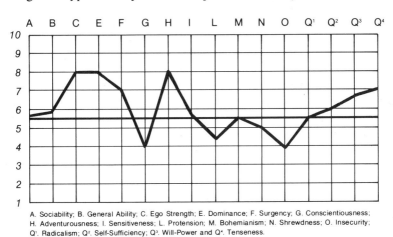

A. Sociability; B. General Ability; C. Ego Strength; E. Dominance; F. Surgency; G. Conscientiousness; H. Adventurousness; I. Sensitiveness; L. Protension; M. Bohemianism; N. Shrewdness; O. Insecurity; Q¹. Radicalism; Q². Self-Sufficiency; Q³. Will-Power and Q⁴. Tenseness.

Figure 1. *Champion athletes.*

by Heusner describes champion athletes as stable (C, L, O traits) and extraverted (A, E, F traits). It is worth noting that subsequent studies have never demonstrated such a definite description of champion athletes. Although this kind of profile analysis has been used mainly to establish fundamental descriptive data of a variety of athletes and activity groups a number of researchers have found that when the activity and level of participation

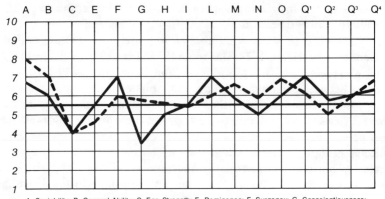

A. Sociability; B. General Ability; C. Ego Strength; E. Dominance; F. Surgency; G. Conscientiousness; H. Adventurousness; I. Sensitiveness; L. Protension; M. Bohemianism; N. Shrewdness; O. Insecurity; Q¹. Radicalism; Q². Self-Sufficiency; Q³. Will-Power and Q⁴. Tenseness.

Figure 2. *Women swimmers and track.*

are held constant, interesting similarities of personality type have been recorded for groups of, for example, racing drivers (Ogilvie 1968), wrestlers (Kroll 1967), soccer players and (see figure 2) women athletes (Kane 1966).

Comparison of profile data has often been reduced to focus on similarities and differences based on the two major Eysenckian dimensions of Extraversion and Neuroticism. In most of these studies, even when significant differences (from the population norms or from other criterian groups) have been established, the problem has been to interpret the real meaning of such group differences. Moreover, group means hide individual differences and in any case the operational implications, for an individual or group, of being, for example, more or less extraverted, tough-minded or emotionally stable has seldom been touched on. This may well have resulted from researchers being more concerned with the personality tests and their popular descriptive meaning than with the theoretical framework which underpins the whole personality assessment procedure being used.

Eysenck (1972) has constantly referred to this point and in particular to the way in which careful attention to the niceties of both personality theory and parameter values are needed in order to interpret experimental findings. As an illustration he refers to the proposed link between extraversion and conditionability and explains the contradictory findings of researches in this area as being a direct reflection of the parameter values used; e.g. weak unconditioned stimulus values favouring quick conditioning of introverts relative to extraverts, while strong unconditioned stimulus values have the opposite effect. It would seem that in the kind of investigation so far described attempting to relate personality to performance, little or no account has been taken of such theoretical subtleties, so that results have tended to be left badly interpreted and unexplained. Lack of reference to a sound theoretical framework has, moreover, caused confusion in trying to explain apparent inconsistencies in findings by different investigators. Nevertheless the better ones of these descriptive studies based on the measurement of traits have been useful in opening up the possibilities for

354

further advanced study. Practically none of them pretended to offer a predictive platform for sports performance.

CORRELATIONAL ANALYSES

Surprisingly few correlational studies have been reported attempting to tease out the nature of the personality/physical performance relationship. If and where a relationship exists it would seem that appropriate correlational procedures could best demonstrate the circumstances under which it is maximized and this in turn could give rise to a better understanding of the nature of the relationship. Some attempts to consider the values of correlational strategies have been reported (Kane 1970, 1972, 1976) and these have included intercorrelation to factor analysis, higher order factoring, multiple regression and canonical analysis. In these correlational studies the two domains — personality and gross physical (athletic) performance — were each assessed by a battery of tests among specialist men and women physical educationists.

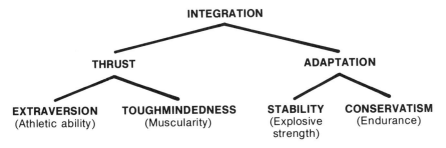

Figure 3. *Personality — athletic ability — hierarchical factor structure.*

Figure 3 summarizes the higher order general factor structure and emphasizes that the largest second order factor links extraversion with general athletic ability (i.e. speed, strength and power). A series of multivariate analyses demonstrated, as expected, the increasing value of the correlation coefficients from simple bivariate techniques (i.e. one personality variable with one physical performance variable) through multiple correlation to canonical correlation. A number of these analyses with multivariate vectors have produced significant coefficients averaging about 0.7 and in many cases permitting a clear interpretation of tough-minded, stable extraversion going with general athletic ability. Notwithstanding the known instability of factor and vector structure these correlational studies have clearly taken the study of the personality physical performance relationship to a serious and useful level. Here again, however, the purpose of the studies using trait measures was not to seek predictive indices of sports performance but rather to search for an understanding of the relationship between the two domains.

THEORETICAL CONSIDERATIONS

Descriptive and correlational studies of the kind so far described are highly valuable if designed and interpreted within the context of a sound theoretical framework and if well standardized measures (with or without trait theory implications) and reasonably sophisticated analyses are used. Few studies so far reported would seem to satisfy these criteria, but as a contribution to seeking an appropriate framework three observations are offered:

A. Is it not unreasonable to expect personality (however measured) to constitute an equally important explanatory or causative dimension in different types of athletic performance being highly important for success in some, of small importance in others, and of no importance at all in the remainder?

B. Eysenck's theoretical and empiric evidence on the nature and antecedents of behaviour appears to represent an attractive general framework to guide investigation of the personality aspects of performance, especially in activities where the perceptual processes (e.g. vigilance, selective attention, kinaesthetic awareness and recall) are of importance. Such a perceptual framework may be elaborated by reference to the work of Witkin (1962) on perceptual styles, and Whiting (1972) on personality and perceptual sampling.

C. If for simplicity we limit our consideration of personality to the two major dimensions Extraversion and Anxiety, and wish to investigate the performance via arousal paradigm, then again we might well consider the Eysenckian version of the causative neurological substrates of behaviour summated in the excitory-inhibitory balance.

2. *The interactional approach.* It is not clear in the recent and generalized attack on the trait approach to personality what precisely is being attacked. Trait theory and trait theorists are referred to regularly though neither is defined or identified. Mischel (1973), who is one of the leading contemporary opponents of traits, refers to 'traditional trait approaches' and to what he assumes to be the implicit assumption in such approaches that "personality comprises broad underlying dispositions which pervasively influence the individual's behaviour across many situations and lead to consistency of behaviour". But even Mischel does not refer specifically to a trait *theory* nor does he name those who are supposed to uphold such a theory. Firstly then, in trying to understand the focus of current concern about traits, it is difficult to see how the concern can be centered on trait *theory* since it is difficult to identify such a theory in the history of personality psychology. Indeed reliance on traits were probably anti-theory originally in the sense that researchers unconvinced about contemporary theoretical postulates decided to content themselves with simply describing behaviour according to derived categories of traits, dispositions, types, etc. Secondly, the attack cannot surely be directed against individual researchers like Cattell, Eysenck and others for having assiduously developed to a thoroughly rigorous level the *measurement* of meaningful personality traits. Mischel at least seems to be objecting to traits as implying broad dispositions predicating behaviour in different situations but nowhere does he appear to deny the existence of traits but only their usefulness in

356

explaining particular behaviour. Again it is not clear what or who is the focus of the attack. Neither Cattell nor Eysenck, for instance, would deny the impossibility of fully and accurately predicting an individual's behaviour in all circumstances on the basis of measurement on broad personality characteristics, such as extraversion and anxiety, or on simpler ones like those incorporated in the 16 PF. Indeed reference has already been made in the earlier part of this paper to Eysenck's constant insistence on the need for researchers to be sensitive to changes in situational parameter values when interpreting their finding in behavioural experiment. Moreover, Cattell (1950, 1957, 1965) whose research and development in the area of personality traits is unmatched has distinguished clearly between 'source traits' (the relatively stable underlying causal entities that determine behaviour) and 'surface traits' (the relatively varying and superficial elements that reflect behaviour in special circumstances), and has suggested the use of 'specifications equations' such as —

$$R(\text{esponse}) = S_1T_1 + S_2T_2 + \text{----} Sn\ Tn$$

where $T_1\ T_2$ etc. are traits and $S_1\ S_2$ etc. the weights relevant to each trait for a given situation.

The notion of personality traits does not require a commitment to completely explaining behaviour in widely differing situations on the basis of broad dispositions.

An interactionist model of behaviour appears to be very much a matter of re-emphasis rather than one incorporating a new mode of thinking. As such, one wonders at the crisis proportions given to the current debate. Indeed the laymen might be forgiven for assuming that to consider both the person and the situation in attempting to explain behaviour was commonsense. Moreover, interactionist explanations of behaviour go back quite a way in the psychology literature. Lewin (1935) it will be remembered, suggested the formula —

$$B = f(P,S)$$

where B refers to the behaviour resulting from a choice of possibilities or a performance measurement on a scale; where P refers to structural dimensions (physiological and psychological) represented in personality measures; where S refers to variable aspects of the situation and f refers to the functional relationship (or interaction between P and S in explaining B.)

There has been a consistant flow of research since Lewin following his general interaction theory of behaviour, emphasizing from time to time different aspects of it. Present day interactionists like Mischel (1976) and Endler and Magnusson (1976) apparently wish to attribute overriding importance in behaviour to the P × S interaction and support their case in two ways — by theoretical postulates concerning the way a person construes a situation and by demonstrating the relatively large size of the P × S variance in selected studies. The analysis of variance is the favoured tool to support the interactionist viewpoint and on the face of it the review of chosen studies by, for example, Bowers (1973) and Argyle (1976) are reasonably convincing demonstrating that person variance tends to fall into the 15 - 30 per cent range, situation variance into the 20 - 45 per cent range and P × S variance into the 30 - 50 per cent range. However, there are a number of unresolved design problems in these studies and Cartwright (1975) has suggested that many of them have been biased against discovering appreciable person variance, while Golding (1975) throws doubt on the appropriateness of variance analysis for seeking out person consistency across situations commending instead the use of Cronbach's coefficient of generalizability!

Nevertheless, the interactionist approach is of undoubted significance to sports psychologists. There had admittedly been a strong campaign over recent years by researchers in this field for the development of sport specific measures of behaviour and there has been a long standing recognition of the variable effects on performance of different sporting situations, particularly where competitiveness and stress are involved. Increasingly researchers have also referred to the importance of the athlete's perception and interpretation of the situation and the way in which such perceptions may be idiosyncratic interactions of relatively stable personal dispositions with experimental factors such as previous experience of such situations, conditioning, and expectation. The attractiveness of interactionist explanations of behaviour seems therefore reasonably assured if only to compliment trait descriptions. Some attempts to follow this line of thinking in sports research are in fact becoming increasingly evident, though Langer (1966) had earlier planned a model design for investigating behaviour and performance in different situations of sporting stress. The study monitored anxiety, as measured by the IPAT scale, of varsity footballers during the off-season (no stress), during the pre-game period (high stress) and immediately after the games (reduced stress) throughout a season and in concluding that anxiety level was a most important determinant of football performance Langer demonstrated the sensitivity of the IPAT anxiety scale for recording changes linked with levels of sporting stress and performance.

Another and more recent attempt to assess a person (trait) x situation model for anxiety in a realistic competitive athletic environment has been reported by Flood and Endler (1976). The measurement of anxiety was based on Speilberger's (1972) state-trait procedures adapted by Endler and Okada (1975) to account for their version of the multidimensional nature of trait anxiety. Although some significant interactions between anxiety state and trait in the anticipation of competition were reported, the results in general were equivocal leaving some doubt as to whether or not the interaction model of anxiety was supportable. In general one is left with some concern in this kind of 'interactionist' study about the methods used for the assessment of personality dimensions. It is almost as if those seeking support for the interaction model too easily and prejudicially discard well-standardized and reliable measures of personal dispositions in favour of superficial and less rigorously developed tests in their reaction against the former trait emphasis. This is a danger that those in sport psychology must avoid in calling for the development of sports specific measures of personality. The futility of employing hastily assembled adjective and observational check lists, questionnaires, self reports and the like should be all too obvious. It is gratifying to note in his connection a few examples of sports specific measures which are being developed systematically with sensitivity to the niceties and scientific rigours of test construction, (e.g. Martens 1976). The problems in allocating the correct amount of importance to the Person, the Situation and the Interaction in sports performance will not be resolved easily or quickly, and certainly not by substituting sound and well-standardized measures of well-rooted personality dimensions for others less carefully developed and more superficial. Neither will fuller understanding of behaviour in sport be achieved by the facile shifting of theoretical perspectives to accommodate all the contemporary moods and 'mini-theories' in psychology.

There is no doubt that behaviour in competitive sport may be properly viewed as a continuous process of multidirectional interaction between the athlete and the situational conditions which prevail and that in this process cognitive factors are critically involved. To this extent the inter-actionist model is in accord with what must be a commonsense interpretation of the competitive environment and is, therefore, attractive. But to establish the superordinate importance of the interaction as opposed to the person or the situation in sport will need a great deal more subtle and supportive evidence than that which is currently available. The current emphasis on interactionism has nevertheless already had undoubtedly beneficial effects on research directions, not least of which has been an orientation to the actual behaviour in situ, a move, as it were, from the laboratory to the field. In the search for the behavioural antecedents of sports performance such a move is essential.

3. *Alternative perspectives.* The study of involvement of the person in the sporting situation has recently become the focus of another psycho-logical approach, one that is much less concerned with the prediction of successful performance than with personal satisfaction, meaning, fulfillment, levels of consciousness, self-actualization, and, above all, joy. This approach owes much to both cognitive and humanistic schools of psychology where man is seen to be in control of his behavioural choices and decisions, and derives personal meaning and interpretation from his experience. The roots of these kind of psychological speculations are in existential philosophy and phenomenology and in such notions as, for example, 'personal knowl-edge' (Polanyi 1958) and 'needs of the mind' (Maddi 1970), which lay emphasis on unique knowledge derived by the individual from his perceptions in the course of satisfying his needs to understand himself, to symbolize, to imagine and to judge. Maslow (1970) perhaps goes nearest to setting out a comprehensive, if speculative, theory to encompass the main elements of this psychological thrust which has sometimes been referred to as third-force psychology.

Maslow categorized human needs into five sets which are placed in a hierarchical arrangement of importance and development, ranging from the lower level of physiological needs through those of security, safety, belonging and respect, to the final capping monarchical need for 'self-actualization'. The self-actualizing person, according to Maslow, would have clear perceptions, be self-accepting, spontaneous, autonomous and natural, appreciate the basic qualities of life, have a deep affection and sympathy for all humans, enjoy peak experiences (i.e. mystical or transpersonal experiences) and know himself in order to maximize his potentialities. For Maslow self-actualization is regarded as the highest and most fulfilled state of human existence.

In somewhat more conventional psychological terms Deci (1975) touches on the processes involved in self-actualizing behaviour in his treatise on intrinsic motivation. Deci, basing his interpretations on the work of Robert White (1959) develops the model of intrinsically motivated behaviours as ones chosen by the person in the pursuit of 'feeling competent' and 'self determining' in relation to his environment. He assumes that in these pursuits the person has access to his own internal states (understanding, orientations, attitudes, etc.) in a way which others cannot, and he effectively argues the importance of cognitions and experiences in changing the individual's internal states.

The psychology of self-actualization and intrinsic motivation, especially when linked with the psychology of the body sensation and perception, would seem to be most attractive to researchers concerned with the experience and personality effects of involvement in physical activity and sport. One interesting analysis of the individual's perception of himself links together these notions in proposing that self-through-body awareness has three dimensions, sensori-spatial, existential and valuative. The sensori-spatial dimension refers to the aspects of body conformation shape and spatial position; the existential dimension is suggested to represent the perceptions related to substantiveness, realness and vulnerability; the valuative dimension is proposed to account for the perceived value, worth and satisfaction of the body's appearance and function. Czikszentmihalyi (1975) investigating the inner experiences concerned with joy and pleasure in play games and life styles described a common form of experience enjoyed by the intrinsically motivated. He called this experience *flow* which incorporated feelings of exhilaration, of creative accomplishment and of heightened functioning. He writes, "they concentrate their attention on a limited stimulus field, forget personal problems, lose their sense of time and of themselves, feel competent and in control, and have a sense of harmony and union with their surroundings. To the extent that these elements of experience are present, a person enjoys what he or she is doing and ceases to worry about whether the activity will be productive or whether it will be rewarded."

One of the most common approaches today towards re-establishing the body as a sensitive vehicle for the recognition and enjoyment of feelings is running or jogging. The experience of runners of all kinds are being increasingly recorded and analyzed, and in the process accounts ranging from mystical and ecstatic interpretations to physiologically sensuous occurrences are to be found. On the back of a general revolution which

360

has 'rediscovered' the body as the source of awareness and vital sensation, running seems to be successfully competing with more elaborate practices involving biofeedback mechanisms, various body therapies and even the martial arts as a means of generating and controlling inner states.

Running, is of course, a very personal activity which over time gives rise to a full spectrum of inner feelings from pain to delight. It represents, therefore, a very special body-mind control system and gives rise to heightened perceptions and appreciation of body-into-mind experiences. For some elite athletes and for unaccountable reasons individuals have experienced a fusing of the body-mind link that has given rise to a gigantic release of bodily energy, a sort of unleashing or disinhibiting mechanism, resulting in an outstanding performance almost impossible to analyze and replicate. Less talented runners have also experiences such occasional releases of energy, but have most often gained 'peak experiences' described variously as 'flow', 'smoothness', 'floating', 'exhilaration' and 'pure joy'. Occasionally the experience has described a projection of self, a separatedness, and extension out of the body to another level of existing and operating. This must be what George Sheeham, the articulate middle-aged doctor/runner meant when he wrote, "We begin in the body and end in a Vision".

For the psychologist, the measurement and assessment of such 'peak experiences' touching on the imagination, the transcendental and the intrinsic states of being, constitute an almost insuperable problem. Joy, delight, fulfillment and ecstacy are indeed hard to record, but their existence is undoubted. They are part of the complex but important system of intrinsic motivation and deserve the serious attention of psychologists. For those involved in physical activities and sports at all levels the intrinsic rewards and personal satisfactions are clear and unmistakably the product of sensitized body experience.

REFERENCES

ALSTON, W. Traits, Consistency and Conceptual Alternatives for Personality Theory in R Harre (ed) *Personality*. Oxford; Blackwell, 1976.

ARGYLE, M. Personality and Social Behaviour in *Personality* (ed. R Harre). Oxford; Blackwell, 1976.

BOWERS, K. Situationism in Psychology: an analysis and critique. *Psychological Review* 1973, 30.

CARTWRIGHT, D. Trait and other sources of variance in the S-R inventory of anxiousness. *J. Pers. Soc. Psychol,* 1975, 32.

CATTELL, R. B. *Personality: A Systematic, Theoretical and Factual Study.* New York: McGraw-Hill, 1950.

CATTELL, R. B. *Personality and Motivation Structure and Measurement.* Yonkers: World Books, 1957.

CATTELL, R. B. Some Psychological Correlates of Physical Fitness and Physique in Cureton J (ed) *Exercise and Fitness.* University of Illinois, 1960.

CATTELL, R. B. *The Scientific Analysis of Behaviour.* Baltimore: Penguin, 1965.

CLARIDGE, G. *Personality and Arousal.* London: Pergamon, 1967.

COFER, C. and JOHNSON, W. Personality Dynamics in relation to Exercise and Sport in (ed. Johnson, W.) *Science and Medicine of Exercise and Sport.* New York: Harper, 1960.

COOPER, L. Athletics, Activity and Personality: A review of the literature *Research Quarterly* 1969, 40.

CORCORAN, D. W. J. Studies of Individual Differences at the Applied Psychology Unit in Nebylitsyn and Gray (eds) *Biological Bases of Individual Behaviour.* London: Academic Press, 1972.

CZIKSZENTMIHALY, M. *Beyond Boredom and Anxiety.* San Francisco: Jossey-Bass, 1975.

DECI, E. L. *Intrinsic Motivation.* New York: Plenum, 1975.

DUFFY, E. *Activation and Behaviour.* New York: Wiley, 1962.

ENDLER, N. S. and MAGNUSSON, D. Personality and person by situation interactions in Endler and Magnusson (eds) *Interactional Psychology and Personality.* Washington: Wiley, 1976.

ENDLER, N. S. and OKADA, M. A multidimensional measure of trait anxiety: The S-R Inventory of General Trait Anxiety. *Journ. of Consult. and Clinical Psychol.,* 1975.

EYNSENCK, H. J. Human Typology, Higher Nervous Activity and Factor Analysis in Nebylitsyn and Gray (eds) *Biological Bases of Individual Behaviour.* London: Academic Press, 1972.

FISHER, S. *Body Consciousness,* New Jersey: Prentice-Hall, 1973.

FLEISHMAN, E. *The Structure and Measurement of Physical Fitness.* New Jersey: Prentice-Hall, 1964.

FLOOD, M. AND ENDLER, N. S. The Interaction Model of Anxiety: An empirical test in an athletic competition situation. *York University Dept. of Psychology Report No. 28,* 1976.

GOLDING, S. L. Flies in the Ointment: Methodological problems in the analysis of the percentage of variance due to person and situation. *Psychol. Bull.,* 1975, 82.

GRAY, J. A. The Psychophysiological nature of Introversion-Extraversion: a modification of Eysenck's theory in Nebylitsyn and Gray (eds) *Biological Bases of Individual Behaviour.* London: Academic Press, 1972.

GROVES, R. Assessing the Characteristics of Top-Level and Recreational Players. *Proceedings of BSSP Conference,* Exeter, 1976.

HARDMAN, K. A dual approach to the study of personality and performances in sport in Whiting et al (eds) *Personality and Performance in Physical Education and Sport.* London: Kimpton, 1973.

HARRIS, D. V. *Involvement in Sport.* Philadelphia: Lea and Febiger, 1973.

HENDRY, L. Assessment of personality traits in the coach — swimmer relationship, *Research Quarterly* 39, 1968.

HENDRY, L. Some notions on personality and sporting ability: certain comparisons with scholastic achievement. *Quest* 13, 1970.

HEUSNER, W. Personality traits of champion and former champion athletes. *MA thesis.* Illinois, 1952.

JOURARD, S. and SECORD, P. Body size and body cathexis. *Jounr. Consult Psychol.* 18, 1954.

KANE, J. E. Personality Description of Soccer Ability. *Res. in Phys. Educ.* No. 1, 1966.

KANE, J. E. Personality and Physical Abilities in Kenyon (ed) *Contemporary Psychology in Sports.* Chicago: Athletic Institute, 1970.

KANE, J. E. *Psychological Aspects of Physical Education and Sport.* London: Routledge and Kegan Paul, 1972.

KANE, J. E. Personality and Performance in Sport in Williams J. and Sperryn P. (eds) *Sports Medicine.* London: Arnold, 1976.

KLEINMAN, S. The significance of human movement: a phenomenological approach in Gerber E. (ed) *Sport and the Body.* Philadelphia: Lea and Febiger, 1972.

KROLL, W. Sixteen Personality Factor Profiles of Collegiate Wrestlers. *Research Quarterly,* 38, 1967.

KROLL, W. Current strategies and problems in personality assessment of athletes in Smith L. (ed) *Proceedings of the Symposium on Motor Learning.* Chicago: Athletic Institute, 1970.

KROLL, W. Athletic Stress Inventory. University of Massachusetts. (in press) 1977.

LACEY, J. I. Psychophysiological approaches to the evaluation of psychotherapeutic process and outcome in Rubenstein (ed) *Research in Psychotherapy.* Washington: Nat. Pub. Co., 1959.

LANGER, P. Varsity Football Performance. *Perceptual and Motor Skills,* 23, 1966.

LEONARD, G. *The Ultimate Athlete.* New York: Viking, 1975.

LEWIN, K. A Dynamic Theory of Personality. New York: McGraw-Hill, 1935.

MADDI, S. R. The search for meaning. *Nebraska Symposium on Motivation,* 18, 1970.

362

MARTENS, R. *The sport competition anxiety test.* Champaign, Illinois: Human Kinetic Pub. 1976.

MASLOW, A. H. *Motivation and Personality.* New York: Harper and Row, 1970.

MISCHEL, W. Towards a cognitive social learning reconceptualization of personality. *Psychol. Rev.* 80, 1973.

MISCHEL, W. *Introduction to Personality.* New York: Holt, Rinehart, 1976.

OGILVIE, B. Psychological consistencies within the personalities of high level competitors. *Journ. Am. Med. Assoc.* 28, 1968.

OGILVIE, B. and TUTKO T. *Problem Athletes and How to Handle Them.* London: Pelham, 1966.

OGILVIE, B. and TUTKO T. *The Athletic Motivation Inventory.* San Jose: Instit. for Study of Athletic Motivation, 1969.

PETRIE, A. Some psychological aspects of Pain and Relief of Suffering. *Ann. of N.Y. Acad. of Science,* 87, 1960.

PHARES, E. and LAMIELL, J. Personality in *Ann. Review of Psych.* 1977, Vol. 28.

POLANYI, M. *Personal Knowledge.* Chicago: University of Chicago Press, 1958.

PONSONBY, D. and YAFFEE, M. Psychology takes the soccer field. *FIFA News,* July 1976.

POULTON, E. On prediction in skilled movement. *Psychol. Bull.,* 54, 1957.

RUSHALL, B. The status of personality research and application in sports and physical education. *Journ. Sports Med. and Physical Fitness,* 13, 1973.

RUSHALL, B. and SIEDENTROP, D. *The Development and Control of Behaviour in Sport and Physical Education.* Philadelphia: Lea and Febiger, 1972.

SINCLAIR, E. Personality of rugby football players. *Thesis* Univ. of Leeds, 1968.

SPEILBERGER, G. D. *Theory and Research on Anxiety.* New York: Academic Press, 1969.

SPEILBERGER, C. Anxiety as an emotional state in Speilberger (ed) Anxiety: *Current trends in theory and research (Vol 1).* New York: Academic Press, 1972.

VANEK, M. and CRATTY, B. J. *Psychology and the Superior Athlete.* London: Macmillan, 1970.

VINCENT W. and DORSEY, D. Body image phenomena and measures of physiological performance. *Research Quarterly, 39,* 1968.

WHITE, R. W. Motivation reconsidered: the concept of competence. *Psychol. Rev.,* 66, 1959.

WHITING, H. T. A. and HUTT, J. The effects of personality and ability on speed of decision regarding the directional aspects of ball flight. *Journal of Motor Behaviour,* 4, 1972.

WILLIAMS, J. Personality traits of Champion Female Fencers. *Research Quarterly, 37,* 1970.

WITKIN, H. A. *Psychological Differentiation.* New York: Wiley, 1962.

WITKIN, H. A. Development of the Body concept and Psychological Differentiation in Werner, H. and Wapner, S. (eds) *The Body Percept.* New York: Random House, 1965.

Motivating the Athlete*

Albert V. Carron, Ed.D.
The University of
Western Ontario

ABSTRACT

Motivation is viewed as a necessary, but not sufficient condition for performance. The total level of motivation of the performer is seen as a combination of factors grouped under the broad categories: the athlete, the athletic competition, the task, and the performance consequences. Selected factors within each category are discussed; emphasis is on the application of information to teaching and coaching.

MOTIVATING THE ATHLETE

Factors which contribute to effective individual and/or team performance include: physical stature, degree of conditioning, personality, level of ability, and motivation. All have a direct impact upon the effectiveness of the athlete's performance; however, if one factor were to be selected as most important it would more than likely be motivation. Despite the research emphasis given the area in psychology and education motivation is still poorly understood, particularly as it relates to teaching and coaching of physical education.

Singer (1975) emphasized the importance of motivation in a simplified, but essentially accurate, equation:

$$PERFORMANCE = LEARNING + MOTIVATION$$
(behavior in a situation) (past experience)

It should be apparent from this equation that motivation is a necessary but not sufficient condition for performance. Motivation in the absence of learning would result in purposeless activity, while learning in the absence of motivation would result in no activity. Without sufficient motivation an athlete will not perform well in competition or train effectively in practice.

Effective application of motivational techniques by the teacher or coach depends upon knowledge of the individual and environmental factors affecting motivation, familiarity with many methods and techniques for motivating individuals, and comprehension of the relative effectiveness of each. Clearly, these aspects are interrelated, since knowledge of individual

* Carron, A. V., "Motivating the Athlete", *Motor Skills: Theory Into Practice*, 1977, *1*, 23-34. Reprinted by permission of the publisher.

and environmental factors affecting motivation can provide a rich source of methods and techniques and can provide insight into the effectiveness of various methods. This paper will focus upon the individual and environmental factors affecting motivation, with emphasis upon application to teaching and coaching.

FACTORS CONTRIBUTING TO LEVEL OF MOTIVATION

Motivation serves to energize, select and direct performance. Although this would seem to be straightforward, the sources of potential motivation for the athlete are numerous and extremely diverse. Unfortunately, the coach or teacher has impact upon only a few of these sources. The task of the teacher or coach is to first be aware of the potential sources of motivation, especially those over which influence may be exerted. Secondly, the coach or teacher must be knowledgeable about the relative effectiveness of each. Finally, decisions must be made regarding where and when each specific technique might be put to best use.

The numerous and diverse sources contributing to the total level of motivation can be subdivided and categorized into four dimensions or classes. These are identified in Figure 1 as: dimensions within the athlete; performance consequences dimension; athletic competition dimension; and task dimensions.

The _dimensions within the athlete_ are factors specific to the athlete which contribute to the total level of motivation. These factors include the athlete's personality, aspiration level, and intrinsic interest, among others. This is a source of motivation which is largely independent of the actions of the coach.

The results or _consequences of performance dimension_ also affects total level of motivation. For example, the outcome of performance usually includes some rewards or punishment and the possibility of that reward or punishment serves as a potential source of motivation for the athlete. The coach or teacher has some influence over this source of motivation.

The _athletic competition dimension_ reflects the dynamics of the athletic situation. Variables such as the relative importance of the event, the absence versus the presence of an audience, the composition of that audience, and the ability of the competition are potential sources of motivation. This source of motivation is generally available and relatively independent of the actions of the coach.

Finally, the task itself contains the potential to be motivating _(task characteristic dimension)._ Two aspects are the information feedback available and the amount of change or special attention in the task, commonly known as the Hawthorne Effect. The coach or teacher can exert considerable influence over these aspects, which are particularly crucial in the practice phase.

Although these dimensions are interrelated, as indicated in Figure 1, they have been examined independently by researchers and, for the remainder of this article, each will be considered in turn.

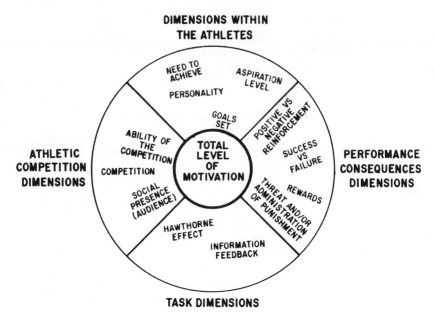

DIMENSIONS WITHIN THE ATHLETES

NEED TO ACHIEVE

ASPIRATION LEVEL

PERSONALITY

GOALS SET

POSITIVE VS NEGATIVE REINFORCEMENT

SUCCESS VS FAILURE

THREAT AND/OR ADMINISTRATION OF PUNISHMENT

REWARDS

ABILITY OF THE COMPETITION

TOTAL LEVEL OF MOTIVATION

COMPETITION

SOCIAL PRESENCE (AUDIENCE)

HAWTHORNE EFFECT

INFORMATION FEEDBACK

ATHLETIC COMPETITION DIMENSIONS

PERFORMANCE CONSEQUENCES DIMENSIONS

TASK DIMENSIONS

Figure 1. *The dimensions of motivation which offset the total level of motivation within the athlete.*

Dimensions within the athlete

Level of aspiration/goal setting. The level of aspiration is the "level of future performance in a task as specified by the individual" (Robb, 1972, p. 79). Research evidence has provided strong support that behavior is controlled by its consequences (Bandura, 1973); thus, success and failure have a tremendous influence upon subsequent goal setting and level of aspiration.

The relationship would appear to be cyclical: previous successes/failures influence present aspiration; present aspiration influences successes/failures. Consider a child who has experienced nothing but failure in every sport attempted. The child will undoubtedly have a low aspiration when faced with yet another new sport. However, the cycle of failure-low aspiration-failure may be broken. The teacher or coach must help the individual to set realistic, progressive goals which lead to small but repetitive successes so that success can beget success. This involves setting intermediate, achievable, realistic goals between the athlete's initial performance and final objective. The success experiences will lead to raised aspirations which will contribute to more effective future performances.

As an example, animals which were formerly noncombative have been trained to become more and more vicious in aggressiveness as a result of positive reinforcement (i.e., repeated victories) in battles with progressively stronger opponents. Similarly, severe repetitive defeats can result in enduring submissiveness even against harmless opponents (Kahn, 1951; Scott and Marston, 1953).

The shaping of behavior through manipulation of the consequences (success and failure) of behavior can be a powerful positive tool when used

366

appropriately by the teacher or coach. Unfortunately, improper use has negative consequences. The theories and applications of this type of approach are cogently presented by Rushall and Siedentop (1972) and the interested coach or teacher would do well to read their book.

On the surface it appears simple, success → raised aspirations → success; however, as in all things, the situation is not as clear as it appears. There are extenuating circumstances which mitigate the relative effects of success and failure. These include: the age at which the initial failure occurs, the absolute number of previous defeats/victories, and the sequence in which these victories/defeats occurred. The theory of need achievement presented by Atkinson (1965) provides a framework to examine the probability that a success or failure experience will result in an increase or decrease in motivation.

This theory reflects the influence of both situational variables, under the coaches' control, and personality variables on the tendency to approach success or failure. The coach has little control over the athletes' motive to achieve but can exert influence over the perceived situational variables of probability for success and incentive value. For example, the relative difficulty of the task influences the athletes' perceived probability of success. Thus, the athlete will have little motivation if the task is perceived as too easy or too difficult. Similarly, the importance of the situation influences incentive level. Little motivation results if there is no incentive value in the task. This has implications for both coaches and teachers with regard to communication with students and types of drills used. Often, teachers use approaches which might seem irrelevant to the student. There is little incentive to achieve the objective by effectively carrying out the drill. The teacher should outline reasons for the drill, thereby increasing the incentive to achieve. If the drill itself is too easy or extremely inappropriate little benefit will accrue because of the low incentive value inherent in the drill.

Anxiety. Need to achieve, just discussed, is one personality variable contributing to the total level of motivation. A second personality variable which has been shown to relate to the general drive level of the individual is *anxiety*. Individuals differentiated into classes of high-anxious and low-anxious on the basis of a paper and pencil personality questionnaire were found to differ on a variety of motor performance tasks. The differences in performance were consistent with what would have been predicted on the basis of differences in drive level/motivation. (Carron, 1968; Castaneda, et al., 1956; Duthie and Roberts, 1968; Farber and Spence, 1953.)

Since anxiety level apparently contributes to general drive level, high anxious individuals inherently have greater initial "motivation" than do low-anxious, on the basis of a paper and pencil personality questionnaire, were found to differ on a variety of motor performance tasks. The differences for a low anxious athlete. In fact, if the task were either extremely difficult, or little learning had occurred, or the athlete was of low ability, the high anxious individual might be too highly motivated initially and the coach or teacher would then need to reduce the athlete's anxiety level in order to obtain optimum performance.

Ability and level of learning. The ability and level of learning of the performer should be considered in determining the optimal level of motivation for a particular task. For example, lower levels of motivation are preferable early in learning when the task is more difficult. Later in learning, higher levels of motivation may be beneficial, depending, of course, on the nature of the task. Ability level is somewhat related to level of learning in that certain individuals find some tasks relatively easy and may begin at a more advanced level. In addition, their initial anxiety may be lower in certain situations than individuials of lesser ability.

Performance consequences dimension

Positive and negative reinforcement/rewards. The characteristics of a reinforcer are that a) it is usually contingent upon a specific preceding behavior and b) it affects the likelihood or probability that a particular behavior will reoccur in a similar situation. While reward is similar to reinforcement, reward has the connotation of being positive, whereas reinforcement may be positive or negative. For example, a hockey coach may temporarily bench a player for going out of position, thus negatively reinforcing the athlete's response. Conversely, the coach might commend a basketball player's attempt to drive inside, positively reinforcing that specific behavior.

What is the relative effectiveness of positive versus negative reinforcement? Singer (1975) observed that both can be effective in specific instances. He also pointed out, however, that the more efficacious of the two would appear to be positive reinforcement. Positive reinforcers inform one when he is doing something right and encourage the continuation of the activity in a specific direction, while negative reinforcement is of little value because it merely indicates that the behavior is incorrect without providing information with respect to the correct response or behavior. Information feedback, because of its greater specificity, may be ultimately more useful in most instances. (Information feedback will be considered under Task Dimensions.)

Rewards (which can be considered analogous to positive reinforcement) can take many forms. Oxendine (1968) suggests that there are three classes of rewards: 1) *symbolic,* including praise, decals on helmets, school grades, team crests, etc.; 2) *material,* including money, promise of team jackets for success, trophies, etc.; or 3) *psychological,* including the sense of belonging, the sense of accomplishment, knowledge of improvement, etc. He notes that psychological rewards are the most desirable.

One of the simplest, most natural, and therefore most frequently used forms of reward, particularly by inexperienced coaches and teachers, is praise. There are some disadvantages which could result from overuse of praise:

The most important disadvantage is the individual's tendency to develop a dependence upon extrinsic rather than intrinsic motivation and therefore, develop false values (interest in the reward rather than the activity itself). Another disadvantage...is that the same few children seem to excel most of the time. It appears that the winners of external rewards are usually the children who need them least for subsequent enthusiasm. (Oxendine, 1968, p. 192.)

In our materialistic society children are taught to expect rewards for achievement. Clearly, the teacher and coach are fighting an uphill battle in attempting to re-educate children to rely upon intrinsic rather than extrinsic types of reward. It is one which must be waged nevertheless and which should stress realistic goal setting behavior and evaluation in terms of one's own performance.

Punishment and/or threat of punishment. If reward is conceived of as one end of a continuum, punishment and/or the threat of punishment is the other. Although positive reinforcement is preferable to punishment as a consequence of performance, punishment, when properly employed, can be effective for *some* athletes in *some* instances. It would appear, however, that the disadvantages and strict methods for application of punishment far outweigh benefits derived from its use. Both Oxendine (1968) and Rushall and Siedentop (1972) stress that to be effective, punishment must: a) be used infrequently; b) be severe when employed; c) have minimal emotionality attached; d) be specific rather than general; and e) be applied consistently.

Success and failure. Success or failure would appear to be a consequence of most competitive athletic performances. Either outcome can have an effect upon subsequent motivation, although complete success and complete failure are rare. Care is taken in setting multiple goals, since both success and failure are relative to the goals that the athlete has set and his/her aspirations for that situation.

Coaches, spectators or parents might make judgments regarding the success or failure of the athlete in a race, e.g. "the athlete came first and that equals success" or "the athlete came last and that equals failure." The problem here is that an *absolute* standard is used which does not take into account the athlete's expectations, aspirations and goals. It is possible that an athlete might consistently run a specific race in 13 seconds. In a competitive situation, however, the athlete might run that race in 12 seconds. If she finishes last this performance might be rated a failure on the absolute scale, in spite of the fact that it is a success relative to past performances.

Clearly, the coach or teacher can manipulate performance consequences through establishing of criteria, choice of opponents, choice of task, assistance in goal setting, and evaluation of performance. Consistent success and consistent failure rarely serve to motivate behavior. High probability of failure, about 0.8, and low probability of success, about 0.2, seem to increase motivation. When either probability of failure or probability of success reaches a chance value (0.5), motivation begins to decrease steadily; it reaches a low when success or failure is assured. Singer (1975) has suggested that the chance level of probability, about 0.5, is the time to increase the difficulty of the task, to choose more difficult opponents, to increase the goals or to establish more stringent criterion. If, for example, a student can achieve a foul shooting score of 5 out of 10, a criterion set by teacher and student jointly, more than half of the time, perhaps it is time to raise the criterion to 6 or 7 out of 10. In terms of evaluation of performance the coach or teacher should become more exacting in their demands or encourage the student to be more exacting in self-imposed demands.

Athletic competition dimension/environment

Social Presence. Organized sport and physical activity is carried out, almost without exception, in the presence of others. These others may be an audience of spectators, fellow competitors, coaches, teachers, teammates or officials. It has been demonstrated repeatedly that the presence of others has an influence upon performance. This performance effect is attributed mainly to increased arousal, activation, and drive/motivation (Zajonc, 1965; Cottrell, 1968).

There are a number of factors which influence the degree to which the social presence of others is motivational. The size and the audience characteristics are two such factors. Audience characteristics is a catch-all for variables such as: age; sex; relationship to player (i.e., fellow teammates, girlfriend, boyfriend, parents); and ability.

Another important factor is the function of the audience. Recent research suggests that it is not the mere presence of an audience that results in increased motivation (Cottrell, et al., 1968; Martens and Landers, 1972), but it is the sense of evaluative apprehension on the part of the competitor. Martens (1975) has suggested that evaluative situations are generally motivating because we learn to expect positive or negative outcomes as a consequence of evaluation.

Teachers especially should be aware that social presence has a different effect upon learning than upon performance. In the sense it is used here performance is behavior occurring after substantial learning has taken place; while learning is the process of changing the most probable response from an incorrect to a correct one (Martens, 1975). Individuals under stress will usually emit the most probable response. Since social presence increases motivation and can be considered a form of stress, it follows that individuals who are in the process of learning might be adversely affected by the presence of others, particularly if they view those others as evaluators. For this reason, learners probably require considerable practice time away from, what they perceive as, the evaluative eye of the teacher.

Competition. The nature of sport is such that it is inherently competitive. The athlete competes against one or more other athletes, against self-imposed standards, or against fixed norms. Since these targets, goals or standards are always available in athletic competition, the situation is generally motivating, although the degree to which it is motivating is highly variable. Athletes differ in competitiveness due to individual variation in motives which contribute to competitiveness. These include: fear of failure, need to achieve, anxiety level, and desire for dominance, among others. Some of these have been considered in a previous section *(Dimensions Within the Athlete).*

A factor which contributes to the athlete's level of motivation that is clearly a part of the environment is the level of ability of the opposing

370

team as perceived by the athlete. The more similar in ability the two competitors (individuals or teams) view themselves, with respect to relative ability level, the greater the probability that competitive behavior will occur. If one athlete does not see any possibility for success there is very little likelihood of competition (Cratty, 1967). In these instances the competition may revert to an attempt to improve the weaker opponent's skill through some form of cooperative performance. For example, if two tennis players or golfers have great disparity in ability, the "game" often reverts to the better player helping the other with tips, coaching instructions, designed to improve the weaker player's game.

If the team or individual appears outclassed, the behavior of the coach must change to fit the situation. It should be obvious that pointing out that "they put their uniforms on one leg at a time, just like us!" is hardly reassuring to an athlete who views the chances for success as nil. Pep talks and other incentives would also be of little benefit in this context. What is needed is for the coach to point out the relative weaknesses of the opponents in contrast to the relative strengths of the athlete or team and indicate how these might best be exploited for potential success. The issue here is that the athlete must perceive some opportunity for success, otherwise little or no competitiveness will be present.

Task characteristic dimension

Information feedback. Information feedback refers to error information which indicates the discrepancy between the completed response and the goal or target, or between the movement as planned and the movement as executed. For example, a teacher or coach may indicate to an archer that the arrow just shot landed two inches to the right of the exact center of the target. In another instance a teacher may inform the learner that the head of the golf club was dropped at the top of the backswing. These two types of information are commonly referred to as knowledge of results and knowledge of performance respectively.[2] As a rule, knowledge of results is available for the performer and so its provision by the coach or teacher is often redundant. On the other hand, knowledge of performance, by definition, is usually unavailable to the learner. (Except, of course, in the instance of kinesthetic feedback which provides knowledge of "how I moved," and is always available to the performer.)

The important issue for the coach to bear in mind is that the most common effect of information feedback is to increase motivation (Ammons, 1956). Athletes receiving feedback tend to pursue the task with greater application and diligence. This may be partly due to the attention given the athlete but it is also due to the fact that the feedback gives the athlete a yardstick by which progress, or lack of it, may be measured. It has also been demonstrated that the effectiveness of the yardstick, particularly for performers with some degree of skill, is directly related to its preciseness. For example, a golfer shooting "blind" to the green can profit from the information that his golf shot was hit over the green. However, for the information to be most effective, the specific distance should be given.

Clearly, the provision for feedback should be one of the major concerns of the coach or teacher, for feedback, properly used, is a crucial factor influencing the learning and/or performance of the individual. Care should be taken to avoid providing information which is readily available so that attention can be given to information the athlete cannot acquire independently. Another function of the coach or teacher concerns the use of feedback. Knowledge of results indicates the effect that a response has upon the environment. The player must learn to use the information to revise the response. For example, a tennis player who serves a ball into the net must consider the possible errors before taking the next serve and adjust it accordingly. Individuals who are encouraged to analyze their behavior in this manner will undoubtedly have an advantage in competition and practice.

Hawthorne Effect. Coaches frequently draw on the principles of the Hawthorne Effect in setting up their practice schedules. The effect is named after a classic series of studies carried out at the Western Electric Company's Hawthorne Plant in Chicago, Illinois (Roethlisberger and Dickson, 1939). The purpose of the experiments was to examine the effect of amount of plant illumination on work output. It was noted that the *productivity of the workers increased whether the level of illumination was increased or decreased. Thus, it was concluded that the level of illumination was not the variable of importance but, rather, the change and special attention given the workers. This phenomenon of an improvement in performance as a result of increased motivation resulting from change(s) in the performance environment has come to be called the Hawthorne Effect.*

Many coaches are sensitive to the need for occasional change in the practice environment, particularly late in a season when individual or team motivation might be low. Thus, football coaches might switch their linemen to the backfield (and vice versa) or have the team play soccer rather than football during the practice. Although the task has been changed and therefore the payoff in football skill acquisition would be negligible, the increased motivational benefits might far outweigh the negative aspects.

While the above examples are among the most extreme illustrations of a coach capitalizing on the well verified Hawthorne Effect, other more subtle examples are available. An example of where the Hawthorne Effect may be applied, but often is not, is in the selection of practice drills. Most coaches who have been involved with a sport for an extended period of time are rather restricted in the number and variety of drills they use. The process is gradual. Through experience in coaching, efficient, effective drills may be added and modified and less utilitarian drills eliminated. The result is that many experienced coaches have a fixed, minimal repertoire of drills which are used repetitively. On occasion, the coach must consider a trade-off. That is, a less effective drill (in terms of teaching potential) might be better in some instances because it is a *change* and therefore is potentially more motivating via the *Hawthorne Effect.*

SUMMARY

At the outset it was stressed that the *factors affecting motivation do not operate independently but, rather, as was illustrated in Figure 1, interact to produce a total level of motivation.* It is important, therefore, that the teacher or coach have information about each of the classes of factors considered: dimensions within the athlete; performance consequences dimension; and task characteristic dimension. Clearly, the teacher or coach cannot hope to encourage optimal motivation unless the four dimensions are taken into account. For example:

—The coach or teacher who applies similar motivational techniques to all performers is in danger of undermotivating some and over-motivating others depending upon their "normal" anxiety levels and upon their particular likes and dislikes.

—Not only should motivational techniques be varied for different athletes but the particular task should dictate the levels to be produced; simpler tasks require higher levels of motivation than more complex tasks.

—The Hawthorne Effect applies to motivational techniques as well as to task characteristics. Therefore, techniques should be widely varied to maintain effectiveness.

—Need achievement theory suggest that coaches and teachers inform students of the rationale behind various drills, keep the task challenging and appropriate to maintain incentive, and help students set multiple goals so that some success will be guaranteed.

—The effect of audience on the performer depends upon the performer's ability. During early learning the effects are generally detrimental; in the intermediate stages the specific effects may depend upon the characteristics of the audience; and, at high levels the effects are generally positive.

It is hoped that these examples, in addition to those in the article, will enable the teacher or coach to generate other examples more specifically matched to their situation and their performers.

REFERENCE NOTES

1. DUTHIE, J. H. and ROBERTS, G. C. Effect of manifest anxiety on learning and performance of a complex motor task. Paper presented at Second International Congress of Sport Psychology, Washington, 1968.

REFERENCES

AMMONS, R. B. Effects of knowledge of performance: a survey and tentative theoretical formulation. *Journal of General Psychology,* 1956, *54,* 279-299.

ATKINSON, J. W. The mainspring of achievement-oriented activity. In J. D. Krumboltz (ed.). *Learning and the educational process.* Chicago: Rand and McNally & Co., 1965.

BANDURA, A. *Aggression: a social learning analysis.* Englewood Cliffs: Prentice-Hall, 1973.

CARRON, A. V. Motor performance under stress. *Research Quarterly,* 1968, *39,* 463-468.

CASTANEDA, A., PALERMO, D. S. and McCANDLESS, B. R. Complex learning and performance as a function of anxiety in children and task difficulty. *Child Development,* 1956, *27,* 327-332.

COTTRELL, N. B. Performance in the presence of other human beings: mere presence, audience and affiliation effects. In E. C. Simmel, R. A. Hoppe and G. A. Milton (eds.), *Social Facilitation and Imitative Behavior.* Boston: Allyn & Bacon, 1968.

373

COTTRELL, N. B., WACK, D. L., SEKERAK, G. J. and RITTLE, R. H. Social facilitation of dominant responses by the presence of an audience and the mere presence of others. *Journal of Personality and Social Psychology,* 1968, *9,* 245-250.

CRATTY, B. J. *Social Dimensions of Physical Activity.* Englewood Cliffs: Prentice-Hall, 1967.

FARBER, I. E. and SPENCE, K. W. Complex learning and conditioning as a function of anxiety. *Journal of Experimental Psychology,* 1953, *45,* 120-125.

KAHN, M. W. The effect of severe defeat at various age levels on the aggressive behavior of mice. *Journal of Genetic Psychology,* 1951, *79,* 117-130.

MARTENS, R. *Social psychology and physical activity.* New York: Harper & Row, 1975.

MARTENS, R. and LANDERS, D. M. Evaluation potential as a determinant of coaction effects. *Journal of Experimental Social Psychology,* $972, *8,* 347-359.

OXENDINE, J. B. *Psychology of motor learning.* New York: Appleton-Century-Crofts, 1968.

ROBB, M. D. *The dynamics of motor-skill acquisition.* Englewood Cliffs: Prentice-Hall, 1972.

ROETHLISBERGER, F. J. & DICKSON, W. J. *Management and the worker.* Cambridge: Harvard University Press, 1939.

RUSHALL, B. and SIEDENTOP, D. *The development and control of behavior in sport and physical education.* Philadelphia: Lea & Febiger, 1972.

SCOTT, J. P. and MARSTON, M. V. Nonadaptive behavior resulting from a series of defeats in fighting mice. *Journal of Abnormal and Social Psychology,* 1953, *48,* 417-428.

SINGER, R. N. *Motor learning and human performance, 2nd Ed.* New York: Macmillan & Company, 1975.

ZAJONC, R. Social facilitation. *Science,* 1965, *149,* 269-274.

The Arousal-Performance Relationship Revisited *

Daniel M. Landers
Pennsylvania State University

When referring to motor performance one of the most frequently used phychological constructs is arousal. Its pervasiveness in the scientific and popular literature is not surprising since a common psychological problem encountered by athletes is their inability to cope with the pressure of competition. This reaction is not of course limited to athletics. It is found in a good many other performance situations, including public speaking and examination pressure.

In the scientific literature arousal is used a motivational construct. According to Murray (1946) motivation is defined as 'an internal factor that arouses, directs, and integrates a person's behavior' (p.7). There are many motivational theories and hypotheses that explain goal-directed behavior but what they have in common is that they conceptualize behavior as varying along two basic dimensions, direction and intensity. The intensity level of behavior is termed arousal. The construct of arousal, which is often used interchangeably with other intensity-related terms such as drive, tension, and activation, refers to the degree of energy release of the organism, which varies on a continuum from deep sleep to high excitement (Duffy, 1957). This energy is sometimes inferred from behavior or self-report measures of behavior, but is more commonly mesasured centrally by means of an electroencephalogram or by peripheral, autonomic measures such as heart rate and muscle tension.

In the present context, the more general arousal and intensity-related terms are merely used to refer to points along this continuum. When arousal levels are high the individual may experience unpleasant emotional reactions associated with arousal of the autonomic nervous system. This maladaptive condition is often referred to as stress or state anxiety. Each person has a slightly different response to stress depending on their learning histories and the type of situation. These responses can be divided into three general categories; cognitive, behavioral, and, of course, physiological since the latter is directly linked to the arousal construct. Response to stress may include one or more of these component categories (see Table 1). Some individuals, for example, will show autonomic arousal and report intense

---

* Landers, D. M. The Arousal-Performance Relationship Revisited, *Research Quarterly for Exercise and Sport*. 1980, *51*, 77-90. Reprinted by permission of the publisher, The American Alliance for Health, Physical Education, Recreation and Dance.

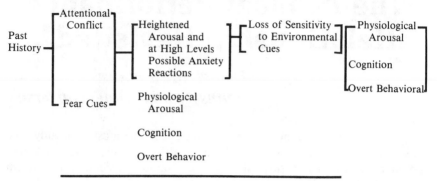

Current Stimulus Conditions	Immediate Reaction	Physiological Arousal	Subsequent Maintaining and Reducing Reactions
⌐Attentional⌐ Conflict	⌐Heightened Arousal and at High Levels Possible Anxiety Reactions	⌐Loss of Sensitivity to Environmental Cues	⌐Physiological Arousal
Past History			Cognition
└ Fear Cues ┘ Physiological Arousal			└Overt Behavioral
Cognition			
Overt Behavior			

Intervention Strategies

Table 1. Descriptive Model of the Arousal-Performance Relation (derived from Borkovec, 1976).

distress in a competitive situation but will show no avoidance behavior of the situation. Other individuals may vary in the degree to which they are aware of their heightened arousal, such as victims of high blood pressure who feel healthy and have few complaints.

In the present paper I would, primarily, like to share with you a descriptive model for explaining the relationship between arousal and motor performance that has guided our recent research and studies. Once this relationship is explained, I will briefly describe a multidimensional research strategy for measuring stress responses characterized by subjective feelings of apprehension and the occurrence of physiological arousal.

EXPLANATIONS FOR THE AROUSAL-MOTOR BEHAVIOR RELATIONSHIP

The Inverted-U and Drive-Theory Hypotheses

Before proceeding with a presentation of the model that I advocate, a brief summary of competing explanations is in order. Martens (1974) has provided an extensive review of the two hypotheses that have frequently been used to explain the relationship between arousal and performance. The first is the drive-theory hypothesis and the second is the inverted-U hypothesis.[1] Drive theory, as modified by Spence and Spence (1966), predicts that performance is a multiplicative function of habit and drive (P $\leq$ H ^{4} D). The theoretical construct of drive is often used synonomously with physiological arousal since the latter is more amenable to scientific measurement. Habit, on the other hand, refers to the hierarchical order or dominance of correct or incorrect responses. According to this theory, one would expect that increases in drive would enhance the probability of the dominant response being made. When performance errors are frequently made, as in the early stages of skill acquisition, the dominant responses are likely to be incorrect responses. Conversely, when performance errors are infrequent, the dominant response is said to be a correct response. Increases in drive (i.e., arousal) during initial skill acquisition impair performance, but as the skill becomes well learned, increases in arousal facilitate performance.

By comparison, the inverted-U hypothesis predicts that as the subject's arousal level increases from drowsiness to alertness, there is a progressive increase in performance efficiency. But, once arousal increases beyond, for example, alertness to a state of high excitement, there is a progressive decrease in task performance. Thus, this hypothesis suggests that behavior is aroused and directed toward some kind of 'balanced' or optimal state.[2]

Notice that the critical difference in the predictions made from these two hypotheses would be for a case when the subject's arousal level was high on a well-learned task. In this situation, drive theory would predict that the quality of performance would be high, whereas the inverted-U would hypothesize it to be low. This distinction is important because, dependent on which hypothesis one accepts, it will lead to different implications for teaching and coaching practice. For example, Oxendine (1970) essentially adopts a position consistent to the drive theory hypothesis for all motor tasks, particularly those involving strength, speed, and endurance. For complex tasks, particularly those involving strength, speed, and endurance. For complex tasks, however, Oxendine (1970) and Coleman (1977) stress that arousal interferes with performance—a position consistent with the inverted-U hypothesis.

Martens (1974) has reviewed the research evidence for the two hypotheses and concluded that:

1. The drive theory hypothesis should be rejected since 'it is not testable for motor behavior because of the inability to specify habit hierarchies for motor performance.'

2. The evidence essentially provided equivocal support for drive theory.

3. The inverted-U hypothesis supersedes the drive theory hypothesis since arousal levels may not have been of sufficient magnitude to cause a performance decrement in studies finding a positive linear relationship between arousal and performance.

4. The psychophysiological theories of activation and attentional theories, such as Easterbrook's (1959) cue utilization theory, are more viable alternatives for explaining the inverted-U relationship.

While I believe that Martens' review has helped to point researchers in the right direction, recent evidence would now suggest that his reasons for abandoning drive theory were not well founded. In the first place very few, if any, of the motor performance studies he reviewed satisfactorily measured habit strength or subject's arousal level. By including these studies in his review, there was no way to avoid the inescapable conclusion of equivocal results. In order to conduct any review of the arousal-motor performance relationship, it is imperative to determine criteria that would define the conditions under which an adequate test of these hypotheses can be made.

Therefore, to test the inverted-U versus drive-theory hypotheses there must be at least three or more levels of a situational stressor applied, and, in addition to employing a motor task in which habit strength can be operational defined, there must be corroborative evidence that an experimental exposure is, in fact, stressful. Burkun (1964) suggests the following three criteria for providing corroborative evience for stress: (1) the performance of subjects assumed to be stressed must be different from a nonstressed-control group, (2) the participants must subjectively report feeling distress in the situation of interest, and (3) there must be an indication of disruption of normal physiological processes. Considering that not one of the motor performance studies reviewed by Martens (1974) satisfied these criteria, it is not appropriate to conclude, based upon the findings of these studies, that drive theory should be abandoned for motor performance.

Martens' conclusion that 'habit strength' is not testable for motor performance is equally indefensible. For some motor tasks habit strength can be operationally defined. For example, Hunt and Hillary (1973) used motor mazes, with known floor and ceiling effects, and found results consistent with drive-theory predictions. Likewise, Landers, Brawley, and Hale (1978) found similar results for physical and psychological stressors with the same maze task (see Landers, 1975, for a detailed description of the simple and complex maze tasks). Carron and Bennett (1976), on the other hand, used a choice reaction-time paradigm to develop habit hierarchies. Although these studies show mixed support for drive theory,[3] they do demonstrate rather clearly that for some motor tasks, at least, habit strength can be operationally defined.

Another obstacle in the way of advocating abandonment of drive theory is the overall success this theory has had in the area of social facilitation research. Here it is generally found that the presence of an audience, or individuals working on similar but independent tasks (coaction), perform in a way that is consistent with drive theory predictions. During the initial stages of learning the arousal created by the presence of the audience detrimentally affects performance, but once the task is well learned, performance is facilitated. As recently as 1977, Geen and Gange concluded their extensive review of this literature with the optimistic appraisal that in spite of numerous competing theories, the drive-theory hypothesis was still the most parsimonious explanation for the research evidence reviewed.

Although the evidence at the time of Martens' review did not support his first two conclusions, the recent research findings do support his last two conclusions. This evidence is derived from studies in which arousal effects on performance have been assessed by means of methodology derived from signal detection theory (see Welford, 1975, for a discussion). This methodology has been employed in three different studies with various types of stressors (Bacon, 1974; Kushnir & Duncan, 1978; Miller & Leibowitz, 1976).

As a case in point, Kushnir and Duncan were able to demonstrate that the effects due to social facilitation are not due to response bias, as would be suggested by the 'response dominance' construct in drive theory. What was affected was subjects' sensitivity, or input bias, to the information presented. The problem appears to be a result of improper reception of information rather than inappropriate output after the information has been processed. Thus, the subjects in the alone condition were better able to distinguish between signals and nonsignals than subjects in the audience condition. These results bring social facilitation research in line with the majority of empirical studies which examine arousal effects on perceptual performance (Broadbent, 1971; Kahneman, 1973).

The results of the Kushnir and Duncan study, and other studies as well (Bacon, 1974; Miller & Leibowitz, 1976), indicate rather directly that response-related constructs such as 'habit' or 'response ceiling' (Broen & Storms, 1961) cannot mediate the arousal-performance relationship. Instead we need to direct our attention to theories which focus on the reception of information.

Elsewhere (Landers, 1978) I have argued that Easterbrook's cue utilization theory, in particular, appears to have heuristic value in understanding the arousal-performance relationship. What has been missing in previous analyses of this relationship (e.g., Oxendine, 1970) is the role that attention plays in most sport skills, including those involving speed, strength, and endurance. In the next section we will examine attention as it relates to arousal and performance.

Attentional Narrowing

One of the commonly reported effects of arousal is its influence on the narrowing of attention. Attention can be directed to a variety of environmental cues, particularly cues detected by the auditory and visual senses. The attentional process to be discussed appear to function the same for auditory and visual cues (Bacon, 1974).

Although research into the attentional narrowing phenomenon spans many different areas, the methodology is fundamentally the same. Employing a dual-task paradigm, studies on this topic generally show that subjects maintaining performance on a central or primarily important task are less able to respond to peripheral or secondary stimuli under stress. In most studies the central task is generally more demanding of subjects' attention than the peripheral task. In such cases, subjects improved performance on a central task, but decreased performance on a peripheral task when under the influence of such stressors as amphetamines, exercise stress, electric shock, sleep deprivation, incentives, hypoxia, and threat of personal injury (see Landers, 1978). Bacon (1974) maintains that the generalization that emerges from these studies is that arousal effects depend upon the degree of attention the stimuli attract with 'sensitivity loss systematically occurring to those cues which initialy attract less attention' (p. 86). The effects of arousal therefore impair one's performance through a loss of sensitivity by interfering with one's capacity to process information.

According to Easterbrook (1959) the behavioral effects due to peripheral narrowing may appear as linear or curvilinear, depending on the degree of arousal and number of levels of stress manipulated. Recall that the inverted-U is merely a relationship which can be explained by Easterbrook's cue utilization theory. Given certain stimulus conditions, such as attentional conflict or the presence of fear cues in the immediate environmental surround, arousal will be heightened. This arousal, particularly if it is high, will often lead to anxiety reactions which are manifest in three general response components: cognitive, overt behavioral, and physiological (see Table 1).

Depending on one's learning history, individuals differ in their degree of reaction to a given stimulus condition. More importantly, Borkovec (1976) maintains that:

individuals differ in terms of the learning history associated with each response component, resulting in individual differences in the intensity and/or functional importance of the response from each component in

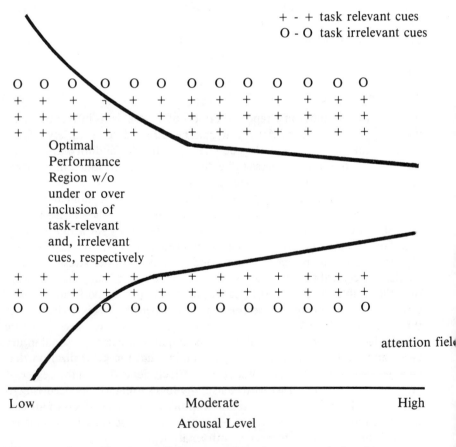

Figure 1. Cue utilization and the arousal-performance relationship

reaction to a particular feared or attentional conflict stimulus. Some individuals, for example, will report intense distress and display rapid avoidance when confronted with feared situations, but no evidence of increases in physiological arousal can be detected. Others may show such autonomic increases but differ in the degree to which they are aware of the arousal, the degree of avoidance behavior, the level of reported discomfort, etc.

For the majority of situations in sport and physical education most individual will at least approach the activity, but often not without some degree of physiological or cognitive anxiety. As a result of heightened arousal in these response components, attentional narrowing occurs accompanied by a loss of sensitivity to environmental cues. Easterbrook's theory predicts that performance under these conditions will depend on the degree of arousal and the available number of task-relevant and irrelevant cues.

As illustrated in Figure 1, a person performing under low arousal has a broad perceptual range and therefore, either through lack of effort or low selectivity, irrelevant cues are accepted uncritically. Performance in this case is understandably low. When arousal increases up to a moderate or optimal level, perceptual selectivity increases correspondingly, and the individual's performance improves, presumably because he/she tries harder or is more likely to eliminate task-irrelevant cues. Arousal increases beyond this optimal point permit further perceptual narrowing and performance deteriorates, in accord with the inverted-U hypothesis. For example, the quarterback in football under high anxiety may be focused too narrowly to detect receivers open in the periphery.

There is some controversy concerning what is actually happening to the performer's attention under high arousal-anxiety. Easterbrook (1959) argues that the range of usable cues is further restricted to the point of eliminating relevant-task cues. High arousal, however, is also associated with distractability, which as Wachtel (1967) has correctly pointed out forces investigators to distinguish not only between the breadth of cues we attend to, but also the amount that we scan the environmental surround. Since the attentional narrowing effect is widespread spanning many different types of stimulus conditions, it is believed to be an adaptive response. Most people display this response but, dependent on their prior history and experience in the situation, they will exhibit it in varying degree. Weltman and Egstrom (1966), for example, detected marked individual differences among beginning divers' exposure for the first time to submergence in the open ocean environment.

The narrowing process outlined in Figure 1 is also influenced by the complexity of the task. Research showing variation in detecting environmental cues as a function of dual-task competition has led Easterbrook to suggest that the task difficulty differences are related to the Yerkes-Dodson Law. To establish this link he assumed that the range of essential task cues is narrower for simple than for complex tasks. Thus, with more relevant task cues to keep track of on a complex task, the probability is greater that a given amount of arousal will lead to a performance decrement on a complex task sooner than it would for a simple task. For simple tasks, the ability to tolerate higher levels of arousal with performance decrements has been empirically supported by research on animals (Broadhurst, 1957) and human motor-skill acquisition. Carron (1965), for instance, has demonstrated that chronically overaroused individuals perform more poorly on complex motor tasks and relatively better on simple motor tasks.

The relationships illustrated in Figure 1 are not intended to indicate that attentional narrowing in fact casuses the inverted-U relationship between arousal and performance. There is always a chance, however remote, that some other variable causes both attention and performance to change as arousal increases. Whatever the cause, the relationships indicated in Figure 1 are empirically supported (see Landers 1978 for a more complete review of this research). The attentional narrowing phenomenon is appealing because of its heuristic value and its ability to account for a wide range of findings from seemingly diverse areas. Geen and Gange (1977) have also suggested cognitively mediated cue-utilization effects as an explanation for a broad range of social facilitation findings. The rationale for such an extension will be presented in the next section.

Social Facilitation and Cue Utilization

The area of social facilitation research is one of the few remaining strongholds for drive-theory explanations for performance effects. In the aftermath of Zajonc's (1965) application of drive theory to account for audience and coaction effects upon performance, there has been a fever of excitement as investigators have been attracted to this seemingly fertile area of research. This 'herd effect' was short lived as many investigators became disillusioned with the weak performance effects and the inconsistent arousal effects which resulted from the presence of audiences and coactors (see Landers, Snyder-Bauer, & Feltz, 1978).

Part of this problem is perhaps due to the lack of well-designed field studies on social facilitation. This point of view has been expressed, perhaps to an extreme by Martens (1979). Although field studies and field experiments may help to enhance the weak effects typically found in the laboratory (see Obermeier, Landers, & Ester, 1977 as an example), there is no guarantee that this approach will increase our understanding of the kind of effects on motor performance that have been the topic of discussion since Zajonc published his important review paper.

A more productive approach in confronting this problem is to use any theoretical or methodological approach (including various research settings) that will increase our understanding of this area. Above all, we must avoid giving up the problem by becoming shackled to a particular method or research setting (Dunnett, 1966; Platt, 1964).

In spite of what Geen and Gange concluded in their 1977 review of social facilitation research, I no longer believe that the best explanation for social facilitation is the drive theory formulation proposed by Zajonc. Recently, arousal-activation theorists have argued that two-factor theories (i.e., drive x habit) are too simplistic to predict performance. There is mounting evidence that subjects' attention must be considered and that this variable may be even more important than the concept of habit strength in predicting the effects of evaluative audiences upon performance.

There are two recent studies which support the conclusion that future research on social facilitation of motor behavior must investigate subjects' level of attention. The first is by Baron, Moore, and Sanders (1978), who found that people were distracted more from the task in the audience condition than in the alone condition. To measure distraction they had subjects try to recall a 'p' printed in red among the nonsense syllables they used for the performance tasks. This measure, more than other measures of distraction, suggests that task recall of subjects with an audience was low because they were attending to others in the situation. Baron et al. conclude that the social facilitation phenomenon is due at least partially to the distracting qualities of others. They propose that the drive-like effects occur because the presence of others creates attentional conflict within subjects; that is, they must reconcile social comparison with the pressure of working diligently on the task. Their distraction-conflict theory does not predict that any form of irrelevant stimulation presented during a task will heighten drive. Drive is only created when conflict with task activity occurs; that is, it is only high when attempting to reconcile two mutually exclusive response tendencies. The distracting qualities of audiences have also been shown for other cognitive tasks (Bruning, Capage, Kozuh, Young, & Young, 1968) as well as motor performance tasks (e.g., Gould, 1974).

The recognition that audiences and coactors do have distracting qualities brings us one step closer to Easterbrook's cue utilization theory and the attentional narrowing process outlined earlier. Although Baron et al. clarified why the evaluative aspects of audiences are arousing for some people but not others, they fall short of bringing the concept of 'attentional conflict' in line with drive theory. Their data did not establish why distractions in the task setting produce drive.

I would suggest that the difficulty encountered by Baron et al. could be alleviated by abandoning the drive theory explanation for social facilitation. I have already described evidence by Kushnir and Duncan (1978) which demonstrates that social facilitation effects are not due to response bias, as suggested by drive theory, but instead are due to sensitivity, or input bias, in the information presented. This of course is only one study and more replication is needed. However, this study was so carefully conceived and designed, à la Platt's (1964) strong inference approach, that it leaves little doubt that sensitivity in the receipt of environmental cues is where we need to search for an explanation for the social facilitation phenomenon.

These studies (Baron et al., 1978: Kushnir & Duncan, 1978) also explain why we have had so much trouble finding consistent and strong audience effects on arousal and motor performance. Our troubles have been precipitated not so much because of failure to operationalize drive or habit, or because of lack of field studies; instead the problem has been in not understanding the phenomena well enough to know where to look for the effects on performance.

It should be clear from what I have presented that future social facilitation research must consider attention as a mediating factor in the arousal-performance relationship. I am also hypothesizing that the arousal created in those individuals who experience attentional conflict will lead to a loss of sensitivity to environmental cues. As with any other research area involving arousal/attention/performance, the performance effects will depend on the individual's past history, the level of arousal experienced, and the difficulty of the task. The latter factor, task difficulty, is where habit strength becomes important since well-learned, task-relevant cues are least likely to be overlooked. In the laboratory, subjects given feedback after numerous training trials can increase their sensitivity to peripherally presented lights as much as a hundred times above their initial threshold values (Abernathy & Leibowitz, 1968). This has practical significance for the teacher or coach because if through extensive training they can make the performer's response to essential task cues automatic, there will be less chance that the performer's sensitivity to these cues will be reduced.

ANXIETY MEASUREMENT AND REDUCTION

Up to this point the effects of arousal on attention and performance have been examined. An equally important problem of contemporary concern is understanding how to control higher levels of arousal or anxiety. Given the negative effects that anxiety has upon performance it is little wonder that this area has recently witnessed an increase in theoretical anxiety research as well as the development of self-regulation techniques.

Currently paper-pencil tests are the primary means of assessing situational anxiety (i.e., state anxiety) in sport and physical education settings. These state anxiety measures include Spielberger's A-state scale and Martens' Competitive Short Form of the State Anxiety Inventory (see Martens, 1977, for a comparative analysis of these measures). These self-report measures sample individuals' perceptions of their overall subjective feelings at a given point in time. Subjects are asked if they feel nervous, tense, secure, calm, etc. The items making up these scales primarily tap the physiological or behavioral dimensions of anxiety.

Unfortunately, most state anxiety questionnaires provide but a single, global score reflecting an unknown mixture of typologically different forms of anxiety. Some of these questionnaires may be designed to be situationally specific (e.g., Martens' Competitive SAI), but they still fail to differentiate between relevant physiological, behavioral, and cognitive components of anxiety. An implicit assumption of these global anxiety scales is that the arousal which is hypothesized to underlie such states as anxiety, is undifferentiated. This assumption by arousal-activation theorists (Duffy, 1972) is now being challenged.

In the remainder of this paper I will briefly summarize a variety of recent factor analytic and psychophysiological evidence which supports the multidimensional nature of fear and anxiety. I will attempt to show that the recognition that anxiety is *not* a diffuse, undifferentiated internal state has important implications for the measurement and understanding of anxiety and also the assessment and treatment of affective disorders. I will argue that we need to redirect our current conceptualization of of sport-anxiety research toward a model of anxiety which emphasizes the reciprocal relationships between cognitions, physiological responses, and behavior.

The multidimensional nature of anxiety has been established through factor analytic studies of traditional anxiety questionnaires. For example, Barrett's (1972) analysis of anxiety items revealed two major subcomponents, one consisting of an awareness of somatic changes (e.g., "I blush often") and the other concerned with conscious awareness of unpleasant feelings about self or external stimuli (e.g., "I frequently find myself worrying about something"). Similar dimensions, labeled psychic (cognitive) and somatic anxiety, were derived from the self-ratings of psychiatric patients (Buss, 1962; Hamilton, 1959).

Recently, Schwartz, Davidson, and Goleman (1978) have developed an anxiety-symptom checklist with separate cognitive and somatic scales. They used this Cognitive-Somatic Anxiety Questionnaire to examine the differential effects of relaxation (physical exercise versus meditation) procedures designed to reduce anxiety in the somatic and cognitive mode,[4] respectively. These investigators found that somatic relaxation through physical exercise was associated with less somatic and more cognitive anxiety than the cognitive relaxation technique of meditation. These studies amply demonstrate the importance of distinguishing between specific subcomponents of anxiety since they may be differentially associated with relaxation techniques engaging primary cognitive versus somatic subsystems.

This evidence together with the psychophysiological evidence, which I will describe later, has prompted a number of contemporary investigators (e.g., Borkovec, 1976; Davidson & Schwartz, 1976; Smith in press) to develop multidimensional models of anxiety and its reduction. Borkovec defines anxiety by the multiple measurement of three *separate but interacting* response components: cognitive, overt behavioral, and physiological (see Table 1). He maintains that there are individual differences in terms of learning history associated with cogniitive behavior, motor behavior, and physiological reactions. In addition, these components may even be separately influenced by different environmental conditions at different points in time and may even obey different learning principles. However, these components may interact such that changes in one response component may ultimately affect subsequent changes in the remaining components.

Therapists are very much aware of this interaction. It is well known that if the physiological component is strongly present in the individual's immediate anxiety reaction, simple manipulation of the cognitive and behavioral components will be ineffective (Borkovec, 1976). This is just one example of how the independent assessment of the subcomponents of anxiety provides a better understanding of conditions which have implications for therapeutic practices for the maintenance or reduction of anxiety. From an applied standpoint, the therapist must also understand which response component is primarily affected since the anxiety coping technique selected should be based on the type of anxiety response displayed by the individual athlete or student.[5]

Several common manipulations may be categorized in terms of which response components are their primary focus (Borkovec, 1976). For example, techniques which deal directly with physiological reactions to anxiety are: relaxation training, autogenic training, systematic desensitization, and biofeedback. Some of the coping techniques for the overt behavioral component are reinforcement of approach behavior and modeling, while cognitive restructuring therapies and thought stopping are specific intervention techniques for the cognitive component (see Meichenbaum, 1977, for a description of these therapeutic techniques).

With the existence of such a variety of recent evidence supporting the multidimensionality of anxiety, it is indeed curious that sport scientists have not considered this model. The reason that they have failed to recognize the merits of a multidimensional model is because of the low intersubject correlations which exists among physiological measures of arousal (Lacey & Lacey, 1958). Martens (1977), for example, maintains that "as general self-report measure of arousal is a better predicator of theoretically related constructs than physiological variables" (p. 104). Statements like these have encouraged most sport psychologists to abandon physiological measures and assess anxiety with a questionnaire which simply yield a single global score.

Although it is true that the correlations among physiological measures or between physiological measures and self-report measures are low, this pattern of findings does not necessarily lead to the assumption by some activation theorists (e.g., Duffy, 1972) that there is poor validity for the measures in question or inadequacies in the measurement procedures. When standard stimulus conditions are employed, some individuals may respond primarily with a specific physiological system (i.e., heart rate) whereas other individuals may respond with quite different physiological systems.

The fact that individuals display different patterns within the physiological components is not an insurmountable problem in the assessment of physiological anxiety. Mandler, Mandler, and Uviller (1958) have shown that the employment of the Autonomic Perception Questionnaire (APQ) provides a promising bridge between the cognitive and physiological subcomponents. Mandler and his associates have shown that subjects who were preselected for reporting high levels of autonomic perception displayed significantly greater autonomic reactivity (heart rate, respiration, etc.) during stress than low perceivers. This study and others (see Borkovec, 1976, for a review) support the view that autonomic perception is an important subject characteristic related to the anxiety process.

The APQ results from several studies have also been factor analyzed resulting in three distinct types of profiles for the female samples and two types of males. Type I males, for example, were characterized solely by high awareness of heart activity and low awareness of headaches and shallow breathing. On the other hand, Type II males were characterized by high stomach activity, perspiration, and frequency of noticing bodily reactions when anxious. Thus, the APQ can be used to indirectly tap, at least for subjects demonstrating high APQ scores, the physiological dimension of anxiety when (1) testing of large groups is required, (2) expensive physiological equipment is not readily available, and (3) the environmental contest is not conducive to obtaining reliable physiological measures (e.g., movement artifacts). For the testing of small samples in the laboratory or limited field contexts, the APQ can be more appropriately used to determine which profile type the individual falls into so the appropriate physiological measures can be identified and subsequently used for research purposes.

The efficacy of the multidimensional nature of anxiety has also been demonstrated in psychophysiological research. As a follow-up to their previous research, Davidson, Davidson, and Freedland (Note 1) found that cognitive and somatic anxiety could be reliably distinguished on the basis of the patterning of cardiovascular, electrodermal, and electromyographical measures. More sophisticated psychobiological partitions of anxiety include studies examining hemispheric asymmetry in emotion, patterning of facial muscle activity in different affective states, and desynchrony in different physiological dependent measures which all have considerable face validity (see Schwartz et al., 1978).

Perhaps the most devastating evidence against the undifferentiated nature of arousal has been the work by Orne and Paskeqitz (1974). They examined the effect of learned control of alpha for reducing stress associated with an aversive stimulus. These investigators observed significant psychophysiological fractionation and specificity. When subjects were confronted with the possibility of receiving an electric shock, there was no significant decrement in learned control of occipital alpha presence, but heart rate and skin conductance responses were elevated. Based on their data, Orne and Paskewitz concluded "that it is possible for the subjects to report the experience of apprehension of fear as well as manifesting the autonomic concomitant of such experiences without associated changes in alpha density" (p. 460).

Because electroencephalogram recordings are considered by most activation theorists to be a *direct* measure of arousal, the findings by Orne and Paskewitz cast considerable doubt concerning the assumed undifferentiated nature of arousal. In referring to the Orne and Paskewitz findings, Schwartz et al. (1978) maintain that:

Instead of assuming, as some activation theorists have occasionally done (Duffy, 1972), that such fractionation is indicative of poor validity for the measures in question or inadequacies in the measurement procedures, we can view data such as these as reflecting meaningful patterns of physiological processes that are associated with particular behavior and experiential states.

The evidence presented supports the conclusion that anxiety is a multidimensional phenomenon and that we should use multimethod procedures to examine it. In sport psychology research, situationally specific self-resport measures are currently the rage! These questionnaires have been an improvement over the more general, nonsport-specific anxiety tests available in the field. Although these scales have enabled investigators to achieve slightly higher correlations than might have been obtained by non-situationally specific scales, they are still global measures and thus have done little to increase our scientific understanding of the multidimensional anxiety process.

We need to use the situationally specific anxiety measures as one of several physiological, behavioral, and cognitive measures. In my opinion, a multimethod approach will go a long way to combat the "little studies" and "little papers" which abound in sport-anxiety research. This also has implications for graduate education. For students interested in anxiety, arousal, and sport performance, we need to discourage total reliance on a single instrument and encourage greater eclecticism in the choice of methods used to examine anxiety. I suspect that what will result from such a redirection of our research efforts will be of considerably greater consquence for furthering our understanding of an individual's anxiety in a sport context.

REFERENCE NOTE

1. Davidson, R. J., Davison, G. C., & Freeland, E. *Psychophysiological specificity and the self-regulation of cognitive and somatic anxiety*. Paper presented at the International Conference on Biofeedback and Self-Control, Tubingen, Germany, November 1977.

REFERENCES

Abernathy, C. N., & Leibowitz, H. W. The effect of feedback on luminance thresholds for peripherally presented stimuli. *Perception and Psychophysics*, 1968, *10*, 172-174.

Bacon, S. J. Arousal and the range of cue utilization. *Journal of Experimental Psychology*, 1974, *103*, 81-87.

Baron, R. S., Moore, D., & Sanders, G. S. Distraction as a source of drive in social facilitation research. *Journal of Personality and Social Psychology*, 1978, *36*, 816-824.

Barrett, E. S. Anxiety and impulsiveness: Toward a neuropsychological model. In C. D. Speilberger (Ed.), *Anxiety: Current trends in theory and research* (Vol. 1). New York: Academic Press, 1972.

Borkovec, T. D. Physiological and cognitive processes in the regulation of anxiety. In G. E. Schwartz & D. Shapiro (Eds.), *Consciousness and self-regulation: Advances in research* (Vol. 1), New York: Plenum, 1976.

Broadbent, D. E. *Decision and stress*. London: Houghton Mifflin, 1971.

Boradhurst, P. L. Emotionality and the Yerkes-Dodson Law. *Journal of Experimental Psychology*, 1957, *54*, 345-352.

Broen, W. E., & Storms, L. H. A reaction potential ceiling and response decrements in complex situations. *Psychological Review*, 1961, *68*, 405-415.

Bruning, J. L., Capage, J. E., Kozuh, G. F., Young, P. F., & Young, W. E. Socially induced drive and range of cue utilization. *Journal of Personality and Social Psychology*, 1968, *9*, 242-244.

Burkun, M. M. Performance decrement under psychological stress. *Human Factors*, 1964, *6*, 21-30.

Buss, A. H. Two anxiety factors in psychiatric patients. *Journal of Abnormal and Social Psychology*, 1962, *65*, 426-427.

Carron, A. V. *Complex motor skill performance under conditions of externally-induced stress.* Unpublished master's thesis, University of Alberta, 1965.

Carron, A. V., & Bennett, B. The effects of initial habit strength differences upon performancein a coaction situation. *Journal of Motor Behavior,* 1976, *8,* 297-304.

Coleman, J. Normal stress reactions in shooting. *The Rifleman,* December 1977, 19-20.

Davidson, R. J. & Schwartz, G. E. The psychobiology of relaxation and related states: A multi-process theory. In D. I. Mostofsky (Ed.), *Behavior control and modification of physiological activity.* Englewood Cliffs, N.J.: Prentice Hall, 1976.

Duffy, E. The psychological significance of the concept of "arousal" or "activation." *Psychological Review,* 1957, *64,* 265-275.

Duffy, E. Activation. In H. S. Greenfield & R. A. Sternbach (Eds.), *Handbook of psychophysiology.* New York: Holt, Rinehart & Winston, 1972.

Dunnett, M. Fads, fashions, and folderol in psychology. *American Psychologist,* 1966, *21,* 343-351.

Easterbrook, J. A. The effect of emotion on cue utilization and the organization of behavior. *Psychological Review,* 1959, *66,* 183-201.

Geen, R. C., & Gange, J. J. Drive theory of social facilitation: Twelve years of theory and research. *Psychological Bulletin,* 1977, *84,* 1267-1288.

Gould, D. R. *Arousal and attentional demands as intervening variables in social facilitation paradigms.* Unpublished master's thesis, University of Washington, Seattle, 1974.

Hamilton, M. The assessment of anxiety states by rating. *British Journal of Medical Psychology,* 1959, *32,* 50-55.

Hunt, P. J., & Hillary, J. M. Social facilitation in a coaction setting: An examination of the effects over learning trials. *Jornal of Experimental Social Psychology,* 1973, *9,* 563-571.

Kahneman, D. *Attention and effort.* Englewood Cliffs, N.J.: Prentice Hall, 1973.

Klavora, P. An attempt to derive inverted-U curves based on the relationship between anxiety and athletic performance. In D. M. Landers & R. W. Christina (Eds.), *Psychology of motor behavior and sport.* Champaign, Ill.: Human Kinetics Publishers, 1978.

Kushnir, T., & Duncan, K. D. An analysis of social facilitation effects in terms of signal detection theory. *The Psychological Record,* 1978, *28,* 535-541.

Lacey, J., & Lacey, B. Verification and extension of the principle of autonomic response-stereotypy. *American Journal of Psychology,* 1958, *71,* 50-73.

Landers, D. M. Social facilitation and human performance: A review of contemporary and past research. In D. M. Landers (Ed.), *Psychology of sport and motor behavior II.* University Park, Pa.: College of HPER, 1975.

Landers, D. M. Motivation and performance: The role of arousal and attentional factors. In W. Straub (Ed.). *Sport psychology: An analysis of athlete behavior.* Ithaca, N.Y.: Mouvement Publications, 1978.

Landers, D. M., Brawley, L., & Hale, B. Habit strength differences in motor behavior: The effects of social facilitation paradigms and subject sex. In D. M. Landers & R. W. Christina (Eds.), *Psychology of motor behavior and sport 1977.* Champaign, Ill.: Human Kinetics Publishers, 1978.

Landers, D. M., Snyder-Bauer, R., & Feltz, D. L. Social facilittion during the initial stage of motor learning: A reexamination of Martens' audience study. *Journal of Motor Behavior,* 1978, *10,* 325-337.

Mandler, G., Mandler, J. M., & Uviller, E. T. Autonomic feedback: The perception of autonomic activity. *Journal of Abnormal and Social Psychology,* 1958, *56,* 367-373.

Martens, R. Arousal and motor performance. In J. H. Wilmore, *Exercise and sport science reviews* (Vol. 2). New York: Academic Press, 1974.

Martens, R. *Sport competition anxiety test. Champaign, Ill.: Human Kinetics Publishers, 1977.*

Martens, R. About smocks and jocks. Journal of Sport Psychology, 1979, *I,* 94-99.

Meichenbaum, D. H. *Cognitive-behavior modification.* New York: Plenum, 1977.

Miller, R. J., & Leibowitz, H. W. A signal detection analysis of hypnotically induced narrowing of the peripheral visual field. *Journal of Abnormal Psychology,* 1976, *85,* 446-454.

Murray, E. J. *Motivation and emotion.* Englewood Cliffs, N.J.: Prentice Hall, 1964.

389

Obermeier, G. E., Landers, D. M., & Ester, M. Social facilitation of speed events: The coaction effects in racing dogs and trackmen. In R. Christina & D. M. Landers (Eds.), *Psychology of motor behavior and sport 1976.* Champaign, Ill.: Human Kinetics Publishers, 1977.

Orne, M. T., & Paskewitz, D. A. Aversive situational effects on alpha feed-back training. *Science,* 1974, *186,* 458-460.

Oxendine, J. B. Emotional arousal and motor performance. *Quest,* 1970, *13,* 23-32.

Platt, J. R. Strong inference. *Science,* 1964, 146, 347-352.

Schwartz, G. E., Davidson, R. J., & Goleman, D. Patterning of cognitive and somatic processes in the self-regulation of anxiety: Effects of meditation versus exercise. *Psychosomatic Medicine,* 1978, *40,* 321-328.

Smith, R. E. Development of an integrated coping response through cognitive-affective stress management training. In I. G. Sarason & C. D. Spielberger (Eds.), *Stress and anxiety* (Vol. 7). Washington, D.C.: Hemisphere, in press.

Spence, J. T., & Spence, K. W. The motivational components of manifest anxiety: Drive and drive stimuli. In C. D. Spielberger (Ed.), *Anxiety and behavior.* New York: Academic Press, 1966.

Wachtel, P. L. Conceptions of broad and narrow attention. *Psychological Bulletin,* 1967, *68,* 417-429.

Welford, A. T. Stress and peformance. Ergonomics, 1975, *16,* 567-580.

Weltman, A. T., & Egstrom, G. H. Perceptual narrowing in novice divers. *Human Factors,* 1966, *8,* 499-505.

Zajonc, R. B. Social facilitation. *Science,* 1965, *149,* 269-274.

REFERENCE NOTES

1. In actuality, the inverted-U hypothesis is not an explanation for the arousal-performance relationship; it merely posits that this relationship is curvilinear without explaining what internal state or process produces it.

2. This optimal state can be assessed for each individual by taking successive anxiety-arousal measures over time and observing performance directly or indirectly through coaches ratings (see Klavora, 1978).

3. The effects due to stress in these studies were either nonexistent or quite small, possibly due to the weak effects which are known to occur when evaluative audiences and coactors are used as stressors (Landers, Snyder-Bauer, & Feltz, 1978).

4. Schwartz, Davidson, and Goleman (1978) further subdivided the somatic into skeletal and autonomic and the cognitive was considered to be either right or left brain mediated.

5. At times, the therapist may not have the time or equipment to determine which component may be affected by response to anxiety inducing manipulations. In this case, it is commonplace to use general intervention strategies, such as stress inoculation and cognitive-affective stress management (Smith, in press), which deal with all response components.

Stress Management Techniques for Sport and Physical Education[*]

Deborah L. Feltz [*]
Daniel M. Landers

In recent years teachers and coaches have become more and more interested in the methods of coping with stress, because of the demonstrated negative effects it has on performance. The term stress, which has been used interchangeably with tension and anxiety, refers to an unpleasant emotional reaction associated with arousal of the autonomic nervous system. Each person has a slightly different response to stress depending on their learning histories and the type of situation. These responses can be divided into three general categories: cognitive, behavioral, and physiological. Response to stress may include one or more of these component categories. (See Figure 1.) Some individuals, for example, will show autonomic arousal and report intense distress in a competitive situation but will show no avoidance behavior of the situation. Other individuals may vary in the degree to which

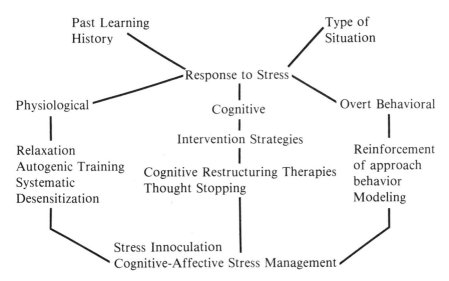

* Deborah L. Feltz and Daniel M. Landers are in the College of Health, Physical Education, and Recreation. The Pennsylvania State University, University Park, PA 16801.

*Feltz, D. and Landers, D., "Stress Management Techniques for Sport and Physical Education," *Journal of Physical Education and Recreation*. 1980, *51*, pp. 41-43. Reprinted by permission of the publisher.

they are aware of their heightened arousal, such as victims of high blood pressure who feel healthy and have few complaints.

Numerous techniques have been developed to cope with anxiety of stress. Some procedures have focused on one particular anxiety-response component, whereas others involve treatment packages that include all three component responses. The coping technique employed should be based on the type of anxiety response displayed by the individual athlete or student. Techniques which deal primarily with physiological reactions to stress are: relaxation training, autogenic training, systematic descensitization, and biofeedback.

Jacobson's (1938) progressive relaxation is based on gaining an awareness of the degree of muscular tension in one's body or body parts. Once individuals can recognize that tension is developing, they can begin to control it through relaxation. The technique generally involves alternating muscular contractions with relaxation of different major muscle groups, usually starting with the muscle groups associated with the wrists and arms working systematically down to the leg muscles. Most experienced teachers of relaxation employ a "discovery method" of tension awareness (Frederick, 1979) rather than using suggestion. For example, they let the student report where and when tension is beginning to develop and what it feels like. This is contrasted with Schultz's autogenic training (1969) which initially resembles Jacobson's technique but relies more on imagery and suggestions by the therapist. An example of this might be, "Imagine yourself lying on a warm beach. The sun is making your body feel warm and relaxed."

Systematic desensitization, as described by Wolpe (1974), basically involves three parts: training in deep-muscle relaxation, which is a brief form of Jacobson's technique; construction of anxiety hierarchies; and relaxation paired with imagined anxiety-evoking stimuli from the hierarchies. For example, a student who is fearful of the water and learning to swim may first be taught deep-muscle relaxation. Then progressively threatening tasks in and around a water environment can be constructed by the therapist in cooperation with the student. Tasks might include climbing down the ladder into the pool, letting go of the side, and walking three feet away from the side. The student would then relax and imagine first the least anxiety-provoking scene. While being relaxed, the mild anxiety which might arise is inhibited by the deep relaxation. Then progressively more anxiety-provoking situations are imagined until the student has worked through the hierarchy.

Biofeedback generally uses electronic equipment to amplify autonomic signals of the body (i.e., heart rate, muscular tension, blood pressure), making them easier to perceive and translating them into observable signals. These feedback signals could be a flashing light, a tone, or the movement of a needle. The same principle is applied in biofeedback as in relaxation training; if you become aware of your physiological responses to stress you can then learn to control it. Respiration biofeedback, in which subjects listen to their amplified breath sounds, has been effectively used to help anxious patients learn to relax (Grim, 1971). Because of the expensive equipment and technical know-how involved, biofeedback has seldom been used in physical education and sport settings.

These techniques assume that once physiological arousal has been controlled anxiety will be eliminated. However, one's anxiety may be maintained beyond an immediate physiological response through subsequent irrational thoughts and images (Borkovec, 1976). Anxiety researchers have, therefore, begun to apply cognitive intervention strategies between immediate anxiety reactions and subsequent maintaining reactions. These cognitively focused techniques include cognitive restructuring therapies and thought stopping.

Cognitive restructuring therapies such as Ellis' (1975) rational emotion therapy or Beck's (1970) cognitive therapy are directed at identifying and modifying irrational beliefs that cause the individual to appraise the situation in a stress-producing manner. Distortions of situations may include drawing certain conclusions when evidence is lacking, exaggerating the importance of an event, rigid perceptions of an event as good or bad, or taking one incident, such as failure, and attributing it to personal incompetence. For instance, a tennis player who has lost his/her last two matches, may believe that he/she has become incapable of playing good tennis, which then has a deleterious effect on future peformances. In employing cognitive restructuring, the therapist would show or guide athletes in discovering their irrational attributions and their negative impact on performance. The therapist would then help particular athletes restructure their attributions.

Dweck's (1975) attributional retraining program for learned helpless children is a type of cognitive restructuring therapy. Dweck's program teaches children to reattribute their failure to a lack of effort rather than a lack of ability. Roberts (1977) has questioned the applicability of attributional retraining in competitive sport situations where success is, in part, determined by the opponent. If a change in one's attributional thinking does not correspond to an increase in successful performance, the individual may give up. Manipulating success in organized athletics is difficult to do. However, in teaching physical education skills, where success is more manipulable, attributional retraining should be helpful to those students who have given up because they feel they are just plain clumsy.

In thought stopping therapy the individual is instructed to think about the stressful-producing cognitions, then taught to shout "Stop!" The overt command eventually becomes covert and can be used by the individual whenever unwanted stressful thoughts occur.

In cases where the student simply avoids the activity, therapists directed towards one's cognitive and physiological reactions may not be effective. Here, reinforcement of approach behavior or modeling may be needed.

Observing a model engaging in threatening activities without adverse consequences can reduce the avoidance behavior in the observer. Modeling techniques can take many forms. The model can be live or covert. In covert modeling, the individual imagines a model performing the threatening activities. The model can also be a mastery or coping model. A mastery model would demonstrate competent performance without any sign of distress or hesitation. A coping model would appear initially anxious but would presevere and overcome this anxiety by determined effort. Investigations have shown that a coping model, who is perceived as similar to the observer, is more effective in reducing avoidance behavior (Kazdin, 1974; Meichenbaum, 1971). Many times coping models incorporate their cognitions into their demonstrations by commenting on their anxiety and accompanying physiological arousal. They then demonstrate their coping ability by instructing themselves to remain relaxed, take one step at a time, and persevere. They may also emit self-rewarding statements upon completion of the task.

Modeling has been combined with guided participation to ensure successful performance in reducing avoidance behavior. In this technique, called participant modeling, the model first demonstrates the task then performs the task jointly with the learner or provides physical guidance to ensure success. Participant modeling has been shown to be more effective than modeling alone with apprehensive learners in swimming and diving tasks (Feltz, Landers, & Raeder, 1979; Lewis, 1974).

Cognitive or behavioral techniques alone may be effective if the physiological component is weak or nonexistent. However, as long as the physiological component is strongly present in the individual's immediate anxiety reaction, techniques to reduce physiological arousal need to be included in the therapy.

Smith (in press), consequently, has proposed a conceptual model of stress which emphasizes the reciprocal relationships between cognitions, physiological responses, and behaivor. His cognitive-affective stress-management training program is a treatment package which teaches a variety of coping skills and provides opportunity for practice in rehearsing and applying the skills. During the skill acquisition phase, the individual is taught muscular relaxation with emphasis on deep breathing, plus emitting the mental command "Relax" during exhalation. This is to teach control of the physiological component response. The individual is then trained in cognitive coping skills, using a form of cognitive restructuring. He/she keeps an "anti-stress" log, listing stress producing self-statements and an anti-stress substitute for each. Individuals are also required to read a book based on rational emotive emotive therapy (Ellis & Harper, 1975) to give them a better understanding of why irrational beliefs affect performance deleteriously.

In the skill rehearsal phase, a psychotherapeutic procedure known as induced affect is used to elicit high levels of emotional arousal by instructing the client to focus on a stressful situation and then using suggestion to generate the intense emotional response. The individual uses his/her relaxation and anti-stress responses, developed in the acquisition phase, to reduce the arousal. This technique has been effective with a number of athletes, from football players to figure skaters. Smith states that this population was able to acquire a number of coping skills more quickly than other groups.

With one exception, Meichenbaum's (1976) stress innoculation proce-

394

dure is a similar treatment package to Smith's cognitive-affective program. The only difference is that in the rehearsal phase Meichenbaum exposes the individual to small, manageable units of stress rather than using induced affect. Meichenbaum (1977) also incorporates modeling and reinforcing self-statements at the completion of performance.

All of the therapy techniques discussed in this article require training in order to properly administer and access which technique would be most effective for the player or student. Even for teaching relaxation or tension control, Frederick (1979) suggests that instructors and coaches enroll in a training course provided by the American Association for the Advancement of Tension Control (AAATC). Most of the other techniques, such as desensitization training, legally require administration by a professional therapist in most states (Harrison & Feltz, 1979). Systematic desensitization administered by an inexperienced individual could actually sensitize rather than desensitize the client. Modeling and the use of reinforcement for approach behavior have been used extensively by coaches and teachers and most have received training in these procedures.

The North American Society for the Psychology of Sport and Physical Activity (NASPSPA) has recently formed a committee to study the qualifications needed to use psychological techniques with athletes; it will then set ethical standards for the practice of sport psychology. If you as a teacher or coach are in serious doubt as to your qualifications to handle an individual's problem, you should contact one of the officers in NASPSPA or refer the individual to a professional therapist.

REFERENCES

Beck, A. T. Cognitive therapy: Nature and relation to behavior therapy. *Behavior Therapy*. 1970, *1*, 184-200.

Borkovec. T. D. Physiological and cognitive processes in the regulation of anxiety. In G. E. Schartz & D. Shapiro (Eds.). *Consciousness and self-regulation: Advances in research*. (Vol. 1). New York: Plenum, 1976.

Dweck, C. S. The role of expectations and attributions in the alleviation of learned helplessness. *Journal of Personality and Social Psychology*. 1975. *31*. 674-685.

Ellis, A. & Harper, R. A. *A new guide to rational living*. Englewood Cliff, N.J.: Prentice-Hall, 1975.

Feltz, D. L., Landers, D. M. & Raeder, V. Enchancing self-efficacy in high-avoidance motor tasks: A comparison of modeling techniques. *Journal of Sport Psychology*. 1979. *I*. 112-122.

Frederick, A. B. *Relaxation: Education's fourth "R."* Washington, D.C.: Eric Clearinghouse on Teacher Education. 1979.

Grim, P. Anxiety change produced by self-induced muscle tension and by relaxation with respiration feedback. *Behavior Therapy*. 1971. *2*. 11-17.

Harrison, R. P., & Feltz, D. L. The professionalization of sport psychology: Legal considerations. *Journal of Sport Psychology*. 1979. *I*. (in press).

Jacobson, E. *Progressive relaxation* (2nd ed.). Chicago: University of Chicago Press, 1938.

Kazdin. A. E. Covert modeling, model similarity and reduction of avoidance behavior. *Behavior Therapy*. 1974. *5*. 325-340.

Lewis, S. A comparison of behavior therapy techniques in the reduction of fearful avoidance behavior. *Behavior Therapy*. 1974. *5*. 648-655.

Meichenbaum, D. H. Examination of model characteristics in reducing avoidance behavior. *Journal of Personality and Social Psychology*, 1971. *17*. 298-307.

Meichenbaum, D. H. A self-instructional approach to stress management: A proposal for stress inoculation training. In C. D. Spielberger & I. G. Sarason (Eds.). *Stress and anxiety in modern life*. New York: Winston. 1976.

Meichenbaum, D. H. *Cognitive-behavior modification*. New York: Plenum. 1977.

Roberts. G. C. Children in competition: Assignment of responsibility for winning and losing. In L. I. Geduilas & M. E. Kneer (Eds.). *Proceedings of the NAPECW/NCPEAM national conference*. Chicago: University of Illinois at Chicago Circle. 1977.

Schultz, J. H., & Wolfgang. L. Autogenic methods. In L. Wolfgang (Ed.). *Autogenic therapy* (Vol. 1). New York: Grune & Stratton. 1969.

Smith, R. E. Development of an integrated coping response through cognitive-affective stress management training. In I. G. Sarson & C. D. Spielberger (Eds.). *Stress and anxiety* (Vol. 7). Washington, D.C.: Hemisphere, in press.

Wolpe, J. *The practice of behavior therapy* (2nd ed.). Elmsford, New York: Maxwell House. 1974.

REFERENCE NOTE

1. Write to Daniel M. Landers, NASPSPA, Sports Research Building, College of Health, Physical Education and Recreation. The Pennsylvania State University, University Park, PA 16801.

Sports, Competition, And Aggression*

Leonard Berkowitz,
University of Wisconsin,
Madison, Wisconsin

You might remember General MacArthur's farewell speech. "Old soldiers never die," he said, "they just fade away." Every once in a while I have the impression that the same thing can be said about certain psychological notions, especially in regard to aggression. Old ideas never die, apparently. They made fade away occasionally, but someone is bound to resurrect them and proclaim them as a newfound truth. This certainly seems to be the case with ventilative conceptions of aggression. We're repeatedly told that civilized man does not have sufficient outlets for his supposedly pent-up aggressive urges. Society would be improved by providing him with safe opportunities to discharge, or sublimate, his aggressive energy. In ventilation there is health.

Sports, and competitive games generally, are frequently recommended as an effective purge. The basic thinking here, as you know, is that an aggressive drive continuously presses for discharge and must have an outlet, either in attacks upon others or against the self, or in efforts to achieve mastery. Sports presumably can furnish this needed release. As an example, one of the leading contemporary exponents of the notion of a spontaneously generated aggressive drive, Konrad Lorenz, has this to say in his recent book On Aggression (1966):

". . . the main function of sport today lies in the cathartic discharge of aggressive urge. . . ." (p. 280).

Extending this reasoning to international relations, he and others believe that international games can promote peace:

"The most important function of sport lies in furnishing a healthy safety valve for that . . . most dangerous form of aggression that I have described as collective militant enthusiasm . . . The Olympic Games are virtually the only occasion when the anthem of one nation can be played without arousing any hostility against another." (p. 281).

The tragic events at the Olympic Games in Munich this past summer

* Berkowitz, L. "Sports, Competition, and Aggression," In L. Wankel and I. Williams (Ed.), *Proceedings — Fourth Canadian Symposium on Psycho-Motor Learning and Sports Psychology.* Fitness and Amateur Sport Canada, Government of Canada, Ottawa, Canada, 1974, 321-326. Reprinted by permission of Fitness and Amateur Sport Canada.

397

must make us wonder about sport as an outlet for "collective militant enthusiasm."

Conventional psychodynamic theorizing also holds that the aggressive "drive," whether it is instinctive or the product of earlier frustrations, can safely be discharged through athletic competition. Writing about 25 years ago, as an illustration, William Menninger (1948) contended that play brings about a healthy release from the tensions supposedly created by "instinctive" aggressive impulses. He also claimed that "competitive games provide an unusually satisfactory social outlet for the instinctive aggressive drive," but believed that some discharge could also be obtained through sports involving "sedentary intellectual competition," such as chess and checkers (p. 343).

It's easy to understand this type of reasoning. We can readily grasp the metaphor of a reservoir of aggressive energy pressing for discharge, like a boiler full of steam, and the idea of games as an outlet for this energy seems to coincide with our experience. But this ease of understanding is a misleading trap. The fit between metaphor and experience is more apparent than real and largely arises from incomplete analyses. A growing body of carefully collected evidence indicates that athletic competition doesn't necessarily reduce the chances of violence and may even increase the probability of aggressive outbursts under some circumstances. Sport is no royal road to peace and social harmony.

In considering the impact of sports it's important to distinguish between the mere observation of a game or competition and active participa-

satisfactory release for its pent-up aggressive urges through watching others beat each other up or through observing competition (Lorenz, 1966; Storr, 1968; Feshbach, 1961), observed sports may not have the same results as actual participation in the game. The individual who only sees the encounter may not enter into it as fully as the actual player, and therefore might not obtain as complete a "release."

EFFECTS ON THE SPECTATORS

Well, what are the effects of watching some competition? There's clearly no single answer to such a question, but on looking at the evidence one thing is puzzling. There are so many reports of spectators becoming violent as a consequence of an athletic match, we have to wonder why the notion persists that the viewers will discharge their aggressive inclinations by seeing the game. Here's a sampling of these reports:

In May, 1964 a referee's decision at a soccer match in Lima, Peru caused a riot, leading to the death of a number of spectators (reported by Goldstein & Arms, 1971, p. 83).

According to some analysts (Lever, 1969), a war between El Salvador and Honduras was precipitated by a soccer game between teams representing these countries.

Athletics didn't improve the relations between Czechs and Russians shortly after the Russians had suppressed the Czechs' attempt to liberalize

398

their government. In March, 1969 when a Czech hockey team defeated the Russian team in the world championship tournament, exuberant Czechoslovakian youths ransacked the Prague offices of the Russian airline; instead of being satisfied, the excited Czechs attacked symbols of those they hated.

In this country, among the many incidents that could be cited, a high school basketball game in New Jersey stimulated a riot in the audience, while another game the same week in a neighboring community brought on a fight between the opposing cheerleaders (Turner, 1970).

Quantitative investigations also show how witnessed athletic contests can arouse hosbility in the spectators. Goldstein and Arms (1971) interviewed men at the 1969 Army-Navy football game in Philadelphia and found a significant rise in feelings of hostility from right before to just after the game regardless of which team the men favored and which side had won. By contrast, spectators at the Army-Temple gymnastics meet held during the same month did not exhibit this increase in hostility.

In this case watching a contact sport had led to heightened aggressive inclinations. This needn't always happen. The tens of millions of people seeing televised football games every Autumn week-end aren't necessarily provoked to violence (unless, of course, they had bet heavily on the outcome of the game and lost). What happens depends upon a variety of factors. I have suggested, for example, that the witnessed event can serve as a stimulus that will elicit semantically-associated responses, but just what reactions occur is a function of the meaning of the stimulus to the observer. If the scene is interpreted as an *aggressive* encounter, in which the competitors presumably are deliberately trying to hurt each other, it is a stimulus having *aggressive* meaning and can then elicit aggressive reactions. Take a football game or a prize fight. A spectator doesn't really have to think of this as an *aggressive* contest, although it is obviously easy to do so. He might regard the opponents merely as players who are trying to win for the money or prestige the victory would bring. When one player knocks someone else down this is viewed as a demonstration of superior strength or skill. The same scene becomes an aggressive match, on the other hand, when the observer believes the contestants want to hurt each other as well as win. However broad or subtle our own definition of "aggression" might be, it's the viewer's interpretation that really matters; the scene isn't really an aggressive stimulus unless he thinks of it as aggression, as the deliberate injury of others.

An experiment by myself and Alioto tested this reasoning using college students as subjects. Each man, who had first been insulted by a paid accomplice, was shown a brief movie either of a prize fight or a professional football game. The introduction to this film "explained" the background of the contest, and portrayed the opponents either as players unemotionally engaged in their professional roles or as aggressors trying to hurt their enemy. When the subject was given an opportunity to shock the insulting confederate at the end of the film, he attacked this person more strongly if he had watched a scene having the aggressive rather than nonaggressive meaning. This was true for both the prize fight and fooball game. More-over, only the men seeing the *aggressive* contest were significantly more punitive to the confederate than a similarly provoked control group shown an exciting but nonviolent film.

This experiment indicates, then, that the spectators' interpretation of a game effects their reactions to it. The contest is more likely to have aggres-sive consequences if it is regarded as an aggressive encounter. But other fac-tors are also important. In our research at Wisconsin, for example, we have found that the observer's readiness to act aggressively at the time he watches the movie influences the probability that he will exhibit overt aggression at the end of the film. This means, obviously that the aggressive game will be most likely to evoke open violence from those spectators who are already in-clined to be aggressive.

But again, I don't think this is all. We also have to consider other things such as the spectators' feeling of anonymity (which would lower their fear of being punished for aggression) and especially now excited as they are. This excitement theoretically should "energize" the aggressive reac-tions elicited by the aggressive scene, heightening the chances of open vio-lence. Green and O'Neal (1969) demonstrated that noise can have this arousing effect. Their subjects who watched our standard prize fight scene and then were exposed to a burst of moderately loud noise were subsequent-ly more punitive towards a fellow student than other subjects not given the noise or who didn't see the film. The arousing noise had evidently strength-ened the implicit aggressive reactions elicited by the witnessed prize fight, leading to the stronger attacks right afterwards.

All in all, this evidence clearly shows that people watching some athle-tic event are unlikely to drain their supposedly pent-up aggressive urges. The game might even heighten the probability of violence under some con-ditions. If the spectators are less aggressive afterwards, I would say they either feel good because their team won or they were so distracted by the ex-citing contest that they forgot about their troubles for the time being and, in not brooding, stopped stirring themselves up.

EFFECT OF PARTICIPATING IN COMPETITION

Earlier I noted the possibility that actual participation in an athletic competition might produce a more satisfactory "release" than the mere observation of such an encounter. In actuality, however, it seems that the persons who take part in the game can also become more aggressive as a consequence of what they see and do.

One reason for this is that the game is exciting, and we just saw, excite-ment can energize whatever aggressive tendencies might be operating at the moment. Zillmann, Katcher and Milavsky (1972) have recently reported that the excitation created by two and a half minutes of strenuous physical exercise (bicycle riding) increased the intensity of the punishment university men administered to a peer. This happened whether or not the subjects were angry with this other person, but the energizing effect was strongest when the men had been provoked by him earlier and now had an opportunity to retaliate. The nonangry men were evidently ready to punish the other person and were therefore already somewhat inclined to attack him when they engaged in the brief exercise. The excitation then strengthened their aggressive inclinations. Needless to say, the angry subjects were even more intent on attacking this other person, and the exercise-created arousal strengthened their aggressive inclinations even more. The angry men didn't discharge their hostile urges through the vigorous physical activity, but instead, became somewhat more violent.

The competition inherent in the game can also be exciting, and again, this can intensify the players' aggressive tendencies. We have some suggestive data in a study of children's play carried out by Christy, Gelfand and Hartmann (1971). The first- and second-graders in this experiment first watched an adult engage in either aggressive-like play (punching and kicking a Bobo doll) or vigorous but nonviolent action (such as jumping around) and then were placed in either a competitive or noncompetitive situation. The arousal created by the competition energized the behavior tendencies activated by the adult's conduct. Whether they had won or lost, the children who had experienced the competition were most likely to imitate the adult's earlier behavior in their own play immediately after the competition. So, if someone starts acting violently for one reason or another, any other people around who are excited because they're competing against others should be particularly likely to do the same thing. The competition heightens, not lessens, their susceptibility to aggressive influence.

I've long suspected (Berkowitz, 1962, 1969) that competition also has some frustrating aspects if there isn't any clearcut victory in sight and especially if the individual loses, and have argued that this frustration can also create a readiness for aggression. This means that competition could increase the chances of aggression specifically as well as heighten the players' susceptibility to external influences generally. There's been a good deal of controversy about this, as you undoubtedly know, but some experimental findings do point to a competition-increased probability of aggression. As just one illustration of this, the well-known "Robber's Cave" experiment (Sherif et al., 1961) dramatically demonstrates how competition between groups of teenage boys can lead to outbreaks of violence. The frustration should be even stronger, obviously, if a person is defeated in the competition, and this thwarting could produce an even greater pre-disposition to aggression. We can see this, as an example, in the research on children's play conducted by Gelfand, Hartmann and their students. In the experiment with Christy that I mentioned earlier as well as in the case of the young boys in an earlier, similar study (Nelson, Gelfand and Hartmann, 1969), those children who had not been subjected to strong environmental influence but then suffered a loss in the competition were especially apt to engage in aggressive-like play afterwards. The pain of the defeat heightened their readiness for aggression.

In all of this I've focused on the temporary impact of sports: the excitement and the aggressive stimulation that might arise. Nothing has been said about more persistent learning, but there's also some suggestive evidence that the aggressiveness learned in play can generalize to other situations as well. In one study (Walters & Brown, 1963) the children given intermittent reinforcement for punching a Bobo doll behaved more aggressively than the controls in a competitive situation some days later. We recognize that this kind of learning may not always occur or may not always become apparent; the reinforced aggression might not transfer to other situations if the reinforcement schedule isn't appropriate and especially if the person learns to discriminate between play and the real world. Prize fighters and football players know that it's alright to knock their opponent down in the ring or on the football field but not in the street or house. Still, I would bet that if they happen to be angry and not thinking on some occasion, the reinforcements they had previously received for aggression in competition will increase the chance that they will act violently in this other setting as well.

The disrciminations the individual learns and the inhibitions he acquires also help restrain the temorary aggressive reactions stimulated by the sight of aggression in the game or by the frustrations in the situation. Those aggressive reactions are usually fairly weak and relatively short-lived (more so in the spectators than in the players, I would guess), and prior learning controls these responses so the people don't attack the others around them indiscriminately. But if these persons are excited enough, stimulated enough, and sufficiently uninhibited at the moment, they could act violently. The game they played or watched has not drained their aggressive energies. Sport has considerable value for our society, but we shouldn't justify it as a safe outlet for pent-up violent urges.

REFERENCES

Berkowitz, L. *Aggression: A Social-Psychological Analysis*. New York: McGraw-Hill, 1962.

Berkowitz, L. "The Frustration-Aggression Hypothesis Revisited." In L. Berkowitz (Ed.) *Roots of Aggression*. New York: Atherton Press, 1969, 1-29.

Christy, P. R., Gelfand, D. M. and D. P. Hartmann. "Effects of Competition-Induced Frustration on Two Classes of Modeled Behavior." *Developmental Psychology, 1971, 5.* 104-111.

Feshbach, S. "The Stimulating Versus Cathartic Effects of a Vicarious Aggressive Activity." *Journal of Abnormal and Social Psychology,* 1969, 63, 381-385.

Green, R. G. and E. C. O'Neal. Activation of Cue-Elicited Aggression by General Arousal." *Journal of Personality and Social Psychology,* 1969, 11, 289-292.

Goldstein, J. H. and R. L. Arms. "Effects of Observing Athletic Contests of Hostility." *Sociometry,* 1971, 34, 83-90.

Lever, J. "Soccer: Opium of the Brazilian People." *Trans-Action,* 1969, 7, 36-43.

Lorenz, L. *On Aggression*. New York: Harcourt, Brace and World, 1966.

Menninger, W. C. "Recreation and Mental Health." *Recreation,* 1948, 42, 340-346.

Nelson, J. D., Gelfand, D. M. and D. P. Hartmann. "Children's Aggression Following Competition and Exposure to an Aggressive Model." *Child Development,* 1969, 40, 1085-1097.

Sherif, M., Harvey, O. J., White, W. R. and C. W. Sherif, *Intergroup Conflict and Cooperation: The Robber's Cave Experiment*. Norman, Oklahoma: University of Oklahoma Book Exchange, 1961.

Storr, A. *Human Aggression*. New York: Atheneum, 1968.

Turner, E. T. "The Effects of Viewing College Football, Basketball and Wrestling on the Elicited Aggressive Responses of Male Spectators." *Medicine and Science in Sports,* 1970, 2, 100-105.

Walters, R. H. and M. Brown. "Studies of Reinforcement of Aggression: III. Transfer of Responses to an Interpersonal Situation." *Child Development,* 1963, 34, 563-571.

Zillmann, D., Katcher, A. H. and A. H. and B. Milavsky. "Excitation Transfer from Exercise to Subsequent Aggressive Behavior." *Journal of Experiment Social Psychology,* 1972, 8, 247-259.

The Relationship Between Aggression and Performance Outcome in Ice Hockey[1] *

W. Neil Widmeyer
Jack S. Birch
Department of Kinesiology
University of Waterloo
Waterloo, Ontario

Widmeyer, W. N., and Birch, J. S. The relationship between aggression and performance outcome in ice hockey. **Can. J. Appl. Spt. Sci.** *4:1:91-94. 1979. - This investigation determined if aggression is a means of obtaining success in amateur ice hockey. Two analyses were undertaken. The first examined the relationship between illegitimate tactics (as measured by penalty minutes accumulated) and team success, while the second compared the penalty minutes accumulated by successful individuals (i.e. all stars) with the penalty minutes accumulated by non-all stars. The sample was comprised of the 87 teams and their 1,667 players who participated in the Ontario University Athletic Association from 1971-72 to 1976-77. The relationship between team aggression and team success was analyzed with a Pearson Product Moment Correlation. A t test was used to compare the mean accumulated penalty minutes of all stars with those of non-all stars. The results failed to support the premise that aggression is a means to success for teams or for individuals.*

aggression; hockey; performance outcome

Cette étude a cherché à déterminer si l'agression est un moyen de gagner une partie de hockey amateur. Deux analyses furent conduites. La première a consisté à examiner la relation entre les actions non-permises (évaluées par la durée des punitions accumulées) et le succes de l'équipe, tandis que la seconde a comparé les minutes de pénalité accumulées par les bous joueurs à celles accumulées par le moins bous joueurs. L'étude a été conduite sur 87 equipes et leur 1667 joueurs, qui participaient aux compétitions de l'Ontario University Athletic Association de 1971-72 a 1976-77. Les relations ont été analysées à l'aide du coefficient de correlation de Pearson. Un test de t de student a été utilisé pour comparer les minutes de pénalité accumulées par

* Widmeyer, W.N. and Birch, J. S. "The Relationship Between Aggression and Performance Outcome in Ice Hockey," *Canadian Journal of Applied Sport Sciences.* 1979, *4,* 91-94. Reprinted by permission of the publisher.

les bous et les moins bous joueurs. Les résultats ne démontrent pas que l'ag-gression est un moyen de gagner pour l'équipe, ni une garantie de succès personnel pour le joueur.

INTRODUCTION

Concern over the increasing violence in society has resulted in a great deal of research into the causes of aggressive behaviour. Aggression has been defined in many ways. However, most would agree that it is behaviour designed to harm another.[2] The world of sport, similar to other domains, is not immune to aggressive behaviour. As a result many researchers and jour-nalists have sought to explain why aggression occurs in sport.

Investigations into the *consequences* of aggression in sport are far fewer than those which have examined the antecedents of this behaviour. Nevertheless some studies have examined the influence of aggressive acts in sport on ensuing levels of aggression (Ardrey, 1966; Berkowitz, 1962; Scott, 1970; Zillman et al., 1974) and on the behaviour of viewers of these acts (Geen and Berkowitz 1966; Goldstein and Arms 1971; Taylor, 1976; Thirer 1978). It is surprising that one of the most commonly researched conse-quences of sport behaviour, namely performance outcome, has rarely been examined as a consequence of aggression in sport.

Before examining the limited research concerning the aggression-performance outcome relationship, the question should be posed: What in-fluence could aggression have on performance outcome in sport? The answer to this question lies in a theory of performance outcome. Perfor-mance outcome in a competitive situation is dependent not only upon the performance of the individual or the group but also upon the performance of the opponent. Steiner (1972) states that group output is a function of group input and group process whereas individual performance depends on-ly on individual input. Thus a group's performance outcome could be altered by changing the group's input, the group's process, the opponent's input or the opponent's process. Individual performance outcome could be changed by altering individual input or the input of the opponent. For ex-ample, aggression could have a positive influence on a group's or on an in-dividual's performance outcome if the aggressive behaviour harmed the op-position either physically or psychologically. Aggression could also improve a group's performance outcome by improving the process of the group. Faulkner (1974) supports this notion when he states that violence can "strengthen existing bonds and establish new ones among players as they deal with their adversaries". Faulkner also suggests that a group's ag-gressive behaviour can help its performance outcome by weakening the op-position's "unity bonds of collective strength" and reducing their "sense of control of the opposition". Aggression could have a negative influence on the performance outcome of a group or an individual if their inputs were weakened because of penalties that they received. Likewise, group cohe-sion, a process variable, is lowered when one or more players are penalized. This forces the other players to work harder and decreases their chance for success while playing shorthanded. Finally, aggression could have no effect on performance outcome if neither a positive influence nor a negative influence was strong, or if both were strong and therefore offsetting each other.

Popular opinion seems to support the notion of a positive influence. People find it difficult to forget the 1973-74 and 1974-75 Philadelphia Flyers whose success is usually attributed to bullying and intimidating tactics. Likewise, many teams through their acquisition of "policemen", appear to be paying homage to Conn Smythe's adage that: "You can't beat them on the ice if you can't beat them in the alley". In addition, the players themselves believe that aggression is a tactic for winning. In a case study based on interviews with two American Hockey League teams Faulkner (1971) was told by the players that they used their elbows and the butt ends of their sticks as a means of persuasion and for finding out "what their opponents were about". Similarly interviews by Vaz (1977) indicated that minor league players believed that they would not be recruited to higher levels unless they "play rough and tough" and have "the ability to take it and dish it out". Such statements and his observations lead Vaz to conclude that rule infractions are functional for team success. Smith (1976) says that violence in hockey becomes legitimate once it has been demonstrated that violent tactics lead to success. However Smith also states that "when official penalties for fighting and other illegal acts of assault are severe enough that victory is jeopardized, athletes may receive negative sanctions from their coaches and teammates for such behaviour."

In one of the first empirical examinations of the relationship between intimidation and success Myers (1966) was unable to support his hypothesis that intimidation helped individuals to succeed in his laboratory designed shuffleboard contest. Russell (1974) examined the aggression and performance of individual players in a six team Alberta hockey league. He found that after 30 games there was a significant correlation at the .001 level between total penalties and the number of assists made as well as a significant relationship at the .05 level between total penalties and goals scored by individuals. Russell himself admits that by treating the offensive outcomes of goals scored and assists made as the indices of performance he ignored other pertinent features of player performance such as defensive skills and qualities of leadership. In a study which examined team data, the National Hockey League's statistician Ron Andrews (1974) compared the order of finish with the penalty minutes accumulated by each team in the N.H.L. during the 1973-74 season. His data revealed that the teams placing highest in the standings were the most penalized. The rank order correlation between team aggression and team success was positive ($r = .64$). His results suggest that penalties do not seriously jeopardize a team's chances for success and that the use of aggression might even improve chances for victory. In a footnote to their paper Cullen and Cullen (1975) stated that they have data (not presented in their paper) which shows that teams who win commit more norm violations than do their losing foes. These researchers do present intercollegiate hockey data which shows that winning teams do take

406

more penalties when the score is very close or when they are so far ahead that the other team is "out of the game". Only when they are behind by 3 or 4 goals do losing teams commit significantly more rule infractions than do winning teams.

These few studies hardly provide a conclusive statement on the relationship between aggression and the performance outcome in sport. Thus, the present investigation was undertaken to shed further light on this topic. Specifically the study examined the relationship between team aggression and team success and the relationship between individual aggression and individual success in ice hockey.

METHOD

Subjects

The sujects were the 87 teams and their 1667 players who participated in the Ontario University Athletic Association from 1971-72 up to and including 1976-77. Information regarding the aggression and performance of players, and their teams, was taken from official news releases issued by the public relations office of the Ontario University Athletic Association.

Assessment of Aggression

Aggression was measured by the average number of penalty minutes accumulated per game by individuals and by teams.

Assessment of Performance

The index used for team performance was the average number of points accumulated per game based upon the system of two points for a victory and one point for a tie. Individual performance was dichotomized into "all star" and "non-all star" categories. "All stars" were individuals who were selected each year by the coaches on an official ballot. In all, there were 128 "all stars" and 1539 "non-all stars".

Treatment of the Data

The relationship between team aggression and team success was analyzed with a Pearson Product Moment Correlation in which average points per game were correlated with the average penalty minutes per game. Correlations were obtained for each division, for each year and over all divisions for all years.

A student "t" test for independent groups was used to compare the mean penalty minutes accumulated by "all stars" with the mean number ac-

Table 1. Pearson Product Moment Correlations for Team Success and Team Aggression.

Division	1976-77	1975-76	1974-75	1973-74	1972-73	1971-72
Western	$r = .6204$	$r = -.6164$	$r = -.0115$	$r = -.4827$	$r = -.2359$	$r = -.2367$
Eastern	$r = .4218$	$r = -.2571$	$r = -.0386$	$r = -.8083*$	$r = -.2275$	$r = -.0197$
Central	$r = .0608$	$r = -.2856$	no. div.	no div.	no div.	

Pearson Product Moment Correlation over all years. $r = .1104$

*$P < .05$

cumulated by "non-all stars". In addition to the overall comparison, separate comparisons were made within each division for each year of the study. The .05 level was selected as the criterion for acceptance of statistical significance in all analyses.

RESULTS

Based upon the limited previous research (Andrews, 1974) and the researchers' interpretations of popular opinion it was hypothesized that the more successful the team the more penalty minutes accumulated. When the relationship between performance outcome and aggression was examined for all teams over all years the Pearson Product Moment Correlation yielded was non significant (r = -.11). Figure 1 presents these results graphically in a scattergram.

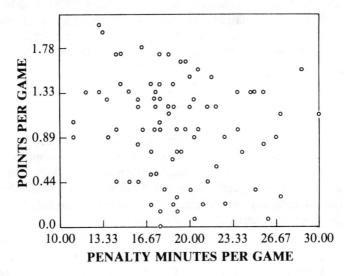

Figure 1. Pearson Product Moment Correlations for Team Success and Team Aggression.

Separate correlations computed for each league in each year of the study are found in Table 1.
Only the negative relationship which existed between team aggression and team success in the Eastern division during 1973-74 was significant.

The relationship between individual aggression and individual success was analyzed by comparing the mean number of penalty minutes accumulated by "all stars" with the number accumulated by "non-all stars". Based upon the findings of Russell (1974) it was hypothesized that "all stars" would accumulate more penalties than would "non-all stars". It was found that over all years and across all divisions the mean penalty minutes for "all stars", normalized for 10 games, was 13.74 whereas the comparable figure for "non-all stars" was 9.56. Nevertheless the t value of 1.16 indicated that the difference between these mean scores was not significant. Although the mean number of penalty minutes of the two groups did not differ significantly the distributions of the penalty minutes by each group were different. The expected normal curve formed by the distribution of penalty minutes accumulated by "non-all stars" is shown in Figure 2. On the other hand, the curve formed by the distribution of penalties accumulated by "all stars" is bimodal, indicating that over 10 games of play "all stars" average either very few penalty minutes (3-5) or receive substantially more penalty minutes (13-15).

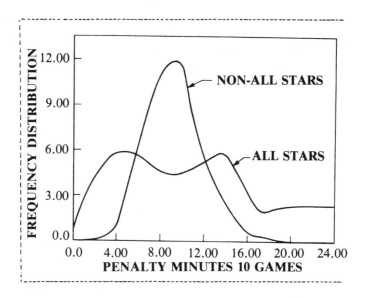

Figure 2. Frequency Distributions of Penalty Minutes Accumulated by All Stars and Non-All Stars.

This suggests that some players may be selected as "all stars" because of very non-aggressive skills such as skating, passing and goal scoring abilities. The distribution also implies that there are a number of "all stars" who are very aggressive. It is interesting to note that the ten most penalized players in the entire study were "all stars". The fact that eight of these players were defensemen suggests that being aggressive is part of the expected role of this position.

DISCUSSION

The non significant relationship ($r = -.11$) between team aggression and team success in this study is quite different from the positive relationship ($r = .64$) that Andrews (1974) found between these two variables. These contrasting results might be due to the fact that Andrews only examined one season of play which might have been atypical. The most successful team that year, the Philadelphia Flyers was definitely the most penalized. In recent years the most successful team in the National Hockey league has been the Montreal Canadians, a team which has received very few penalties while the highly penalized Chicago Black Hawks has not been very successful. It is therefore recommended that the team aggression-team performance outcome relationship in the National Hockey league should be examined over several years before definitive conclusions are stated.

The discrepant results between the present study and the Andrews' investigation may also be due to differences between the style of hockey played in the professional ranks and that played at the college level. Because spectator appeal is a major objective of professional hockey it may well be that aggressive play is encouraged more and penalized less. If such were the case the positive effects of aggression would be more likely to prevail. This suggests that the examination of the aggression-performance outcome relationship should be extended to other levels of hockey such as non-college amateur leagues and to minor hockey teams. Indeed an examination of this relationship in minor hockey might show that the beliefs that individuals hold regarding the link between these two variables is learned through very early experiences.

It is equally difficult to compare the non significant results found in this study for the relationship between individual success and individual aggression with the significant findings of Russell (1974). In this study a successful individual was an "all star" whereas in the Russell study success as an individual was measured in terms of goals scored and/or assists made. As already stated such measures of individual performance are quite inadequate in that they do not consider important defensive skills and leadership qualities. Being an "all star" often entails possessing defensive skills and leadership abilities as well as the offensive skills of assisting and scoring goals. Thus designation as an "all star" or "non-all star" seems to be a better method of identifying individual success than does the method used by Russell (1974). This does not mean that the present method is ideal. Success is not an all or nothing variable and therefore it would be better if levels of success could be identifed for all players by trained observers.

Similarly the method used to assess aggression is not without flaws. Undoubtedly many aggressive acts go unpenalized whereas on the other hand penalties are often awarded for non aggressive behaviour such as delay of game. It would appear that the latter problem is easier to correct than is the former. In this regard McCarthy and Kelly (1978) advocated the separation of what they referred to as "non aggressive norm violations" from "aggressive penalties". Likewise Wankel (1973) distinguished between instrumental and reactive aggressive penalties. Unfortunately there is not agreement by these researchers as to what penalties should be considered aggressive. For example, Wankel treats interference as an aggressive penalty whereas McCarthy and Kelly do not. Thus before researchers separate some penalties from others, agreement must be reached by some panel of experts (i.e., players, coaches, referees and researchers) as to what penalties are indeed "aggressive penalties".

CONCLUSION

While the present study does not provide a conclusive statement on the aggression-performance outcome relationship, it does suggest that the often held assumption that aggression leads to success in hockey may not always be true. Furthermore, failure to find a positive or negative linear relationship between these two variables does not mean that no relationship exists. Indeed there may very well be some sort of curvilinear relationship between aggression and performance outcome. Future investigations of this topic should consider such a possible relationship.

REFERENCES

Andrews, R. A. Spearman Rank Order Correlation for 18 NHL teams. *National Hockey League Guide.* NHL Publications, 1974.

Ardrey, R. *The territorial imperative.* New York: Atheneum, 1966.

Berkowitz, L. *Aggression: A social psychological analysis.* New York: McGraw-Hill, 1962.

Cullen, J., and Cullen, F. The Structural and Contextual Conditions of Group Norm Violation: Some Implications from the Game of Ice Hockey. *Int. Rev. of Spt. Sociol.* 10:2-1975.

Faulkner, R. R. Violence, camaraderie and occupational character in hockey. Paper presented at the Conference on Deviancy in Sport. Brockport, New York, 1971.

Faulkner, R. Making Violence by Doing Work: Selves, Situations, and the World of Professional Hockey. *Sociology of Work and Occupations* 1:3:1974.

Geen, R. G., and Berkowitz, L. Name mediated aggressive cue properties. *J. Personality* 34:456-465, 1966.

Goldstein, J. H., and Arms, R. L. Effects of observing athletic contests on hostility. *Sociometry* 34:1:83-90, 1971.

Lorrenz, K. *On aggression.* London: Methuen and Co. Ltd., 1966.

Martens, R. *Social psychology and physical activity.* New York: Harper and Row, 1975.

McCarthy, J., and Kelly, B. Aggressive behaviour and its effect of performance over time in ice hockey athletes: An archival study. *Int. J. Spt. Psych.* 9:2:90-96, 1978.

Myers, A. F. Performance factors contributing to the acquisition of a psychological advantage in competition. *Human Relations* 19:283-295, 1966.

Russell, G. W. Machiavellianism, Locus of Control, Aggression, Performance and Precautionary Behaviour in Ice Hockey. *Human Relations* 27:9:825-837, 1974.

Scott, J. P. Sport and aggression. In G. S. Kenyon (Ed.) *Contemporary Psychology of Sport,* Chicago: The Athletic Institute, 1970.

Smith, M. D. The Legitimation of Violence: Hockey Players' Perceptions of Their Reference Groups' Sanctions for Assault. In Gruneau and Albinson (Eds.), *Canadian Sport: Sociological Perspectives,* Don Mills, Ontario: Addison-Wesley, 1976.

Steiner, I. *Group Process and Productivity.* New York: Academic Press, 1972.

Taylor, I. Spectator violence around football: The rise and fall of the "working class weekend." *Research Papers in Physical Education* 3:2:4-9, 1976.

Thirer, J. The effect of observing filmed violence on the aggressive attitudes of female athletes and non-athletes. *J. Spt. Behav.* 1:1:1978.

Vaz, E. W. Institutionalized rule violation in professional hockey: Perspectives and control system. *C.A.H.P.E.R.J.* 43:3:June-February, 1977.

Zillman, D., Johnson, R. C., and Day, K. D. Provoked and unprovoked aggressiveness in athletics, *J. Research in Personality* 8:1974.

REFERENCE NOTES

1. Paper present at the Tenth Canadian Psycho-Motor Learning and Sport Psychology Congress, Toronto, November, 1978.

2. In response to a reviewer's comment we examined a number of papers and found that not one elaborated on the definition of aggression. Most authors freely interchanged synonyms for aggression.

Perception And Sport Skill

Fran Allard, Ph.D.

Dr. Allard is a professor lecturing in both the Kinesiology and Psychology departments at the University of Waterloo where she has been conducting research in the acquisition of motor skill and the role of perception in sport. Dr. Allard has played and coached basketball at different levels and is currently a member of the Canadian Volleyball Association's research committee.

The visual system of highly skilled athletes does not differ substantially from that of less skilled performers. The performance differences are due in part to the different methods in how the brain processes the information available from the sport environment. This difference in picking up information is a result of the athlete's experience in the particular sport environment, and is specific to that particular sport environment. This article will explain the importance of perception in sport, describe some of the experiments that provide scientific support for the value of perception and finally, present some implications and applications of these concepts.

PERCEPTION IN SPORT

Approximately 99.9% of the world thinks of sport skill as being the smooth execution of the set of motor patterns appropriate to the particular sport. Consequently, there are "objective" tests of sport skill, consisting of a set of skills that, in the mind of the developer of the test, constitute the elements of sport. However, a sport skill is much more complex than the execution of motor responses. The important word in the last sentence is *responses*. A movement is performed in response to something in the environment (i.e., the sport setting). Indeed, a great many different types of sporting contests are won or lost according to how successful the team or individual is in causing something to happen in the environment: shooting the puck into the net, jumping over the high bar, finishing the race before the others. In these reaction (or environmental) sports, the primary goal of the performer is to produce the desired outcome consistently. Thus, in these sports, the movement pattern used by the athlete is the means to an end; it doesn't so much matter how the puck gets into the net, as long as it gets there. There do exist sports in which the movement pattern is both an end and a means; for example gymnastics, diving, or figure skating. In these sports, the winner is determined by a judge, rather than by an environmen-

* Allard, F. "Perception and Sport Skill," *Coaching Science Update, 1980-81.* 1981, 52-55. Reprinted by permission of the publisher.

tal outcome. The focus of this paper will be on environmental sports rather than judged skills since the role of perception appears to be more obvious for those sports requiring the athlete to react to aspects of a rapidly changing environment.

The important fact to be remembered from this section is that skill in an environmental sport is not simply the execution of motor patterns: the performer must react to the environment and select the most appropriate response in his or her repertoire for the situation. The study of the relationship between perception and skill is currently a popular topic in cognitive psychology (the study of perception and knowing). In the next section some of the current experiments in the study of chess skill will be described. These experiments are important because they are applicable to the sport situation.

The execution of sport skills can be classified in two ways. Either the winner of the contest is decided by some objective, external measure — i.e., the score in basketball or baseball — or the winner is decided by a judge — i.e., gymnastics or diving. The perceptual demands placed on the athlete are very different in each classification.

Much of the interest in perception and skill stems from the work of the Dutch psychologist de Groot. De Groot did extensive investigation into the nature of the skill of the Master chess player. Among the tasks invented by de Groot to study chess skill is an experimental task that has proven to be very useful in a variety of skill situations outside chess. This procedure is called the five second recall task. For chess players, the task consists of studying a chess board set up in a game situation for five seconds, after which time the player attempts to reconstruct the game position on a second board. As would be expected, de Groot found chess Masters do very well on such a task. Two American researchers, Chase and Simon repeated de Groot's experiment, and added a second recall condition consisting of presenting subjects with a chess board containing pieces arranged in a random fashion. If chess skill was attributable to superior memory as would be suggested by de Groot's experiment, chess Masters should show superior performance on the random boards as well as on the game boards. Chase and Simon found that chess Masters were better than A level players only when recalling game boards. The same relationship existed between the A level players and novice players. All the subjects were virtually identical in recall accuracy for the random boards. The superior recall of Master players is specific to real chess games, showing that Master players are sensitive to the structure present only in game boards. Further experiments showed that chess Masters are able to *chunk* game information for recall; that is, they *put the pieces of game information into memory in configuration rather than as individual pieces.* A close analogy to the chess Master would be skilled readers of English attempting to recall strings of letters. If the letter strings were to form words, a reader would be able to recall many more individual letters than if the letters have been selected at random from the alphabet. Game chess positions for the Master player are like words for the skilled reader. The entire word (or game configuration) can be recognized and retained without reading each individual letter.

Chess Masters were capable of recalling game situations because they were able to chunk the information. That is, they were able to recognize patterns or configurations of play rather than recalling where each individual chess piece was located.

The five second recall task has been extended to a variety of other skill situations, with much the same results. Skilled bridge and Go (Japanese board game similar to chess) players show the same recall superiority for structured situations as do chess players. Skilled musicians, medical practitioners, and electronic technicians are similarly superior to less skilled individuals for structured examples of their particular skills.

The work done by cognitive psychologists in their studies of skill and perception has shown that skilled subjects differ from their less skilled counterparts in the way they store information about their specialty. This storing superiority has important consequences for performance. Using the chess Master as an example, the Master is able to compare the information he is receiving from the board to previous games he has played or studied and stored in his memory. Rather than have to search through a variety of possible lines of play in order to discover the best move, the chess Master is able to recognize the situation and generate an appropriate move. It has been estimated that the chess master may store up to as many as 50,000 chess patterns in long term memory.

But what do chess skill and sport skill have in common? Quite a bit, as it turns out.

PERCEPTION AND SPORT

The relationship between perception and sport has been under investigation at the University of Waterloo for some time. The research has attempted to determine if skilled athletes would exhibit the same encoding (storage and recognition) of structure for their sport as do the chess Masters just described. Consequently, the five second recall test was employed in a study with basketball players as subjects. The varsity basketball players and the non-skilled basketball playing subjects were shown slides of basketball games and instructed to memorize the position of the players on the court. One half of the slides used depicted structured situations — an offensive play in progress — and the other half depicted unstructured situations — turn-overs or loose balls. The subjects recalled the player positions by placing magnets representing the players on a metal board representing the court. It was found that basketball players were indeed sensitive to *structure*. The varsity players' recall was better than the non-skilled basketball playing subjects only when viewing the structured slides, suggesting that encoding and chunking (storing and recognizing) information is an important element of basketball skill.

The next series of tests attempted to determine how far this information *chunking* could be generalized in other sport situations by testing volleyball players on the same five second recall test. The basketball experiment was repeated by changing the slides to volleyball situations and the subjects to skilled volleyball players and non-skilled volleyball players. The subjects were given a booklet of schematic drawings of a volleyball court and instructed to recall the location of the players on the court by placing marks on the paper corresponding to their positions.

It appears that basketball players perceive patterns and configurations in their game much the same way that chess Masters perceive the game of chess. Superior performance is due in part to recognizing the pattern and reacting accordingly. The player needs to be able to recognize the situation before selecting the appropriate reaction.

The volleyball players did not show the same sensitivity to structure as did basketball players. The possibility remains that this was not the best way to do the experiment, or that structure may be important only for some positions in volleyball (i.e., setters). The experiment could also have been inappropriate because the *structured* slides did not capture the crucial elements of volleyball structure. It seems however, that the volleyball players were not being asked the right question. In viewing game slides the players always recognized the action — they could tell if they had just seen a hitter attempt to go through a double block for example — but they showed little concern for where the action was taking place on the court. It was decided to change the task that the subjects were being required to do. Rather than recalling the court action, the volleyball players were asked to detect the presence of a volleyball in a slide. To make the task more challenging, the slides were flashed to subjects for an extremely brief period of time — 16 milliseconds. As well as measuring how accurate subjects were at detecting volleyballs, the speed with which subjects made their response was also recorded. In summary then, the experiment consisted of volleyball players and non-volleyball playing subjects looking for volleyballs in rapidly flashed slides. A ball was actually present in half the slides. One set of slides was game situations, while the second set of slides was non-game volleyball situations — time out or warm-ups.

There was no difference in accuracy of ball detection between players and non-volleyball playing subjects, but a tremendous difference in speed of detection existed. The players were about twice as fast in the ball detection task, a superiority that held for both game and non-game slides. As well, players were slowed down only a little in ball detection for non-game slides. Rather than being *chunkers,* volleyball players seem to be perceptual *focusers,* ignoring background information to do a rapid ball detection.

Volleyball players perceive their sport in relation to the ball rather that the patterns and configurations inherent in the game. Rather than recognizing and reacting to the patterns of the game — *chunking* their environment — they *focus* on the ball and react accordingly.

In an attempt to determine whether athletes could turn themselves into *chunkers* or *focusers* at will or according to the demands of the experimental situation, we looked at the focusing abilities of basketball players. We performed the ball detection task changing the slides to basketball slides and the subjects to basketball players. We found the basketball players were no different from control subjects in speed of basketball detection; in fact, players tended to be slower than controls, perhaps, reflecting an inappropriate use of chunking (recognition of patterns).

IMPLICATIONS AND APPLICATIONS

These experiments provide support for the idea that perception is an important aspect to performance in sport. Both basketball players and volleyball players showed clearly superior performances over control subjects in the experiments described.

Secondly, the experiments show that the nature of the perceptual skill is very different for the two sports. Basketball seems to demand *chunking,* an encoding of as much information as possible about the position of players on the court. Volleyball seems to demand virtually the opposite sort of perception, a rapid *focusing* on the ball that requires a player to ignore the background information. It will be indeed interesting to determine how many other types of perceptual skills emerge as important for specific sports.

What does all this mean to the coach? First of all, there can be little doubt that perceptual skill is a function of experience in a situation. This implies that perception might be trainable by having athletes simply watch films or tapes of their sport.

Secondly, this research would argue against player assessment purely on the basis of physical skills. For environmental sports, skill cannot be divorced from a player's ability to perceive the sport environment in a manner appropriate for the sport.

Thirdly, these experiments suggest that a coach might learn a great deal about their athletes by studying the errors they make. According to available scientific evidence, performance = perception + execution. In other words, performance consists of the *selection* of an appropriate motor response to conform to environmental demands and the *execution* of the selected response. The athlete, then, could foul up for two very different reasons. The athlete could make a selection error implying a problem in perceiving, or he/she could make an execution error implying a problem in generating the motor response. It is crucial for a coach to understand what is behind the performance error, selection or execution. If an athlete has a selection problem, all the drilling in the world on fundamental skills will not solve the problem.

A specific example of the selection problem in sport is in the translating of plays drawn on a blackboard by the coach into actual plays executed by the players. To carry out the diagrammed play, an athlete first has to understand it; then remember it; then recognize the situation in the real time of the game; co-ordinate his or her movements with the rest of the team; and translate the movements of the players from the blackboard to the court. All this must be done before the simple execution of the skill can occur.

Successful performance involves skill in perception as well as in execution. The perceptual side of skill is both trainable and assessable, and should be an important consideration for a coach in player selection and correction of performance errors.

REFERENCES

Allard, F., Graham, S., & Paarsalu, M. Perception in sport; basketball. *Journal of Sport Psychology,* 1980, *2, 14-21.*

Allard, F., & Starkes, J. L. Perception in sport; volleyball. *Journal of Sport Psychology,* 1980, *2,* 22-23.

Chase, W. G., & Simon, H. A. Perception in chess. *Cognitive Psychology,* 1973, *4,* 55-81.

de Groot, A. D. *Thought and choice in chess.* The Hague: Mouton, 1965.

For the Coach — Recall and Insight

1. Volleyball players and basketball players differ in their perceptions of their particular sport environments. What are the differences in their responses.?

2. Would it be possible to use the perceptual facts presented in this article to simplify skill teaching in your particular sport? What type of perceptual demands exist in your particular sport?

Social Facilitation of Speed Events: The Coaction Effect in Racing Dogs and Trackmen *

George E. Obermeier,
Daniel M. Landers
Mark A. Ester
The Pennsylvania State University

The effects of the presence of other individuals who work simultaneously and independently on the same task as the subject has been termed coaction (Zajonc, 1965). Coaction research has a long history which began with a study now regarded as the first experiment ever conducted in social psychology. Prior to undertaking his laboratory work, Triplett (1897) studied the effect of competition on the elapsed time of cyclists. He found that the best times were recorded for races involving simultaneous competition with one or more coactors, while the next best times were for paced races against the clock, and the poorest times were for cyclists racing alone against the clock. The results of subsequent laboratory studies by Triplett (1897), Moede (1914), Hurlock (1927), Leuba (1933) and Church (1962), generally showed that coaction increased the speed or strength of a response. It should be noted that, although relatively consistent findings were evident for single response type tasks (e.g., those involving strength and speed), the coaction effects found in these laboratory studies were much smaller than the differences in cycling performance noted by Triplett (1897). It has not been determined if the relatively subtle coaction effects found in the laboratory studies were due to the control of contaminating variables or if these manipulations were less powerful than those used in field studies (e.g., Hillery & Fugits, 1975; Triplett, 1897).

The purpose of the two field experimental studies reported here was to re-examine coaction effects in selected naturalistic stituations found in

The completion of Experiment 1 would not have been possible had it not been for Albert Whigman, manager of the Florida Kennel, Inc., who allowed the dogs to be used as subjects and supervised the collection of the running times.

* Obermeier, G. E., Landers, D. M., and Ester, M. A. "Social Facilitation of Speed Events: The Coaction Effect in Racing Dogs and Trackmen," 1975. In D. Landers and R. Christina (Eds.), *Proceedings of the North American Society for the Psychology of Sport and Physical Activity.* 9-23. Reprinted by permission of the publisher.

sport. The sport activities selected were based on Zajonc's (1965) drive theory reinterpretation of the coaction literature and Cottrell's (1972) clarification of the habit strength construct as used by learning theorists. Cottrell (1972) distinguished between simple, single response situations and competitional situations where one habit does not sufficiently override other habits that may be incompatible with the desired response. Although some success has been achieved in examining competitional task situations in the laboratory, these situations have not been examined in field settings (see Landers & McCullagh, 1976). The difficulty in applying the competitive response situation to sport skills prompted the initial examination of the conceptually simpler single response situation. The task chosen was running. This task clearly involves a single response which was well developed in the subjects under investigation.

Previous research has shown coaction effects for animals and humans. In the first field experimental study, coaction effects were examined among racing dogs. Based on Zajonc's (1965) drive theory formulation for tasks of this type, the hypothesis was that the times for dogs racing in coaction are faster than the same dogs' times when running alone.

EXPERIMENT 1

Method

The subjects were 84 greyhound racing dogs housed at Florida Kennels, Incorporated, Hialeah, Florida. The dogs chosen for the study were selected by their trainer. Their training regimen was not altered for this study. The dogs ate a light meal before their run and a big meal following each run. Each dog was run alone and in a coacting group of two, three or four runners. The times were taken with a manually controlled stopwatch, and all alone and coaction trials were conducted on the same 400-m track. The distance at which most of the dogs ran was 1,650 ft. (500 m).[1] Greyhounds generally run as hard as they can for approximately half this distance and then depend more and more on the pacer (rabbit) to maintain their original speed. The mechanical pacer was operated manually by the trainer and set at a variable speed 10 ft. (3.05 m) ahead of the lead dog in the race. The number of dogs running alone and in coaction at this distance was 65.

Results and Discussion

Means were computed for each group. The mean for coaction was summed across group size. For this distance the alone group had an average time of 32.84 sec. while the coaction group averaged 32.58 sec. A dependent t test was employed and the difference between these means was found to be statistically significant, $t(63) = 3.92$, $p < .05$. This difference was in the predicted direction with faster times for the coaction than for the alone condition.

The significant difference found between the alone and coaction times was in support of Zajonc's hypothesis. This result is consistent with other well-learned animal behaviors reported in the literature. Coaction, for example, has been found to enhance the speed of nest building among ants

(Chen, 1937) and eating behavior in various animals (Harlow, 1932; James, 1953; Stamm, 1961; Tolman & Wilson, 1965). Of greater relevance to the findings of the present investigation are the studies examining running speed of animals (see Table 2). Zajonc, Heingartner and Herman (1969) found that times run by cockroaches in coaction were faster then times run alone. These cockroaches traversed a simple, straight runway 20 in. long (.51 m) to escape a light that had been turned on at the start of the runway. Also, Sanford (Note 1) found that the average times of four race horses were faster by 1.70 sec. in coacting conditions than when timed running alone. In horse racing the influence of the jockey on these times cannot be ignored — a potentially confounding variable which was not present with racing dogs.

Although the difference between dogs run in coaction and alone conditions was significant, the magnitude of the difference was not large with the average difference being only .26 sec. Over the 500 m distance 21 dogs increased their times (performance decrement) from the alone condition and 44 other dogs decreased their times in the coaction condition as compared to the alone condition. One reason for some of the dogs running slower in a group was the arrangement of the course for running. The dogs ran on an oval track. Therefore, some dogs may have been slowed down due to bumping and fighting in the pack.

The result of this study indicate general support for Zajonc's hypothesis for performance increases involving competitive coaction of well-learned skills. This result is consistent with other animal studies previously cited. Little, however, is known about this effect on human performance in naturalistic settings. Even though Triplett's (1897) analysis of cyclists records were suggestive of coaction effects on performance, the ex post facto nature of his archival data makes interpretation of the extremely large effects for the paced race (34.4 sec/mile faster than unpaced cyclists) problematic. The purpose of Experiment 2, therefore, was to examine various facets of the coaction effect for experienced track runners under conditions that approximated "all out" performance during training ("time trials").

EXPERIMENT 2

Of particular concern was the effect of coaction in a naturally occurring field situation. The 400-m (400-yard) dash was the field situation that was chosen. This running event had two vital aspects of interest to the present investigators. First, the dominant response being measured for the trackmen under investigation was a biomechanically correct response for which they had developed a well formed habit. Second, the 400-m dash event started from a staggered start may contain inherent differences in evaluative cues which may exist among runners in different lanes. It has been previously proposed (Cottrell, 1968) that coaction effects would not occur unless coactors evaluate each other's performances. In the case of running this evaluation may heighten competitive motives or provide directive cues by way of audio or visual information that may affect race

420

strategies designed to enhance performance outcomes. The 400-m dash beginning with a staggered start provides a natural situation in which runners on the inside lanes have greater access to visual cues (at least early in the race) than runners in the outer lanes. The advantage of the inside lane assignment has been shown for reaction times in leaving the starting blocks, but has not been investigated for 400-m running performances (Bradtke & Oberste, 1975). The purpose of Experiment 2, therefore, was twofold: (a) to investigate the effects of coaction versus alone performance of a 400-m dash and (b) to investigate performance variability (pacing) for each 100-m (110-yard) of a 400-m dash of subjects on an inside lane as compared to the pacing of the same subjects running on the outside lanes.

Because previous laboratory studies have shown that coacting performances were better than alone performances when measuring a predominantly correct response, it was hypothesized that the performance of subjects running in coaction would be significantly better than the performance of the same subjects in the alone condition. Due to the differences in the amount of visual information inherent in the staggered start of the 400-m dash, it was so hypothesized that subjects would prefer to run on the inside lane and that the performances in this lane would differ in pacing over each 100-m segment ("splits") of this distance when compared to these same subjects running on the outside lane.

Method

Subjects and design. The 14 subjects were high school and college men between the ages of 15-20. They had been participating in track and field all-comer meets in the State College area of Pennsylvania. Most of these runners were middle distance and long distance runners; one of the subjects specialized in the sprint events (including the 400-m dash). Of these volunteer subjects, two served as alternates. The alternates did not complete all of the test trials and were, therefore, not included in data analysis.

Each subject ran a series of nine 400-m dash trials under three different conditions; coaction outside, coaction inside and alone. Subjects in the coaction outside condition ran in Lane 4 and subjects in the coaction inside condition in Lane 2. Subjects in the alone condition ran singly in Lane 2. Subjects ran three trials in each condition. The sequence of the alone runs among coacting runs was distributed on a counterbalance order. Subjects were then assigned to one of the 12 counterbalanced running sequences with consideration being given to matching subjects of similar ability. Each runner's running ability in the 400-m dash was previously determined by the investigator (G.E.O.). In this initial trial preceding the nine test trials runners ran singly, but with other subjects present.

Measures of arousal. In order to determine potential increases in arousal, Thayer's (1967, 1971) Activation-Deactivation Adjective Check List-Short Form (AD-ACL), was employed. The AD-ACL is an objective self-report measure of transient levels of activation which has been used in previous social facilitation studies (McCullagh & Landers, 1976; Thayer & Moore, 1972). In order to disguise the true intent of the test, 15 nonactivation adjectives were integrated with the five activation adjectives. The activation adjectives had previously been correlated with physiological variables. These correlations have been moderate to low depending on the techniques employed to obtain physiological measures and the activation manipulations used (Dermer & Berscheid, 1972). Subjects rated their immediate feelings on a 4-point scale ranging from definitely feel to definitely do not feel.

To obtain a physiological measure of subjects' arousal levels, pulse rates were taken by the experimenter using a stethescope and stop-watch. The pulse rates were taken for 1 min. prior to any warming-up procedures. In order to obtain baseline arousal measures, subjects filled out the AD-ACL and had their pulse rates taken prior to their intitial run. This run was used to determine their ability level.

Instrumentation. In order to obtain the 100-m split times, all subjects under all conditions were filmed by a 16-mm Arriflex camera with a split image add-on lens (.5 diopter, 72-mm). The camera was mounted on a tripod. Attached to the tripod, mounted in half of the split lens field, was a continually running stopwatch which was accurate to .1 sec. As the camera turned on the tripod, the stopwatch, which was mounted on an extension in front of the lens, remained in view. In a pilot study the film speed and stopwatch were tested for accuracy. The number of picture frames were counted per second elapsed on the stopwatch and this was found to be consistent at 24 frames/sec for each reel of film.

A .22 caliber starting pistol with smoke blanks was used in starting all trials. This was done so that the smoke would be clearly visible on the film to establish a consistent procedure for designating the time of the start. The stopwatch was running before the gun was fired so that later when the smoke was seen on the film it signaled the beginning of the timed interval.

Experimental arrangement. The actual filming took place from a fixed point in the approximate center of the infield of the track area. This filming arrangement provided an unobstructed view of the entire track and possibly provided additional incentive for subjects who were aware that their run was being filmed. By means of this filming arrangement, all 100-m split times for each 400-m were recorded simultaneously for all coacting performances. This was done by placing 7-ft. (2.13-m) poles every 100-m for each testing lane in a position off the track and in line with the camera. The poles were painted florescent orange to assist the investigator in consistently determining the exact location of each runner's 100-m split times when viewed on film (Fig. 1).

Procedure. The nine 400-m dash trials were run within a two-week period. This schedule functioned to minimize practice effects, while also controlling as much as possible for fatigue effects. The weather conditions for the trials run on each day were recorded. All trials were during the month of August and conducted around noon for efficient lighting. Prior to the study, subjects were instructed to wear the same running shoes for each day's testing to insure some degree of consistency in their performances. They were also told that the purpose of the study was to establish some very

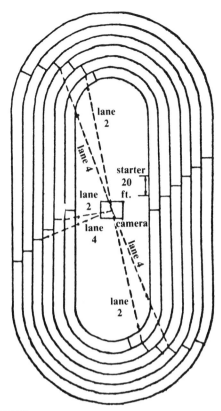

= POLE MARKINGS

Figure 1. Experimental arrangement.

important norms in running the 400-m dash. The investigator emphasized the importance of the "bogus" norms and as added inducement told them that they would also be able to view themselves on film after the investigation was completed.

When each subject arrived for testing, the investigator met him and informed him as to the condition he would encounter on that day. Each subject was then asked to fill out the AD-ACL questionnaire. The experimenter then took the subject's pulse rate. Following the taking of these measures, the subject was directed to warm-up for approximately 10 min. outside the track area and report to the track when it was his turn to run.

After this brief warm-up, coaction subjects were directed by the starter to their predetermined lane starting postions. The investigator gave some last minute remarks as to the importance of their running as fast as they could and then proceeded to start the trial. The start count went, "Runners take your mark" and then the gun fired. When they had finished they were given their approximate time of finish and were asked that they inform the next runner that his trial was to begin.

Because only one subject at a time was to be tested in the alone condition, subjects other than the one being tested were directed to warm-up or wait outside the track area. After the subject was ready the starter directed him to the Lane 2 starting position. All other directions were the same as given for the coaction condition. On the last trial day following their 400-m run, subjects were asked to fill out a final questionnaire concerning their reactions to conditions and testing sessions.

Results and Discussions

Performance raw scores. To test for differences among conditions, a Subjects x Treatment Conditions x Split Times (12 x 3 x 4) within-subjects analysis of variance was calculated by a method described by Dayton (1970, pp. 268-270). The result for the treatment condition main effect was significant $F(2,22) = 9.11$, $p < .001$. In addition, the split times main effect was significant, $F(3,33) = 17.40$, $p < .001$. The Treatment Conditions x Split Times interaction was also significant, $F(6,66) = 8.62$, $p < .001$.

Table 1. Mean Splits for Each Condition.

Splits	1	2	3	4	M	Total
Alone	16.3	16.9	17.2	17.5	17.0	67.9
Coaction Outside	15.8	15.8	16.5	17.3	16.3	65.4
Coaction Inside	15.9	15.9	16.5	17.4	16.4	65.7
Mean	16.0	16.2	16.7	17.4	16.6	

The mean split times for each treatment condition are presented in Table 1. As can be seen from these results, the sum of the split times for the two coaction conditions were faster by 2.2 and 2.5 sec. than times run under the alone condition. These differences were particularly notable for the first three 100-m splits (300 m), but were diminished by the fourth split. This result supports the first hypothesis which states that subjects would run significantly faster in the coaction condition (see Fig. 2).

To test for differences between splits within conditions, a post hoc analysis for simple effects was calculated using the Newman-Keuls procedure. All the differences between the splits of the coaction inside and outside conditions were significant, except between Splits 1 and 2. In the alone condition only the first 100-m split was found to be significantly different from the other three. Subjects, therefore, ran more evenly paced trials in the alone condition. This result did not support the second hypothesis of the study which stated that subjects running in coaction inside and outside conditions would differ in their pacing over the four 100-m splits.

Arousal measures. To measure arousal increases that were hypothesized to result from coaction, the AD-ACL scores were blocked for each treatment condition. A Subjects x Treatment Conditions (12 x 3) analysis of variance on this self-report activation measure was nonsignificant, $F(2,33) = 0.07$, $p > .05$.

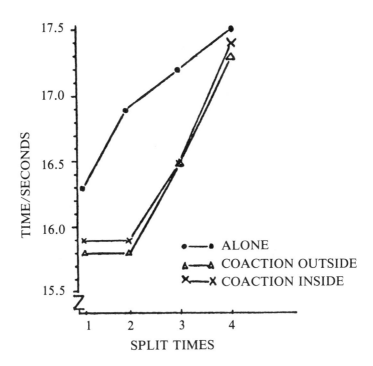

Figure 2. Alone, coaction outside, and coaction inside means for each 110-split.

The pulse rates taken before each trial were blocked and analyzed in the same way as the AD-ACL scores. The results revealed that the differences between treatment conditions were nonsignificant, $F(2,33) = 1.16$, $p > .05$.

To further clarify subjects' arousal levels, three yes-no answer-type questions relating to arousal were given to subjects in their final questionnaire. One question asked if subjects felt arousal and, if so, under what running condition did they most often feel this way. A binominal test, computed for the resulting 10 "yes" and 2 "no" answers, was significant, $p < .05$. Of those answering "yes", one subject indicated being most aroused before running in the outside lane, four subjects indicated that it was before running in coaction conditions and five indicated being aroused before running in all treatment conditions, alone as well as coaction. Other questions about the starting gun creating arousal and about the subjects' arousal levels at the end of a trial were nonsignificant.

The pulse rate and self report measures did not support the arousal mechanism proposed by Zajonc (1965) to underlie the coaction effect. Subjects rated their highest AD-ACL arousal during the initial trial before the actual testing sessions. After this initial trial, however, subjects' ratings decreased and leveled off to remain relatively constant through all conditions. One explanation which may account for the constant self-report scores across conditions lies in the early time of reporting by subjects. Even though subjects were told under what condition they would run before fill-ing out the check lists, they still had to have their pulse rates taken, and warm up before actually running. On the first day when everything was new, the environment itself could have been arousing. As testing progressed, however, these stimuli may have lost their arousing effect.

A similar occurrence was found with the pulse rate measures where the differences among conditions were also nonsignificant. Added to the problems cited above for the self-report measures, was the fact that many of the runners were running early in the morning and depending on how hard they ran, their pulse rate would fluctuate.

Additional self-report ratings. Each subject rated his preference for each treatment condition on a 9-point scale after their 9th and final test trial. The preference scale ranged from 1, which was extremely disliked, to 9, which was extremely preferred. The Subjects x Treatment Conditions (12 x 3) analysis of variance which was computed for the preference scores was significant, $F(2,33) = 24.53$, p .001. Post hoc analysis indicated that all conditions were significantly different from each other. Subjects preferred running on the inside lane most ($M = 7.42$). Their second preference was to run alone ($M = 5.83$) and their last preference was to run on the outside lane ($M = 3.42$). The results provided strong support for the preference prediction stated as part of the second hypothesis.

Two additional questions on the questionnaire given after Trial 9 were designed to assess subject's awareness of information cues in the coaction situation and also his motivation to perform in all treatment conditions. One question asked if subjects watched the person in the outside lane when running in the coaction inside condition. Only one person answered "no". The answer "yes" was recorded significantly more often ($p < .05$).

Another question asked the subject to indicate how reliable it was to assume that he had run all trials to the best of his ability. Nine of the subjects reported running "all" trials to the best of their ability. Three subjects reported running "most" trials to the best of their ability. No subject reported a "didn't care" response. It can be assumed, therefore, that subjects at least perceived that they most often performed their best.

GENERAL DISCUSSION

The significant performance differences in Experiments 1 and 2 between coaction and alone conditions supported the first hypothesis that performance of subjects running under coaction conditions would be facilitated by the presence of others. These results conform to previous coaction findings where the measuring criteria have been speed of response. Table 2 contains a summary of the experimental coaction results for cockroaches, greyhound racing dogs, race horses and trackmen. In each case the times in coaction are faster than times run alone. Such consistency is rarely achieved in coaction studies conducted in a laboratory setting. In most cases the time differences between coaction and alone conditions are quite large lending some degree of practical importance to statistically significant differences evident in these studies. Only among the greyhound racing dogs are the differences between conditions less than 1 sec. It must be

426

noted, however, that unlike the other groups tested for speed of response, racing dogs were paced so as to off-set performance decrements toward the end of the race. The time difference for trackmen, however, was substantial because a 2.4 sec difference at this speed gives coacting subjects an approximately 13.4 yd (12.16 m) advantage over their comparable run under alone conditions.

Individual gains among the racing dogs and trackmen were also quite impressive. Two-thirds of the greyhounds and 10 out of 12 of the trackmen experienced faster times in coaction than they had when running alone. As indicated in Table 3, one trackman had exactly the same time in both conditions. Interestingly, the one trackman who did better in the alone condition was also one of two subjects who indicated on the final questionnaire that he was not aroused by any of the conditions in the investigation. His performance results seem to substantiate this. Therefore, even though coaction effects occurred generally among the racing dogs and trackmen, individual differences were evident.

Due to the design of Experiment 2, the arousal measures used may not have been sensitive enough to differentiate among the treatment conditions. Then again, possibly arousal was not the underlying cause for the coaction effect. When subjects were asked if they focused their attention on the person in the outside lane when running in the coaction inside condition, only one person answered "no". Coaction effects have been found to occur when coactors evaluate each other's performances. The subjects in Experiment 2 were not instructed to watch the person in the outside lane, yet almost all did.

Table 2. Coaction Effects Involving Speed of Response.

Study	Coaction Time	Alone Time	Difference Time	Distance
Cockroaches (Zajonc et al., 1969)	32.96 sec.	40.48 sec.	+ 7.52 sec.	.51 m
Greyhound-Racing Dogs (Experiment 1)	32.58 sec.	32.84 sec.	+ 0.26 sec.	500 m
Racehorses (Sanford, Note 1)	56.8 sec.	58.5 sec.	+ 1.70 sec.	800 m
Trackmen (Experiment 2)	65.5[a] sec.	67.9 sec.	+ 2.4 sec.	440 yds. (400 m)

Note. Triplett's (1897) archival data on cyclists indicated a 34.4 sec. average/mile advantage of paced records as compared to records for cycling alone against the clock.

[a] Mean time for both coaction conditions.

This result indicates that the coaction effect may have been a result of evaluation which could have led to subjects using directive cues in order to vary their pace. The faster times of coacting trackmen on the second and third 100-m splits occurred after the first turn when the distance between

Table 3. Mean Times for Each Condition.

Subject	Coaction	Alone	Difference
1	68.43	73.80	+ 5.37
2	62.76	65.50	+ 2.72
3	69.33	70.20	+ 0.87
4	65.58	68.00	+ 2.42
5	64.80	67.10	+ 2.30
6	59.26	59.26	0
7	61.42	62.66	+ 1.24
8	66.75	67.86	+ 1.11
9	67.85	69.70	+ 1.85
10	82.86	90.76	+ 7.90
11	84.20	86.10	+ 1.90
12	66.06	65.73	− 0.33

This result indicates that the coaction effect may have been a result of evaluation which could have led to subjects using directive cues in order to vary their pace. The faster times of coacting trackmen on the second and third 100-m splits occurred after the first turn when the distance between runners that existed in the staggered start had narrowed. These directive cues or perhaps the demand characteristics of this naturalistic setting may have led the trackmen to compete. Further study is needed to clarify the constructs of evaluation, arousal, directive cues and competition as processes underlying coaction effects in naturalistic sport settings.

runners that existed in the staggered start had narrowed. These directive cues or perhaps the demand characteristics of this naturalistic setting may have led the trackmen to compete. Further study is needed to clarify the constructs of evaluation, arousal, directive cues and competition as processes underlying coaction effects in naturalistic sport settings.

The second hypothesis of Experiment 2 received only partial support. Lane assignment for coaching runs only affected subjects' preferences, but not their pacing throughout the 400-m distance. There have been reports of some reaction time differences between runners occupying different lanes at the start of a 400-m race (Bradtke & Oberste, 1975). These reaction time differences were quite small but were statistically significant. The results of Experiment 2 suggest that the small reaction time advantage for runners in the inside lane seems to disappear rather quickly once movement has been initiated in the beginning of the race. In fact, the coaction inside and outside group means are practically identical at the end of the first 100-m split. Caution needs to be exercised, however, in comparing the results of Experiment 2 with those of Bradtke and Oberste (1975). Their results were recorded in .001 sec. with the greatest discrepancies in reaction time noted for runners in extreme inside and outside lanes (e.g., lane 1 vs. 8). The timing device in Experiment 2 was only accurate to .1 sec. and only one lane could be used to separate coaction inside and outside conditions so that both runners could be viewed simultaneously at each 100-m split. Therefore, the reaction time advantage noted by Bradtke and Oberste (1975) may have been present at the start of the race, but the equipment and procedures used did not allow the possibility of detecting these small differences.

Although performance differences showed no particular performance advantage for inside or outside lane assignment, subjects showed a strong preference for running in the inside lane. Least preferred by subjects was running in the outside lane. Possibly, even though there was no performance difference between the two conditions, there may have been a difference in the psychological or mental stress involved between the two conditions. This suggesion is supported by subjects' responses to a question on the final questionnaire. Most subjects indicated that it was easier to "kick" at the end of a 400-m dash when running with someone. Because the kick comes at the end of the race when runners come in view of each other, possibly running is easier when watching someone else. Previous research by Meumann (1904) dealing with speed of finger ergograph response, where subject responded faster when watching faster performers, would seem to support this notion. Further work in this area, however, must be conducted before any conclusions can be drawn.

1.A few dogs were run at distances of 1,940 ft. (600-m) ($N = 16$) and 2,310 ft. (700-m) ($N = 4$). The means (39.03 and 47.27) for the two coaction runs at these distances were faster than the alone performances (39.29 and 48.13). The small sample together with the relatively large variability negated any chance of obtaining statistically significant results (t's $= 1.30$ for 600-m and .74 for 700-m).

REFERENCE NOTE

1. Sanford, J. Unpublished data, 1975 (Available from J. Sanford, Wyeth Laboratories, Huntercombe Lane South, Taplow, Maidenhead, Berkshire, England SL6 OPH).

REFERENCES

Bradtke, M., & Oberste, W. Equality of the start in races with a staggered start, *Die Lehre der Leichtathletik,* 1975, *43,* 1565, 1568.

Chen, S. C. Social modification of the activity of ants in nest-building. *Physiological Zoology,* 1937, *10,* 420-436.

Church, R. M. The effects of competition on reaction time and palmar skin conductance. *Journal of Abnormal and Social Psychology,* 1962, *65,* 32-40.

Cottrell, N. B. Performance in the presence of other human beings: Mere presence, audience and affiliation effects. In E. C. Simmel, R. A. Hoppe, & G. A. Milton (eds.), *Social facilitation and imitative behavior.* Boston, Mass.: Allyn & Bacon, 1968, 91-114.

Cottrell, N. B. Social facilitation. In C. G. McClintock (Ed.), *Experimental social psychology.* New York: Holt, Rinehart & Winston, 1972.

Dayton, C. M. *Design of educational experiments.* New York: McGraw-Hill, 1970.

Dermer, M., & Berscheid, E. Self-report of arousal as an indicant of activation level. *Behavior Science,* 1972, *17,* 420-429.

Harlow, H. F. Social facilitation of feeding in the albino rat. *Journal of Genetic Psychology,* 1932, *41,* 211-221.

Hillery, J. M., & Fugita, S. S. Group size effects in employment testing. *Educational and Psychological Measurement,* 1975, *35,* 745-750.

Hurlock, E. B. The use of group rivalry as an incentive. *Journal of Abnormal Social Psychology,* 1927, *22,* 278-290.

James, W. T. Social facilitation of eating behavior in puppies after satiation. *Journal of Comparative and Physiological Psychology,* 1953, *46,* 427-428.

Landers, D. M., & McCullagh, P. D. Social facilitation and motor performance. In J. F. Keogh (Ed.), *Exercise and sports science reviews* (Vol. 4). Santa Barbara, Calif.: Journal Publishing Affiliates, 1976.

Leuba, C. J. An experimental study of rivalry in young children. *Journal of Comparative Psychology,* 1933, *16,* 367-378.

McCullagh, P. D., & Landers, D. M. A comparison of the audience and coaction paradigms. In D. M. Landers, D. V. Harris, & R. W. Christina, *Psychology of sport and motor behavior* (Vol. 2). University Park, Pa.: College of HPER, 1975.

Moede, W. Der Wetteifer, sein Strucktur and sein Ausmann. *Zeitschrift Pedagogishe Psychology,* 1914, *15,* 358-368, & 369-393.

Stamm, J. S. Social facilitation in monkeys. *Psychological Reports,* 1961, *8,* 479-484.

Thayer, R. E., & Moore, L. E. Reported activation and verbal learning as a function of group size (social facilitation) and anxiety-inducing instructions. *Journal of Social Psychology,* 1972, *8,* 427-437.

Tolman, C. W., & Wilson, G. F. Social feeding in domestic birds. *Journal of Animal Behavior,* 1965, *13,* 134-142.

Triplett, N. The dynamogenic factors in pace-making and competition. *American Journal of Psychology,* 1897-1898, *9,* 507-533.

Zajonc, R. B. Social facilitation. *Science,* 1965, *149,* 269-274.

Zajonc, R. B., Heingartner, A., & Herman, E. M. Social enhancement and impairment in the cockroach. *Journal of Personality and Social Psychology,* 1969, *13,* 83-92.

Attitudes, Beliefs, Behavioral Intentions, and Behaviors of Women and Men Toward Regular Jogging *

Patricia K. Riddle**
University of Nebraska-Lincoln

Fishbein's Behavior Intention Model was examined in a study of the beliefs, attitudes, and behavioral intentions of women and men toward regular jogging. Data were collected for 296 female and male joggers and nonexercisers who were 30 years of age and older using a mail questionnaire which was constructed according to Fishbein's specifications. Significant and meaningful differences were found between joggers' and nonexercisers' beliefs. Nonexercisers thought jogging would require too much discipline, take too much time, and make them too tired. Joggers were more likely than nonexercisers to believe that regular jogging would have positive effects, and joggers evaluated being in good physical and mental condition more positively than nonexercisers. Nonexercisers indicated it was unlikely their referents (particularly physicians) thought they should jog regularly. The results supported the theory upon which the model was based: the relationship between the intention to jog and jogging behavior was high ($r = .82$) and behavioral intention was predicted from an attitudinal and a normative component alone ($R = .742$). The results of the study suggest that educators can develop behavior change strategies by focusing on change of beliefs and attitudes identifiable through the model.

Health educators have long sought a means of understanding human behavior with the hope that once behavior is understood it can be changed. To change behavior it is necessary to ascertain those components that influence and determine it. The Health Belief Model (Rosenstock, 1974) has been used frequently in the past by health educators, but there is also an interest in studying other behavior models to determine their usefulness. Jac-

---

* Riddle, P. K. Attitudes, Beliefs, Behavioral Intentions, and Behaviors of Women and Men Toward Regular Jogging, *Research Quarterly for Exercise and Sport.* 1980, *51*, 663-674. Reprinted by permission of the publisher.

** Patricia K. Riddle is in the School of HPER, University of Nebraska, Lincoln, NE 68588. This research was completed in partial fulfillment of the requirements of the Ph.D. degree at the University of Illinois at Champaign–Urbana under the direction of D. Stone.

card (1975) has suggested an investigation of the utility of Fishbein's Behavioral Intention Model (Fishbein & Ajzen, 1975) which has previously been used in marketing research. This paper reports a study in which Fishbein's model was employed to examine the beliefs, attitudes, and behavior intentions held by female and male joggers and nonexercisers regarding regular jogging. Also included are a comparison of behavioral intention with actual jogging behavior and an examination of the prediction of behavioral intention from an attitudinal and a normative component.

Social psychologists and health educators have debated the relationship of attitudes to behavior, of beliefs to behavior, and of attitudes to beliefs for many years. According to Fishbein's model, beliefs are the precursors of attitude, behavioral intention, and behavior. Fishbein defines beliefs as the probabilistic linkages of an object or behavior to an attribute. An attitude is a person's learned affect toward an object or behavior. Fishbein theorizes that as a person formulates a belief about an object or behavior, the person also develops an attitude toward that object or behavior. Further, the attitude predisposes the person to behave in accordance with that attitude. Thus the underlying key to a person's attitude and behavior is the person's beliefs about the relevant object or behavior. This is a critical point for health educators who are involved in behavior change. Once the person's salient beliefs are determined, educational strategies can be aimed at changing beliefs and thereby changing behavior.

THEORY AND APPLICATON OF THE MODEL

According to the model's conceptual framework, a person's specific behavior (B) is determined by his or her intention (BI) to perform that behavior. Furthermore, the behavioral intention can be adequately predicted by a combination of the attitude toward performing the behavior (A_B) and the subjective norm (SN). Thus. the model is symbolically represented as follows:

$$B \simeq BI = (A_B) w_1 + (SN)w_2$$

where B is the behavior, BI is behavioral intention, A_B is attitude toward the behavior, SN is subjective norm, and w_1 and w_2 are the empirically determined weights.

Behavior (B) refers to an overt, observable behavior being studied in its own right (e.g., participation in regular jogging in the next two weeks). The measure of behavior is obtained through self-report, as in this study, or observation.

Behavioral intention (BI) is defined as a person's subjective probability that he or she will engage in the behavior of interest. The prediction of a person's behavior can be obtained by asking the person whether or not he or she intends to perform the behavior. The correlation between behavior (B) and the behavioral intention (BI) should be high; this has been found in studies regarding voting (Fishbein & Coombs, 1974), family planning (Davidson & Jaccard, 1975), various type of cheating in college (DeVries & Ajzen, 1971), blood donation (Pomazal & Jaccard, 1976), and attending football games (Holman, 1956). Behavioral intention (BI) is measured on a scale which indicates the probability that the person will perform the specified behavior. In this study the behavioral intention, "I will take part in regular jogging in the next two weeks," was measured on a scale with endpoints of "likely" and "unlikely."

Direct Measures of Behavioral Intention Components

Behavioral intention (BI) is a function of two components: (1) the attitude toward performing the behavior (A_B) and (2) the subjective norm (SN). Both components can be measured directly and indirectly: according to Fishbein's theory the direct measures should have a higher correlation with BI than do the indirect measures.

Attitude toward the behavior (A_B) is defined as a person's predisposition to respond in a consistently favorable or unfavorable manner with respect to the behavior. The direct measure of A_B is derived by having subjects rate the behavior on bipolar scales with adjectival endpoints such as "good-bad" and "wise-foolish." Fishbein emphasizes the importance of use of attitude toward performing the behavior (e.g., "my taking part in regular jogging in the next two weeks") instead of attitude toward the object associated with the behavior (e.g., "regular jogging"). Davidson and Jaccard (1975), in their study of family planning behaviors, found attitude toward the behavior (A_B) a better predictor of behavioral intention than attitude toward the object (A_O).

The second component of behavioral intention, the subjective norm (SN), is defined as the various normative (external) pressures concerning the performance of the behavior. The direct measure of SN is obtained by asking subjects to rate the likelihood that significant referents think the subject should engage in the behavior (e.g., "most people important to me think I should jog regularly in the next two weeks").

Indirect Measures of Behavioral Intention Components

Although Fishbein's theory states that the direct measures of A_B and SN should predict BI better than the indirect measures, the indirect measures are more useful in that their subcomponents provide the researcher with more information that can be used to develop strategies for behavior change. In addition, Fishbein and Ajzen (1975) report that in practice the indirect measure of SN results in better prediction of BI than the direct measures.

The indirect measure of A_B utilizes two subcomponents: beliefs about the consequences (b_l) and the evaluation of those consequences (e_l). Beliefs about the consequences of a behavior (b_l) are the probabilistic linkages between the behavior and a consequence. Beliefs represent the information a person has incorporated about an object or behavior (Fishbein & Ajzen, 1975). People hold beliefs of varying strengths; some beliefs are strongly held and some are attached with ambivalence. Using a bipolar "likely-unlikely" scale, the strength of the linkage between behavior ("my taking part in regular jogging in the next two weeks") and a consequence ("will benefit my health") can be measured. If a person believes that a behavior is

433

quite likely to result in a particular consequence (e.g., "regular jogging is quite likely to benefit my health"), the person is said to have a positive belief strength.

The second subcomponent of A_B is the evaluation of the consequences of performing the behavior (e_i). In the example above, the consequence of regular jogging is "benefiting my health." If a subject believes that "benefiting my health" is an extremely *good* consequence, this evaluation is indicated by marking "extremely good" on a "good-bad" evaluation scale.

A sum of the product of the beliefs (b_i) weighted by their respective evaluations (e_i) produces the indirect measure of the attitude toward the behavior (A_B):

$$A_B = \sum_{i=1}^{n} b_i e_i$$

where n is the number of consequences. Therefore, if a subject has a high positive belief strength ("regular jogging is extremely likely to benefit my health") and a strong positive evaluation of that consequence ("benefiting my health is extremely good"), and if the subject's other beliefs about the consequences (b_i) are strongly held and positive, and the consequences (e_i) are seen as favorable, the subject should also have a positive attitude toward the behavior (A_B). This means there should be a high correlation between the direct measure of A_B and its indirect measure, $\sum_{i=1}^{n} b_i e_i$

Given a strong positive A_B, and provided the subjective norm (SN) is also positive, the subject should have a positive behavioral intention (BI). A subject has a positive subjective norm (SN) when two conditions are met: the subject's normative beliefs (nb_i) are positive, and his or her motivation to comply (mc_i) is high. Normative beliefs (nb_i) refer to a person's beliefs regarding a referent's expectations and are treated like other belief measures: subjects indicate how likely or unlikely it is that each relevant referent thinks the subject should engage in the behavior. The motivation to comply (mc_i) refers to the subject's tendency to accept or reject the expectations of the relevant referent groups or individuals. The measure of mc_i is obtained from the subject's rating of their motivation to comply with each referent's expectation concerning the subject's participation in the behavior. The scales in this measure have "want to comply-want to do the opposite" endpoints. Normative beliefs (nb_i) and motivation to comply (mc_i) combine to provide the indirect measure of the subjective norm as follows:

$$SN = \sum_{i=1}^{n} nb_i mc_i$$

where n is the number of referents.

Summarizing Fishbein's model, behavioral intention (BI) correlates highly with actual behavior (B), and attitude toward the behavior (A_B) and subjective norm (SN) are sufficient predictors of BI. The direct measure of

434

A_B has a high correlation with the sum of the products of b_i and e_i, and the direct measure of SN has a high correlation with the sum of the products of nb_i and mc_i.

METHODOLOGY

Following Fishbein's protocol, a pilot study was conducted to elicit beliefs about participation in regular jogging (B). Regular jogging was defined as jogging or running three or more times a week for one mile, 1.5 kilometers, or more for two weeks. Forty subjects including an equal number of female and male joggers and nonexercisers, listed their beliefs concerning the consequences (advantages and disadvantages) of their participation in regular jogging. They also listed those referents who might approve or disapprove of their jogging regularly.

From the consequences and referents elicited in this pilot study, a survey instrument of 68 scales was developed. Of the 68 scales, 19 measured the beliefs about the consequences (b_i) listed most frequently by subjects in the pilot study, and 19 scales measured the evaluation of the consequences (e_i) corresponding to those beliefs. Seven scales were developed to measure beliefs about the expectations of the seven referents (normative beliefs, nb_i) most frequently mentioned by respondents in the pilot study. A scale was also included to measure the motivation to comply (mc_i) with regard to each referent. In addition, the instrument contained seven adjectival scales for the attitude toward the object (A_o) and seven scales for attitude toward the behavior (A_B). Finally, one scale for behavioral intention (BI) and one for subjective norm (SN) were included. All 68 items were seven-point bipolar scales containing a variety of endpoints. The belief and intention scales (B_i, nb_i, SN, and BI) had endpoints of "likely-unlikely." Attitudinal scales (A_B, A_o, e_i) had "good-bad" endpoints. The A_B and A_o scales had six additional endpoints ("wise-foolish," "convenient-inconvenient," "delightful-disgusting," "exciting-dull," "beneficial-harmful," and "enjoyable-unenjoyable"). The motivation to comply (mc_i) scales had endpoints of "want to comply" and "want to do the opposite."

The survey instrument was distributed to 369 women and men, 30 years and older. Subjects were informed verbally and in writing that participation was completely voluntary. Nonexercisers and joggers from social service clubs in Champaign County, Illinois, as well as joggers found jogging in parks, offered to complete the questionnaire. Joggers and nonexercisers were similar in age, occupation, educational status, and income. The volunteers classified themselves as either regular joggers or nonexercisers according to their jogging behavior prior to the study. Regular joggers were defined as people who jogged or ran three or more times a week for one mile, 1.5 kilometers, or more. Nonexercisers were defined as people who did not participate in physical activity (more strenuous than walking) three or more times a week for 30 or more minutes at a time. Those people who exercised regularly (3 times a week or more) but did not fit the criterion for regular jogging were excluded from the study. A total of 98 females (49 joggers and 49 nonexercisers) and 198 males (100 joggers and 98 nonexercisers) took 15 to 45 minutes to complete the entire survey instrument; it was returned by mail. Reminder telephone calls at one and two weeks following questionnaire distribution resulted in a total return rate of 80%.

All subjects who returned a completed questionnaire were telephoned two weeks after returning their individual questionnaire and asked if they had jogged regularly (three or more times per week) during those two weeks. Their self-reports of "yes" or "no" were used as the single measurement of their actual jogging behavior (B) during the study.

In the course of the telephone interview a random group of 64 respondents was asked to complete the questionnaire again. A total of 63 subjects complied, and this retest was used to determine the consistency of the instrument. The correlation coefficients for four summary scores were as follows:

$$\Sigma\, b_i e_i = .867. \ \Sigma nb_i mc_i = .775, \ A_o = .739, \text{ and } A_B = .718$$

All scales were weighted from $+3$ for "extremely good" and "extremely likely" to -3 for "extremely unlikely" and "extremely bad." Responses on the seven scales measuring A_B and A_O were averaged to obtain a mean A_B and mean A_o score.

The data were treated in the following ways:

(1) Multiple correlations and regression statistical procedures were used to predict BI from a combination of A_B and SN and to predict BI from a combination of A_B and $\Sigma nb_i mc_i$.

(2) Intercorrelations between components of the model were determined.

(3) Hotelling's T-square analysis and the multivariate extension of Hays' omega square were computed for the four subcomponents (b_i, e_i, nb_i, and mc_i).

(4) One-way ANOVAs were determined for each of the 68 individual variables to ascertain the significance of the differences in responses between joggers and nonexercisers. Due to the expected inflated error rate, Hays' omega square technique was used to determine the meaningfulness of these differences by ascertaining the amount of variance accounted for in each comparison.

RESULTS

The major test of Fishbein's behavioral intention model is whether or not the behavioral intention (to jog regularly) can be predicted from a linear combinaton of attitudinal and normative components. In this study, the model provided high prediction of behavioral intention (BI) from a combination of A_B and $\Sigma nb_i mc_i$ with a multiple correlation of $.742\ (Sy.x = 1.885)$. Fifty-five percent of the behavioral intention variance between joggers and nonexercisers was accounted for using the two-predictors A_B and $\Sigma\, nb_i mc_i$. The attitudinal component (A_B) was a better predictor of BI than was the normative component ($\Sigma nb_i mc_i$). The standarized regression coefficient for A_B was $.643$ and for $\Sigma nb_i mc_i$ was $.157$, both significant

(p < .05). All other significant results were reported at $p < .001$.

The results also supported the model in several other respects. The intercorrelation between B and BI was .820. There was substantial intercorrelation between the two predictors and their respective subcomponents. The intercorrelation between A_B and $\Sigma\, b_i e_i$ was 764 and between SN and $\Sigma\, nb_i mc_i$ was .726. Consistent with the theory, there was a higher intercorrelation between A_B and BI (r = .730) than between $\Sigma\, b_i e_i$ and BI (r = .646).

Contrary to the theory but consistent with past findings (Fishbein & Ajzen, 1975), there was a lower intercorrelation between BI and SN (r = .432) than between BI and $\Sigma\, nb_i mc_i$ (r = .515), and the prediction of BI was lower with a combination of A_B and SN (r = .683) than with a combination of A_B and $\Sigma\, nb_i mc_i$ (r = .742). The present study also failed to support Fishbein's emphasis on the importance of using A_B instead of A_o to predict BI; the difference in correlation between A_B and BI (r = .730) and between A_o and BI (r = .700) was negligible.

The multivariate extention of Hays' omega square (Sachdeva, 1973) was used to determine the amount of variance accounted for between joggers and nonexercisers on the model's four subcomponents. The beliefs about the consequences (b_i) distinguished joggers from nonexercisers more than any other subcomponent, accounting for 62% of the variance. The variance accounted for by normative beliefs (nb_i) was 30%; evaluations of the consequences of the behavior (e_i), 25%; and motivation to comply (mc_i), 12%. The sum of the variance of the four subcomponents totaled more than 100%, possibly due to lack of independence between subcomponents.

The mean differences in responses of joggers and nonexercisers were determined for each of the variables which comprised the four subcomponents. The fact that a large number of comparisons were made inflated the error rate and resulted in significance ($p < .001$) for many variables. To offset this, Hay's omega square was used to determine which variables accounted for the largest amount of variance between groups.

Table 1 contains the mean beliefs about the consequences (b_i) and the mean evaluations of the consequences (e_i). The scores reported in Table 1 range from a possible $+3$, indicating "extremely likely" and "extremely good," to -3, indicating "extremely unlikely" or "extremely bad." All but two of the 19 beliefs about the consequences differed significantly between joggers and nonexercisers. The two beliefs on which the groups varied most were the beliefs that jogging would "require too much discipline for me" (44.8% of the variance) and "take up too much of my time" (40.2% of the variance). Nonexercisers had weak positive ("slightly likely") beliefs about these two factors and joggers had strong negative ("quite unlikely") beliefs about them. Other beliefs accounting for more than 20% of the variance were the beliefs that jogging would "make me feel good mentally" (28%), "make me feel too tired" (27%), "help me work off tensions and frustrations" (24%), and "be unpleasant" (24%). As Table 1 shows, joggers generally had strong beliefs about the positive consequences of jogging, and nonexercisers had neutral beliefs about the positive and negative consequences. In particular, joggers thought regular jogging would benefit their mental and physical health, and nonexercisers though regular jogging would require too much time and discipline and make them too tired.

As can be seen in Table 1, the evaluation of the consequences (e_i) did not acccount for as much variance between the two groups as did the beliefs about the consequences (b_i). However, once again joggers rated the positive consequences of jogging ("helping my physical condition" and "benefiting my cardiorespiratory endurance") more positively than did nonexercisers.

Table 2 shows the comparison between joggers' and nonexercisers' mean ratings of normative beliefs (nb_i) and motivation to comply (mc_i). Scores are reported from a possible $+3$, indicating "extremely likely" and "want to comply very much," to -3, indicating "extremely unlikely" and "want to do the opposite." The normative beliefs measured the respondents' beliefs about how likely it was that each of the seven referents thought they should jog regularly. The differences between the responses of the joggers and nonexercisers were significant for all seven referents. The nonexercisers believed it was slightly unlikely that their referents thought they should jog; the only referents excepted were friends who jog. All the joggers believed it was quite or slightly likely their referents thought they should jog.

On the fourth subcomponent, motivation to comply, joggers indicated they wanted to comply more with their referents as a whole than did the nonexercisers. The main difference between groups concerned compliance with the perceived desires of friends who jogged; the joggers wanted to comply more then did nonexercisers. Both groups indicated a fairly strong desire to comply with their physicians, although their normative beliefs relative to their physicians were opposite.

Finally, significant differences between joggers and nonexercisers were demonstrated on each of the seven scales measuring the attitude toward the behavior (A_B). The highest univariate omega square was found in the "good-bad" scale and accounted for 41% of the variance between joggers and nonexercisers. Joggers consistently had significantly more positive attitudes then nonexercisers. Joggers rated their taking part in regular jogging as extremely good, wise, and beneficial and as slightly delightful and enjoyable. On the other hand, nonexercisers scored their taking part in regular jogging as dull and inconvenient.

DISCUSSION

The theoretical tenets underlying Fishbein's behavioral intention model were supported in the study of regular jogging behavior. There was a high correlation between behavior (B) and behavioral intention (BI). Behavioral intention (BI) was adequately predicted from an attitudinal and a normative component. There was also a high correlation between the direct (A_B) and indirect (sum of the products beliefs about the consequences and the evaluation of the consequences) measure of the attitudinal component. In addi-

438

Table 1. Mean Beliefs and Evaluation of Consequences of Joggers and Nonexercisers

Taking part in regular jogging in next two weeks would . . .	Beliefs				Evaluations			
	Joggers (N = 149) $\overline{X}$	SD	Nonexercisers (N = 147) $\overline{X}$	SD	Joggers (N = 149) $\overline{X}$	SD	Nonexercisers (N = 147) $\overline{X}$	SD
Make me feel too tired	-1.84*	1.23	-0.04[b]	1.67	-1.09	1.08	-1.22	0.99
Lead to my having good companionship	0.30*	1.93	-0.90[a]	1.57	2.14	0.90	2.16	0.75
Make me have a fatal stroke/heart attack	-2.67*	0.58	-1.88[a]	1.43	-2.56	1.02	-2.16	1.09
Take too much time from family responsibilities	-1.84*	1.34	-0.48[a]	1.60	1.42	0.97	-1.69	0.94
Make me feel good mentally	2.19*	0.70	0.80[b]	1.42	2.65	0.57	2.54	0.61
Help in controlling weight	1.57*	1.15	0.92	1.44	2.12*	0.98	1.58	1.34
Help my physical conditioning	2.34*	0.70	1.78	1.04	2.29*	0.66	1.55[a]	1.06
Benefit my overall health	2.30*	0.69	1.42[a]	1.33	2.52*	0.60	2.04	0.92
Take too much time	-1.83*	1.24	0.54[b]	1.62	-0.83	0.94	-1.05	1.05
Help work off tension	1.98*	0.96	0.55[b]	1.54	2.00*	0.85	1.43	1.14

Table 1. Mean Beliefs and Evaluation of Consequences of Joggers and Nonexercisers

Help me tone my muscles	2.18*	0.84	1.77	1.00	2.00*	0.80	1.48	1.12
Make me feel uncomfortable when others watch me jog	-2.03*	1.28	-0.90[a]	1.72	-0.13	0.83	0.41	0.91
Lead to my getting a muscle or joint injury	-1.75*	1.16	-0.85	1.62	-1.52*	0.92	-1.36	1.10
Benefit my cv endurance	2.40*	0.75	1.49[a]	1.39	2.49*	0.61	1.91[a]	0.93
Require too much discipline	-2.03*	1.18	0.58[b]	1.66	-0.14	1.26	-0.52	1.20
Be unpleasant	-1.87*	1.35	-0.10[b]	1.76	-0.98	0.91	-0.98	1.08
Make me feel good physically	2.33*	0.63	1.33[a]	1.27	2.50*	0.55	2.23	0.67

*Difference between means for joggers and nonexercisers is significant $p \leq .001$

[a] Amount of variance accounted for 10-20%

[b] Amount of variance accounted for > 20%

440

Table 2. Mean Normative Beliefs and Motivation to Comply of Joggers and Nonexercisers

	Normative Beliefs				Motivation to Comply			
	Joggers (N = 149)		Nonexercisers (N = 147)		Joggers (N = 149)		Nonexercisers (N = 147)	
Referent	$\overline{X}$	SD	$\overline{X}$	SD	$\overline{X}$	SD	$\overline{X}$	SD
My physician	0.83*	1.40	-0.29[a]	1.60	1.09	1.04	1.12	1.08
My spouse	1.54*	1.33	-0.36[b]	1.80	0.91	1.10	0.63	1.16
My friends who jog	1.78*	1.20	0.58[a]	1.59	0.68	0.92	0.15	0.80
My children	0.94*	1.24	-0.12[a]	1.57	0.50	0.95	0.37	0.95
My friends	0.49*	1.08	-0.31	1.52	0.40	0.76	0.21	0.85
My business associates	0.40*	1.14	-0.32	1.47	0.24	0.73	0.01	0.73
My parents	0.08*	1.03	-0.61	1.36	0.18	0.81	0.13	0.94

*Difference between means for joggers and nonexercisers is significant p< .001.
[a] Amount of variance accounted for 10-20%
[b] Amount of variance accounted for ⩾20%

tion, the correlation between the direct (SN) and indirect (sum of the product of normative beliefs and motivation to comply) measure of the normative components was high. The direct measure of A_B was a better predictor of BI than was the indirect measure.

Two findings were incompatible with Fishbein's theory. The indirect measure of the normative component correlated better with BI than did the direct measure. Also, the differences in the two attitudinal measures, attitude toward the behavior (A_B) and attitude toward the object (A_o), were negligible, although A_B did have a slightly higher correlation with BI than did A_o.

In this study, over half of the variance between intenders (joggers) and nonintenders (nonexercisers) was accounted for using an attitudinal (A_B) and normative ($\Sigma nb_l mc_l$) variable. A similar level of prediction was found in the studies of family planning (Davidson & Jaccard, 1975) and cheating in college (DeVries & Ajzen, 1971), but other studies did not result in such high multiple correlations. Of the two predictors, the attitudinal components of this study contributed more to the prediction of BI than did the normative component. This finding was also documented in other studies using Fishbein's model (Davidson & Jaccard, 1975; Jaccard, 1975; Pomazal & Jaccard, 1976).

The correlation between B and BI found in this study ($r = .82$) is comparable to the correlations reported in other studies which range from an r of .89 for political voting (Fishbein & Coombs, 1974) to an r of .54 for blood donation (Pomazal & Jaccard, 1976). It is interesting to note that the behavior investigated in this study required repeated actions (jogging three or more times a week) to meet the single behavioral criteria for regular jogging. In most of the other studies only a single action (e.g., donating blood) was required to fulfill the behavioral criteria. The fact that so mush of the theory was supported in regard to a multiple action behavior could have important implications for health education since much of health-related behavior requires repeated actions such as regular exercise or eating nutritious food.

Perhaps the most useful findings in this study are the differences in beliefs about the consequences of regular jogging (b_l). These beliefs distinguished the joggers from the nonexercisers more than did evaluation of the consequences (e_l), normative beliefs (nb_l), or motivation to comply (mc_l). The overall attitude toward taking part in regular jogging was significantly different between the two groups of respondents but it is the beliefs themselves and the difference in belief strength that are the most important findings. On the whole, joggers had strong beliefs about the consequences (b_l) of regular jogging, and these beliefs reflected positive consequences of jogging. The joggers had stronger positive evaluations (e_l) of beneficial consequences than did nonexercisers. The nonexercisers tended to hold more neutral beliefs about the consequences of regular jogging, they were not as convinced about the benefits of regular jogging, and their beliefs refuting the negative aspects of jogging were not as strong as the joggers' beliefs.

442

Fishbein's model should be useful to health educators in their attempts to motivate volitional behavior change. This particular study focused on only one of a variety of exercise behaviors that health educators are trying to encourage. Jogging is certainly not the best type of exercsie for all people. However, it is hoped that the suggestions offered here for changing jogging behavior can be applied in the study of other types of exercise.

Fishbein suggests that the best strategy for changing behavior is to determine and influence target beliefs. It is likely that those beliefs accounting for the largest amount of variance between joggers and nonexercisers should be the target beliefs. Thus, from the present study, nonexercisers would be best persuaded to jog by convincing them of the positive consequences of regular jogging (e.g., feeling good mentally and physically, working off tension, and benefiting cardiorespiratory endurance) and convincing them to evaluate these consequences more positively. Also, their beliefs refuting the negative consequences of jogging (e.g., taking too much time and requiring too much discipline) should be strengthened.

These beliefs, which accounted for the greatest amount of variance between joggers and nonexercisers, are similar to the reasons respondents in the National Adult Physical Fitness Study (1974) gave for exercising: "good health," "weight control," "enjoyment," and "relaxation." Reasons for not exercising included, "not enough time" and "too lazy." Goodrick (1975) found similar reasons for exercising: women exercised to feel better and to reduce weight, sleep, and relaxation problems. The men in his study emphasized the preventive effects of fitness on heart disease.

In another study of beliefs about physical activity, Harris (1970) found that the beliefs and attitudes of a sedentary-made-active group shifted during a year-long exercise program and approached those held by a volitionally active group. Harris made no attempt to change target beliefs but after a year of behavior change found a change in two beliefs; beliefs about the physiological values of exercise and beliefs about the subjects' physical abilities to participate in vigorous activity. Although a causal relationship was not established, this study provides some substantiation for use of these beliefs as target beliefs for effecting behavior change. These two beliefs are similar to some of the target beliefs indentified in the present study. This suggests that target beliefs might be identifiable prior to behavior change and might be used in developing behavior change strategies.

Beliefs obtained from the model's normative component might also be used in developing behavior change strategies. However, in the present study, the model's normative component did not predict behavioral intention as strongly as did the attitudinal component, although it did significantly contribute to the prediction of BI. Joggers, and nonexercisers held different normative beliefs (nb_j) but similar motivations to comply (mc_j). In general, joggers thought their referents expected them to jog and wanted to comply with their referents' expectations. On the other hand, nonexercisers thought their referents expected them not to jog, but they too wanted to comply with their referents' expectations. In particular, both groups wanted to comply with their physicians; however, joggers believed their physician thought they should jog, while nonexercisers thought that unlikely. The same normative influence of the physician was reported in the National Adult Physical Fitness Survey (1974). Using the normative component from the present study, strategies for behavior change include convincing nonexercisers that their referents expect them to jog. Perhaps the best strategy from a health standpoint might be to convince physicians of the benefits of jogging and other types of exercise so they can encourage their patients to jog or exercise regularly.

The results of this study indicate that jogging *BI* can be predicted using Fishbein's model. This model should be tested using other health-related behaviors including other types of exercise, to augment current understanding of human health behavior.

REFERENCES

Davidson, A. R., & Jaccard, J. J. Population psychology: A new look at an old problem. *Journal of Personality and Social Psychology,* 1975 *31*(6), 1073-1082.

DeVries, D. L., & Ajzen, I. The relationship of attitudes and normative beliefs to cheating in college. *Journal of Social Psychology,* April 1971, *83,* 199-207.

Fishbein, M., & Ajzen, I. *Belief, attitude, intention and behavior.* Reading, Mass.: Addison-Wesley Publishing Company, 1975.

Fishbein, M., & Coombs, F. S. Basis for decision: An attitudinal analysis of voting behavior. *Journal of Applied Social Psychology,* 1974, *4*(2), 95-124.

Goodrick, G. K. *Becoming physically fit: Behavioral intention and behavioral intervention.* Unpublished doctoral dissertation, University of Houston, 1975.

Harris, D. V. Physical activity history and attitudes of middle-aged men. *Medicine and Science in Sports,* 1970, *2*(4), 203-208.

Holman, P. A. Validation of an attitude scale as a device for predicting behavior. *Journal of Applied Psychology,* 1956, *40,* 347-349.

Jaccard, J. A theoretical analysis of selected factors important to health education strategies. *Health Education Monographs,* Summer 1975, *3*(2), 152-167.

National adult physical fitness survey. *Physical Fitness Research Digest,* 1974, *4*(2), 1-27.

Pomazal, R. J., & Jaccard, J. J. An informational approach to altruistic behavior. *Journal of Personality and Social Psychology,* 1976, *33*(3), 317-326.

Rosenstock, I. M. Historical origins of the health belief model. *Health Education Monographs,* Winter 1974, *2*(4), 328-335.

Sachdeva, D. Estimating strength of relationship in multivariate analysis of variance. *Educational and Psychological Measurements,* 1973, *33,* 627-631.

Changes In Attitudes Toward Physical Activity As A Result Of Individualized Exercise Prescription [*]

Homer Tolson
John M. Chevrette

SUMMARY

College freshmen ($n = 193$) were subjected to a daily physical education and intramural program for six weeks. The physical education program centered around individualized prescription. Significant changes in attitude toward physical activity as assessed by the Kenyon Inventory for Determining Attitude Toward Physical Activity were obtained for four of the six scales of the instrument.

A. INTRODUCTION

There are a multitude of factors other than the approach to the program of physical education that may influence the student's attitude toward physical activity. Brumbach[2] found that certain situational actions on the part of the teachers, such as his or her participation with the student in the exercise, might be a substantial cause for the change in attitude. Mista[7] investigating the attitudes of college women toward their high school physical education program found significant differences in attitudes among the letter winner and nonletter winners, among those students from farms and cities, among students from varying size high schools, and among many other factors relating to the student's previous experiences.

Alden[1] and Bullock and Alden[3] concluded in their studies in the area of attitude that such factors as the inconvenience of changing clothes, poor program planning, the physical education instructor, and the number of hours of physical education per week could affect attitudes of students.

The purpose of the present study was to ascertain the effect of a daily program of exercise upon six scales for assessing attitude toward a physical activity as a sociopsychological phenomenon.

[*] Tolson, H. and Chevrette, J. M. "Changes in Attitudes Toward Physical Activity as a Result of Individualized Exercise Prescription," *Journal of Psychology,* 1974, *87,* 203-207. Reprinted by permission of the publisher.

445

B.   METHOD

1. Subjects

The subjects were 193 college freshmen males enrolled at Texas A&M University. The subjects' ages ranged from 16 to 20 with a mean age of 17.8 years.

2. Program

A daily physical education period of one hour and 20 minutes duration was required of all subjects six days a week. Subjects were assigned at random into eight classes of approximately 25 students each. The program was administered by two instructors, each teaching four of the eight sections to which the subjects were assigned. The same procedures and teaching approaches were used in all sections of the program. Each student was required to participate in intramural activity one hour each day as a member of his group. The program was based on the capabilities and needs of each student as far as these could be assessed by the evaluative techniques available. An individual profile was developed for each student on the basis of selected tests. Basic parameters measured included height, weight, % body fat, total body strength, strength/pound of body weight, somatotype, cardiovascular fitness, reaction time, speed, and agility.[4] Data on these variables were collected during the first and sixth weeks. After initial data profiles were scrutinized, ability groups were formed and exercise was prescribed on either an individual or a group basis. Each week the subjects devoted three days to the program prescribed, two days to skill learning, and one day to a lecture period centered around the basic concepts of physical education.

3. Attitude Scales

The Kenyon Inventory for Determining Attitude Toward Physical Activity was the measuring instrument used in the study[6]. Form D for men was administered to all subjects during the first and sixth weeks. The six dimensions evaluated in the study were as follows: (a) social experience, (b) health and fitness, (c) pursuit of vertigo, (d) aesthetic experience, (e) catharsis, (f) ascetic experience. Test administrators emphasized that the best answer to each statement in the inventory was the student's personal opinion and that the response would have no effect on the student's final grade.

Validity of all scales used, except catharsis, has been developed.[5] The validity of the catharsis scale has not been established, and further work in this dimension is needed. Hoyt's reliabilities for each of the six scales are as follows[6]: social experience, .72; health and fitness, .79; pursuit of vertigo, .89; aesthetic experience, .82; catharsis, .77; and ascetic experience, .81.

The scales were scored with use of a *priori* weights. Maximum score in each domain was 70 on the basis of 10 statements, except for the response to the "physical activity as catharsis" scale which had a maximum score of 63. Each scale was scored individually, and the results of the test were not cumulative. Pre and protest scores were submitted to a paired observation *t* test to determine any significant differences. All tests were conducted with use of an alpha level of .01.

446

C. RESULTS

The results of the study are presented in Table 1. The program of exercise employed in the study elicited significant increases in four of the six scales of the Kenyon Attitude Inventory. Significant differences were found in the dimensions of catharsis ($t = 3.21$), ascetic ($t = 4.58$), vertigo ($t = 4.19$), and health and fitness ($t = 5.16$). No significant difference was observed on the dimensions of aesthetic ($t = -.46$) and social ($t = -.36$) experience.

D. DISCUSSION

An aspect of the program which could possibly account for improved performance and attitude was the fact that at the end of the first week each student's individual profile of pretest scores was presented to him in the form of a T-score bar graph. The meaning and interpretation of T-scores were explained to the students. The students were also informed that their programs would be prescribed on the basis of these charts. Since the profiles were marked with a heavy red line at the average T score of 50, a student could quickly observe those areas in which he was deficient. The realization that one has scored considerably below the rest of his peer group might provide ample incentive for improved performance and attitude.

Table 1. Pre and Posttest Means and t Values

Scale or dimension	Pre		Post		
	Mean	*SD*	**Mean**	*SD*	*t*
Catharsis	41.5	7.5	43.4	8.3	3.21*
Ascetic	41.4	8.8	42.9	9.7	4.58*
Vertigo	46.1	10.9	49.1	10.8	4.19*
Aesthetic	37.5	8.4	36.8	10.4	− .46
Health and fitness	43.4	7.8	46.9	8.4	5.16*
Social	45.2	6.6	45.1	6.9	− .36

* Significant at .01 level.

Another factor which according to Brumbach[2] may have enhanced the attitudes of the students was the fact that the instructors took part in all of the running and jogging parts of the program.

Since the subdomains of social and aesthetic experience were the least affected, one may wonder what some of the causes might be. Although little planned emphasis was placed on the aesthetic subdomain, it would appear that the attitude of the subject toward physical activity as a social experience would be affected positively. The planned intramural program, recreational opportunities offered, and the informal atmosphere of the physical education class all seem to point in that direction. It would appear that additional research, particularly directed to the use of the social experience scale of the Kenyon Inventory, or the use of a different scale, might provide some enlightening results.

E. CONCLUSIONS

The following conclusions appear to be in order within the limitations of the study:

1. Attitudes of college freshmen toward physical activity as a sociopsychological phenomenon can be affected in a relatively short period of time.

2. The attitudes of the subjects toward physical activity for health and fitness can change significantly as a result of planned programs.

3. The attitudes of the subjects toward physical activity as the pursuit of vertigo can be affected significantly.

4. The attitudes of college freshmen toward physical activity as catharsis can be improved as the result of a planned program.

5. Attitudes toward physical activity as an ascetic experience can be improved significantly.

6. Attitudes in the aesthetic and the social subdomains of physical activity do not appear to be as susceptible to change by an individual prescription program of the nature presented in this study.

REFERENCES

1. Alden, M. A. The factors in the required education program that are least attractive to the college girl. *Res. Quart.,* 1932, *3,* 97-107.
2. Brumbach, W. B. Effects of a special conditioning class upon students' attitudes toward physical education. *Res. Quart.,* 1968, *39,* 211-213.
3. Bullock, M., & Alden, F. Some factors determining the attitudes of freshmen women at the University of Oregon toward required physical education. *Res. Quart.,* 1933, *4,* 60-70.
4. Chevrette, J. M., & Tolson, H. Individual prescription. *J. Health, Physical Educ., & Recreat.,* 1970, *41,* 38-39.
5. Kenyon, G. S. A multidimensional scaling approach to validating an *a priori* model for characterizing values held for physical activity. Paper presented at The American Association for Health, Physical Education and Recreation Convention, Dallas, Texas, 1965.
6. _____. A conceptual model for characterizing physical activity. *Res. Quart.,* 1968, *39,* 96-105.
7. Mista, N. J. Attitudes of college women toward their high school physical education programs, *Res. Quart.,* 1969, *39* 166-174.

Motivation And Performance Of Sports Groups *

Alvin Zander
Research Center For Group Dynamics
The University Of Michigan

Since the beginning of history people in positions of authority have valued coordinated effort in a group, especially in athletic teams. Romans were excellent in social organization and every Roman city, so carefully planned, had an area set aside for sports. Where Plato and Aristotle once collaborated in Athens, just a few blocks from the parliament building, is now a basketball court. The New Testament in the Bible urges subordinates (slaves and servants) in any organization to work hard for their superior no matter how unfair he may be; thereby establishing an ethic for obedience to leaders (and coaches) that confounds us to this time. Nowadays, cooperation among members of a team is so widely respected that invocation of the idea through such terms as team work, team spirit, unselfish desire, clicking, or precise execution, are uttered in a reverent tone; they are especially precious virtues (next to cleanliness) in the eyes of the priests for athletics, the sports reporters.

Such concepts about team work and the nature of group-oriented motivation are familiar and practical matters to athletes, coaches, and spectators. Most psychologists, in contrast, tend to think of these notions as mystical or romantic trivia that are not worthy of study. I propose that motivation in teams warrants better psychological research than it has received thus far and I intend to give some reasons for this belief.

I have three objectives: 1) To describe the characteristics of a group-oriented motivation called the desire for group achievement; 2) to indicate the effects of this desire on team performance; and 3) to suggest ways in which this motivation may be aroused by coaches and teammates. Before taking up the desire for group achievement, however, it will be useful to remind ourselves that a sports team is a unique institution, and to review several methods widely used in arousing personal motivation in individuals.

AN ATHLETIC TEAM

An athletic team has special properties, and a special environment, that

* Zander, Alvin. "Motivation and Performance of Sports Groups," In D. Landers, D. Harris and R. Christina (Eds.), *Psychology of Sport and Motor Behavior II*. University Park, Pennsylvania: Pennsylvania State University Press, 1975, 25-40.

449

make it similar to other groups, such as a symphony orchestra, the cast of a play, a set of glass blowers creating handsome objects, or the crew of a submarine, but unlike any other organization in most respects. These qualities are worthy of attention because they press teammates and coaches in several different directions at once, thereby threatening the stability of their rationale for joint endeavor. Here are some of these properties:

1. A team conducts its major business (engaging in athletic contests) before the eyes of observers who see all that goes on and who may later also read news reports about these events. (Imagine how different some political units or business firms might be if they were monitored as thoroughly.)

2. The observers are deeply (even emotionally) involved in the team's fate. They experience as much elation after a team's success, or as much depression after a team's failure, as they would if they had been in the contest themselves.

3. The observers want a victory, not mere improvement in skill, or better development of the athletes' moral fiber. Yet, they also believe there can be too much emphasis on winning which, of course, is not everything, especially in certain unhappy seasons.

4. The observers freely provide unrequested advice to higher management (the coach) on how he should do his job, and freely blame the management (not the team) for a poor performance by the participants.

5. Observers often bypass management and direct their messages to the participants on how they should conduct themselves: the observers also give applause and rewards (often mindless) to players they like for crowd-pleasing reasons.

6. There is a rigid code of behavior that all must follow, and officials (who are at once both policemen and judges) are present to see that these rules are obeyed.

7. The team members are fully able to evaluate their performance because the repeat their major business many times and receive ample feedback after each trial, from their score, their rivals, the observers, the press, friends, and from films made during the contest.

8. The team undergoes wide extremes of emotional reaction during its existence, from boredom to pride to shame.

9. Members of the team and management are inspired by some of the above conditions to want to do well. It becomes evident to them, furthermore, that winning is indeed not the only thing that counts (except when job security is needed for certain persons). A success must be one that engenders pride, a loss must be one that causes no shame.

An athletic team, in sum, is a very public thing. Many forms of influence act upon it, and within it. These forms provide conflicting bases for the motivation of team members, which means that there are no simple and consistently effective practices for arousing motivation in all participants on all teams at all times.

Three different approaches are rather commonly used in building motivation of individuals by those who have the responsibility to do so. I do not know how frequently coaches use these approaches, or how often anyone uses them for that matter. A very brief review of them will serve to underscore the point that teachers or coaches, like business managers, use any of several styles on different occasions. None of these approaches are directly concerned with how well a team performs as a unit, only with how well each individual performs, or, what is more important perhaps, with how hard each individual works to improve his own skill and his own rewards.

The supportive approach. The logic in this method is that a well satisfied person, more than a less satisfied one, puts out more effort on the tasks assigned to him. Accordingly, in the business world he is given good pay, fringe benefits, housing, bonuses, and security. In college athletics he is given room and board, tuition, help in studies, a cash allowance, and one long distance call a week to Mom. These satisfiers are given, it should be noted, regardless of the recipient's performance, or changes in that performance. The high producer and loafer share alike, which is one of the reasons for its appeal. It is egalitarian, compassionate, and paternalistic. In the light of Title IX, it must now be maternalistic as well. This approach clearly improves the rate of recruiting and reduces absenteeism and turnover, but there is no good evidence that it affects the quality of performance. It does not help us understand, furthermore, why individual incentives work and why there are individual differences in motivation even though all individuals are treated the same.

The reinforcement approach. The logic here, as you know, is that a reward is given to a person if some agent thinks he deserves it, otherwise it is not given, or a punishment is administered instead. An important point is that the reward is contingent upon the quality of the recipient's behavior, and the rewarder sets the standard of excellence to be met if one is to qualify for that reward. In the world of work this reward is the raise in pay, the promotion, or the gold pin for good service. In the world of sports it is the star pasted on the back of the football helmet, or being named wrestling-team champion of the week. Being "benched" is the ultimate punishment, and some well known coaches are famous for their ability to terrify players by use of sarcasm and towering rages.

Reinforcements are known to enhance learning, or unlearning, and are the basis of behavior modification in psychotherapy. Over the long haul, however, the value of rewards will fade, and the price, so to speak, rises as a reward loses its value. Many costs likewise lose their sting. When these contingencies weaken, a coach must invent tailor-made appeals for the case in hand: suggesting, for example, that a player might qualify for a professional career or that a runner can set a new record if he works hard, or the coach makes changes in the schedule of reinforcements he is using. When rewards are given to some team members but not to others, they are a potential source of rivalry, not of team spirit. Because the athlete's motivation is based on things offered by another person, this approach does not account for intrinsic motivation — the zeal a person develops for himself alone. An example of the latter was the daily walk taken by former President Truman or my own daily exercises. Neither of us have taken these workouts to please someone else. The motives are private.

The pride-in-performance approach. Individuals develop personal motivations in which they seek to obtain social power, affection, nurturing, information, or other states that have significance for them. In sports, the most obvious motivation of this kind is the desire for pride in what one accomplishes, commonly called the need for achievement. We will concentrate on that need.

Psychologists usually assume that the need for achievement is learned in childhood as a result of particular parental practices. I am willing to wager, however, that this need can be developed (in principle at least) at any age, for any specific task, under appropriate conditions. What is wanted, to do this, is a task that can be repeated many times, which provides a score (in time, points, or distance) for each repetition. Gradually, a participant develops some idea about what level of accomplishment he can attain with ease, with some stretching, or not at all. He is then encouraged to see how well he can do, which ordinarily leads him to choose a goal that is a bit harder than the best level he has thus far reached. When he accomplishes that, he feels pride in his performance, and he is then asked to set a new goal. It is best if this again is a moderate challenge, not too hard. We should note that his goals become more precious to him if he knows that other persons depend on his attainments.

A coach is arousing need for achievement when he asks a player to select a private goal for each of many separate activities for the season and asks the player periodically to evaluate his behaviors in reference to each goal. Sometimes a coach and athlete jointly select a number of goals to guide the athlete in an upcoming contest because the athlete is thereby made aware of what he can reasonably ask of himself and, as a result, becomes more involved in those actions. Regardless of the source of the goals, whether they are handed down, jointly decided, or privately developed, the important thing is that the athlete use them to evaluate his own performance, which in turn determines his pride in his output. It is evident that this approach is more tasteful at an educational institution than are others.

GROUP MOTIVATION

The latter two approaches stimulate personal effort because they are based on the satisfaction one derives from either a reward or a sense of pride. Such motives are clearly effective in sports, especially those in which solo actions occur, as in track, golf, swimming, or wrestling, and where much of the training is an individual effort. But there is a further kind of satisfaction that teammates can deeply value — the pride they develop in their team.

Let us consider two group-oriented motives. The *desire for group success* is a disposition on the part of a participant to experience pride and satisfaction with his group if it successfully accomplishes a challenging group task. *The desire to avoid group failure* is a disposition on the part of a member to experience embarrassment or dissatisfaction with his group if it fails on a challenging task. Either group-oriented desire is not an impulse for action; it is rather a disposition that will influence those actions that are perceived to be ways of attaining preferred consequences, that is, to attain pride in the group or to avoid shame in it. The impulse to take part or not to take part in a given activity is called a *tendency*. The tendency to achieve success is thus an inclination to have the group approach a task with interest and the intent of performing it well. The tendency to avoid group failure, in contrast, is an inclination to have the group resist performance of the activity because it is expected to lead to failure. Because a precise description of these tendencies becomes too complicated and abstract to take up here, we will devote our attention to the desire for group success and the desire to avoid group failure — assuming they invoke the appropriate tendencies (Zander, 1971, see Chapters 4 & 10).

A team, by definition, is a social unit with a task that requires a set of persons to accomplish; no individual member can do it all alone. It is perfectly reasonable, therefore, that teammates become involved in their team's outcome, not only in their individual products. This team-centered interest is most likely to develop, of course, when the team gets a score, but an individual member does not. Deep appreciation of the importance of team pride is developed as members become concerned about the excellence of their team in numerous respects, not only in its winning record. One coach I know has his team (through group discussion) set a number of challenging goals, for various statistical matters, at the outset of the season, and he presses them to be realistic about these. The goals, he says, must stretch the players but must not be pipe dreams. He does this because he wants his players to believe that winning is not the only standard of excellence and that it is important above all for him and the athletes to have pride in their team's effort in many ways. There are times when the members of a team prefer to avoid engaging in an athletic contest altogether because they expect to fail. When they are nevertheless constrained to compete, they prepare themselves and their observers to minimize the effects of failure (i.e., the noble try against impossible odds) or they set easy goals so a failure is not likely to occur. All in all, a team will be more alert when the desire for group success is stronger than the desire to avoid group failure, instead of the other way around.

Although he is a member of a team, an individual retains his own personal motive to achieve success, to some degree. I believe (on the basis of good evidence) that person-oriented and group-oriented motives are separate variables and are not the same thing at all (Forward, 1969; Medow & Zander, 1965; Zander & Forward, 1968). This means that a team member may be more interested in his own outcome than in the team's, or more interested in the fate of the team than his own, or, that both interests may be strong and additive, or that both may be weak. In some sports it is crucial that the desire for group success be stronger than the personal motive. In

453

others it does not matter much, but it would help.

EVIDENCE OF GROUP-ORIENTED DESIRES

If group oriented desires are to be taken seriously in theory or in practice, we must be able to examine their effects on group behavior under various conditions, which in turn requires that we be able to say with confidence whether these desires are present or absent in a group at a given time. It would be best if we did not have to ask people whether they care about their group's fate because their reports may not be credible. Fortunately, we do not have to ask because there is a behavioral measure we can use to determine the presence of a desire for group success. It is based on the observation that individuals with different degrees of the *personal* motive to approach success choose different kinds of personal goals. More specifically, a person with a strong motive to succeed chooses a moderately challenging goal, one that is neither so easy as to make success certain (because that would not be satisfying) or so difficult as to make failure certain (because that also would not be satisfying). And, individuals in which the motive to avoid failure is strong will choose either very easy goals (where success is certain to occur) or very hard goals (where failure is not embarrassing). We assume that decisions about group goals are parallel to the individual choices just described and for the same reasons. That is, groups with a strong desire for group success will prefer challenging group goals, whereas groups with a strong desire to avoid group failure will prefer either very easy or very hard group goals.

My first efforts to create variations in the strength of the desire for group success, in accord with the above ideas, were based on earlier findings by Emily Pepitone (1952). She had observed that individual members of a group produce more quantity and better quality if their function is said to be important, even though all members (unknown to them) were performing exactly the same task. In accordance with this observation, we assumed that a central member of a group, in contrast to a peripheral member, would have a stronger desire for group success and that a central member, in contrast to a peripheral one, would therefore favor a more challenging goal for his group.

In an early experiment (Medow & Zander, 1965), small groups, three members in each, were asked to construct geometrical designs out of small blocks of wood. The teammates were seated at a single table but concealed from one another by screens. They were told that each member was to construct on the table before him, in a limited period of time, an exact duplicate of a design. The group's score was determined by the length of time taken for all three members to complete all three solo designs. On the wall of the room there were 14 large poster cards, each displaying a geometrical pattern. These designs varied in complexity from very simple to very hard. After each trial a group chose which design it wished to attempt on the next turn. The boys drew lots to determine who was to be the central person and who were to be the two peripheral ones. The group was told that the peripheral persons could not put a block in place until the central one had

454

done so and had announced that fact. Thus, his actions were central in the structure of the task because he led the way and set the pace, even though all three were doing exactly the same thing at the same time.

The results were that the central person perceived himself as having the more responsible position and that the peripheral persons saw their jobs as less important. More significantly, the central person, in contrast to the peripheral ones, chose challenging designs reliably more often. Analysis of separate treatments that also were part of this experiment indicated that this last contrast was stronger when the central member chose the goal for the group all by himself than when the three members jointly participated in making this choice.

In a replication of this study (Zander & Forward, 1968) the central character was the only member who laid out the chosen design while the two peripheral persons provided particular pieces as the central member called for them. Halfway through the experiment central and peripheral persons changed places, in order to control on effects of personal disposition. Each design of blocks was limited to just five pieces and the goal was speed of completion, not complexity of design. Here again, a central player chose a challenging goal (time in seconds) more often than did the peripheral person. In a later naturalistic study, comparing the responses of central and peripheral members on Boards of Trustees for United Funds in 46 cities, the results were substantially similar to those found in the laboratory (Zander, Forward & Albert, 1969). Members with greater commitment to the group seemed to have greater desire for group successes.

In another early experiment to examine further if variations in the strength of members' desire for group success could be detected, weak groups were developed on the one hand and strong groups on the other (Zander & Medow, 1965). The weak groups were simply a set of strangers seated on randomly arranged chairs who were addressed as individuals ("you") during the opening instructions of the session. The members of the strong groups, in contrast, were seated tightly around a table, were addressed as "this group," were asked to choose a name for their team, and in other ways were helped to see themselves as within a single entity. Each group then performed the same task while all members were seated at a table. Here, the stronger groups chose challenging goals more often than did the weaker groups while working for many trials on an activity that required cooperative speed and accuracy.

In an additional investigation, desire to avoid group failure was generated, as was the desire to achieve group success, by telling subjects in one treatment that every group failure in a series of trials would cost them points while a success would not be rewarded at all; and, in a different treatment, that a success would be rewarded but failure would cost them nothing (Zander & Medow, 1965). As you might expect, the groups in the cost-only condition chose less challenging (and more erratic) goals than did those in the reward-only condition. It appears, in sum, as though something like a desire for group success and something like a desire to avoid group failure may have been operating in these experiments. The crucial question now is,

455

so what? Do groups with different degrees of desire for group success behave differently in ways that are interesting to us?

DESIRE FOR GROUP SUCCESS AND THE PERFORMANCE OF A GROUP

The effect of desire for group success upon a group's performance has been examined in nine studies, six of them in the laboratory and three in natural settings. While none of the group activities can be called athletic, they often required coordination of motor movements among members and demanded some individual skill. There is no doubt, however, that the relevance of the following results to your interests remain to be investigated.

In the laboratory, variations in the strength of the desire for group success have been created by the several methods already mentioned. In addition, variations have been sought by making the group's task more or less important to the outcomes members may obtain when they are away from the group (Forward & Zander, 1971; Thomas & Zander, 1959), by reporting that the group had succeeded or failed (when the subjects did not know these facts themselves) (Zander & Forward, 1968), or by giving questionnaires that were alleged to measure the members' desire for group success and then reporting average scores for the group on these tests (high or low) to the members (Zander, 1971, p. 148). In general, the desire for group success, created in one or another of these ways, had quite consistent relationships with one or another of the following measures of group performance.

Different aspects of group performance were investigated. In one case expenditure of energy was the central interest. Each subject held a hand dynamometer and all members were asked to "squeeze" simultaneously (Zander, 1971, p. 149). The meters were joined by wires in order, it was said, to create a group-strength score, calculated by a small and clicking "computer" to which these wires ran. In four other studies, performance was measured by speed of movement, as in making the designs of wooden blocks or in marking IBM cards (Horwitz, Exline, Goldman & Lee, 1953; Zander & Medow, 1965; Zander & Ulberg, 1971; Zander, 1971, p. 150). In another case it was persistence, as shown by the number of times a group repeated a jig-saw puzzle, working against time, when they were free to stop at any trial (Horwitz, et al., 1953). In two cases the measure of performance was greater accuracy, as in counting holes in IBM cards (Forward & Zander, 1971; Zander & Ulberg, 1971). In two unexpected instances, less accuracy accompanied more desire for group success, probably because the group task (one that required speed in ordering dominoes by number when each person had some of the necessary pieces) caused much talking and confusion as the task had not been previously rehearsed (Zander, 1971, p. 150). And finally, as just noted, stronger desire for group success caused more oral chatter among members (Zander, Fuller, & Armstrong, 1973).

In "real life" greater desire for group success was associated with more sales of insurance policies in separate districts of a large company (Bowers & Seashore, 1966), with more speed and skill when groups of military officers were on a four and a half day trek in the snow (Thomas & Zander,

1959), and with more production on 28 assembly lines (manned by women) in a factory making slippers (Zander & Armstrong, 1972).

Because, as we have noted, challenging goals are more often chosen by members who have a stronger desire for group success, it should follow that groups produce better when they have challenging goals than when they have less challenging ones. This result was observed in two laboratory experiments in which the speed of coordinated movement improved, step by step, as the group's goal was made harder, step by step (Zajonc, 1962; Zajonc & Taylor, 1963). In two studies of United Fund campaigns it was also found that goals placed just a bit harder than previous income levels generated more money than did goals placed much higher or lower than previous levels of performance (Zander & Newcomb, 1967; Zander, *et al.,* 1969). A goal that causes a group to stretch, but is attainable, in short, appears to stimulate a better group effort than either a very easy or a very hard goal.

TALKING AMONG MEMBERS AND DESIRE FOR GROUP SUCCESS

While the American team was climbing Mount Everest, Richard Emerson, a member who was interested in both team motivation and communication under stress, made standard pre-planned comments to his colleagues and recorded their answers on a small tape machine he lugged through the snow (Emerson, 1969). He found that the responses to his comments were typically such that motivation was maximized through emphasizing that the changes of making it to the top were 50-50. If Emerson made a discouraging comment, they cheered him up; if he made an optimistic comment, they dampened his ardor — in both cases the future was made to appear uncertain. Talk among teammates ought, then, to bear some relevance to interest in the group's job. In athletics it is well known that "talking it up" is valuable. Indeed, in wrestling and in baseball good chatter is a true skill, an art form. Through team meetings members may also arouse one another's desire for group success and may establish a joint view that all agree to share, and live by. In a few investigations, therefore, we watched the effect of communication among team members, with these results.

1. After a group had finished its work on a group test of motor skill, in one experiment, members privately completed questionnaires that measured their feelings about their team and the work it had done. After that they had a group discussion in which they were to reach a unanimous decision on the same matters. During these discussions the participants became more approaching if that was their original inclination and more avoiding if that was their prior perference before the discussion had begun. Thus, the discussion strengthened private dispositions (Zander, 1971, p. 22).

2. Members were allowed to talk freely in one condition of an experiment and were denied any opportunity to talk whatsoever in a contrasting condition, while all participants worked on a group assignment that required very close and simultaneous coordination of motor movements. The groups that were allowed to talk set more challenging goals than did the groups that were not allowed to talk. Thus, group discussion aroused

stronger desire for group success (Zander, Fuller, Armstrong, 1973).

3. Some remarks made by teammates can be conceived as *approaching* (for example, encourageing, praising, giving suggestions on how to do the group's task), while other remarks can be conceived as *avoiding* (criticizing, blaming, suggesting that less vigor be used). When remarks among members are coded under these headings we note that (Zander, Fuller, Armstrong, 1973):

    a. Members generally make more approaching remarks than avoiding ones, which means that an interesting task stimulates the kind of talk that arouses a desire for group success.

    b. Approaching remarks are made more often while working on the group's assignment than when discussing it during periods between trials.

    c. Approaching remarks caused (that is, were followed by) more approaching comments as often as they were followed by avoiding ones. In general, then, avoiding remarks are avoided.

All in all, more group stimulates more enthusiasm for what needs to be done by a group.

SHIFTS IN GROUP GOALS

We have used the term goal a good deal in the foregoing as a shorthand way of describing any of a variety of actions a person may want himself or his group to complete in accord with a given degree of excellence. Because improvement in skill and the attainment of new degrees of excellence are important in all sports, and because output on any given trial can be placed somewhere on a scale of difficulty from very easy to very hard, the term goal is a convenient way to keep all this in mind.

We should emphasize, however, that the goal teammates prefer may change over time, which is not news to those who know the literature on personal levels of aspiration. You can assume that groups will change their goals, if they have the freedom to make this decision on their own (which is not the case in most settings, including athletics) and they will make these changes in accord with the simple rule: raise the goal after a success and lower the goal after a failure. You can also anticipate that the tendency to raise after a success is much stronger than the tendency to lower after a failure because, as earlier implied, success on a harder goal is more attractive and failure on an easier goal is more repulsive. It follows that there are strong pressures on a group to raise its goals as its performance improves, and not to lower them as its performance worsens. Observers and others who have influence over a team also want higher goals and their desires are usually more telling on the group's choices than are the group's own scores, according to half a dozen studies into that matter. Group goals, as a result, usually tend to get harder and harder (Zander, 1971, Chapter 2).

It is interesting, then, that groups with a stronger desire for group success follow the "succeed-raise" part of the rule with greater care, because they wish to make it possible for their team to have a success and to have that success be one that is satisfying. Groups with a stronger desire to avoid group failure, in contrast, are more erratic in setting their goals, because it is not entirely clear to them how they can best avoid that failure.

How do group goals affect the personal objectives of individual members? Under what conditions are members of a group more willing to set an individual goal that is congruent with what the group expects of them? The answers to these questions are what your experience as group leaders cause you to expect. In three different experiments it was found that members are more likely to set their personal goals at levels similar to ones being pressed on them by groupmates (a) as members perceive their actions to have greater significance for the group's attainment, and (b) as members are more attracted to membership in that group. In ordinary language, if a teammate wants to be on the team and thinks what it does is important, he will ask of himself the things he knows his colleagues expect of him (Zander, 1971, pp. 164-167).

EVALUATION OF GROUP

The moment that members of a team establish a goal for their unit, they simultaneously create a criterion for evaluating their group's performance. Thereafter, when the group does better than this goal, members give the unit a favorable evaluation and when worse than this goal, an unfavorable evaluation. This practice occurs with such reliability that we can use it to judge whether the goal was internalized by the members. If the goal is used as the basis for evaluation of the team, it has really been accepted. But, if the goal is ignored and evaluation of the group is determined by some other standard of excellence instead, the goal has not been accepted — members only pretended to hold it dear. For example, a failing performance that is given a favorable evaluation reveals that the members did not employ the relevant goal for the team in making their judgment. Not uncommonly, some unexpressed aspiration is used by members as their standard of excellence (Zander, 1971, Chapter 7).

In an athletic team the importance of winning is what most often confounds matters. Clearly, being able to defeat other teams is the most laudable and visible kind of success and thus it doubtless is given most weight — expecially among teams that have a winning record. Other kinds of excellence probably become more important as winning occurs less often, but I cannot think of any research that bears directly on this issue.

There are data that are indirectly related to these matters. They concern the amount of pride or shame members feel in their group, and themselves as individuals, when they try to understand a good or a poor group performance. We asked members of groups to rate the amount of pride or shame they felt in their group's score as the competence of members, and the effort exerted by them, were varied. Several findings are notable (Zander, 1974; Zander, Fuller, Armstrong, 1972):

    a. An excellent performance by a group generates much more pride among members if they had tried hard than if they had not tried at all, regardless of how much ability members brought to the group's assignment.

b. A poor performance by a group generates more shame if the members are very able but did not try on the group's task than if the members are not competent but tried very hard. Thus, shame in a group after it fails is determined by the degree to which members waste their competence by not exerting themselves.

c. A success, if achieved without effort, is not a strong source of pride, if it is achieved after much effort, it is a source of pride.

d. Lack of effort is a greater source of shame in the group than a source of shame in self.

DEVELOPING A DESIRE FOR GROUP SUCCESS

Suppose you have by now developed some interest in the desire for group success and you wish to try your hand, more consciously than heretofore, at arousing it within a team. How would you go about it? If I were in your shoes, I would attempt to generate a commitment to the group by doing the following things. These will come at you like beads on a string, but there is no help for it. Listen to them as variations on a theme: making pride in team an important thing.

1. Emphasize the importance of pride in the group, its sources and its consequences for the team. One coach I know makes his seniors responsible for developing these ideas as well as for enthusiasm during practice and games.

2. Make sure that each member understands that his contribution to the team is valued.

3. Use various means to underscore how each teammate depends upon the work of each other for the success of their unit.

4. Emphasize the unity of the group, the score as a product of team effort, and the perception that all members are within the group's boundary.

5. Indicate to members separately how membership helps each individual, so that each will see the group as an attractive entity.

6. Take care in the selection of group goals so that these are realistic challenges, not unreasonably hard or easy ends. Set standards of excellence for all skills and activities.

7. Don't be afraid to change goals that are found to be unreasonably difficult. The warmest pride comes from living up to reasonable expectations for that group, not in failing impossibly difficult ends.

8. Once goals have been set, consider what obstacles might prevent fulfillment of these goals and how the obstacles might be overcome by the team.

9. Encourage talk in the group about how performance can be improved and how the boring parts of athletics can be made more involving.

10. Avoid fear of failure and the tendency to evade challenges that are engendered thereby.

SOME FINAL COMMENTS ABOUT THE DESIRE FOR GROUP SUCCESS

When the desire for group success is strong among members, they have a keen awareness of their mutual social responsibility, which causes them to help one another, to coordinate their efforts with maximum efficiency (provided the work to be done is well practiced) and to be friendly. All members of a team, regardless of whether they are superstars or bench-riders, can attain satisfaction of a desire for group success. Society accepts it, moreover, as an appropriate and praise-worthy aspect of group purposes.

Finally, there are questions to be raised about these ideas. One is that not every person can become concerned about a group and this motivation will therefore not work for asocial types who prefer to be alone — they must be allowed to be soloists or not at all. Repeated failures by a team can make it difficult for members to arouse a desire for group success unless they have developed strong beliefs ahead of time about what they expect of themselves, aside from victories. For that matter, emphasis on winning can distract from efforts to achieve any goal other than a championship, but the distraction is not as great for a winning team as it is for a losing one. Doubtless, it is harder to develop a desire for group success in sports that require little coordination among team members than in the so-called interactive team sports that demand smooth blending of the movements of several persons.

SUMMARY

In summary, we have taken seriously what every coach knows — the desire for success of the team as a unit can be a powerful motivating force on the participants. We have talked about the origins and consequences of this group-oriented motivation. It seems reasonable to suggest that this approach warrants further study in athletic settings. It is no panacea, but it can be useful as a means of understanding, predicting, and furthering the attainment of excellence, one of the prime values of athletics in all cultures.

REFERENCES

Bowers, D. & Seashore, S. Predicting organizational effectiveness with a four-factor theory of leadership. *Administrative Science Quarterly*, 1966, *11*, 238-263.

Emerson, R. Mount Everest: A case study of communication feedback and sustained goal striving. *Sociometry*, 1966, *29*, 213-277.

Forward, J. Group achievement motivation and individual motives to achieve success and to avoid failure. *Journal of Personality*, 1969, *37*, 297-309.

Forward, J. & Zander, A. Choice of unattainable group goals and effects on performance. *Organizational Behavior and Human Performance*, 1971, *6*, 184-199.

Horwitz, M., Exline, R., Goldman, M. & Lee, R. *Motivational effects of alternative decision making processes in groups.* Technical Report to U.S. Office of Naval Research, Bureau of Education Research, University of Illinois, 1953.

Medow, H. & Zander, A. Aspirations for group chosen by central and peripheral members. *Journal of Personality and Social Psychology* 1965, *1*, 224-228.

Pepitone, E. *Responsibility to Group and its Effects on the Performance of Members.* Unpublished doctoral dissertation, The University of Michigan, 1952.

Thomas, E. J., & Zander, A. The relationship of goal structure to motivation under extreme conditions. *Journal of Individual Psychology*, 1959, *15*, 121-127.

Zajonc, R. The effects of feedback and probability of group success on individual and group performance. *Human Relations,* 1962, *15,* 149-161.

Zajonc, R. & Taylor, J. The effects of two methods of varying task difficulty on individual and group performance. *Human Relations,* 1963, *16,* 359-368.

Zander, A. & Medow, H. Strength of group and desire for attainable group aspirations. *Journal of Personality,* 1965, *33,* 122-139.

Zander, A. & Newcomb, T. M., Jr. Group levels of aspiration in United Fund campaigns. *Journal of Personality and Social Psychology,* 1967, *6,* 157-162.

Zander, A. & Forward, J. Position in group, achievement motivation, and group aspirations. *Journal of Personality and Social Psychology,* 1968, *8,* 282-288.

Zander, A., Forward, J., & Albert, R. Adaptation of board members to repeated success of failure by their organizations. *Organizational Behavior and Human Performance,* 1969, *4,* 56-76.

Zander, A. & Ulberg, C. The group level of aspiration and external social pressures. *Organizational Behavior and Human Performance,* 1971, *6,* 362-378.

Zander, A. *Motives and goals in groups.* New York: Academic Press, 1971.

Zander, A. & Armstrong, W. Working for group pride in a slipper factory. *Journal of Applied Social Psychology,* 1972, *2,* 193-207.

Zander, A., Fuller, R., & Armstrong, W. Attributed pride or shame in group and self. *Journal of Personality and Social Psychology,* 1972, *23,* 346-352.

Zander, A., Fuller, R., & Armstrong, W. Communication among members during a challenging group task, 1973 (unpublished report).

Zander, A. Alone versus together: Attributed pride or shame in self, 1974 (unpublished report).

When Cohesion Predicts Performance Outcome in Sport*

W. Neil Widmeyer
Rainer Martens

This study determined whether the measure of cohesion employed and the ability level, participation motivation, and sex of team members mediated the cohesion-performance outcome relationship in sport. The basketball ability of 117 male and 81 female university student volunteers was assessed and three-person teams of equal ability were formed within each of three ability levels for each sex. Following two practice sessions, self-report measures of participation motivation and cohesion were taken. Teams played two half-hour games weekly for 5 weeks. Multiple regression analyses revealed that when cohesion was directly assessed through players' ratings of their team's closeness and the team's overall attraction, 18% of the variance in performance outcome was accounted for by cohesion. When cohesion was assessed by summing individuals' evaluations of their teammates' contributions to the task and the group's enjoyment, only .7% of performance outcome was predicted. Knowing a member's self-motivation improved cohesion's prediction of performance outcome 7%. The task motivation, affiliation motivation, ability level, or sex of the players did not improve cohesion's prediction of performance outcome. Thus, the cohesion measured used influenced cohesion's prediction of performance outcome more than did the ability level, participation motivation, and sex of the team members.

Many athletes, coaches, and spectators believe that cohesiveness is often a deciding factor in winning or losing in team sports. "The team that stays together plays together and wins together" and "players play, but teams win" are locker room slogans indicative of the significance attached to cohesiveness in sport.

Does team cohesiveness actually help win games? Many psychologists believe that high-cohesive teams perform better than low-cohesive teams because: (a) high-cohesive teams need not expend as much time and energy on group maintenance and therefore have more energy to devote to task

* Widmeyer, W. N. and Martens, R. "When Cohesion Predicts Performance Outcome in Sport," *Research Quarterly*, 1978, *49*, 380-388. Reprinted by permission of the publisher.

W. Neil Widmeyer is with the University of Waterloo, Waterloo, Ontario, and Rainer Martens is with the University of Illinois, Urbana, IL 61801.

performance than low-cohesive teams (Cattell, 1948); (b) team members who are attracted to a group work harder to achieve the goals of that group (Shaw, 1971); (c) the superior communication within cohesive teams enables them to coordinate their resources better, thus improving the quality of performance (Lott & Lott, 1965); (d) cohesive teams possess a willingness to interact, making group resources available to a degree not enjoyed by less cohesive groups (Davis, 1969); and (e) membership loyalty and group longevity, characteristic of cohesive groups, make it easier for team members to persist at a task and therefore increase the team's chances of performing well (Cartwright, 1968). On the other hand, Fiedler (1954) has argued that highly cohesive teams may not perform as well as less cohesive teams because individual members may allow the maintenance of group cohesion to interfere with the group's task performance.

What does the experimental evidence show for sport teams? Arnold and Straub (1973), Klein and Christiansen (1969), Martens and Peterson (1971), and Vander Velden (1971) found that highly cohesive basketball teams were more successful than less cohesive teams. Similarly, Smith (1968) reported a positive relationship between group cohesion and basketball shooting performance; cohesive teams not only took more shots, they made more baskets. Stogdill (1963) found that "team integration" on each play during a football game was as positively related to success on that play. Recently Ball and Carron (1976) foud a positive relationship between the mid-season cohesion and postseason success of intercollegiate hockey teams.

In contrast, the study of high school basketball teams by Fiedler (1954); Fiedler, Hartman, and Rudin (1952); and Grace (1954) and the investigation of rifle teams by McGrath (1962) revealed a negative relationship between cohesion and performance outcome. Lenk (1969) reported that West German Olympic rowing crews were very successful despite internal strife among crew members. Landers and Leuschen (1974) observed that unsuccessful bowling teams had higher mean interpersonal attraction than successful team. Finally, Melnick and Chemers (1974) found that cohesiveness had neither a positive nor a negative relationship to group success in basketball. Thus, there is evidence in sport settings not only that high cohesiveness is related to high performance outcome, but also that high cohesiveness is related to poor performance outcome, that low cohesiveness is related to high performance outcome, and that cohesiveness and performance outcome are unrelated.

Two obvious explanations for the equivocality of the results are (a) the inconsistency in the measurement of cohesiveness, with several operational definitions having questionable validity, and (b) that the relationship between cohesiveness and performance outcome is likely altered by different task demands, by certain group input variables, and by other group processes (Steiner, 1972). The purpose of the present study therefore, was to investigate further the cohesion-performance outcome relationship by examining the influence of three possible mediating variables — ability, pariticipation motivation, and sex of the team members.

The ability of the group members commonly is thought to be the most important determinant of group performance. Five professional basketball players undoubtedly would outperform five recreational players regardless of the cohesion of either group. The question, however, of whether cohesion is a more crucial variable in the professional ranks than it is in amateur leagues has never been examined. It is thought that the ability of the experienced professional players does not fluctuate greatly from game to game and therefore nonability factors such as cohesion play a greater role in determining team victory in high ability teams than in low ability teams.

In reviewing the cohesion literature, Stogdill (1972) concluded that high cohesiveness by itself does not lead to high productivity. He stated that since "group drive or motivation is the variable most consistently related to productivity,' cohesiveness and productivity tend to be positively related under conditions of high-group motivation and negatively related under conditions of low motivation. The only motivation examined by Stogdill was task motivation (concern with performing the task), but individuals participate in groups, including sport groups, for reasons other than performing the task. Bass (1967) theorized that individuals not only participate in groups to perform the task, but that they participate in groups to affiliate (affiliation motivation) and to obtain direct rewards such as esteem and prestige (self-motivation). In comparing the influence of these three types of participation motivation, Cooper and Payne (1972) found that task-oriented football teams were not as successful as self-oriented teams. Martens (1970) found that high affiliation-motivated basketball teams were less successful than moderate or low affiliation-motivated teams. These results suggest that participation motivation (task, affiliation, and self-motivation) is likely to mediate the cohesion-performance outcome relationsip.

The third mediating variable examined in this study was the sex of the participants. To date only one study (Bird, 1977) has examined the cohesiveness of female groups. Although her study and the few that have been done outside of sport with female groups (Darley, Gross, & Martin, 1952; Schachter, Ellerston, McBride, & Gregroy, 1951) have shown a positive cohesion-performance outcome relationship, none of the studies have compared the relationship for males and females to determine if cohesion is a more powerful variable for one sex than the other.

METHOD

Subjects

Subjects were 117 male and 81 female undergraduates from the University of Waterloo representing all years and all fields of study. These indiviudals volunteered to participate in a 3-on-3 basketball league which was advertised as providing opportunities both for playing basketball and for socializing with fellow university students.

Procedures

Subjects were given a basketball ability test, the results of which were used to classify players as above average, average, and below average ability. Three players within each category were then grouped together to form a team whose ability score was equal to that of other teams within their league. Separate leagues were formed for males and females. Prior to participating in their first game each team held two 40-minute practices. Two days before their first game all participants completed a questionnaire designed to determine their motives for participating in the league and the cohesion of their team at that point in time. Each team then played one or two games per week for 4 to 5 weeks. Games consisted of two 12-minute halves with a 5-minute half-time break. The percentage of games won represented team performance outcome.

Assessment of Basketball Ability

Although basketball ability has been assessed formally since the turn of the century, there are no recognized ideal tests. Based upon the tests reviewed and the 3-on-3 half court game being used, a 3-item test was devised. Shooting skill was measured by the number of baskets scored from the five shots that were taken from each of five floor positions which were 16 feet from the basket for males and 12 feet for the females. "Dribble-drive" ability was measured by the number of lay-up shots scored after dribbling around a chair positioned 16 feet from the basket. Subjects dribbled and shot from the right side of the basket for 30 seconds and after a 15-second rest duplicated the activity from the left side. Lastly, each subject played 60 seconds of offense and 60 seconds of defense in a 1-on-1 drill with one of the research assistants. Three observers, using a 1-to-5 scale, gave each player a separate score for offense and defense. Scores on each of the three test items were converted to a score ranging from 1 to 9. Subjects whose scores on the three test were above 21 were classified as high ability, those between 9 and 20 as average, and those below 9 as below average.

Assessment of Participation Motivation

A subject's task, affiliation, and self-motivation for joining the 3-on-3 basketball league were assessed by his or her response to the following three-part question:

There are many specific reasons for participating in an activity such as basketball. These specific reasons may usually be classified according to three broad categories: (1) the opportunity to associate with others, (2) the intrinsic enjoyment of playing basketball, and (3) to have others admire your ability. Using the scale below as a reference, indicate how important each of these reasons is for your participation in this program.

A. To be with the guys (girls)

1	2	3	4	5	6	7	8	9
Very Important								Not at all Important

B. I enjoy playing basketball

1	2	3	4	5	6	7	8	9
Very Important								Not at all Important

C. To be admired

1	2	3	4	5	6	7	8	9
Very Important								Not at all Important

All team members' scores for each type of participation motivation were summed to obtain separate team scores for task-, self-, and affiliation-motivation.

Assessement of Cohesion

In view of the problems associated with past attempts to define cohesion operationally, and in keeping with more recent cohesion research (Martens & Peterson, 1971), four different approaches were used to assess team cohesiveness. First, each team member rated his friendship with every other member of his team. Secondly, each member assessed the contribution that each other member of his team was likely to make to the success and to the enjoyment of the team. Next, each individual assessed the overall attractiveness of the group for himself in light of his expectations and available alternatives by responding to questions which asked: "How strong is (a) your liking for playing with this team, (b) your sense of belonging to this team, and (c) the value you place on your team membership?" Finally, each individual gave his direct assessment of the cohesion of his team by indicating how "close-knit" he felt the team was and how strong the "teamwork" of the group was. Eight separate measures of cohesiveness resulted from these four approaches. Team cohesion scores were computed for each measure by averaging the responses of each of the three team members.

The data were analyzed with multiple regression techniques using the cohesion variable, ability, participation motivation, and sex as predictor variables and win percent as the criterion variable. Because there were too many cohesion variables to maintain adequate statistical power for the sample tested, and because the cohesion variables were substantially correlated with each other, a principal component factor analysis followed by a varimax rotation was undertaken. This procedure provided a satisfactory solution to these problems by yielding two independent factors (see Table 1). The first factor, labelled "descriptive cohesion" was loaded heavily with those measures which asked an individual to describe his group's cohesion and with those questions measuring the total attraction that the group held for the individual. The second factor was highly loaded with the members' ratings of each teammate's contribution to the group's enjoyment and to the group goal. This factor was labelled "inferential cohesion" because the group's attractiveness had to be inferred from the ratings which players

467

gave to other individuals. It is noteworthy that interpersonal attraction, the most frequently used single measure of group cohesion, contributed little to either of the cohesion factors.

RESULTS

Factor scores were used for the two cohesion factors in all multiple regression equations. The first regression analysis, using only the two cohesion variables as predictors and win percent as the criterion variable, significantly predicted performance outcome (see Table 2). The descriptive cohesion factor accounted for 18.7% of the variance in performance outcome and the inferential cohesion factor accounted for only 0.7% of the variance.

Including ability level with the two cohesion factors in the regression equation did not change the multiple R at all in the prediction of performance outcome. Similarly the addition of the interaction of cohesion and ability level in the regression equation had no significant influence on the multiple R, increasing it only .03.

Table 1. Orthogonally Rotated Factor Matrix

	Factor Loadings	
Cohesion Measures	Descriptive Cohesion	Inferential Cohesion
1. Friendship	.25	.30
2. Contribution to Task Based on Ability	.19	.93
3. Contribution to Enjoyment	.19	.89
4. Enjoy Playing with This Group	.75	.32
5. Sense of Belonging	.81	.15
6. Teamwork	.85	.26
7. How Close-knit is the Group	.77	.36
8. Value of Membership	.88	.12
Variance	3.45	2.08
Variance Percent	62.36	37.64

A regression analysis with the three types of participation motivation as predictors did not significantly predict performance outcome, but the inclusion of participation motivation with the cohesion factors significantly improved the prediction of performance outcome (see Table 3). The three forms of participation motivation along with the two cohesion factors accounted for 28% of the variance in performance outcome. A t test of the individual regression coefficients indicated that it was descriptive cohesion and self-motivation that were contributing significantly to the variance in performance outcome. A stepwise multiple-regression analysis showed that descriptive cohesion and self-motivation alone predicted 26% of the

Table 2. Summary of the Regression of Performance Outcome on Team Cohesion		Table 3. Summary of the Regression of Performance Outcome on Cohesion and Participation Motivation.	
Performance Outcome		**Performance Outcome**	
Standarized Regression Coefficients		*Standarized Regression Coefficients*	
Descriptive Cohesion	.43	Affiliation Motivation	− 0.06
Inferential Cohesion	− 0.7	Task Motivation	− 0.00
		Self Motivation	0.29
		Descriptive Cohesion	0.47
		Inferential Cohesion	− 0.09
Multiple R	.44	Multiple R	.52
R^2	.19	R^2	.28
F Ratio ($df = 2,63$)	7.52[a]	F Ratio ($df = 5,60$)	4.55[a]
t Test for Testing Significance of Coefficients (df = 63)		*t Test for Testing Significance of Coefficients (df = 60)*	
Descriptive Cohesion	3.83[a]	Affiliation Motivation	− 0.51
Inferential Cohesion	− 0.63	Task Motivation	− 0.00
		Self Motivation	2.55[a]
		Descriptive Motivation	4.00[a]
		Inferential Cohesion	− 0.83
[a]p < .01.		[a]p < .01.	

variance in performance outcome, with descriptive cohesion predicting 19% and self-motivation 7%.

When the sex of the group was added as a predictor variable, along with the two cohesion factors, the sex variable did not significantly change the prediction of performance outcome. Also, the addition of the interaction of sex with each cohesion factor did not improve this prediction. Females had higher ($p < .07$) descriptive cohesion scores. ($M = .28$) than did males ($M = .17$); however, this result did not meet the established criterion level for significance ($p < .05$).

DISCUSSION

The results supported the observation that the greater the cohesion of the group the better is performance outcome. This relationship held true only when cohesion was assessed directly by having subjects rate their team's cohesion and the value of their group membership, raising the question as to what the inferential-cohesion factor measures. The items contributing most to the inferential-cohesion factor were those which asked each individual to rate the contribution of each of his teammates to the task and to the enjoyment of the group. An individual's rating of his group was obtained by summing his ratings of individual members. This procedure assumes that an individuals's relationship with each of his teammates is of equal worth, a questionable assumption. Second, since the inferential-cohesion factor involves only ratings of other members, it ignores the values that individuals place on the goal, activities, or instrumentality of the group, as well as membership in one group as compared with alternate groups.

Of the previous investigations conducted within sport settings only the study by Arnold and Straub (1973) found a positive relationship between cohesion and performance outcome when inferential type measures of cohesion were used. All studies which found a negative relationship between cohesion and performance outcome, however, employed inferential measures. Also, it is worth repeating that the interpersonal attraction measure, one of the inferential measures in the latter group of studies and probably the most frequently used single indicator of cohesion, did not load high on either cohesion factor. While there are so many difficulties with previous cohesion-performance outcome studies that it is impossible to attribute the discrepancy of results solely to the use of descriptive or inferential cohesion variables, certainly there is cause to suspect that the different operational definitions of cohesion are not measuring the same construct.

Although this study was not concerned with the relationship between ability per se and performance outcome, it did determine how the general ability level of teams mediated the cohesion-performance outcome relationship. Thus, three different ability level leagues were created. The failure to find that cohesion predicted performance outcome better in high-ability groups than it did in low-ability groups is difficult to explain. The only explanation of some plausibility is that the three ability levels used were not sufficiently different. The teams certainly did not represent either very high or very low ability levels, but were of a somewhat homogeneous college-age, nonvarsity ability level.

The contention that participation motivation together with the two cohesion factors predict performance outcome better than the two cohesion factors alone was supported. However, the only regression coefficient other than the descriptive cohesion factor which was significant was self-motivation. The failure of task motivation to significantly predict performance outcome was due likely to the extremely small variation in task motivation among subjects ($M = 8.23$, $SD = .88$). The combination of the positive relationship between affilation motivation and initial cohesion and the absence of a relationship between affiliation motivation and performance outcome suggests that affiliation motivation's relationship to cohesion is simply paralleling rather than contributing to cohesion's relationship with performance outcome. Similarly, self-motivation's significant improvment of cohesion's prediction of performance outcome can be attributed to both the positive relationship between self-motivation and performance outcome ($r = +.23$) and to the lack of relationship between self-motivation and both descriptive cohesion ($r = -.09$) and inferential cohesion ($r = +.11$).

Another significant aspect of the result of the regression of perfor-

470

mance outcome on cohesion and participation motivation is that they contradict the finding of Schachter et al. (1951) that group induction is more powerful than group cohesion and Stogdill's (1972) conclusion that "group drive or motivation is the variable related to productivity." Stogdill was making the point that the combination of high cohesiveness and high drive make for high productivity, but that of the two, it is drive or motivation that is making the major contribution. It should be recognized that Schachter et al. were dealing with laboratory-induced cohesion and that the studies reviewed by Stogdill primarily employed indirect measures of cohesion and that the motivation he assessed was primarily "task motivation" and not affiliation or self-motivation. The present study indicates that cohesion, when measured directly, is a better predictor of performance outcome than is participation motivation.

Sex was expected to mediate the cohesion-performance outcome variable, but failed to do so. The notion that cohesion predicts performance outcome better in male groups than it does in female groups was based upon achievement motivation studies that suggested females are less task motivated than males, plus the assumption that high-task motivation leads to superior performance outcomes. Since task motivation in this study was not a significant predictor of performance outcome, and since males were not more task motivated than females, it is not surprising that the sex of the group did not affect the cohesion-performance outcome relationship.

In conclusion this study provides further evidence that the descriptive measures of cohesion, particularly the questions asking subjects to directly evaluate the team's cohesiveness, are better predictors of team success than are individuals' assessments of their teammates' contributions to the task and to group enjoyment. Furthermore, ability level, within the range manipulated in this study, and sex did not affect the cohesion-performance outcome relationship. Both affiliation and task motivation also failed to significantly affect this relationship. Although self-motivation contributed a significant 7% to the prediction of performance outcome and, combined with the cohesion factors, accounted for 26% of the variance, the cohesion-performance outcome relationship was more dependent upon how cohesion was measured than on the presence of this mediating variable.

REFERENCES

Arnold, G., & Straub, W. Personality and group cohesiveness as determinants of success among interscholastic basketball teams. In I. Williams & L. Wankel (Eds.) *Proceedings of Fourth Canadian Psycho-Motor Learning and Sport Psychology Symposium.* Ottawa: Department of National Health and Welfare, 1973.

Ball, J., & Carron, A. The influence of team cohesion and participation motivation upon performance success in intercollegiate ice hockey. *Canadian Journal of Applied Sport Sciences,* 1976, *1,* 271-275.

Bass, B. Social behavior and the orientation inventory: A review. *Psychological Bulletin,* 1967, *68,* 260-292.

Bird, A. Development of a model for predicting team performance. *Research Quarterly,* 1977, *48,* 24-32.

Cartwright, D. The nature of group cohesiveness. In D. Cartwright & A. Zander (Eds.) *Group Dynamics* (3rd ed.). New York: Harper and Row, 1968.

Cattell, R. Concepts and methods in the measurement of group syntality. *Psychological Review*, 1948, *55*, 48-63.

Cooper, R., & Payne, R. Personality orientations and performance in soccer teams. *British Journal of Social and Clinical Psychology*, 1972, *1*, 2-9.

Darley, J., Gross, N., & Martin, W. Studies of group behaviour: Factors associated with productivity of groups. *Journal of Applied Psychology*, 1952, *36*, 396-403.

Davis, J. *Group performance.* Reading Mass.: Addison-Wesley, 1969.

Fiedler, F. Assumed similarity measures as predictors of team effectiveness. *Journal of Abnormal and Social Psychology*, 1954, *49*, 381-388.

Fiedler, F., Hartman, W., & Rudin, S. *The relationship of interpersonal perception to effectiveness in basketball teams* (Suppl. Tech. Rep. No. 3, Contract N60T1-07135). Urbana: Bureau of Records and Service, University of Illinois, 1952.

Grace, H. Conformance and performance. *Journal of Social Psychology*, 1954, *40*, 233-237.

Klein, M., & Christiansen, G. Group composition, group insurance, and group effectiveness of basketball teams. In J. Loy Jr. & G. Kenyon (Eds.), *Sport, culture and society: A reader on the sociology of sport,* London: MacMillan, 1969.

Landers, D., & Lueschen, G. Team performance outcome and cohesiveness of competitive co-acting groups. *International Review of Sport Sociology, 2* (9), 57-69.

Lenk, H. Top performance despite internal conflict: An antithesis to a functionalistic proposition. In J. Loy, Jr. & G. Kenyon (Eds.), *Sport, culture and society: A reader on the sociology of sport,* London: MacMillan, 1969.

Lott, A. J., & Lott, B. R. Group cohesiveness as interpersonal attraction: A review of relationships with antecedent and consequent variables. *Psychological Bulletin*, 1965, *64*, 259-309.

Martens, R. Influence of participation motivation on success and satisfaction in team performance. *Research Quarterly*, 1970, *41*, 510-518.

Martens, R., & Peterson, J. Group cohesiveness as a determinant of success and member satisfaction in team performance. *International Review of Sport Psychology*, 1971, *6*, 49-61.

McGrath, J. The influence of positive interpersonal relations on adjustment and effectiveness in rifle teams. *Journal of Abnormal and Social Psychology*, 1962, *65*, 365-375.

Melnick, M., & Chemers, M. Effects of group social structure on the success of basketball teams. *Research Quarterly*, 1974, *45*, 1-8.

Schachter, S., Ellertson, N., McBride, D., & Gregory, D. An experimental study of Cohesiveness and Productivity. *Human Relations*, 1951, *4*, 229-238.

Shaw, M. *Group dynamics: The psychology of small group behavior.* New York: McGraw-Hill, 1971.

Smith, G. *An analysis of the concept of group cohesion in a simulated athletic setting.* Unpublished masters thesis, University of Western Ontario, London, Canada, 1968.

Steiner, K. *Group process and productivity.* New York: Academic Press, 1972.

Stogdill, R. *Team achievement under high motivation.* Columbus: The Bureau of Business Research, College of Commerce and Administrtion, Ohio State University, 1963.

Stogdill, R. Group productivity, drive and cohesiveness. *Organizational Behavior and Human Performance*, 1972, *8*, 26-43.

Vander Velden, L. *Relationships among members, team and situational variables and basketball team success: A social-psychological inquiry.* Unpublished doctoral dissertation, University of Wisconsin, 1971.